Constitutional Culture and Democratic Rule

This volume investigates the nature of constitutional democratic government in the United States and elsewhere. The editors introduce a basic conceptual framework, which the contributors clarify and develop in eleven essays organized into three separate sections. The first section deals with constitutional founding and the founders' use of cultural symbols and traditions to facilitate acceptance of a new regime. The second discusses alternative constitutional structures and their effects on political outcomes. The third focuses on processes of constitutional change and why founders might choose to make formal amendments relatively difficult or easy to achieve. The book is distinctive because it provides comprehensive tools for analyzing and comparing different forms of constitutional democracy. These tools are discussed in ways that will be of interest to students and readers in political science, law, history, and political philosophy.

John Ferejohn is Carolyn S. G. Munro Professor of Political Science at Stanford University and serves as a Visiting Professor of Law at New York University. He is the author, coauthor, or coeditor of five books, including *The New Federalism: Can the States Be Trusted?* (1997, with Barry Weingast), *Information and Democratic Processes* (1990, with James Kuklinski), and *The Personal Vote: Constituency Service and Electoral Independence* (1987, with Bruce Cain and Morris Fiorina), and author or coauthor of 100 articles in leading academic journals.

Jack N. Rakove is William Robertson Coe Professor of History and American Studies and Professor of Political Science at Stanford University. He received the Pulitzer Prize in History in 1997 for *Original Meanings: Politics and Ideas in the Making of the Constitution* and has written or edited five other books, including most recently *James Madison: Writings* (1999) and *Declaring Rights: A Brief History with Documents* (1997). Professor Rakove is a member of the American Academy of Arts and Sciences and the American Antiquarian Society, and he is currently preparing a new edition of the major essays of *The Federalist* and a brief history of the origins of judicial review.

Jonathan Riley is Professor in the Department of Political Science and the Murphy Institute of Political Economy at Tulane University and holds the Laurance S. Rockefeller Fellowship in the University Center for Human Values at Princeton University for 2000–1. He is the author or coeditor of six books, including *Mill's Radical Liberalism: An Essay in Retrieval* (2001), *J. S. Mill: Principles of Political Economy and Chapters on Socialism* (1994), and *Liberal Utilitarianism: Social Choice Theory and J. S. Mill's Philosophy* (Cambridge University Press, 1988), and author of more than thirty articles in academic journals and collections. Professor Riley is currently completing a study of pluralistic liberalisms, with a focus on the theories of Isaiah Berlin, John Rawls, and Mill.

Murphy Institute Studies in Political Economy

General Editor: Richard F. Teichgraeber III

The books in this series are occasional volumes sponsored by the Murphy Institute of Political Economy at Tulane University and Cambridge University Press, comprising original essays by leading scholars in the United States and other countries. Each volume considers one of the intellectual preoccupations or analytical preoccupations or analytical procedures currently associated with the term "political economy." The goal of the series is to aid scholars and teachers committed to moving beyond the traditional boundaries of their disciplines in a common search for new insights and new ways of studying the political and economic realities of our time. The series is published with the support of the Tulane-Murphy Foundation.

Also in the series:

Gordon C. Winston and Richard F. Teichgraeber III, eds., *The Boundaries of Economics*

John Dunn, ed., *The Economic Limits to Modern Politics*

Thomas L. Haskell and Richard F. Teichgraeber III, eds., *The Culture of the Market: Historical Essays*

James L. Regens and Ronald Keith Gaddie, *The Economic Realities of Political Reform*

Praise for *Constitutional Culture and Democratic Rule*

"This excellent set of essays will be of great value to all of those who are interested in the origins of constitutions and their role in the democratic process. It has something for every student of constitutions from analytic discussions of the origins and workings of actual constitutions to game-theoretic analyses of the properties of abstract constitutional forms and processes. A must read for all scholars interested in 'constitutionalism' broadly defined."

– Dennis C. Mueller, *University of Vienna*

"Constitutionalism . . . an otherwise vague concept . . . is brought into sharp focus by this penetrating and comprehensive set of essays. This volume should not only be required reading for any class on democratic principles, but also by anyone who might participate in designing institutions, constitutional or otherwise, for a new democracy."

– Peter Ordeshook, *California Institute of Technology*

Constitutional Culture and Democratic Rule

Edited by
JOHN FEREJOHN
Stanford University

JACK N. RAKOVE
Stanford University

JONATHAN RILEY
Tulane University

CAMBRIDGE
UNIVERSITY PRESS

32 Avenue of the Americas, New York NY 10013-2473, USA

Cambridge University Press is part of the University of Cambridge.

It furthers the University's mission by disseminating knowledge in the pursuit of
education, learning and research at the highest international levels of excellence.

www.cambridge.org
Information on this title: www.cambridge.org/9780521790222

© John Ferejohn, Jack N. Rakove, Jonathan Riley 2001

This publication is in copyright. Subject to statutory exception
and to the provisions of relevant collective licensing agreements,
no reproduction of any part may take place without the written
permission of Cambridge University Press.

First published 2001

A catalogue record for this publication is available from the British Library

Library of Congress Cataloguing in Publication data

Constitutional culture and democratic rule / edited by John Ferejohn, Jack N.
Rakove, Jonathan Riley.
    p. cm. – (Murphy Institute studies in political economy)
    1. Constitutional law – United States.   2. United States – Politics
and government.   I. Ferejohn, John A.   II. Rakove, Jack N., 1947–
III. Riley, Jonathan, 1955–   IV. Series.
KF4552 .C66   2001
342.73 – dc21

                                  00-046794

ISBN 978-0-521-79022-2 Hardback
ISBN 978-0-521-79370-4 Paperback

Cambridge University Press has no responsibility for the persistence or accuracy of
URLs for external or third-party internet websites referred to in this publication,
and does not guarantee that any content on such websites is, or will remain, accurate
or appropriate.

To Sam Beer
a constitutionalist for the ages

Contents

List of Contributors		*page* xi
Editors' Introduction		1

PART ONE. CONSTITUTIONAL BEGINNINGS AND TRANSITIONS

1	**Constitutional Problematics, circa 1787** *Jack N. Rakove*	41
2	**Inventing Constitutional Traditions: The Poverty of Fatalism** *James Johnson*	71
3	**The Birth Logic of a Democratic Constitution** *Lawrence G. Sager*	110

PART TWO. CONSTITUTIONAL STRUCTURE AND DESIGN

4	**Constitutional Democracy as a Two-Stage Game** *Jonathan Riley*	147
5	**Imagining Another Madisonian Republic** *Jonathan Riley*	170
6	**One and Three: Separation of Powers and the Independence of the Judiciary in the Italian Constitution** *Pasquale Pasquino*	205
7	**A Political Theory of Federalism** *Jenna Bednar, William N. Eskridge Jr., and John Ferejohn*	223

PART THREE. CONSTITUTIONAL CHANGE AND STABILITY

8	**Designing an Amendment Process** *Sanford Levinson*	271
9	**Constitutional Theory Transformed** *Stephen M. Griffin*	288

x *Contents*

10 Constitutional Economic Transition 328
Russell Hardin

11 Institutionalizing Constitutional Interpretation 361
Jack Knight

Name Index 393

Subject Index 399

Contributors

Jenna Bednar
University of Michigan

William N. Eskridge Jr.
Yale University

John Ferejohn
Stanford University

Stephen M. Griffin
Tulane University

Russell Hardin
New York University

James Johnson
University of Rochester

Jack Knight
Washington University in St. Louis

Sanford Levinson
University of Texas, Austin

Pasquale Pasquino
New York University

Jack N. Rakove
Stanford University

Jonathan Riley
Tulane University

Lawrence G. Sager
New York University

Editors' Introduction

Martin Diamond, the late political theorist, closed a famous essay by reflecting on the "profound distinction" that the essays of *The Federalist* "made between the qualities necessary for Founders and the qualities necessary for the men who come after" (1992, 35). Whereas the act of founding the American constitutional republic had demanded an exceptional exercise in reason, he observed, the conduct of politics thereafter would depend on nothing more exalted than the ordinary play of interest. Diamond's distinction nicely captures the idealized image of constitution making that many scholars still intuitively, and perhaps even uncritically, share. In this view, considerations of stability and justice alike should encourage constitution makers to transcend the particular interests they represent. If they cannot be expected to step behind a Rawlsian veil of ignorance, where they will be uninformed of the social position they will occupy in the new regime, they should at least recall (to borrow a phrase from John Marshall) that it is a constitution they are drafting, not some ordinary piece of legislation. The establishment of a successful constitutional regime thus demands substantial self-restraint; its authors have to expect more of themselves than they do of their successors, the "posterity" for whose benefit framers, in the heroic account, struggle.

A satisfactory political theory of constitutionalism can well agree, with Diamond, on the importance of the initial deliberative processes through which a constitution is adopted. But such a theory can hardly stop there. It also calls for a satisfactory interpretation of constitutional history. That is, it has to ask not only how constitutions are adopted, but also how the norms they embody first gain acceptance and then retain legitimacy amid the political buffetings of those "who come after." Much of that constitutional history can doubtless be written in conventional terms, as a story of the resolution of early disputes, the setting of essential precedents, and the evolution of procedures for adjudicating later controversies. But each of these facets of constitutional theory and history presupposes something

1

2 *Editors' Introduction*

else: a commitment to constitutionalism as important in itself. How that commitment takes hold can be described as the production of a constitutional *culture*, which may well prove as vital to the stability of a constitutional regime as any of the more familiar factors scholars routinely analyze.

The further we stand in time from the foundation of the particular constitutional regime we are studying, the easier it may be to accept Diamond's sharp distinction between founders and followers. But founders are usually the first to follow themselves. Even when, as in the American case, the very authority of a constitution depends on its having been framed and ratified by bodies specially convened for those purposes alone, constitution makers must assume that they will attempt to exercise power under the document they are framing and/or ratifying. When they do, they face the fundamental challenge that the creation of a constitutional culture must answer. On the one hand, they must feel some obligation to promote the constitutional norms that they have just sought to establish. On the other, to advance the policies they favor, they have strong incentives to treat the constitution instrumentally, typically by stressing the authority of whichever branch or department seems most conducive to their interests or most amenable to their influence.

Among the constitutional founders who wrestled with this dilemma, the best known may well be James Madison – whose contributions to *The Federalist* were, of course, the basis for Martin Diamond's reflections. A brief consideration of Madison's concerns during the decade following the adoption of the federal Constitution will illustrate the general themes that many of the essays in this volume address.

A MADISONIAN PARABLE

In April 1787 Madison described his pet scheme to vest Congress with an unlimited negative on all state laws as "the least possible encroachment on the State jurisdictions" that a new constitution might make. The rejection of this proposal by the federal convention in Philadelphia was one reason why Madison initially believed that the Constitution would "neither effectually answer its national object nor prevent the local mischiefs which every where excite disgusts ag[ain]st the state governments."[1] A decade later, however, Madison found himself drafting the Virginia Resolutions, which urged the state legislatures to embark on a campaign to oppose the offensive Alien and Sedition Acts of 1798. Over time, these resolutions, along with the even more militant Kentucky Resolutions drafted by Vice-

---

[1] Madison to Washington, April 16, 1787, in Rakove 1999, 81; Madison to Jefferson, September 6, 1787, in ibid., 136.

President Thomas Jefferson, came to be regarded as the locus classicus of exactly the sort of states' rights theories that Madison, the nationalist of 1787, would have rejected out of hand (and did in fact roundly criticize in the years to come). How Madison seemingly moved so far in his thinking within the space of a decade obviously poses a serious question for Madison's biographers. But more than that, it offers a revealing early commentary on the problem of adjusting constitutional intentions and expectations to the messy uncertainty of political life and the lessons of experience.

The course of politics during the first decade of government under the Constitution challenged Madison's initial assumptions in two crucial ways. First, the ongoing foreign policy crises generated by the wars of the French Revolution revealed that the executive posed a far greater danger to the stability of the constitutional order than Madison had calculated. In his original view, the popularly elected House of Representatives was the one institution most likely to "encroach" on the just powers of the other branches; but from 1793 on, Madison increasingly realized that the executive could exploit crises of national security to gain a decided advantage over Congress. Second, and more important, the success of the Federalist Party in gaining control of all three branches of the national government called into question the fundamental premise of the Madisonian federalism of 1787–8: that durable factious majorities would be far less likely to coalesce at the national level of politics than within the smaller compass of the individual states. Once he recognized that a factious party, "whether amounting to a majority or a minority of the whole," had seized control of the government, Madison had no choice but to reconsider his starting positions. Whatever this process of reconsideration indicates about his theoretical consistency, it speaks well for his intellectual honesty – as well as his ongoing concern with securing the authority of the Constitution (rightly interpreted).

It would be easy to explain Madison's problems in the 1790s in primarily political and biographical terms, as the result, say, of his falling under the dark star of Thomas Jefferson, with his Frenchified nonsense; or of a genuine Anglophobia; or of his envy of Alexander Hamilton's success in gaining the ear and confidence of President Washington; or of the continued political strength of Anti-Federalism in his home state of Virginia.[2] Plausible as these explanations might be, none of them will help us to grasp the distinctively constitutional aspects of Madison's trajectory in the 1790s, much less measure their significance for our own understanding of how constitutional regimes take hold even when their

---

[2] For some examples, see McDonald 1974, 68–81; Elkins and McKitrick 1993, 79–92.

4   *Editors' Introduction*

establishment immediately gives way to periods of intense partisan competition. What do Madison's reconsiderations reveal about the process of converting the textual Constitution of 1787 into a working set of practices and understandings?

Let us begin by stating the basic challenge that events posed to Madison's original constitutional theory. That theory rested on at least these crucial positions. First and foremost, the creation of an extended national republic embracing a diversity of interests would secure the essential liberties that Americans cherished by providing the long missing cure for the peculiar propensity of republican government to fall prey to the "mischiefs of faction." Second, "auxiliary precautions" against the abuse of national power could be found in the various modifications of the pure separation of legislative, executive, and judicial power that the Constitution had engineered. Officials in each of the major institutions of national government would have both a jealous stake in protecting their particular functions against the "encroachments" of their rivals, and the means to do so. Third, the most likely sources of impolicy, injustice, and encroachment lay in those institutions that were most susceptible to the fluctuating interests and passions of the people: the national House of Representatives and the state legislatures. If that was the case, it seemed unlikely that the people at large could be expected to protect the landmarks of constitutional government against disequilibrial encroachments. Fourth, and somewhat more synthetically, against these dangers, mere statements of constitutional principle (such as formulaic affirmations of the separation of powers or bills of rights) were only so many "parchment barriers," of marginal use at best if institutions were not designed to channel the real swirling forces of republican politics.

By 1798 nearly all these propositions, except the last, had been tried in the balance and found wanting. The passage of the Alien and Sedition Acts indicated either that the likelihood of a minority tyranny was higher than he had supposed, or that the protection that the extended nature of the republic was supposed to supply against the danger that a factious majority might capture the government was grossly inadequate. With the Federalists firmly in control of all three branches of the national government, the structural, ambition-checking-ambition protections of *Federalist* 51 seemed no more effective. Under these conditions, there seemed no choice but to attempt to mobilize the people not simply to reverse unwise Federalist policies but also to rally around the Constitution itself.[3] If the people were to be mobilized, Madison understood that the

---

[3] To be sure, this position posed much less of a problem to Jefferson than it did to Madison. In *Federalist* 49 and 50, Madison had gone out of his way to criticize Jefferson's proposals for appealing to the people to correct errors in constitutional interpretation.

"parchment barrier" of the Bill of Rights would have to play the traditional role that he had once been skeptical it could actually fulfill in a republic: providing the people with a standard against which they could judge the excesses of their governors.[4] But with Federalists using the Sedition Act to make war on that "palladium of liberty," the free press, how could the people get a clear view of that standard – unless the state legislatures, the institutions Madison had once been so quick to condemn, could in turn be prevailed upon to protest Federalist misrule? That, of course, was the political strategy to which Madison and Jefferson turned in 1798, drafting the Virginia and Kentucky resolutions that respectively urged the other state legislatures to mount an effective political opposition or even to impede the operation of the protested acts.

That strategy had not been manufactured from whole constitutional cloth, however. Madison had in fact anticipated it, at least in academic terms, in *Federalist* 46. There he had argued that "ambitious encroachments of the federal government on the authority of the State governments would not excite the opposition of a single State, or of a few States only. They would be signals of general alarm. Every government would espouse a common cause. A correspondence would be opened. Plans of resistance would be concerted." In 1788 Madison had clearly imagined that the states might indeed provide an effective recourse to the abuse of national power – though then he had doubted whether such a recourse would prove necessary. Now events suggested that he had been even more prescient than he had realized at the time. But even here, his proto–states' rights position was found wanting. For the other states – generally dominated by Federalists, too – did not rise to the occasion. They spurned the Virginia-Kentucky invitation, leaving the fate of the constitutional republic to ride on the outcome of the election of 1800. In response to the rebuff of the other states, Madison drafted the so-called Report of 1800, defending the original resolutions, and suggesting that the states, in "their sovereign capacity" as the original parties to the federal compact, could never renounce their authority "to decide in the last resort, whether the compact made by them be violated."[5] Whatever the fair meaning of these remarks, they and the original resolutions they defended acquired a life of their own, providing John C. Calhoun with a foundation for his doctrine of nullification.[6]

Madison's trajectory after 1787 is replete with the ironies, unintended consequences, and agonizing reappraisals that make constitutional history

---

[4] Madison to Jefferson, October 17, 1788, in Rakove 1999, 418.

[5] Report of 1800, in Rakove 1999, 608–63.

[6] For Madison's repudiation of Calhoun's doctrine of nullification, see Madison, "Notes on Nullification, 1835–36," in Hunt 1900–10, 9:573–607.

6   *Editors' Introduction*

so inherently interesting a subject – but which also illustrate why the birth pangs of a constitution involve more than the labor of delivering it into the political world. At the outset, Madison had hoped that the unavoidable ambiguities in the meaning of the Constitution would be "liquidated" gradually as the new government plotted its initial course and set key precedents. But history, in its cunning, made that process more difficult and divisive than he anticipated. In part this was because interpretive questions proved more difficult and divisive than he had foreseen, even allowing for his disappointment over the plan as adopted. But it was also because political events did not stand still while constitutional procedures were ascertained and tested. Had political controversies been confined to issues like the assumption of state debts and the establishment of a national bank, it is possible that Madison's original hope for constitutional gradualism would have been fulfilled. But the French Revolution created a host of more pressing questions, rich with symbolic possibilities and ideological overtones, that reopened earlier disputes with a new urgency. Federalists and Democratic-Republicans quickly came to regard each other as partisans of foreign powers and the dangerous ideologies they represented. Under such circumstances, not only was any effort to create stable norms of constitutional interpretation bound to be deeply politicized; the defense of one view of the Constitution or another could easily become a mere instrumentality of political conflict.

The striking aspect of this first decade of constitutionalized politics and politicized constitutionalism, however, is that it did not destroy the underlying American inclination to idealize the authoritative stature of the Constitution. By contrast, in revolutionary France a very different attitude toward the authority of constitutions prevailed. With the American example(s) before them, the members of the National Assembly also ventured to "fix" a constitution for their new republic. But that effort repeatedly failed, because the imperatives of the revolutionary emphasis on the ongoing sovereignty of the national will always prevailed over the prudential desire to establish a durable institutional framework of government.[7] However sharply the former American revolutionaries divided over the interpretation of their Constitution, and however much these divisions might have sparked speculation about its durability, the fundamental American concept of a constitution as an extraordinarily authoritative instrument of government remained unshaken.

That fact, taken by itself, may well identify one crucial component of what it means to establish a constitutional culture (at least on the American model). But that in turn should not disguise or relegate the importance of another facet of constitutionalism. In the abstract, a con-

---

[7] Baker 1990, 252–305.

stitution should operate to constrain the costs of political conflict by fostering fundamental confidence in its institutions and procedures. But until its meaning is itself settled, and a satisfactory set of precedents established, disagreements about a constitution may do as much to exacerbate controversy as to restrain it. In the context of the 1790s, the tendency of each party to view its antagonists as advocates of Anglo-monarchical or Gallo-Jacobin principles raised the potential costs of constitutional disagreement by suggesting that their positions, if adopted, would subvert the Constitution's true meaning. In 1793 and again in 1796, the absence of an underlying consensus about the constitutional allocation of national security powers added a fresh dimension or layer of conflict to the existing disagreements over policy. Far from dispelling suspicion about the rival motives of the opposing parties, constitutional disagreement, or simple uncertainty, operated to inflame suspicions and raise the stakes of conflict.

Yet even amid the presumed "paranoia" of the 1790s, with insidious motives being ascribed all around, both Federalists and Republicans opted to seek advantage not through a strategy of exit but rather by exploiting potential opportunities within the Constitution itself. Both parties quickly discovered a strong incentive to convert the untested mechanisms of presidential election into an occasion for political innovation. In 1787 no one had expected the presidency to emerge as the crucial focus for national political competition, but by 1796, and even more so by 1800, it was evident that control of the executive was essential to control of the government. If one purpose of the Constitution was to advance a process of national integration, the invention of successive electoral games to capture the presidency was an essential ingredient in fashioning a constitutional culture. With some qualification, the same claim can be made for the defensive strategies that both parties had to pursue in their bleaker moments: Republicans by turning to the state legislatures in 1798, Federalists by packing an expanded federal judiciary in 1801. American constitutionalism does not require one set of political actors to be consistent in favoring one forum of decision over another; indeed it should benefit from circumstances that force political competitors to exchange strategies, so long as they remain committed to finding the constitutional niche that will best protect their interests.

The original American experience, and James Madison's trajectory within it, thus illustrate why constitutionalism can never be described as a mere matter of founding, no matter how wise the founders or how principled their deliberations. The acceptance of a constitutional text which must be in its nature incomplete or open-ended requires the development of interpretative canons that are themselves likely to reflect political, historical, and cultural factors as much as legalistic methods of textual analysis. These features of constitutionalism underscore the fragility of

8 *Editors' Introduction*

any nation's constitution, however it is represented textually, by revealing how its interpretation lies hostage to future fluctuations in meanings and shared understandings. In the United States, interpretative disputes did not, of course, end with the Civil War. Indeed, battles over constitutional interpretation have resulted in other critical "moments" of constitutional change: Reconstruction, the New Deal, the "rights revolution" of the midtwentieth century. As Bruce Ackerman has noted, only a few of the changes we associate with these "moments" have left textual marks on the Constitution, and these textual changes underdescribe the changes that occurred. More often, more profoundly, what changed is how the Constitution was understood. This circumstance is not peculiar to the United States and alerts us to the necessity of understanding constitutionalism or constitutional politics as an ongoing and continuous process. This is not to say beginnings are unimportant. But they are only beginnings.

The contributors to this volume analyze and discuss various aspects of the ongoing process of constitutional democracy. Before outlining the concerns of the respective chapters, however, we first attempt to clarify some basic ideas that we think are central to any understanding of constitutional government and, in particular, constitutional democracy. These basic ideas compose a common conceptual framework which is more or less taken for granted by the contributors. Our clarification does not pretend to settle all important questions pertaining to constitutional democracy. Rather, it is intended to promote further thinking, including critical assessment of the contributors' arguments.

SOME BASIC IDEAS

Constitutionalism as a Social Process of Interpretation

Constitutionalism, in practice, is largely a process of interpretation conducted within a community whose members share political power and jointly seek to determine what a constitution permits or requires in specific instances. But interpretation of what? And by whom? It is much too narrow a view, we think, to identify constitutional interpretation with the exegesis of one or more documents by courts, although that is certainly an important aspect in many countries. The place of some founding document within a political system is itself fixed by prior or background conventions or understandings and does not flow from any properties of a piece of parchment. By the same token, constitutionalism does not require a commitment to a particular methodology of textual construction. As American practice amply illustrates, a variety of interpretative strategies can flourish within a single constitutional system, helping to generate the constrained level of conflict that maintains the vitality of the constitutional commitment itself. Constitutionalists may, without self-contradiction, adopt either literalist or open-ended modes of textual construction. We think it is important to understand the interpretation of constitutional *texts* as only one part, and perhaps not always the most significant part, of constitutionalism.

Constitutionalism must be understood as involving historical and cultural interpretation, as well as textual exegesis, in that the meaning of a constitutional text depends on the context to which it is to be applied. For example, when deciding whether campaign spending is like political speech, courts need to consider actual campaign practices themselves, as well as public beliefs and expectations about these practices. It is not that texts are unimportant. Everyone would agree that texts can constrain plausible interpretation. Words, if they are to retain any useful social purpose, cannot mean just anything we say. But how they constrain depends, intrinsically, on how their meanings are construed in practical circumstances.

Constitutionalism must also be understood as involving political theorizing. Even if no one actually recognizes campaign spending as speech, it is necessary to understand how it functions within the electoral regime. If campaign spending generally conveys information, and if its regulation prevents some people's views from entering public debate – if, in effect, it operates like speech in unrecognized ways – that is surely a (defeasible) reason for courts to treat it like speech. Which regulations on spending or contributions should stand or fall should, moreover, consider the purposes that the First Amendment is supposed to serve (itself a deeply controversial matter). Perhaps even more controversially, the constitutionality of regulations might also depend on a consideration of their consequences for the political system more generally. Brutally put, a campaign regulation might be constitutionally justified in terms of its desirable effects on the political system.

Thus, constitutionalism has both backward- and forward-looking elements. It looks backward in that it necessarily involves historical and cultural interpretation to construe the force of constitutional texts (whether they are thought to enhance or limit governmental authority). It looks forward in considering the effects of proposed laws on the functioning of our political system and public life. The backward-looking element is sometimes considered the province of justification and legality, whereas the forward-looking aspect is seen as the domain of the practical and useful.

Constitutional systems differ greatly in how they divide constitutional from ordinary law. Systems with written constitutions often rely on procedural tests that identify as constitutional norms those which have entered the text according to accepted higher-order rules of

10 *Editors' Introduction*

ratification and amendment. But such a formal test cannot be necessary. Constitutional norms can be "implied" or can arise interpretatively. Moreover, the higher-order rules that govern constitutional development are themselves in need of interpretation. Procedural tests are probably not sufficient either. Again, the American example contains numerous procedurally legitimate clauses that seem without normative force, at least as they are currently understood. For these reasons, the determination of constitutional norms seems unavoidably to involve substantive judgment and interpretation within the interstices of the formal rules. The text and the formal procedures for changing it are a starting point for this effort. They may constrain it but they are not the end of it. We think of the discourse by which such determinations are made as that of constitutional theory.

Constitutional Governments and Cultures

Any particular form of constitutionalism makes reference (at least implicitly) to a constitutional political system or government, a constitutional culture, and a constitutional theory. We shall define a *constitutional political system* as a two-level system of political norms and rules such that the higher-level elements (called "constitutional") are supposed to be superior in legal and/or moral force to the lower-level elements (called "ordinary"); and such that the "constitutional" norms and rules place binding legal and/or moral limits on the scope of authority granted to any group of government officials (including legislators, administrators, and judges) to create "ordinary" norms and rules (including statutes, regulations, and orders) or to settle the meaning of "constitutional" ones when conflicts arise. This basic idea of a constitutional government is complex and requires further elaboration. But it is distinct from any idea of the constitution as a mere blueprint of how power is actually allocated among existing institutions. The actual allocation of power in a society may deviate significantly from the allocation prescribed by the higher-level norms and rules composing the constitution as we understand it.

A *constitutional culture* is a web of interpretative norms, canons, and practices which most members of a particular community accept and employ (at least implicitly) to identify and maintain a two-level system of the appropriate sort. We might speak of various cultures (or levels of culture) correlating to different communities within society, including a highly sophisticated culture associated with judges and other members of the legal profession as well as a perhaps cruder popular culture associated with the community at large. In any case, the line between constitutional culture and constitutional government will not always (or perhaps even often) be sharp. The concept of culture is the more encompassing of the two, we think, meant to include norms and rules of interpretation as well as the institutions and practices of the government. But we do not insist on a sharp distinction and, indeed, wish to emphasize how blurry any line must be.

A *constitutional theory* seeks to explain or justify a constitutional culture and its associated form of government. It seeks to identify the higher-level norms and rules that are accepted as "constitutional" in a particular society, for example, and to provide insights into the various mechanisms that are employed – or could be introduced – to limit the authority of any group of government officials. As the diverse essays in this book suggest, there are many different forms of constitutionalism in the world today and there is every reason to think that abundant untried possibilities remain to be explored. When it comes to constitutional governments, cultures, and theories, diversity is the order of the day.

A constitutional government, as we understand it, is a distinctive type of political and legal system. Not every political and legal system displays the two-level structure of norms and rules that we regard as essential to constitutionalism. Even if H. L. A. Hart is correct to claim that every legal system presupposes a "rule of recognition" by which valid laws in that system are identified by the courts and others, for example, it would not follow that every legal system is a constitutional system in our sense.[8] Hart's two-level structure is distinct from ours: a "rule of recognition," as he understands it, can be associated with a political and legal system that does not involve any binding limits – legal or moral – on the authority of government officials to create statutory norms or settle the meaning of the constitution. According to his approach, for instance, the rule of recognition accepted by the courts and by the community might stipulate that every command of Brutus the King is a valid law. Such unlimited government authority is incompatible with constitutionalism, in our view. Thus, although our idea of a constitutional government is "thin" and can accommodate a wide variety of more specific forms and structures, it is not empty.

The difference between Hart's framework and ours is important and worth spelling out a bit further. In our view, a political and legal system is a constitutional one if and only if it distinguishes between constitutional and ordinary political rules such that the former constrain what can count as valid examples of the latter and also place binding limits – legal or moral, as the case may be – on the share of authority that any group of government officials has either to create valid ordinary rules or to settle the meaning of constitutional rules. The constitutional rules – legal or moral – cannot properly be ignored or dismissed by government officials

---

[8] See Hart 1961; 1982, 220–68; and 1983, 343–64, esp. at 359–62.

12 *Editors' Introduction*

in a constitutional culture. The cultural norms and practices accepted by most people in the community generally contradict any claim by some officials that they have unlimited authority to pass statutes and regulations or to dictate constitutional meanings when conflicts arise. Granted, officials may have some room for maneuver. After all, they do have a share of authority, and constitutional rules must be interpreted on a continuing basis. But the interpretative norms and practices composing the culture also have bite to some extent, and no group of officials has all the authority to resolve conflicts.

In contrast, a Hartian rule of recognition, though it is superior in an important sense to the ordinary laws of the community (because it supplies the criteria of legal validity), does not necessarily place any binding limits – legal or moral – on the authority of a group of officials to pass valid laws or settle the meaning of the constitution in the face of opposition from others. As already indicated, any command issued by an absolute ruler might be recognized as a valid law or a proper interpretation of the frame of government. Alternatively, unlimited legal and moral authority might be recognized as residing within an elected assembly. Absolute rule by elected representatives is no more a constitutional government than is absolute rule by Brutus, in our view. Rather, any group of officials must have limited authority and the limits must somehow be enforced by suitable mechanisms – separated powers, independent judicial review, formal barriers to constitutional amendment, or some other mechanism – even if no particular one of these various possible mechanisms is viewed as essential to a constitutional government per se.

We have argued that a constitutional government features constitutional norms and rules that are superior in force to ordinary laws. This superiority does not imply, however, that constitutional imperatives nullify ordinary legal commands when conflicts arise. A statute inconsistent with a state's written constitution may or may not be illegal. Whether illegality follows from unconstitutionality depends on other features of a governmental system. In some constitutional systems, such as the United Kingdom, the constitutional framework involves (in addition to some basic statutes) a set of conventional normative restrictions and expectations that Parliament and government should generally, but need not invariably, respect. Acts of Parliament that violate such constitutional norms retain their legal force and indeed can have the effect of changing the constitution itself.

In fact, there is a range of intermediate positions between what might be called "legal" and "normative" constitutionalism. Only part of a particular constitution might consist of legally enforceable rules, while the rest contains statements that have only normative or aspirational force. The U.S. Constitution's "guarantee clause" (assuring the states of a republican form of government) and, arguably, the Ninth and Tenth Amendments (reserving unenumerated rights and powers to the people and the states) stand as examples of constitutional provisions that historically have enjoyed little legal force. While there remains controversy on this issue, most commentators regard them as constitutional norms, or principles of interpretation, rather than as rules that either have or could have legal effect. Some also take a similar view of some aspects of the Fourteenth Amendment, seeing in (parts of) it aspirational welfare "rights" that are not fully legally enforced but retain their status as guiding principles of constitutional law nevertheless. Even in a system of government that permits the judicial review of statutes, some constitutional norms, as Lawrence Sager (1978) has argued, may necessarily remain underenforced by the courts. There is always a gap, Sager suggests, between a constitution, conceived of as a set of norms, and the results of constitutional adjudication – between what is constitutional, and what courts have chosen to enforce. The gap arises as much from the practical demands of judging as from the open-ended (abstract or aspirational) nature of many constitutional norms.

For these reasons, it would be a mistake to identify or equate constitutionalism with judicial review. Empowering courts to enforce constitutional clauses is neither a necessary nor a sufficient condition for the development of a constitutional regime. The example of British constitutionalism, like the underenforcement thesis, shows that constitutional norms can have force without any judicial pronouncement, as long as the norms are widely understood and shared within the community of political actors. Officials and citizens alike may guide their actions and expectations according to shared constitutional norms, without needing to resort to courts or judicial process. Even in systems with judicial review, courts must generally rely on the willing compliance of other, more powerful parts of government to enforce their directives. Judicially enforced constitutionalism depends on the same widespread acceptance of certain conventional constitutional norms required for regimes operating without judicial review. In effect, the question of whether a political system can be understood as a constitutional regime depends on the existence of a constitutional culture that contains shared normative expectations about appropriate governmental conduct.

Even in constitutional regimes that authorize judicial review, the courts typically develop ways to limit the legal enforcement of constitutional norms. The U.S. Supreme Court severely limits its jurisdiction, for example, by exercising its complete discretion to grant or deny writs of a certiorari (requests from petitioners to review lower-court decisions). Courts also develop doctrines of justiciability that permit them to limit their role as interpreters of the constitution. Notions of standing, ripeness,

14   *Editors' Introduction*

administrability, and the political question doctrine have all provided the Supreme Court with ample license to remain silent on constitutional issues it prefers to avoid.[9] Even in America, the Court has not claimed – in fact, it has often disclaimed – a monopoly on constitutional interpretation. American constitutionalism, rather than being an extreme example of judicially enforced constitutionalism, is more appropriately located on the continuum between legal and normative constitutionalism, in the same general neighborhood where many other modern constitutional states may be found. As much here as elsewhere, constitutionalism rests on a complex and only partly visible collection of norms and practices of constitutional interpretation – what we are calling a constitutional culture.

We need not assume that a constitutional culture is completely coherent. Widely shared interpretative canons may conflict with one another, and conflicting interpretative ideologies may exist within a well-functioning constitutionalism. Indeed, we are willing to postulate that a degree of conflict is *essential* to the vitality of a constitutional culture.[10] A lack of principled dispute within a culture is more probably evidence of disease than of health. In the absence of systemic coherence, the regulative effect of constitutional law and convention on governmental action may sometimes be uneven and unpredictable but such effects may, nevertheless, still be felt. Ordinary law can be understood to be separate from and subordinate to constitutional norms, and to be limited by these norms, even if everyone does not agree, in all instances, how exactly this is so.

Constitutionalism, in this sense, is a system of interpretative canons, practices, and expectations, in which governmental commands may appropriately be evaluated and justified in terms of higher or deeper principles that themselves are not necessarily sanctioned by courts. Whether constitutionality is ultimately determined by courts or resolved by political debate and whether the relevant choices exhibit much systemic coherence matter less than the idea that statutes and executive orders need this kind of justification. In a constitutional culture, it is not enough that a governmental action has generally good consequences; the action must plausibly be seen as constitutionally permitted in some way. In this sense, in spite of conflict and uncertainty within their constitutional cultures, we

---

[9] Some writers offer a political explanation for internal restraints on judicial review, arguing that courts are wisely or cravenly sidestepping dangerous political issues, but these doctrinal restraints also serve more mundane legal purposes, such as allowing for experimentation and evolution of new legal rules in unsettled areas.

[10] On the other hand, conflict is certainly not *sufficient* for the vitality of constitutional culture. Conflicting interpretative ideologies may well paralyze and even destroy the constitutional system: incompatible northern and southern readings of the constitutional culture eventually erupted in the Civil War.

may think of the United States, Canada, and the United Kingdom as exemplary constitutional governments.

Admittedly, many modern political systems can be considered as constitutional systems on our approach. We think this is a virtue because it allows us a broad platform to examine the diversity of constitutionalisms in the modern world. As long as a government systematically evaluates its laws and actions with reference to higher-level norms and rules (legal or moral) that – among other things – place limits on the authority granted to any group of officials to resolve interpretative disputes, it will be counted as constitutional. As we have already emphasized, however, our approach is not vacuous. To be regarded as constitutional, a political system must affirm that constitutional norms can be separated in principle from ordinary legal commands; and those constitutional norms must distribute power among officials such that no group of them has absolute power to fix the line of separation over the objections of others. Whether or not there is some canonical text, the specification of constitutional norms in the context of a suitable decentralization of authority is necessary to a constitutional regime.

Identifying a Constitution

Much of the action in creating the structures of government and delimiting their authority takes place outside constitutional texts, however conceived, sometimes in statute law, often in interpretations by judges and other officials, and, less visibly, by the establishment of informal conventions or understandings. In short, we must look to a constitutional culture – the practices that a people follow in instituting and constraining their government – rather than to a constitutional text to describe both how a polity actually operates and (something typically quite different) how its citizens believe it should operate. Indeed, in an important sense, the interpretative practices that form much of the substance of constitutionalism must be seen to reach "all the way down" and to involve the citizenry at large, through the people's more or less willing compliance with governmental commands, their involvement in electoral decisions, their participation in governmental actions in juries, and so on.

This point may be illustrated by a brief consideration of the operation of American government today. If one were to ask a political scientist to identify the distinctive or characteristic elements of contemporary American government – the ones that provide the best explanation of its structure and functioning – she would probably point to single-member districts, plurality-rule elections, the structure of the political parties and the party system, the administrative-regulatory state, the interest group system, the president's role as chief legislator, and perhaps the

16   *Editors' Introduction*

development of an extensive civil liberties jurisprudence by the courts. What these governmental features have in common, aside from their explanatory importance, is that they are not fixed or specified in the text of the Constitution. Each arose from the successful assertion of authority, usually by some governmental institution, or sometimes by private citizens or groups, and each subsequently took on a life and importance of its own. Each has a claim to be a part of our constitutional system. Each must be taken account of in any adequate explanation of how power is actually allocated among institutions and of which liberties are or are not securely held by individuals. Each must be evaluated in any adequate justification of how power should be allocated and of which liberties ought to be secured.

So what is in a constitution? What, if anything, is characteristic of a constitutional government? It seems clear that a constitution cannot simply be identified with text: some constitutions, such as Britain's, have only limited textual reference, while others, such as that of the United States, can be identified with the written text only on certain highly implausible theories. We may describe ordinary statutes, executive orders, and administrative regulations as first-order rules – instances of substantive policies – whereas constitutional norms and rules establishing the jurisdiction and powers of governmental departments and agencies (including the judiciary) might be called higher-order rules (or rules about rules). In constitutional government, the determination of higher-order rules is distinguished from that of first-order rules. A constitutional culture recognizes these different orders of rules and includes conventions that facilitate identification of the higher-order rules, as well as interpretation of their scope, operation, and effect. A constitutional theory explains or justifies a constitutional culture. In particular, the theory explains or justifies the considerations surrounding the making, revising, and sustaining of the higher-order rules and distinguishes these considerations from those surrounding ordinary rules and policies.

To describe constitutionalism in this way is not to make the much stronger, and obviously incorrect, assertion that first-order considerations do not, as a matter of fact, enter into the choice of higher-order rules. When choosing a constitutional provision, drafters appropriately try to anticipate the consequences that alternative higher-order rules would have for the production of policies and no doubt they are sometimes successful in this. Still, a constitutional polity does not put its basic institutions up for grabs every time an unpopular or undesirable policy outcome is anticipated.[11] Such polities exhibit a reluctance to engage in constitutional

---

[11] Our defining idea of a constitution does not preclude the possibility that constitutional procedures are selected, and justified, with reference to the general *pattern* of outcomes

rule making, a conservatism of the kind that Madison recommended and Jefferson deplored.

It might be useful to follow A. V. Dicey (1982) and adopt a functional definition of a constitution that permits us to identify (though non-exhaustively) the essential elements that compose a constitution by reference to the aims or purposes that any constitution may be taken to have. Such an approach would permit us to place all constitutions on the same scale, allowing us to identify not only constitutional contents but also functionally equivalent elements of constitutions. In particular, we might propose the following defining idea. A *constitution* is defined as the set of formal procedures for establishing governmental agencies, specifying their limited jurisdictions, establishing how these agencies may take authoritative action, appointing and removing their officers, and specifying how conflicts among constitutional entities are to be resolved. Constitutions may or may not contain explicit provisions for protecting the rights of individuals or such constitutional rights may be located interstitially among the authorized powers of constitutional agencies. This approach allows us to identify certain kinds of norms and rules, whether written or not, as constitutional in the sense of constituting or limiting governmental authority.

But the functional conception of a constitution, however useful it may be for comparative purposes, is restrictive in the sense that, on its account, many textual provisions of particular constitutions – first-order or substantive rules such as the slavery provisions of the U.S. Constitution or the Eighteenth Amendment – appear to be out of place.[12] Such provisions are too narrowly aimed at achieving particular policy outcomes to belong in the normative system aimed at regulating how policy outcomes may properly be achieved. True, such textual statements do, in effect, limit the jurisdiction or authority of constitutional agents, but they do this more or less incidently as a means of achieving a substantive purpose. More controversially, at least nowadays, the functional approach seems to be

---

that they are predicted to generate. But the higher-order procedures cannot be continually revised, even in separate fora and at separate times, merely to produce a desired first-order result in any particular situation.

[12] James Buchanan's constitutional theory, like Dicey's, is proceduralist insofar as he assumes that the content of any constitution will consist of higher-order rules or rules for making rules. Like Dicey, Buchanan makes no explicit attempt to justify this assumption with specific normative argument, but one could imagine a conceptual argument running something like this. In any functioning governmental system one can identify how it is that rules are changed and we simply call the best explanatory account of this phenomenon the constitution of that government. Of course, the problem with this conception is that it imposes powerful conceptual limits on the capacity of a people to achieve constitutional change. Or Buchanan could adopt a normative argument that says that well-functioning constitutions ought not to contain substantive or first-order rules. See Buchanan 1984, 444.

18   *Editors' Introduction*

incompatible with what is sometimes called a "moral reading" (or what we would call a substantive reading) of a constitution. Ronald Dworkin (1986) has argued that the U.S. Constitution should be understood as embodying certain moral principles (treating everyone with equal concern and respect) and constitutional disputes should be resolved in ways that elucidate and give force to this reading. Although Dworkin's moral reading might often have the effect of authorizing or limiting constitutional agencies, it does this only incidently as a means to achieving certain substantive ends.

These considerations suggest that identifying a constitution is not a neutral enterprise but entails accepting if not embracing certain substantive commitments. Constitutional definition depends, unavoidably we think, on constitutional theory – on some particular conception of constitutional culture and of what it is that a constitutional government (or, perhaps, *this* constitutional government) is aimed at achieving. Dicey's functional conception is, then, only one of several candidates for such a theory.

Constitutional Theories

A constitutional theory is, in effect, a way of seeing, or modeling, a constitutional culture. Such a theory explains and justifies what is in a constitution and indicates, in particular, the relationship between the constitutional text (if any) and constitutional contents. Some constitutional theories see constitutions as collections of substantive principles and norms while others regard constitutions as collections of substantively empty procedural norms. The functional theory discussed earlier is a purely proceduralist view of a constitution, whereas Dworkin's moral reading of a constitution is a purely substantive conception. All textual constitutions are theoretical embarrassments in that they plainly contain both procedural and substantive elements, and (pure) constitutional theories need to work hard to suppress disfavored interpretations.[13] Of course, every actual constitutional culture must be understood as embodying both substantive and procedural norms that are found nowhere in constitutional texts. Thus, according to virtually every constitutional theory, the constitutional text will not be coextensive with the constitution.

There are, of course, theories whose proponents claim to be an exception to this observation. Such theories seek to identify the constitutional with what is in the canonical text, using only the contemporary understandings available to its adopters to parse clauses. Textualist theories, in this sense, lack the resources to distinguish procedural from substantive

---

[13] Dicey was at liberty to take a purely procedural view of the British Constitution precisely because of the loose connection of that constitution to particular texts.

Editors' Introduction 19

constitutional elements. A constitution is just what it is. Any particular textual provision simultaneously confers substantive and procedural rights on individuals or agencies, and, lacking an extratextual basis for deciding which procedural and which substantive rights belong in the constitution, strict textualists can only read each clause literally.[14]

But other constitutional theories do distinguish substantive and procedural norms and can, as a matter of construction, give interpretative priority to one or the other. For example, John Hart Ely's (1980) influential theory of the U.S. Constitution sees it largely (though not completely) in procedural terms, as aimed at guaranteeing fair process, legal or democratic, to all citizens who are free to use it to pursue their own substantive agendas (within broad constitutional limits). Courts, for Ely, should confine themselves to ensure that constitutionally mandated processes work in a fair way in the sense of being available to all those subject to the law (as they may or may not have been originally intended to work). Of course, cashing out the underlying conception of fairness at the base of Ely's proceduralism entails putting some (relatively thin) substantive conceptions into his constitutional theory. In this sense, Ely's theory is an example of an impure or imperfect proceduralist theory.

By contrast, Ronald Dworkin (1986) sees constitutions as consisting in norms directed at achieving substantive justice. While courts, for Dworkin, should regulate procedures to ensure fair and equal access, they have a further role to play in ensuring that just results are achieved as well. Indeed, the point of good procedures is to secure substantive values and liberties. Ely's emphasis on procedural aspects of the constitutional text seems plausible if we assume that substantive limits on outcomes (what it is that procedural fairness requires) are likely already to be found within the generally accepted constitutional culture.[15] Dworkin, by contrast, seeks to connect these substantive limits to a conception of justice, by reading the text in light of a particular conception of justice, which he does not take to be already commonly understood or widely accepted. This underlying conception of justice must "fit" with the received constitutional tradition but it must also be grounded in more fundamental moral theory. For him, constitutional law is largely a matter of doing the hard work of determining what justice requires in specific factual circumstances and then using the

---

[14] Textualists are often accused of adopting their interpretative theory for strategic reasons – seeking, for example, a means to restrain judges from imposing their own views on the constitution. We make no such attribution here.

[15] That Ely builds his theory out of Justice Stone's assertion of a judicial role in providing constitutional protections for "discrete and insular minorities" suggests that both Justice Stone and Ely took the identification of these minorities and the violation of their rights as largely self-evident.

20 *Editors' Introduction*

devices of constitutional adjudication to incorporate these requirements into law.

Originalist Theories: Constitutions as Bargains

Constitutions are often thought of as contracts or bargains, reflecting a particular distribution of bargaining power among social entities that may alter (resulting in pressure for renegotiations) over time. Constitutionalism of this kind has a very long tradition, flourishing certainly in the Middle Ages, if not long before, where the idea of the "mixed constitution" expressed a balance of regal, aristocratic, and popular elements. Sometimes, as in the Magna Carta, this balance is located in historical time as a signed deal, struck under circumstances of conflict, among representatives of two or more of these "estates." Often the dispute is between government's desire for revenues or military support, and people's desire to live secure and prosperous lives. Generally, the mixed constitution is thought of as combining the energy and efficiency of "top down" rule with the sensitivity of "bottom up" consent (expressed in the ancient maxim: "quod omnit tangit...."). The mixed constitution is then thought to be a representational structure that appropriately balances these virtues.

Other constitutions have been thought of as bargains among preexisting geographic units, claiming some sovereign dignity and/or regional economic, cultural, or linguistic interests. Constitutional legitimacy in such cases is inherited from the (delegated) juridical authority of previously sovereign units, or located in the fidelity of the newly constituted state to preexisting regional interests. John Calhoun's constitutional theory is a good example here – transmuting constitutional justification from the medieval ideal of balancing "estates" into classical ideas of balancing regional forces.[16]

More recently, at least in liberal states, the constitutional bargain has been seen as involving all the people (We the People, as the preamble to the U.S. Constitution has it), as separate and autonomous individuals. Such a popular bargain is conceived either as an actual historical compact or as a hypothetical deal that never was, but would have been, agreed to by suitably rational agents. Justification of specific constitutional authority then arises from some specific act of consent, whether direct or indirect.

Many traditions see the constitutional bargain as essentially pregovernmental. The contracting parties agree among themselves on a bargain that constitutes a government, endowing it with some powers and

---

[16] Other examples include the ancient Greek federations discussed by Madison and the emerging institutions of the European Community.

placing limits on its authority. Presumably, constitutional violations in such a tradition must ultimately be checked by the people or their agents, because government officials per se are not parties to the deal. Even so, the people may designate certain governmental officials (including an independent judiciary) to act as their agents for this purpose. Alternatively, a constitution may be conceived of as a contract between the people and their government, indicating what powers the people "agreed" to delegate to government officials in return for valued governmental services. Here governmental officials would seem to have obligations to keep to the agreement, and, possibly, some officials may be counted on to keep others in line.

Many writers, and probably most citizens, suppose that the origins of a constitution ought to influence (or even to determine) how it should be construed. This idea – constitutional originalism – has played a major role in constitutional interpretation in American history but it features in other constitutional traditions as well. Originalism comes in many flavors: some variants place the original textual understandings of constitutional bargainers in a privileged position – examining clauses in minute and historically situated detail to see what might have been meant by "cruel and unusual" punishment or "due process" of law. Other originalisms focus more broadly on what the original players were attempting to accomplish in setting up a new constitution. Originalism can be more or less forward looking in this sense: if the purpose of a constitution is to permit a people to balance liberal rights with democratic rule, current moral conceptions may outweigh earlier understandings.[17] Thus, this brand of "purposive" originalism is a dynamic as opposed to static textual originalism.

Originalists also differ in their interpretations of the mechanics of the bargaining process. The American case is, again, instructive. How do we weigh the relevant authority of the actual framers of the Constitution, who often acted as if they were bargaining agents for their individual states, against the understandings of the delegates in the separate state ratification conventions? Whose understanding of the reputed bargain that produced the original amendments to the Constitution matters more: that of the Anti-Federalists, who insisted that an unamended text would be dangerous to liberty, or that of their condescending Federalist opponents, who finally and reluctantly

---

[17] The classic example here is whether the Fourteenth Amendment should be understood, as the *Brown* Court understood it, to prohibit legally segregated public schools. That it was not understood to have that effect by its drafters is evident from the facts that public schools in the post–Civil War era were generally segregated, and that there is no evidence that any of the amendment's proponents suggested that this circumstance would change after the amendment was adopted.

22   *Editors' Introduction*

added a "bill of rights" to the text largely to still the Anti-Federalist clamor?[18] How well can we in fact identify the contracting parties in any constitutional bargain?

Whatever form an originalist doctrine may take, it remains just one kind of constitutional theory – one way that a constitutionalism may evolve that regulates and anchors ordinary legal commands – and it underdetermines such a culture. Saying that a constitutional theory is originalist is to leave open many important questions about it. For one thing, we would still have to ask why later generations continue to profess fidelity to the perceived original meaning of their constitutional charter, rather than develop circumlocutions and circumventions to avoid the dead hand of the past. Nevertheless, some originalist assumptions seem to undergird most constitutional traditions. The constitutionalisms discussed here mostly share the assumption that constitutional norms are somehow anchored in what particular people at some earlier time said, agreed, and understood they were doing. Each contains the idea of a founding bargain – mythic or not – that helps to fix at least the form of constitutional inquiry. Even the nontextualist English Constitution has often been understood in these terms: the constitution of post-1689 Glorious Revolution England supposed that some particular set of "founding moments," including 1215, 1642, and 1689, had set liberty-loving Englishmen on their special course.

Constitutionalism and Democracy

If the constitution (textual or otherwise) is seen as a popular compact, whether between citizens in a prepolitical situation or between the people and government officials, two rather different views of the goals of the constitutional system may be taken. What might be called a pessimistic perspective sees the constitution largely as a device to restrain, if not thwart, government. According to this perspective, the main purpose of constitutions is to limit government power, including the authority of elected officials to work their will. Here jealousy of state power, suspicion of official motivation, and anxiety to protect individual liberties should all be the watchwords of constitutional construction. Government, on this account, is a dangerous business, made necessary perhaps by the fallibility of human nature or the dangers of a treacherous world, but requiring the utmost vigilance. As such, there is an argument to construe constitutional norms – at least those rules that surrender authority to governors – narrowly, in terms of an explicit charter. Other norms – those which

---

[18] For further discussion of some of the problems involved in ascertaining the original meaning of the U.S. Constitution, see Rakove 1996, esp. 7–22, 94–160.

declare individual liberties or which specify how officials are required to make themselves accountable to the electors – ought, on the other hand, to receive a more generous or expansive construction, even if they do not find their way into a written document. Indeed, if the constitution is seen as a text proposed by officials themselves to a relatively uninformed public, the pessimistic view recommends construing the whole document against the "adventurer," understood as the party who offered the contractual terms. Just as in commercial law, where courts commonly construe contracts against the adventurer, governmental powers under a constitutional contract should be construed against government officials, who may reasonably be assumed to be the parties most interested in unduly expanding those powers.

Against this pessimistic (or "antifederalist") view of constitutionalism stands another more optimistic perspective. That other ("federalist") view sees a constitution as a compact in which the people give up (at least conditionally) some of their precontractual rights to create an instrument of government that will enable them to undertake valuable projects collectively that they might otherwise have to forgo. A constitution, on this view, creates and lends vigor to governmental institutions and permits them to work on behalf of the people to deal with a future that is filled with unknown and unanticipated problems. Although there may be a need for protection against official malfeasance, governmental powers ought to receive a more generous construction, one that is open to revision as the future unfolds. Reliance should be placed on elastic open-ended interpretations that permit a people to face and solve their common problems. Rights and liberties are vulnerable to official machinations, of course, but rather than putting faith in the power of a mere (judicially enforced) parchment barrier to protect these liberties, the structure of the constituted government should be arranged to trigger automatic defenses. The defense of liberties on this account rests on the separation of powers, checks and balances, federalism, political competition, and the like. Clauses of a text, however ancient, would in any case be inefficacious against a government turned rapacious or tyrannical. Limiting official powers and protecting individual rights are on this view not matters of written provisions literally interpreted but of the political science of institutional design. Besides, to put too much emphasis on particular powers and rights is to ossify these claims and, often, to unduly privilege people and groups that have done well in the past, against new claimants. Entrenched powers and rights tend to protect existing structures of power and wealth, and to limit the capacity of a people to shape their destiny.

These two strands of constitutionalism are firmly embedded within American political history, though both are usually not simultaneously

24 *Editors' Introduction*

visible to most observers of our politics. Both can be traced to the very beginning of the republic. On the one hand, we see repeated displays of popular suspicion not only of federal institutions but also of state and local officials, from Shays to the Sagebrush rebellions. On the other, we also see intermittent popular enthusiasms for affirmative governmental programs, illustrated by Henry Clay's American Plan, the New Deal, and the Great Society. Moreover, depending on which strand we emphasize, constitutional democracy will tend to be viewed either as a muddled form of government at war with itself or as a liberal form of popular government that is likely to be more effective and fair than popular government without constitutional constraints. From the pessimistic perspective, separated powers, independent judicial review, and other checks and balances tend to appear as essential brakes on a dangerous government that, however democratic in form, is inclined to violate the rights of the people. From the other perspective, however, these same mechanisms tend to be seen as more or less prudent devices that may activate and energize a better sort of democratic government, by making officials as well as the popular majority itself more informed and concerned about *everyone's* rights and interests (including those of minorities).

There is, of course, nothing in this dualism that is peculiar to the United States. An analogous interpretive battle occurred between James I and his chief justice and parliamentary rival, Edward Coke, as to the nature of the "ancient" English Constitution (and as to whether subsequent events had compromised it). Constitutions, in every place they exist, simultaneously create and limit governmental institutions, place them in circumstances of competition and cooperation, endow their occupants with motivations and perspectives, and situate them in relation to the people. Or at least so it seems. The bargaining perspective on constitutions is, then, a powerful one within the Western tradition because it provides a way of going beyond texts to make use of other historical materials. How exactly it does so turns on identifying the nature of the bargain, the parties involved, and how their interests were engaged in the bargain. These issues are deeply political in that their resolution fixes much about the nature of the polity itself.

We think it important to stress that a constitution serves as much to create and empower governmental institutions as to place limits on the actions of governmental officials. Indeed, modern work in game theory and economics suggests that by placing limits on official action, a constitution can actually increase, not diminish the capacities and powers of governmental agencies. By restricting the ability of officials to renege on agreements, a constitution may permit a government to make credible commitments to repay its debts, to maintain a stable money supply, and to make credible threats of retaliation.[19] By limiting governmental discretion, a constitution may also permit government to do justice to individuals and minority groups, even in the face of momentary political passions pointing in another direction, thereby ensuring their allegiance to the state where it would otherwise be uncertain. In this way, a constitution may simultaneously enhance the capacity of a people to embark on courses of action that would otherwise be foreclosed to them, and protect fundamental rights and liberties. Constitutions can thus empower and legitimize the state by placing restrictions on the actions of its officials.

Of course, a constitution cannot create commitment capacity unless it is relatively difficult to change. Herein lies a fundamental problem of constitutional design. Constitutional change can be effected in two ways: through formal amendment or through interpretation. If a constitutional text is difficult to amend, those officials in a position to interpret the document – whether courts, legislatures, or agencies – may have a great deal of latitude to change the meaning of the text through interpretation. In that case, there may be no great difference between a system with a text and one without. If, on the other hand, the text is easy to amend, interpretative latitude may be diminished at the price of an increased frequency of amendment. But then the text itself mirrors more or less frequent changes in interpretative conventions and practices. In either case, the constitution (including nontextual elements) will be relatively changeable and therefore relatively ineffective in creating commitment capacity. How to develop a democracy-enhancing constitution – one that enhances the powers of the people to achieve their shared purposes without subjecting

---

[19] The characteristic problems of dynamic planning received early attention by Strotz (1956) in the context of a Robinson Crusoe economy. He showed that except under very special and unusual circumstances, Crusoe's optimal dynamic consumption plan was necessarily unstable in the sense that, when the time arrived for him to consume something prescribed in the plan, Crusoe would prefer some alternative choice and therefore revise his plan. Dynamic plans were shown to be, in this sense, incredible because Crusoe would foresee that he would not consume according to his plan when the time came to eat. The implication of Strotz's article was that because rational agents could not commit to executing plans in the future, they could not achieve optimal policies and would have to settle for a "credible" plan: one that would rationally be executed. Kydland and Prescott (1977) showed that because optimal plans cannot generally be executed by rational agents, they would rationally choose among sustainable plans, which often entails using rigid rules rather than more flexible policies. More recently, the game-theoretic literature on the intractability of the "sovereign debt" problem, which points to the incapacity of sovereigns to commit to debt repayment and therefore to attract financing for their investment schemes, suggests that the absence of commitment capacity is a barrier to economic development. See, e.g., Bulow and Rogoff 1989. More generally in the context of the theory of constitutional democracy, see also Holmes 1988.

26 *Editors' Introduction*

them too much to the arbitrary shackles of a past electorate – is therefore a delicate question of political science.

No matter how these issues are resolved, there remains the question of how an original bargain, however it is described, is relevant for us today. Why should a historicist theory of a constitution, any more than a text, have any normative force for us? By what authority do parties to the original contract, if one exists, bind their heirs or followers? We stand in the relation of third parties to the deal and cannot reasonably have had our precontractual rights (if we have any) transferred by the mere fact of a contract, to which we did not consent. True, the value of commitment capacity is that it permits the people of a nation to attain the benefits of policies that they would otherwise have to forgo. The problem is sometimes posed as one of continence or self-control, in which an agent may increase his capacity to achieve goals by preventing himself from yielding to certain temptations, as in Jon Elster's *Ulysses and the Sirens* (1979). But in the case of a nation, the people whose actions are restrained by a constitution are not necessarily those who adopted it; and those "who come after" (in Martin Diamond's phrase) may well be made worse off by prior constitutional choices, especially when they lack effective political influence. While a constitution may provide commitment capacity, it may do so only by limiting the capacity of future generations to make their own choices as to what kind of a collective life they wish to live. Entrenching constitutional provisions or making them difficult to amend diminishes the capacity of "The People" today to take responsibility for their nation's actions and is, in that respect, undemocratic.

In fact, it seems that the only way to leverage the bargaining metaphor into actual legality is through its being a good idea – a deal by which, in the cool light of deliberate reflection and without the distractions of private interest, we ourselves would have agreed to be bound. Once we make such a move, a constitutional contract can be viewed as an ongoing bargain, an evolving hypothetical agreement among different generations of rational persons who at any time share certain interpretative norms and practices. Such persons, of any generation, may repeatedly reaffirm, as well as renegotiate, the agreement as their shared culture evolves, even if there is no single actual text from which the series of hypothetical contracts emanates. Thus, beneath the vision of the constitution as contract, there must stand a deeper willingness to adhere to a constitutional culture that produces good results. This willingness should reflect something more than an aversion to the uncertainties of substituting a new constitutional bargain for the old one; ideally, it should also express a positive commitment to the existing constitutional arrangements on their merits.

Good results can be understood in two ways: substantively or procedurally. A constitution may command its political creatures to produce

Editors' Introduction

substantively just outcomes, however understood, and that it does so is a reason to respect its commands. Or, a constitution may establish procedures that enable us to deliberate and make decisions as morally autonomous members of a political community. Whether the outcomes of these decisions are substantively just will depend on our virtue and care as citizens.

These central themes of constitutional culture and democratic rule are discussed from various critical perspectives by the contributors to the present volume. No attempt will be made to summarize the eleven chapters, which are organized into three separate parts. But an indication of the nature of the arguments is provided by way of conclusion.

PART ONE: CONSTITUTIONAL BEGINNINGS AND TRANSITIONS

As our opening allusion to Martin Diamond's essay suggests, scholars often set up a sharp distinction between the foundation of a constitution and its subsequent implementation and interpretation. The enterprise of framing a constitution involves one kind of politics, making it stick and work another. But this dichotomy may well ignore or undervalue two essential components of the process of establishing and legitimating a constitutional regime: first, the extent to which residual uncertainties about how a constitution will work in practice shape its inaugural period of operation; and, second, the need to deploy existing traditions within a culture or even invent new ones to provide the formal mechanisms of governance with deeper sources of popular support and attachment.

The first of these concerns lies at the heart of Rakove's opening chapter, where the problems to be solved fell under the heading of what Madison called the "vices of the political system of the United States." Most efforts to recover the essential tenets of Madisonian theory begin (and usually end) with the classic essays from *The Federalist* that are commonly regarded as authoritative statements of the original theory of the Constitution. By examining the mixture of political and constitutional concerns on which Madison was acting in 1787–8, Rakove identifies a number of uncertainties in his thought that complicate the meaning of these familiar extracts from *The Federalist*. As hard as Madison worked to convince his colleagues of the merits of his own constitutional proposals, he met defeat on a number of key issues, and these in turn left him fearful that the proposed Constitution might prove far more problematic than the public language of *The Federalist* might suggest. For the purposes of this book, this account of Madison's political thinking has several significant implications. First, the paradigmatic influence that Madison's writings exert over modern commentaries on the American Constitution

28 *Editors' Introduction*

– which is itself illustrated in the chapters by Riley and Pasquino – makes any well-grounded historical effort to recover the complexities of his thinking worthwhile in itself. Second, historical evidence that this exemplary model of a constitutional founder was intensely aware of the uncertainties of any scheme of institutional design confirms our basic supposition of the difficulty, not to say impossibility, of treating the establishment of a constitutional regime as a onetime achievement. As Madison well understood, all sorts of political problematics remained to be resolved after the Constitution was formally ratified. But, in the third place, it was this experientially informed awareness of the difficulty of fashioning satisfactory constitutional settlements that also alerted Madison to the importance of placing the original Constitution on as high and secure a pedestal as possible. Leery of the capacity of the people at large to abide by the constitutional norms he valued most, fearful of the costs of energizing popular politics around constitutional controversies, and doubtful of the capacity of the weaker branches of the executive and judiciary to withstand the "impetuous vortex" of legislative encroachments, Madison would certainly have welcomed cultural veneration of the founding as an essential component of constitutional stability.

A recognition of the importance of developing cultural traditions to maintain the authority of new constitutions is also the central question that Johnson addresses in Chapter 2. As his point of departure, Johnson disputes the "fatalist" view of post-1989 Eastern European politics, which predicts that resurgent ethnic tribalism is likely to triumph, sooner or later, over efforts to establish liberal democratic constitutions of the kind that Western Europeans and Americans would prefer. But why should we assume that these ostensibly primitive blood loyalties should prevail, he asks? Drawing on the recent writings of historians and anthropologists who have described how seemingly venerable cultural traditions were in fact invented at particular moments in historical time, often for explicitly political reasons, he proposes that the project of establishing stable constitutional regimes must include a strategy of redeeming older symbols of attachment, or creating new ones, if it is to withstand the recourse to ethnic chauvinism that rival political actors will predictably make. While conceding the difficulty of this challenge, Johnson concludes that the historical resources available to constitutionalists are far less impoverished than the pessimists would suggest; and in any case, if the strategic use of cultural traditions (long-standing, recovered, or invented) is ineluctably a component of any constitutional transition, there seems to be little alternative to considering how they might be deployed.

In Chapter 3, Sager reminds us that the framers of the U.S. Constitution invented their own ratification procedure, which required the consent of nine of the original thirteen states for the Constitution to come into effect for the ratifying states, as a way around the legal formalities of the Articles of Confederation, which required unanimous consent among the states to amend the terms of the Confederation. The successful deployment of this novel ratification formula was associated with the rise to prominence of a powerful symbol of popular sovereignty, namely, the idea of special ratifying conventions or assemblies elected by the people solely to consider proposed constitutional rules, which, if ratified, would thereby be recognized as legitimately superior in cases of conflict to ordinary legal rules (including statutes as well as the Articles) enacted by legislatures.[20] The apparent willingness of the founding generation to allow, if not encourage, simple majorities in nine special state conventions to transcend the standing legal requirements of the Articles approved unanimously by the state legislatures has led some modern commentators to argue that the U.S. Constitution itself can be amended or even replaced by a suitable process of simple majority rule, independently of the formal requirements of Article V.[21]

Sager offers many cogent criticisms of this modern simple majoritarian view of what he calls "the birth logic of a democratic Constitution," that is, the view that a commitment to democracy requires a political community to admit that its constitutional arrangements can be altered at the will of a simple majority after suitable discussion and deliberation. He argues that the legal requirements of Article V are an appealing part of "the pragmatic, justice-seeking quality of our constitutional institutions." Against the idea that a simple majority has a general right to amend a democratic constitution by extraconstitutional means, he defends the rather Lockean idea that the majority has a limited right to revoke a constitutional regime when there is widespread agreement that the regime has broken down. In his view, the founders must have (rightly or wrongly) "believed themselves at the point of breakdown or something very much like it" to have acted as they did, on the one hand relying on popular sentiment to justify ignoring the legal formalities of the Articles and, on the other hand, insisting on a complex supermajoritarian procedure to

---

[20] A special convention in a single state can, by ratifying proposed state constitutional rules, confer legal supremacy on those rules over conflicting enactments of the state legislature. But no legal supremacy is thereby conferred on state constitutions over conflicting enactments of Congress (at least if we ignore the discredited state compact theory of the union advocated by Calhoun and other southern radicals prior to the Civil War). At the national level, ratification by special conventions in a supermajority of states is required to confer supremacy on proposed national constitutional rules over conflicting enactments of Congress or of the state legislatures.

[21] See, e.g., Amar and Hirsch 1998, 3–47. They argue for the legitimacy of amending the Constitution by a national initiative and referendum process. Proposed amendments would become part of the Constitution if approved by a simple majority in a national referendum.

30 *Editors' Introduction*

legitimately amend the new Constitution. Still, when it comes to popular support for proposed changes in written constitutional rules, Article V makes demands similar to those of the novel ratification formula. Members of the founding generation demanded of themselves what they demanded of subsequent generations on this score, it seems.

PART TWO: CONSTITUTIONAL STRUCTURE AND DESIGN

Our authors here are concerned mainly with the effects of alternative constitutional arrangements, and, ultimately, with the choice of an appealing constitutional structure. The perspective adopted is essentially that of the constitutional designer – the interested citizen as much as the lawgiver – who attempts to assess the effects of alternative systems of rules, with a view to understanding and perhaps reforming whatever constitutional code prevails in the given cultural context.

Riley, in Chapter 4, the first of two contributions, sketches an abstract two-stage game-theoretic framework for analyzing any form of constitutional democracy. At the first stage, rational individuals jointly select a constitutional code from some set of possible codes, by imagining themselves behind a suitable veil of ignorance. The cultural norms that shape their constitutional consensus may be specified in a wide variety of ways. But Riley assumes (for the sake of illustration) that the norms are utilitarian. At the second stage, individuals compete to achieve their respective personal aims, by playing strategies permitted by the constitutional rules. To select an optimal constitutional code for their society, individuals at the first stage must be able to predict how individuals at the second stage will interact under the alternative codes up for consideration. Alternative constitutional structures can then be compared in terms of the equilibrium outcomes that are predicted to arise under their respective rules.

A question of broad interest concerns the elements of an optimal constitution in any given social context. Which forms of election systems and legislative voting rules should be established? Which individual rights (if any) should be protected in the constitution? Riley goes on to outline different versions of the general transactions cost approach to these matters, which require much further study. The general approach seeks to design institutions so as to minimize the sum of such costs as decision-making costs, costs of being excluded from winning coalitions, and costs of acquiring information.

In Chapter 5, Riley makes use of the two-stage framework to analyze a distinctive Madisonian form of constitutional democracy and to compare it with more familiar American and parliamentary alternatives. Remarkably, Madison and other leading figures at the Philadelphia

Convention favored a constitutional structure in which Congress would have ultimate control over constitutional interpretation but would also be checked by a constitutional council of revision, comprising both the chief executive and the supreme court judges. If the council arrangements had been established, the federal judiciary would not have any legitimate claim to have final say over the meaning of the constitutional text. Riley's comparative analysis provokes us to consider the possibility that such a Madisonian option might foster a more stable and effective liberal democracy than that associated with the U.S. Constitution. The more general point is that even our most settled constitutional rules and practices should not be viewed as sacrosanct. Rather, they ought to be assessed critically and tested against potentially superior alternatives.

In Chapter 6, Pasquino also points us toward comparative exercises of this sort, by investigating the distinctive version of separation of powers that enters into the design of the modern Italian Constitution. He suggests that the Italian version of the doctrine is a hybrid of traditional French and American doctrines, in which American-style checks and balances are absent and there is no traditional French-style hierarchy with judges serving as the mouth of a sovereign legislature.[22] In his view, the three branches of Italian government are more or less equally powerful, with the caveat that the independent judiciary includes both prosecutors and judges. Moreover, the constitutional structure is safeguarded by an extraordinary Constitutional Court, to which any ordinary judge may refer cases for review if he thinks unconstitutional laws are implicated.[23] According to Pasquino, the fate of liberal democracy in Italy may well depend on the incentives of this powerful judiciary to check increasingly aggressive partisan majorities. This invites us to critically assess the Italian constitutional structure and consider whether more appealing structures might be feasible in that social context.

Bednar, Eskridge, and Ferejohn in Chapter 7 are interested in the conditions under which federalism, understood as a constitutional division of sovereign authority among distinct governmental units, can flourish, yielding efficacious national government in combination with the advantages of local autonomy. When rules of federalism may reasonably be expected to produce the effects they are designed to produce, they suggest, society's

---

[22] The traditional French understanding of separated powers has apparently undergone considerable modification under the Fifth Republic. The emerging new understanding is arguably some distinctive mixture of incongruous American and traditional French ingredients as well. See Rohr 1995, 44–67, 93–137, 189–206, 242.

[23] Like the Constitutional Council created under the Fifth Republic of France, the modern Italian Constitutional Court is reminiscent in some ways of the federal council of revision recommended by Madison for America. But there are also important differences among these review bodies.

32   *Editors' Introduction*

commitment to a decentralized political structure is credible, and the federal bargain is likely to endure. After examining political practices in Britain, Canada, and the United States, they argue that two conditions are necessary (and perhaps jointly sufficient) for durable federalism.

First, national forces must be restrained from infringing on the federal bargain, often, if not always, by a suitable fragmentation or separation of powers. The necessity of this condition is illustrated by the case of Britain after 1832, when decentralized political practices (which had emerged earlier, despite the absence of any explicit federal bargain) largely disappeared with the rise of an unrestrained (both legally and structurally) national Parliament. Second, provincial temptations to renege on federal arrangements must be checked as well, possibly by the application of legal rules enforced by an independent judiciary.[24] The necessity of this condition is illustrated by the case of Canada after 1949, when the termination of the Judicial Committee of the British Privy Council as a final court of appeal for federal-provincial conflicts arguably led to increased provincial anxiety and dissatisfaction over the federal compact and its enforcement.

Bednar et al. claim that both conditions have been satisfied (with some local variation) in the United States since the time of founding, and that this circumstance has contributed substantially to the durability of American federalism. They imply that America's rare success in this regard is linked to its peculiar hybrid of structural and juridical protections for federalism. More specifically, the national government and the states are *each* restrained from violating the federal bargain, by a "double whammy" of separation of powers (present within both levels of government) and an independent federal judiciary willing to interpret the legal terms of the bargain (perhaps contrary to the wishes of both national and state officials). That double whammy may well explain, at least for the most part, why American political practices have successfully evolved to permit continuing cooperation between national and state governments.

PART THREE: CONSTITUTIONAL CHANGE AND STABILITY

Constitutional texts are usually difficult to change. Article V of the U.S. Constitution is perhaps extreme in requiring numerous special majorities to form at separated moments in time to amend the Constitution's text. While other kinds of constitutional change can occur without such action

---

[24] The use of judicial checks on the provinces is probably only one method of restraining them. The provinces might themselves develop fragmented systems of power that prevent them from opportunistic behavior. While such a system might be possible, it seems hard to believe that every province will be sufficiently restrained over the long run to solve the credibility problem.

Editors' Introduction 33

– through shifting meanings of words as well as by means of changes in background assumptions and conditions of application – these other kinds of change seem to occupy a different place in the constitutional firmament than change brought about through formal amendment. As Bruce Ackerman (1991; 1998) has reminded us, it is not so clear that changes wrought through interpretation or changing circumstances are any less profound or any more controversial than those that come about according to amendment processes. But it does seem likely that constitutional amendment, because it provides a formal and democratic process by which the people may purposely change their laws, deserves a special kind of respect. Yet how much respect is due to extraordinary processes that are freighted with requirements for special majorities, aimed explicitly at limiting direct input by the people?

Our authors propose several ways of thinking about this issue. In contrast to Sager, who sees nothing intrinsically antidemocratic in the difficult Article V procedures and indeed sees these procedures as devices that enhance and solidify democratic rule, Levinson, in Chapter 8, argues that there is no good normative or interpretative reason to make our Constitution as difficult to amend as it is. For him, Article V places far too many restrictions on the people's ability to amend their Constitution and the cost of doing this is to create numerous other modalities of constitutional change. These other modes of constitutional change are, in their own fashion, as undemocratic as the Article V requirements are.

Levinson goes on to ask whether the Article V procedures should be reformed and, if so, how. Should Article V be supplemented or replaced by a national initiative and referendum system, for example? Should the states continue to be involved as states in the national amendment process? Should congressional simple majorities be sufficient to propose amendments, unless the president vetoes? Is it necessary to follow Article V in order to make any legitimate changes to Article V itself? In his exploration of these matters, Levinson suggests that multiple amendment rules might coexist in a constitution. In particular, he seems to favor "a two-tier system" in which basic rights such as freedom of speech would remain difficult to amend, whereas term limits and "other structural features" could be amended more easily. Although fights are likely to erupt over what counts as a "basic right," such a system might encourage judicial control over changes in basic rights while discouraging it over changes in other political matters.

Whereas Sager writes of a constitution as a legal instrument for seeking and maintaining just arrangements, and Levinson sees it as an instrument for permitting a people to exert maximal influence on their collective affairs, Griffin views a constitution in terms of the norms and practices of

34 *Editors' Introduction*

the three branches of government as well as other surrounding institutions. In a wide-ranging discussion in Chapter 9, he deflects our attention away from normative questions relating to the ease and frequency of formal amendments, toward normative and practical questions concerning informal processes of change in the broader institutional norms and practices. He contrasts his own "historicist, state-centered perspective on the development of constitutional institutions" with a "legalistic" perspective that overemphasizes the importance of formal amendments and/or putatively impartial judicial interpretations. The legalistic approach depicts both amendments and judicial interpretations as being on a higher plane than the play of ordinary interest-group politics. Both are seen as preserving a sacred text from corruption by biased everyday political forces.[25]

To illustrate his thesis that the legalistic approach has given rise to a fundamentally misleading vision of an "unbroken American constitutional tradition" centered on judicial interpretation, Griffin focuses on the New Deal. He claims that the New Deal amounts to a "constitutional revolution," involving crucial changes in our understanding not only of the constitutional role of the central government in managing the national economy but also of the powers of the presidency and of federal-state relations, and that this great break in the tradition was engineered by the political branches in response to popular sentiment. A revolution occurred in our everyday democratic norms and practices, even though it was not reflected in formal amendments and should not be treated (as Ackerman would have it) as being on a par with Article V amendment. This democratic revolution eventually forced the judiciary to adapt its reading of the legalized Constitution to fit with these fundamental political changes. Griffin argues that the judiciary did not begin as of 1937 to "restore" some earlier legal tradition of the Marshall Court, as some legal scholars maintain, but rather adapted the legal rules to conform to the new political reality manifested by the Depression generation's overwhelming support for expanded government regulation of the economy. His more general point is that the judiciary cannot be expected to control innovations in democratic institutional norms and practices that take place "off text." Rather than serve as a powerful gatekeeper, it must ultimately bend to the political branches and popular sentiment. Even so, it seems clear that the judiciary can exert some influence over broader constitutional understandings through its recognized authority to expound the legal text, especially when basic rights and other legal norms are implicated.

Like Griffin, Hardin sees a constitution as part of a larger political economy. For him, a key aspect of a constitution is whether it enhances

---

[25] Griffin (Chapter 9, in this volume) reads Ackerman as subscribing to a subtle version of the "legalistic" perspective.

or limits the powers of governments relative to other social and economic agents. If the American and a few other experiences are indicative of current and future prospects of successful constitutionalism, he maintains in Chapter 10, we must conclude that the best constitutional arrangement for handling economic transitions is to leave the economy relatively free of government management. Constitutional flexibility is, from this perspective, undesirable in that it permits the government of the day the opportunity to intervene too often in economic processes. A government that attempts to run the economy is likely to be tarnished with economic failure because state interference will put the nation at a competitive disadvantage to other nations whose economies are less encumbered. Although he does not ask whether a constitution that permits the development of a prosperous economy is democratic, he leaves little doubt that the people would generally have better lives if they lived under such a constitutional regime. For example, it was impending economic failure that finally broke the Soviet regime, he suggests, rather than seven decades of sometimes brutally illiberal social and political control.

Knight's purpose in Chapter 11 is to try to provide an explanation for how amendable a constitution is. He notes, rightly, that the world's constitutions are enormously variable in this regard, with a few like the U.S. Constitution requiring arduous procedures that are rarely successfully invoked and many others that require only the actions of legislatures without ratification. He argues that a key to understanding why some constitutions are made hard to amend is the level of political heterogeneity of the founding generation. Homogeneous founders are likely to produce abstract and hard-to-change constitutions, while more heterogeneous constitution writers will tend to write more specific constitutional provisions and make them easier to change. Knight's explanatory framework may help to understand the deep disagreement between Sager and Levinson, in that Sager's emphasis on justice, something that presumably we all agree to seek, emphasizes the social consensus that is found at the root of even modern societies. Levinson's insistence that democracy comes first reflects a belief that it is up to the people themselves to decide what it is that government should and should not do, and this decision will depend on the divergent preferences of citizens in a modern society. The implications for Hardin's argument are that constitutions drafted in modern pluralistic conditions are unlikely to place sufficiently firm restraints on governmental powers to permit the people to flourish economically. Moreover, according to Griffin's historicist state-centered approach to constitutional change, we cannot expect the judiciary to preserve impartially any firm restraints that may have been drafted and ratified in earlier times, when citizens were more homogeneous.

REFERENCES

Ackerman, Bruce. 1991. *We the People: Foundations.* Cambridge, Mass.: Belknap Press of Harvard University Press.

1998. *We the People: Transformations.* Cambridge, Mass.: Belknap Press of Harvard University Press.

Amar, Akhil Reed, and Alan Hirsch. 1998. *For the People: What the Constitution Really Says about Your Rights.* New York: Free Press.

Baker, Keith Michael. 1990. *Inventing the French Revolution: Essays on French Political Culture in the Eighteenth Century.* Cambridge: Cambridge University Press.

Buchanan, James M. 1984. "Constitutional Restrictions on the Power of Government." In James M. Buchanan and Robert D. Tollison, eds., *The Theory of Public Choice II,* 439–52. Ann Arbor: University of Michigan Press.

Bulow, Jeremy, and Kenneth Rogoff. 1989. "A Constant Recontracting Model of Sovereign Debt." *Journal of Political Economy* 97: 155–78.

Diamond, Martin. 1992. "Democracy and *The Federalist*: A Reconsideration of the Framers' Intent." In William A. Schambra, ed., *As Far as Republican Principles Will Admit: Essays by Martin Diamond,* 17–36. Washington, D.C.: AEI Press.

Dicey, Albert V. 1982. *Introduction to the Study of the Law of the Constitution.* Indianapolis: Liberty Fund.

Dworkin, Ronald. 1986. *Law's Empire.* Cambridge, Mass.: Belknap Press of Harvard University Press.

Elkins, Stanley, and Eric McKitrick. 1993. *The Age of Federalism.* New York: Oxford University Press.

Elster, Jon. 1979. *Ulysses and the Sirens: Studies in Rationality and Irrationality.* Cambridge: Cambridge University Press.

Ely, John Hart. 1980. *Democracy and Distrust: A Theory of Judicial Review.* Cambridge, Mass.: Harvard University Press.

Hart, H. L. A. 1961. *The Concept of Law.* Oxford: Clarendon Press.

1982. *Essays on Bentham: Jurisprudence and Political Theory.* Oxford: Clarendon Press.

1983. *Essays in Jurisprudence and Philosophy.* Oxford: Clarendon Press.

Holmes, Stephen. 1988. "Precommitment and the Paradox of Democracy." In Jon Elster and Rune Slagstad, eds., *Constitutionalism and Democracy,* 195–240. Cambridge: Cambridge University Press.

Hunt, Gaillard, ed. 1900–10. *The Writings of James Madison.* Vols. 1–10. New York: G. Putnam Sons.

Kydland, Finn, and Edward Prescott. 1977. "Rules Rather than Discretion: The Inconsistency of Optimal Plans." *Journal of Political Economy* 85: 473–91.

McDonald, Forrest. 1974. *The Presidency of George Washington.* Lawrence: University Press of Kansas.

Rakove, Jack N. 1996. *Original Meanings: Politics and Ideas in the Making of the Constitution.* New York: Knopf.

1999. *James Madison: Writings.* New York: Library of America.

Rohr, John A. 1995. *Founding Republics in France and America.* Lawrence: University Press of Kansas.

Sager, Lawrence G. 1978. "Fair Measure: The Legal Status of Underenforced Constitutional Norms." *Harvard Law Review* 91: 1212–64.

Strotz, Robert. 1956. "Myopia and Inconsistency in Dynamic Utility Maximization." *Review of Economic Studies* 23: 165–80.

PART ONE

CONSTITUTIONAL BEGINNINGS AND TRANSITIONS

1

Constitutional Problematics, circa 1787

Jack N. Rakove

Modern commentators on the U.S. Constitution of 1787 generally share two broad but closely related sets of assumptions about its origins. First, we tend to ascribe a high measure of coherence and purpose to the original intentions and understandings upon which the framers and ratifiers of 1787–8 acted. We regard the Constitution not only as the bundle of bargains required to replace the "imbecile" union of the Articles of Confederation with an effective national government, but also as the expression of a deeper body of norms, values, and expectations that together constituted a coherent and integrated theory of a federal republic. This belief has in turn sustained seemingly endless searches for the true sources of these norms in different intellectual traditions, modes of thinking, or "discourses." Second, in reconstructing this theory, scholars often emphasize the extent to which the Constitution was designed to establish a set of self-enforcing and self-correcting mechanisms that would preserve the general stability of the constitutional system against the vicissitudes of time and fortune. The constitutional scheme of checks and balances (embracing both the separation of powers and federalism) was contrived to maintain an enduring equilibrium while permitting gradual adjustments to take place (through either Article V amending procedures or judicial review) without blunt trauma. This scheme would neutralize the "mischiefs of faction" that so alarmed James Madison and other framers, thereby demonstrating that it was entirely realistic to extend the republican form of government to the dimensions of an expanding national empire of quasi-sovereign states.

Together, these two broad sets of assumptions provide the basis for what might be called a pure theory of the American Constitution. I use the term "pure theory" advisedly – and admittedly quite loosely – to capture the somewhat abstracted way in which many modern commentators, especially legal scholars and political scientists, have described the original intentions and understandings of 1787–8. This pure theory places

42   *Jack N. Rakove*

a remarkable (though not undeserved) emphasis on the ideas of James Madison, especially as they were encapsulated in his best-known writings, the essays of *The Federalist*. It assumes that these views represent an authoritative, accurate, and relatively unproblematic account of the underlying concerns that gave meaning and purpose to the spare prose of the constitutional text. This conviction of the representative character of Madison's ideas may itself be not only arbitrary but highly problematic, but it has become such a convention in the modern interpretation of the Constitution that one can hardly imagine what an alternative account of "the founding" would look like.[1]

As a historian, I propose to offer a more complicated account identifying sources of uncertainty and contingency in the original constitutional design. From the vantage point of two centuries, practitioners of other disciplines may feel that the most authoritative and celebrated statements of the founding are sufficient for our purposes, but historians have a nasty knack for insisting that a more complicated story always merits telling. Accordingly, after an initial account of some of the uses to which a "pure theory" may be put, the succeeding sections of this chapter consider several potential sources of "impurity" in the original theory of the Constitution. The chapter first considers which elements of the institutional design of the Constitution were originally regarded as most problematic or uncertain. It then identifies those sources of political tension within the early American union that posed the greatest threat to its stability, and asks whether these were as susceptible to the Madisonian solution of an extended republic as the pure theory, stated independently of particular conflicts, might suggest. The final section examines how the framers approached the problem of securing the legitimacy of the Constitution as a partial remedy mitigating the potential institutional defects and political tensions that the debates of 1787–8 exposed. Each of these questions is treated in a way that will make Madison a more complicated, and therefore more interesting, thinker than he sometimes appears.

THE FEDERALIST AND THE PURE THEORY
OF THE CONSTITUTION

The belief that *Federalist* 10 and a handful of the other essays that Madison and Alexander Hamilton wrote as Publius offer a paradigmatic

---

[1] For a noteworthy dissent, see Kramer 1998–9, which argues at some length that this emphasis on Madison is misplaced. In my view, Kramer places too great an emphasis on the absorption of Madison's ideas during the public debates over ratification and not enough on the agenda-shaping role he played in the actual drafting of the Constitution. For a different view, see Rakove 1996, 35–93.

statement of the original theory of the American Constitution is a twentieth-century construct. Earlier readers of *The Federalist* had neglected the essays we now examine with painstaking care, while directing their attention instead to topics that modern commentators largely ignore.[2] The conviction that Madison's best-known essay was the interpretive key that would unlock the deepest purposes of the framers of the Constitution can be traced largely to Charles A. Beard, who made it into something of a proof text in his *Economic Interpretation of the Constitution* (published in 1913, and still arguably one of the most influential works of American history ever written). But in the years following its publication, more subtle interpreters took a different tack. As the late Paul F. Bourke (1975) argued in a brilliant essay in intellectual history, the absorption of *The Federalist* as a serious work of political theory occurred when a distinguished cadre of social scientists, beginning with Harold Laski, developed what came to be known as the pluralist theory of democracy. The culmination of this approach to *Federalist* 10 came in the opening chapter of Robert A. Dahl's *A Preface to Democratic Theory* (1956, 4–33), which converted Madison's eighteenth-century distinctions into a set of determinate hypotheses that modern political scientists (like Dahl) could rigorously test. While conceding that it was "a little unfair to treat Madison as a political theorist" when he was "up to his ears in politics, advising, persuading, softening the harsh word," Dahl nonetheless analyzed *Federalist* 10 as a "compactly logical, almost mathematical, piece of theory" (1956, 5), and he thereby set a precedent that other scholars have followed.[3]

Even while Dahl was writing, however, two other scholars – one a historian, the other a political theorist of the Straussian persuasion – were launching important efforts to restore *The Federalist* to its historical context. Commentators sometimes disagree whether Douglass Adair deserves greater credit for this than Martin Diamond, but there is no need to quibble over this point when the net result seems evident. Operating from somewhat different perspectives, both struggled to locate Madison's writings within the context of a venerable debate, running from the writers of classical antiquity to Montesquieu and Hume, over the comparative virtues and vices of republican and democratic forms of government. It was Adair, in particular, who worked hardest to challenge Beard's reading of *Federalist* 10, just as other revisionists were undermining Beard's claims about the actual propertied interests at play in

---

[2] For a discussion, see Rakove 1987c. A case can be made that the early authority of *The Federalist* rested primarily on the extensive use that Justice Joseph Story made of them in his *Commentaries on the Constitution of the United States* (1833).

[3] For a critique of Dahl's reading of Madison, see Riley 1990.

44 *Jack N. Rakove*

1787–8.[4] In their different ways, however, both Adair and Diamond anticipated what soon became the dominant motif in historical writing about the events that political theorists portentously call "The Founding," and which historians prefer to label as the "republican experiment" of the revolutionary era.

Together, Adair, Diamond, and Dahl laid the groundwork for a veritable cottage industry of commentary and reinterpretation revolving around *Federalist* 10 and the other seminal essays that codify the theory of the Constitution, especially Madison's reformulation of the separation of powers in essays 47–51 and Hamilton's discussion of judicial review in *Federalist* 78. Other essays come under review only when some pressing issue of contemporary concern requires a quick interpretive foray into the "original meaning" of the Constitution.[5] But recourse to the entire corpus of eighty-five essays became serious enough to convince a major university press to publish a concordance of *The Federalist* – surely a remarkable (if now obsolescent) tribute to its authority (Engeman, Erler, and Hofeller 1988).

What purpose does this scholarly preoccupation with *The Federalist* serve? Our interest does not rest on the belief that these essays played a major role in the ratification of the Constitution, for there is little evidence that they exerted any influence over the public debate. Americans responded much more directly to the concise statements that a handful of other framers published in the months after the convention adjourned.[6] We get closer to an answer when we consider the authoritative status that Madison and Hamilton command not only as leading framers and ratifiers in 1787–8 but also as partisan adversaries during the great political falling-out of the 1790s. But the deeper sources of the authority of *The Federalist* lie elsewhere. When all is said and done, its eighty-five essays are the most comprehensive and lucid commentary on the Constitution that the debates of 1787–8 produced; there is no rival to *The Federalist* in the entire corpus of Federalist and Anti-Federalist writing. Because that is so, these essays enjoy a great virtue of convenience; they offer a defined point

---

[4] The case for Diamond's greater importance is made by Kesler 1987, 14. Diamond's leading essay, "Democracy and *The Federalist*" (1959), was published two years after Adair's Hume essay, which was itself the sequel to his "The Tenth *Federalist* Revisited" (1951). But, then again, we do not expect political theorists to be as scrupulous about the importance of chronology as historians.

[5] Thus in the recent impeachment of President Clinton, *Federalist* 65 and 66 enjoyed a sudden surge in popularity, with predictably meager results.

[6] These would include James Wilson's public speech outside the Statehouse in Philadelphia on October 6, 1787, as well as the dissents of the nonsigning delegates George Mason, Elbridge Gerry, and Luther Martin. For further discussion, see Rakove 1996, 34–8, 142–5.

of departure – a baseline – against which the workings of the contemporary constitutional system can be measured. Much scholarly time and energy are saved by taking *The Federalist* as an accurate statement of American constitutional theory, especially when our true interests lie in the present, not the past.

Viewed in this way, the preeminent power of *Federalist* 10 and 51 also rests on their relative abstraction, which was, after all, what enabled Dahl to convert Madison's propositions into disembodied, notational hypotheses. As Adair and Diamond both understood, Madison was seeking to overturn the received wisdom that held that socially complex and geographically extensive states were inconsistent with the republican form of government, and which also preferred the stability of a mixed government of distinct social estates to a more functional balancing of mere departments and branches of government. He directed much of his argument to circumscribing, qualifying, and co-opting the appeals that could be made to "the oracle who is always consulted and cited on this subject . . . the celebrated Montesquieu."[7] At times, Madison and Hamilton both used empirical data drawn from the American states to intimate that Montesquieu was less relevant to the American case than uncritical admirers believed.[8] But the crucial passages in Madison's essays lack any specific historical referent. In *Federalist* 10 Madison speaks of faction as a problematic factor in "all civilized societies," and *Federalist* 51 operates at a similar level of generality. Is Madison speaking of America in the 1780s, Britain circa 1750, Cromwellian England a century earlier, or the Italian city-states of the Renaissance or the Greek city-states of antiquity? Madison's pretensions for his theory do seem universalist, and if so, Dahl was well within his rights to give the hypotheses of *Federalist* 10 their abstract due.

Nor has Dahl been alone in treating these essays as a sort of pure statement of the original theory of the Constitution. The scholarly literature of law and political science is replete with discussions of Publian theory (or its Madisonian and Hamiltonian variants), some quite sophisticated and insightful,[9] some largely regurgitative, and others so simple and uninformed as to verge on caricature.[10] What nearly all these ventures share is the ambition to extract from these essays, and other supplementary

---

[7] *Federalist* 47, 337. All page references are to Wright's (1961) edition.

[8] Cf. Hamilton's comparison in *Federalist* 9 of the size of the American states with Montesquieu's optimal republic, and Madison's survey of the separation-of-powers provisions of the individual states in *Federalist* 47, 126–9, 338–42.

[9] By way of example, see Nedelsky 1990, 16–66, 141–202, which does not confine itself to *The Federalist* alone; or Epstein 1984.

[10] See Bork 1990, 139–41, which presents a statement of "the Madisonian dilemma" that Madison would be hard pressed to recognize.

materials, not only a coherent statement of an underlying theory, but one that is also either largely depoliticized or overly conceptualized. That is, such interpretations either pay little attention to the immediate political concerns on which the framers and ratifiers acted, or else they assume that the proper context within which these sources are to be read takes the form of a conversation between the founders and other similarly abstract and conceptually powerful authorities (Locke or Montesquieu or Blackstone or Hume being the usual suspects).

These strategies make sense when the imperatives of contemporary writing in law and political science warrant juxtaposing the wisdom of 1787 with matters of more pressing concern. Again, the original theory of the Constitution is viewed primarily as a baseline against which the current operations of the constitutional system or the contending doctrines about its proper functioning can be assessed. This is true even in the case of those "originalists" who argue that the only true meaning of the Constitution is that which was attached to it at the moment of its adoption. For no one in the endless present of democratic society – and especially in a society as nonpatriarchal as America's – proposes to defer to the wisdom of the past merely because it is past; appeals to the past are more likely to operate as clubs to bludgeon the objectionable principles and practices of the present.

Historians have a different agenda. Their obligation is less to present a usable version of the past than to explain and interpret its complexity; less to smooth over the dissonances of old debates than to identify their discordant elements. As Gordon Wood has observed, "It may be a necessary fiction for lawyers and jurists to believe in a 'correct' or 'true' interpretation of the Constitution, in order to carry on their business, but we historians have different obligations and aims." The foremost of these tasks is to explain why "contrasting meanings" were attached to the Constitution from its inception.[11] Insofar as cognate disciplines may feel a need for "pure theories" of the American Constitution, the historian's task is to muddy the waters by introducing unruly streams of contingency and doubt into what would otherwise be too smooth and placid an account.

THE FILTRATION OF TALENT REVISITED

During the debates over the Constitution, both Federalists and Anti-Federalists issued numerous appeals for citizens to be moderate and prudent in their judgments. But only rarely did the participants bother to reflect on the nature of the science of politics, or the inherent difficulties

---

[11] Wood 1987. Wood here draws on an important article by Nelson (1986).

of thinking about political phenomena. Anti-Federalists, perhaps, would not have conceded that political science really was so difficult a discipline. As faithful heirs of the radical Whig ideology that carried the Americans from resistance to revolution in the decade before independence, they tended to think that the basic axioms of politics were well known and universal (Bailyn 1990). The Federalists, as the political entrepreneurs in this process, had the more daunting task of explaining why innovation, and therefore risk taking, were unavoidable; but few even of them bothered to reflect, self-consciously, on what made that enterprise so problematic. The most notable exception to this reluctance can be found in *Federalist* 37 – not one of the classic essays in the canon, perhaps, but well worth reading. In this essay Madison offered a transition from the general advantages and necessity of union that had been the central theme of nearly all the preceding essays, and toward the more clause-bound explication of the Constitution that Publius would pursue thereafter.

With his usual penchant for branching problems in twos and threes, Madison identified three general difficulties that the Federal Convention had met: first, "combining the requisite stability and energy in government, with the inviolable attention due to liberty and the republican form"; second, "marking the proper line of partition between the authority of the general and that of the State governments"; and third, adjusting "the interfering pretensions" of different "combinations" of states. In the midst of the second of these points, Madison compared the essential constitutional task of line drawing between levels (and also among departments) of government with analogous efforts at delineating the "faculties of mind" in metaphysics or the variety of material forms in the natural sciences. Like these other fields, Madison reasoned, political science had to contend with the inherent complexity and "indistinctness" of the phenomena to be studied. In nature those distinctions were (it had to be assumed) "perfectly accurate" – that is, they really existed, and were muddled only by the inadequacy of human senses. When one turned to "the institutions of man," however, "obscurity arises as well from the object itself as from the organ by which it is contemplated," teaching us "the necessity of moderating still further our expectations and hopes from the efforts of human sagacity." Madison illustrated this point by extending his analysis of the difficulty of drawing the lines of federalism to the comparable problem of delineating the three forms of power.

Experience has instructed us that no skill in the science of government has yet been able to discriminate and define, with sufficient certainty, its three great provinces – the legislative, executive, and judiciary; or even the privileges and powers of the different legislative branches. Questions daily occur in the course of practice, which prove the obscurity which reigns in these subjects, and which puzzle the greatest adepts in political science.

48   *Jack N. Rakove*

Similar obscurity reigned in distinguishing the limits of various forms of law. Moreover, Madison continued, language itself interposed a third fundamental problem muddying the clarity of political science. The "perspicuity" that Madison desired in law must always prove elusive because "no language is so copious as to supply words and phrases for every complex idea, or so correct as not to include many equivocally denoting different ideas."

Madison distilled the moral to be drawn from this analysis into a single sentence that speaks volumes to those who think that the meaning of a legal text can be fixed at the moment of its adoption. "All new laws, though penned with the greatest technical skill, and passed on the fullest and most mature deliberation, are considered as more or less obscure and equivocal, until their meaning be liquidated and ascertained by a series of particular discussions and adjudications." Although it might well be true that the processes of constitutional interpretation would diverge from the norms of statutory construction to which Madison alluded, the deeper point he was making remains no less valid. Constitutional meaning, in 1787 and 1788, was no more than a set of predictions and hypotheses that could be validated or falsified only by experience. And that was at least as true of the great principles that determined the underlying constitutional design as the lesser clauses that were more hurriedly adopted or less thoroughly debated.[12]

Reconstructing Madison's ideas about the three departments of government thus suggests that he was less confident of the self-enforcing character of the Constitution than uncritical views of its original theory might imply. Whether one looks at his expectations for the nature of national representation and legislation, or the capacity of the executive and judiciary to withstand the "encroachments" of legislative power, intriguing disparities appear between the prognostications of *The Federalist* and the reservations they bypassed.

A great deal of recent commentary on Madisonian thinking has emphasized his hope to improve the quality of law making in America by recruiting a superior class of lawmakers.[13] This hope was expressed not only in *Federalist* 10 but also in both private writings and speeches *in camera* at Philadelphia, and it certainly was an important element in his thinking. In his reaction against the "vices" he ascribed to the legislators and legislative processes of the states, Madison invoked a mixture of Burkean and republican ideals to offer an image of national legislators who would

---

[12] Quotations in this and the preceding paragraph are taken from *Federalist* 47, 265–72. For further elaboration, see Rakove 1996, 156–60.

[13] The most important statement is Wood 1969, 506–18; for a less tempered statement, see Wills 1981.

transcend the parochial interests of their electors in order to frame laws embodying a true public good representing more than the aggregated preferences of the general population. For Madison, then, a Burkean ideal of deliberation still defined the duty of the legislator, while the republican conception of a general public good remained the object of legislative decisions. Madison thought that a system of elections in which representatives would be chosen by relatively large districts while senators emerged from a more indirect procedure would secure the desired end.

Madison's commitment to bicameralism, of course, presupposed some doubt as to whether these two electoral tracks would operate equally well. Going into the convention, he was probably more concerned with creating a true senate than he was convinced that a popularly elected lower house would withstand the populist impulses of American politics. After all, the belief that large electoral districts would enable distinguished, disinterested candidates to prevail over the wiles of the parochial demagogues he detested in the state legislatures was only a hypothesis, plausible in its arithmetical reasoning but as yet untested. On the other hand, as early as 1785 he had concluded that the most promising solution to the vices of legislation lay in creating upper houses that would be genuinely senatorial;[14] and the importance he placed at Philadelphia on the character of the proposed national Senate was fully consistent with that desire. Yet at the convention, his hopes for the Senate were undercut by the very compromises we are taught to revere. Irked as he was by the idea that the states should have an equal vote in the Senate, Madison was probably more troubled by the convention's early decision allowing senators to be elected by the same state assemblies whose power and influence he hoped to reduce.

Madison failed on this point for several reasons. He had no way to reconcile his commitment to proportional voting in the Senate with the idea that each state deserved to be represented *and* that the Senate should be a small, intimate chamber capable of deliberating in the most sober way. Equally important, he had not solved the problem of how senators were to be elected. In his view, and that of James Wilson, any method was preferable to election by the state legislatures.[15] But nearly every other framer thought that legislative election was the simplest and politically most appealing option the convention could adopt, and Madison and Wilson simply could not convince their colleagues otherwise. Whether a Senate elected by these parochial bodies would acquire

[14] For his early criticism of state legislation, see Madison to Caleb Wallace, August 23, 1785, in Rutland et al. 1962–91, 8:350–5.
[15] On this point, see their comments during the crucial debate of June 7, 1787, in Farrand 1966, 1:150–6.

50 *Jack N. Rakove*

the cosmopolitan character Madison sought for it remained an open question.

A different set of uncertainties surrounded the decisions about the House. Although the delegates often spoke as if they expected the states to adopt a system of district elections, and although the convention could certainly have made such a system a constitutional mandate, the debate over the construction of the lower house was always about the apportionment of representation *among* the states, not *within* them. Rather than insist that the states adopt a district system, the framers merely gave Congress a power to alter state electoral laws in the interest of remedying gross malapportionment. In fact, as Rosemarie Zagarri (1987) has noted, large- and small-state delegations tended to think about mechanisms of popular representation in different ways. Large states were already more comfortable with the idea that states were complex societies that had to be subdivided for electoral purposes if representation was to meet norms of accountability. But small states could still think of themselves as more cohesive, integral units, and thus preserve the idea that it was the people of the state, rather than of lesser communities, that deserved representation. For all his concern with the importance of maintaining equitable apportionment and purifying republican politics, even Madison seemed prepared to allow the states to experiment with the crucial details of electoral law. "Whether the electors should vote by ballot or vivâ voce, should assemble at this place or that place; should be divided into districts or all meet at one place, shd all vote for all the representatives; or all in a district vote for a number allotted to the district; these & many other points would depend on the Legislatures," he observed on August 9 (Farrand 1961, 2:240–1). The general arithmetical logic underlying his theory of the advantages of large districts would still apply; but as with the Senate, Madison's position seems to concede that a potential would always exist for state legislatures to manipulate national elections through their control of rules of voting and districting.

Nor did Madison appear convinced that the shift in the scale of representation from state to national districts would produce the qualitative improvement in the character of legislators that *Federalist* 10 predicted. His writings elsewhere in *The Federalist* imply that members of the House would act much like their counterparts in the states. They were likely to serve a single term, much of which would be spent being brought up to speed in their knowledge and understanding of public issues – and in overcoming the provincial orientations Madison expected most of them would share. In *Federalist* 62, Madison rightly predicted that the House would likely experience the same high rate of turnover, with an accompanying instability in policy, that was already manifest in the states. Nor was this an argument he felt compelled to make solely to justify the existence of a

Constitutional Problematics, circa 1787 — 51

high-toned Senate. For in private letters written as the First Congress was due to assemble, he predicted that it would have many of the same democratic features of the state governments.[16]

THE IMPETUOUS LEGISLATIVE VORTEX

These qualifications suggest the need to treat the extravagant claims made on behalf of the likely superior character of national representatives with some caution. Modern commentators tend to express greater confidence in this theory than did Madison. Moreover, too great an attention to the question of representation may lead us to slight an equally important facet of his thinking: his obsession with the danger of legislative misrule, which was a function both of his concern with the political advantages that representatives would exploit, and of his acutely modern grasp of the fundamental nature of legislative power per se. These dual concerns drove Madison's thinking about the problem of the separation of powers, leading him to doubt whether the new distribution of authority proposed by the Constitution would protect the two weaker branches of the executive and judiciary against "encroachments" emanating from the "impetuous vortex" of Congress. Madison's reasons for fretting over the likely political superiority of the legislature are well known and can be quickly summarized; his concern with the nature of legislative power bears closer examination because it reflects a shift in the purposes for which representative assemblies were convened.

Madison succinctly summarized the political advantages that representative lawmakers would enjoy in *Federalist* 48 and 49. In a republic, he argued in the first of these essays, the greatest "jealousy" should be directed against the "enterprising ambition" of the legislature, "which is inspired, by a supposed influence over the people, with an intrepid confidence in its own strength; which is sufficiently numerous to feel all the passions which actuate a multitude, yet not so numerous as to be incapable of pursuing the objects of its passions" (*Federalist* 21, 343–4). Here Madison addressed, in effect, the psychology of legislative ambition, but in the next essay he turned more directly to the question of influence when he discussed the defects in his friend Thomas Jefferson's proposal to allow two aggrieved departments to call a convention to remedy the constitutional infractions of a third. Believing that the legislature was the most likely perpetrator, Madison concluded that Jefferson's proposal missed the mark because the two weaker branches would almost always lack the political resources of the dominant branch, with its more numerous

---

[16] On this point, see Madison to Edmund Randolph, March 1, 1789, and to Jefferson, March 29, 1789, in Rutland et al. 1962–91, 11:453, 12:38. See my discussion (Rakove 1987a) of this transition from theoretical prediction to practice.

membership. "They are distributed and dwell among the people at large. Their connections of blood, of friendship, and of acquaintance embrace a great proportion of the most influential members of the society. The nature of their public trust implies a personal influence among the people, and that they are more immediately the confidential guardians of the rights and liberties of the people" (*Federalist* 49, 350). How would the less numerous and customarily less trusted branches of executive and judiciary rally similar sources of support?

The superiority of the legislature was not merely political, however. It also "derives," Madison argued, "from other circumstances. Its constitutional powers being at once more extensive, and less susceptible of precise limits, it can, with the greater facility, mask, under complicated and indirect measures, the encroachments which it makes on the coordinate departments. It is not unfrequently a question of real nicety in legislative bodies, whether the operation of a particular measure will, or will not, extend beyond the legislative sphere" (*Federalist* 48, 344–5). This was the deeper problem to which Madison had already alluded in *Federalist* 37 when he lamented the recurring difficulties of distinguishing the proper boundaries of the three departments of power. Its very rule-making authority gives the legislature a potentially decisive legal advantage in compelling the weaker branches to do its bidding, or in circumscribing the proper exercise of their own powers. The pressing need of republican constitutionalism was accordingly to fortify these two inferior departments against the meddlesome intrusions of an overbearing legislature.

Madison's criticism of legislative power was closely tied to his theory of faction in one other respect. Intent as he was on protecting rights of property against the populist tendencies of American politics, he doubted whether any formal limitation of legislative power could prevent willful lawmakers and the majorities they represented from enacting measures inimical to those rights. Madison closed his famous paragraph in *Federalist* 10 describing the sources of faction with a revealing observation: "The regulation of these various and interfering interests forms the principal task of modern legislation." He then proceeded to reflect on the reasons why all such acts were susceptible to the pull of faction. "What are many of the most important acts of legislation, but so many judicial determinations, not indeed concerning the rights of single persons, but concerning the rights of large bodies of citizens?" he asked. "And what are the different classes of legislators but advocates and parties to the causes which they determine?" And the examples he then gave – laws governing debtors and creditors, encouraging manufactures, imposing import duties, and taxes of all kinds – indicate that he regarded *all* forms of economic regulation as potentially intrusive of private rights, and likely to lie beyond the corrective power of courts and executive officials. For as he reminded Jefferson five weeks after the convention adjourned, willful law-makers could always exploit an "infinitude of legislative expedients" to circumvent formal limitations on their power. Moreover, even impartial judges would find it difficult to determine when, if ever, the legislative had exceeded its authority.[17]

This was, on the whole, a strikingly modern notion of what legislatures could do, for it assumed that the chief task of representative assemblies was to make law. It was not a notion that Madison had to piece together from whole cloth. His criticisms of the dangers of republican legislation strongly echoed, and may well have been informed by, the comparable criticism that leading British authorities (Mansfield, Kames, Blackstone) had directed against the upsurge of parliamentary law making in the eighteenth century (Lieberman 1989). It was even more certainly driven by his criticism of the quantity and quality of the legislation that the exigencies of the Revolutionary War and its aftermath had inspired the states to enact, for it was the "multiplicity" or "luxuriancy," the "mutability" and the "injustice" of these acts that led him to question the fundamental majoritarian premises of republican government.[18] Nonetheless, it is equally important to note that this perception of the legislature as a continuous regulator of economic activity carried Madison well beyond the traditional view that saw the legislature more as a check on the executive and a sounding board for local petitions than as the active or dominant force in government. As recently as 1770, as shrewd a commentator as Edmund Burke had repeated the traditional formula when he observed that the House of Commons was originally "designed as a control *for* the people," and that its "true characteristics" remained to provide "a vigilant and jealous eye over executory and judicial magistracy; an anxious care of public money; an openness, approaching towards facility, to public complaint."[19]

From our vantage point, the conviction that its rule-making powers give the legislature a decisive advantage over the executive in the conduct of government would certainly have to be qualified by the experience of mass bureaucracy. Which department has the greater staying power and discretion in supervising the actual implementation of law and policy: the legislature that adopts the basic policy and its accompanying regulations,

---

[17] *Federalist* 10, 131–2; Madison to Jefferson, October 24, 1787, in Rutland et al. 1962–91, 10:211–12. Madison's concern with the security of property is well treated in Nedelsky 1990 and McCoy 1989.

[18] Madison, Vices of the Political System of the U. States, [April 1787], in Rutland et al. 1962–91, 9:353–4.

[19] Burke, *Thoughts on the Cause of the Present Discontents* [c.1770], in Kurland and Lerner 1987, 1:391 (excerpt). My general interpretation owes much to the work of Reid (esp. 1989), although he cannot be held culpable for the uses to which I have put it.

54 *Jack N. Rakove*

or the executive agencies that carry these measures out?[20] But Madison's concerns still represent a telling response to the evisceration of executive power that was the most conspicuous feature of the state constitutions written in conjunction with independence (Wood 1969, 132–61). To enable the executive and the judiciary – newly recognized in American thinking as a third independent department of government – to discharge their responsibilities free from improper legislative encroachment was thus the dominant goal shaping Madison's approach to the separation of powers.

Yet here, too, Madison left Philadelphia doubtful whether the Constitution had solved the problem to his satisfaction. Going into the convention, Madison was far from certain how the executive should be constituted, and the "tedious and reiterated discussions" from which the presidency finally emerged fell short of his desires.[21] The framers were equally perplexed, and as a result, they reached the crucial decisions giving the presidency its constitutional form only during the final fortnight of debate. The framers were generally agreed that the executive should be rendered constitutionally independent of the legislature, but how to achieve that end required solving a complex equation in which rules of election, tenure, length of term, and reeligibility all acted as mutually dependent variables.

The weightiest of these variables was the question of election. Although a sort of popular mythology holds that the electoral college was the product of an elitist aversion to democracy, other considerations in fact led the framers to adopt this seemingly quaint institution. Popular election, though supported by Wilson and Madison, proved unacceptable for two reasons: first, because the delegates were generally skeptical that the people would be well informed about likely candidates to make an effective choice without having to go through a protracted and inconvenient series of elections; and, second, because the national electorate that popular election would create would leave the free white voters of the South in a permanent minority. By contrast, an election by Congress had the great advantage of placing the choice in the most informed constituency available. But to reconcile that method with the desire for executive independence would require either rendering the president ineligible

---

[20] This is hardly a profound observation, of course; but for at least one noteworthy historical study of this process, see the treatment of the landmark Civil Rights Act of 1964 and its transformation by the "subversive bureaucracy" of the Equal Employment Opportunity Commission in Graham 1990, 125–254.

[21] Madison to Washington, April 16, 1787, and to Jefferson, October 24, 1787, in Rutland et al., 1962–91, 9:385, 10:208. For a fuller discussion of the points developed in this and the following paragraphs, see Rakove 1996, 256–68.

for reelection, which in turn disturbed those who felt that the promise of reelection would be a spur to all the right ambitions, or giving the executive a lengthy term that might encourage monarchical pretensions. The electoral college emerged as an attractive if problematic alternative to the greater defects of popular or legislative election.

Even then, however, few delegates thought it would actually make a decisive choice in the first round. Anxious to avoid the "cabal" that would ensue if repeated rounds of voting were required – whether the faculty of this college met in one place, or in the satellite campuses of the states – the framers recognized that the final right of election had to reside somewhere in Congress. The (so-called) committee of postponed parts that proposed this solution muddied the issue by placing this power in the Senate at the same time as it linked the upper house with the president in the exercise of the treaty and appointment powers, thereby implying that the executive would become the "tool" of an "aristocratic" clique of senators. It took the framers three days of debate (September 4–6) to stumble on the solution of having the House act as the contingent electors (with the vote being taken by delegations to preserve the "compromise" of giving the large states the advantage in the first round, while the small states exerted disproportionate influence in the second, decisive phase).[22]

What seems most striking about this prolonged debate is that none of the framers anticipated the two dominant facts of American politics for the next two centuries: that control of the government would depend on control of the presidency, and that this in turn would require the creation of political alliances or coalitions running across state lines.[23] Whether the struggle to control a bicameral Congress would have provided a similar stimulus for national parties is an open question. But among the framers, only Madison seems to have sensed that the real challenge was "to render an eventual resort to any part of the Legislature improbable" by encouraging the large states "to make the appointment in the first instance conclusive" – that is, to adopt rules that would encourage the electoral college to produce a majority on its own account. Most of the delegates seemed to agree, with George Mason, "that nineteen times in twenty" the electoral college would fail to make a choice.[24] Even if that expectation proved wrong (as, of course, it did), it testifies to the overwhelming difficulty the framers faced in imagining the political dimensions of presidential leadership and influence. Nor were Anti-Federalists any more sophisticated in this respect. Notwithstanding their occasional alarms over the specter of incipient monarchy, they were more inclined to view the president as a

---

[22] The best account of these decisions is Slonim 1986.
[23] See, generally, McCormick 1982.
[24] The debate can be followed in Farrand 1966, 2:499–502, 511–15, 521–7.

56   *Jack N. Rakove*

potential coconspirator with the Senate than an independent source of political power (Rakove 1966).

To compile all the uncertainties under which the framers labored in designing the political branches of the new government thus reminds us what an extraordinarily novel enterprise they were conducting in establishing a national polity. As Professor Beer has often noted, that is also what makes their achievement all the more impressive. It was nevertheless one thing to propose workable solutions to all the problems of political design the framers faced, another matter entirely to predict how those solutions would work in practice, or what level of innovation would be required to convert constitutional aspirations into the ordinary habits and procedures of politics and governance.

That caution extends as well to the nonpolitical, judicial branch of government that was an equally innovative feature of the framers' Constitution. Too much of this part of the story has been told in ways that emphasize the emergence of a doctrine of judicial review – such as Hamilton espoused in *Federalist* 78 – over the prior and arguably more important problem of developing a full conception of judicial independence. Many Americans still shared a traditional animus against the dangers of allowing an elite corps of national judges to exercise broad appellate jurisdiction over the law- and fact-finding powers of juries. In local practice, judges were little more than glorified bailiffs. That was why the otherwise absurd charge that the Constitution had effectively abrogated the "inestimable" right to trial by jury resonated so deeply during the ratification debates of 1787–8. The framers and many of their Federalist supporters had begun to think differently. They were now prepared to regard judges as independent sources of a legal expertise not available to the citizen-jurors who were responsible for many of the key governing decisions taken within the realm of local communities. But again, this was a relatively novel conception, and many Federalists, including Madison, were far from certain that the judiciary would be willing to challenge the politically powerful voice of the legislature.[25]

THE PLAY OF FACTION

Thanks to Adair, Diamond, Dahl, and others, generations of American college students have learned that *Federalist* 10 offers the paradigmatic solution to the problem of faction. That was why this essay has become the locus classicus of the theory of the Constitution, and why it ranks with the Declaration of Independence and the Gettysburg Address in the canon of American political literature. Nor can there be any question whether

[25] For elaboration of these points, see Rakove 1997.

Madison would have thought this status well deserved. By recurring to it in the concluding paragraphs of his discussion of the separation of powers in *Federalist* 47–51, he signaled later readers (far more than contemporary ones) how great an importance he attached to the central argument of *Federalist* 10. Even so, as a "pure" statement of Madisonian theory, it is defective, or at least partial, on two grounds. First, it does not offer a satisfactory solution to the continuing problem of factional misrule *within* the states; it only explains why a national republic should be less susceptible to this vice than the existing governments of the states. Second, its level of abstraction offers no solution to the gravest threat that American federalism was most likely to (and in fact did) face: that the centrifugal force of sectionalism would reduce the play of a multiplicity of interests and opinions into two sharply antagonistic factions, each dominant within one region of the country, and each unable to imagine how the union could endure unless significant concessions were extracted from the other.

Madison's entire approach to the task of constitutional reform in 1787 was driven by his observations of the play of faction within the realm of state politics. Frustrated in his efforts to convince the Virginia assembly (in which he served in the mid-1780s) either to adopt a consistently "federal" policy supporting the Continental Congress or to complete the comprehensive revision of the state legal code that Jefferson had initiated, Madison took further alarm from the progress of paper money legislation in other states. By the summer of 1785 he was convinced that the *state* constitutions should be reformed in ways that would give their legislation the "*wisdom* and steadiness" it sorely lacked, perhaps through the establishment of truly senatorial upper chambers or of select committees of draftsmen to make pending bills technically competent, or even by extending the terms of lawmakers beyond the republican norm of a single year.[26] Over the course of the next two years, he sharpened these criticisms into the program for reform he carried to Philadelphia.

The crucial lessons were distilled in his preconvention memorandum on the "Vices of the Political System of the United States" and the concurrent letters Madison sent in March and April 1787 to Jefferson (then in France), Edmund Randolph (his close friend and governor of Virginia), and Washington (whose participation in the convention he assiduously courted). His analysis was predicated on the inability of either the legislatures of the states or the popular majorities whom they represented all too well to pursue measures that would respect the general interests of the union, the true public good of their own communities, or the rights of minorities and individuals within their boundaries. Here Madison identified two sets of causes that explained why the state legislatures were so

---

[26] Madison to Caleb Wallace, August 23, 1785, in Rutland et al. 1962–91, 8:350–5.

58 *Jack N. Rakove*

prone to "vicious" decisions. The first pertained to the vices of legislators: their personal ambitions and interested motives, their occasional demagoguery, or their frequent inexperience. But the more important set of causes steered attention away from the elected to their electors. In Madison's view, "a still more fatal if not more frequent cause" of unjust legislation "lies among the people themselves." It was their instrumental use of government, rather than the caprices of lawmakers, that best explained why the law codes of the states were marked by an "injustice [that] betrays a defect still more alarming . . . not merely because it is a greater evil in itself, but because it brings more into question the fundamental principle of republican Governments, that the majority who rule in such Governments, are the safest guardians both of public Good and of private rights."[27]

Madison drew two programmatic conclusions from this analysis. The first, and ultimately more persuasive, was that any plan of reform that left the national government dependent on the voluntary compliance of thirteen state legislatures was doomed to failure. Rather than having to continue to rely on the states, the national government had to be reconstituted as a completely articulated government in its own right, capable of enacting, executing, and adjudicating its own laws. This simple though decisive move enabled the Philadelphia Convention to rethink all the structural aspects of republican government for which the original state constitutions provided the necessary experimental data. And here it was, too, that Madison deployed his well-known reasoning about the comparative merits of large republics to explain why the quality of policy deliberations at the national level of government should be superior to those he denounced within the states. Popular factions bent on injustice would be much less likely to form, while an enlarged scale of political competition should foster the recruitment of a more cosmopolitan class of lawmakers.

Madison's second great conclusion addressed the residual problem of the character of republican governance within the states. Madison was no consolidationist; he recognized that even the most ambitious constitutional reform would still leave the state governments to regulate most of the ordinary business of government and the daily activities of the American people.[28] Within the states, the same factious pressures that produced the "vicious" legislation he distrusted would continue to operate, leaving minorities and individuals vulnerable to infringements of their rights. In this highly reactionary phase of his political career, Madison was most obsessed with the danger to rights of property, but he was far from

---

[27] Vices of the Political System of the U. States, in Rutland et al. 1962–91, 9:345–57.

[28] For the strongest exposition of the authenticity of Madison's underlying commitment to a federalism of this kind, see Banning 1995.

certain that his other great cause, religious liberty, was as yet secure. Demonstrating that a national republic would be relatively immune to the mischief of faction was therefore not the same thing as purging the evils of faction from the larger Republic of which the union *and* the states were the constituent parts.

To reach the problem of republican misrule within the states, Madison favored nothing less than an unlimited congressional veto on all state laws. This, too, was a proposal whose implications he had not thought through. Not only did it raise all sorts of problems of practicality – would the national government not need to establish some sort of proconsular authority in the states, to approve necessary laws pending congressional review? – but it also seemed as impolitic a measure as the convention could conceivably propose. How could Madison's own region accept a measure that gave the national government authority to oversee the most important and innovative class of legislation its assemblies had adopted: the slave codes that governed fundamental aspects of social relations in the plantation states?

Although Madison gained some noteworthy adherents to this proposal, they could never overcome the objections it raised. In place of the veto, the convention ultimately substituted the supremacy clause of the Constitution and a modest set of prohibitions on the legislative powers of the states. Madison was convinced that this substitution would leave the Constitution seriously flawed. Judicial protection of rights was likely to prove far less effective than the form of legislative preemption that Madison favored; nor did it seem likely that the partial enumeration of rights in the Constitution would be able to restrain the "infinitude of legislative expedients" to which willful lawmakers could always resort. Most important, even if the national government scraped by in a nonfactious way, the states would be left free to follow their erratic, rights-impairing course. A month after the convention adjourned, he sent Jefferson a lengthy defense of his pet scheme in his remarkable letter of October 24, 1787; but then, with the campaign for ratification gathering steam, he put these reservations aside as he drafted *Federalist* 10, which appeared a month later. There was no need to defend a proposal the convention had rejected, nor to betray his deeper doubts about the security of rights within the states.

The implications of this concern for a "pure theory" of the Constitution (as expressed in *Federalist* 10) should now be apparent. In one sense, of course, no theory of the Constitution need take account of what was not in the document. Yet there is a deeper irony in this issue which goes to the heart of much of the contemporary discourse of American constitutionalism. Although the legal wing of the academy has a vested interest in treating the problem of judicial review as an aspect of the separation of

60 *Jack N. Rakove*

powers, bringing the judiciary into parity with the other coequal branches of national government, in the matter of rights judicial review is as much a weapon or vector of federalism. Most judicial decisions treating claims of constitutional rights are concerned with acts of state and local government; most therefore follow the logic of the Madisonian critique of republicanism, in assuming that factious majorities are more likely to form within their compressed compass than at the level of national politics. A powerful argument could accordingly be made that the most Madisonian elements of the Constitution are the Fourteenth Amendment and the incorporation doctrine to which it belatedly gave rise, for these are what have provided the national government with the capacity to intervene within the states as Madison originally hoped it would: as a "disinterested & dispassionate umpire in disputes between different passions & interests in the State" – that is, within the individual states.[29]

When Madison thought about the particular interests most deserving protection, two categories of rights headed his list: those of property and those of conscience. He was, in many ways, far more confident about the latter than the former. More than Jefferson, who half-expected that the progress of reason would eventually move most Americans toward his own deistic beliefs, Madison better understood that Protestant fractiousness would continue to generate that multiplicity of sects that would make it ever more difficult for the state to find a consensus for the regulation or repression of dissenters. The security of property was less certain; here Madison was a proto-Malthusian pessimist. "An increase of population will of necessity increase the proportion of those who will labour under all the hardships of life, & secretly sigh for a more equal distribution of its blessings," he warned the convention. "These may in time outnumber those who are placed above the feelings of indigence. According to the equal laws of suffrage, the power will slide into the hands of the former. No agrarian attempts have yet been made in this Country, but symptoms of a leveling spirit . . . have sufficiently appeared in certain quarters to give notice of the future danger." The danger could be guarded against by establishing a well-constructed senate, Madison concluded, or perhaps by fixing constitutional requirements for the suffrage that would appear liberal now but work more prudentially in the future.[30]

---

[29] Compare this language in Madison's letter to Washington, April 17, 1787, with the penultimate paragraph of his memorandum on the Vices of the Political System; Rutland et al. 1962–91, 9:384, 357. For a more refined view of the relation between the Fourteenth Amendment and the original amendments, see Amar 1998, which, however, rests on treating Madison, the principal author of the amendments of 1789, as an unrepresentative thinker precisely because of the protoliberal quality of his positions on rights.

[30] See his speeches of June 26 and August 7, in Farrand 1966, 1:421–3, 2:203–4.

Constitutional Problematics, circa 1787

These are the concerns that best illustrate how much Madison's theory of faction was tied to the defense of property that Charles Beard and his intellectual followers insisted provided the key to the Federalist agenda of 1787. There was, however, an entirely different way to pose the problem of faction in the political context of the 1780s – and one that Madison himself had confronted at the convention and afterward. In contrast to his somewhat abstract fear about the future security of property, Madison had more pressing reasons to worry about the durability of an intersectional union built on the different social systems of northern and southern states. One of the crucial considerations that led him to shift from a strategy of incremental reform of the Articles of Confederation to wholesale constitutional change was the conviction that the union might soon devolve into two or three regional confederacies. This concern reflected the Mississippi controversy of 1786, a dispute that split the Continental Congress into two sectional blocs when Secretary of Foreign Affairs John Jay asked Congress to abjure American claims to the free navigation of the Mississippi in order to secure a commercial treaty with Spain, which had closed American access to the Gulf of Mexico in 1784 (Rakove 1979, 349–50, 353–4). (It is noteworthy that Madison's first recorded objection to the republican principle that the majority was best qualified to determine the true public interest arose in the context of this issue, rather than his assessment of the internal vicissitudes of the states.)[31]

The Mississippi issue loomed large in the thinking of southern leaders because, like other Americans in the 1780s, they assumed that the arc of postrevolutionary migration would carry inland settlers southwest toward New Orleans rather than due west along the Great Lakes. In regional terms, as the historian Drew McCoy has noted, this assumption in turn suggested that the parity required to maintain political harmony among the regions of the new republic would develop over time as the emerging frontier became more an extension of southern than northern society. Nor were regional differences yet constructed primarily in terms of slavery and freedom, McCoy suggests; the South was thought of more as a "landed" interest, the North as a "commercial" one (McCoy 1987). Going into the convention, Madison knew that this question of sectional balance had to be solved because concern over the Mississippi ran high among his Virginia countrymen – and was felt with special fervor by Patrick Henry, the great demagogue of Virginia politics.

Yet Madison's sectional calculations reached the question of slavery as well, and they did so in terms that at least partly qualified his general theory of faction. One purpose of that theory was to provide a principled basis for challenging the predicted claim of the small states that states, as

---

[31] Madison to Monroe, October 2, 1786, in Rutland et al. 1962–91, 8:141.

62 *Jack N. Rakove*

such, were valid interests deserving an equal vote in at least one house of the new Congress (Rakove 1987). By locating the sources of factious behavior in the attributes of individuals, Madison was in effect also arguing that theirs were the true interests that a republican polity had to balance; states had no interests other than the aggregates of those of their citizens. Size was an interest, Madison argued, only when the question of basing representation on size was itself under review. Once the union was reconstituted, representatives would vote never again on the basis of the size of their states but rather in pursuit of all the other interests each state (or constituency) contained.

When this argument failed to make headway against the persistent claims of the small states, however, Madison was driven to evoke the specter of sectional difference as a further means of challenging the "vicious" principle of representing states equally without regard to population. In his speech of June 30, Madison reminded the delegates

that the States were divided into different interests not by their difference of size, but by other circumstances; the most material of which resulted partly from climate, but principally from the effects of their having or not having slaves. These two causes concurred in forming the great division of interest in the U. States. It did not lie between the large & small States: it lay between the Northern and Southern[,] and if any defensive power were necessary, it ought to be mutually given to these two interests.[32]

The obvious rhetorical advantage of this appeal was that it identified lasting interests that would have to be accommodated if the union were to prove durable. The division between small and large states would not survive the convention; that between slave and free states might outlast the union itself. If this argument failed to have the effect Madison intended for it vis-à-vis the Senate, it surfaced in another form over the next fortnight as the convention approved the three-fifths clause as an expedient to reassure southern delegates and their constituents that their regional interests would be reasonably protected in the new Congress.

The candor with which Madison invoked slavery in this debate raises a troubling question for all who want to read *Federalist* 10 as the definitive prescription for faction. Its cure still seems promising if American society is imagined as a bustling commercial republic peopled by disputatious Protestants, pursuing their economic ambitions and spiritual aspirations in ways that could only multiply their factional allegiances, dissolving old loyalties and creating new ones as individuals migrated across state boundaries, took up new occupations, or fell under the sway of new notions of divinity. The theory appears much less promising, however, when we

---

[32] Madison, speech of June 30, 1787, in Farrand 1966, 1:486; reprised July 14, in ibid., 2:9–10.

imagine the new republic as a society half slave, half free. Perhaps the course of migration westward would work, Madison may have assumed, to mitigate sectional differences. Western states might enter the union not as a new field of sectional rivalry but as a source of sectional balance; or if they did fall more within the ambit of southern than northern influence, as a factor promoting political parity. Yet when all is said and done, it is difficult to avoid the suspicion that Madison understood that the theory of faction broke down when slavery was recognized as a peculiar interest unlike any other (in just the way that the three-fifths clause identified slaves as a form of property unlike any other). A factional politics based on the emergence of two great and mutually incompatible commitments to slavery and freedom, each rooted in and dominating one great region of the country, would belie the sanguine promises of *Federalist* 10 – but not the sanguinary threat that darkened the unionist dream.

FROM RATIFICATION TO LEGITIMATION

If Madison and his allies had reason to worry about the durability of the Constitution, then the conditions of its adoption would arguably become all the more important, not only to produce an unequivocal act of ratification, but also to provide a measure of legitimacy upon which the new government could draw. In practice, however, few Federalists seem to have reflected on the processes that would have to unfold for the Constitution to secure an acceptance transcending its initial approval. The two notable exceptions to this were, fittingly, Hamilton and Madison – and the different ways in which they approached this question anticipated the political and constitutional disputes that soon led to the invention of a political party system that no one in 1787 could have conceived possible.

Shortly after the convention adjourned, Hamilton jotted down a set of "Conjectures about the new Constitution" that bear all the marks of his own brand of political realism. After assaying the different *political* factors that would weigh on one side or another in the debate over ratification, he commented on both the likely consequences of rejection and the steps needed to convert a legally approved Constitution into a popularly accepted government. "If the government is adopted," he wrote,

it is probable general Washington will be the President of the United States – This will ensure a wise choice of men to administer the government and a good administration. A good administration will conciliate the confidence and affection of the people and perhaps enable the government to acquire more consistency than the proposed constitution seems to promise for so great a Country – It may then triumph altogether over the state governments and reduce them to an entire subordination, dividing the large states into smaller districts. The *organs* of the general government may also acquire additional strength.

64 *Jack N. Rakove*

But should this salutary beginning not take place, Hamilton cautioned, it was equally possible that "the *momentum* of the larger states" would give them the advantage over the national government and in turn "produce a dissolution of the government. This after all seems to be the most likely result," he concluded inauspiciously.[33]

Hamilton had not quite reached the well-known position inscribed by Alexander Pope:

> For forms of government let fools contest,
> That which is best administered is best.

Still, he had come close enough, even though in *Federalist* 68 he labeled Pope's verse a "political heresy."[34] Adoption of the Constitution was a mere point of departure; the true proof of its capacity would take the form of a test of strength (or momentum) between rival levels of government, in which the decisive factor would be the character of its initial administration (and presumably legislation as well, especially the fiscal measures that Hamilton hoped to take a leading hand in drafting). Legitimation would come only as the government demonstrated its effectiveness; until then the Constitution would remain an untested promise.

Madison shared Hamilton's concern that the state governments would retain real political advantages that the new national government would have to struggle to overcome.[35] He, too, was convinced of the importance of getting the new government – especially Congress – under way, quickly adopting the legislation necessary to gain popular confidence. But in Madison's view, a crucial component of legitimacy should be the outcome of the ratification process itself. Madison was the leading designer of the ratification procedures the framers fixed upon to allow the Constitution to be approved by nine popularly elected conventions, rather than the thirteen state legislatures, thereby evading the formal requirements of the Articles of Confederation. He supported this step not only because it solved the liberum veto problem of Rhode Island – unrepresented at the

---

[33] Jensen, Kaminski, and Saladino 1976–, 13:277–8. Hamilton's position rests on the same zero-sum notion of the future competiton between national and state governments that he had described in his famous convention speech of June 18, 1787 (Farrand 1966, 1:282–93), and which was commonly shared by Anti-Federalists, who predicted that adoption of the Constitution would necessarily end in the creation of a "consolidated" union in which the states would be mere cyphers. For further discussion, see Rakove 1996, 181–8.

[34] *Federalist* 68, 443; see the discussion in Stourzh 1970, 82–3, 234 n. 23. John Adams also made Pope his point of departure in the opening paragraphs of his influential *Thoughts on Government* (1776).

[35] We find this concern voiced not only in the lengthy defense of the national veto over state laws contained in Madison's letter to Jefferson of October 24, 1787 (note 24), but also in *Federalist* 45 and 46.

convention, and a sure vote against ratification – but also because he appreciated the deeper legal authority it would bestow on the Constitution in subsequent disputes over its authority. Although such legal scholars as Richard McKay, Akhil Amar, and Bruce Ackerman have recently debated the "legality" of these procedures, implying that the adoption of the Constitution was in some sense a revolutionary act not acceptable under the standing law of 1787, it is at least as true that Madison was attempting to replace a defective standard of legality with a new and powerful set of norms more in keeping with American constitutional principles.[36]

Recognizing that both the state constitutions and the Articles of Confederation had received no sanction higher than the approval of the state legislatures, Madison understood that a constitution adopted through some process of popular ratification could be said to have attained a superior authority – to have become fundamental law in a way that the state constitutions were not (with the precedential exceptions of the Massachusetts Constitution of 1780 and the New Hampshire Constitution of 1784, which had been popularly ratified). As Jefferson had argued and others recognized, constitutions adopted legislatively were vulnerable to the objection that they enjoyed no status superior to that of any other statute; they could therefore be violated with impunity (under the doctrine *quod leges posteriores priores contrarias abrogant*). On this basis the Constitution could not only circumvent the procedural obstacles embedded in the Confederation; it could also lay a strong foundation for the principle of national supremacy.[37]

Popular sovereignty was potentially a two-edged sword. In theory, Anti-Federalists could have used this doctrine to convert the ratification conventions into something more than a referendum on acceptance or rejection of the Constitution. If these conventions did indeed embody the political will of a sovereign people, why could they not approve or reject the Constitution in part, or make its acceptance contingent on the actual adoption of the particular amendments they sought, perhaps by calling the second general convention that Madison's wavering friend, Edmund Randolph, favored? Well aware that the genie of popular sovereignty could all too easily escape the narrow vessel within which the framers hoped to keep it confined, Madison and other Federalists insisted that popular sovereignty could be exercised only to approve or reject the Constitution

---

[36] See McKay 1987; Amar 1994; Ackerman and Katyal 1995; and Rakove 1998–9. This and the following paragraphs draw heavily on the discussion in Rakove 1996, 94–130.

[37] For Madison's early recognition of this point, see his letters to Washington, April 16, 1787, and to Pendleton, April 22, 1787, in Rutland et al. 1969–91, 9:385, 395; and compare point 8 in the Vices of the Political System, in ibid., 352–3. For Jefferson's development of this point, see Peden 1955, 121–5.

in toto. When Anti-Federalists finally achieved the strength to push the case for amendments (as they first did in Massachusetts), Federalists similarly struggled, with striking success, to confine the resulting resolutions to the mere recommendation of amendments, rather than some other form of conditional ratification pending further action by other states, Congress, or a second convention. To follow any other procedure than that recommended by the convention and endorsed by Congress would lead, Federalists warned, to procedural chaos at best. At worst, if a second convention was called, it would likely be attended by delegates forewarned and forearmed to protect local interests, and thus unlikely to reach consensus on anything.

In retrospect, the Federalists' success in limiting their adversaries to the recommendation of amendments must be adjudged as bold a stroke as their earlier maneuvers to produce the convention had been. It meant, in the end, that the decision for ratification was relatively clean and completely unambiguous. That did not prevent outflanked Anti-Federalists from grumbling about the impropriety of abandoning the Confederation, but it meant that the transition from one regime to another could proceed as smoothly as even Hamilton might have hoped. The elegance of the ratification decision helped to confine most subsequent political disputes with constitutional overtones within the four corners of the founding text, when the alternative might have been to challenge the Constitution itself. That was legitimation, as it was conceived and executed in the Federalist démarche.

For Madison, however, the problem of legitimacy had a deeper meaning. No one had a more acute sense of how difficult or close the whole enterprise had been, or how unlikely it was that any subsequent effort at wholesale constitutional reform could meet similar success. In part, this attitude reflected the underlying conservatism evident in both his political theory and his personality. But it was also a mark of his extraordinarily keen perception of the foibles of popular politics. Madison was a Federalist, not a neo-Federalist of the Bruce Ackerman persuasion, and his reservations about the possibilities of "constitutional politics" were well recorded in the two essays of *The Federalist* that preceded his restatement of the problem of separated powers in *Federalist* 51.

Federalist 49 and 50 are a surprising digression in the argument, for they take as their subject an idea that was *not* before the American public in 1787–8 – and their inclusion thus suggests that Madison had an independent concern he was anxious to insert into the public debate. The idea at hand was Jefferson's proposal, appended to the *Notes on the State of Virginia*, to empower any two departments of government to summon a popularly elected convention to correct breaches in the constitution. Such an idea might seem theoretically correct, Madison conceded, because "the people are the only legitimate fountain of power," but it would not remedy the most likely source of encroachment – the legislature – whose superior political resources would prevail nearly every time. But Madison also seized this occasion to develop a further point.[38]

Frequent constitutional appeals to the people would have a pernicious effect, he warned in *Federalist* 49, for they would "deprive government of that veneration which time bestows on every thing, and without which perhaps the wisest and freest governments would not possess the requisite stability." Perhaps in "a nation of philosophers" this concern might be waived; but "in every other nation, the most rational government will not find it a superfluous advantage to have the prejudices of the community on its side." But that acceptable version of prejudice in the form of veneration was to be distinguished from the variety that would flourish if Jefferson's scheme was adopted. The circumstances that prevailed in America in 1776 – and perhaps again in 1787–8 – would not always be present to promote popular confidence in their leaders and consensus about the ends of government. Once ordinary politics got under way, it would never again be possible to replicate these conditions. A "public decision" on an agitated constitutional question "could never be expected to turn on the true merits of the question. It would inevitably be connected with the spirit of preëxisting parties, or of parties springing out of the question itself." It would, in short, always be a product of the "passions" and "not the *reason*, of the public."

To treat the original decision of 1787–8 as the only possible exercise in rational constitutional choice the American public could ever make was a breathtaking move. Perhaps it resonates faintly today in the conviction that theirs was indeed a relatively pure choice – or at least that it produced a relatively pure theory. But it testifies as well to Madison's concern with the problem of legitimating the Constitution for the long haul, and his desire to guard it against the vicissitudes of ordinary politics by distinguishing this one decision from all that would follow. Over the long haul, perhaps it would prove more important to develop this popular attachment to the Constitution writ large than to worry overmuch about the merits and defects of its particular provisions. The fact that all but a handful of hard-boiled academics and gadfly intellectuals treat our eighteenth-century Constitution with such respect, or that they regard the idea of wholesale constitutional change – as opposed to piecemeal amendment and revision – as

---

[38] The quotations in this and the next paragraph are taken from *Federalist* 49, 348–51. The first of these essays discusses the idea of "occasional" appeals to the corrective authority of the people; the second simply extends the argument to "periodical" (regular) appeals.

68 *Jack N. Rakove*

something like anathema, demonstrates the staying power of the Madisonian aspiration.[39] Yet this attitude may also expose another problem in our understanding of constitutionalism more broadly: that Americans have an inherent bias that makes it difficult for them to think of constitutions in non-Madisonian terms.

REFERENCES

Ackerman, B., and N. Katyal, eds. 1995. "Our Unconventional Founding." *University of Chicago Law Review* 62: 475–573.

Adair, D. 1951. "The Tenth *Federalist* Revisited." *William and Mary Quarterly*, 3rd ser., 8: 48–67. Reprinted in Trevor Colbourn, ed., *Fame and Founding Fathers: Essays by Douglass Adair*, 75–92. Chapel Hill: University of North Carolina Press.

Adams, J. 1776. *Thoughts on Government*. Philadelphia: John Dunlap.

Amar, A. 1994. "The Consent of the Governed: Constitutional Amendment outside Article V." *Columbia Law Review* 94: 457–508.

    1998. *The Bill of Rights: Creation and Reconstruction*. New Haven: Yale University Press.

Bailyn, B. 1990. "The Ideological Fulfillment of the American Revolution: A Commentary on the Constitution." In B. Bailyn, ed., *Faces of the Revolution: Personalities and Themes in the Struggle for American Independence*, 232–46. New York: Alfred A. Knopf.

Banning, L. 1995. *The Sacred Cause of Liberty: James Madison and the Founding of the Federal Republic*. Ithaca: Cornell University Press.

Bork, R. H. 1990. *The Tempting of America: The Political Seduction of the Law*. New York: Free Press.

Bourke, P. F. 1975. "The Pluralist Reading of James Madison's Tenth *Federalist*." *Perspectives in American History* 9: 271–95.

Burke, E. 1987. *Thoughts on the Cause of the Present Discontent* [c. 1770]. In P. Kurland and R. Lerner, eds., *The Founder's Constitution*, 1: 391. Chicago: University of Chicago Press.

Dahl, R. A. 1956. *A Preface to Democratic Theory*. Chicago: University of Chicago Press.

Diamond, Martin 1959. "Democracy and *The Federalist*: A Reconsideration of the Framers' Intent." *American Political Science Review* 53: 52–68.

Engeman, T. S., E. J. Erler, and T. B. Hofeller, eds. 1988. *The Federalist Concordance*. Chicago: University of Chicago.

Epstein, D. 1984. *The Political Theory of the Federalist*. Chicago: University of Chicago Press.

Farrand, M., ed. 1966. *Records of the Federal Convention of 1787*. 3 vols. Rev. ed. New Haven: Yale University Press.

Graham, H. D. 1990. *The Civil Rights Era: Origins and Development of National Policy, 1960–1962*. New York: Oxford University Press.

---

[39] For the most recent populist counterblast, see Lazare, 1996.

Jensen, M., J. Kaminski, and G. Saladino, eds. 1976. *The Documentary History of the Ratification of the Constitution*. Vol. 13. Madison: State Historical Society of Wisconsin.

Kesler, C. R. 1987. "*Federalist* 10 and American Republicanism." In C. R. Kesler, ed., *Saving the Revolution*, 14. New York: Free Press.

Kramer, L. 1998–9. "Madison's Audience." *Harvard Law Review* 112: 611–79.

Lazare, D. 1996. *The Frozen Republic: How the Constitution Is Paralyzing Democracy*. New York: Harcourt Brace.

Lieberman, D. M. 1989. *The Province of Legislation Determined: Legal Theory in Eighteenth-Century Britain*. Cambridge: Cambridge University Press.

McCormick, R. P. 1982. *The Presidential Game: The Origins of American Presidential Politics*. New York: Oxford University Press.

McCoy, D. 1987. "James Madison and Visions of American Nationality in the Confederation Period: A Regional Perspective." In R. Beeman, S. Botein, and E. C. Carter II, eds., *Beyond Confederation: Origins of the Constitution and American National Identity*, 226–58. Chapel Hill: University of North Carolina.

1989. *The Last of the Fathers: James Madison and the Republican Legacy*. Cambridge: Cambridge University Press.

McKay, R. 1987. "The Illegality of the Constitution." *Constitutional Commentary* 4: 57–80.

Nedelsky, J. 1990. *Private Property and the Limits of American Constitutionalism: The Madisonian Framework and Its Legacy*. Chicago: University of Chicago Press.

Nelson, W. E. 1986. "History and Neutrality in Constitutional Adjucation." *Virginia Law Review* 72: 1237–96.

Peden, W. 1955. *Notes on the State of Virginia*. Chapel Hill: University of North Carolina Press.

Rakove, J. N. 1979. *Beginnings of National Politics*. New York: Knopf.

1987a. "The Structure of Politics at the Accession of George Washington." In R. Beeman, S. Botein, and E. C. Carter II, eds., *Beyond Confederation: Origins of the Constitution and American National Identity*, 261–94. Chapel Hill: University of North Carolina Press.

1987b. "The Great Compromise: Ideas, Interests, and the Politics of Constitution-Making." *William and Mary Quarterly*, 3rd ser., 44: 424–57.

1987c. "Early Uses of *The Federalist*." In C. R. Kesler, ed., *Saving the Revolution: The Federalist Papers and the American Founding*, 234–49. New York: Free Press.

1996. *Original Meanings: Politics and Ideas in the Making of the Constitution*. New York: Knopf.

1997. "The Origins of Judicial Review: A Plea for New Contexts." *Stanford Law Review* 49: 1031–64.

1998–9. "The Super-Legality of the Constitution, Or, A Federalist Critique of Bruce Ackerman's Neo-Federalism." *Yale Law Journal* 108: 1931–58.

Reid, J. P. 1989. *The Concept of Representation in the Age of the American Revolution*. Chicago: University of Chicago Press.

70 *Jack N. Rakove*

Riley, J. 1990. "American Democracy and Majority Rule." In J. W. Chapman and Alan Wertheimer, eds., *Majorities and Minorities*, 267–307. *Nomos* 32. New York: New York University Press.

Rutland, R. A., et al., eds. 1962–91. *The Papers of James Madison*. Charlottesville, Va.: University of Virginia Press.

Slonim, S. 1986. "The Electoral College at Philadelphia: The Evolution of an Ad Hoc Congress for the Selection of a President." *Journal of American History* 73: 35–58.

Story, J. 1833. *Commentaries on the Constitution of the United States*. Boston: Little and Brown.

Stourzh, G. 1970. *Alexander Hamilton and the Idea of Republican Government*. Stanford: Stanford University Press.

Wills, G. 1981. *Explaining America: The Federalist*. Garden City, N.Y.: Doubleday.

Wood, G. S. 1969. *The Creation of the American Republic, 1776–1787*. Chapel Hill: University of North Carolina Press.

1987. "Ideology and the Origins of Liberal America." *William and Mary Quarterly*, 3rd ser., 44: 632–3.

Wright, B., ed. 1961. *The Federalist*. Cambridge: Belknap Press of Harvard University Press.

Zagarri, Rosemarie. 1987. *The Politics of Size: Representation in the United States, 1776–1850*. Ithaca: Cornell University Press.

2

Inventing Constitutional Traditions:
The Poverty of Fatalism

James Johnson

In his reflections on the nineteenth-century British Constitution, Walter Bagehot remarks: "It is often said that men are ruled by their imaginations; but it would be truer to say that they are governed by the weakness of their imaginations" ([1867] 1963, 82). In this chapter I take the politics of post-Communist Eastern Europe as a point of departure from which to explore Bagehot's suspicion. More specifically, I hope to show that, contrary to what Bagehot insinuates, popular political imagination is not so much constrained by inherent deficiencies as it is differentially sustained by political possibilities that occupy the intersection of symbol and strategy.[1]

What I offer is an exploration of political possibility occasioned by historical events, rather than a detailed report on those events.[2] I am especially concerned to examine the rapidity with which assessments of Eastern European politics shifted, in the aftermath of the revolutionary events of 1989, from a sense of enlarged, perhaps limitless, possibility to more or less rampant fatalism.[3] The primary focus for my argument is the impact of such fatalism on assessments of the prospect of establishing enduring constitutional democracy in post-Communist Eastern Europe.[4] I thus am more concerned with the politics of constitution making than with the substantive features of the resulting constitutions. However, compared with those who view the politics of constitution making primarily

---

[1] For more detailed arguments on the ways that symbol and strategy intersect in politics, see Johnson 1997; 1999.

[2] My understanding of politics in post-1989 Eastern Europe rests heavily on the descriptions provided by Glenny 1993a, 1993b; Brown 1994; and Woodward 1995.

[3] Timothy Garton Ash (1990) offers a provocative firsthand account of the sense of enlarged possibilities that gripped participants in the 1989 revolutions.

[4] I assume both that liberal constitutionalism and democracy are mutually dependent (Elster 1993, 172–3) and that they remain in considerably greater tension than most discussions of contemporary political transitions recognize (Arato 1993).

72   *James Johnson*

in terms of the fairly narrow compass of bargaining over institutional
arrangements and legal provisions, I focus on what is an analytically separate and, for political purposes, arguably prior question.[5] In the competition for the attention and imagination of large political constituencies in
contemporary Eastern Europe, do purveyors of ethnic nationalism hold a
necessary, irreversible advantage over political leaders committed to the
project of designing, ratifying, and implementing constitutional arrangements? In this sense, it is perhaps more accurate to say that I am concerned
with constitutionalism as an especially pressing instance of the politics of
possibility.

Fatalism, Webster tells us, consists in an "attitude" toward the world
that holds "that events are fixed in advance for all time in such a manner
that human beings are powerless to change them." In thinking about post-
Communist Eastern Europe, fatalism comes in two primary variants. The
first, especially stark, variant sees "tribalism" as an irresistible threat to
the chances of constitutional democracies in post-Communist states
(Walzer 1992; 1994).[6] The second variant identifies an only slightly less
dire "logic of rational political nihilism" underlying ethnic nationalism in
the region (Offe 1997, 79).

The bulk of my argument entails reconstructing plausible versions of
tribalism, rationalist fatalism, and of several derivative positions and then
demonstrating why they are unpersuasive. In order to differentiate these
views, and thereby see what they entail, it is helpful to distinguish between
what I call the hydraulic thesis and the impoverishment thesis. The
hydraulic thesis holds that ethnic nationalism in Eastern Europe is driven
by the resurgence of long-suppressed primordial ethnic attachments. The
impoverishment thesis holds that nationalist revival in the formerly
Communist states is particularly menacing because political actors in
those states lack alternative political traditions on which to draw. Among
fatalists, those who endorse tribalism subscribe to both theses, whereas
those who endorse the rational nihilism variant subscribe only to the
impoverishment thesis. I argue that, because both theses are erroneous,
neither brand of fatalism is persuasive.

In the next section, I portray tribalism more fully and show how it
trades upon the hydraulic and impoverishment theses. In the third and
fourth sections I offer first theoretical and then empirical reasons for
finding the hydraulic thesis and, by extension, tribalism, unconvincing. In
the fifth section I portray the rational nihilism variant of fatalism more

---

[5] In the former category, see, for instance, Elster 1993 and Howard 1993.

[6] "Tribalism names the commitment of individuals and groups to their own history, culture,
and identity, and this commitment (though not any particular version of it) is a permanent feature of human social life" (Walzer 1994, 81).

fully, focusing, in particular, on the ways that this variant of fatalism trades, unsuccessfully, upon the impoverishment thesis. In the sixth and seventh sections I show first how nothing in either the rational nihilism account or the history of Eastern Europe precludes the construction of alternatives to the constructed traditions of ethnic animosity and then how, given a particular understanding of the politics of constitutionalism, invented political traditions are especially important.[7] In the final section I briefly address two views that contend to fill the theoretical void that opens once we acknowledge the poverty of fatalism.

TRIBALISM

Rampant uncertainty, fluidity, and indeterminacy are central, perhaps defining, features of politics in post-Communist Eastern Europe (e.g., Bunce and Csanadi 1993). Analyses of politics in the region rightly stress what one writer refers to as "the helter-skelter of post-communism, . . . the bewilderment of life since 1989." Because in such circumstances "the old political labels" are "anachronistic and misleading" and the entire political world therefore is "in flux," there are both an urgent need for and intense struggles to impose "new political definitions" (Brown 1994, 17, 35).[8] The situation in Eastern Europe is, in this sense, an instance of a more general pattern in transitional polities where identities and options – in short, political possibilities – are not just extraordinarily fluid, but are actively contested (O'Donnell and Schmitter 1986, 3–6).

In this context many observers are alarmed both by the appearance of particularistic ethnic attachments and the nationalist ardor that they fuel and by the threat this poses to the prospects for constitutional democracy in the region.[9] Such observers worry not just because these political impulses – what they label "tribalism" – are inimical to liberal democratic politics but because they appear to be irresistible (e.g., Walzer 1992; 1994). Yet, as I hope to show, the premises that supposedly support widespread alarm about resurgent tribalism – and, consequently, deep pessimism over possible alternatives to it – are flawed.

---

[7] Insofar as the tribalism variant of fatalism trades upon the impoverishment thesis, my arguments in these sections tell against it as well.

[8] Thus, "post-socialist change" not only "involves the redefinition of virtually everything," it involves social and political actors in intense struggles over such redefinition (Verdery 1999, 34–5, 50–3, 108–9, 125–7).

[9] For present purposes I follow Elizabeth Kiss, for whom "*ethnic nationalism*" consists in "a politics of identification with and allegiance to a nation, a collectivity defined by what its members regard as a shared descent, history and culture." She insists that such identification is, at bottom, subjective and notes, rightly, that it is difficult to draw a precise, general line between the everyday experience of ethnicity and this sort of *political* identification (1996, 290–2). On the relation between ethnicity and nationalism, see also Kiss 1995, 370–4.

74 *James Johnson*

Worries about the threat of tribalism seem well warranted. Tismaneanu (1992, 3–4, 279–88) depicts the situation as one in which the prospects for liberal democracy are jeopardized by the rise of "ethnocracy."

Following the euphoria of the first postrevolutionary months, it appeared that the old problems were back: Croatians protesting Serbian hegemony, Serbs indicting Croatians and Slovenes for their secessionist drive, ethnic Hungarians in Romania denouncing infringements on their minority rights, ethnic Turks in Bulgaria scapegoated by advocates of a homogenous Bulgarian nation, Slovaks jeering President Havel as a champion of Czech supremacy, Czechs deploring the nationalism of Slovaks, Lech Walesa using anti-semitic innuendo during his presidential campaign against his critics and challengers, and so forth. (Tismaneanu 1992, 3)

This sketch, if a bit dated in its particulars, still resonates.[10] Among subsequent efforts to navigate this terrain, the partitioning of the Czech and Slovak republics appears as a "success," whereas the worst excesses in the Balkans are perhaps yet to be glimpsed.

Fatalism emerges here not from the sheer fact of widespread and potent ethnic nationalism but, worse, from the prevalent perception that in contemporary Eastern Europe alternatives to this politics of tribalism are at best feeble, at worst nonexistent. So, for example, despite the inspiring events of 1989, the common reference point of a popular, founding "revolution" has been discredited as a potential source of political identity and legitimacy in Eastern Europe by the use that Communist regimes made of that theme (Arato 1993). Likewise, and perhaps more important, the countries of the region apparently lack a pre-Communist tradition of constitutional democracy. Observers bemoan the "backwardness" of political traditions in Eastern Europe. As compared with the West, the countries of the region have only a very rudimentary history of checks on political power, protection of individual autonomy, or institutions of popular participation (Schopflin 1990; Pognay 1996). Thus the complaint that, with "the exception of Czechoslovakia, none of these countries could invoke a consistently democratic tradition" seems both justified and, in the unsettled postrevolutionary circumstances, ominous (Tismaneanu 1992, 3).

The actual circumstances in Eastern Europe are considerably more complex, and so – potentially, at least – less dire than those who see the region besieged by tribalism allow. The sort of apprehension that these observers articulate nevertheless sustains a fatalism that consists of two

---

[10] Thus "every day brings us additional news of the degeneration of the old communist world into an arena of ethnic rivalries, witchhunting, chauvinistic nationalism, and other sorts of frantic self-assertion, whether it is war in Bosnia or Azerbaidjan, clericalization in Poland, attacks on gypsies in Hungary and Romania, or witchhunting former bureaucrats in Berlin and Prague" (Ost 1993, 454). The persistence of this sort of "frantic self-assertion" is also a sustained theme in Brown 1994 and Tismaneanu 1998.

reinforcing theses. I call these the hydraulic thesis and the impoverishment thesis. According to the hydraulic thesis, what we are witnessing in post-Communist Eastern Europe is the resurgence of nationalist impulses fueled by long-simmering ethnic animosities that, until 1989, Communist regimes in the region had suppressed but not eliminated. Ethnic nationalism, on this view, has emerged "after long periods of submergence, subjection, or constraint" and, as a result, is especially virulent in the sense that for large populations in post-Communist states it is "not just a priority aim but an all-consuming impulse or passion" (Brown 1994, 14). Fatalists see tribalism as fueled by just such passion.

All over the world today, but most interestingly and frighteningly in Eastern Europe and the former Soviet Union, men and women are reasserting their local and particularistic, their ethnic, religious, and national identities. The tribes have returned, and the drama of their return is greatest where their repression was most severe. It is now apparent that the popular energies mobilized against totalitarian rule, and also the more passive stubbornness and evasiveness that eroded the Stalinist regimes from within, were fueled in good part by "tribal" loyalties and passions. (Walzer 1994, 62)

Tribalism, on this view, is inevitable and perhaps irresistible insofar as it draws sustenance from hitherto stifled primordial ethnic attachments.

According to the impoverishment thesis, resurgent ethnic nationalism in the region is singularly threatening because the countries of Eastern Europe are almost entirely bereft of the sort of powerful, preexisting "traditions" needed to sustain liberal democratic politics.[11] And because such political traditions are inherited and immutable, tribalism threatens to spread unimpeded across the region. The lack in Eastern Europe of long-standing liberal democratic traditions, according to this version of fatalism, is a standing, perhaps insuperable, obstacle to the prospects for establishing and maintaining stable constitutional democratic polities in the region.[12]

---

[11] "With the exception of the Czechs, therefore, the Central and East European states can be said to lack any real or extended experience of functioning as democratic societies governed by the rule of law before sovietization excluded even the possibility of democratic and constitutional development. This fact remains of critical importance to a proper understanding of the difficulties which beset efforts to constitutionalize post-Communist societies. Thus, it is not simply a matter of 'returning to Europe,' as some have suggested. A 'return' to *their* pre-Communist past would, in reality, be a return not to some mythical golden age of liberal enlightenment and economic contentment, but to political authoritarianism, economic underdevelopment and an often stifling social stratification" (Pognay 1996, 570).

[12] Howard (1993, 107–8) insists, for instance, that this is because constitutionalism "*requires*," in the sense that it can only successfully develop within, a supportive preexisting cultural context. For the contrary view, see Przeworski 1991, 23–4.

76   *James Johnson*

This strong variety of fatalism holds that because the political choice in contemporary Eastern Europe is between tribalism and constitutionalism, the prospects for enduring liberal democracy are especially bleak.[13] Although this is far from the only available perspective, it nevertheless provides an auspicious point of departure from which to explore the politics of possibility.

CONTESTABLE ASSUMPTIONS

Apprehensions about tribalism trade upon contestable underlying assumptions. Fatalists who endorse tribalism are committed to both the hydraulic and impoverishment theses. These theses, in turn, tacitly trade upon at least two reinforcing, faulty premises. First, they presume that ethnic attachments are somehow "primordial." Second, they presume that traditions are inert and immutable – that they either exist or do not. Together these assumptions sustain a rather massive misunderstanding of the genesis and nature of political traditions, which, in turn, sustains the defects of tribalism.

Ethnic Attachments as Primordial

Among the continuing areas of contention in the Balkans, relations between what, under the former Yugoslav regime, were the Republic of Serbia and the autonomous province of Kosovo (with a large population of ethnic Albanians) are especially volatile (Brown 1994; Woodward 1995).[14] When traveling between the two regions, however, official boundaries often are less clear than symbolic ones. "There is no sign marking the border between Serbia proper and Kosovo. The most reliable marker is the first *plis*, the egg shaped white cap that older Albanian men wear" (Glenny 1993a, 134). It is by now a commonplace that the boundaries of all particularistic communities are "constructed," that they are marked and sustained symbolically in just this manner (Cohen 1985). This is true, in particular, of ethnic and national communities (Mach 1993).

By contrast, those who, like Walzer, see tribalism as an unavoidable, if deeply disturbing, social fact understand populations across Eastern Europe as divided and driven by deeply internalized, archaic antipathy toward those unlike themselves. Tribal attachments and the antipathies

---

[13] This dichotomous interpretive framework is quite common. Arato surveys a range of analyses of 1989 and its aftermath, most of which assume that the relevant possibilities reduce to "either the relatively easy victory in East Central Europe of liberalism . . . or the danger which can come from the revival of nationalist-populist politics" (1993, 631).

[14] This chapter was written and revised well before the conflagration in Kosovo reached its peak in 1998–9. I have not altered the essay to reflect subsequent events. I am convinced, however, that those events do not challenge my basic argument.

Inventing Constitutional Traditions

77

that they fuel are, on this view, "primordial." This presumption is perhaps clearest in journalistic accounts of the sources of ongoing ethnic conflict in the Balkans (e.g., Kaplan 1993).[15] Yet the preoccupation with primordial attachments has roots among more sophisticated social theorists.

Clifford Geertz affords an especially visible example here. In an early essay he ascribes the acute difficulty of establishing "new states" to an enduring tension between what he calls "civil sentiments" and "primordial attachments."[16] The former category consists in "a generalized commitment to an overarching and somewhat alien civil order" that revolves around practical demands for political efficacy, social justice, and economic progress. The latter category includes such "specific and familiar identifications" as kinship, race, religion, geographic proximity, language, and so on that are grounded in an "insistence on recognition." Primordial "sentiments" of this sort, on Geertz's account, are ancient in the sense that they are "the product, in most cases, of centuries of gradual crystallization" (1973, 268). Primordial attachments also are deeply irrational in the sense that they are transmitted and persist in inarticulate and unselfconscious ways.[17] Geertz explains that, "for virtually every person, in every society, at almost all times" ties of this sort "seem to flow more from a

[15] If Kaplan is the poster boy for this view, it is difficult to identify other scholars willing to endorse it explicitly. Nonetheless, in his survey of theories of cultural pluralism, Young (1993) devotes considerable attention to this position. Analysts of the former Yugoslavia also find it necessary to debunk the notion that ethnic conflict there results from "primordial" hatreds. In the process they suggest how deeply this view has penetrated into policy debates (Donia and Fine 1994; Woodward 1995, 7–8, 426n6). See, more generally, Rudolph and Rudolph 1993 and Bowen 1996.

[16] Geertz is talking about how this tension is intensified by "the transfer of sovereignty from a colonial regime to an independent one." He points out that this involves "more than a mere shift of power from foreign hands to native ones." It "is a transformation of the whole pattern of political life, a metamorphosis of subjects into citizens" (1973, 269). In this respect, the analogy from postcolonial politics in the Third World to contemporary events in Eastern Europe is, while not perfect, still quite apt. Indeed, one might map Geertz's distinction between "civil" and "primordial" quite neatly onto the one that Tismaneanu (1992) draws between "democracy" and "ethnocracy."

[17] One recent survey concludes that: "In its extreme form, 'primordialism' wanders into the zoological gardens of sociobiology" (Young 1993, 23). This may seem a caricature. Indeed, Geertz lately has complained that "the idea of primordial loyalty has been quite often misunderstood by social scientists." He insists that while his original use of the term was intended "to expose the artifactual, or as we would say now 'constructed' (and, indeed, often quite recently constructed), nature of social identities, and to disaggregate them into the disparate components out of which they are built, the idea of primordial loyalty was often seen to be doing quite the opposite – reifying them, archaizing them, and removing them to the realm of the darkly irrational" (1993, 57–8).

Nevertheless, consider the following characterization. "By a primordial attachment is meant one that stems from the 'givens' – or, more precisely . . . the assumed 'givens' – of

78 *James Johnson*

sense of natural – some would say spiritual – affinity than from social interaction" and that, as a result, such primordial attachments "tend . . . to be repeatedly, in some cases almost continually, proposed and widely acclaimed as preferred bases for the demarcation of autonomous political units." Due to their seeming naturalness and the insistence with which they are pressed, primordial attachments give rise to an unruly "tribalism" that represents an "ominous and deeply threatening" challenge to civil politics (1973, 255–61).

At this juncture fatalists commit a significant theoretical error. They infer from this depiction of certain attachments as primordial that such ties are *in fact* inert, immutable, inherited, and deeply irrational. The fatalist, however, mistakes appearance for reality here. There is little doubt that for many people, much of the time, certain attachments, in Geertz's words, "seem" to be not artifacts sustained by social convention but, rather, "natural." There is, however, even less doubt that political leaders and politically motivated intellectuals go to considerable lengths to depict certain, notably "ethnic," attachments as primordial in precisely this sense (Kiss 1996, 302–3; Mostov 1995; Hobsbawm 1993).[18] In short, political leaders deploy the symbolic force of ritual, myth, and tradition to *construct* certain ties as "primordial." This is the case across much of contemporary Eastern Europe as political leaders of various types endeavor, in hopes of reaping strategic political advantage, to reorient political identities in particular, partial ways.[19]

Traditions as Inherited

Fatalists preoccupied with the threat of tribalism despair at what they take to be the absence of political traditions that might inhibit ethnic animosities. In particular, they lament the absence of liberal democratic

---

social existence." Such attachments, which consist of "congruities of blood, speech, custom, and so on, are seen to have an ineffable, and at times overpowering, coerciveness in and of themselves." They are the "result not merely of personal affection, practical necessity, common interest, or incurred obligation, but at least in great part . . . of some unaccountable absolute import attributed to the very tie itself." Primordial ties thus consist in an "unreflective sense of collective selfhood" that, in turn, is "rooted in the nonrational foundations of personality" (Geertz 1973, 259, 277).

[18] Rudolph and Rudolph (1993, 26) make this point in their reflections on purportedly primordial animosities that animate politics in contemporary South Asia: "Ancient hatreds are thus made as much as they are inherited. To call them ancient is to pretend that they are primordial forces, outside history and human agency, when often they are merely synthetic antiques. Intellectuals, writers, artists and politicians 'make' hatreds." See also Bowen 1996.

[19] This process is not new in Eastern Europe. Niederhauser (1981) describes, country by country, how "awakeners" fabricated national histories across Eastern Europe in the eighteenth and nineteenth centuries.

Inventing Constitutional Traditions 79

traditions in Eastern Europe. But what is a tradition? Consider the answer provided by one sociologist unlikely to be sympathetic to the view I defend. Minimally, a tradition is something "handed down from one generation to the next." This "decisive criterion," however, settles very little.

It makes no statement about what is handed down or in what particular combination or whether it is a physical object or a cultural construction; it says nothing about how long it has been handed down or in what manner, whether orally or in written form. The degree of rational deliberation which has entered into its creation, presentation, and reception likewise has nothing to do with whether it is a tradition. The conception of tradition as here understood is silent about whether there is acceptable evidence for the truth of the tradition or whether the tradition is accepted without its validity having been established; the anonymity of its authors or creators or its attribution to named and identified persons likewise makes no difference as to whether it is a tradition. (Shils 1981, 12)

Fatalists tacitly take reinforcing positions on many of these issues. They presume that an "authentic" tradition emerges anonymously from the very distant past; that it is irrational or, at best, nonrational; that it is uniformly shared; that it is largely if not entirely unquestioned; that it is unalterable; and that, for those reasons, it is especially constraining. Based on this view of tradition, fatalists presume that if a group has a particular tradition, it pretty much is stuck with it; whereas if a group lacks a tradition, it pretty much is doomed to proceed without it.[20]

Nothing in the basic criterion for identifying traditions, however, entails any of the characteristics that fatalists attribute to them or the lesson that fatalists derive from their analysis. We might alternatively depict a tradition as a symbolically constructed practice, or set of practices, established, altered, and enacted by social and political agents in the effort to impose conceptual order on an otherwise indeterminate world (Lukes 1977).[21] Indeed, there is considerable historical evidence that suggests that many allegedly "authentic" and "ancient" traditions were, in fact, *invented* by particular actors for specific, often political purposes (Hobsbawm and Ranger 1983).

Consider an example here. In 1867 Walter Bagehot distinguished between the "*dignified* parts" and the "*efficient* parts" of what he called the English Constitution. He located the monarchy in the first category and the cabinet system in the latter. And he insisted that both parts were essential to any constitutional arrangement. "These are the two great

---

[20] Putnam 1993 is an exemplar of this view.

[21] "Traditions are not independently self-reproductive or self-elaborating. Only living, knowing, desiring human beings can enact them, reenact them and modify them. Traditions develop because the desire to create something truer and better or more convenient is alive in those who acquire and possess them" (Shils 1981, 14–15).

80 *James Johnson*

objects which every constitution must attain to be successful, which every old and celebrated one must have wonderfully achieved: Every constitution must first *gain* authority, and then *use* authority; it must first win the loyalty and confidence of mankind, and then employ that homage in the work of government" ([1867] 1963, 61, emphasis in the original).

The important point for present purposes is not Bagehot's analysis of the English Constitution or of its more general relevance. Rather, it is important to note that, like contemporary Eastern European intellectuals and political leaders who regularly are accused of distorting or abusing history, Bagehot here is engaged as much in advocacy as in analysis. For although he claims subsequently that "the characteristic merit of the English Constitution is that its dignified parts are very complicated and somewhat imposing, very old and rather venerable; while its efficient part, at least when in great and critical action, is decidedly simple and rather modern" ([1867] 1963, 65), recent historical studies suggest that this was not, at least as far as the dignified parts are concerned, actually the case.

The "dignified" character of the British monarchy, in fact, is a decidedly recent invention. Indeed, Bagehot's own portrait is, strictly speaking, false insofar as it predates the ability or willingness of British monarchs to engage in the sort of "theatrical" endeavor that he deems necessary to the task of elevating the masses to "an interest higher, deeper, wider than that of ordinary life" ([1867] 1963, 63–4). As late as the mid-nineteenth century in Britain gestures toward royal pomp and pageantry of the sort that Bagehot extols were incompetent and inconsequential. In the words of one recent historian, until the period between 1870 and 1914 the now "traditional" splendor and popularity of the British monarchy "oscillated between farce and fiasco" and was of distinctly "limited appeal" among the public (Cannadine 1983, 117, 120). More important, the upsurge and increased sophistication of royal ritual during the final decades of the nineteenth century was not a naive process. It quite clearly was a calculated response by political elites to a novel set of political exigencies – the appeal of socialism to the domestic working class, the demands of controlling the empire, and heightened international rivalry (Cannadine 1983, 126–8, 131–2, 137). Thus, the process by which British monarchs came to present themselves not merely as rulers of society but as symbols of nation and empire represents, Bagehot notwithstanding, the quite purposive, intensely political instance of the "invention of tradition."

As this example suggests, the effort to fabricate a tradition is a "strategic move" (Schelling 1960, 106). It represents an effort to transform the political game, to recast the understandings of extant political circumstances that relevant constituencies embrace by capturing their attention or commanding their imagination. Precisely because it has symbolic force – and *only* to the extent that it does – invented tradition affords strategic

Inventing Constitutional Traditions 81

actors with a powerful resource for shaping the expectations of relevant others (Johnson 1997; 1999). Moreover, once we properly grasp the strategic structure that informs the politics of constitutionalism, it becomes plain that, contrary to a fatalist view, which holds that a preexisting, well-established constitutional tradition is a necessary prerequisite to the effort to establish and sustain liberal democracies in Eastern Europe, the invention of constitutional traditions is a crucial part of that process.

Conclusion

Recall, in conclusion, that fatalism consists of a pair of complementary theses. The hydraulic and impoverishment theses draw in what I hope are obvious ways on the reinforcing assumptions I have challenged in this section. If ethnic ties are indeed primordial, and if tradition and other cultural practices are inert and inherited, then the hydraulic and impoverishment theses would seemingly provide fatalism with a solid theoretical footing. From this vantage point, not only do the virulent, ancient animosities that fuel ethnic nationalism in Eastern Europe seem irresistible, but the feeble edifice of liberal and democratic traditions in the region appears entirely inadequate to the task of sustaining resistance to tribalism.

For the reasons I advance, however, each of these hypothetical claims is contestable. We have serious theoretical warrant for assuming both that ethnic ties are constructed and that tradition and other cultural practices are neither inert nor inherited, but invented. It remains to elaborate the criticisms that I level in this section into an alternative account of the dynamics of ethnic nationalism and constitutional politics in Eastern Europe.

CONFOUNDING TRIBALISM

In offering some empirical ballast for the preceding theoretical discussion, I sketch an example that directly challenges the hydraulic thesis on what, for the fatalist, is the apparently very favorable terrain of Bosnia-Herzegovina. If ever there were a case where the hydraulic thesis of long-suppressed but newly resurgent ethnic animosity should have purchase, Bosnia-Herzegovina in the period following 1990 would seem to be it. Yet the case confounds the fatalist's expectations.[22]

---

[22] "While many outsiders cling to the insupportable generalization that tribal hatreds and ethnic warfare have characterized Bosnia for centuries, those familiar with Bosnian history and culture more typically have the opposite perception. They ask how Bosnians, who lived together in relative tranquility and mutual tolerance for many centuries, can suddenly turn on neighbors and friends and commit vicious and murderous acts that have become commonplace in the current Bosnian Conflict" (Donia and Fine 1994, 84). Here,

82   *James Johnson*

Bosnia-Herzegovina became, in the first half of the 1990s, perhaps the paradigmatic example of ethnic enmity and violence. Yet it was by no means obvious, at the start of the decade, that this should be the case.

Despite the claims made by nationalist leaders, the reality of multi-ethnic Yugoslavia still existed in the lives of individual citizens in 1990–91 – in their ethnically mixed neighborhoods, villages, towns, and cities; in their mixed marriages, family ties across republic boundaries, and . . . in their conceptions of ethnic and national coexistence and the compatibility of multiple identities for each citizen; and in the idea of Bosnia-Herzegovina. (Woodward 1995, 225)

Nationalist leaders, then, confronted the arduous task of rendering ethnic ties primordial, of making ethnicity a salient dimension for political mobilization and conflict. This task was arduous because, as late as the fall of 1991, Bosnian citizens did not, by and large, entertain the possibility of a politics based on ethnic animosity. Such a politics was, according to one observer, "simply unthinkable" for typical Bosnians (Glenny 1993a, 238; 1993b, 153–4, 157–8).[23] Nationalists, therefore, needed to convince both

---

as elsewhere, fatalism leads us to ask the wrong question. "The question, in other words, is not why old conflicts are flaring up anew, but rather why traditionally harmonious mosaics have been shattered" (Rudolph and Rudolph 1993, 25).

[23] It is difficult to establish systematic empirical support for this strong and important claim. I offer some anecdotal evidence later in the text, but existing quantitative studies are ambiguous on this point. For instance, analysis of survey data gathered in 1989–90 on the eve of the breakup of Yugoslavia shows that, together with Vojvodina, Bosnia-Herzegovina had both the most diverse population and the highest levels of tolerance of the republics (Hodson, Sekulic, and Massey 1994, 1543, 1547). The question remains, however, whether this was a matter of what we now think of as Serbs, Croats, and Muslims living in close proximity and tolerating one another or whether it exemplifies how ethnicity lacked, for many, any particular social or political salience. Behavioral indicators also are difficult to interpret. For instance, consider the following common observation. "By 1990 some 40% of Bosnian urban couples were ethnically mixed. In many instances the children of mixed marriages thought of themselves as Yugoslavs or Bosnians without ethnic allegiances" (Donia and Fine 1994, 186, 9). This remark raises questions about rates of intermarriage and other possible indicators of ethnic self-identification. One statistical study suggests that, in fact, rates of intermarriage in Yugoslavia generally and in Bosnia-Herzegovina in particular were both relatively modest and constant in the period 1961 through 1989 (Botev 1994). However, the data upon which the study is based do not allow for controls on such relevant variables as education or place of residence (e.g., urban vs. rural). Moreover, the author compares rates of intermarriage in Yugoslavia to those in countries such as the United States and Canada that are very different in terms of both economic development and patterns of immigration. So it is difficult to know what it means to say that the Yugoslav rates were relatively low. With respect to a further indicator a comparatively large and increasing number of residents of Bosnia-Herzegovina identified themselves as "Yugoslav" on the national census in the period from 1961 to 1991 (Sekulic, Massey, and Hudson 1994). See also Kiss (1996, 304n48). Given the chance, respondents in this category explicitly declined to identify themselves with any ethnic

Inventing Constitutional Traditions 83

domestic constituencies and international audiences that ethnic coexistence was impossible and that only separate, nationally defined states were politically viable.[24] Their effort to redefine political possibilities required an intense, prolonged campaign that revolved around the task of establishing a tradition of ethnic animosity and strife.[25]

The nationalist campaign encountered significant symbolic impediments. But when extant realities proved recalcitrant, nationalist forces responded ruthlessly.

> The towns and cities presented a formidable obstacle to the nationalist propaganda aimed at making national states appear the natural condition. With their mixed populations, which were living proof of multiethnic coexistence and multicultural civilization, they could not be taken psychologically. They would also, as a result, put up stronger resistance to military takeover by armies loyal to ethnic parties. . . . As a result, the cities were filled with people who had something to defend, and they were ready to resist an attack on even the idea of mixed communities. . . . The siege of Sarajevo, drawn out over more than seventeen months – from April 5, 1992, to August 1993, and revived with a vengeance in November 1993 until a cease-fire was negotiated in February 1994 – was the most dramatic example, along with Mostar in Herzegovina, of the campaign to destroy the symbol of Bosnian identity and to weaken the physical resistance of citizens still committed to living together. Far more than a military target, Sarajevo stood as a mockery to national exclusiveness. (Woodward 1995, 234–5)

Serbs, Croats, and Muslims all connived in this brutal symbolic contest (Woodward 1995, 235–6). Serb and Croat leaders tacitly colluded in the division of militarily valuable positions around Sarajevo from which they could bombard the city. Muslim leaders, meanwhile, cynically traded on the symbolic status of Sarajevo by provoking Serb attacks which they then used to keep the Muslim plight before the eyes of both putative Western sponsors and the international media. For present purposes, however, it is

---

nationality (Hodson et al., 1994, 1542–3). But, as in the country as a whole, this number remained relatively modest in absolute terms. Finally, there is the question of whether and how such social indicators translate into politics. Electoral support for nationalist parties in the first multiparty, republic-level elections in 1990 affords some indication. Yet such parties did not gain a majority in any republic (Woodward 1995, 117–25). And the order and timing of the elections themselves may well have contributed to exaggerated support for nationalists (Linz and Stepan 1992).

[24] In this sketch I ignore the way that inept Western responses contributed to – usually exacerbating – the disintegration of Bosnia-Herzegovina specifically and Yugoslavia more generally. But such ineptitude commonly is recognized (e.g., Glenny 1993a, 253; Woodward 1995).

[25] Donia and Fine (1994, 12) insist that the notion that Bosnia-Herzegovina has been plagued by "a centuries long past of ethnic and/or religious hatred and fighting" is "sheer myth." The question I explore here is how this myth was constructed. Verdery (1999) offers grisly insight into the process.

84   *James Johnson*

important to recognize that this campaign had important, far-reaching domestic consequences. It shifted ethnic attachments and identities from the realm of the "unthinkable" to the center of political conflict in Bosnia-Herzegovina in particular and in other republics of the former Yugoslavia more generally.

This was a considerable strategic accomplishment precisely to the extent that symbolically constructed political identities sustain some possibilities at the expense of others. Croat journalist Slavenka Drakulic, for example, depicts how, after 1991, politics and war rapidly transformed ethnically based nationalism – in her case, "being Croat" – from an at best partial ascription that, for herself and many of her fellows, held "no special meaning," into a suffocating new political identity.

I am living in a country that has had six bloody months of war, and . . . being Croat has become my destiny. . . . [W]hereas before, I was defined by my education, my job, my ideas, my character – and, yes, my nationality too – now I feel stripped of all that. I am nobody because I am not a person anymore. I am one of 4.5 million Croats. . . . But I am not in a position to choose any longer. Nor, I think, is anyone else. . . . What has happened is that something people cherished as part of their cultural identity – an alternative to the all-embracing communism, a means to survive – has become their political identity and turned into something like an ill-fitting shirt. You may feel the sleeves are too short, the collar too tight. You might not like the colour, and the cloth might itch. But there is no escape. One doesn't have to succumb voluntarily to this ideology of the nation – one is sucked into it. . . . Before this war started, there was perhaps a chance for Croats to become persons and citizens first, then afterwards Croats. But the dramatic events of the last twelve months have taken away that possibility. (Drakulic 1993, 50–2)

Drakulic is not alone in feeling that this new identity constricted her range of choice and action. When transported to and imposed with equal ruthlessness in Bosnia-Herzegovina, this same inexorable, one-dimensional identity afforded such a narrow range of possibilities that, for example, members of Croat paramilitary groups insisted that they had no choice but to slaughter Muslims and Serbs.[26] Muslim targets of Serb and Croat violence experienced their newly imposed identities in similar, if more extreme, ways. An American correspondent quotes one, now decidedly Muslim, resident who survived the repeated bombardment of Sarajevo as follows: "We never, until the war, thought of ourselves as Muslims. We

---

[26] Thus one such Croat "said he wanted to avoid taking part in the war but that this was impossible. The situation in Mostar caught up with him, labeled him, made him choose: stand with your own or leave your city like a dog and a traitor. 'I no longer have any of the friends I grew up with. They are all on the other sides. Serbs among Serbs. Muslims among Muslims. If I met them again I would not know what to say to them. There is no turning back now'" (Block 1993).

were Yugoslavs. But when we began to be murdered because we were Muslims, things changed. The definition of who we are today has been determined by our killers. In a way this means that these Serbs have won, no matter what happens in the war" (Hedges 1995, A4). In Bosnia-Herzegovina apparently "primordial" identities and hatreds appear for what they are – as symbolic artifacts, fabricated at immense cost by political leaders intent on securing strategic advantage.

The point in all this is not to assign blame. There is surely enough and more to go around. Rather, the point is to establish why fatalists who endorse tribalism should find this sketch discomfiting. In what sense does this scenario confound tribalism? It seems that the sort of ethnic enmity and violence that erupted in Bosnia-Herzegovina supports the hydraulic thesis and therefore is just what the fatalist would predict in Eastern Europe. There is a difference, however, between a prediction and an explanation.[27] And the most plausible explanation for the scenario I just sketched runs counter to the hydraulic thesis to which tribalism is committed.

In the first place, contrary to the hydraulic thesis, ethnicity explicitly was recognized and institutionalized, not suppressed, in pre-1989 Yugoslavia. It was institutionalized in a set of constitutional protections for individuals of various ethnic backgrounds and in the loose federal structure of the state (Woodward 1995, 45; Verdery 1996, 83–103). As a result, and as Drakulic suggests, politically salient cleavages in the period from 1961 through 1991 in Yugoslavia reflected social divisions along lines of occupation, social status, and place of residence (Woodward 1995, 44, 225).

The violence that engulfed Bosnia-Herzegovina was not, as tribalism would have it then, caused by pent-up, allegedly "primordial" ethnic animosity. Rather, "it was a political construction built and encouraged by reactionary leaders prepared to consolidate their power by sacrificing tens of thousands of lives" (Glenny 1993a, 238). This assessment leaves open important, obvious questions regarding "the conditions that made such leaders possible and popular" (Woodward 1995, 15). But when we turn to those questions we find that, again contrary to the fatalist expectation, ethnic enmity and violence were produced by, rather than being the cause of, the disintegration of political and economic institutions.[28] Fatalists who

---

[27] I set aside questions regarding the scope of the fatalist's prediction. As I argue here, the sort of violent ethnic nationalism that fatalism predicts is an exception in post-Communist states. This is true elsewhere as well (Bowen 1996).

[28] This is true not only in the case at hand (Woodward 1995, 13, 15) but also is true more generally (Przeworski et al. 1995, 20–2). Interestingly, Geertz points to institutional disintegration as the proximate cause for the virulence of allegedly "primordial" politics in postcolonial nations (Geertz 1973, 269–70, 274–6).

86 *James Johnson*

endorse tribalism, in short, reverse the direction of causality. To understand why, we need to attend to the particular political and economic uncertainties and indeterminacies of post-Communist Yugoslavia.

In the Yugoslav case, starting at least as far back as the late 1970s, international economic reforms and consequent domestic austerity had the effect of shifting the economic fortunes of republics and of powerful leaders and contributing to popular uncertainty and suspicions (Woodward 1995, 47–81). These economic pressures were exacerbated by constitutional revisions – first at the republic level in 1989, and subsequently at the national level in 1990 – that redefined the bases of popular sovereignty (Woodward 1995, 123, 210). Prior to 1989, because sovereignty had a dual basis in territorially based republics and in only partially overlapping historical nations, individuals had rights both as residents of republics and as members of constituent nations. The constitutional revisions collapsed sovereignty into a more unitary understanding of national self-determination within territorial boundaries (Hayden 1992). This redefinition had the effect of disrupting the delicate system of shared sovereignty that sustained Yugoslav federalism and, crucially, of defining certain groups as de jure minorities within political units dominated by other ethnic groups (Woodward 1995, 30–41, 199–222). Thus, it was economic uncertainty and suspicion, compounded by political insecurity, all of which were generated by institutional disarray, that afforded the conditions that made "possible and popular" the now infamous leaders who first incited and then superintended brutal ethnic violence in Bosnia-Herzegovina.[29]

I return to the important role of political leaders in the next two sections. Here it is important to note that such leaders were quite rational to resort to ethnic nationalism as a basis from which to mobilize popular support and, thereby, to solidify political and economic power (Offe 1992; 1993). Moreover, it is important to recognize how this strategy depended on their ability to deploy – or, more accurately in this case, to destroy – the force of particular symbolic forms. The success of nationalist leaders hinged crucially on the politics of possibility. Their task was to render conceivable what for many of their putative constituents was, initially at least, "unthinkable." This meant symbolically recasting the political world in such a way that exclusionary ethnic nationalism might command the attention and capture the imagination of prospective constituencies. The

---

[29] This brief sketch is overly simple in – at least – the obvious sense that those same leaders who prosecuted the ethnic violence in Bosnia-Herzegovina also were involved directly or indirectly, for instance, in the constitutional revisions of 1989 and 1990 that created the very unsettled political circumstances that they subsequently exploited after 1991. I return to this theme later. See generally Hayden 1992.

Inventing Constitutional Traditions

built environment of urban, cosmopolitan Bosnia-Herzegovina, however, emerged as a standing material and, more importantly, symbolic hindrance to this project. The cities and towns, by their brute existence, embodied ethnic coexistence and cooperation and thereby exhibited the very possibilities that nationalist leaders were determined to deny. In this sense Sarajevo, Mostar, and other cities and towns of Bosnia-Herzegovina occupied what turned out to be one very perilous intersection of symbol and strategy and so became contested resources – symbolic as much as military – in a particularly tragic episode. Serb, Croat, and Muslim political leaders, pursuing a strategy of ethnic nationalism, simultaneously recognized the potency of symbolic force and, by their relentless military attacks on Sarajevo and other cosmopolitan centers, demonstrated that such force also is quite precarious.

A RATIONALIST GROUNDING FOR FATALISM?

The fatalist might find the sketch I offer in the preceding section reassuring. The former Yugoslavia did, in fact, descend into a seemingly irreversible dynamic of ethnic violence. Fatalists might claim that it hardly matters whether that violence traded on primordial enmities or on the self-serving strategies of political leaders seeking to consolidate their power and prerogatives. For, even if the hydraulic thesis misfires, thereby undermining tribalism, fatalists might think themselves vindicated by a second, less extreme but, from their perspective, nonetheless persuasive argument. This alternative, succinctly stated by Claus Offe, identifies a "logic of rational political nihilism" that compels political leaders to manipulate ethnic and nationalist themes as a way of exploiting popular atomization and insecurity (Offe 1992; 1993; 1997).

One legacy of communism in Eastern Europe is that societies in the region are "atomized" in the sense that "people have no cognitive, ideological or organizational patterns to help them encode the social universe and guide their decisions as to whom to trust and with whom to cooperate" (Offe 1997, 70–1). This "associational wasteland" is a major component of the uncertainty, fluidity, and indeterminacy that is, as mentioned earlier, a defining feature of post-Communist political and economic relations.[30] It is exacerbated by several additional factors. In the first place, the stakes in the current transitional period are enormous. It is common knowledge that "this is the decisive time at which a new game is being started and the 'original endowment' of territory and legal resources is being distributed which will determine the relative position of the actors

---

[30] Linz and Stepan (1992, 132–3) similarly stress the "flattened landscape" of post-Communist states.

88 *James Johnson*

involved for the indefinite future" (Offe 1993, 13). Second, the economies across the region are in various states of disarray (Brown 1994, 121–71). This generates heightened economic insecurity and induces very low expectations among relevant populations regarding the prospects for sustained recovery (Offe 1992). Thus, even if adopting a constitution enhances the prospect of enacting economic reform, insecurity and low expectations among the populace about the possibility for economic gains to coordination deflate the attractiveness of constitutional politics.[31] Third, weak political institutions and "minority" populations that traverse official political boundaries generate internal and external insecurity, respectively.[32] Such political insecurity provides a strong impetus to ethnic identification (Walzer 1992; Offe 1997, 66–7). Finally, ethnicity, to the extent that it remained untainted by connections to prior Communist regimes, "provides for a 'clean' identity" (Offe 1993, 9). In a setting characterized by weak political institutions and immature civil society, ethnicity and nationalism afford – almost by default – a focal point for mobilization (Ost 1993; Offe 1992).[33]

Offe argues that, under these conditions, political leaders rationally adopt a strategy of ethnic mobilization and that this strategic imperative sustains the threat of violent conflict in post-Communist Eastern Europe. Because they operate in the sort of highly indeterminate but economically and politically pivotal environment just described, political leaders will look to the past in the attempt to "reappropriate history" (Offe 1992, 22–3).[34] Among the prominent lessons they extract from the history of Eastern Europe is a litany of evils perpetrated and justified in the name of this or that ethnic chauvinism (Verdery 1999). These lessons, in turn,

---

[31] Preliminary empirical studies suggest that although they are "not a precondition for economic reforms, constitutions do appear to contribute to the political capacity to adopt economic reform measures" (Hellman 1996, 56).

[32] Brown (1994, 176–7) offers a typology of various forms of ethnic nationalism that exist or threaten post-Communist Eastern Europe.

[33] I presume, following Przeworski (1991, 28), that only the noncompliance of groups is a threat to institutional arrangements. Nationalist claims afford an especially attractive basis for mobilization because they are comparatively simple and because they consequently can be communicated easily and inexpensively (Woodward 1995, 124). Moreover, the sort of particularistic, exclusionary attachments upon which ethnic nationalism draws arguably have greater, more immediate force than universalist claims (Hardin 1995, 140–1, 151).

[34] It should come as no surprise that nationalist leaders are especially attuned to history. For example, after spending several years in prison for his nationalist leanings under the Tito regime in the early 1960s, Croatian nationalist leader Franjo Tudjman "found work as an archivist at the Zagreb Museum of Military History. There he developed his broad knowledge of Croatian history and his obsession with Croatian military figures. His party's paraphernalia is characterized by heroes of Croatia's history, symbols and flags" (Glenny 1993a, 128).

afford political leaders with what they take to be warrant, minimally for sowing seeds of distrust and, beyond that, for actively advocating more or less extreme, exclusionary brands of ethnic nationalism.

A fatalist might argue that, because the impoverishment thesis still holds, the nihilistic logic that Offe identifies is very nearly irresistible. How, in the sort of indeterminate circumstances that prevail in post-Communist societies, could political leaders proceed otherwise? In order to advance this argument the fatalist must suppose that in indeterminate circumstances political leaders *necessarily* will succumb to nihilism. Failing that, they might defend the weaker supposition that political leaders in post-Communist Eastern Europe lack the resources to proceed otherwise. The fatalist cannot, however, sustain either of these suppositions.

What reason do we have to believe, as rationalist fatalism must suppose, that political leaders necessarily resort to nihilism? A casual glance at the record in post-Communist states suggests that the sort of extreme, violent ethnic nationalism that erupted in Yugoslavia is exceptional.[35] Moreover, even when we examine the Yugoslav case more closely, the appearance that political leaders more or less uniformly and enthusiastically embrace the nihilist political strategy that Offe identifies proves deceptive. Rather than inevitable, the emergence of violent ethnic politics in what, for the fatalist, remains the strongest case, appears highly contingent.

In the late 1970s and 1980s the Yugoslav Communist Party systematically suppressed any manifestation of liberal political opposition. The party thus inadvertently eliminated in advance much of the competition that opportunistic nationalist leaders might have encountered.[36] In order

---

[35] When we survey post-Communist Eastern Europe we surely see points of nationalist tension of various sorts. See Brown (1994, 176–8). Yet the dynamic in Bosnia-Herzegovina stands out. "In one respect, the experience of the former Yugoslav federation can be considered positive. For until now its disintegration has been the exception proving the rule. Irrational and violent nationalism has not succeeded throughout Eastern Europe and the majority of nations have easily avoided descent into armed conflict" (Glenny 1993a, 238). See Laitin (1995) and Bowen (1996) on the contingent relation between ethnic nationalism and violence more generally.

[36] "The party's concern for social order thus produced a conservative, habitual response: to try to strengthen the party while preventing the perceived threat to the political system posed by political liberals, critical intellectuals, and civil libertarians. The real danger, in the party's view, lay in the activities of nonparty liberals and social democrats who were fighting for greater rights of expression in general, independent organization, and individually based voting rights. . . . The consequence of this rearguard action, however, was the opposite of what was intended. . . . Instead of viewing the right-wing revivals of unresolved historical issues from previous wars, of religious fervor, of fascist tendencies, and of ethnic conflict as a danger to both the state and the economic reforms, the party made the task of the political right easier by seriously undercutting the efforts of political liberals and moderates who could have built a political center throughout the country, and thus an alternative to the republic centered nationalists" (Woodward 1995, 76–7).

to show successfully that the "logic of rational political nihilism" *inevitably* drove the disintegration of Yugoslavia, then, the fatalist must persuasively dismiss the counterfactual claim that, if it had not been decimated by the Communists, the liberal opposition might have successfully embraced an alternative political strategy. This is slippery ground. I do not mean to suggest that such a counterfactual claim is thoroughly defensible. I surely have not defended it here. Instead, I wish to suggest only that fatalists have considerable work to do if they hope to sustain the supposition that the nihilistic strategy is irresistible.

Fatalists might, of course, resort to a weaker position. They might take the impoverishment thesis as warrant to argue that even if liberal political actors would seek to formulate a strategy that would compete with the rational nihilism of ethnic nationalism, the paucity of powerful alternative symbolic resources means that any such strategy is severely disadvantaged in the sort of circumstances that Offe depicts. Here the claim is not that rational ethnic nihilism is irresistibly attractive, but that, for practical purposes, there simply is no alternative. The logic that Offe identifies, however, allows for a much less gloomy interpretation. To see why this is so I must challenge the impoverishment thesis more directly.

INVENTING CONSTITUTIONAL TRADITIONS

The impoverishment thesis, you will recall, consists in the claim that ethnic nationalism is especially dangerous in the formerly Communist states because political actors in those states lack competing political traditions upon which to draw as part of the effort to establish and consolidate liberal democratic politics. The position to which we now turn is committed to a version of this thesis. It holds that although political leaders in post-Communist Eastern Europe may not *necessarily* embrace the "logic of rational ethnic nihilism," the paucity of alternative symbolic resources means that, practically speaking, ethnic nationalism affords an extremely tempting basis for political mobilization.

Those who adopt this view subscribe to the impoverishment thesis but are not, properly speaking, fatalists. I call them pessimists. Unlike those fatalists who endorse tribalism, pessimists do not subscribe to the hydraulic thesis. And they do not treat political traditions as inherited and immutable. Moreover, unlike the brand of rationalist fatalism just discussed, pessimists claim that political leaders in post-Communist states are committed to ethnic nationalism in an opportunistic but contingent way. Pessimists merely suggest that, in any case, the impoverishment thesis casts doubt on the availability of resources from which rational political agents might construct alternatives to the invented traditions of ethnic nationalism.

Inventing Constitutional Traditions 91

Pessimists bemoan the "cult of the past" that, on their view, is a "ubiquitous" feature of politics in post-Communist Eastern Europe. From their perspective political actors draw on the past in "manipulative" ways in order to create "new historical mythologies" that can function simultaneously to obscure complicity with the old regime and to justify self-serving political ambitions (Gyani 1993). Pessimists thus acknowledge that political traditions can be invented and deployed for strategic purposes. They see in this possibility, however, the seeds of irrationalist demagoguery of the sort that, on their account, informs ethnic nationalism.[37] It would be foolish to deny that political actors in Eastern Europe in fact invent traditions for precisely such purposes. The thrust of my argument to this point has been that they, in fact, do just that. Yet the question remains as to whether invented traditions can serve ends other than duplicity, self-deception, and manipulation.[38] An affirmative reply to that question – one that deflates the pessimist stance – requires that I squarely confront the impoverishment thesis.

The most obvious way to challenge the impoverishment thesis might be to examine historical cases of polities that, while internally heterogenous and lacking conducive preexisting constitutional traditions, nevertheless constructed such a tradition as an integral part of political transformations through which they repudiated authoritarianism, navigated the perils of both economic crisis and ethnic nationalism, and consolidated a working liberal democratic order. Perez-Diaz (1993), for instance, argues that this was the case in post-Franco Spain. Although he offers a descriptive account of the events of Spain's transition, he offers scant theoretical purchase on the processes underlying the events that he describes. He attributes an "important role" in the Spanish transition to "the invention of a democratic tradition." He also insists that this tradition was, in large measure, "a deliberate institutional and cultural construct" (1993, 5–6, 21). Yet Perez-Diaz neglects the mechanisms at work in this process and so, in particular, does not adequately appreciate the ways that symbol and strategy intersect in the invention of tradition.[39] While he asserts that

---

[37] Jaworski (1985) seems to share this view. For charges of demagoguery, see, e.g., Walzer 1992, Hobsbawm 1993, and Mostov 1995.

[38] At a minimum the pessimists' apprehension seems to entail that relevant actors are engaged in manipulation – setting the parameters of political debate behind the backs of participants. And it presumes that there is some more normatively defensible way of, for example, drawing political boundaries. I am not saying that these conditions do not hold in contemporary East Central Europe, only that they need to be spelled out.

[39] In fairness, with reference to political actors in the Spanish case, Perez-Diaz claims in passing that newly constructed traditions shaped "their preferences and their sense of what can be done." But, at the same time, he insists that by and large, political actors are not rational agents (Perez-Diaz 1993, 28, 7). As a result he fails to appreciate the extent to which

92   *James Johnson*

"symbolic politics" informed the creation of new political traditions in the Spanish case, his own account provides little understanding of why invented tradition is important or how it is constructed. This is problematic because, absent a persuasive theoretical account of this process, it is difficult to discern the relevance of the sort of case that Perez-Diaz describes for more general political analysis. In short, the fact that historically an invented political tradition was crucially important to the Spanish transition may be strictly irrelevant to, for instance, current circumstances in post-Communist Eastern Europe.

Many political leaders in contemporary Eastern Europe symbolically sustain the ethnic nationalism that they promote with traditions invented for the purpose in the sense that, when pressing their case, they not only deliberately reappropriate and reinterpret history, but (as in Bosnia-Herzegovina) also seek, more or less forcefully, to efface extant possibilities not in keeping with the newly rewritten historical record.[40] Nationalist leaders in the former Yugoslavia aimed in this way simultaneously to establish precedent for their own vision of political possibility and to eradicate competing possibilities. Offe identifies the strategic logic that animates these attempts to trade upon history and presents that logic as unavoidably nihilistic. Pessimists commonly respond to these efforts by condemning them – even where they are not violent – as demagoguery. Such condemnation, though perhaps warranted in particular instances, is unduly sweeping and unlikely to be effective. It is overly sweeping because all political leaders, nationalist or otherwise, confront very much the same strategic task.[41] The condemnation is likely to be ineffective because, if Offe's account is correct, "instead of moral exhortations," the remedy for ethnic nationalism "is a change in the parameters and rules of action of these leaders and strategists that would make it both preferable and affordable for them to refrain from pursuing or supporting otherwise perfectly rational strategies of ethnification" (Offe 1993, 6; 1992, 21).

The strategic task of political leaders is to establish focal points around which relevant constituencies can coordinate (Schelling 1960, 91; Calvert 1992).[42] In indeterminate social and political circumstances like those

---

political agents have both incentive and opportunity to try to deploy symbolic force to their strategic advantage. I offer just such an account elsewhere (Johnson 1997; 1999).

[40] On the lengths to which political actors pursue this task, see Verdery 1999.

[41] This does not, of course, imply that constitution making will rely on violence, only that it does rely on the ability of relevant political actors to define political possibilities in particular ways. And that is a thoroughly strategic enterprise. I return to the ways that symbolic contests figure in the process of constitution making in the next section.

[42] This is a departure from the perhaps canonical rational choice view that "political entrepreneurs" largely provide a source of "selective incentives" to constituents. Indeed, some argue that coordination is prerequisite to the production of the resources needed to

Inventing Constitutional Traditions

which obtain in post-Communist states, this task is especially difficult. Such circumstances present political leaders, nationalist or otherwise, with a "derived coordination problem" where what is at stake are common understandings of the nature of the political game itself. In strategic settings of this sort actors are uncertain about the nature of their ongoing interaction. That is, they are unsure about the identities and interests of relevant players, about what alternative courses of action are available, about the various outcomes that might ensue, and so on (Calvert 1992, 12–13).[43] Political leaders, as a result, have both the opportunity and motivation to try to recast the social and political world and the possibilities that it affords in particular, partial ways. In so doing they, not surprisingly, seek to exploit "the *symbolic* contents of the game" generally and engage "in the creation of *traditions*" more particularly (Schelling 1960, 106–7). The destruction of Sarajevo, Mostar, and other urban centers of Bosnia-Herzegovina is only the most recent, glaring reminder of just how far political leaders will press such symbolic contests.

On this account, moral exhortation, as Offe suggests, is likely to be entirely ineffectual. Instead, if we accept that even political leaders who would define the political world otherwise face powerful, widespread "'rational' motivations to engage in ethnic politics," the appropriate and crucial response is to encourage them to identify and deploy symbolic resources that will enable relevant constituencies to entertain political possibilities that embody identities and options that run counter to ethnic nationalism.[44] In the case at hand, of course, this means encouraging efforts to tap the potential, essentially symbolic "power of constitutional legitimacy to command popular support in times of anarchy or political vacuum" (Schelling 1960, 74). Here it is not enough to preach the virtues of democracy, the rule of law, human rights, and economic development. Political leaders confront a task that, analytically at least, is prior to that. They must endeavor to define the political world to their own ends where this amounts to rendering constitution making central to the political game. They must formulate and advance a vision of the political world on which relevant constituencies might draw to interpret and assess their strategic situation. This is a task of coordination that, like the appeals to historic injustice that animate ethnic

---

distribute selective incentives (Hardin 1995, 28–37). Moreover, this view allows us to see the strategic underpinnings of the concept of "charisma" (Hardin 1995, 36). The latter in this sense refers not to an irrational attachment but to the capacity of political leaders to identify themselves symbolically with the central preoccupations of society (Geertz 1983, 122–3).

[43] This sort of "derived" problem may suggest an unavoidable limit to any effort to represent social relations in the framework of repeated games (Taylor 1987, 107).

[44] The quoted phrase comes from Offe 1993, 13.

94   *James Johnson*

chauvinism, will draw upon a "tradition" invented for the purpose. It remains to be seen what sort of resources might be available to political leaders who, intent on designing constitutional arrangements and, thereby, on countering the call of ethnic nationalists, seek to construct alternative political traditions.

Fatalists and pessimists alike no doubt will here throw up their hands in exasperation. Their response, however, is ill-conceived. On their account the debilitating political problem in post-Communist polities is, precisely as the impoverishment thesis holds, that those states are devoid of resources from which political actors might construct constitutional traditions. A cursory inspection, however, reveals that the situation is not nearly so bleak as the impoverishment thesis allows.

Suppose, as seems likely, that the Soviet-era constitutions, which, with more or less substantial revision, remain in force in most post-Communist states, are so compromised as to be meaningless in the longer term. It still is relatively easy to identify both formal institutional arrangements and informal traditions that actors seeking to invent constitutional traditions might summon as precedent. Consider some examples. Minimally, most post-Communist states "had more or less democratic constitutions for much of the period between the two wars" (Elster 1993, 193). Such a precedent is perhaps clearest in the former Czechoslovakia (Stein 1993). Even fatalists, however, concede that Czechoslovakia has a tradition of demo-cratic constitutionalism, so this example perhaps provides no terribly impressive warrant. Yet Hungary too – with significant interruptions and limitations – has an intermittent history of parliamentary constitutional government stretching back to 1848 (Ilonszki 1993). More surprisingly still, Poles have a constitutional history traceable – once again despite disruptions due to partition and occupation – to the twelfth century (Brzezinski 1991). And even where political leaders cannot point to formal constitutional arrangements, they might well invoke historical patterns of informal norms and practices. Thus, prior to 1991, Bosnia-Herzegovina displayed precisely this sort of informal heritage of toleration and coexistence.[45]

The point of these examples is not to suggest that constitutional regimes dominate Czech, Polish, or Hungarian political history or that Bosnia-Herzegovina has been a land of uniform, uninterrupted harmony and that, therefore, such historical precedents somehow constitute the real,

---

[45] Historians of Bosnia-Herzegovina trace a "centuries long tradition of accommodation and mutual coexistence of different religious communities and nationalities" that existed not just in the rarefied realm of ideas but also in "historical patterns of coalition and com-promise, coupled with deeply rooted traditions of cooperation and coexistence in every-day life" (Donia and Fine 1994, 280).

Inventing Constitutional Traditions 95

authentic political tradition of the region. The point, rather, is that, even under the seemingly most inauspicious circumstances, political actors might identify and appropriate symbolic resources from which to construct constitutional traditions.[46] If successful, they might thereby lend salience to constitutional politics as a focal equilibrium in what otherwise is a highly indeterminate, very hazardous, derived coordination problem. The strategic task, in short, is to render constitution making a possible basis for political interaction.

The suggestion that political leaders deploy invented traditions in order to redefine political possibility may appear to be an especially nebulous, if not entirely fantastic and, pejoratively, utopian enterprise. I believe such a conclusion is mistaken for at least three reasons. First, the fact that ethnic animosity and violence emerged as an equilibrium in the former Yugoslavia says nothing about whether and how such an outcome might have been avoided. Second, even if political leaders successfully establish constitution making as the primary dimension of strategic interaction, ethnic nationalism remains a threat. Finally, it is important to note that invented traditions are arbitrary in the sense that they need not reflect actual historical trajectories in any direct way. I develop these observations in turn.

First, I do not claim that the sort of symbolic politics involved in the invention of traditions can counter massive material asymmetries or withstand violent assault. The symbolic force that governs political possibility for particular actors in particular settings is subject to material and physical constraints. The ruins and casualties of Sarajevo, Mostar, and other Bosnian cities testify to that. It is hard to imagine political leaders who could invoke with any credibility a tradition of toleration and cooperation, no matter how robust, while their putative constituents are under bombardment. Once underway, the dynamic of violent ethnic nationalism that emerged in Bosnia-Herzegovina might, in that sense, have been very nearly irreversible.[47] That in no way implies that that dynamic was unavoidable. The theoretical account that I offer allows us to draw lessons from the experience of post-Communist Eastern Europe quite at variance with the sort of resignation that fatalists and pessimists recommend. Yet those lessons apply, where they do, largely

---

[46] On the historical precedents for democratic institutions even in Russia which, after the Balkans, is perhaps the post-Communist country least hospitable to constitutional democracy, see Starr 1989.

[47] Here I have in mind resistance by indigenous actors. I leave aside whether international pressure might have been effective. I only mean to suggest that, once initiated, ethnic violence *may* emerge as an equilibrium (Laitin 1995). There nevertheless is anecdotal evidence that even this sort of equilibrium can be subverted by the spontaneous, decentralized action of indigenous populations. See, e.g., O'Connor 1996.

96 *James Johnson*

before nationalist leaders demonstrate their willingness to resort to violence.[48]

Second, if politicians designing a constitutional regime expect it to endure, they must include provisions that protect internal religious, linguistic, and ethnic minorities (Ordeshook 1993a). Clearly, one necessary part of this task is to promote the virtues of democracy, human rights, and economic development. Another necessary part of the task is to resist the strategies of nationalist politicians who, as in the former Yugoslavia, seek to manipulate the formal apparatus of liberal constitutionalism in order to heighten the salience of ethnicity that they might then exploit for purposes of political mobilization (Hayden 1992, 673). This, in particular, requires vigilance against constitutional provisions that expound the sort of "constitutional nationalism . . . that privileges the members of one ethnically defined nation over other residents in a particular state" (Hayden 1992, 655).[49] Nationalist leaders

---

[48] The difficulties involved here are captured in the following story. "On April 6, 1992, a crowd of demonstrators estimated at over 50,000 gathered in front of the Bosnian Parliament building in Sarajevo to demonstrate for peace in Bosnia and Hercegovina. The demonstrators were members of all three of Bosnia's largest nationalities: Serbs, Croats and Bosnian Muslims. Directly across the street, from the upper floors of the ultra-modern Holiday Inn built for the 1984 Winter Olympics, heavily-armed militiamen fired randomly into the crowd, killing and wounding dozens of the peace demonstrators. This cavalier killing spree dispersed the crowd and marked the demise of the few remaining hopes that moderation and compromise might prevail in Bosnia and Hercegovina.

"The Sarajevo massacre of April 6 contained many elements that would recur in the Bosnian war in subsequent weeks and months. The victims were unarmed civilians who hoped for the preservation of a multiethnic Bosnian society which had roots and traditions dating back many centuries. The perpetrators were nationalist extremists, organized and heavily armed by political and paramilitary leaders intent on destroying Bosnia's multiethnic society and replacing it with the national supremacy of a single ethnic group, in this case the Serbs. Symbolically, the Sarajevo massacre stilled the voices of peace and mutual tolerance; the shrill shouts of ethnic hatred and national divisiveness triumphed by force of arms" (Donia and Fine 1994, 1).

[49] A variation on this phenomenon appears in constitutional provisions that articulate a "protective nationalism" that purports to safeguard ethnic nationals who reside beyond officially recognized borders (Brown 1994, 176). A good example here is the current Hungarian Constitution, embodied in the *Hungarian Rules of Law in Force* (December 31, 1990). Chapter I: General Provisions (Article 6.3) of that document explains: "The Republic of Hungary bears a sense of responsibility for what happens to Hungarians living outside its borders and promotes the fostering of their relations with Hungary." Given the large numbers of ethnic Hungarians currently residing in Slovakia, Transylvania (Romania), the Ukraine and Vojvodina (Serbia), and the unsettled history of relations between these minorities and their home states, such language can readily be interpreted as incendiary (Brown 1994, 192–3, 213). This same problem could easily arise elsewhere. Thus, even Poland, which is relatively homogeneous internally, might articulate similar inflammatory claims about ethnic Poles living in Lithuania, Belarus, Russia, and the Ukraine (Brown 1994, 204–13).

introduced provisions of this sort in the new or amended constitutions adopted in the formerly Yugoslav republics of Croatia (1990), Slovenia (1989), Macedonia (1991), and Serbia (1990) (Hayden 1992, 656–65). In this way the process of constitutional revision itself hastened the descent into violent ethnic nationalism. Conversely, by opposing such constitutional provisions political leaders can help to defuse the political salience of ethnicity and nationalism as competing ways of organizing the political world.

Finally, as Hobsbawm points out, the link between invented traditions and actual historical trajectories is peculiarly arbitrary.[50] Here we might recall Bagehot's effort to depict the "dignified parts" of the British Constitution as "very old and rather venerable." Or, to take a more recent example, we might once again consider the way that, in the 1970s and 1980s, the typically beleaguered Polish opposition constructed a "tradition of resistance" to the Communist regime.[51] In both cases, the "tradition" that political actors invoke is at some considerable variance with the historical record.

It is difficult, perhaps impossible, to identify with any great confidence the factors that might constrain the arbitrariness at work in such cases. Material factors of the sort just mentioned provide one obvious, relatively broad source of constraint. A second possible source of constraint on the arbitrariness of invented tradition might operate on analogy to the first of the imperatives that Ronald Dworkin claims confront agents engaged in legal interpretation.[52] Dworkin argues that we must assess the adequacy of any interpretation along two dimensions. The first, and for present purposes, the relevant one of these, is what he calls "the

---

[50] "Invented tradition is taken to mean a set of practices, normally governed by overtly or tacitly accepted rules and of a ritual or symbolic nature, . . . which automatically implies continuity with the past. . . . The historic past into which the new tradition is inserted need not be lengthy, stretching back to the assumed mists of time. . . . However, insofar as there is such reference to an historic past, the peculiarity of 'invented' traditions is that the continuity with it is largely factitious. In short they are responses to novel situations which take the form of reference to old situations, or which establish their own past by quasi-obligatory repetition" (Hobsbawm 1983, 1–2).

[51] It is extremely difficult, in terms of objective historical description, to portray the political trajectory of postwar Poland as having been dominated by what were basically episodic outbursts of concerted political opposition (e.g., in 1956 and 1970–1). This is especially the case to the extent that the regime systematically suppressed the opposition. In terms of the strategic problem of political mobilization, however, an invented "tradition of resistance" appears to have been extremely important. On the latter, see Laba 1991 and Kubik 1994. I return briefly to this example later.

[52] I thank John Ferejohn for this suggestion. These constraints on interpretation are a running theme in Dworkin's portrait of legal interpretation (e.g., Dworkin 1986, 230–1, 255–8, 410–11).

98   James Johnson

dimension of fit."[53] According to Dworkin, any interpretation must, if it is to conform to this imperative, "claim an adequate grounding in past practice" in the sense that it "must be rejected if actual legal practice is wholly inconsistent with the legal principles that it recommends; it must, that is, have some considerable purchase on or grounding in actual legal experience" (1993, 111). We might restate this demand in the following terms. A potential constituency will find some effort to portray some understanding of the political world as "traditional," credible, or acceptable only if the range of possibilities that that understanding encompasses is not wholly inconsistent with the actual political experience, past or present, of that constituency. Otherwise the proposed "tradition" will have little force for the constituency whose imagination it is designed to capture.

It is important to note two things here. First, the invention of tradition, as a strategic process, aims to establish a distinctive account of what counts as past practice. It is not meant to bring some proposed interpretation of the political world and the possibilities that it contains into line with an independently existing commonly accepted set of precedents. Rather it is meant to establish just what counts as precedent in the first place.[54] Here, arbitrariness emerges once again. This is because, second, as I restate his claim, Dworkin makes a relatively modest demand. What might it mean for some understanding of the political world to be *wholly inconsistent* with actual experience? Consider in this regard the episodic, if concerted, opposition to the Polish regime in the period between the imposition of communism and its collapse in 1989. Such episodes, however inspiring, surely were both relatively fleeting and quite distant from the everyday experience of most Poles during the otherwise bleak decades of Communist rule. Nevertheless, not only *did* the Polish opposition mount

---

[53] "Any interpretation of the Constitution must be tested on two large and related dimensions." I discuss the first of these, "the dimension of fit," in the text. "The second is the dimension of justice. If two different views about the best interpretation of some constitutional provision both pass the test of fit . . . we should prefer the one whose principles seem to us best to reflect people's moral rights and duties, because the Constitution is a statement of abstract moral ideals that each generation must reinterpret for itself" (Dworkin 1993, 111). This second dimension is not obviously relevant to the sorts of strategic interactions with which I am concerned here.

[54] Elster alludes to this in the context of constitution making in post-Communist states. "It seems that sometimes the pre-Communist constitution is invoked in defense of an idea that has no good substantive justification; sometimes it serves as a convenient focal point among a plethora of possible arrangements; and sometimes it is harnessed to a genuine need to assert the continuity of the nation's life and the parenthetical character of the Communist regime" (1993, 193). In any case, on Elster's account, the pre-Communist constitutional tradition of a nation can provide either constructive examples to be imitated or negative examples to be avoided.

episodic, overt resistance to the regime, but studies of how Solidarity mobilized its supporters show that the "tradition of resistance" that the opposition invented out of those transitory events was an extremely potent strategic resource (Laba 1991; Kubik 1994). There is no reason why invented tradition cannot play an analogously important strategic role in the constitution-making processes of post-Communist states. In order to see just why constitutional traditions are important, it is necessary to examine the strategic structure of constitutional politics.

THE STRATEGIC STRUCTURE OF CONSTITUTION MAKING

Constitutionalism, as standardly understood, embodies "ideas about how the powers of government and state officials are to be limited" (Ten 1993, 394). On this view the "essence of constitutionalism" consists in "a system of effective restraints upon governmental action" (Friedrich, 1941, 20–1; Buchanan 1994). From here it is but a short step to strategies of political justification that take constitutions to be contracts – based on, if not un-animous, at least very substantial, ex ante agreement – that establish rules to govern parties to exchange relations that are in some way uncertain, and therefore potentially susceptible to ex post opportunism (Brennan and Buchanan 1985; Mueller 1991).[55]

There are at least two difficulties with this standard view. The first is a rather obvious empirical observation. Historically, the essentially negative notion of "effective restraint" fails to capture anything like the full range of operative constitutional provisions. More important, however, especially outside of the United States, that negative criterion does not even obviously capture what might be called the "essence" of constitutionalism as embodied in political texts and legal documents. If we widen our view of constitutionalist thought and practice beyond America to include Europe as well, we see that constitutionalism regularly imposes not just constraints but duties and obligations on both citizens and governments (Casper 1989).

The second difficulty is more properly theoretical. It arises from the insight that the value of even such canonical "restraints" on government action as the establishment clause in the First Amendment to the U.S. Constitution perhaps resides in the extent to which, by removing especially contentious issues from the political arena, such "restraints" actually *facilitate* effective democratic government (Holmes 1988). This point is general. Indeed, recognition that constitutions operate to facilitate future political and economic interaction, significantly undermines the com-monly accepted contractarian justification sketched earlier. A constitution

---

[55] Hence the preoccupation with the difficulties involved in establishing "credible commit-ments" in constitutional regimes (e.g., North and Weingast 1989; Weingast 1993).

100   James Johnson

on this view is as much a mechanism for enabling as for constraining government.

This last observation provides initial warrant for the revisionist view that a constitution is best understood not as "a social contract that creates rules to commit later selves and later generations to various specific things" but as a coordinating mechanism that "merely raises the costs of trying to do things some other way through its creation of a coordination convention" (Hardin 1989, 111). I will not rehearse the details of this revisionist account here.[56] For present purposes, it is important only to recognize three relevant analytical differences between constitutions and contracts. First, a constitution and a contract solve different strategic problems. The former is a mechanism for resolving a coordination problem, whereas the latter induces cooperation in a prisoners' dilemma. Second, constitutions typically rely more on ex post mass compliance than on the sort of explicit ex ante consent or agreement entailed in a contract. Finally, unlike contracts, which require exogenous enforcement, constitutions, if they are to be effective, must be self-enforcing (Hardin 1989, 101–2). A constitution, on this view, is an equilibrium institution that, by coordinating the expectations of relevant parties, enables them to realize potentially large gains through long-term patterns of social, political, and economic interaction.

This revisionist view allows us to recognize several important, related contingencies in constitution-making processes. These contingencies, in turn, are germane to challenging the impoverishment thesis. First, constitutional arrangements, if they are to be successful, must be a self-enforcing equilibrium. A coordination problem is, by definition of course, a setting in which multiple equilibria are available.[57] An equilibrium solution to such a problem, however, not only need not, but typically is not, either symmetrical (in the sense that all relevant parties are indifferent between available equilibria) or efficient (Ordeshook 1993a, 147).[58] Consequently the equilibrium solution to a coordination problem commonly – and rather modestly – simply represents the best outcome any actor can hope for given her expectations about how relevant others will proceed. This raises the issue of how power enters into constitution making specifically and into processes of institutional creation and

---

[56] See Hardin 1988; 1989; and Ordeshook 1993a; 1993b. I address the problems that this revisionist account raises in some detail elsewhere (Calvert and Johnson 1999).

[57] In this sense, although perhaps not for reasons the original author would endorse, it is correct to say that "the transformation of the post-Communist societies should be understood as an inherently uncertain process with a plurality of possible outcomes, particularly in the short and medium term" (Pognay 1996, 569).

[58] Knight (1995) specifies the empirical conditions necessary for symmetrical, efficient coordination.

change more generally. There is little doubt that coordination itself generates power.[59] Yet insofar as coordination equilibria need be neither symmetrical nor efficient, it seems reasonable to anticipate that power asymmetries among relevant actors (reflecting differential levels of risk aversion, time preference, and credibility) enter into the coordinating process itself as differentially endowed actors seek, by shaping the expectations of others, to focus the coordination process in advantageous ways (Knight 1992).[60]

Second, the revisionist view of constitutions as solutions to large-scale coordination problems calls attention to still further vicissitudes of the equilibriating process (Calvert and Johnson 1999). It identifies compliance as problematic in ways that contractarian conceptions – premised as they are on widespread, ex ante agreement – neglect. Consider the following view of the American Constitution.

> The Constitution of 1787 worked in the end because enough of the relevant people worked within its confines long enough to get it established in everyone's expectations that there was no point in not working within its confines. The agreement of certain people to it may have been important for those people to work within the Constitution, but agreement was not the only motivator. Many must have worked within the Constitution simply because it was the most useful thing for them to do in their own interests. They may as soon have continued to work within the Articles of Confederation and their respective state constitutions. (Hardin 1989, 117–18)

At least two things follow from this sketch. In the first place, it should be clear that on this view the equilibriating process is not instantaneous. Any proposal that emerges as a potential coordination equilibrium from constitutional bargaining is precarious precisely because it takes time to establish widespread, stable, reciprocal expectations. And if, as seems to be the case in post-Communist Eastern Europe, time is at a premium, then the process of coordinating on any constitutional arrangement will be especially susceptible to disruption.[61]

In the second place, compliance with a constitutional arrangement does not derive simply from mutual expectations. For any expectations that actors form rest, in turn, on their assessment of what alternatives are available and, within that set, of the attractiveness and accessibility of

---

[59] Schelling (1960), Calvert (1992), and Hardin (1995), for example, all concede that coordination can generate power.

[60] This, of course, is an empirical claim for which I here offer no evidence. But it is important to understand that the conditions under which pure, symmetrical coordination problems exist are extremely limited as compared with the circumstances of asymmetry just described in the text. Knight (1995) specifies these conditions in a simple, stark, and persuasive way.

[61] On the time constraints in post-1989 Yugoslav politics, see, e.g., Woodward 1995, 144–5.

102 *James Johnson*

alternatives.[62] In the strategic structure of constitution making, other, usually many other, feasible coordination points are available. Whether and to whom they might be attractive are other issues. In the American case, for example, the Articles of Confederation provided a relatively plausible, if not terribly efficient, status quo. Yet, in this respect the current situation in Eastern Europe, where the status quo ante is seriously discredited, is considerably less determinate. Prior to 1989 the Eastern European countries were "governed" by Soviet-style constitutions that, in the post-Communist period, occupy a very ambiguous position. On the one hand, in the years immediately following 1989, citizens of the newly post-Communist states properly viewed these constitutions with considerable suspicion – as hollow documents and largely vestiges of Soviet domination. On the other hand, Hungary, Poland, and Czechoslovakia, for example, did not initially seek to write wholly new constitutions. They instead simply amended the existing constitutional documents.[63]

Here we begin to see why, in the current Eastern European context, the threat to constitutionalism from ethnic nationalism is especially acute. Not only is it the case that numerous constitutional arrangements exist that might serve to coordinate political action in a society. There also exist other competing "extraconstitutional" equilibria around which relevant constituencies might coordinate their political activities. Ethnicity, religion, and so on afford obvious possible alternative focal points for political mobilization and interaction. The strategic structure of constitution making thus does not just require that any proposed arrangement be robust relative to competing constitutional arrangements. It also requires that any such arrangement must be stable against a variety of extraconstitutional equilibria, any one of which might serve, however destructively, as an alternative focal point for political activity. Moreover, politicians engaged in constitutional design must anticipate that their rivals have both good reason and ample opportunity to render some competing dimension of political mobilization more salient and to try, thereby, to coordinate the expectations of relevant constituencies around it.[64]

Thus, finally, and perhaps most importantly, the revisionist view of constitutions as coordination mechanisms highlights the vagaries of political leadership in the constitution-making process. Political leaders, as noted earlier, generally seek to coordinate the expectations of relevant constituencies by establishing the relevance and attractiveness of one among

---

[62] "The forms of commitment that are especially important for constitutional and even for conventional social choice . . . are those that derive from the difficulties of collective action and of recoordination from one coordination outcome to another" (Hardin 1989, 117).

[63] See Elster 1993, 171; and Howard 1993.

[64] See Offe 1992, 23; 1993; and Ordeshook 1993a, 148–51, 161; 1993b, 215–16.

the available equilibria. In constitution-making processes this is most obvious in the sort of negotiations through which political leaders settle on one from among the available packages of constitutional provisions.[65] Thus, in the American case, the framers might well have defended numerous alternatives to the document that they arrived at in Philadelphia. Yet once the political leaders assembled in the convention in fact produced a document, it became the focal point for all subsequent political disagreement and debate (Hardin 1989, 108). Similarly, in contemporary Eastern Europe reformers might propose entire new constitutions or, as they in fact have done, they might negotiate a package of more or less systematic revisions to the Soviet-style constitutions inherited from the period of Communist rule.

Unfortunately, as the discussion in this section intimates, this portrait of relatively straightforward constitutional bargaining leading to coordination is far too simple. Political leaders instead face a much more arduous task. They must successfully resolve the prior derived coordination problem posed by the difficulty of establishing constitutionalism as a central political preoccupation for relevant constituencies. In this sense their strategic problem does not differ in any qualitative way from the problem faced by nationalist politicians in the former Yugoslavia who sought, at great cost and with considerable success, to shift ethnicity from the realm of the "unthinkable" to the center of the political world.

CONCLUSION

Bagehot speculates that compliance with political arrangements typically depends on the limits of popular political imagination. In one sense he is correct. Political arrangements and projects trade upon some vision of the political world and the possibilities that it contains, and such views, to the extent that they exercise force over relevant constituencies, tend to be coercive. But my arguments in this chapter suggest that, because possibilities materialize and dissipate at the intersection of symbol and strategy in politics, we ought not to take his remark as identifying an absolute limit to or inherent feebleness of political imagination. We should, rather, appreciate more fully the politics of possibility.

Even if my arguments defuse fatalists and the somewhat less despairing pessimists, there are others – who defend what I call dismissive and idealist positions – whom I must briefly address in this conclusion. Consider first a dismissive position. From this perspective one might, for

---

[65] Thus, recalling the earlier discussion of power asymmetries, bargaining is "essentially a coordination problem" (Miller 1992, 47). On bargaining of this particular context, see Elster 1993.

104 *James Johnson*

instance, simply deny the relevance of preexisting political traditions to the problem of democratic transformation and consolidation. Adam Przeworski (1991) offers a prominent but not unique example of this position.[66] This dismissive approach, however, is no more plausible than fatalism. Indeed, the two views are very nearly mirror images. Each treats political tradition as a largely inert inheritance. The two views differ only in the weight that they attribute to the causal efficacy of this historical legacy. To the fatalist, tradition is determining; for those who are dismissive it is largely irrelevant. Unfortunately for those who adopt a dismissive posture, a revisionist account such as the one I sketch in the preceding section – one that conceives of a constitution as a negotiated solution to a large-scale coordination problem and recognizes the exigencies of constitution making that emerge from that conception – suggests that their position is untenable.[67]

Consider now the idealist position. Like those pessimists discussed earlier, idealists acknowledge that political traditions can be invented and deployed for strategic purposes. The idealists hold out the possibility that rationalist liberals might engage in such a strategic undertaking, but they neglect to explore either the strategic dimension of this program or the implications it holds for their own normative commitment to constitutionalism. Bruce Ackerman (1992) is, for my purposes, a paradigmatic idealist.[68] In his own reflections on 1989 and its aftermath in Eastern Europe he suggests in passing that those activists who pursue a "rationalistic liberal revolution" of the sort that he advocates "may well make imaginative use of indigenous precedents and symbols as they struggle to push history in a progressive direction" (1992, 29). If successful, such revolutionaries might well provide a robust constitutional framework that can serve as a focal symbol of political identity for citizens in the emergent regime (1992, 61–2). As should by now be clear, I think that this is correct. But if the argument I present has any force it raises several important points. First, if they are to have any hope of success, Ackerman's liberal rationalists have no choice but to engage in the sort of enterprise

---

[66] Shapiro (1993, 126) surveys several recent writers who, despite their differences, each disparage "claims about the importance to democracy of something called 'democratic political culture' or 'democratic civil society.'"

[67] This is true whether one speaks of constitution making or, as Przeworski does, of democratic consolidation. If we conceive of institutional design as an ongoing strategic interaction, and model it – as Przeworski suggests we should – as a repeated game, then it is necessary to address coordination problems of the sort I mention in the preceding section.

[68] He is not a *naive* idealist, for he fears that his liberal program can and may well fall short in political competition. But he is optimistic that liberals might construct the sort of constitutional tradition I discuss here and he is, in my view, overly sanguine about the implications of this prospect for his liberal program.

he describes. Second, in so doing they will be engaged in a strategic interaction with other political leaders whose aim is to construct and impose alternative categories of political action and identity. Finally, if Ackerman's liberal rationalists succeed, it will be because they are more *strategically* creative and adept than their rivals. Whatever constitutional regime they manage to implement will be the product of this strategic contest and so can derive scant legitimacy or normative force from the process by which it was established. I suspect that this means that those who wish to justify any constitutional regime emerging from the sort of process I sketch will have to do so in terms of a pragmatic consequentialism that Ackerman would find unappealing. Like the pessimists, idealists such as Ackerman rightly focus our attention on whether and how, in particular situations, political agents might justify constitutional traditions that they invent for strategic purposes.

I hope my arguments will prompt analysis of the ways that symbols and strategy converge and sustain one another in the process by which political actors attempt to create and foreclose possibilities. This is an especially pressing issue. "In a sense, the union of men can only be symbolized; it has no palpable shape or substance. The state is invisible; it must be personified before it can be seen, symbolized before it can be loved, imagined before it can be conceived" (Walzer 1967, 194). This is a lesson that those hoping to design and implement liberal democratic constitutions need to learn. Whether they learn it on their own or from adversaries who seek to organize politics around alternative visions of the past and future remains to be seen.

REFERENCES

Ackerman, Bruce. 1992. *The Future of Liberal Revolution.* New Haven: Yale University Press.

Arato, Andrew. 1993. "Interpreting 1989." *Social Research* 60: 609–46.

Bagehot, Walter. [1867] 1963. *The English Constitution.* Ithaca: Cornell University Press.

Block, Robert. 1993. "Killers," *New York Review of Books,* November 18, 9–10.

Botev, Nikolai. 1994. "Where East Meets West: Ethic Intermarriage in the Former Yugoslavia, 1962–1989." *American Sociological Review* 59: 461–80.

Bowen, John. 1996. "The Myth of Global Ethnic Conflict." *Journal of Democracy* 7: 3–14.

Brennan, Geoffrey, and James Buchanan. 1985. *The Reason of Rules.* Cambridge: Cambridge University Press.

Brown, J. F. 1994. *Hopes and Shadows: Eastern Europe after Communism.* Durham, N.C.: Duke University Press.

Brzezinski, Mark. 1991. "Note: Constitutional Heritage and Renewal – The Case of Poland." *Virginia Law Review* 77: 49–112.

Buchanan, James. 1994. "Notes on the Liberal Constitution." *Cato Journal* 14: 1–9.

106 *James Johnson*

Bunce, Valerie, and Maria Csanadi. 1993. "Uncertainty in the Transition." *East European Politics and Societies* 7: 240–75.

Calvert, Randall. 1992. "Leadership and Its Basis in Problems of Social Coordination." *International Political Science Review* 13: 7–24.

Calvert, Randall, and James Johnson. 1999. "Interpretation and Coordination in Constitutional Politics." In Ewa Hauser and Jacek Wasilewski, eds., *Lessons in Democracy*, 99–138. Cracow: Jagiellonian University Press.

Cannadine, David. 1983. "The Context, Performance, and Meaning of Ritual: The British Monarchy and the 'Invention of Tradition,' c. 1820–1977." In E. Hobsbawm and T. Ranger, eds., *The Invention of Tradition*, 101–64. Cambridge: Cambridge University Press.

Casper, Gerhard. 1989. "Changing Concepts of Constitutionalism: 18th to 20th Century." In G. Casper and D. Hutchinson, eds., *Supreme Court Review*, 311–32. Chicago: University of Chicago Press.

Cohen, Anthony. 1985. *The Symbolic Construction of Community*. London: Tavistock.

Donia, Robert, and John Fine. 1994. *Bosnia and Hercegovina: A Tradition Betrayed*. New York: Columbia University Press.

Drakulic, Slavenka. 1993. *The Balkan Express*. New York: Harper.

Dworkin, Ronald. 1986. *Law's Empire*. Cambridge, Mass.: Harvard University Press.

1993. *Life's Dominion*. New York: Vintage.

Elster, Jon. 1993. "Constitution-Making in Eastern Europe." *Public Administration* 71: 169–217.

Friedrich, Carl. 1941. *Constitutional Government and Democracy*. Boston: Little, Brown.

Garton Ash, Timothy. 1990. *The Magic Lantern: The Revolutions of '89 Witnessed in Warsaw, Budapest, Berlin and Prague*. New York: Random House.

Geertz, Clifford. 1973. *The Interpretation of Cultures*. New York: Basic Books.

1983. *Local Knowledge*. New York: Basic Books.

1993. "Ethnic Conflict." *Common Knowledge* 2: 54–65.

Glenny, Misha. 1993a. *The Rebirth of History*. 2nd ed. New York: Penguin.

1993b. *The Fall of Yugoslavia*. New York: Penguin.

Gyani, Gabor. 1993. "Political Uses of Tradition in Postcommunist East Central Europe." *Social Research* 60: 893–913.

Hardin, Russell. 1988. "Review Article: Constitutional Political Economy." *British Journal of Political Science* 18: 513–30.

1989. "Why a Constitution?" In B. Grofman and D. Wittman, eds., *The Federalist Papers and the New Institutionalism*, 100–20. New York: Agathon.

1995. *One for All: The Logic of Group Conflict*. Princeton: Princeton University Press.

Hayden, Robert. 1992. "Constitutional Nationalism in the Formerly Yugoslav Republics." *Slavic Review* 51: 654–73.

Hedges, Chris. 1995. "War Turns Sarajevo Away from Europe." *New York Times*, July 28, A4.

Hellman, Joel. 1996. "Constitutions and Economic Reform in Postcommunist Transitions." *East European Constitutional Review* 5: 46–56.

Hobsbawm, Eric. 1983. "Introduction: Inventing Traditions." In E. Hobsbawm and T. Ranger, eds., *The Invention of Tradition*, 1–14. Cambridge: Cambridge University Press.

———. 1993. "The New Threat to History." *New York Review of Books*, December 16, 62–4.

Hobsbawm, Eric, and Terence Ranger, eds. 1983. *The Invention of Tradition*. Cambridge: Cambridge University Press.

Hodson, Randy, Dusko Sekulic, and Rath Massey. 1994. "National Tolerance in the Former Yugoslavia." *American Journal of Sociology* 99: 1534–58.

Holmes, Stephen. 1988. "Gag Rules and the Politics of Omission." In Jon Elster and Rune Slagstad, eds., *Constitutionalism and Democracy*, 19–58. Cambridge: Cambridge University Press.

Howard, A. E. Dick. 1993. "Constitutional Reform." In R. Staar, ed., *Transition to Democracy in Poland*. New York: St. Martin's Press.

Ilonski, Gabriella. 1993. "Tradition and Innovation in the Development of Parliamentary Government in Hungary." *Journal of Theoretical Politics* 5: 253–66.

Jaworski, Rudolf. 1985. "History and Tradition in Contemporary Poland." *East European Quarterly* 19: 349–62.

Johnson, James. 1997. "Symbol *and* Strategy in Comparative Political Analysis." *APSA-CP: Newsletter of the APSA Organized Section in Comparative Politics* 8 (Summer): 6–9.

———. 1999. "Why Respect Culture?" *American Journal of Political Science* 44: 405–18.

Kaplan, Robert. 1993. *Balkan Ghosts*. New York: Vintage.

Kertzer, David. 1988. *Ritual, Politics, and Power*. New Haven: Yale University Press.

Kiss, Elizabeth. 1995. "Is Nationalism Compatible with Human Rights? Reflections on East-Central Europe." In A. Sarat and T. Kearns, eds., *Identities, Politics and Rights*, 367–402. Ann Arbor: University of Michigan Press.

———. 1996. "Five Theses on Nationalism." In I. Shapiro and Russell Hardin, eds., *Political Order*, 288–332. New York: New York University Press.

Knight, Jack. 1992. *Institutions and Social Conflict*. Cambridge: Cambridge University Press.

———. 1995. "Models, Interpretations and Theories." In J. Knight and I. Sened, eds., *Explaining Social Institutions*, 95–120. Ann Arbor: University of Michigan Press.

Kubik, Jan. 1994. *The Power of Symbols against the Symbols of Power*. University Park: Penn State Press.

Laba, Roman. 1991. *The Roots of Solidarity*. Princeton: Princeton University Press.

Laitin, David. 1986. *Hegemony and Culture*. Chicago: University of Chicago Press.

———. 1995. "National Revivals and Violence." *European Journal of Sociology* 36: 3–43.

Linz, Juan, and Alfred Stepan. 1992. "Political Identities and Electoral Sequences." *Daedalus* 121: 123–39.

Lukes, Steven. 1977. *Essays in Social Theory*. New York: Columbia University Press.

108 *James Johnson*

Mach, Zdzislaw. 1993. *Symbols, Conflict and Identity*. Albany: SUNY Press.

Miller, Gary. 1992. *Managerial Dilemmas*. New York: Cambridge University Press.

Mostov, Julie. 1995. "The Use and Abuse of History in Eastern Europe." *East European Constitutional Review* 4: 69–73.

Mueller, Dennis. 1991. "Choosing a Constitution in East Europe: Lessons from Public Choice." *Journal of Comparative Economics* 15: 325–48.

Niederhauser, Emil. 1981. *The Rise of Nationality in Eastern Europe*. Budapest: Corvina Kiado.

North, Douglass, and Barry Weingast. 1989. "Constitutions and Commitment." *Journal of Economic History* 49: 803–32.

O'Connor, Mike. 1996. "Serb Village Is Reborn in Muslim Zone." *New York Times*, December 8, A20.

O'Donnell, Guillermo, and Phillip Schmitter. 1986. *Transitions from Authoritarian Rule: Tentative Conclusions about Uncertain Democracies*. Baltimore: Johns Hopkins University Press.

Offe, Claus. 1992. "Strong Causes, Weak Cures." *East European Constitutional Review* 1: 1–23.

1993. "The Rationality of Ethnic Politics." *Budapest Review of Books* 3: 6–13.

1997. *Varieties of Transition*. Cambridge, Mass.: MIT Press.

Ordeshook, Peter. 1993a. "Constitutional Stability." *Constitutional Political Economy* 3: 137–75.

1993b. "Some Rules of Constitutional Design." *Social Philosophy and Policy* 10: 198–232.

Ost, David. 1993. "The Politics of Interest in Post-Communist East Europe." *Theory and Society* 22: 453–86.

Perez-Diaz, Victor. 1993. *The Return of Civil Society: The Emergence of Democratic Spain*. Cambridge, Mass.: Harvard University Press.

Pognay, Istvan. 1996. "Constitution Making or Constitutional Transformation in Post-Communist Societies?" *Political Studies* 44: 568–91.

Przeworski, Adam. 1991. *Democracy and the Market*. Cambridge: Cambridge University Press.

Przeworski, Adam, et al. 1995. *Sustainable Democracy*. Cambridge: Cambridge University Press.

Putnam, Robert. 1993. *Making Democracy Work*. Princeton: Princeton University Press.

Rudolph, Susanne Hoeber, and Lloyd Rudolph. 1993. "Modern Hate: How Ancient Animosities Get Invented." *New Republic*, March 22, 24–9.

Schelling, Thomas. 1960. *The Strategy of Conflict*. Cambridge, Mass.: Harvard University Press.

Schopflin, George. 1990. "The Political Traditions of Eastern Europe." *Daedalus* 119: 55–90.

Sekulic, Dusko, Garth Massey, and Randy Hodson. 1994. "Who Were the Yugoslavs?" *American Sociological Review* 59: 83–97.

Shapiro, Ian. 1993. "Democratic Innovation." *World Politics* 46: 121–50.

Shils, Edward. 1981. *Tradition*. Chicago: University of Chicago Press.

Starr, S. Frederick. 1989. "A Usable Past." *New Republic*, May 15, 24–7.

Stein, Eric. 1993. "Post-Communist Constitution Making." *New Europe Law Review* 1: 421–75.

Taylor, Charles. 1985. *Philosophy and the Human Sciences*. Cambridge: Cambridge University Press.

Taylor, Michael. 1987. *The Possibility of Cooperation*. Cambridge: Cambridge University Press.

Ten, C. L. 1993. "Constitutionalism and the Rule of Law." In R. Goodin and P. Petitt, eds., *A Companion to Contemporary Political Philosophy*, 394–403. Cambridge: Blackwell Publishers.

Tismaneanu, Vladimir. 1992. *Reinventing Politics: Eastern Europe from Stalin to Havel*. New York: Free Press.

1998. *Fantasies of Salvation*. Princeton: Princeton University Press.

Tocqueville, Alexis de. 1987. *Recollections: The French Revolution of 1848*. New Brunswick, N.J.: Transaction Publishers.

Verdery, Katherine. 1996. *What Was Socialism, and What Comes Next?* Princeton: Princeton University Press.

1999. *The Political Lives of Dead Bodies*. New York: Columbia University Press.

Walzer, Michael. 1967. "The Role of Symbolism in Political Thought." *Political Science Quarterly* 82: 191–204.

1992. "The New Tribalism." *Dissent* (Spring): 164–71.

1994. *Thick and Thin: Moral Argument at Home and Abroad*. South Bend, Ind.: University of Notre Dame Press.

Weingast, Barry. 1993. "Constitutions as Governance Structures." *Journal of Institutional and Theoretical Economics* 149: 286–311.

Woodward, Susan. 1995. *Balkan Tragedy*. Washington, D.C.: Brookings Institution.

Young, Crawford. 1993. "The Dialectics of Cultural Pluralism." In C. Young, ed., *The Rising Tide of Cultural Pluralism*, 3–35. Madison: University of Wisconsin Press.

3

The Birth Logic of a Democratic Constitution

Lawrence G. Sager

THE BIRTH OF THE CONSTITUTION

The birth of the U.S. Constitution was marked by two prominent and connected features. First, the process by which the Constitution was proposed and ratified differed radically from the means for constitutional change specified in the extant legal order that preceded the Constitution. At the national level, the Articles of Confederation announced themselves to be perpetual and required for amendment the vote of the Continental Congress followed by confirmation in the state legislature of each of the compacting states. In contrast, Article VII of the Constitution provided for ratification by special state conventions and required the ratification of only nine of the states to launch the Constitution as the highest law (binding only in the ratifying states but fully destructive of the confederated regime nonetheless). At the state level, each of the thirteen state constitutions specified a procedure for amendment. Included were requirements that the state legislature initiate an amendment, that a supermajority of the electorate approve, and that the amendment take place after a certain year or in a specified cycle of years. Article VII's ratification procedure depended on special state conventions rather than legislatures, contained no intrastate[1] supermajority requirement, and paid no homage to temporal requirements in the extant state constitutions. Thus, the Articles of Confederation were annulled and replaced, and the constitutions of the states were subordinated to a national government, all by a careful and elaborate process that ignored the specified channels for foundational change.[2]

---

[1] There were, however, two interstate supermajority requirements: Article VII required the support of nine states (three-fourths rounded down) for the Constitution to take effect; and only those states which so ratified were bound (in effect a unanimity requirement).

[2] Although it is clear that the ratification of the Constitution was inconsistent with the terms of both the Articles of Confederation and the constitutions of the ratifying states, there is

The Birth Logic of a Democratic Constitution

Second, the process by which the Constitution was ratified was self-consciously democratic and driven – at least in part – by a common democratic mechanism, simple majority rule. Elections were held in each state for representatives who met in special conventions. Although Article VII did not so specify, each of these conventions proceeded to make its ultimate decision by simple majority vote. In some states, the ratification vote was quite close; but simple majority will prevailed in these states and the Constitution was in fact launched.

This familiar history[3] certainly deserves a place on the shelf of constitutional folklore. But does it deserve more? Does the birth of the Constitution offer important guidance for our contemporary understanding of constitutional choice and change? In particular, does this history suggest that the elaborate and intentionally burdensome requirements for amendment in Article V of the Constitution are no more secure than were the procedures for change specified in the Articles of Confederation or in the constitutions of the states prior to the launching of the Constitution?

Some commentators think so; they believe that the actual birth of the Constitution was consistent with and revealing of what we might call the birth logic of a democratic constitution. They believe that an appropriately engaged, deliberative process culminating in an expression of majority will was sufficient to legitimate the dramatic revision of the foundations of government in the United States. Accordingly, they further believe, the enacted Constitution itself is subject to replacement or amendment by an appropriately engaged and deliberative process, whether or not that process conforms to the requirements of Article V.

This view of constitutional change is, to be sure, startling, but it is offered by those who hold it as a means of making our constitutional

---

some debate as to whether the Constitution is best understood as having been *illegal* in its inception. Amar (1994) argues that the Articles of Confederation created only external treaty obligations, obligations that were severed for all states when repudiated by any one state; as to the state constitutions, he regards these as having been understood as specifying nonexclusive means of amendment and implicitly embracing amendment by the popular sovereign of the relevant state by any appropriate means. Ackerman and Katyal (1995) argue the Articles were a constitution for the United States and binding on all, and that most of those in the founding generation who concerned themselves with the question understood the launching of the Constitution to be illegal on a variety of grounds. For my purposes, nothing turns on this nice question. Both Amar on the one hand and Ackerman and Katyal on the other take their respective readings of history to advance the claim that extra–Article V amendments to the Constitution are appropriate. I disagree, and I think that the grounds of my disagreement remain constant and equally strong as against either of these characterizations of the birth of the Constitution.

[3] Familiar in rough, at least. Akhil Amar, Bruce Ackerman, and Neal Katyal have done constitutional commentators a substantial service in their fine-grained and reflective history of the process of the Constitution's founding.

arrangements more rather than less congenial. We can see how this might be so. Suppose our understanding of the Constitution were deeply originalist, and driven by a particular view of the requirements of popular sovereignty: pursuant to this understanding, the value and legitimacy of the Constitution would be crucially dependent on its embodying the expressed, detailed, and authoritative will of past constitutional majorities; and pursuant to this understanding, the essence of the job of interpreting the Constitution would lie in the recovery of that will. Were this our view, we would want constitutional adjudication to be fundamentally backward looking, an exercise in what one commentator, Bruce Ackerman, has called "principled positivism." If this were the best way to think of the Constitution, we should be skeptical about the narrow and arduous prescriptions for constitutional change offered by Article V. At best, they would offer only one possibility among many for the registration of the prevailing deliberative judgment of a political generation; at worst they would be an indefensible barrier to popular control of our constitutive arrangements.

Birth logic aside, there are good reasons to believe that the originalist account of the U.S. Constitution and its constitutionalism is wrong. The best account of our constitutional institutions regards them as forward looking and justice seeking. The combination of popular constitutional decision making through the ratification of constitutional text and judicial decision making through the wide-bodied interpretation of that text is pragmatically well suited to the job of identifying the central features of political justice. The Constitution's text is fixed by the process of popular constitutional decision making and, wisely, that text at its most critical points speaks at a high level of generality, inviting and requiring the active partnership of the constitutional judiciary in the enterprise of shaping the contours of constitutional justice.

On this account, in turn, the requirements of Article V for the amendment of the Constitution are an attractive part of the pragmatic, justice-seeking quality of our constitutional institutions. By design, they make the Constitution hard to amend, and by design, they require not just large majorities, but a broad geographic consensus. The obduracy of the Constitution to amendment requires of members of the ratifying generation that they choose for the Constitution principles and provisions not just for themselves but for their children and their children's children; and the geographic diversity demanded by Article V works as a reasonable proxy for a broad diversity of circumstance among those who must join in endorsing changes in the text of the Constitution. The result is a structural tendency in popular constitutional decision making toward the choice of general principles attractive and acceptable to persons in a variety of actual human circumstance, imagining their

The Birth Logic of a Democratic Constitution

application over time to generations unborn in circumstances unknown (Sager 1990).

So we have what seems a mismatch: an otherwise appealing account of our constitutional institutions that favors a pragmatic, justice-seeking Constitution, with a proactive constitutional judiciary in partnership with a popular, constitutional amendment process shaped by Article V; but a birth logic that, it is claimed, favors instead a backward-looking constitutional judiciary and an amendment process ultimately requiring only the determined will of deliberative majorities.

In this essay, I hope to dispel this illusion of mismatch by offering a different, and, I believe, better understanding of the birth logic of a democratic constitution. The stakes here overreach our own national circumstance: if determined majorities are free to overturn the constitutive arrangements that restrain their considered will, then all democratic constitutional arrangements are more fragile – even in theory – than is commonly supposed.

BIRTH LESSONS

We need at the outset to understand what sort of guidance we can and cannot plausibly expect from the birthing of the Constitution. In particular, we need to set aside the clearly false idea that there is a necessary symmetry between the conditions under which a regime of government is born and those under which it can be changed or replaced, that the "sovereign" that birthed a constitution is thereby entitled to revoke or remake its work, or that the precedent of a constitution's birth stipulates the conditions of its demise.

There is no logical or necessary connection between the formal provenance of a constitution, its legitimacy, and the circumstances under which it can be revoked and changed. Imagine a country ruled by generations of despotic monarchs until the moment that Queen Liza assumes the crown. Liza is a democrat through and through, and she commissions the leading thinkers of her land to fashion a democratic constitution, which constitution she then imposes by decree upon her people. The people respond by participating in the decreed elections; the congress is formed and the president elected; and the government is launched. If it is a well-formed democratic government, and the population salutes, it is legitimate by democratic lights. Once democracy thus takes hold, Liza has an assured place among her nation's heroes, but she does not have ongoing sovereign authority to revoke or amend the constitution. Were Liza to suffer a change of heart, and wax nostalgic for the days of the monarchy, the democratic government to which she gave birth would (we imagine), and certainly should, treat her impulse as an unfortunate, undemocratic, and unconstitutional attempt to usurp the authority of the people, their elected representatives, and the constitution itself. A democratic constitution can name and create the popular sovereign; it can render obsolete and even repugnant its own nondemocratic parent.

So too, an imperfect democratic order can irreversibly work itself fine, and a significantly flawed democratic process can launch a constitutional order that from the first or eventually overcomes its flaws. We need no imagined or exotic example of this proposition at work: the ratification of the U.S. Constitution, though wonderfully democratic by the standards of its time, involved an exclusive electorate of white, propertied males. It would be preposterous to suggest that the exclusionary features that marked the group that gave birth (à la Zeus) to the Constitution also confer on contemporary white, propertied males the power to alter or abolish our constitutional order by a preponderance of judgment – however thoughtful it might be – among themselves.

To make sense of arguments about the birth logic of the Constitution, accordingly, we have to understand them as claiming something other than a natural symmetry or normative identity between the circumstances that launched the Constitution and those that would legitimate contemporary attempts to change the Constitution. We must understand claims about the birth logic of the Constitution as arguing for something less strong and direct than that.

Two possibilities suggest themselves on behalf of those who argue that the machinery for amendment specified in Article V of the Constitution is not exclusive. A normative claim about political justice holds that a democratic people have the endemic authority to remake their constitutive arrangements at will and uses the founding as example rather than binding authority. An interpretive claim holds that Article V is best read as merely offering suggestions about the process for amending the Constitution, not as stipulating an exclusive protocol for so doing; and it uses the founding as evidence of the framers' collective state of mind. The normative claim implies that the framers were at least in general wise and argues that in this instance they were indeed right – right to ignore extant constraints and to submit the draft Constitution to an ad hoc, democratically composed process. The interpretive claim argues that – whether or not they were actually right in believing themselves to have the license to ignore extant constitutive law – the framers must have meant for succeeding generations to have the same license to amend their constitutive arrangements that they took themselves to have, and that Article V should be read to reflect their intention in this regard.

The normative argument must do the lion's share of the work for Article V revisionists. The text of Article V – in isolation and in the context of the Constitution as a whole – is far from congenial to the claim that Article

The Birth Logic of a Democratic Constitution 115

V is not the exclusive means of amending the Constitution. The same is true of our constitutional practice over time, which has consistently named Article V as the exclusive source of popular amendment of the Constitution.[4] This is not to say that imaginative interpretive efforts to find room for an extra–Article V amendment of the Constitution are doomed to failure, but rather, that the possibility of their success is crucially dependent on our being persuaded that an important principle of political justice is vindicated by this strained reading of text and history. The idea that we can or should read the Constitution through the lens of the framers' rhetoric or behavior is doubtful at best. But even if we set these formidable general doubts aside, the most that we can gain from the events surrounding the launching of the Constitution is that the framers apparently believed that they were justified in effectuating constitutional change in the course of their fight for national survival. But should the license to disregard extant legal constraints toward which the words and the acts of the founding generation gestured be read broadly as the license of all democratic peoples at all times, or much more narrowly, as the license of a democratic people under the exceptional circumstances of constitutional breakdown? The choice between these readings can only be justified by a prior normative judgment. Thus, the normative argument for disregarding Article V must have first claim on our attention.

[4] The most determined and elaborate attempt to find historical support for popular authority to amend the Constitution by non–Article V means is that of Bruce Ackerman. Ackerman points to the founding, of course, and invokes the highly manipulated ratification of the Reconstruction amendments and an unacknowledged New Deal amendment as instances of the exercise of such authority. I have never failed to be engaged and educated by Ackerman's efforts to harness constitutional history in service of his project; but I have never been persuaded of its conceptual infrastructure, either. The founding is a special case and can be justified on the far narrower grounds of constitutional breakdown, if justified at all. Reconstruction also courts understanding as a breakdown, of course, and is in any event garbled precedent for these purposes: after all, it was the importance of preserving the form of the Article V amendment that drove the reconstructionists to such questionable lengths. The New Deal conversion of the Supreme Court is the most interesting case, and here Ackerman's history is at best equivocal between there having been an informal amendment to the Constitution that obliged judges to follow suit, and what is commonly thought to have taken place, namely, a change in the prevailing judgment of the members of the Court as to the best understanding of the Constitution. In this choice between a positivist and judgmental account of the New Deal transformation, Ackerman could not possibly prevail without first persuading us of the normative claim underlying his interpretation, the claim that insists that the legitimacy of our government depends on the Constitution being more permeable to change than Article V standing alone permits it to be. See Ackerman 1998, 344. At times, both Ackerman and Amar write as though they thought they could make their cases on grounds of "fit" alone, that the underlying normative claim is not essential. But interesting questions about the Constitution are seldom answered by text and history alone; and the positions of Ackerman and Amar are in particular need of normative assistance.

The normative argument from the founding does not make the mistake of equating the conditions of a regime's birth with the preconditions of legitimate change of that regime. Read in this way, birth logic claims can be rescued from plain error. But this merely gets us to the point of interesting disagreement. So read, after all, these claims still take from the example of the founding of the U.S. Constitution the lesson that in a democracy a constitution is freely amendable by an appropriately deliberative democratic process, notwithstanding express provisions – like Article V itself – which offer narrow and rather burdensome requirements for any amendment.

Some would take the normative lesson of the Constitution's birth still further, and argue that simple majority rule is an appropriate metric of consensus for constitutional change. Here, of course, the example of the founding itself, even if read for all that it could be worth, is less helpful to Article V revisionists. Article VII's requirements for ratification are roughly congruent with the heart of Article V's requirements for amendment: where the agreement of nine-thirteenths of the states was necessary to launch the Constitution, the agreement of three-fourths is required for its amendment; in both cases the Constitution is silent on the question of what metric of consensus within each state is appropriate, and simple majority rule has been the uniform norm in lieu of a more demanding constitutional stipulation.

But even if the example of the founding falls considerably short of endorsing majority rule, it is the disparity between majority rule and the requirements of Article V that lies at the heart of the normative claim. In the end, the argument is a simple one: the fact that reflective political majorities cannot effectuate constitutional change is an embarrassment to the democratic foundations of our constitutionalism. I hope to demonstrate that this argument is false.

AMENDMENT AND CHANGE

There is one other preliminary matter that will clarify our discussion. No one denies that judicial understandings of the Constitution have changed – sometimes rather sharply and dramatically – over time, and that many of these changes in understanding have occurred without formal, Article V amendment of the text of the Constitution. The most prominent of these alterations of judicial course is the "switch in time" – those few months in 1937 in the space of which the Supreme Court effectively repudiated the substantive due process tradition of which *Lochner v. New York* has become the reviled symbol, and reshaped the prevailing jurisprudence of the Commerce Clause – in the course of which the Court stepped aside and permitted Congress to pursue its New Deal agenda. If each relatively

The Birth Logic of a Democratic Constitution

evulsive and apparently enduring change in constitutional doctrine counted as an "amendment" of the Constitution, then obviously Article V could not be regarded as the exclusive means of amending the Constitution.

But the challenge to the exclusivity of Article V is meant to have more bite than that. We can better understand the source of that bite if we think about the prospect of a change in constitutional understanding from the standpoint of a judge. Imagine that it is 1937, and all that actually happened has happened. A justice of the Supreme Court, heretofore a champion of a rather restrictive view of the Commerce Clause, sits in his study, and decides that, notwithstanding his prior judgment, Congress should have broad, largely unfettered authority to pursue its New Deal agenda. Now we can imagine two very different sort of reasons our justice might have for this conversion. Having been educated by experience of and reflection upon the Great Depression and its aftermath, he might have altered his judgment as to the best understanding of the Constitution in the time and place he finds the nation and its economy. Or, looking back over the political events of the last months or years, he might believe that an appropriately formed and expressed political consensus had emerged and produced a popular amendment to the Constitution, just as though the text was formally amended in accord with Article V. In the first story, the Constitution has remained constant but the judge's understanding of it has changed; we can call this the judgmental account. In the second, the Constitution itself has changed, and this is the reason that the judge has altered his understanding of what it permits; we can call this the positivist account.

Now it is important to note that both the judgmental and the positivist account can and are likely to be sensitive to history and social context. Both might even be sensitive to the same features of the practical world on occasion. For example, both the judgmental and the positivist account might focus on an increasingly broad and sustained view among the members of our political community that the commerce clause was being improperly invoked by the Supreme Court to impede the national recovery effort; for the justice in the judgmental account, this mounting consensus might be an important reason to reconsider his views. But the difference between these accounts is profound, and profoundly important. In the judgmental account, the judge's own judgment governs her interpretive obligation; in the positivist account, the formation of a popular consensus under stipulated extra–Article V circumstances governs her interpretive obligation.

Article V revisionists are committed to some form of the positivist account of non–Article V constitutional change. They believe that an appropriately formed non–Article V consensus changes the Constitution

118 *Lawrence G. Sager*

and binds conscientious judges and all other constitutional actors accordingly. This is what makes their view worth arguing about.

CHOOSING VOTING RULES IN THIN AIR

Suppose that, in the meeting of a more or less democratically run faculty of law, a motion is made to conduct a particular vote by secret ballot. This is an irregular and controversial proposal, and the inevitable question arises: how is the secondary, procedural vote – the vote, that is, on how the principal vote is to be conducted – itself to be conducted? Questions of this sort are latent in any vote about how to vote; within a regime of rules they are typically resolved by reference to rules – explicit or implied, particular or general – about changing the rules. But when a choice of this sort must be made outside any existing system of rules, when the root governing rules are themselves being chosen, matters become conundral.

This is what makes the question of how a democratic constitution gets started so interesting. A theocratic community has a great conceptual advantage: a vision is seen, a heavenly voice heard, or a sacred tablet unearthed; by one means or another the divine force announces its presence and dictates ground rules for the holy. But in a community committed to self-rule, the constitutional details of democratic government must be chosen by a process that is itself at least roughly democratic. In such a setting the problem of what preconstitutional rules should be followed for choosing the constitutional rules for postconstitutional political choices has real bite. Actually, the problem starts somewhat further back, at the stage of the constitutional convention.

Suppose that we are in the remarkable position of forming a new government, unencumbered by our legal past. (We need not fill in the hypothetical details, but we can imagine a constitutional convention held after revolution has deposed an unpopular monarch, or on the occasion of a group of persons gathered to form an ongoing society on virgin territory, with no lingering allegiances to or fondness for the governmental arrangements in our states of origin.) And suppose that we are elected delegates,[5] charged with the job of drafting a constitution and submitting it to our fellow citizens for ratification. Among us, there is broad agreement that the government must be democratic, and a shared, general picture of what qualifies a government as democratic; but, of course, there are important details about which there is not wide agreement.

Our first question will be how to resolve our substantive disagreements at the convention stage, where we are fashioning a draft constitution to

---

[5] Still more questions of the voting-about-voting sort are implicated in the election of delegates, of course.

propose to the broader population for ratification. Various internal procedural issues that may have important consequences will arise. Among these is the question of what voting rule we should follow in making our substantive decisions. Imagine that three protocols emerge as rivals: simple majority rule, supermajority rule (pegged at two-thirds of those voting), and unanimity.

The question is this: by what voting protocol will we make the election between the rival protocols (and, probably, make our other decisions about procedures at the convention as well)? We might well choose simple majority rule. The reflex in democratic assemblies to act on simple majority rule is so entrenched and common that we might not even recognize that we have any other possibility. But even if we were reflective about this first question, the choice of simple majority rule at this default stage is supported by pragmatic, epistemic, and equitable concerns. First, simple majority rule will almost certainly produce answers to these initial procedural questions, as opposed to locking us in possible stalemate. Second, as we make various procedural choices in order to get our convention going, there is no apparent reason to adopt a rule that deflects close choices toward the status quo, no policy or epistemic reason for preferring inaction to action supported by a majority of those who attend. Third, simple majority rule has the equitable virtue of counting each voter as one and giving each one equal weight; any supermajority rule confers on those who favor the status quo a minority veto over change. (We see this most vividly in a regime of unanimity, which confers on any one resister-to-change authority over all of her colleagues' contrary inclinations.)

But this hypothesized selection of simple majority rule as the mechanism for choosing, inter alia, among voting rules at this stage in our proceedings must not be read for more than it is worth. On a comparatively superficial level, there is this obvious but nagging question: who were the "we" that chose simple majority rule, and by what voting rule did "we" act? Presumably, we were the totality of the delegates, representing in turn the totality of the parties who are recognized as members or putative members of the forthcoming polity; and presumably, in some sense or another – informally perhaps or by implication – we *all* gave our consent to the choice of simple majority rule for the purpose of our first official decisions. We did so by showing up and participating, at least, and possibly by more explicit means as well.

Lurking behind this observation is the deeper sense that, in principle, a constitution – and before the constitution, the constitutive process by which the constitution is drawn – ought to be acceptable to every member or group within the polity-to-be. Theoretical unanimity is the basal condition of political legitimacy. Gathering together to form our community, we agree to be bound by a process that we hope will eventually lead to the adoption of a constitution, and, as the first step, we adopt what seems a fair and effective voting process – a seemingly natural process – to get us started, namely, simple majority rule. But behind even this first step is the requirement of consent to go forward; and in front of this step is the reasonable prospect that decisions taken by a majority of those assembled, taken as a whole, ought to be acceptable to each member of the political community. As against this basal aspiration of the constitutional project, the intra-assembly equitable virtues of majority rule must be seen as comparatively superficial and contextual.

Back in our constitutional convention, we next confront the question of which voting rule – simple majority, super majority, or unanimity – we will pursue in resolving the substantive questions that are bound to divide us as we go about the business of drafting a constitution. Much the same general concerns confront us as we vote – by simple majority rule – on this question, but the picture has changed somewhat. Initially, we were choosing a pump-priming mechanism to get us started; we were, in effect, constituting the "we" that would deliberate about the new constitution. Now we are in a position to think as a group about what ongoing mechanism will best suit our enterprise of drafting a constitution. We may have reason to resist the rush to simple majority rule. The two-thirds majority or unanimity rules would encourage reflection and deliberation, and press toward compromise and consensus – toward constitutional arrangements that can enjoy the support of a broad range of the group that will live under the constitution; they would do so, however, at the risk of delay, possibly even the collapse of our constitutional convention in stalemate. Equitable concerns among ourselves as delegates may continue to favor simple majority rule, but they are comparatively superficial; deeper is the concern that our process lead to a constitution that in principle can be acceptable to all the members of the new political community.

For all of this, given the urgency in getting the job of constitution making done and the process of governance underway, simple majority rule may well be the preferred alternative, but that is not what is important when we step back from our hypothetical world to our inquiry into the birth logic of a democratic constitution. What is important is this: first, our choice of simple majority rule to make our choices about procedure at our constitutional convention did not foreclose the possibility that we would choose the two-thirds rule as the protocol for our subsequent choices about the constitution itself; and, second, neither of these choices turned on some deep and essential truth about fair democratic processes. Simple majority rule, at its strongest, sponsors a fair and reasonable process, one that ought to commend itself to the representatives of a free and democratic people under some circumstances.

The Birth Logic of a Democratic Constitution   121

It bears emphasis that the point is *not* that having adopted simple majority rule as our initial mechanism of choice we have thereby legitimated any set of mechanisms that we choose to put in place. The democratic provenance of governing arrangements does not certify those arrangements. A hereditary monarchy chosen by a perfectly composed democratic process is neither democratic nor just. Rather, the point is stronger and perhaps more provocative: the pragmatic, epistemic, and normative features of voting rules need to be evaluated in context, and while democracy is a necessary feature of just and sensible arrangements for governance, simple majority rule is not.

CONSTITUTING "THE PEOPLE"

We are not through, of course (with either our constitution-drafting fiction or our birth logic analysis); in fact, we have barely begun. Most of our work at the convention stage will concern the substantive provisions of our constitution. In the most general of terms, these provisions will have at least two features of interest: first, they will parse between those matters that are decided in the constitution itself and those that are directed to the ordinary, ongoing political process of our nascent state; second, they will put in place the machinery of ordinary politics. For our purposes here, we assume that the substance of the constitution is much like the substance of the U.S. Constitution, that relatively few matters are concluded in the constitution itself, and that the machinery of ordinary politics is more or less appropriately democratic.

In our role as drafters of the constitution, we will also need to set the terms by which the constitution will be ratified, the kind of approval our draft will have to receive from the population of our political community before it becomes – by its own, formal terms – valid and binding. (I add the qualifying phrase because no document and accompanying process can literally command its own authority; Hans Kelsen's "Grundnorm" or H. L. A. Hart's "ultimate rule of recognition" are constructs that reflect the conceptual shape of a regime of rules that has come to enjoy social acceptance.) We also need to set the terms by which the constitution can subsequently be amended. By now you will have anticipated the direction in which I hope to extend the argument: As with the two choices of voting rules we made at the convention stage, these two choices at the constitution stage need not be the same; and as with our earlier choices, these choices are not rigidly preordained by fundamental requirements of democracy or justice. More pointedly and clearly, the choice of simple majority rule is not insisted upon by either democracy or justice.

Let us begin with ratification. Suppose for a moment that our proposed government is rather small; imagine, for example, that we are all independent settlers who have carved up a small island geographically into our respective parcels, the boundaries of which we more or less regularly respect as a modus vivendi; our proposed constitution is intended to replace this temporary arrangement with the machinery for systematic governance. We might well take the view that only those of us who support the constitution should be bound by it – that simple majority rule was fine for drafting, but that in the end the root formation of a political community requires actual consent. This would lead us to a voting rule requiring unanimous support among those who will become part of our new constitutional community, and probably the support of a large percentage of the island population before the constitution becomes effective at all.

Or, in contrast, we might think that a simple majority vote is the best mechanism for ratification, on the same sorts of grounds that have attracted us to that rule in our earlier discussion. Here, majority rule is no more decisive than any other rule, but it does make acceptance of the constitution more likely. The same back-and-forth epistemic arguments can be made, and the limited form of fairness offered by majority rule remains in place, although offset rather directly and powerfully by the claim that actual consent is requisite to inclusion in a new political community.

Or, yet again, we might believe that while the consent of each new member is not required to form our political community, a supermajority requirement nevertheless is appropriate: to the general advantages of reflection and deliberation of a supermajority process, there would be added the practical and normative virtues of broad consensus as the predicate for the formation of a new political community. The normative virtues of broad consensus should be obvious: consensus points in the direction of theoretical unanimity.

Now things are getting problematic for our constitution-drafting enterprise, with serious and conflicting contenders for what might seem to be the most crucial voting event of all, the ratification or rejection of our proposed constitution. There is no obvious rule offered by the concept of democracy from which deviation must be justified, but rather various views of how a new political community is appropriately launched. Ironically, the judgment between these views will not be made directly by the members of the political community at all but rather by us, delegates of the community. We are either voting by simple or supermajority rule, and none of us, presumably, thinks that our consensus should actually serve to ratify the draft constitution. Yet we are going to have to make the election between these ratification rules for the community as a whole, using only the general voting rule we have chosen to operate with in convention.

Even if we were to pass the choice of the appropriate ratifying protocol on to the community as a whole as an open question, we could not really avoid the conundral aspects of the situation. What voting mechanism should the community as a whole use for making this choice between ratifying protocols? Suppose, for example, the community as a whole voted by simple majority vote that the ratification protocol should itself be simple majority vote – that alone could not satisfy those committed to another voting protocol that they were wrong.

If our proposed constitutional community was larger in scale than our island community, and already divided into groups that enjoyed geographic contiguity and cultural affinity, we might think that what best suited the ratification vote was a procedure that elicited the consent of these extant groups, rather than the consent of each individual. The actual ratification requirements of the U.S. Constitution had some of this flavor, but in an interestingly mixed form. Only those states that ratified the Constitution would be bound by it as members of the United States, and further, the Constitution would become effective only if ratified by nine of the thirteen states. What is curious about the ratification protocol of Article VII is that, although it depends heavily on the extant states as the relevant units of consent, it is at considerable pains to avoid the existing machinery of governance in those states, calling for ratification by special state constitutional conventions rather than by the state legislatures. Hence a hybrid process emerged in which simple majorities would ultimately determine state ratification outcomes but only those states that consented would be bound, and a supermajority of states (three-fourths, rounded down) would have to consent for the Constitution to be operative at all. This is far different than a mere simple majority requirement, and much more like the state supermajority requirements of the Article V amendment process than birth-logic, simple-majority-rule theorists commonly recognize.

And what of the amendment procedure for our new community's constitution? As I suggested early on, we have good reason for wanting the constitution to be obdurate to change. If popular constitutional decision making proceeds on the assumption that constitutional provisions will endure for a very long time, salutary tendencies will be encouraged: the range of circumstance over one's own life, the life of one's children and their children in turn, encourages a generality of perspective that draws away from self-interest and toward the choice of reasonable ground rules for all; and the need to fashion the liberty-bearing provisions of the constitution in ignorance of many of the details of social life to which they will come to be applied in the future encourages a generality of description that invites and requires the partnership of a constitutional judiciary, and discourages attempts by the founding generation to overconstitutionalize political choice. If it is understood from the outset that the constitution will be obdurate to change, these effects of well-formed rules for

124 *Lawrence G. Sager*

amendment kick in long before the first effort to amend the constitution; the anticipation of the durability of the constitution will impact not just the decision whether to ratify the proposed constitution but the substance of the proposed constitution itself. If, as we have reason to hope, an obdurate constitution will in this fashion inspire careful, general, long-range reflection, then we can regard it as a virtue, not a liability, that in its domain the constitution resists the passions of the moment.

There is, of course, an additional, less savory, incentive (we will not call it a reason) that we as the founding generation have for making our constitution hard to amend. We may have a natural desire to resolve the questions of constitutional structure not just for ourselves but for posterity. We trust ourselves, perhaps, but not those who will succeed us in stewardship of our political community. This is not a particularly attractive picture, perhaps; but both the appeal and the liability of this generational chauvinism, it should be observed, are much blunted by the very act of making our constitution obdurate to change. We, the founding generation, have to live with this constitution for many years ourselves, and after us, our progeny; precisely because our constitution is obdurate to change, we are constrained to broad issues of structure and general propositions of political justice. In effect, by electing to extend our influence over time, we are required to reduce its substantive scope.

As with ratification, if our constitutional community is reasonably large, procedures for amendment may take account of groups – like states, of course – that enjoy geographic contiguity and cultural affinity. This might be so on either of two conceptually distinct grounds. We might hold the view that these groups have so much in common that they reflect the relevant *units* of agreement; we might hold, that is, that these groups are themselves entities that are entitled to have a say – a vote or veto – about constitutive arrangements. Even if we did not believe that, we might well believe that, by insisting on agreement among such groups, we introduce a diversity of value and circumstance, a diversity in sum of perspective, that makes for judgments better suited to the project of doing justice among a diverse people – considered from the perspective of the present population and future populations who presumptively will be living under the same or similar constitutional arrangements. In the latter case we would make group votes the *measure* of constitutive agreement, even though it was individuals rather than the group who were the pertinent units.

Now all this speculation about the voting procedures we might deploy at various stages in the process of constitution making is meant to be in aid of four propositions. First, there are various voting protocols that a political community deeply committed in principle to democracy and democratic procedures might choose. Second, a democratic community might quite sensibly choose different procedures for different purposes, and hence for different stages in the process of establishing and maintaining a written constitution. Third, the conundrum of what voting protocol a group should employ in order to decide what voting protocol it should employ becomes a serious matter at tender intervals like the ratification of a constitution. And fourth, ratification and amendment protocols more or less like those specified in Articles VII and V of the U.S. Constitution make reasonably good sense for a constitutional regime committed to the project of seeking political justice. I mean for these purposes to be modest about this last point: I do not claim that a political community requires a constitution that is obdurate to change, or that it requires a written constitution at all; nor do I claim that a polity with a written, enduring constitution is necessarily superior to one that lacks such an amenity. What I do mean to claim is that an enduring constitution is a sensible institutional design for the ongoing pursuit of political justice in a political community, and that an amendment procedure like that in Article V is a sensible way, inter alia, of making the Constitution an enduring one.

CHANGING THE RULES?

Now let us suppose that we have passed through both the convention and ratification stages. We have in place a constitution; for convenience, we'll imagine that its provisions are very close to those actually chosen in the U.S. Constitution. Not only has our constitution been formally ratified, it has taken hold firmly as a matter of social practice. Our constitution has provisions that permit amendment but only under circumstances considerably more arduous than formal deliberation followed by simple majority support for change (its provisions are more or less like those of the actual Article V). At the convention stage we framers proposed these amendment procedures and at the ratification stage the members of our political community accepted our proposal. Whatever choice among the competing voting mechanisms was made, it is fair to say that the provisions for amendment were a reasoned choice, in service of democratic justice. They were perceived as making more likely that the collaboration of popular and judicial constitutional decision making for which the new constitution provided would produce good results.

After a time, a movement for constitutional change takes form in our political community. The proposed change appears to enjoy substantial popular support, but to the frustration of those who favor the change, it appears that the attempt to comply with the constitution's requirements for amendment will fail. Accordingly, the leaders of the movement for

126 *Lawrence G. Sager*

change call on congress, by simple majority vote, to convene a special national convention of elected representatives, who after a careful deliberative process, will in turn vote by simple majority to approve or disapprove the proposed change. (Or perhaps they ask congress to authorize a process in which a national referendum figures prominently. What is important is that they ask for a process other than those authorized in the amendment provisions of our constitution.) Now the question arises: must our constitution's stipulation of the requirements for amendment be followed, or can an alternative deliberative process, ultimately keyed to a simple majority vote, be substituted?

We should take a moment to be clear about what we are asking. The question is not how history in our community might actually go: whether congress is likely to call a special national convention or institute a national referendum, whether an amendment would be approved, whether the courts would endorse an amendment created outside the terms of the constitution, or how the population at large would respond to this event. Rather, the question is how conscientious political actors should act: whether the leaders would be right to call on congress to act in this unusual way, whether congress should consider itself free to agree, whether the courts should respect an amendment created in this way, and whether we as citizens should celebrate or protest this enlargement of the amending power.

This is a good moment to leave behind our hypothetical world with its hypothetical constitution and turn to our world, with the U.S. Constitution, complete with Article V, as it actually is. The question we arrived at in our hypothetical world is precisely the question on which the validity of the normative claim advanced by the Article V revisionists turns.

ARTICLE V AND "THE PEOPLE"

What can be said in support of the idea that the amending procedures of Article V can be freely circumvented? We can begin with a particular understanding of popular sovereignty in a democratic state: the government belongs to the people; it was created by them and it owes its legitimacy to their initial and ongoing acceptance. The people cannot bind themselves to a constitution entrenched against their decision to amend it. If they could do this, they could bind themselves to a constitution entrenched against all change, or to the rule of a hereditary leadership. The democratic provenance of a constitutional regime is not enough to make it democratic. There must be ongoing power vested in the people; and the majority of the people must enjoy the power to remake their government when the need arises. That is the lesson of the founding of the

Constitution. On this account, it follows that the people can always change their government by simple deliberative majority action.

There is an important truth in this argument. In a democracy government does indeed belong to the people, and that proposition is more fundamental than the mechanical framework of government through which the democratic ideal is sought to be realized at any given time or place. Furthermore, there are surely constitutional arrangements that could be arrived at democratically that would be unacceptable from the vantage of political justice, precisely because of their undemocratic substance. Our earlier example of the democratic enthronement of a hereditary monarch was intended to make precisely that point.

But to invoke "The People" is to invoke what is at best a metaphor, and here, as is often the case in constitutional discourse, that metaphor obscures rather than reveals many important questions. Modern democracies consist of persons who to some, quite possibly substantial, degree share a cultural and political identity, to be sure, but among those persons are groups and individuals who differ in significant ways over serious matters. Every protocol for revealing the state of popular judgment or preference – including the deployment of elaborate measures of electoral outcomes over a period of time – offers at best one possible depiction of the sensibilities of the people as a whole.

For the moment, let us set aside the obvious problem of how a particular arithmetic division among the national population should be resolved into a choice among competing options, and assume that we are concerned only with the full picture, with a complete report of the divergent votes. Even such a complete report, taken on its own terms, is at best only one possible representation of the people. How many people actually voted? What were the choices offered them? How were issues joined or severed, and how were they functionally ordered? What information and arguments were available? Was debate free and extensive? Did the circumstances of the vote conduce to reflection or reflexion? And on and on: we know enough about human nature, group choice, and the complexities of political events more generally to recognize that no encompassable electoral event or sequence of events can give us the ineffable substance of the people, even if we have in mind the actual persons who are alive and citizens of our polity within a relatively cabined period of time.

When we take up the problem we laid aside a moment ago, the point deepens. Competing mechanisms for converting division into choice are just that. Even ignoring the nonarithmetic difficulties of the previous paragraph, when have the people spoken? When 51 percent of the voting population expresses a uniform choice, or perhaps 66 or 75 percent? Or – to introduce some of the problems of our actual constitutional world – if simple majorities in three-fourths of the states support option x but that option falls slightly short of majority support in the nation as a whole, where a small overall majority favor option y, does option x or option y better represent the people? This is why we had hard choices among voting protocols to make at every step along the way in the launching of our constitution in the first place.

The point of all this is not that there are no reasons sounding in the values of democracy for preferring one protocol of political choice over another but rather that choice of protocols must be defended, and further that the defense of a given protocol must be seen in the context of a rather thick understanding of the circumstances in which it is meant to operate. We never have the people in a very interesting or durable sense; what we have are various mechanisms for doing the best we can to get reports or representations of the people. More accurately, we have various mechanisms for treating the competing and shifting judgments and preferences of the members of a *political community* fairly, and for doing justice among those members.

Within these competing mechanisms, simple majority rule has no a priori claim to pride of place. Simple arithmetic intuition cannot do the work being asked of it by those who want to treat democracy, rule-by-the-people, and simple majority rule as synonymous. Imagine our reaction if one of our friends returned from a tennis match and announced that the player who was treated by all the other spectators and the officials as having lost had in fact played much the better game and, further, that the scoring of the tennis match was poorly calculated to award the win to the better player. Our friend's rationale for this pair of propositions is simply this: given the game-set-match scoring protocol of a tennis match, it is entirely possible that the person who wins the most points can lose the game. Now our friend might prove in the end to be right, of course. But even in a matter as simple as tennis, the question of whether the game would be better or worse if the person with the most single points won – even the narrower question of whether the game would then be a better measure of the ability of contending players – is surely complex enough to require more than the blind invocation of arithmetic. When we are considering the elaborate institutional arrangements that compose an ongoing democratic government and the array of concerns that go into an evaluation of those arrangements, the superficial appeal of simple arithmetic is far more misleading.

It is possible, of course, that upon reflection we would conclude that tennis would be a better game if played on a simple highest-number-of-points basis; and, likewise, possible that we would come to think that some mechanism centering on simple majority rule would be the most democratic – or the most just, or both – way of connecting the members of a political community with the ultimate destiny of their community. But

The Birth Logic of a Democratic Constitution 129

either of these judgments needs support from an argument that puts the protocol it champions in contest with other possible or suggested protocols and defends it as superior. An appeal to "The People" is only interesting as a rhetorical way of presenting the result of such a contest; it does not take us behind or above the contest.

The claim that Article V can be displaced spontaneously by a less onerous procedure for amendment, accordingly, must depend on more than simple arithmetic. What is required is support for the proposition that – in light of the overall structure of governance contemplated by the Constitution – it is anathema to democracy for the people to be separated from the substance of their Constitution by the rigors of Article V.

DEMOCRATIC OBJECTIONS

In order to evaluate the claim that a commitment to democracy requires a political community to make its constitutive arrangements vulnerable to change at the will of deliberative majorities, we need to have some understanding of the rationale and requirements of democracy. Suppose we begin with a reasonable sketch of what features are essential to a well-formed democratic community, and then ask what call these features make upon the protocol for constitutional change in such a community.

As a first pass, let me offer these features. First, there is the requirement of equal membership – that is, membership in the community is open to all within its enduring sovereign authority, and that the interests and concerns of all members of the community are treated with equal regard. Second, there is the requirement of voice, which requires both that individuals and groups within the society have the opportunity to be heard in debates about matters of public choice, and that the population as a whole have the ability to direct the outcome of decisions about such matters. Third, there is the requirement of independence: a well-formed democratic community must respect the ability of its members to make basic choices about what is valuable to them in shaping the course of their private lives and in directing the course of the community of which they are a part.

Membership, voice, and independence . . . I hope readers will agree that this is a reasonably satisfactory description of the requirements of a well-formed democratic community. More to the immediate point, I hope that ultimately we can agree that, on the one hand, a thinner, more mechanical description of democracy would be inadequate and, on the other, that an appropriately rich but better description of democracy would be no more congenial to the claim that a well-formed democratic community must make its constitutive arrangements vulnerable to change at the will of deliberative majorities.

With this working sketch of the requirements of democracy in hand, we can now ask whether and when simple majority rule is an entailment of those requirements. It is useful to distinguish two different sorts of connection between these requirements and majority rule: epistemic and direct. An epistemic claim for majority rule at the constitution-shaping level in the name of democracy would be at one remove; it would argue that we are more likely to realize and maintain the features of a well-formed democratic community if our constitutive arrangements are guided by majority will. A direct claim would argue that majority control over constitutive arrangements is itself a necessary subfeature of a well-formed democratic community, that the conditions of membership, voice, and independence entail such control.

The epistemic insistence on majority control of the constitutive arrangements of a democratic community is simply implausible. Remember that we are not considering the possibility that majority constitutional control would – all things considered – be a sensible means of getting right answers to questions about the shape of a well-formed democratic community, or the more telling possibility that majority constitutional control would be a better strategy than, say, actual constitutional arrangements under Article V. The epistemic claim has to be a good deal stronger than that: it has to insist that an amendment protocol like that specified in Article V so cripples our capacity to shape our institutions as to seriously threaten our democratic commitments. This seems an insupportable claim. Earlier, I argued that requirements like those in Article V are well suited to getting good answers to constitutional questions, especially in combination with a constitutional tradition like that present in the United States, a tradition that contemplates a partnership of a certain kind between the popular constitutional sovereign and an active constitutional judiciary. Roughly, the claim is that by making the Constitution obdurate to change we encourage spare and apt popular constitutional decision making: spare in that most matters are confided to the machinery of popular politics for resolution; apt in that general and enduring precepts of political justice are likely to commend themselves to the popular constitutional decision maker who understands herself to be writing in stone. The Article V demand for broad interstate consensus has the additional virtue of drawing on the diversity of contemporary circumstance for which the states are a reasonable proxy. Overall, our constitutional institutions are justice seeking and depend upon a collaboration between popular constitutional decision makers and judicial constitutional decision makers, a collaboration that works best when popular constitutional decision makers speak in terms of general principle, as they are encouraged to do by Article V.

The Birth Logic of a Democratic Constitution

It does not follow that the Constitution would be inexcusably defective if Article V were otherwise, only that there are good reasons to have chosen requirements like those in Article V. But the contrary proposition, that somehow Article V intolerably interferes with collective judgment about the shape of our democratic institutions, is simply out of bounds.

But to dismiss the epistemic claim is not to dismiss the democratic objection to Article V. The democratic argument against Article V may be more persuasive when it comes into the debate earlier, as the claim that a well-formed democratic community would have as one of its features majority control over its constitutive arrangements. This is the direct claim, that membership, voice, and independence are not adequately realized in a community that does not have majority constitutional control.

Two versions of this claim suggest themselves. In the first, the equal regard aspect of membership is invoked: only simple majority rule treats each person equally, because any other voting protocol cedes to some minority the capacity to block the will of the majority, and this must mean that the votes of those in the minority count for more. In the second, the objection focuses on voice: here the partnership between Article V majorities (typically from the remove of a century or two) and an unelected judiciary is made the villain, on the grounds that it excludes the voice of contemporary political majorities.

In thinking about equality of membership and Article V, it is useful at the outset to observe the distinction between the distribution of agency and the differential weighing of votes. The formidable Article V requirement of ratification by three-fourths of the states is a distribution of agency, and it is distinctly odd to object to it as a failure of equal regard. Consider the requirement in municipal law that a community's effort to annex a particular area be supported by electoral majorities in both the annexing community and the target area. Suppose that the annexation is strongly supported by the voters in the annexing community, but rejected by a majority of the much smaller electorate in the target area. We could characterize the annexation rule as a unanimity requirement, because both electoral entities must agree; and it would be true that a comparatively small number of voters could defeat the will of a much larger group. But the voters in the target area are not being preferred in any illuminating sense of that verb; they are merely being accorded agency over their own municipal destiny.

True, Article V makes it harder to amend the Constitution than would other possible rules, including a majority vote among the entire national electorate, or a more or less ordinary legislative act by Congress standing alone; and true, the mutual-agreement-to-annexation rule makes it harder to annex a target area than would other possible rules. But that does not, without more, give rise to any objection, and if either of these rules is objectional for this reason alone, the objection must be based on something other than equal regard.

Perhaps the relevant comparison is not between Article V and other possible voting protocols, but rather between possible outcomes under Article V. Certainly it requires a much broader base of support to amend the Constitution than to defeat a proposed amendment. Because the population of the fifty states varies so radically, it is not possible to measure the differential burden in terms of numbers of voters, but the differential is very great, and under many plausible scenarios, comparatively few voters could indeed defeat a constitutional amendment.

This suggests a second distinction, implicated by the distinction between the differential weighing of votes and the distribution of agency – namely, the distinction between disfavoring persons and disfavoring positions. Any voting regime that disfavors persons is suspect on equal regard grounds and requires a substantial justification. But a voting regime that disfavors positions is not, without more, in tension with equal regard. Depending on its form and rationale, we might consider a position-disfavoring vote rule a good or bad thing, but without more, our concern about such a rule would not turn on equality of membership. This is true even of straightforward supermajority rules where the differential burden on those favoring the nondefault position is concrete and quantifiable in terms of the number of voters required to overcome that burden.

There may be situations in which the interests of some classes of persons or groups are so deeply and pathologically associated with some issues that a position-favoring rule would be inconsistent with equal regard. This would be true, for example, in a society where there was a durable distinction between farmers and ranchers: we imagine that the ranchers dominate in their wealth and stature; that mobility between the careers is, as a practical matter, difficult; that ranchers require open ranges to thrive; and that farmers, conversely, require fences. In such a society, a voting rule that made open ranges the default and required a supermajority vote as a precondition to any permission to fence might well be an affront to equal regard. But this functional inequality of membership is a special case, born of special circumstances; the mere formal disfavoring of a position does not put equal regard at hazard.

On the contrary, a voting protocol that formally disfavors a position may functionally improve equality of membership. That is precisely what we have to hope for in Article V in the U.S. Constitution and the reason for the adoption of Article V's twin in our hypothetical constitutional community. The idea, you will remember, is that the insistence on a supermajority of states is a reasonable proxy for the demand that constitutional precepts be acceptable to persons in a wide variety of circumstances, while the general difficulty of amending the constitution causes popular constitutional decision makers to take account of their own future interests and those of their children and their children's children – all of which should conduce toward the selection of constitutional principles fair to all members in the community. Again, there may be other ways of organizing a well-formed and well-functioning democratic community, but the amendment strategy of Article V is a promising mechanism to that end; and, again, it should be clearer still that an amendment protocol like Article V is not inconsistent with equality of membership.

That leaves the charge that Article V is unacceptable because it interferes too drastically with the ability of the people to control their government, that it inappropriately muffles the democratic voice. We have celebrated Article V in part precisely because it makes amendment of the Constitution difficult, thereby encouraging a generality of perspective and expression in the text and, in turn, facilitating an active judicial role in making the generalities of the text concrete. The practical result is that authority over most constitutional choices is distributed between political generations long since departed, on the one hand, and the constitutional judiciary presided over by the Supreme Court, on the other. Conspicuously missing, of course, is the voice of contemporary members of our political community – us.

This is not a wholly unfounded observation. Before we take its measure, it is useful to set aside two responses on behalf of Article V that move too quickly and conclusively to its defense. The first is the point on which we have already relied rather heavily, which may seem apt here as well: the observation that simple majority rule has no presumptive claim to represent "The People" in matters of constitutional choice, whereas Article V may well have. That observation, in its place, is telling; however, it was meant to invite or insist upon the consideration of rival amendment protocols in terms of the requirements of democracy, not to conclude such consideration. The claim from voice against Article V does not presume the shape of an appropriate protocol to represent the people but rather argues for it, and such a claim must be met.

The second response on behalf of Article V that must be set aside – at least in its strongest form – is more familiar. Various defenses of judicial review assume a common abstract form: the robust adjudicatory tradition of the U.S. Supreme Court is best understood as pointed toward the perfection of the democratic features of our political community; a complaint against that tradition in the name of democracy, accordingly, will not lie. In some extreme circumstances, this would be entirely true. In a political community that was egregiously deficient in the essential features of a well-formed democracy, it could not be objectionable on democratic grounds for a court to insist on changes that brought the community closer to the requirements of democracy. It would be wrong to prefer the results of a grossly flawed popular political process to those of a judiciary engaged in serious democratic reform, or to see in the displacement of the outcome of the deeply infirm process a significant democratic cost. But things change in a political community where the essential features of a well-formed democracy are reasonably well realized. In such a working democracy, it is at least sensible to remand the question of what constitutes a democratic improvement in the popular political process or its outcomes to that process itself, and in such a working democracy it is at least sensible to think that there is some cost entailed in displacing the results of the popular political process. We are a working democracy, and the strong tendency of Article V to take constitutional questions out of the hands of the present members of our community cannot be sweepingly excused on the grounds that improvements in membership, voice, and independence form much of the corpus of modern constitutional adjudication.

If we believe, as I think we should, that our constitutional institutions – Article V, the spare and abstract text of the liberty-bearing provisions of the Constitution it has encouraged, and the role the judiciary has assumed in giving concrete content to those provisions – play an important part in maintaining and improving the conditions of democracy in our community, then that fact is of course significant to our evaluation of Article V. But we are now in the somewhat shaggy domain of the pragmatic evaluation of how institutions work in practice and in context. And in the appraisal of our constitutionalism generally or of specific constitutional outcomes, it should not be crucial that acknowledged improvements in political justice are or are not appropriately regarded as improvements in democracy per se. What is important is the judgment, backed by experience, that our constitutional institutions are well suited to the job of identifying and realizing the precepts of political justice, including the necessary features of democracy.

In thinking about Article V in these terms, it must be remembered that we are not evaluating Article V in isolation, or even Article V, the often abstract text of the Constitution, and our tradition of judicial responsibility for giving concrete content to the generalities of the text. In considering whether our constitutional arrangements are critically defective in the way that they connect the members of our political community with choice over its destiny, we need to consider not just the machinery of constitutional amendment but the whole of the governmental arrangements specified in the Constitution. The U.S. Constitution directs most governmental business to popular political institutions and distributes the power

The Birth Logic of a Democratic Constitution 135

among these institutions in complex ways. At the federal level there is both the House of Representatives, which is population-apportioned and subject to frequent elections, and the Senate, which is neither. There is also the president, and, de facto, the vast administrative establishment of the modern welfare state. This complex array of federal authority, in turn, shares the day-to-day business of government with state and local governmental entities.

Some of this distribution of popular political authority is actually specified in the Constitution; some is clearly contemplated, and some is merely tolerated. But all is part of the overall structure of government under the regime of constitutional authority we are evaluating. Not all matters are open to the popular political process, however. The Constitution – or more exactly our constitutional traditions, including the Constitution itself, and the relatively robust role of the judiciary in giving the Constitution meaning and application – treats some questions as matters for constitutional resolution, and decides them through a combination of a textual stipulation and wide-bodied judicial interpretation. Finally, the Constitution provides for ongoing popular constitutional decision making by specifying the circumstances under which its textual terms can be amended.

The question of whether choice over the destiny of our political community is properly connected to the members of the community under our extant constitutional arrangements thus includes but is not limited to the protocol for constitutional amendment. It embraces the whole complex scheme of governance that has developed under the aegis of and in the name of the Constitution. The particular question of what steps must be taken to amend the Constitution must be considered against the backdrop of the scheme of governance as a whole.

In our political community, there is great opportunity for the expression of popular will and the control of popular political institutions by various configurations of the people. Even as to questions of constitutional substance, Article V itself does not absolutely entrench the Constitution's text but merely discourages its amendment. And the president and the Senate have an ongoing capacity to shape judicial decision making at the margins at least by means of the appointment of the justices of the Supreme Court. Article V and the constitutional arrangements it promotes do narrow the discretion of popular political institutions somewhat, but that narrowing is entirely consistent with our commitment to democracy.

The simplest defense of this proposition would speak of the trade-off between the value of popular political choice and other fundamental values of political justice, and insist that – given room for the substantial play of popular political judgment – such a trade-off is entirely

136 *Lawrence G. Sager*

appropriate for a democracy. While this formulation may literally be correct, however, it conceals a more complicated and interesting picture.[6]

We can begin to reveal this picture by imagining the following: suppose Britain still maintained its historic structure of governance,[7] which to a modern constitutionalist looks remarkably nonconstitutional, with no written constitution and no interference by the judiciary with the will of the Parliament in the name of enduring practices and values of the sort associated with the U.S. Constitution. And suppose further that an exhaustive inventory revealed that, bracketing the question of parliamentary sovereignty versus judicial review in the name of the Constitution, Britain and the United States were identical in their conformity with the fundamental requirements of political justice. Now the question is this: would we be tempted to say that Britain, which got to be as it is without the intervention of a constitutional judiciary, was for that reason the more just (or at least the more democratic) political community? I think that the answer is no, and that is what makes the trade-off defense of an obdurate constitution a little too simple.

To begin with, there is the question of what we can call the democratic threshold. Imagine a modern political community that moves from town meeting governance by the whole to governance by elected representatives; later, it adds institutions that further deflect the immediacy of popular reflection and choice: a senate with members elected every six years, or even a central bank with important authority over day-to-day monetary policy like the setting of interest rates. What I want to suggest is that one can be committed to democracy as a crucial element of

---

[6] My general debt to my colleague Christopher Eisgruber is particularly strong here, as he has more than once pushed me to better understand and defend my view of this question.

[7] At the turn of the millennium, the United Kingdom in fact finds itself acquiring a constitution by stealth. Transnationally, the United Kingdom, as a signatory of the European Convention on Human Rights, is open to the scrutiny and judgment of the European Court of Human Rights in Strasbourg. Nationally, the rights and freedoms guaranteed under the convention are given significant weight in British domestic law by virtue of the Human Rights Act of 1998, which requires British courts to give legal effect to the convention in legal disputes not implicating acts of Parliament; to interpret acts of Parliament so far as possible to make them compatible with the convention; and – failing interpretive space to accomplish that – to declare those acts to be incompatible with the convention, thus triggering a "fast track" amendment procedure in Parliament. The Human Rights Act, though nominally merely a statute and with variegated force at that, is likely to come in time to function much as a judicially enforced bill of rights. Subnationally, authority recently has been devolved by statute from Westminster to parliaments or assemblies in Scotland, Wales, and Northern Ireland, thus creating a legally prefigured structure of quasi federalism. Constitutional theorists, accordingly, will in future have only the memory of historic Britain as a counterexample to the flourishing of constitutionalism; parliamentary sovereignty is likely to become a theoretical possibility rather than a practical reality.

political justice, and committed to popular control over matters of public choice as crucial to democracy, without believing that these moves toward modern governance represent diminutions of either justice or democracy. In a generally well functioning democracy, with a fairly distributed franchise and robust opportunities for political debate, a limited set of public choices can be placed in the hands of bodies whose decisions are not immediately and easily revisable by popular political mechanisms. To be sure, there are limits both as to the range of the matters that can be so committed and the degree to which committed matters can be made obdurate to popular revision. But an important part of what makes it seem odd and abstract to suggest that, in our hypothetical comparison of Britain and the United States, the United States would have an innate deficit of justice by virtue of its hard-to-amend Constitution is the sense that our constitutional practice does no violence to the democratic threshold.

There is a deeper point as well. To see it, we will have to take a small excursion into the realm of democratic theory, with the promise that we will return to our line of march. The democratic virtues of membership, voice, and independence converge on the idea that in a democracy the people rule themselves, that they choose the structures and substance by which they are governed. But as many democratic theorists have observed, there is something deeply troubling about this naive formulation of the democratic ideal. If there were an entity, "The People," that could sensibly be seen as the agent to which the ideal of self-rule could attach, then we could undertake to design our institutions so as to be assured that this entity had the proper degree of control over public choices. But, of course, there is no such entity, or at least no such entity this side of agreement on the part of all the members of our political community as to the appropriate course of action. Short of unanimity, there will be some persons, possibly a large number of persons, who disagree with the course of action chosen by the applicable voting protocol or representative mechanism. As to any such decision – as to *any* decision, as a practical matter – there will surely be persons who are not ruling themselves; and there may, in fact, be many such people, and even many who often find themselves on the losing side of public choices that are of considerable importance to them. Hence, ideas like "the tyranny of the majority" are perfectly sensible, while the notion of self-governance is in chronic jeopardy.

Some theorists who have confronted this deep problem of democratic governance have responded by thickening the requirements of democracy. Frequently, this thickening has been directed to the question of how members of a democratic political community are to regard each other, and, as consequence, the kind of reasons they must have for supporting public choices. Common to this line of democratic thought is the starting point that members of a democratic community must regard each other

138   *Lawrence G. Sager*

as equals. From this stipulation there flow two others: each member of the community must have an opportunity to be heard – in the strong sense of having his or her arguments taken seriously for what they are worth, without regard to his or her power or position – on each contested question of community choice; and each member of the community should support only those community choices that he or she believes are reasonable from the vantage of every other member of community regarded as an equal. Even if this idealized account could be realized in practice, of course, there would almost certainly be substantial disagreements. But these would be disagreements of a particular sort: they would be disagreements about what was the right thing to do. Deliberation followed by a vote would produce "a pooling of judgments," not a "vector sum" of aggregated preferences.[8] The majority would win, but by the postdeliberation assemblage of individual judgments (we could think of them as adjudications, but that is getting ahead of ourselves); and, in this sense, it would be "reason" rather than "power" that would prevail. Each member of the community would be heard, and the interests of each taken into account by all.

But this idealized account is so far from being realized in practice as to be almost unrecognizable, and the structure of popular political institutions seems better suited to the negotiated summation of preferences than the deliberative pooling of judgments. This is not a prospect that should be greeted with dismay, because the competition for support will often push the powerful to include the interests of the less powerful in their political agendas. Driven in part by their location at the margins of power, "discrete and insular minorities" may through coordination of their determined energy acquire genuine political muscle (Ackerman 1985). But this is a function of what is expedient in shifting political circumstances, of the wavering hand of a process that is not accidental, but which proceeds far more readily by the logic of accumulated power than by that of reflective justice. No one can demand to be heard or to have his interests taken into account unless he can make himself strategically valuable. In the real world of popular politics, power, not truth, speaks to power.

Consider again, in this light, the impact of a constitution that is obdurate to change, and obdurate in the way that the U.S. Constitution is obdurate. The framing generation, for its part, is encouraged by the demands of space (the requirement of a supermajority of states) and time (the

---

[8] The apt phrases are from Michelman (1989), who distinguishes between "deliberative" and "strategic" politics. More generally, the broad model of popular politics that I am referencing here is often referred to as "deliberative democracy." In another context, Lewis Kornhauser and I have tried to draw and inform the distinction between preferences and judgments (Kornhauser and Sager 1986).

The Birth Logic of a Democratic Constitution 139

practical resistance to change) to populate the Constitution with propositions that prescind from immediate self-interest, are widely shared within the political community as a whole, and are expressed at a level of generality that invites and requires the collaboration of constitutional judges in giving concrete content to the text's lofty generalities. Within the constitutional judiciary, adjudication is reflective of the egalitarian logic of idealized democracy: every claimant before a court stands on equal footing; the force of her claim is the force of reason – the strength of its connection to an articulate scheme of principle – not her wealth, popularity, or social stature (Sager 1984).

Courts, of course, are far from perfect, and I do not mean to invite the comparison of the real world of popular politics – its blemishes made prominent – with a pollyannaish vision of the constitutional judiciary at its best. The point, though, is this: popular politics and constitutionalism represent fundamentally different faces of democracy, different democratic modalities. In an important sense, these two institutional arrangements aspire to different democratic virtues. The demands of the democratic threshold surely hold, and no society without a robust place for popular politics can be counted as democratic. And it may be sensible to speak of trade-offs between these democratic virtues in the space for institutional choice above or beyond that threshold. But it is a mistake to think that there is a blunt opposition between process and outcome – between the fair and democratic process of popular politics and the potential for just results offered by constitutional practice in the United States. Constitutional practice embodies a distinct process that is itself fair and democratic, fair and democratic in a way that popular political institutions cannot realistically be – hence, to complete our most recent excursion, my reluctance to move too quickly to the idea of trade-off; and, hence, the grounds for declining to think that a country with parliamentary supremacy would, if we were to stipulate substantive parity, enjoy an edge in political justice over a constitutional democracy like our own.

A DEMOCRATICALLY DEFICIENT CONSTITUTION: RESPONDING TO BREAKDOWN

But suppose we were dealing with a constitution that in its time and place exacted too great a cost in voice. Suppose we return to our hypothetical constitutional world and stipulate that it is credible to believe that our constitution there is deficient in this way. Even so, how could the claim that this is true become an argument for circumventing the amendment requirements of our constitution? Why isn't this simply an argument for amending the amendment provisions? After all, our constitution is law, and it specifies exclusive procedures for its own amendment. And we arrived at

140   *Lawrence G. Sager*

our constitutional arrangements, including the procedures for amending the constitution, in the course of an elaborate and careful series of events, events aimed at securing sound results themselves fairly arrived at from the vantage of constitutional democracy.

To have grounds for circumventing the constitutionally stipulated requirements for amendment, the leaders of the movement for constitutional change in our hypothetical political community must insist that their objection is deeper than a mere disagreement about whether a rival mechanism is a better amendment procedure. Their claim must be that the constitution as it stands is in some important sense inconsistent with the sound governance of the community; that the amendment procedures specified in the constitution are a more or less decisive barrier to constitutional change and are an inappropriate means for a democratic community to make constitutional choices; and, further, that these procedures are functionally self-entrenching, that the same qualities that make them undemocratic made them immune to change as a practical matter. If the constitutionally specified procedure for amendment is radically infirm and defeating of efforts to change it, then it is futile to submit the question of how the constitution should be amended to it, and wrong to accept that futility and requiring continued support of the misshapen and unyielding representation of the people offered by the extant amendment procedure.

On the other hand, if the complaint of those who want to circumvent the constitutionally specified procedure for amendment does not satisfy these conditions of entrenched, radical infirmity, then they face the problem we have already hinted at, the problem of having no democratic grounds on which they can rely. They argue that we as a political community would be better off if our protocol for constitutional amendment were different; others strongly disagree. The matter, all agree, should be referred to the people, and the constitution stipulates the representation of the people that should govern constitutional choices. If those who would disregard that representation claim only that it could be improved upon, they have not given us a reason to disregard it, only a reason to change it in conformity with its requirements. This is not a matter for the court or the legislature, but rather the people, acting in accord with the constitution's stipulated procedure for amendment to amend that procedure.

So we have made some headway. We have sketched, in effect, the circumstances of constitutional breakdown and determined that these are the conditions of a license for a democratic polity to ignore its own constitution's requirements for constitutional change: aspects of the constitutional regime are critically deficient, in that they are an obstacle to sound governance at a moment of considerable need; the specified amendment

The Birth Logic of a Democratic Constitution 141

procedures make amendment of the regime impossible or extremely unlikely, inducing a kind of paralysis; and the specified amendment procedures are, in some deep sense, a failed representation of the people.

By now you may have anticipated the regressive nature of the problem. Suppose that the leaders of the movement for constitutional change in our hypothetical community believe that the amendment provisions of the constitution are both radically infirm and entrenched by virtue of that infirmity. Not everyone agrees that either or both of the propositions are true, we may assume. Who is to decide?

This is like our earlier problem of how to choose the mechanism for ratifying the constitution, but with a particular bite: we find ourselves in the unhappy position of having to decide a prickly question of democratic choice in order to select the mechanism for deciding a prickly question of democratic choice. How ought we proceed?

It might seem that the circumstances dictate the choice of decision maker. In our story, the leaders of the movement for constitutional change turn first to congress for authorization of their proposed unorthodox amendment process. Should congress grant their request and launch such a process, citizens will surely be involved – informally as a matter of debate, and formally when something or someone is put to the vote. And if anything purporting to be a constitutional amendment ultimately emerges from the renegade process, the supreme court will almost certainly be called upon to pass on its validity. Are not each of these groups – congress, citizens, supreme court – nominated by circumstance as the constitutional decision maker in its time and place?

Matters are not quite that simple, of course. Each of these groups may indeed become the decision maker, in a sense, but as to any of these groups it might be the case that the appropriate course involves firm deference to another group or process. Here there is good reason for deference to the people, because popular control of some sort is the abiding commitment of the amendment requirements in our hypothetical constitution, just as in Article V in the actual Constitution. But the constitution's representation of the people for purposes of amendment is being challenged as deeply infirm and impossibly entrenched. What can replace that representation as the appropriate representation of the people?

Perhaps we can do no better than to suggest this prescription: no political actor – member of congress, justice of the supreme court, or conscientious citizen – should lightly or independently reach the conclusion that the circumstances of constitutional breakdown obtain. Thus far, we have defined the conditions of constitutional breakdown as these: (1) aspects of the constitutional regime must be critically deficient, an obstacle to sound governance at a moment of considerable need; (2) the specified amendment procedures make amendment of the regime impossible or

142 *Lawrence G. Sager*

extremely unlikely, inducing paralysis; and (3) the specified amendment procedures must be in some deep sense a failed representation of the people. To these three there must be added a requirement of obviousness and consensus: (4) only when there is widespread agreement that these three conditions obtain should any political actor feel free to disregard the constitutionally stipulated protocol for amendment. Note that last condition does not insist that there be widespread agreement on what changes must be made, only widespread agreement that changes must be made and that the constitution is a failed mechanism for making those changes.

Together, these four conditions can be thought of as specifying a limited right of a democratic people, the right to revoke a failed constitutional regime. This is in sharp distinction to the idea that a democratic people enjoy a general right to amend a constitution extraconstitutionally. The requirement of breakdown is meant to respect the representation of the people – the strategy for governing themselves – that they themselves chose in their constitution and have actually lived in their political lives under the constitution. Under anything like ordinary circumstances, the specified means for constitutional amendment ought to be understood as enjoying the strongest possible claim for representing the people, and questions of constitutional change, including change of the requirements for amending the constitution, ought to be submitted to the people in this privileged form. But when it is widely perceived that the specified means for amending the constitution prevent a necessary constitutional change, and have in contemporary context become a failed representation of the people, the privilege may be revoked.

If the constitution has, in fact, broken down, members of the political community are once again faced with the menu of choices we considered at the beginning of our constitution-making story: the selection of representatives to a convention or some other mechanism for drafting changes, the voting protocols at the convention stage, the substance of the constitutional changes to be proposed, and the protocol for their acceptance by the polity. The process, whether it aims at relatively modest constitutional changes or complete displacement of the current constitutional scheme, is in an important sense a popular revocation of a (at least partially) failed constitution; what these choices have in common is the rejection of the specified requirements for constitutional change.

THE PUZZLE OF THE CONSTITUTION'S BIRTH REVISITED

The idea of constitutional breakdown helps to make sense of the otherwise quite puzzling situation of the men who drafted the U.S. Constitution and the members of the founding generation who ratified it. On the one hand, they asserted and acted on the proposition that as a democratic people they were entitled to revoke their extant governmental arrangements without following the procedures for change specified in those arrangements. On the other hand, they undertook to bind successive generations to Article V's requirements for amending the Constitution. How could they reconcile the free-form liberty of constitutional choice that they assumed for themselves with the narrow preconditions of constitutional choice that they imposed on the future?

They might have seen themselves as giants and assumed that lesser persons would walk our part of the planet in the future. They might have consciously engaged in an odd kind of political drama, in which the founding generation knows that its successors are fully justified in disregarding their instructions, but nonetheless do their very best to persuade them that this is not the case. Or they might have understood that under the extraordinary circumstances of constitutional breakdown a democratic people have full license to revoke their constitutional arrangements. Only something very much like the distinction between amendment and revocation – with the latter dependent on the widely shared perception of breakdown – can make sense of a thoughtful group of men who apparently believed that a democratic people own their government and can replace it when it becomes necessary, and yet carefully included Article V in their own Constitution.

I do not mean either to assert or to deny that the founding generation actually faced constitutional breakdown under the Articles of Confederation, but rather, that we can best make sense out of their views and actions by supposing that they believed themselves at the point of breakdown or something very much like it. The historians among us can no doubt set me right, but I imagine that reasonable persons among the founding generation might well have concluded the following: that sound governance of the nascent republic was impossible under the Articles of Confederation; that meeting the requirements for change under both the Articles of Confederation (which required unanimous state consent) and the respective state constitutions would at best be a process of many years and was quite possibly a doomed venture; and that the representation of the people under the extant regime of law was a failed one in that it made the states rather than the people the units of national government.

If these speculations about the founding generation are true, then the model of breakdown-revocation explains the way the otherwise odd discrepancy between the founding generation viewed the legal past and the legal future. But I do not mean to belabor or depend on this possible understanding of history. As we were at some pains to observe early on, the example of the founding generation is only that, and if this attempt to explain that example fails, then we may simply have to grant that our constitutional past has its share of warts.

REFERENCES

Ackerman, B. 1985. "Beyond *Carolene Products*." *Harvard Law Review* 98: 713–46.
   1998. *We the People: Transformations.* Cambridge, Mass.: Belknap Press of Harvard University Press.

Ackerman, B., and N. Katyal. 1995. "Our Unconventional Founding." *University of Chicago Law Review* 62: 478–512.

Amar, A. R. 1994. "The Consent of the Governed: Constitutional Amendment outside Article V." *Columbia Law Review* 94: 462–87.

Kornhauser, L. A., and L. G. Sager. 1986. "Unpacking the Court." *Yale Law Journal* 96: 82–117.

Michelman, F. I. 1989. "Conceptions of Democracy in American Constitutional Argument: The Case of Pornography Regulation." *Tennessee Law Review* 56: 291–319.

Sager, L. G. 1984. "What's a Nice Court Like You Doing in a Democracy Like This?" *Stanford Law Review* 36: 1087–105.
   1990. "The Incorrigible Constitution." *New York University Law Review* 65: 951–3.

PART TWO

CONSTITUTIONAL
STRUCTURE AND DESIGN

4

Constitutional Democracy as a Two-Stage Game

Jonathan Riley

Constitutional democracy can be modeled as a complex game involving two general stages of political decision making. One stage (sometimes labeled the constitutional phase or higher track) is a cooperative game in which moral (i.e., rational and fair-minded) players jointly agree to promote their common good by unanimously accepting a (written or unwritten) constitutional code. The code typically sets out fundamental political institutions (including legislative procedures, modes of election and appointment, amendment processes, and the like), delineates a system of checks and balances (though not necessarily one that undergirds an American-style separation of powers), and lists some basic rights of the people. Unanimous consent to *some* such constitution is effectively guaranteed through suitable definition of what it means to be a moral agent. For example, it might be supposed that, for this higher track of politics, any moral agent is an expected utility maximizer who imagines himself in a hypothetical position (or state of nature) behind a veil of ignorance, where he is uncertain as to his actual position in society and thus assigns equal probabilities to occupying each of the possible positions. Given these assumptions, moral agents will consent to a utilitarian constitution whose rules of conduct maximize the general welfare.

The second stage (also called the postconstitutional phase or lower track) is a noncooperative game in which the veil of ignorance is lifted and each moral player freely pursues his particularistic interests in competition with other people under the constitutional rules chosen at the first stage. Each person may be assumed for this lower track of politics to have full knowledge of his own actual circumstances (including power, wealth, and so on) relative to those of the other members of his society. General compliance with the constitutional rules is expected because the players continue to recognize a binding moral commitment to the constitution that they have unanimously endorsed during the constitutional phase, a phase that any moral player of any generation (not merely the founding generation) can enter in his imagination at any time.[1] A moral agent ideally exhibits sufficient virtue and honor to prevent him deviating from the rules, where virtue and honor might amount to nothing more than long-term self-interest or what Tocqueville called "self-interest rightly understood."

To the extent that these agents fear that they or others may not always display the requisite portion of virtue and honor at the second stage, however, they will allow, when choosing a constitutional code at the first stage, for the possibility of some degree of noncompliance with the constitutional rules. In particular, they will endorse a constitutional system of credible threats and rewards designed to give amoral agents, who feel little if any moral commitment to the constitution, "external" incentives to comply with its rules. Some such system of checks and balances is evidently needed to mitigate if not thwart the unconstitutional activities of opportunistic government officials who lack a conscientious desire to follow the rules. Legislators might be subjected to frequent elections, recall procedures, and other popular checks, for example, to encourage them to implement democratic legislative procedures, as Bentham (among others) recommended. Or power might be divided and shared among distinct groups of officials (including legislators, administrators and judges) in such a way that each group has incentives (at least partially) to check the other groups' improper encroachments on its authority. By thus checking each other, even amoral officials might largely prevent each other from trampling on each other's authority or on authority reserved to the people in the form of basic rights, a general strategy made famous by the framers of the U.S. Constitution.

This abstract two-stage conception of constitutional democracy is not entirely free from ambiguity. Are formal amendments to fall within the category of constitutional politics or within that of postconstitutional politics? If moral agents at the constitutional stage jointly establish a simple majoritarian amendment procedure, for example, then amendments can be effected at the postconstitutional stage by smaller groups than the grand coalition of society as a whole. Interested majorities are authorized to impose new constitutional provisions on unwilling minorities. If the agents jointly establish a unanimity rule for amendments, however, then

---

[1] A moral agent can thus be committed to the constitutional code, even though he is not one of its actual framers (all of whom may be long deceased). All that matters is that he (and every other moral person in his society) would consent to the constitution (as amended) when suitably imagining himself in the hypothetical state of nature under the veil of ignorance. Given the assumption that common knowledge exists of each other's moral agency, everybody would know at any time that the constitution is unanimously accepted. The players can change with the generations, therefore, without creating special compliance problems.

amendments are a species of constitutional politics, on a par with the framing and ratification of original documents. The two-stage model can accommodate either of these possibilities. Indeed, it can even accommodate both over time. After initially establishing a unanimity rule for amendments, agents might unanimously amend that amendment formula to establish a majoritarian or supermajoritarian formula, and subsequently switch back to unanimity rule again.[2]

In any event, moral agents clearly display an uneasy mixture of motivations in a two-stage constitutional democracy as sketched. When selecting or endorsing a constitutional code, such a person forgets his actual social position and becomes impartial in that he chooses general rules or principles that appear reasonable from behind his assumed veil of ignorance (which can be of varying degrees of thickness). One way of explaining why he does this is to focus on the long-term nature of the constitutional code (Buchanan and Tullock 1962). If he projects into the indefinite future, the agent may agree that individuals about whom he cares (including his children, their children, and so on) could someday find themselves in any of the actual positions occupied by members of society. When conceiving of his own interests, such an agent assigns present value to the future utility payoffs of his progeny by imagining himself in their respective positions. Because he cannot be certain that these members of his extended family will always be in his existing circumstances, he finds it prudent to act as if he does not know his actual position when selecting a constitutional code to coordinate and constrain what are in effect indefinitely repeated political interactions among people like himself, who take a long-term view of self-interest while tending to remain biased in favor of friends and kin.

Another way to explain why agents place themselves behind a veil of ignorance for constitutional purposes is to appeal directly to virtuous motives rather than to long-term self-interest (without necessarily asserting that virtue is incompatible with all conceptions of long-term self-interest). According to Rawls (1971), for example, any rational person with a sense of fairness will put himself behind a veil so thick that probabilities cannot be assigned to his occupying actual social positions. From this vantage point, the agent chooses constitutional principles so as to maximize the life chances of any member of society who is in a worst-off position (in terms of an index of primary goods). According to Harsanyi

---

[2] I do not discuss the possibility of constitutional amendment by popular consent outside the formal amendment procedure, except to say that it would seem to defeat the purpose of jointly committing to a formal amendment procedure. Ackerman (1991; 1998) and Amar and Hirsch (1998) defend the possibility of amendments to the U.S. Constitution outside the Article V procedure.

150 *Jonathan Riley*

(1977; 1992), in contrast, any rational agent who seeks social justice will imagine himself behind a veil where he assigns equal probabilities to his occupying any social position and chooses a code that maximizes the average (expected) utility of the members of society.

Whether prompted by virtue or by long-run prudence, moral agents are assumed to display a degree of impartiality sufficient to enable them to cooperate mutually to establish a constitutional code. At the same time, however, these agents are assumed to be partial to their own narrow concerns when engaging in postconstitutional politics. Impartiality and cooperation extend only so far. At best, people can be expected to comply with the constitutional rules and no more, as they seek all manner of advantages for themselves, their families, and friends as compared to strangers. In fact, some of them can be expected to lapse from what they know are their obligations under the rules. Recognizing their own fallibility and potential weakness of will, moral agents have a justified fear that people like themselves will at times behave as amoral agents. Such agents will bend if not break the rules to personal advantage unless suitable external checks and balances are established.

The idea that rational and fair-minded agents in the two-stage model are driven by this delicate balance of motivations is to be contrasted with two cruder ideas of agency. The first is that rational agents are necessarily amoral agents motivated solely by their own immediate narrow concerns. Myopic expected utility-maximizers preoccupied with their own circumstances can hardly be expected to place themselves behind a veil of ignorance in order to select or endorse a constitutional code. Even if they are supposed to be mutually cooperative, they will only strike a bargain in light of what they know about each other's actual positions, as, for example, under Nash bargaining.[3] Any constitutional code selected as a Nash bargaining solution would be Pareto-optimal, that is, nobody could be made better off under an alternative constitution without making somebody else worse off. But it generally would not have a liberal democratic content with impartial appeal. The content of its rules would reflect inequalities in the existing distribution of bargaining power. Indeed, it is conceivable that no constitution (let alone a liberal democratic one) would be Pareto-superior to a state of war in this case. Some family or group may accumulate relatively great wealth and military might, for example, and then veto every attempt to move away from that status quo, preferring its existing advantages (however "nasty, brutish, and short") to those of any constitutional peace.

---

[3] On the mechanics of Nash bargaining, see Sen 1970, 126–8; and Harsanyi 1977, 141–67, 196–211.

The other crude idea is that moral agents are motivated solely by an impartial concern for the public good, even to the extent of sacrificing their particularistic interests whenever this seems necessary to confer greater benefits on other people. Such strictly impartial agents cannot be expected ever to lift the veil of ignorance. They would never leave room for individuals to pursue their particularistic concerns freely in a post-constitutional phase. Rather, these godly creatures can be expected to do one of two things. They might directly frame an extremely broad and intrusive constitutional code, its general rules so detailed as to identify and sanction every possible action (including collective actions) that citizens are obligated to perform for the public good. Or, if such an illiberal *one-stage* constitutional democracy is simply not feasible, they could delegate absolute power to some body of likewise virtuous representatives to guide everyone's political actions, in place of any constitution that limited government authority.

Whereas the assumption that people are motivated exclusively by immediate personal interests seems more fit for devils than ordinary humans, the assumption that people are motivated exclusively by an impartial concern for public good seems fit only for moral saints. A liberal democratic constitution has dubious appeal in either context. Rational devils, if they agree to adopt any constitution, may be expected to tailor their constitutional institutions to a historically given, typically unequal (perhaps highly unequal) distribution of bargaining advantages. Liberal democratic institutions would be a rare and temporary phenomenon, observed, perhaps, only where bargaining power happened to be widely dispersed across competing groups. Moral saints would not bother with liberal democratic institutions either. They could trust any one of their number to dictate laws and policies as he saw fit, given that the dictator would remain as saintly as anyone else.

Even if liberal democratic constitutionalism makes little sense for societies of devils or of saints, however, there are good reasons why it makes sense for societies of human beings conceived as moral agents with a reasonable fear of their own tendency to lapse into amorality in some circumstances. These circumstances include situations in which any humans are given something like absolute power to rule over others.

WHY A LIBERAL DEMOCRATIC CONSTITUTION?

A constitutional code that simultaneously authorizes a democratic government and limits its authority to interfere with certain basic liberal freedoms is arguably better than the alternatives for moral agents with our natures.

152 *Jonathan Riley*

The Value of Freedom

One general argument is that the alternatives are associated with what Harsanyi calls "intolerably burdensome negative implementation (or compliance) effects" (1992, 688). Moral agents with our volatile blend of partial and impartial inclinations will not comply with any constitutions but liberal democratic ones. Undemocratic or illiberal alternatives must be imposed by devils or saints on humans, who will tend to resist the imposition.

A liberal democratic constitution recognizes that great value attaches to any moral person's *freedom* to pursue his own particularistic concerns under the rules in postconstitutional politics. Value attaches to his negative freedom to choose without being unduly coerced by others in many "private" areas of life, even if his personal actions are not impartial and do not maximize social value in saintly (say, act utilitarian) terms. Value also attaches to his positive freedom to participate in government on a more or less equal basis with his fellow citizens, even if democratic political choices are not the best ones conceivable in terms of act utilitarian criteria. These elements of liberal democratic freedom are not adequately recognized under illiberal or nondemocratic political arrangements, of the sorts we would expect to find in societies of rational devils or moral saints.

In a society of rational devils, for example, Nash bargaining might result in a highly inegalitarian constitution, where political authority is concentrated in the hands of some wealthy families (because such a political system could maximize the product of all citizens' respective utility gains in relation to a given status quo point). But human beings are not wholly devils, according to the two-stage model, and, when considering things from behind the veil of ignorance, they would find "intolerably burdensome" a political system that failed to secure basic rights of personal choice and democratic self-government. Because they are not motivated entirely by the prospect of immediate personal gain but rather are willing to be impartial for the purpose of framing constitutional rules that secure their liberal and democratic freedoms, moral humans can be expected to implement liberal democratic constitutional rules as general constraints on everybody's pursuit of narrow personal concerns at the postconstitutional stage. Codes that do not secure basic liberal and democratic rights will tend to be rejected as too burdensome. Not just any system of constitutional conventions will do as a way to coordinate and constrain postconstitutional interactions.

In a society of moral saints, on the other hand, constitutional deliberations behind the veil might result in a highly demanding and illiberal constitution that prescribes every action that citizens are obligated to perform to maximize social value in, say, act utilitarian terms. Saints may be driven

Constitutional Democracy as a Two-Stage Game   153

to this kind of constitutional extremism in light of Plato's point that philosopher-kings would prefer to let their fellows be rulers rather than themselves take on the burdens of administering the state.[4] Given that none of the saints would take on the burden of ruling unless threatened with some form of social punishment, all might agree instead to frame and ratify jointly an all-encompassing act utilitarian code that leaves no room for any postconstitutional politics or freedom. Constitutional rules would then fully anticipate and become coextensive with the impartial demands of act utilitarianism. No deviations from those demands would be permitted.

But the constitutional extremism of saints hardly promises to be more tolerable than the constitutional arbitrariness of devils is for humans. Because humans do have particularistic concerns, it would simply be too demanding to require all citizens to act with rigid impartiality in all situations. Even if constitutional framers could be assumed to have the information needed to identify and sanction in the constitution all of the actions called for by act utilitarian criteria in the given social context, moral agents with our natures would value the freedom to deviate from such saintly constitutional demands. Humans would prefer the freedom to make at least some personal and collective choices of their own at a post-constitutional stage, even though such choices may appear mistaken from the perspective of saints of any generation.

Alternatively, if it proves impossible to frame and ratify the requisite constitutional code, moral saints may be expected to delegate absolute power randomly to one or more of their fellows to govern in the public interest. Even if Plato is right that saints would be reluctant to rule over one another, absolute rule by some may be essential because the information required to fix an all-encompassing code is lacking. In that case, some form of absolute rule would replace constitutional democracy. There would be no constitution but rather a benevolent dictator or assembly issuing saintly decrees as different political choice situations arise.

Even if such a grant of absolute power is generally expedient for saints, however, it is surely not expedient for moral humans, who remain biased to some degree in favor of their own personal concerns and need equal

---

[4] Like Plato's philosopher-kings, moral saints may be reluctant to hold political office at all, doing so only to avoid the greater likelihood of incompetence and oppression associated with less virtuous rulers. If all in society were saints, a penalty may have to be imposed for refusal to take office because otherwise none would rule: "For we may venture to say that, if there should be a city of good men only, immunity from office holding would be as eagerly contended for as office is now, and there it would be made plain that in very truth the true ruler does not naturally seek his own advantage but that of the ruled, so that every man of understanding would rather choose to be benefited by another than to be bothered with benefiting him" (*Republic*, I, 347d, in Hamilton and Cairns 1961, 597).

154 *Jonathan Riley*

freedom to pursue those concerns under general rules. Moreover, experience suggests that even moral humans can be corrupted into devils by a grant of absolute power. It is unreasonable to assume that humans given unlimited power will *invariably* act impartially in accord with fair procedures that all would accept behind some veil of ignorance. Given our natural inclinations, any grant of absolute power is akin to abandoning constitutional rules altogether. Absolute rulers, never having to defend their decisions through discussion and debate with opponents, will tend to lose their intellectual and moral capacities and eventually refuse to countenance impartial limitations on their immediate self-interest.

Part of the problem with a grant of absolute power is the intolerable burden placed on political leaders who are not saints. Even if possessed of the intellectual capacities required to predict and evaluate the consequences of alternative government actions for the public good, any human legislator with absolute power would have to suppress voluntarily his natural biases in order to avoid trampling on the vital interests of others, which rational humans behind a suitable veil of ignorance can be expected to regard as basic liberal and democratic freedoms. As Harsanyi suggests, such suppression of natural impulses "could be done, if it could be done at all, only by extreme efforts and at extremely high psychological costs" (1992, 688). Unless it is done, however, the biases of absolute rulers will trump any impartial concern for the public at large, given the absence of external checks on the rulers.

Another part of the problem with a grant of unlimited power is the intolerable burdens placed on ordinary citizens. It is not merely that substantial anxiety will accompany their credible beliefs that rulers who are not saints will abuse unchecked power. Even if the rulers were saints who invariably exercised power to maximize the public good in act utilitarian terms, any ordinary citizen would have to suppress *his* natural inclinations in order to comply with, and help finance, such saintly acts of government. Even if rulers exhibited an extraordinary degree of public virtue, compliance with their rigidly impartial actions would be too demanding for citizens as opposed to saints. By implication, rulers commonly known to be saints would be unelectable in a representative democracy where elected leaders enjoyed absolute power between elections. A fortiori, absolute power should never be granted to human beings.

Rather than adopt the illiberal or undemocratic alternatives that might be found in societies of devils or of saints, moral agents with our delicate balance of motivations should commit themselves to a constitutional code that secures certain liberal democratic freedoms for all. Such a code permits both leaders and ordinary citizens to choose freely in some situations, even though their actions may not be the best ones possible for promoting some saintly notion of the public good that is incredibly demanding for humans. It recognizes the value of individual freedom, by identifying and protecting by right certain sets of personal actions that the individual is permitted to choose in accord with his particularistic inclinations at the postconstitutional stage. It also recognizes the value of collective self-determination, by identifying and protecting by right certain sets of collective actions that the popular government is permitted to perform in accord with the particular constitutional and cultural imperatives of the given society. Such a constitution reflects a reasonable judgment that these sorts of freedom are valuable for moral agents with our natures.

Thus, a liberal democratic constitution assigns certain basic individual rights, as well as correlative duties not to interfere with anyone else's rights. Given that these rights include familiar democratic rights, any citizen who chooses to run for political office, and who is elected or otherwise duly appointed, may also incur "special obligations" (akin to the special obligations associated with promises, contracts, or trusts) to perform or exercise the constitutional powers or rights of that office. At the same time, the constitution must take due precautions to minimize the danger that government officials, naturally inclined to be biased in favor of their own short-term interests, will abuse their constitutional powers. In addition to the primary precaution of more or less frequent popular elections, "auxiliary precautions" are generally held to be prudent – for example, mechanisms whereby government officials can be recalled by their constituents, or rules that divide political authority among different groups of officials and give each group some power to check or balance the authority of others.

As well, a liberal democratic constitution implies certain basic collective liberties, even if it cannot impose any correlative duties on other collectivities to respect the relevant society's freedom of self-determination. This freedom of social groups to develop in their own ways, without undue interference by other collectivities, is held to be valuable for moral humans, who are situated in particular cultural traditions if not prone to discriminate on the basis of particular ethnic, racial, sexual, and other group characteristics. Such considerations might encourage federal arrangements, such that the different levels of government operate to check each other's attempts to encroach on each other's local jurisdictions. Moreover, foreigners who are temporarily resident in any state may be afforded liberal and democratic freedoms similar to those guaranteed for citizens under the constitution. But the idea of a global constitution, whose rules are chosen behind a veil that renders the chooser ignorant as to which of many societies he actually belongs to, is rejected as too demanding, even though moral saints might well act to maximize the general welfare of all people of the world independently of particular state boundaries.

The Value of Secure Expectations

In addition to its less burdensome implementation effects (associated with its capacity to recognize the value of liberal and democratic freedoms for humans), there is a second general argument for the relative appeal of a liberal democratic constitution, namely, its socially valuable "expectation effects" for moral persons (Harsanyi 1992, 689–91; 1995, 327–30). In particular, such a constitution can produce positive "incentive effects" and "assurance effects" that cannot be realized if political leaders (however saintly) face no suitable external checks on their power to act.

For example, a code that subjects legislators and other officials to frequent elections, term limits, recall by their constituents, and so on, can create socially valuable incentives for leaders to enact laws and policies that mirror popular opinion. Socially valuable assurances that government will generally respect any basic rights of religious liberty, private property, due process, and the like that are commonly recognized are also thereby provided to citizens. These kinds of incentives and assurances can hardly be expected if ambitious officials have the capacity to act arbitrarily without being effectively checked by popular opinion.

To take another illustration, constitutional rules that suitably divide power among distinct groups of ambitious political leaders can provide socially valuable incentives for the leaders to check, at least partially, each other's attempts to usurp authorities of offices other than their own. This separation (and sharing) of powers, made possible in practice by a system of checks and balances within the government's structure, tends to encourage the maintenance of some reasonable interpretation of the constitutional plan of government. It also gives citizens some assurance that their constitutional rights will be upheld even if their leaders are far from being moral saints. In Madison's words: "Ambition must be made to counteract ambition. The interest of the man must be connected with the constitutional rights of the place. . . . [T]he constant aim is to divide and arrange the several offices in such a manner as that each may be a check on the other; that the private interest of every individual, may be a centinel over the public rights" (*Federalist* 51, in Cooke 1961, 349). Any absolute concentration of government power in the same hands must destroy these incentives and assurances. Individual citizens will lack any adequate way to protect their vital interests from the holders of such power, for example, even if the holders are subject to elections, term limits, recall procedures, and so on. The latter checks may give *majorities* of constituents effective power to curb abuses by their rulers. But checks of that sort cannot protect *minorities* from abuses tolerated if not encouraged by those same majorities. Some individuals may well be unduly exposed to unreasonable government demands and interpretations of their constitutional rights, if there are not suitable intragovernmental checks and balances designed to encourage majorities and their elected representatives to reconsider.

Any declaration by omnipotent officials that they will voluntarily bind themselves to follow liberal democratic constitutional procedures and respect the equal rights of all is simply not credible. It cannot replace the incentives and assurances created by a liberal democratic code that divides power such that one group of government officials has recognized rights to check others, and such that citizens have rights to throw at least some officials out of office at regular intervals. Without entrenched constitutional checks and balances (whether popular, intragovernmental, or federal) on the rulers, only the expectation effects of particular government actions can be considered because the unrestrained rulers can freely deviate from any self-imposed rules at any time. But those expectation effects are typically negligible.

Admittedly, if government officials and ordinary citizens were invariably moral saints, none would miss the expectation effects of a liberal democratic constitutional code. The relevant incentives and assurances are really only socially valuable if moral agents are naturally inclined to be partial toward their own narrow concerns (both as individuals and as collectivities). Unlike a saint, for example, an ambitious leader may lack motivation to respect basic rights or to otherwise exercise power impartially unless he is permitted to appropriate the fame, honor, and other benefits attaching to his political office. Saintly leaders, however, would rigorously carry out any government acts required to promote the public interest, independently of any rights and privileges of office. Similarly, an ordinary citizen has little political security, as well as little incentive to support the government, unless he has assurance that the leaders will satisfy the obligations of their respective offices. But saintly citizens would be willing to sacrifice their vital interests for the public good and would support elected leaders who ignored obligations of office to bring about some saintly moral ideal such as act utilitarianism.

THE TWO-STAGE MODEL

The two-stage game of constitutional democracy can be formulated with more precision.[5] For convenience, all players may be assumed to have complete and perfect information, although they choose to imagine themselves

---

[5] The two-stage model is analogous to Harsanyi's (1992, 682–94) model of a rule utilitarian society, with the important caveat that an optimal constitutional code need not be seen as utilitarian in form.

158 *Jonathan Riley*

behind a veil of ignorance at the constitutional stage in order to choose and ratify a constitution.[6]

At the constitutional stage, these moral agents unanimously agree to choose an optimal (written or unwritten) constitutional code M* from some given set M of feasible codes. Recall that a moral agent of any generation (not merely the founding generation) can imagine himself at the constitutional stage and replicate for himself the reasoning that underlies the selection of M*, including its amendment procedures by which M* is legitimately altered in response to changing circumstances. The optimal code maximizes a social welfare functional w. The precise form of w can be left open so long as each person's interests are treated impartially in some sense. For convenience, however, I assume with Harsanyi that w is utilitarian in form.

Any optimal constitutional code $M^* \in M$ selected by the moral cooperators gives rise to a permissible strategy set $P(M^*)$, which is the same for all agents committed to that constitution.[7] At the postconstitutional stage, any player k (including government officials) is free to choose a (pure or mixed) personal strategy s_k from his feasible strategy set S_k so as to maximize his own particularistic utility function u_k, subject to the requirement that:

$$\forall k: s_k \in P(M^*).$$

I have suggested that M* has a broadly liberal democratic content. Any person's constitutional rights and obligations are included among his permissible strategy choices.

The idea of equal rights for all is reflected in the fact that $P(M^*)$ is the same for every person. Of course, any person's permissible strategy moves may vary with his personal circumstances (including his past behavior). A person's rights and special obligations will vary as he leaves the position of a child for that of a citizen, for example, or as he leaves the position of ordinary citizen for that of a duly elected legislator, or as he leaves the

---

[6] Complete information implies that agents are fully aware of all the information contained in the (extensive form of the) game, including the rules of the game as well as each other's strategy sets, utility payoffs, and rational and moral agency. All of those elements are assumed to be "common knowledge." Perfect information implies that actors are aware at each stage of the game of the history of play. For further clarification of the distinction between complete and perfect information, see Harsanyi 1977, 87–94. Harsanyi (1992, 694) also suggests extensions of the basic model, including dropping the assumption of complete information as well as the assumption that all players are fully committed to the chosen code.

[7] Harsanyi (1992, 693) assumes that, for all $M \in M$, $P(M)$ is a nonempty compact subset of the feasible strategy set S which is conveniently assumed to be the same for every player, i.e., $S = S_1 = \ldots = S_n$. The latter assumption could be dropped to permit each player to have a distinct strategy set, however, in which case $S = \Pi S_k$.

position of a legislator for that of a convicted felon. Everybody also has the same general obligations to refrain from impermissible strategy choices. He must not neglect his special political obligations, for example, or otherwise violate the constitutional rights of others.

Similarly, the permissible strategy set $P(M^*)$ itself will vary as society amends the optimal constitution M^* in accord with its amendment procedures. Thus, recognized constitutional rights and obligations may alter as social circumstances change over time.

To choose an optimal constitution M^* at the first stage, the players must predict an equilibrium point $\bar{s} = (\bar{s}_1, \ldots, \bar{s}_n)$ of any noncooperative game at the second stage. Different noncooperative games will emerge for different constitutional codes and their respective permissible strategy sets. Even under a given code and its permissible strategy set, distinct noncooperative games will emerge as we vary the given set of players' utility payoffs over outcomes. Given an appropriate concept of equilibrium (some refinement of Nash equilibrium, for example),[8] a "predictor function" π may be defined that selects, for every possible noncooperative game $g(M)$, an equilibrium point $\bar{s} = \pi(g(M))$.

Harsanyi suggests that any person k's utility function u_k may be assumed to take the form $u_k = u_k(\bar{s}, M)$. He includes M as a variable "because the players may derive some direct utility by living in a society whose [constitutional] code permits a considerable amount of free individual choice" (1992, 693). Thus, a player's utility may vary with the different degrees and types of freedom permitted by distinct codes, as well as with the distinct equilibrium strategy combinations selected by the players. Since the social utility functional w is defined in terms of the personal utility functions $u_1, \ldots, u_n$, however, we must have:

$$w = w(\bar{s}, M) = w(\pi(g(M)), M).$$

A best form of political system (one that maximizes w) is achieved by joint commitment to an optimal liberal democratic constitutional code M^* such that each person k freely chooses any permissible personal strategy $\bar{s}_k \in P(M^*)$ that is a best reply to the given permissible strategy choices of his fellows.

The implementation effects of an optimal code are represented in the model "by the fact that the players' strategies will be restricted to the permissible set $P(M^*)$ defined by this [constitutional] code M^*" (Harsanyi 1992, notation altered). That restriction "will produce both utilities and disutilities for the players and, therefore, will give rise to both positive and negative implementation effects" (ibid.). Compared with a saintly

---

[8] See, e.g., Harsanyi and Selten 1988.

160   *Jonathan Riley*

constitution such as an all-encompassing act utilitarian code that gives the individual no freedom to depart from the acts that it defines as obligatory, M* produces utilities for the players by distributing equal liberal and democratic rights. The obligations correlative to those rights are less burdensome than act utilitarian obligations fit only for saints. Such obligations also produce less general disutility for the players than may reasonably be expected under political systems (including a state of war of all against all) that lack any suitable constitutional checks on the power of rulers. This point holds whatever the motivations (benevolent or malevolent) of those who wield absolute power. Only devils or saints will accept absolute rule: moral humans need assurance that their vital interests will be equally protected by right.

The expectation effects of an optimal code M* are represented "by the fact that some players will choose different strategies than they would choose if their society had a different [constitutional] code – not because M* directly requires them to do so but rather because these strategies are their *best replies* to the other players' expected strategies, on the assumption that these *other players* will use only strategies permitted by the [constitutional] code M*" (Harsanyi 1992, 693–4, emphasis in original, notation altered). If he has assurances that his fellows will respect his property rights, for example, a player with particularistic motivations may choose to work and invest at the postconstitutional stage in ways that he would not choose if he had no such assurances. Or if he has assurances that political procedures and rights will be respected, such a player may choose to participate in democratic politics to an extent that he would refuse to consider under a different code that offers no such assurances. More specifically, if he is confident that his vote will be fairly counted, that legislators will be thrown out of office if they lose an election, that any winning candidate will generally satisfy the special obligations of his political office, and so on, he may decide to vote, contribute to campaigns, run for office, and the like. Under a different code that creates no such expectations, though, the same agent may well display political apathy.

Through their joint commitment to an optimal constitution M* that secures valuable liberal and democratic freedoms, moral humans in a constitutional democracy can gain "an important advantage" over those in any political system in which leaders are unconstrained by suitable constitutional checks on their actions. It is not merely that their constitutional commitment prevents liberal democratic citizens (including leaders) from damaging the public interest by deviating from the optimal code merely to increase their own personal utilities at the expense of their fellows. Part of the advantage is that their constitutional commitment will also prevent them from violating the other players' constitutional rights or their own special obligations as a way to maximize some saintly conception of social

Constitutional Democracy as a Two-Stage Game

utility. Impartial deviations from the constitutional rules in the name of some saintly conception of the public good are no less impermissible than selfish deviations. They equally detract from the mutual benefits made possible by the optimal code.[9]

DESIGNING AN OPTIMAL CONSTITUTION

The two-stage model reflects a general hypothesis that rational and fair-minded people with our frailties will jointly establish a liberal democratic constitutional code in order to secure the valuable freedoms, incentives, and assurances that can be created by such a code. Such a code maximizes an impartial conception of social good such as Harsanyi's rule utilitarian conception, I have suggested, if proper account is taken of the value that moral humans place on equal freedom and security of expectations. If this much is accepted, we might attempt to say something more definite about the elements of an optimal constitution. We might try to fix a particular combination of election system and legislative voting rule as optimal, for example, and specify an optimal system of checks and balances for discouraging misrule (especially government violations of recognized basic rights) in this or that social context.

The game-theoretic framework is quite open to suggestion in this regard. It invites consideration of what rational and fair-minded constitutional designers would choose in the given social context. This in turn depends on the given criteria of moral choice. Whatever else is assumed, such framers must be capable of assessing the consequences of their choices. Anyone who seeks to design the best possible form of constitution for his society must be able to analyze and compare the effects of the different feasible constitutions. Different constitutional codes may yield different political outcomes because the different systems of rules have different implementation and expectation effects for the humans who will be competing with one another in postconstitutional politics. To select an optimal code, therefore, constitutional designers must be able to infer how these agents will behave under the different possible codes. From behind the veil of ignorance, they must be able to predict equilibrium points of any noncooperative game that arises at the postconstitutional phase, after satisfying themselves that most if not all citizens (including those who may at least occasionally wish to ignore their constitutional obligations) will have adequate incentives to comply with the constitutional rules.

Beyond this, I have followed Harsanyi in conceiving of moral agents as rule utilitarian agents. But the two-stage model can accommodate different ideas of moral agency. Moreover, even if rational and fair-

---

[9] For related discussion, see Riley 2000.

162   *Jonathan Riley*

minded conduct is spelled out in terms of Harsanyi's brand of rule utilitarianism, many different liberal democratic constitutional plans can plausibly be defended as optimal. Thus, different societies might accept as optimal different legislative voting rules, for example, or different election methods.[10]

For purposes of illustration, let us continue to view moral agents in Harsanyi's terms, as expected utility maximizers who, when choosing a constitutional code to regulate their political interactions, imagine themselves having an equal probability of being in anybody's social position. Which sorts of voting rules, election systems, amendment rules, and so on might be chosen by such people?

Minimizing Transactions Costs

An influential general approach to these matters posits that fair-minded rational agents, who suppose that they have an equal probability of winning or losing on any binary issue or pair of options, will be concerned to minimize aggregate transactions costs (measured in common units) at the postconstitutional stage (Buchanan and Tullock 1962; Rae 1969; Buchanan 1984; Mueller 1996). Given that *decision-making costs* rise whereas *external costs* on people outside the winning coalition fall with the size of the legislative majority required to pass a law, for example, the optimal voting rule in the legislature is a majoritarian one that minimizes the sum of decision-making and external costs (on the assumption that they exhaust transactions costs).[11] At the same time, there may well be different *kinds* of binary issues such that the optimal size of the majority required for legislative action will vary across the different kinds. Thus, Mueller argues that the normative case for *simple majority rule* is strong in the context of a type of binary issue for which we can assume that "the gain to an individual on one side of this issue is the same as to a person on the other side"; in his view, simple majority rule proceeds "as if the intensities of preferences on both sides of the issue are equal" (1996, 159). It operates as if the expected utility gain of winning on the issue is equal to the expected utility loss of losing for every rational individual.[12]

---

[10] For critical surveys of the vast literature on alternative democratic voting rules and election methods, see, e.g., Riker 1982; Ordeshook 1986; Mueller 1996; Sartori 1996, pt. 1, 1–79; and Myerson 1999.

[11] Minority rule can never be optimal because it is indecisive over any pair of options. Because both options can be chosen simultaneously by different legislative minorities, transactions costs effectively become infinite. See, e.g., Mueller 1996, 209–11.

[12] As Mueller (1996, 172 n14) notes, this "equal-intensity assumption" also plays an important role in the justifications for simple majority rule offered by Buchanan and Tullock (1962, 128–30) and Rae (1969), among others. Remarkably, the assumption presupposes that interpersonal comparisons of cardinal utilities are possible: different persons' prefer-

More generally, because minority rule is a nonstarter, the case for simple majority rule remains strong for that "large group" of issues where the expected loss of being on the losing side is small relative to the expected gain of being on the winning side. In contrast, the case for a *supermajoritarian rule* (such as two-thirds majority vote or three-quarters majority vote for enactment of a law) becomes strong in the context of a different type of issue for which "the expected loss to those on the losing side is large relative to the gain for the winners" (Mueller 1996, 211). At the limit, the *unanimity rule* is justified if the ratio of the expected loss of any loser to the expected gain of the winners approaches infinity.

Mueller (1996, 212–23; 1991) suggests that *constitutional rights* are devices for reducing decision-making costs associated with the unanimity rule. "[T]here would *never* be a need to define constitutional rights if all decision-making costs were zero," he says. "No institution other than the unanimity rule itself would be required" (1996, 212). Under the unanimity rule, given that any person on the losing side stands to lose much more than anyone on the winning side stands to gain on the issue, potential losers would veto legislation that threatened to impose such a loss. Anticipating this, the constitutional designers can reduce transactions costs by recognizing individual rights in place of the unanimity requirement: "A constitutional right to undertake certain actions provides the same protection, with lower decision-making costs, as does the implicit veto each citizen possesses under the unanimity rule" (1996, 214). In effect, the individual who stands to lose so much is given the authority to decide the issue as he wishes, without interference or coercion from others. The designers do this because they judge, from behind the veil, that anyone in

---

ence *intensities* must be comparable to be deemed *equal* in value. In effect, any rational and fair-minded constitutional designer must be able to place himself in every citizen's position, empathize with each citizen by adopting his preference intensities while in his shoes, and then make interpersonal comparisons by constructing a cardinal comparable extended utility ranking over the relevant pair of options. The assumption of equal intensities on both sides of an issue can not always be maintained, however, if individuals have conflicting complete and transitive preference orderings over *three or more options (i.e., two or more distinct binary issues)*. Still, if he can make interpersonal utility comparisons, the constitutional designer can always in principle avoid the well-known inconsistencies that can arise when majority rule is used to decide among three or more options. In that case, as Mueller (1996, 169) also suggests, Arrow's (1963) famous impossibility theorem no longer applies because it presupposes that interpersonal comparisons are *not* feasible. (It should be noted that Sen [1970, 129–30] extends Arrow's negative result to *cardinal noncomparable* utilities.) By implication, if he recommends majority rule even though he knows that the agents who employ it at the postconstitutional phase will experience inconsistencies that *they* can not remove because they do not make interpersonal comparisons, then the constitutional designer seems to be saying that it is essentially a matter of constitutional indifference how these inconsistencies are "removed."

164   *Jonathan Riley*

that person's shoes reasonably has such an intense preference not to lose on the issue that the preference intensity of anyone else to win is infinitesimal by comparison. Thus, by delineating rights, the designers "protect an intense minority from the majority by effectively requiring the use of the unanimity rule in these particular externality situations" (1996, 215).

Given the basic freedoms protected by a liberal democratic constitution, it is also reasonable to suggest that the unanimity rule must be used for amendments that would limit those basic freedoms.

The question of how to minimize transactions costs can also be pursued in the design of competitive party systems and electoral methods. For example, a case can be made for constitutional designers to establish a two-party system in conjunction with majority or plurality elections based on single-member districts. The goal is to produce a disciplined legislative majority that can smoothly pass legislation subject to the approval of electoral majorities, who will have an opportunity to cast their votes for members of the opposition party in subsequent elections. Alternatively, the designers might select a multiparty system (or even a system without parties) in combination with some method of proportional representation (PR). By allowing virtually every citizen's vote to count in the sense that it helps to elect a legislator, PR can minimize the frustration of wasted votes and contribute to a goal of broad consensus on legislation. It is far from straightforward to decide which of these options minimizes transactions costs in any social context. The more narrowly majoritarian option attempts to minimize legislative decision-making costs but does not give popular minorities a legislative voice in proportion to their numbers, whereas the consensus option attempts to minimize the external costs associated with exclusion from the legislature but perhaps makes more difficult the formation of any winning legislative coalitions. It is sometimes suggested that the one is preferable in relatively homogenous societies, where legislators are unlikely to violate the basic rights of those citizens excluded from representation, whereas the other is preferable in more diverse social settings, where lack of a voice in the legislature is likely to translate into ethnic or racial discrimination.

If constitutional designers focus relentlessly on the minimization of legislative decision-making costs, it seems natural to extend the narrowly majoritarian option to include simple majority voting in the legislature. If they focus relentlessly on minimizing the external costs of being excluded from winning legislative coalitions, however, the consensus option might be extended to include supermajoritarian voting rules in the legislature. But these extensions are not logically required and do not exhaust the possibilities in any social context. Hybrids might be defended as minimizing transactions costs overall. Mueller argues, for example, that designers of a utilitarian constitution could settle on PR combined with "point voting" in the legislature (1996, 171). In any case, legislators would be required to respect any constitutional rights recognized by the constitutional designers.[13]

This transactions cost approach to constitutional design can be further extended in many ways. At a general level, how should power be divided and shared among distinct groups of officials (legislators, executives, and judges) so as to promote effective democratic government that is responsive to electoral majorities without violating certain basic rights of the individual? Are all relevant costs likely to be minimized by adopting a parliamentary system, a presidential system, or some mixture of the two such as a semipresidential system on the model of the French Fifth Republic or an "alternating presidential" system of the sort proposed by Sartori (1996)? Which intragovernmental systems of checks and balances are best? Under what conditions should federal arrangements be established? These issues are at the heart of constitutionalism. But discussion of them must be left for another occasion.[14] Before concluding, however, a variation on the transactions cost approach merits attention.

A Variation on the Theme

Under the transactions cost approach as usually interpreted, interpersonal comparisons of cardinal utility play a key role in justifying the elements of an optimal constitution. The equal-intensities assumption is used to justify simple majority voting in the legislature, for example, just as constitutional rights are tied to the assumption that a reasonable individual's expected utility loss from losing on the issue vastly outweighs anyone else's expected utility gain from winning. The implication seems to be that, to work the institutions of a utilitarian constitution, rational individuals at the postconstitutional stage will need to possess the requisite cardinal comparable utility information. Otherwise, they may lack adequate motivations to comply with the relevant institutions – for example, they will not be able to confirm for themselves whether any given binary issue is properly decided by majority voting or viewed as a matter of constitutional right.

A variation on the usual approach takes for granted that individuals at the postconstitutional phase will not possess such rich utility information. Unlike the constitutional designers who rely on such information to frame and ratify the rules, postconstitutional agents competitively pursue their

---

[13] Mueller (1996, 160–1) discusses the mechanics of point voting. More generally, see also ibid., 101–74.

[14] For an introduction to the vast literature, see Lijphart 1992; Shugart and Carey 1992; Mueller 1996, pt. 4, 175–296; Sartori 1996, pts. 2–3, 83–202; and Gordon 1999.

own narrow concerns by acting in accord with the given rules. They have no need to make interpersonal comparisons by extending sympathy to each other while imagining themselves with equal probability in each other's actual position. Moreover, moral agents at the constitutional stage agree that it is too costly in terms of time and effort to engage in interpersonal comparisons at the level of particular actions as opposed to the level of rules and institutions. Rather than rely on cardinal comparable utility information to calculate which particular (individual or collective) actions are best, these moral agents design the constitutional code to protect certain liberal and democratic freedoms to act. Such freedoms permit postconstitutional agents to choose certain permissible actions without interference or coercion from others and, thus, are independent of interpersonal comparisons at the level of particular actions.

Under this variant approach, the cost of acquiring utility information is a species of transactions cost. In particular, the cost of acquiring the cardinal comparable utility information essential to calculating optimal acts may be prohibitive in many situations. To minimize transactions costs, the constitutional designers must recognize that agents at the postconstitutional stage have no need of such rich utility information in any case to act as permitted under the chosen constitutional rules. Even as moral agents who voluntarily comply with the rules, these postconstitutional agents can only be expected to work with ordinal noncomparable utility information, that is, their own preference orderings over issues. Thus, the designers should select optimal rules and institutions that can be worked by agents who might be assumed to have common knowledge of each others' preference rankings, strategy sets, and so on but not of cardinal comparable utilities. Such institutions can be implemented by rational and fair-minded individuals who lack any motivation to make interpersonal utility comparisons, even when they are not too costly to make.

In light of Harsanyi's ultimate goal of maximizing a utilitarian social welfare functional, constitutional designers seeking to minimize transactions costs with constitutional institutions whose operation does not depend on interpersonal comparisons will arguably establish simple majority rule as an optimal legislative voting procedure. As I have shown elsewhere (Riley 1990), majority rule can be treated as a purely ordinalist utilitarian calculus, in the sense that norms of anonymity, neutrality, Pareto optimality, and so on that together characterize a classical utilitarian procedure in the context of cardinal comparable utilities map onto similar norms that together characterize majority rule in the context of ordinal noncomparable utilities. In this regard, the justification of majority rule does not depend on the assumption that the individual preferences being counted on both sides of any binary issue are of *equal intensities*, despite the prominence of the equal-intensities assumption in the literature. Indeed, the assumption that individual preferences for x over y are equally as intense as different individual preferences for y over x can become impossible to maintain if individuals have conflicting complete and transitive preference orderings over *three or more options* x, y, z . . . Rather, majority rule may suppose that the different individual preferences are noncomparable and then count them in an unbiased manner, where "unbiased" has a precise meaning in terms of procedural conditions of anonymity, neutrality, and so on.[15]

The utilitarian designers may also combine simple majority decision making in the legislature with Hare's (1859) "single-transferable vote" method of PR (Riley 1990).[16]

Constitutional rights can also be delineated without the assumption that the right holder's preference intensity vastly outweighs the intensities of others on the relevant issue. Even if we are confined to ordinal noncomparable utilities, every moral agent at the postconstitutional stage can be assumed to confirm for himself that violations of his basic liberal and democratic rights would push his ordinal utility below some minimal threshold level that he finds essential for his continued support of the political system. His loss of utility from such violations need not be supposed to be greater than any utility gains to the violators. Each person's utility and minimal threshold level can be noncomparable. Yet every person reiterates that his peculiar threshold level – associated with certain vital types of personal interests, which turn out to be similar in content for all reasonable human beings – must be protected by constitutional right. Every rational agent can see (without engaging in interpersonal utility comparisons) that violations of his rights of this sort must throw him into a state of war with the violators, just as his violations of others' similar rights must throw them into a state of war with himself. That does not mean that such agents will not violate others' rights, of course, in the absence of suitable checks and balances designed to preserve everyone's constitutional rights.

It remains plausible to think that supermajoritarian if not unanimous amendment procedures will be established to make it relatively difficult to limit basic individual rights recognized in the constitution.

Whichever version of the transactions cost approach is held to be most defensible, much more needs to be said about such matters as an optimal system of institutional checks and balances designed to prevent misrule and foster constitutional democracy. Moreover, it bears repeating that the two-stage game-theoretic framework is not tied to the imposition of utilitarian criteria at the constitutional stage. Rawlsian criteria might be

---

[15] A formal axiomatization of simple majority rule is provided by Sen 1970, 71–4.
[16] On Hare's "single-transferable vote" method of PR, see Tideman 1995.

168   *Jonathan Riley*

assumed instead, for example, and their implications for optimal institutions and rules investigated.

REFERENCES

Ackerman, Bruce. 1991. *We The People: Foundations*. Cambridge, Mass.: Harvard University Press.

1998. *We The People: Transformations*. Cambridge, Mass.: Harvard University Press.

Amar, Akhil Reed, and Alan Hirsch. 1998. *For the People*. New York: Free Press.

Arrow, Kenneth. 1963. *Social Choice and Individual Values*. 2nd ed. New York: Wiley.

Buchanan, James M. 1984. "Constitutional Restrictions on the Power of Government." In James M. Buchanan and Robert D. Tollison, eds., *The Theory of Public Choice II*, 439–52. Ann Arbor: University of Michigan Press.

Buchanan, James M., and Gordon Tullock. 1962. *The Calculus of Consent*. Ann Arbor: University of Michigan Press.

Cooke, Jacob E., ed. 1961. *The Federalist*. Middletown, Conn.: Wesleyan University Press.

Gordon, Scott. 1999. *Controlling the State: Constitutionalism from Ancient Athens to Today*. Cambridge, Mass.: Harvard University Press.

Hamilton, Edith, and Huntington Cairns, eds. 1961. *Plato: The Collected Dialogues*. Princeton: Princeton University Press.

Hare, Thomas. 1859. *A Treatise on the Election of Representatives, Parliamentary and Municipal*. London: Longman, Green.

Harsanyi, John C. 1977. *Rational Behavior and Bargaining Equilibrium in Games and Social Situations*. Cambridge: Cambridge University Press.

1992. "Game and Decision Theoretic Models in Ethics." In R. J. Aumann and S. Hart, eds., *Handbook of Game Theory*, 1: 669–707. Amsterdam: North-Holland.

1995. "A Theory of Prudential Values and a Rule Utilitarian Theory of Morality." *Social Choice and Welfare* 12: 319–33.

Harsanyi, John C., and Reinhard Selten. 1988. *A General Theory of Equilibrium Selection in Games*. Cambridge, Mass.: MIT Press.

Lijphart, Arend, ed. 1992. *Parliamentary versus Presidential Government*. Oxford: Oxford University Press.

Mueller, Dennis C. 1991. "Constitutional Rights." *Journal of Law, Economics and Organization* 7: 313–33.

1996. *Constitutional Democracy*. New York: Oxford University Press.

Myerson, Roger. 1999. "Theoretical Comparisons of Electoral Systems." *European Economic Review* 43: 671–97.

Ordeshook, Peter C. 1986. *Game Theory and Political Theory*. Cambridge: Cambridge University Press.

1992. "Constitutional Stability." *Constitutional Political Economy* 3: 137–75.

Rae, Douglas W. 1969. "Decision Rules and Individual Values in Constitutional Choice." *American Political Science Review* 63: 40–56.

Rawls, John. 1971. *A Theory of Justice*. Cambridge, Mass.: Harvard University Press.

Riker, William H. 1982. *Liberalism against Populism*. San Francisco: W. H. Freeman.

Riley, Jonathan. 1990. "Utilitarian Ethics and Democratic Government." *Ethics* 100: 335–48.

　2000. "Defending Rule Utilitarianism." In Brad Hooker, Elinor Mason, and Dale Miller, eds., *Morality, Rules and Consequences*, 40–70. Edinburgh: University of Edinburgh Press.

Sartori, Giovanni. 1996. *Comparative Constitutional Engineering*. 2nd ed. New York: New York University Press.

Sen, Amartya K. 1970. *Collective Choice and Social Welfare*. San Francisco: Holden-Day.

Shugart, Matthew S., and John M. Carey. 1992. *Presidents and Assemblies: Constitutional Design and Electoral Dynamics*. Cambridge: Cambridge University Press.

Tideman, Nicolaus. 1995. "The Single Transferable Vote." *Journal of Economic Perspectives* 9: 27–38.

5

Imagining Another Madisonian Republic

Jonathan Riley

INTRODUCTION: WHO SHOULD CONTROL CONSTITUTIONAL INTERPRETATION?

Madison, in a letter sent to John Brown during October 1788 discussing Jefferson's 1783 draft of a constitution for Virginia, pointed to a flaw in the U.S. Constitution, which has never been remedied by formal amendment: "In the State Constitutions & indeed in the Federal one also, no provision is made for the case of a disagreement in expounding them" (Meyers 1981, 42). Writing as Publius in *The Federalist* some eight months earlier, he had noted that the legislature is supposed to be supreme in a constitutional democracy: "In republican government the legislative authority, necessarily, predominates" (*Federalist* 51, 350).[1] But the flawed design of American constitutions allowed the judiciary to claim supremacy over the legislature: "[A]s the Courts are generally the last in making the decision it results to them by refusing or not refusing to execute a law, to stamp it with its final character. This makes the Judiciary Department paramount in fact to the Legislature, which was never intended and can never be proper" (Meyers 1981, 42–3). Madison thus seems opposed in principle to one of the most salient features of American constitutionalism as it has evolved, namely, the doctrine of judicial supremacy,[2] which

[1] All page references are to Cooke's (1961) edition.

[2] The doctrine of judicial supremacy, as I understand it, means supremacy of the judiciary over the elected branches in matters of constitutional interpretation. It implies the power of judicial review, that is, the authority of the courts to veto legislative acts or bills as unconstitutional. But judicial review is not necessarily linked to judicial supremacy, even though the two are conjoined in American practice. Courts might be given a review authority akin to the president's veto, for example, in which case any judicial veto of proposed bills could be overridden by legislative supermajorities. The distinction is important for present purposes because Madison endorses judicial review while rejecting judicial supremacy. For similar distinctions between judicial review and judicial supremacy, see Wills 1981, 131–3; and Murphy, Fleming, and Barber 1995, 264–8.

(whatever its origins) was enunciated by the federal Supreme Court as early as 1803.[3]

This is not to say that Madison regarded federal judicial supremacy in matters of constitutional interpretation as a catastrophic development, unacceptable in comparison to, for example, a state legislature claiming final say over the meaning of the national constitution.[4] He may well have grown more receptive to the doctrine with experience.[5] But, if he had had his way at the Philadelphia Convention, it seems clear that the Constitution would have explicitly provided for Congress rather than the judiciary to have final say in case of a disagreement over the meaning of the document.

Perhaps for strategic reasons, Madison did not allow his objections to judicial supremacy to surface when he wrote as Publius. Nor did he explicitly defend the federal judicial arrangements as acceptable for a constitutional republic.[6] Rather, he left that task to Hamilton. As is well known, Hamilton argued as Publius that the framers can reasonably be assumed to have granted the courts a "peculiar" authority to expound the Constitution because otherwise the legislature would be the judge of its own cause. No effective check exists against unconstitutional acts of Congress, he claimed, unless the judges can nullify statutes that are

---

[3] American-style judicial review is commonly viewed as stemming from Chief Justice Marshall's famous opinion in *Marbury v. Madison*, 5 U.S. (1 Cranch) 137. For a more sophisticated discussion of the admittedly murky origins of judicial review, see Rakove 1997. Among other things, Rakove emphasizes that review by independent federal judges emerged largely as a check on state rather than national government, even though Marshall's opinion is concerned with separation of powers at the national level.

[4] See, e.g., his three letters (dated, respectively, September 2, 1819; May 6, 1821; and June 29, 1821) to Spencer Roane, in Meyers 1981, 357–69; and his letter of August 1830 to Edward Everett, in Rives and Fendall 1865, 4:95–7.

[5] J. S. Mill (1861, 556–7) claimed that the "natural apprehensions" felt by the founding generation toward judicial supremacy were "entirely quieted" by the time of his writing. Like Tocqueville, he generally defends this role for the federal judiciary as "eminently beneficial," although he admits that popular confidence in it "was for the first time [greatly] impaired" by the notorious decision in *Dred Scott v. Sandford*, 60 U.S. (19 How.) 393 (1857).

[6] In *Federalist* 39 Madison defines the idea of a republic sufficiently loosely to accommodate American political institutions, including judicial supremacy (251). But his loose definition may have been strategic, given the need in that context to present the plan of the convention as "strictly republican" in form. "It is evident that no other form would be reconcileable with the genius of the people of America" (250). Insistence on his own strict republican principles would imply that the framers' plan "depart[ed] from the republican character." Such a departure would tend to destroy the legitimacy of the plan in the eyes of the people. Indeed, his insistence would be needlessly provocative because it would imply that "every government in the United States" (including the existing state governments) must be "degraded from the republican character" (251).

contrary to the "manifest tenor" of the Constitution. He went on to emphasize that this peculiar judicial authority to check the legislature is not improper in a republic. Elected representatives can still enact suitable constitutional amendments to override highly unpopular constitutional interpretations pressed by the judiciary. In effect, the people can delegate to appointed courts a peculiar authority to interpret the constitution, without alienating that authority. Even if Congress and the president have no power to override the judiciary, override by formal amendment, however awkward, remains feasible.[7]

This conflict between Publius (Hamilton) and Madison over the proper division of power in a constitutional republic deserves further study.[8] Two quite different forms of constitutional democracy emerge, which may be termed, respectively, "American" and "Madisonian." The fact that a Madisonian option may be opposed to an American one is likely to seem counterintuitive to many. It should remind us, however, that the so-called father of the U.S. Constitution had no illusions about its perfection as an instrument of republican government. I am also interested in comparing and contrasting these two forms of constitutional democracy with a parliamentary alternative. Of course, many other forms of constitutional democracy, such as the complex "semipresidential" system of the Fifth Republic of France, might also be brought into the mix.[9] Indeed, part of my purpose is to suggest the importance of that broader comparative constitutional exercise. In the meantime, though, I confine attention to the three forms.

[7] Madison agrees that sovereignty in the American political system resides outside government in the people and their constitutional code (*Federalist* 53, 360–1). Popular sovereignty in that sense is inalienable, though portions of it may be delegated temporarily to various groups of "representatives" for specific purposes. Even ratification and amendment are performed for the people by special bodies of elected delegates, on this view, but the authority of those special bodies supersedes and limits that of the ordinary government branches under the Constitution. The sovereignty of the people consists of a set of basic inalienable rights, including the extraconstitutional right to rebel against unjust government and establish a new constitution that in the majority's estimation is more likely to preserve basic rights. On American democracy, see also Riley 1990.

[8] I refer to Publius rather than Hamilton to allow for the strong possibility that Hamilton may not have believed all he said as Publius. Like Madison, he may have tailored his contributions to *The Federalist* to put the best possible face on the convention's work, so as to appeal to the people of New York (who had still to ratify the Constitution at the time he wrote). For present purposes, however, it is unnecessary to clarify the extent to which Hamilton's personal views are reflected in his discussion as Publius.

[9] On the modern debate over the various forms of constitutional democratic government, see, e.g., Lijphart 1992 and Sartori 1996. Rohr (1995) offers a useful comparison of American and French constitutional systems.

LEGISLATIVE SUPREMACY VERSUS JUDICIAL SUPREMACY

Parliamentary Democracy

As a familiar point of reference, it may be useful to recall that legislative majorities have control over constitutional interpretation in traditional parliamentary democracies such as Britain. Given that the constitution comprises certain fundamental acts of parliament as well as various unwritten customary norms and practices, the sovereign legislature can always pass legislation to interpret or otherwise alter the constitutional rules as a majority sees fit. The judiciary is subservient in principle to the will of parliament and confines itself to expounding the intentions of the legislature.

Despite the subservience of the judiciary and the partial fusion of legislative and executive powers in the hands of the prime minister (PM) and cabinet, checks and balances do exist to create a partial degree of separation of powers between the executive and legislature within the British parliamentary system. By convention, the PM can dissolve the legislature and call new elections in case of a disagreement between the cabinet and the legislative majority on some fundamental issue; and the legislative majority can also vote nonconfidence in the executive, forcing the PM to resign or to call new elections. As Mill (1849, 361–3; 1861, 523–6) argued, this system of reciprocal checks creates some independence between legislature and executive, even though the PM remains a member of the legislature and is responsible to the legislative majority. In addition to political conventions of this sort, the Parliament can create structures that facilitate legislative oversight of the executive, as occurred with the establishment, in 1979, of the system of bipartisan select committees composed of backbench members of the House of Commons (Drewry 1989). Again, the select committees promote some degree of separation of power between the legislative majority and the cabinet as an executive body. Such checks and balances are entirely compatible with the idea of parliamentary sovereignty because duly passed acts of parliament are binding on all and cannot be altered legally by any institution except parliament itself. There are no legal limits on its law-making authority, no constitutional courts or assemblies with legal authority to nullify its statutes against its wishes.

That the resulting division of powers within the parliamentary system is only partial in degree should not be disparaged from an American perspective. Madison himself emphasized that separation of powers can never be complete because the sharing of power implicit in intragovernmental checks and balances is required for any degree of separation in practice: "[U]nless these departments be so far connected and blended, as to

174　　　　　　　　　　　　　*Jonathan Riley*

give to each a constitutional controul [*sic*] over the others, the degree of separation which the maxim requires as essential to a free government, can never in practice, be duly maintained" (*Federalist* 48, 332). A due independence of the legislature and executive cannot be achieved by "a mere demarkation on parchment of the constitutional limits" (ibid., 338), he says, or by "occasional" or "periodical" appeals to the people, whether through popular referenda or constitutional conventions (*Federalist* 49–50, 338–47). Rather, "the interior structure of the government" must be suitably designed such that "its several constituent parts" have power to check one another, thereby "keeping each other in their proper places" (*Federalist* 51, 347–8). Some sharing or fusion of powers is inescapable. Moreover, a degree of separation can be created even if the chief executive is chosen by the legislature.[10]

Thus, legislative supremacy in a pure parliamentary democracy does not imply that a legislative majority or the chief executive has absolute power to interpret the constitution. They share power and must agree before fundamental legislation can be enacted. On the other hand, the judiciary has no authority to review the constitutionality of acts of parliament. Judicial review does not exist as a constitutional check on the political branches.

American Democracy

By contrast, it is commonly accepted that constitutional democracy in the United States today features a federal judiciary with supreme authority to expound the Constitution (subject to duly enacted amendments). The Supreme Court itself now claims "the authority to . . . speak before all others for constitutional ideals" (*Planned Parenthood v. Casey*, 120 L Ed 2nd 674 [1992], 709). Its claim of this peculiar authority finds support, of course, in the classic argument of Publius.

According to that argument, the Supreme Court and Congress are coordinate constitutional agents of the sovereign people, with distinct functions to perform. The function of the legislature is to enact policies that do not violate the "manifest tenor" of the Constitution. But the courts are assigned an equally valuable function: "The interpretation of the laws [including the Constitution] is the proper and peculiar province of the courts" (*Federalist* 78, 525). The legislature has no authority to enact statutes contrary to the manifest tenor of the Constitution. The courts are empowered by the people to strike down such unconstitutional acts. In the absence of this judicial check, the legislative deputies of the people could

---

[10] Even under the U.S. Constitution (Twelfth Amendment), the president is chosen by the House of Representatives if no candidate wins a simple majority of the votes in the electoral college.

substitute their views for those of the people themselves as manifested in the Constitution. Thus, in a clash between legislative and judicial interpretations of what the Constitution as "fundamental law" requires, the judiciary (as agent of the people with peculiar authority to interpret their constitutional intentions) ought to prevail over the legislature:

Nor does this conclusion by any means suppose a superiority of the judicial to the legislative power. It only supposes that the power of the people is superior to both; and that where the will of the legislature declared in its statutes, stands in opposition to that of the people declared in the constitution, the judges ought to be governed by the latter, rather than the former. They ought to regulate their decisions by the fundamental laws, rather than by those which are not fundamental. (ibid.)

Evidently, despite his assertion that "a superiority of the judicial to the legislative power" is not implied, Publius *does* imply that the judiciary should have authority paramount to that of the legislature for the peculiar purpose of constitutional interpretation. Indeed, he claims that the framers should not be assumed to have intended Congress to control the constitutional interpretation of its own acts, because that would enable legislators to substitute their will for that of the sovereign people. "It is far more rational," he says, "to suppose that the courts were designed to be an intermediate body between the people and the legislature, in order, among other things, to keep the latter within the limits assigned to their authority" (ibid.). In effect, when it comes to constitutional interpretation, all members of government are properly instructed by the sovereign people, whose general will is revealed by the manifest tenor of the Constitution; and the people have delegated peculiar authority to independent judges to help ensure that the constitutional instructions are observed.

By implication, it is a good thing that American democracy does not give the elected branches an opportunity to override the court's opinions as to the constitutionality of government acts. The judiciary *should* claim supremacy over the legislature and executive with respect to constitutional interpretation.

Publius admits that the Constitution itself does not say anything about judicial supremacy over constitutional interpretation: "[T]here is not a syllable in the plan under consideration, which *directly* empowers the national courts to construe the laws according to the spirit of the constitution" (*Federalist* 81, 543, emphasis in original). He insists, however, "that the constitution ought to be the standard of construction for the laws, and that wherever there is an evident opposition, the laws ought to give place to the constitution." In cases of "evident opposition," the court's constitutional interpretations should override acts of Congress: "But this

176 *Jonathan Riley*

doctrine [of judicial supremacy] is not deducible from any circumstance peculiar to the plan of the convention; but from the general theory of a limited constitution" (ibid.). The framers did not explicitly affirm judicial supremacy, he implies, because nobody committed as they were to constitutional democracy would even think to dispute such a power (Wills 1981, 130–50). There is no real "danger of judiciary encroachments on the legislative authority." That putative danger "is in reality a phantom," mainly because the Court has "total incapacity to support its usurpations by force" and Congress retains the impeachment power (*Federalist* 81, 545–6).

Madison contra Publius

Nevertheless, Madison does dispute judicial supremacy. He argues that the Congress ought to be supreme with respect to both policy and constitutional interpretation, subject to formal amendments.[11] Yet he also realizes that the framers failed to include any clear statement of such legislative supremacy. He makes clear that the omission mars the Constitution's design from his republican perspective. At the same time, he never pretends that the framers did something they did not do. Rather than claim that they could only have intended legislative supremacy over constitutional interpretation, for example, he admits that they did not speak to the issue and unwittingly left open the possibility of judicial supremacy. Then he rationalizes their silence in such a way that the legislature can generally be expected to predominate over the judiciary.

Madison agrees with Publius that the framers made no explicit provision "for a particular authority to determine the limits of the constitutional division of power between the branches of the government" (Murphy, Fleming, and Barber 1995, 280, quoting from Madison's June 1789 speech during the House debate over the scope of the president's removal power, as reprinted from *Annals of Congress*, 1:519–21). But he rejects Publius's rationalization of the framers' silence in the matter. While recognizing that the justices would be able to claim that they had

---

[11] Congress might be legally supreme over the other branches, of course, without being a sovereign parliament. A sovereign has *unlimited* legal authority. But congressional authority is limited by the written Constitution. Properly interpreted, the doctrine of popular sovereignty implies that no branch of government has undivided sovereignty in the American system. At the same time, however, even a sovereign parliament can be limited morally by unwritten constitutional conventions that have no legal status. Similarly, a parliament can be limited morally or politically by its various international agreements, as the British Parliament is, for example, by its ratification of the human rights conventions enforced by the European Court of Human Rights, in Strasbourg. As a strictly legal matter, however, the British Parliament retains authority to revoke its ratification of international conventions and "laws," and even to opt out of the European Union.

been granted the supreme authority, he suggests that it is more reasonable to suppose that the framers' silence implies that no one branch has been granted any more authority than the others to expound the meaning of the Constitution. By implication, constitutional meaning remains ambiguous in the absence of agreement among the leaders of the branches.[12]

At the same time, Madison seems to take for granted that Congress has so many bargaining weapons – the power of the purse, the impeachment power, and so on – that agreements will tend in practice to be struck on terms predominantly to the liking of legislative majorities. Thus, the framers' silence would translate more or less into de facto legislative control of constitutional interpretation, even though no branch was granted de jure control.[13] In this way, the flawed constitutional plan could be reconciled with republican principles calling for legislative predominance.[14]

Still, Madison clearly believed that the framers' silence created a flaw in American constitutional design. Both at the Philadelphia Convention and in his private writings, he consistently emphasized his support in principle for legislative control over constitutional interpretation as well as policy.[15] Indeed, he and other leading members of the convention

---

[12] Murphy et al. (1995, 269–70) use the term "departmentalism" to refer to this view that none of the three departments was granted control over constitutional interpretation. As they note, many legislators and presidents seem to have held the view, including Jefferson, Jackson, Lincoln, and Franklin Roosevelt in addition to Madison. For a normative defense of departmentalism, see Burt 1992. Evidently, Madison's endorsement of departmentalism as a positive theory of American constitutional interpretation does not imply that he thinks it ought to be adopted in an optimal constitutional democracy.

[13] Even Publius admits that Congress has so many bargaining chips that the Court will generally be too weak to abuse its supreme power with respect to constitutional interpretation.

[14] In an otherwise illuminating discussion, Wills (1981, 126–61) refers to popular ratification of the constitution as a "legislative" (rather than a constitutive) act, merely to support his conclusion that American political institutions exhibit legislative supremacy despite the Court's veto power. But the people's power to establish a written constitution should not be conflated with Congress having control over policy and constitutional interpretation. The Constitution does *not* give control over constitutional interpretation to Congress; it is silent on the issue of which branch has control. Congress may have many weapons at its disposal to bully the judiciary but it has no authority to specify standards of constitutional interpretation that are binding on the justices.

[15] Murphy et al. (1995, 269) assert that Madison's commitment to departmentalism "fluctuated" over time, whereas Burt (1992) suggests that Madison consistently defended its normative appeal. Neither claim is persuasive. Madison clearly believed that legislative control over constitutional interpretation had more normative appeal than departmentalism in a republican form of government. At the same time, he recognized that the framers had not actually given such legal supremacy to Congress, much to his chagrin. Rather than accept Publius's defense of judicial supremacy, however, he and Jefferson adopted

178   *Jonathan Riley*

advocated a form of constitutional democracy in which legislative supermajorities would have final say yet also be checked by a powerful national
"council of revision," comprised of the president and the Supreme Court
justices.[16] The national council would be analogous to the New York
council created under that state's constitution of 1777.[17] This Madisonian
form of constitutional democracy is quite distinct from its American
cousin.

Madisonian Democracy

In a truly Madisonian democracy, legislative supermajorities would be
supreme over constitutional interpretation. But the national council would
serve as "a check to precipitate, to unjust, and to unconstitutional laws"
(Meyers 1981, 42). Like the state council that he envisioned for Kentucky
in his October 1788 letter to Brown, it would have a complex qualified veto
against legislative proposals:

[R]equir[e] bills to be separately communicated to the executive and judiciary depts.
If either of these object, let 2/3, if both 3/4 of each House be necessary to over-

---

departmentalism as a positive theory of American constitutional design. But the American
design was flawed from a proper republican perspective, he indicated, and departmentalism would not be found in an optimal constitutional democracy.

[16] The national council idea was included in section 8 of the Virginia Plan debated at the
convention (Farrand 1966, 1:21). Although the idea was rejected, it was repeatedly brought
forward and ably defended by some of the leading intellects, including Madison, James
Wilson, George Mason, and Gouverneur Morris. As first envisaged in the Virginia Plan,
the council's qualified veto would also have applied against the proposed (but ultimately
rejected) congressional veto of state legislation. For the main discussions, see Farrand
1966, 1:108–12, 138–40; 2:73–80, 298. There is no evidence that Madison ever ceased to
find the council idea appealing. He defends it as late as 1817, in a letter to James Monroe
(Farrand 1966, 3:424). For further discussion of the council arrangements, see Street
1859; Wills 1981, 151–6; Nedelsky 1990, 59–66; and Rakove 1988, 490–7; 1996, 252–3,
261–2.

[17] New York's council of revision is described in section 3 of the state's first constitution of
1777, reprinted in Schechter 1990, 175–6. The council was in place during 1777–1822 and
was unique to that state. Comprised of the governor, chancellor (chief judge of the Court
of Chancery), and Supreme Court judges, it had authority to revise or veto by a majority vote of its members "all bills about to be passed into laws by the legislature," subject
to override by two-thirds of both the Senate and House of Assembly. It was abolished by
the state constitutional convention of 1821, at which time the veto authority was given to
the governor. For the relevant details, see the Ulshoeffer Reports reprinted in appendix A
of Street 1859, 453–79. Madison speaks favorably of New York's council as early as August
1785, in a letter to Caleb Wallace offering guidance on the design of a constitution for
Kentucky (Meyers 1981, 28). More generally, Schechter claims that "the New York tradition of constitutionalism . . . provided a laboratory for Federalist constitution-makers, a
prototype for the U.S. Constitution of 1787, and proof that a republic could be based on
a respect for diversity and the pursuit of commerce" (1990, 166).

rule the objection; and if either or both protest against a bill as violating the Constitution, let it moreover be suspended notwithstanding the overruling proportion of the Assembly, until there shall have been a subsequent election of the House of Delegates and a repassage of the bill by 2/3 or 3/4 of both Houses as the case may be. It should not be allowed the Judges or the Executive to pronounce a law thus enacted unconstitutional and invalid. (Meyers 1981, 42–3)[18]

These council arrangements would preclude judicial supremacy, which involves judicial nullification of legislative acts. As Madison emphasized in a letter to Monroe dated December 27, 1817, the council's "controul [*sic*], restricted to constitutional points, besides giving greater stability & system to the rules of expounding the instrument, would have precluded the question of a judiciary annulment of legislative *acts*" (Farrand 1966, 3:424, emphasis in original). Rather, a qualified judicial veto would be involved, analogous to the executive veto that applies only against legislative bills and can be overridden by legislative supermajorities. That qualified veto would not "disarm . . . the legislature of its requisite authority," in his opinion, because legislative supermajorities would retain the power of override.[19]

In such a Madisonian democracy, the justices would not be regarded as agents to whom the people have delegated "peculiar" control over constitutional interpretation. The president would be authorized to give constitutional reasons for his veto, for example, and double legislative supermajorities (i.e., three-fourths of both chambers before and after an intervening election) would have final say.

Moreover, Congress and the president would not have exclusive jurisdiction with respect to policy matters. The Court would be authorized to exercise its veto solely on policy grounds. At the same time, however, a distinction would be recognized between policy and constitutional interpretation, such that vetoes based on constitutional reasons would have more weight (because less easily overridden) than mere policy vetoes.[20]

---

[18] For a similar description of the national council, see Madison's record of the convention debates for August 15, 1787, reprinted in Farrand 1966, 2:298.

[19] The council arrangements were rejected by the framers for reasons that remain ambiguous, although a prominent criticism was that the arrangements violated separation of powers by improperly giving judges a voice in the making of laws that they might also be called upon to interpret in cases subsequently brought before the bench. That criticism is a weak one and reveals a misunderstanding of the separation-of-powers doctrine, as council defenders pointed out (Farrand 1966, 2:73–80). Indeed, an analogous criticism is applicable to the president's veto power, yet the executive veto was approved.

[20] The New York State model set a precedent for giving the executive and judges broad authority to veto bills "inconsistent with the spirit of this constitution, or with the public good" (Schechter 1990, 175). But no distinction between policy and constitutional interpretation was recognized by the state as two-thirds of both houses were required to override council vetoes in any case.

180   *Jonathan Riley*

Madison's preferred form of constitutional democracy would differ from American democracy in many other respects as well. He seems to have wanted a far stronger national government than that provided for in the Constitution, for example. Thus, he argued in 1787 that Congress (or perhaps the Senate alone) should be granted a power to disallow or veto all state laws (Rutland and Hobson 1977, 12–18, 41–3, 102–3, 205–20; Hobson 1979). He also expressed doubts that the federal judiciary could effectively protect the central authorities from inevitable encroachments by the more powerful state governments.[21] He never ceased to fear that the national government had been granted insufficient power to check the states. During the 1830s, for example, he adamantly rejected the "South Carolina heresy" generated by Calhoun that a single state had the radical right to nullify within its borders any act of Congress that the state in convention determined was unconstitutional.[22] The states' rights he had endorsed in the Virginia Resolutions of 1799 were limited to those found in the Constitution, he insisted, and included the right to protest against national legislation under the First Amendment, as well as the right to jointly amend the Constitution through the national convention route of

---

[21] Despite Madison's preference for a congressional veto on state laws "in all cases whatsoever," the veto proposed at the convention as the sixth resolution of the Virginia Plan was expressly limited to "all laws passed by the several states, contravening in the opinion of the national legislature the articles of Union." In any case, the proposed veto was defeated despite repeated efforts by Madison and James Wilson on its behalf. Rutland and Hobson conclude that Madison "clearly regarded the loss of the negative as a serious, perhaps fatal, omission from the Constitution" (1977, 6). In his letter to Jefferson of October 24, 1787, he seems to dismiss the idea "that the judicial authority under our new system will keep the states within their proper limits, and supply the place of a negative on their laws." He argues "that it is more convenient to prevent the passage of a law, than to declare it void after it is passed; that this will be particularly the case, where the law aggrieves individuals, who may be unable to support an appeal against a State to the supreme Judiciary; that a State which would violate the Legislative rights of the Union, would not be very ready to obey a judicial decree in support of them, and that a recurrence to force, which in the event of disobedience would be necessary, is an evil which the new Constitution meant to exclude as far as possible" (Rutland and Hobson 1977, 211).

[22] It is worth emphasizing that Madison's commitment to departmentalism as a positive theory of American constitutional design (both at the national level and at the state level) does not imply any (positive or normative) commitment to what Murphy et al. (1995, 348–9) call "confederational departmentalism," that is, the doctrine that each state government and the national government have coequal authority to interpret the national constitution. Madison consistently denied that an individual state government has – or should have – any authority to override the federal judiciary's interpretations of the national constitution, although he also recognized that amendments can be passed, more or less independently of the national government, by the requisite supermajorities of state governments involved in the national convention route of Article V. But any defense of Madison's consistency on that score must await another occasion.

Article V.[23] Moreover, in letters to Jefferson and Everett dated, respectively, June 27, 1823 and August 28, 1830, he goes so far as to reject any analogy between separation of powers and the federal principle, suggesting that the latter (unlike the former) may not be for him an essential instrument of constitutional democracy.[24]

On the other hand, it would be surprising if Madison's preferred constitutional republic displayed no institutional overlap with its U.S. counterpart. He apparently favored a minimal rate of formal amendment, for example, so that the written framework of government might eventually acquire "that veneration, which time bestows on every thing" (*Federalist* 49, 340). By implication, an amendment formula of a high degree of difficulty, such as the Article V formula (Lutz 1994), has appeal for him. He also takes for granted the inevitability of a process of informal constitutional revision, however, and prescribes supermajoritarian legislative control (rather than judicial control) of that interpretive process. Thus, his preferred "stable republic" would combine relatively infrequent constitutional conventions and amendments with a supreme Congress and the council of revision.[25]

PREDICTING OUTCOMES IN POSTCONSTITUTIONAL GAMES

As I have suggested in Chapter 4, constitutional democracy can be formulated as a two-stage game comprised of a cooperative constitutional stage, in which a constitutional code is unanimously selected from feasible alternatives by rational and fair-minded agents, and a noncooperative postconstitutional stage, in which rational and possibly amoral agents compete for personal advantages in light of the chosen rules. Any moral agent can be assumed to be playing these two stages simultaneously. He is capable of imagining himself behind the veil of ignorance at the constitutional stage at any time, to consider alternative constitutions and affirm an optimal one. To assess any given constitutional code impartially, he must be able to predict Nash equilibrium points of any game played according to its rules, while pretending ignorance of his own actual position in society. At the same time, once an optimal code is established, he can be assumed to follow its rules as he competes with his fellow citizens at the postconstitutional stage. At that stage, with full knowledge of each

---

[23] See esp. Madison's draft note on nullification, reprinted in Meyers 1981, 417–42; and McCoy 1989, 119–70.

[24] See, respectively, Rives and Fendall 1865, 3:325–6; and Hunt 1900–10, 9:393–4.

[25] For insights into Madison's normative constitutional theory as revealed by his critical discussions of American constitutions, see, e.g., Rakove 1987; 1988; 1990; 1991; 1996; Beer 1993; Banning 1996; McCoy 1989; and Sorenson 1995.

182 *Jonathan Riley*

person's actual circumstances, strategies, utility payoffs, and so on, he is able to understand and confirm for himself the Nash equilibria of any postconstitutional game in which he finds himself.

The two-stage model can be viewed as having both pragmatic and normative purposes. It can be used pragmatically in the context of an established constitution, for example, to predict the outcomes of any game played according to those given constitutional rules. The given constitution need not be supposed optimal in any sense. For pragmatic purposes, it simply happens to exist in the actual society under consideration. In effect, we leave open whether such a constitution could have been the object of unanimous consent among suitably rational and impartial framers. On the other hand, we might also ask whether the given constitution is optimal in terms of some criteria – for example, general welfare or social justice. The two-stage framework can then be used with those criteria to evaluate predicted outcomes under the given constitutional rules.

Alternative forms of constitutional democracy, including parliamentary, American, and Madisonian forms, can be compared in pragmatic as well as normative terms. I focus for the most part on the pragmatic exercise, although the discussion is also relevant to any normative assessment.

Some Simple Cases

To illustrate, consider the three-period noncooperative law-making game that Eskridge and Ferejohn (1992) suggest captures the American framers' intent (keeping in mind that the framers did not include in the Constitution any mention of judicial review). First, House and Senate majorities choose whether to propose a new law or to rest content with existing policy designated as the status quo (SQ). If a bill is endorsed by majorities of both chambers, the president then decides whether to sign or veto the bill presented to him. If the bill is vetoed by the president, then House and Senate supermajorities choose at last whether to override the veto (thereby making the bill into law) or to let the veto stand (so that SQ results). The Supreme Court is assumed to passively endorse whatever outcome emerges.

To simplify the analysis, it is assumed that alternative policies (including SQ) can be arranged along a single dimension (e.g., liberal to conservative), that any rational actor's policy preferences can be represented as a well-behaved function of Euclidean distance on that dimension,[26] and that solutions are expressed as subgame perfect equilibria under

---

[26] Where rational actors are collectivities such as the House or Senate or even the citizenry as a whole, the set of individual members' preferences may be suitably restricted such that the median voter theorem applies.

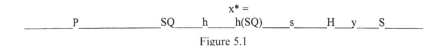
Figure 5.1

conditions of complete and perfect information.[27] A possible configuration of preferences is given in Figure 5.1, where H signifies the top-ranked policy alternative (or "ideal point") of the median representative, S is the ideal point of the median senator, P is the ideal point of the president, h is the ideal point of the veto median representative (whose vote is needed to override the presidential veto), and s is the ideal point of the veto median senator.

The subgame perfect equilibrium is located at x*. No rational agent has an incentive to depart from that postconstitutional outcome. It may be calculated as follows. In the initial period of the game, House and Senate median voters agree to propose a bill y that is in the core of a cooperative bargaining game within Congress, that is, y = g(H,S) such that H ≤ y ≤ S. The form of the bargaining game may be left open but its outcomes are assumed to be Pareto-efficient and thus Pareto-superior to SQ. In the second period, the president vetoes y because he prefers SQ to any policy (including y) to the right of SQ. In the final period, Congress overrides the veto by choosing a policy x* = h(SQ), where h(SQ) is the point at which the veto median member of the more propresident chamber (in this case, the House) is just indifferent between SQ and the new law. Given our simplifying assumptions, however, Congress will foresee and implement x* = h(SQ) immediately so that the presidential veto and subsequent override need not actually be exercised. Note that his veto power allows the president to have an influence on the outcome: x* is closer than y is to P (and SQ) in this case.

Still ignoring judicial review, consider next a contrast between American and parliamentary procedures in a situation where sharp ideological conflict exists between legislative majorities and the chief executive. Figure 5.2 illustrates the "gridlock" that can emerge in the U.S. procedure if Congress is unable to override the presidential veto. In this case, where the veto median member of the more propresident chamber (again, the

---

[27] Subgame perfection implies that a Nash equilibrium of the game remains an equilibrium if we limit attention to the restricted game at the final period, to the restricted game at the penultimate period, and so on. Given that "the players perfectly anticipate the future course of play, that no one is able to commit to future courses of action, and that all the actors in the model prefer that their decisions not be overturned," rational actors with the initial move will calculate and implement equilibrium outcomes without play in later periods having to take place (Eskridge and Ferejohn 1992, 529).

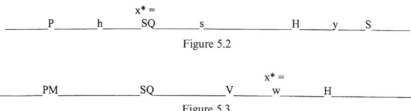

Figure 5.2

Figure 5.3

House) prefers SQ to the bargain y struck by a congressional majority, the legislature and executive are unable to agree on a change from the status quo. Thus, if SQ reflects a massive federal budget deficit or perhaps an inadequate health care system that fails to assure poor citizens of basic medical benefits, the inability of the legislative majority to effect change is likely to strike many democrats as perverse. Moreover, the absence of any indication of popular majoritarian sentiment in Figure 5.2 drives home the point that executive and legislative leaders may have little if any incentive to respond to the median citizen during a considerable period between the fixed dates of elections. Even if well defined, in other words, popular majority preferences are unlikely to resolve gridlock, unless perhaps a midterm or presidential election happens to be impending. This is not to deny the possibility that customs of civility and compromise might evolve between the legislature and executive to facilitate coordinated political action. But such conventions are not guaranteed and may break down in the face of intense partisan conflict.

Figure 5.3 illustrates a distinct parliamentary law-making procedure in a similar situation where the median member of a unicameral legislature sharply opposes the preferred policy of the prime minister and his cabinet. In this case, where a popular majority is assumed to prefer the policy of the legislative majority to that of the PM, an equilibrium emerges that is in the core of a bargaining game between the electorate and the legislature, that is, $x^* = w = g(V,H)$ such that $V \leq w \leq H$, where V is the ideal point of the median voter among the citizenry, and H is the preferred policy of the median legislator. In the first period of the game, the PM proposes his preferred policy PM. At a second period, the median legislator refuses to enact the PM's bill and demands that the PM endorse H instead. When the PM refuses to act, the third period is triggered: the legislative majority votes nonconfidence in the PM, forcing him to resign or call new elections.[28] If he resigns, the legislature can replace him with the

---

[28] I view the political conventions governing the nonconfidence vote as (unwritten) constitutional rules that limit the (moral and political if not legal) authority of a parliamentary government. Strictly speaking, parliament is legally unlimited yet leaders generally recog-

Figure 5.4

median legislator and enact H at a fourth period. If new elections are called instead, the electorate might be able to select a new assembly whose median member reflects the preference of the median citizen, in which case that median legislator will be made PM by the new parliament and V enacted. At worst, the electorate can simply return all incumbents, so that the original median legislator replaces the previous PM and enacts H. More generally, given some possibility of entry into election races, incumbents have reason to assure voters that, if reelected, they will enact $x^* = w$. Assuming rational behavior under complete and perfect information, however, the PM will introduce w in the first place, without any elections actually taking place: the standing legislature's credible threat of a nonconfidence vote is sufficient to produce an equilibrium outcome.[29]

Figure 5.4 illustrates the parliamentary process in a case where the median citizen's ideal point happens to coincide with that of a PM facing ideological conflict with a legislative majority. Despite its preference for SQ over V, the legislative majority has no choice in this case but to support the PM. First, the PM proposes his preferred policy PM. Next, the legislative majority refuses to enact the PM's bill and demands that the

---

nize the conventional limits on their authority. Of course, nonconfidence in the government is not implied every time the cabinet is defeated on a proposed measure. As Norton says: "Defeats involving questions of confidence in the Government are very much the exception, not the rule" (1978, 370). See also Norton 1991. Indeed, aside from explicitly worded motions of nonconfidence (usually tabled by the opposition) or motions on issues that the government itself declares are so important that the vote is a question of confidence, leaders have significant discretion as to how to interpret a defeat on a given motion and have strong incentives to minimize the importance of such defeats so as to continue in office. At the same time, as Norton suggests, there may be times when leaders can get their way strategically by making motions on fairly minor matters into questions of confidence, thereby forcing their own backbenchers and even the opposition to back down to avoid an unwanted resignation by the PM or a call for new elections. In any case, the point is that conventions of nonconfidence have force without requring the PM to step down or call new elections every time the government is defeated on a proposed bill.

[29] By implication, we must be careful before accepting any suggestion that "the noconfidence vote is so drastic an alternative" that it has little practical relevance. Arthur Schlesinger Jr. seems to dismiss it because "in Britain, for example, it succeeds in forcing a new general election only two or three times a century" (in Lijphart 1992, 91). But the threat of a nonconfidence vote may act as a powerful check on the executive, even though the vote is rarely observed. Indeed, its actual use implies that the prime minister and/or the legislative majority are mistaken about the preferences of the median voter or otherwise nonrational.

186 *Jonathan Riley*

PM endorse H instead. When the legislature refuses to act, the PM then dissolves the legislature, provoking new elections. Given that the electorate can return a new assembly whose median member supports the shared preference of the PM and the median citizen, the PM will be confirmed in office by the new parliament and V = PM enacted. Moreover, as before, the PM's credible threat of dissolution is sufficient to produce this equilibrium, without the need for actual elections.

But to compare parliamentary, American, and Madisonian constitutional structures, we need to go beyond these simple cases by bringing in a constitutional court or other body with authority to check the legislature in the law-making process.

Bringing in Judicial Review

Reconsider the Eskridge-Ferejohn game in Figure 5.1. Suppose now that the Supreme Court, having successfully claimed judicial supremacy with respect to constitutional interpretation, decides in a case brought before it at a fourth period whether to affirm a new act of Congress or nullify it (thereby restoring SQ). To simplify matters, it is assumed that alternative constitutional doctrines (or canons of constitutional interpretation) can be arranged along a single dimension distinct from the policy dimension, that the judiciary alone has authority to choose among constitutional doctrines, that the interpretive preferences of the median justice are a well-behaved function of Euclidean distance on the constitutional dimension, and that a one-to-one correspondence exists between constitutional interpretations and policy outcomes so that the median justice's ideal point j on the constitutional dimension maps to an ideal point J on the policy dimension.[30] Figure 5.5 indicates the two-dimensional nature of the Court's choices.

Given the simplifying assumptions, the constitutional dimension may be conveniently suppressed in what follows to focus attention on the influence of the judiciary on policy outcomes. Figure 5.6 reproduces the configuration of preferences found in Figure 5.1 among rational legislative

---

[30] Less restrictive ways of modeling the Court's behavior are conceivable. For example, it might be assumed that a one-to-many correspondence exists between constitutional interpretations and policies such that the median justice's choice of a constitutional doctrine maps to a range of admissible policy choices (in effect, a choice set among the elements of which the elected branches then bargain and pick a winner). Even less restrictively, it might be assumed that the choice of a constitutional interpretation results in a significant reduction of the dimensionality of the multidimensional policy space confronting the elected branches, for example, a reduction from two dimensions to one with no further restrictions on outcomes along the remaining dimension. For further clarification of the latter modeling option, see Spiller and Spitzer 1992; and Spiller and Tiller 1996. More generally, see also Spiller and Tiller 1997.

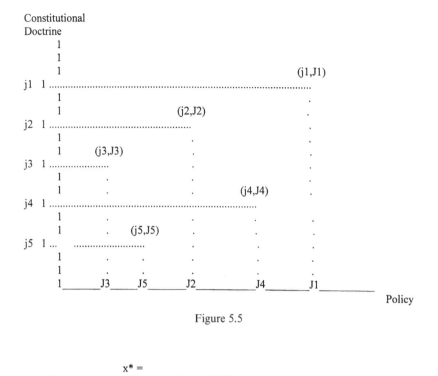

Figure 5.5

Figure 5.6

and executive actors but illustrates the case where the ideal point J of the median justice is to the left of SQ, for example, J = P.

The subgame perfect equilibrium is now located at x* = SQ. At the new final period, the Court reviews and vetoes h(SQ) because (like the president) the median justice prefers SQ over any policy outcome (including h(SQ) and y) to the right of SQ. Unlike the president, however, the Court links its veto to a constitutional interpretation that is accepted by the elected branches as supreme over competing interpretations. Congress accepts that it has no authority to override that judicial veto of its acts. Thus, given the requirement of subgame perfection under complete and perfect information, the legislators will simply decide not to act, thereby obviating any need for the Court to nullify the law in a case subsequently brought before the bench.

With due caveats about the delegation by Congress of law-making authority to modern administrative agencies, Figure 5.6 is an illustration

188 *Jonathan Riley*

$$x^* =$$

| | C | SQ | h2 | h1 | h2(SQ) | s1 | s2 | H2 | H1 | S1 | S2 |

Figure 5.7

of the American law-making process that has evolved despite the framers' silence about judicial supremacy. Consider now a Madisonian law-making process in which a bill proposed jointly by House and Senate median voters is presented to a council of revision for signature or veto, with any veto being subject to legislative override. More specifically, suppose that the president and median justice (as members of the council) have identical preferences and choose to exercise their respective vetoes for constitutional reasons, in which case legislative override requires the support of three-quarters of both House and Senate before and after an intervening election. Figure 5.7 incorporates the preference configuration found in Figure 5.1, where H and S in the latter figure are reproduced in the former as the preelection House H1 and preelection Senate S1, respectively. Assuming that the membership of the council remains fixed before and after the election, C is the ideal point of the council, h1 and h2 are the veto median members of the preelection House H1 and postelection House H2 respectively, and s1 and s2 are the veto median senators of the preelection Senate S1 and postelection Senate S2 respectively.

The equilibrium $x^* = h2(SQ)$ is located at the point h2(SQ) where the veto median member of the more procouncil chamber (in this case, the House) in the more procouncil Congress (in this case, the Congress *after* the intervening election) is just indifferent between SQ and the new law. For reasons that should be apparent to the reader, x^* must now be closer to SQ than in Figure 5.1. In terms of outcomes for the given preference scenario, therefore, the Madisonian procedure is something of a compromise between the framer's design (illustrated in Figure 5.1) and the American procedure with judicial supremacy (illustrated in Figure 5.6).

More generally, the game-theoretic approach can be used to compare many distinct law-making procedures for a wide variety of preference scenarios. That comparative exercise would enable us to see more clearly what is at stake when choosing among alternative constitutional rules for distributing power within a republican government. The remainder of this chapter is devoted to a much less ambitious exercise. Without pretending to be exhaustive, I employ the approach to clarify some of the main reasons that Madison seems to have had in mind when arguing against American law-making rules (including judicial supremacy) in favor of the council arrangements, namely: (1) judicial obstructionism and activism can in principle always be checked by the supreme legislature under the council scheme; (2) the justices and president may have stronger incentives to veto arbitrary legislation when they are united in the council; and (3) the rule of law can be expected to exhibit more stability under the Madisonian procedure. I do not mean to imply that he had no other reasons for his preferred law-making rules. As Rakove (1987) has remarked, for example, he may well have endorsed the council arrangements partly to facilitate more competent drafting of legislation by means of the judiciary's systematic review of bills.[31] In any case, it remains open to debate whether Madison's preferred law-making process *ought* to be chosen over all alternatives as an effective instrument of constitutional democracy, even if the relevant normative criteria (including justice in the sense of protection of basic rights) can be agreed upon.

WHAT IS DISTINCTIVE ABOUT MADISONIAN DEMOCRACY?

Supermajoritarian Legislative Supremacy

Madison's argument for legislative supremacy under the council scheme depends in part on a claim that elected legislators have stronger incentives than appointed judges do to respond positively to broad and persistent changes in public opinion. As he emphasizes as Publius, elections are the primary check against misrule in a representative democracy: "A dependence on the people is no doubt the primary controul [*sic*] on the government" (*Federalist* 51, 349). Under the council scheme, as Figure 5.7 illustrates, independent judges cannot block statutory (re)interpretations of constitutional rules and rights demanded by "the great body of the people" and their requisite supermajorities of elected legislators. Despite the extraordinary double supermajorities required, Congress has authority to override council vetoes offered on constitutional grounds. Thus, great swings in public opinion are likely to be quickly transmitted into the law-making process and constitutional interpretation. At least in principle, sufficiently united and determined voters can frequently and repeatedly replace recalcitrant legislators.[32]

---

[31] Madison's concern that some expert body should be appointed to help draft legislation is expressed in his August 1785 letter to Caleb Wallace, for example, where he mentions both the New York council and a "standing committee" with power to initiate bills "on all subjects" and to draft bills as requested by the legislature during its sessions (Meyers 1981, 28). The latter idea was subsequently elaborated in interesting ways by Mill 1861, 430–2; Wilson 1885; and others.

[32] I ignore but do not deny the serious social choice theoretic problems of aggregation and manipulation that bedevil any attempt to ascertain the public will, as emphasized by Riker (1982), among others. Even social choice theorists must admit, however, the possibility of a more or less unanimous grand coalition of enraged voters determined to get its way on a single decisive issue, say, term limits for legislators or a balanced federal budget. Riker

In contrast, as Figure 5.6 makes clear, the possibility arises under American arrangements that the courts may stubbornly ignore national sentiment and choose to obstruct legislative reforms overwhelmingly supported by the people. That the courts have such a power of obstruction is improper in principle, Madison insists, even if rarely exercised and gradually self-corrected as new judges are appointed by elected officials.[33] However short-lived, judicial obstructionism may create the sort of widespread contempt for the courts observed during, say, the New Deal period (Leuchtenburg 1995). Indeed, blatant judicial defiance of legislative compromises reflective of divided and volatile national sentiments might even contribute to civil disorder and violence as, for example, the *Dred Scott* decision seems to have done. Even if violence is avoided in such situations, the people and their elected representatives have no recourse in the short run but to take extraordinary measures, including amendments, impeachments, and/or court "packing" schemes, when more ordinary measures (specifically, statutes passed by the requisite congressional supermajorities) would seem to be more expedient.[34]

The argument that legislative supremacy is needed to implement effectively the primary check against arbitrary government may be bolstered by considering Figure 5.8, which contrasts American, Madisonian, and

himself maintains that elections can provide an effective, if largely random and perhaps even perverse, check on political leaders.

[33] According to an influential view associated with Dahl (1957; 1989), the Court "regularly" bends its opinions to the views of persistent national majorities largely because the elected branches can suitably control its membership through appointments. He cites two "egregious" examples where the Court finally gave up its "rearguard delaying action," namely, dock workers' compensation laws and child labor legislation (1989, 190n8). For recent empirical studies that (with some caveats) tend to support Dahl's view that the Court offers at best a temporary check against national majoritarian sentiment, see Marshall 1989 and Mishler and Sheehan 1993.

[34] Under Roosevelt's doomed court-packing bill, the president would have been authorized to nominate a new federal judge if an existing one who had served for at least ten years waited more than six months beyond his seventieth birthday to resign or retire. As many as six new justices could be added to the Supreme Court (for a total of fifteen Justices) and forty-four new judges added to the lower federal courts. Before proposing this plan to reorganize the federal judiciary, Roosevelt had considered with his advisors various other ways to combat the doctrine of judicial supremacy over constitutional interpretation (Leuchtenburg 1995, 82–162). For instance, he apparently took seriously the possibility of an amendment that would confer explicit power on the Court to declare acts of Congress unconstitutional subject to override by Congress after an intervening congressional election. If the postelection Congress reenacted (perhaps over a presidential veto) the legislation deemed unconstitutional by the Court, then "'the taint of unconstitutionality would be removed and the law would be a valid one'" (Leuchtenburg 1995, 95, quoting from a December 27, 1935, diary entry made by Harold Ickes). This scheme bears some similarities to the council scheme favored by Madison, although there are also important differences.

Imagining Another Madisonian Republic 191

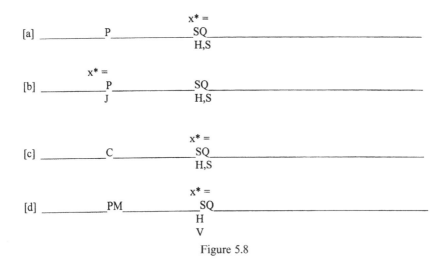

Figure 5.8

parliamentary law making in the context of another preference scenario. In panel (a), under the framers' procedure (no judicial review), the equilibrium $x^* = SQ$ because median legislators in the House and Senate agree to maintain the legislative status quo. Similarly, in Madisonian law making depicted in panel (c), the equilibrium $x^* = SQ$. Congress chooses not to present any bill to the council for its signature or veto. Again, in the parliamentary system of panel (d), where the judiciary has no authority to declare acts of parliament to be beyond the authority of the legislators, $x^* = SQ$. No incentives exist for elected officials to alter the status quo.

But, in panel (b), under American law making with judicial supremacy, the equilibrium $x^* = J$ because the Court, when deciding some case(s), seizes the opportunity both to nullify SQ as unconstitutional and to "legislate" the ideal point of the median justice. Judicial supremacy here allows the Court to destabilize the status quo and lead elected legislators along some path of reform that they would not choose to take by themselves. The question arises why Congress ever chose to enact SQ in the first place. This points in turn to the legislators' uncertainty about how courts will exercise the supreme power over constitutional interpretation, an issue to which I return later in the chapter.

Figure 5.8 suggests that Madison is warranted in fearing unpopular judicial forays into law making if judicial supremacy rather than legislative supremacy prevails. Under the council scheme, the courts can never veto SQ in cases brought before them because they have no authority to nullify legislative *acts* (as opposed to bills). The same holds for a parliamentary system. In contrast, as panel (b) makes clear, the courts under

192 *Jonathan Riley*

American arrangements can overturn existing statutory deals and interpretations of rights to initiate changes that "the great body of the people" and their elected representatives oppose. Again, that judges have such a power of initiating legislative reform is improper in principle, Madison insists, however rare and temporary its exercise or whatever its normative appeal in particular instances.[35] Until elected representatives are sufficiently impressed by the breadth and persistence of national sentiment to enact new legislation, he implies, the policy status quo should not be nullified by the Court. Even if prevailing national sentiment supports a status quo that is unjust toward certain minorities, blatant judicial defiance of that unjust national sentiment is unlikely to be helpful and may produce widespread discontent. More generally, judicial activism, however tempting in the short run, may be expected to invite resistance by the elected branches, "politicization" of the Court (e.g., ideological "litmus tests" for appointments), public distrust of technical legal reasoning, and eventually a majoritarian backlash in favor of restoration of the status quo ante.[36]

Nevertheless, this Madisonian critique of judicial supremacy may itself be dismissed as overly cautious from a republican perspective, as shown in Figure 5.9. Panel (a) reproduces Figure 5.2: the equilbrium $x^* = SQ$ because Congress is unable to override the presidential veto under the framers' procedure. Panel (b) extends Figure 5.2 such that the Court "legislates" the preference of its median member: $x^* = J (= V \neq SQ)$. Panel (c) reproduces the situation in Figure 5.2 in the context of Madisonian law making: $x^* = SQ$ because Congress is unable to override the council veto. Panel (d) reproduces the parliamentary system of Figure 5.4: $x^* = PM (= V)$.

---

[35] Dahl suggests that it is difficult to find examples of this sort of judicial activism in American political experience. He points out that "most of the famous cases of the Warren Court [including *Brown v. Board of Education*, 347 U.S. 483 (1954) and *Cooper v. Aaron*, 358 U.S. 1 (1958)] involved state or local laws, not acts of Congress" (1989, 190). Even so, the Court's judgments and orders might have influenced national opinion sufficiently that Congress and the president eventually were led to pass the Civil Rights Act of 1964 and the Voting Rights Act of 1965. Dworkin (1994, 20–1), for example, emphasizes the Court's leadership on abortion rights as well as racial integration. For a pessimistic view of the Court's ability to lead public sentiment and effect reform, however, see Rosenberg 1991.

[36] It may not be implausible to suggest that the apparent upsurge of "radical conservative" public sentiment since 1980, for example, is at least in part a reaction against "liberal" judicial activism of the sort epitomized by the Court's opinions in *Roe v. Wade*, 410 U.S. 113 (1973), and the *Brown v. Board of Education* cases, 347 U.S. 483 (1954) and 349 U.S. 294 (1955), whatever the justice of those opinions. Mishler and Sheehan, it should be noted, see an increasingly conservative Court during the Reagan-Bush years. In their view (1993, 95, 97–8), however, that Court's opinions run counter to an observed upsurge in "liberal" national sentiment since 1980.

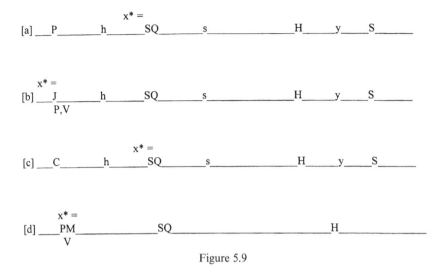

Figure 5.9

As a comparison of panels (b) and (d) shows, judicial supremacy in the U.S. context can mirror parliamentary outcomes in accord with the preferences of the median voter. Such outcomes are thwarted by checks and balances in the other two procedures. As panels (a) and (c) illustrate, Congress cannot muster the supermajorities required to override the veto of the president and council, respectively, even though the legislators are supported by popular majorities.

Effective Checks on the Legislature

Madison insists that "auxiliary precautions" are needed in a republic to supplement the primary electoral check against misrule: "[E]xperience has taught mankind the necessity of auxiliary precautions" (*Federalist* 51, 349). The presidential veto and judicial review are familiar auxiliary precautions to Americans.[37] Yet Madison seems to have believed that the qualified vetoes of the council of revision would be more effective checks against Congress. As he put it: "Whether the object of the revisionary power was to restrain the legislature from encroaching on the other coordinate departments, or on the rights of the people at large; or from

---

[37] Bicameralism is also essential in a republic, Madison argued, to remedy the tendency of the predominant legislature to usurp the authority of the other branches. Indeed: "It may even be necessary to guard against dangerous encroachments by still further precautions." Given that the House is the stronger chamber of the legislature, for example, prudence may demand that it should be checked by uniting the Senate and the executive for certain purposes, including appointments and foreign treaties (*Federalist* 51, 350).

194 *Jonathan Riley*

passing laws unwise in their principle, or incorrect in their form, the utility of annexing the wisdom and weight of the judiciary to the executive seemed incontestable" (Farrand 1966, 1:139).

Why might the American combination of executive and judicial vetoes not provide such an effective check against legislative misrule, including violations of basic rights? In this regard, it must be recognized that the executive and judiciary exercise their respective vetoes separately at different periods of the law-making process, and generally for different purposes. Given that the one veto is exercised against *bills* for merely expedient or partisan purposes whereas the other is exercised against *acts* for constitutional reasons, conventions have not evolved to encourage the two branches to form a coalition against the legislature. Under the council arrangements, however, it may make sense to model council actions as cooperative bargains between the president and justices. Rather than make their respective veto decisions independently, the members of the council may develop a practice of deciding jointly whether to veto bills for constitutional and/or policy reasons because, for example, they view the prestige of the council as being at stake. Conventions that evolve within the council might thus enforce veto agreements among its members.

This sort of cooperation can have important implications if, in the larger noncooperative game with Congress, the executive and judiciary are far more likely to play their veto strategies when they are united in the council rather than separated as under American arrangements. When united, the president and justices might believe that their power to check Congress has both constitutional and democratic justification because it is associated with the legal expertise of the highest court as well as the popular mandate of the chief executive. When separated, however, the president and justices might be very reluctant to exercise their veto powers against Congress, especially when they think that the legislators are supported by a popular majority. The independent courts might be sufficiently uncomfortable with the claim of judicial supremacy in what is supposed to be a representative democracy, for example, that they choose relatively rarely to nullify acts of Congress.[38] If so, the president might feel less

---

[38] Since 1787, the U.S. Supreme Court has nullified all or part of less than one federal law per year on average, although it has struck down more than a thousand state statutes. The reasons for the judiciary's apparent reluctance to invalidate acts of Congress remain open to debate. The judges have attempted to define categories of "political questions" that, in their view, are properly settled by the other branches through bargaining. On the political question doctrine, see Scharf 1966, Henkin 1976, and Murphy et al. 1995, 270–3, 485–97, 769–75, reprinting relevant sections of opinions from *Baker v. Carr*, 369 U.S. 186 (1962), *Gilligan v. Morgan*, 413 U.S. 1 (1973), *INS v. Chadha*, 462 U.S. 919 (1983), and *Dalton v. Specter*, 114 S.Ct. 1719 (1994)). Spiller and Tiller (1996) argue that it may often be to the strategic advantage of the Court to employ "statutory review" (where Congress can over-

inclined to stand up alone against Congress even for mere policy reasons, let alone constitutional ones.[39] In any case, the presidential veto alone is easier to override than the council veto would have been.[40]

If we suppose that the executive and judiciary will not actually exercise their checks unless united in the council, then the U.S. law-making process appears in a very different light. Given common knowledge that the executive and courts are unwilling to cast their separate vetoes, the process effectively becomes a legislative tyranny in which congressional majorities have absolute power to enact statutes. Bicameralism becomes the sole remaining check against arbitrary rule. When contrasted with such a system of legislative despotism, of course, Madisonian law making seems a paragon of liberty because the council is assumed to exercise its veto power whenever its members agree.

On the other hand, the Madisonian alternative may seem far too biased in favor of recognized minority interests to defenders of parliamentary democracy. For example, it might seem too difficult for Congress to muster the double supermajorities (before and after an intervening election) required to override the council's veto of any legislation on constitutional grounds, including legislation seeking to reform or modify constitutional rights. Sustained, virtually unanimous popular support for the legislation would be essential to its success. In contrast, under parliamentary procedures, bare majorities ultimately control constitutional interpretation. True, the parliamentary model should not be confused with the corrupted version of American democracy, which results if executive and judiciary fail to exercise their powers to check Congress. Some independence between legislature and executive is maintained within parliamentary democracy by its distinctive system of reciprocal checks, to wit, the legislative majority's power to vote nonconfidence and the executive's power of dissolution. But, in the absence of compromise, electoral majorities will decide any constitutional conflict by virtue of the legislators returned to office. It is thus easier to reform – but also to violate – recognized rights than it is under Madisonian democracy.

---

ride the opinion) rather than nonoverridable constitutional review (interpreted as reduction of the dimensionality of admissible policy space). Since 1995, however, the Court has been more active in striking down federal legislation, usually on federalism or separation-of-powers grounds.

[39] The presidential veto has been exercised relatively frequently on policy grounds, however, and has arguably had a significant impact on legislation (at least since the Civil War). For an analysis that focuses on the effects of its use from Franklin Roosevelt through Jimmy Carter, see Watson 1993.

[40] Indeed, at the convention, Madison, Wilson, and Morris each favored a stronger executive veto that could be overridden only by three-fourths rather than two-thirds of both House and Senate (Farrand 1966, 2:587).

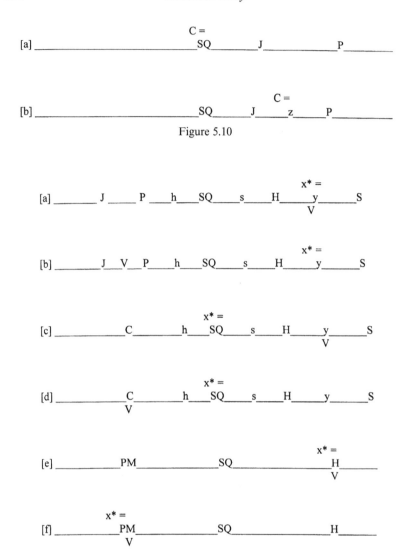

Figure 5.10

Figure 5.11

These various points can be sharpened in terms of Figures 5.10 and 5.11. Figure 5.10 depicts the assumption that checks are exercised under the council arrangements when not exercised under American law making. Panels (a) and (b) illustrate the idea that the president and justices cast a veto if (but only if) they can strike a bargain $z = f(J,P)$ to their mutual advantage when united in the council. By contrast, the executive and judiciary are simply assumed never to exercise their separate vetoes under

American arrangements. In effect, their respective preferences or demands, P and J, are not politically effective because they are unwilling to spend the requisite constitutional currency.

Consider now Figure 5.11. Panel (a) illustrates a case of the American process as a legislative despotism: the equilibrium $x^* = y$ because everyone knows that the executive and judiciary will not cast their vetoes despite their opposition to Congress. Panel (b) illustrates a similar case where the checks remain idle even though Congress is now assumed to act in opposition to the median voter. This perverse situation is conceivable because the executive and judiciary have no power to dissolve the Congress between the fixed dates of elections. Panels (c) and (d) illustrate the Madisonian system in two comparable scenarios. Evidently, given that $x^* = SQ$ in both of these latter panels, the checks on Congress are now far more powerful under the council than under American arrangements.

Panels (e) and (f) provide comparable parliamentary scenarios to facilitate comparison. In contrast to the scenario of legislative despotism depicted in panel (b), for example, the parliamentary system in panel (f) is associated with a distinct equilibrium $x^* = PM (= V)$ that reflects popular majority preferences. A popular majority might support violations of basic rights, of course, in which case the Madisonian system of checks in comparable panel (d) is associated with protection of liberty. Or perhaps the legislative despots of panel (b) seek to violate basic rights in opposition to popular majority preferences, so that the comparable Madisonian procedure is again associated with security of rights. In any case, whether majorities prefer to act unjustly or otherwise, the Madisonian system provides the strongest checks against legislation.

In brief, Madison's suggestion that the council arrangements seem superior to American ones for checking arbitrary legislation may have been based on an idea that the president and Court would be more willing united than alone to engage in conflict with Congress. United, under arrangements where the legislature retained its supremacy, they might be more confident of the legitimacy of exercising their checks.[41] Indeed, the council arrangements provide a very powerful check on Congress if the

---

[41] The New York council of revision used its veto far more frequently than contemporary presidents and justices used their vetoes. According to Street (1859, 7), the New York council rejected 169 bills and the legislature overrode the veto 51 times during 1777–1821. Schechter (1990, 176n3) also cites Street (1859) but gives different totals for unexplained reasons. Street describes and lists the council vetoes as well as legislative overrides at 199–402, 481–98, 517–22, 525–47. In contrast, presidents vetoed only 10 bills (Madison alone vetoed 7 of these) during 1789–1829. None of the vetoes were overridden by Congress (Watson 1993, 13–17). The Court nullified no acts of Congress during that period.

198   *Jonathan Riley*

president and justices unite to exercise their vetoes on constitutional grounds.[42] Still, Madison's strictly republican principles are not compromised. If legislators can muster three-fourths majorities of both chambers before and after the intervening election, Congress can override and thereby have final government say over constitutional interpretation.[43]

A Stable Rule of Law

The approach employed up to now cannot adequately capture another concern expressed by Madison. He claims that the rule of law is likely to be more stable under his supreme-legislature-cum-council process than under American arrangements. Council vetoes are confined to legislative proposals and thus can never disappoint certain legitimate expectations that may have formed around legislative acts of long duration. Security of legal expectations is central to key social goals, he implies, including economic efficiency and political order. The security of expectations made possible by stable and transparent laws of private property and contract, for example, is essential to economic efficiency and perhaps distributive justice. To the extent that judicial supremacy upsets this security by nullifying (or even threatening to nullify) acts of Congress long after their dates of enactment, it may detract from key economic and social goals. As Madison emphasizes, such instability discourages investments of every sort. Moreover, unstable laws of property give an "unreasonable advantage ... to the sagacious, the enterprising and the moneyed few" who "watch the change, and can trace the consequences." That minority of speculators is thereby enabled to capture "a harvest reared not by themselves but by the toils and cares of the great body of their fellow citizens" (*Federalist* 62, 421).

Madison's concern here can be illustrated by modeling the American law-making process as a problem of decision making under uncertainty faced by a Bayesian median legislator. Congress and the Court are no longer seen as playing a game in which each has the capacity to calculate

---

[42] Wills (1981, 152–4) argues that "this [council] scheme was a stronger limit on the Congress than either the executive veto or judicial review. . . . It is easier for the present Congress to amend the Constitution, impeach a justice, pack the Court, . . . refuse funding, or have other recourse to popular opinion, than it would have been to defeat 'suspension' of a bill by Madison's double-veto scheme."

[43] At the convention, Wilson initially favored giving the "executive and judiciary jointly an *absolute* negative" (Farrand 1966, 1:98, emphasis added). This would give the council rather than the legislature final government say. Such council supremacy is improper in terms of Madison's idea of republican government (which demands legislative supremacy). The impropriety would not be removed even if, as Wilson favored, the president were directly elected.

and know for certain how the other will react to its choices. Rather than playing a game under complete and perfect information, Congress is choosing nonstrategically between SQ and a proposed deal y = g(H,S) under conditions of imperfect information about what the Court will do when it hears cases implicating y or SQ sometime in the future. The legislators are uncertain about the preferences of the median justice because, for example, the membership of the current Court may alter before a relevant case is heard. Different ideological types of Court are feasible in the future, each with a distinctive median preference J in relation to SQ and y. Whereas the justices know for certain which type of court exists when the time comes for them to decide whether to sustain or veto, Congress does not possess such knowledge when choosing between SQ and y. That information is private to the justices. The justices also know for certain what Congress has already done. As such, the median justice chooses to nullify or affirm as he sees fit, unconstrained by how Congress might react to his constitutional interpretation.

To illustrate, consider the decision tree depicted in Figure 5.12. The historical chance node at the root of the tree indicates that "nature" has already made a choice that constrains Congress. More specifically, nature determines a probability distribution over distinct types of courts, one of which the current Court will have evolved into by the time the justices must choose to sustain or veto. Assume that two types of courts are feasible. The current Court evolves into type A with probability $\wp$ and into type B with probability $1 - \wp$, $0 \leq \wp \leq 1$. The membership of a type A court is assumed to be such that the median justice has "right-wing" views, that is, his ideal point J lies to the right of SQ. Thus, for example, J might be assumed to coincide with y in a Figure 5.1 scenario. In contrast, a type B court is assumed to display "left-wing" views, that is, J lies to the left of SQ. Thus, J might be assumed to coincide with P in a Figure 5.6 scenario so that the median justice opposes Congress and prefers to maintain SQ rather than affirm y. Given complete information, legislators and judges both are aware of the probability distribution as play unfolds. But the legislators, unlike the justices, are ignorant of the type into which the Court has actually evolved when the time comes to sustain or veto whatever Congress has done.

Because they do not know which type of court has actually evolved (although they do know the probability distribution) by the time they must choose between SQ and y, the legislators have imperfect information. The bracketed line drawn around the two congressional nodes of the tree represents an "information set" to show that the legislators cannot distinguish between these nodes when making a choice. If he cannot distinguish between the nodes, a median legislator must make the same decision at both. Given $\wp = 0.6$ and the cardinal payoff structure indicated in Figure

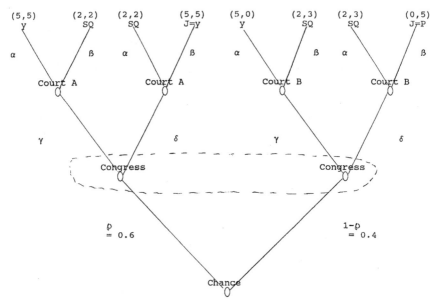

Figure 5.12. Congressional strategies are denoted as γ ("enact new legislation y") and δ ("do nothing"). The Court's strategies are denoted as α ("sustain") and β ("veto"). If the Court vetoes SQ, however, the median justice is assumed to "legislate" J. By vetoing SQ, the Court creates a legislative void in the sense that no existing legislative policy is constitutional. But, given the one-to-one correspondence between constitutional interpretations and policies as depicted in Figure 5.5, the Court's veto must implicitly refer to an ideal point J. Since no constitutional act of Congress is in place, the Court's veto is taken to imply that J has been "enacted."

The median legislator maximizes expected utility by choosing γ in this case. If Congress enacts y, a type A court will sustain y with probability ρ whereas a type B court will veto y with probability 1 − ρ. Thus, by choosing γ, Congress can expect 3.8 units of utility, that is, [5 × 0.6 + 2 × 0.4]. If Congress does nothing, however, a type A court will veto SQ and "legislate" J = y with probability ρ, whereas a type B court will veto SQ and "legislate" J = P with probability 1 − ρ. Thus, by choosing δ, Congress can expect only 3 units of utility, that is, [5 × 0.6 + 0 × 0.4].

5.12, a Bayesian median legislator maximizes expected utility by enacting the new policy y rather than leaving SQ in place.

Unlike Congress, however, the justices have perfect information because they know which type of court exists and what Congress has done when the time comes to sustain or veto the median legislator's choice. The justices can thus distinguish among the four Court nodes when making a choice. Given that a Bayesian Congress has enacted y, a type A Court will sustain y (so that y is the outcome) whereas a type B Court will veto y (so that SQ is the outcome). Given the 40 percent chance that a type B Court

Imagining Another Madisonian Republic

has evolved, however, Congress must expect to be disappointed two times out of five in this case. More generally, some instability in the rule of law must be expected under American arrangements as modeled.[44]

This sort of legislative decision problem under uncertainty does not arise in a parliamentary regime, where there is no judicial review. Nor does it arise in a Madisonian democracy. Such instability in the rule of law is avoided because council vetoes can only be exercised against legislative bills. Neither the president nor the justices can nullify *acts* of Congress.

CONCLUSION

I have focused attention on Madison's defense of a form of constitutional democracy in which the legislature would be supreme in case of conflict among the departments of government with respect to constitutional interpretation. This Madisonian democracy is distinct from American democracy as it has evolved, in which the judiciary has claimed final say over constitutional meaning. At the same time, a supreme Madisonian legislature would still face a formidable system of checks and balances giving rise to a distinctive separation of powers between Congress and a national council of revision. With the help of some game theory, I have tried to indicate what is distinctive about such a Madisonian regime in comparison to American and parliamentary alternatives.

Of course, the comparative constitutional exercise must be considerably broadened for pragmatic or normative purposes. For instance, the Fifth Republic's highly complex form of constitutional democracy, in which bills supported by legislative majorities can be – and typically are – referred by various officials (including the president, prime minister, and legislative

---

[44] To minimize such instability, Congress has strong incentives to control suitably the membership of the Court so as to be able to predict its median preference. Moreover, both the legislators and justices have incentives to develop conventions or canons of interpretation that enable improved coordination of mutual expectations. For example, given that the current Court is of type A, the justices might develop a convention of following precedent (*stare decisis*) as a way of assuring Congress that a type A Court will persist for some time. Congress would then rely on that understanding when choosing y rather than SQ. Sets of coordinating conventions might be termed "expectations regimes" (Rasmussen 1994). If entirely successful in developing an expectations regime, Congress and the Court would always know how the other will behave in any situation. By implication, a single ideological type of Court would persist indefinitely. For the case considered in our simple model, Congress would try to control the Court's membership and encourage formation of an expectations regime such that the probability of a type A Court becomes unity, i.e., $\wp = 1$. If entirely successful, Congress would never suffer any "disappointments" as a result of judicial annulments of its acts. Needless to add, however, it is implausible to think that the branches could be so successful in coordinating their mutual expectations across all scenarios.

202 *Jonathan Riley*

minorities, among others) to a constitutional council with an absolute veto over their enactment, is sufficiently distinctive to be of great interest.[45] My larger purpose has been to suggest that the two-stage game-theoretic framework can be a useful tool for citizens and constitutional designers in conducting this sort of comparative exercise.

REFERENCES

Banning, Lance. 1996. *The Sacred Fire of Liberty*. Ithaca: Cornell University Press.

Beer, Samuel H. 1993. *To Make a Nation: The Rediscovery of American Federalism*. Cambridge, Mass.: Belknap Press of Harvard University Press.

Burt, Robert A. 1992. *The Constitution in Conflict*. Cambridge, Mass.: Belknap Press of Harvard University Press.

Cooke, Jacob E., ed. 1961. *The Federalist*. Middletown, Conn.: Wesleyan University Press.

Dahl, Robert A. 1957. "Decisionmaking in a Democracy: The Supreme Court as a National Policymaker." *Journal of Public Law* 6: 279–95.

1989. *Democracy and Its Critics*. New Haven: Yale University Press.

Drewry, Gavin, ed. 1989. *The New Select Committees: A Study of the 1979 Reforms*. Oxford: Clarendon Press.

Dworkin, Ronald. 1994. "Mr. Liberty." *New York Review of Books* 41 (August 11): 17–22.

Eskridge, William N., Jr., and John Ferejohn. 1992. "The Article I, Section 7 Game." *Georgetown Law Journal* 80: 523–64.

Farrand, Max, ed. 1966. *The Records of the Federal Convention of 1787*. Vols. 1–4. Rev. ed. New Haven: Yale University Press.

Henkin, Louis. 1976. "Is There a 'Political Question' Doctrine?" *Yale Law Journal* 85: 597–625.

Hobson, Charles F. 1979. "The Negative on State Laws: James Madison, the Constitution, and the Crisis of Republican Government." *William and Mary Quarterly* 36: 215–35.

Hunt, Gaillard, ed. 1900–10. *The Writings of James Madison*. Vols. 1–9. New York: G. P. Putnam's Sons.

Leuchtenburg, William E. 1995. *The Supreme Court Reborn: The Constitutional Revolution in the Age of Roosevelt*. New York: Oxford University Press.

Lijphart, Arendt. 1992. *Parliamentary versus Presidential Government*. Oxford: Oxford University Press.

---

[45] For clarification of the Constitutional Council's authority and a comparison with the U.S. Supreme Court, see Rohr 1995, 22–3, 138–77. Among other things, the council is charged with policing the striking division of power between Parliament (which has exclusive power to make general laws restricted to certain subjects) and the prime minister as leader of the government (which has exclusive power to make regulations). Remarkably, a separate Council of State has authority to review the constitutionality of the latter executive regulations. On the French understanding of separation of powers and associated checks and balances, see Rohr 1995, 44–67, 93–137, 189–206, 242.

Lutz, Donald S. 1994. "Toward a Theory of Constitutional Amendment." *American Political Science Review* 88: 355–70.

Marshall, Thomas. 1989. *Public Opinion and the Supreme Court*. New York: Longman.

McCoy, Drew R. 1989. *The Last of the Fathers: James Madison and the Republican Legacy*. Cambridge: Cambridge University Press.

Meyers, Marvin, ed. 1981. *The Mind of the Founder: Sources of the Political Thought of James Madison*. Rev. ed. Hanover: University Press of New England for Brandeis University Press.

Mill, John Stuart. 1849. "Vindication of the French Revolution of February 1848." In J. Robson, ed., *Collected Works of J. S. Mill*, 20: 317–63. Toronto and London: University of Toronto Press and Routledge, 1985.

1861. *Considerations on Representative Government*. In J. Robson, ed., *Collected Works of J. S. Mill*, 19: 371–7. Toronto and London: University of Toronto Press and Routledge, 1977.

Mishler, William, and Reginald S. Sheehan. 1993. "The Supreme Court as a Countermajoritarian Institution? The Impact of Public Opinion on Supreme Court Decisions." *American Political Science Review* 87: 87–101.

Murphy, Walter F., James E. Fleming, and Sotirios A. Barber. 1995. *American Constitutional Interpretation*. 2nd ed. Mineola, N.Y.: Foundation Press.

Nedelsky, Jennifer. 1990. *Private Property and the Limits of American Constitutionalism: The Madisonian Framework and Its Legacy*. Chicago: University of Chicago Press.

Norton, Philip. 1978. "Government Defeats in the House of Commons: Myth and Reality." *Public Law* (Winter): 360–78.

1991. "The Changing Face of Parliament: Lobbying and Its Consequences." In *New Directions in British Politics? Essays on the Evolving Constitution*, 58–82. Aldershot: Elgar.

Rakove, Jack N. 1987. "The Great Compromise: Ideas, Interests, and the Politics of Constitution Making." *William and Mary Quarterly*, 3rd ser., 44: 424–57.

1988. "The Madisonian Moment." *University of Chicago Law Review* 55: 473–505.

1990. *James Madison and the Creation of the American Republic*. Glenview, Ill.: Scott, Foresman.

1991. "Parchment Barriers and the Politics of Rights." In Michael J. Lacey and Knud Haakonssen, eds., *A Culture of Rights: The Bill of Rights in Philosophy, Politics, and Law – 1791 and 1991*, 98–143. Cambridge: Woodrow Wilson International Center for Scholars and Cambridge University Press.

1996. *Original Meanings: Politics and Ideas in the Making of the Constitution*. New York: Knopf.

1997. "The Origins of Judicial Review: A Plea for New Contexts." *Stanford Law Review* 49: 1031–64.

Rasmussen, Eric 1994. "Judicial Legitimacy as a Repeated Game." *Journal of Law, Economics, and Organization* 10: 63–83.

Riker, William. 1982. *Liberalism against Populism*. San Francisco: W. H. Freeman.

Riley, Jonathan. 1990. "American Democracy and Majority Rule." In John W. Chapman and Alan Wertheimer, eds., *Majorities and Minorities*, 267–307. Nomos 32. New York: New York University Press.

Rives, William C., and Philip R. Fendall, eds. 1865. *Letters and Other Writings of James Madison*. Vols. 1–4. Philadelphia: J. B. Lippincott.

Rohr, John A. 1995. *Founding Republics in France and America*. Lawrence: University Press of Kansas.

Rosenberg, Gerald N. 1991. *The Hollow Hope: Can the Courts Bring About Social Change?* Chicago: University of Chicago Press.

Rutland, Robert A., and Charles F. Hobson, eds. 1977. *The Papers of James Madison*. Vol. 10. Chicago: University of Chicago Press.

Sartori, Giovanni. 1996. *Comparative Constitutional Engineering*. 2nd ed. New York: New York University Press.

Scharf, Fritz W. 1966. "Judicial Review and the Political Question." *Yale Law Journal* 75: 517–97.

Schechter, Stephen L., ed. 1990. *Roots of the Republic*. Madison: Madison House.

Sorenson, Leonard R. 1995. *Madison on the "General Welfare" of America: His Consistent Constitutional Vision*. Lanham, Md.: Rowman and Littlefield.

Spiller, Pablo T., and Matthew L. Spitzer. 1992. "Judicial Choice of Legal Doctrines." *Journal of Law, Economics, and Organization* 8: 8–46.

Spiller, Pablo T., and Emerson H. Tiller. 1996. "Invitations to Override: Congressional Reversals of Supreme Court Decisions." *International Review of Law and Economics* 16: 503–21.

Spiller, Pablo T., and Emerson H. Tiller. 1997. "Decision Costs and the Strategic Design of Administrative Process and Judicial Review." *Journal of Legal Studies* 26: 347–70.

Street, Alfred B. 1859. *The Council of Revision of the State of New York*. Albany: William Gould.

Watson, Richard A. 1993. *Presidential Vetoes and Public Policy*. Lawrence: University Press of Kansas.

Wills, Garry. 1981. *Explaining America: The Federalist*. London: Athlone Press.

Wilson, Woodrow. 1885. *Congressional Government*. Baltimore: Johns Hopkins University Press, 1981.

6

One and Three: Separation of Powers and the Independence of the Judiciary in the Italian Constitution

Pasquale Pasquino

Funiculus triplex difficile rumpitur
(A threefold cord is not easily broken)
Ecclesiastes 4.12

INTRODUCTION

In contemporary democracies electors can choose their representatives, reward them by reelection, or turn them out of office; no appeal can be made against a judgment as final or conclusive as an election. However, electors cannot bind representatives, once elected, in the choices they make as legislators. Representatives have a power constitutionally unbound from any promise they may have made during the campaign; a freedom that also entails a risk, because they may be punished at the next election,[1] but only if the voters hold them to their promises. The ban on "imperative mandates" is one of the central tenets of modern representative government.[2]

Rousseau famously held, not without reason, that the citizens of representative governments – which we call democracies with a small abuse of language[3] – are, like the English, free only for one day, the day of the

---

I owe the original impulse to write this chapter to my friend Stefano Nespor. I am grateful to Luigi de Ruggiero, Alessandro Pizzorno, Larry Kramer, and John Ferejohn for their comments, and to Jack Rakove for the care with which he read previous drafts and helped me to avoid errors and misconceptions.

[1] This is the only sense in which one can claim that contemporary democracies are "mixed regimes" since they combine the aristocratic principle of elections with the democratic principle of popular choice of the elites. See Manin 1995.

[2] An imperative mandate obliges the representative to follow strictly the will expressed by the electors, without any possibility of modifying it. The ban on imperative mandates was one of the first important decisions taken by the French Constituent Assembly in 1789 and is still one of the tenets of representative government.

[3] The proper meaning of the Greek word democracy is "government by the poor"; *demos*, indeed, inside the Greek polis, is not the equivalent of our word "people," but designates

206 *Pasquale Pasquino*

elections, and slaves the rest of the time.[4] Unfortunately, Rousseau failed to suggest any clear or sensible alternative to that extreme and bleak verdict. Perhaps unintentionally, he eventually opened a path that leads nowhere, or rather, toward the utopia that some still vaguely call "direct democracy."[5]

In addition to the rejection of representative government, another aspect of Rousseau's theory of democracy deserves emphasis: its nonconstitutionalist thrust. Rousseau in fact did not distinguish between ordinary and constitutional laws. He had no conception of the supremacy or "superlegality" of the constitution;[6] nor did he notice the critical difference, pivotal in any contemporary *Rechtstaat*, between the constituent power that establishes the constitution and the subordinated powers, such as the legislative, that carry out their constitutionally delegated duties. Those distinctions were introduced into the public positive law only at the end of the eighteenth century, during the era of the American and French revolutions,[7] which placed at the basis of the state organization a *written constitution*, governing the exercise of political power, and so opened the way to modern liberal constitutionalism. The American Constitution of 1787 and the French Constitution of 1791 have their foundation in a principle held to be an essential element of the constitutional *Rechtstaat*: the separation of powers. The elective principle, the preeminence of the constitution, and the separation of powers are the three pillars of this tradition and they cannot be taken apart without destroying the basis of representative democracy.

The people are sovereign only on the day of the elections; but the government as well as the parliament should not violate the constitution,[8] even though they are not bound by the people's (imperative) mandates and are free to disregard their campaign promises. The defense of the constitution, which the French charter of 1791 entrusted to the "watchfulness of the fathers, to the wives and mothers,"[9] became in the twentieth century,

---

only one part of it: the poor or those who live on the countryside as opposed to the *eudaimones* (the rich) and to the *dunatoi* (the powerful). See Chantraine 1968, 1: 273.

[4] *Du contrat social*, book III, ch. 15: "Le peuple anglais pense être libre, il se trompe fort; il ne l'est que durant l'élection des membres du parlement: sitôt qu'ils sont élus, il est esclave, il n'est rien."

[5] See Böckenförde 1991 for a final criticism of that concept.

[6] This expression points at the supremacy of constitutional norms over laws enacted by Parliament.

[7] Larry Kramer drew my attention to previous examples of those distinctions in English customary law, like the *Calvin's Case* in the very early seventeenth century.

[8] In a manuscript where he comments on his book on the Third-Estate, Sieyes wrote explicitly that "the body of the ordinary representatives of the people, that is those who are in charge of the ordinary legislation, cannot without contradiction and absurdity modify the constitution" (Archives Nationales, Paris, 284 AP 4 Doss. 8).

[9] Art. 8 of *Titre* (section) VII.

through the judicial review of parliamentary laws, the specific and explicit function of nonelective organs, whose prestige and authority have continued to increase in nearly all the Western countries.

A central element of modern constitutionalism is *liberalism*, meaning here the doctrine that preeminently emphasizes the *limitation of state* power to the end of guaranteeing individual rights. Before considering the meaning, the rationale and the different interpretations of this principle – the same principle that justifies the separation of powers – it may be useful to say a few words about the institution of the state as a central political agency, and about its origin and necessity. In order to understand the limitation of the powers of the state, we first have to ask why we need a state, or in other words, why liberalism is not an "anarchy," the absence of political power, but simply its regulation and limitation.

From the late medieval era on, European monarchies struggled to centralize and consolidate their control of the fiscal and judicial authorities of governance. Nonetheless, it was only during the religious wars of the sixteenth and seventeenth centuries that the state emerged as the dominant political agency monopolizing the exercise of fiscal, judicial, and legislative power, as well as the ability to wield coercive force through its command of a standing army. It acquired this stature because it was the only institution capable of establishing peace and guaranteeing a minimal degree of security (preservation of life) to its subjects. Only an overwhelming power concentrated in a single institution seemed likely to impose an adequate measure of reciprocal tolerance on the different Christian sects, which had perpetrated hideous crimes, like the massacre of the Huguenots by the French Catholics on the eve of St. Bartholomew 1572, or any of the many other acts of persecution that accompanied the civil conflicts sparked by the Reformation.

The type of political power that we call Absolutism arose in Europe[10] from the necessity of ending the catastrophic violence of religious warfare.[11] From the mid-sixteenth until the mid-seventeenth century, nearly all of Europe was the theater of a tragic experience similar to the one that we have witnessed in the country now regrettably known as "the former Yugoslavia."

Civil peace was achieved in those centuries at a very high price: the emergence at the center of society of the Leviathan state, creator and defender of peace. Only against this background is it possible to understand the birth of the liberal project to find some means of limiting the powers of this new

---

[10] Absolutism has not been a specific characteristic of monarchies. The power of the English Parliament after the Glorious Revolution was exorbitant as well.

[11] See the important book by Crouzet (1990).

state. The exorbitant power of the central political agency, which had seemed necessary to bring an end to the disorder produced by religious conflicts, began in turn to pose a dangerous threat to the good order of society, and to the security and freedom of citizens. Different means were used to limit that threat and to reorganize the exercise of the state's functions on safer grounds. One involved appealing to those customary institutions and practices of governance that the new centralized state was discarding: here the idea of the "ancient constitution" as a prescriptive restraint on the sovereign authority of the consolidated monarchy acquired its allure. The concept of the separation of powers, which had its roots in English constitutional history, also began to play a central role, especially with the publication of Montesquieu's *Esprit des lois* in 1748. In the final quarter of the eighteenth century, the first constitutional states[12] were established in republican America and revolutionary France, and in both societies, as is well known, the legacy of Montesquieu was substantial. Thus the principle of the separation of powers finds explicit expression in Articles XXIX and XXX of the Massachusetts Declaration of Rights of 1780 and again in Article 16 of the French Declaration of Rights of 1789: "Any society in which there is no fixed guarantee of rights nor separation of powers, has no constitution." From that point onward, the constitution and the separation of powers became virtually synonymous. But what exactly does it mean to equate a constitution with separated powers? To answer that question, we need to take a step backward and consider briefly Montesquieu's political theory.

The core of Montesquieu's doctrine of forms of government was the distinction he introduced into political theory between "despotic" and "moderate regimes." Montesquieu defined despotism as the type of political power where a single agency or institution concentrates all of the three powers that exist in each state: the legislative, the executive,[13] and the judiciary. The minimal guarantee for the existence of a moderate regime consists, by contrast, in the establishment of an independent body with the power to enforce the laws with reference to concrete cases. Some form of independence of the judiciary (like that established by the Italian Constitution of 1948)[14] represents indeed the hallmark of any government that could legitimately claim that it is not "despotic."

---

[12] That means characterized by the existence of a written constitution.

[13] Concerning the relationship between legislative and executive power of which I am not going to speak here, see Bognetti 1994. The book gives a useful introduction to that problem, though I do not agree with its conclusions and proposals.

[14] "The Judiciary (*la magistratura*) is an autonomous order independent of any other power" (Art. 104). Later I shall come back to the meaning of that expression in the Italian Constitution.

This doctrine, expounded by Montesquieu in the famous chapter of his *Spirit of Laws* devoted to the English Constitution, is one of the fountains of modern constitutionalism, and it found its fulfillment in the American and the French constitutions of the late eighteenth century. Yet this same doctrine or principle has been the object of two markedly different interpretations in France and the United States.[15] In order to understand those two different and partly divergent interpretations of the same constitutional tenet – the separation of powers – we need to consider some of the founding texts. The view of the separation of powers that came to prevail in Europe in the wake of the French Revolution, while accepting the principle, presented a hierarchical interpretation of the Rousseauian type, with the legislative power (the direct expression of the popular sovereignty) at the top and the executive and judiciary occupying distinct but subordinate positions. Something like that hierarchical ordering of the powers also characterized the initial American view of the doctrine circa 1776. But by 1787 Americans had begun to develop another, more liberal (and less populist) version of the separation of powers, which stresses the "sovereignty" of the constitution over all three departments of government. The emergence of this version of the principle marked the true foundation of the American model of "checks and balances." The latter envisages the three state organs as active counterpowers, capable of acting as instruments of intervention in the specific field assigned to the other powers, in order to produce a dynamic equilibrium and avoid despotism.

Those two models do not exhaust the typology, as we shall see when considering the Italian Constitution. Nonetheless, they are the two classical patterns from which it may be useful to start.

Before discussing the Italian case, however, I shall briefly present the two models I have just mentioned, which I shall respectively call "la bouche de la loi" (following Montesquieu) and "ambition counteracting ambition" (following James Madison's famous formulation in *Federalist* 51). Moreover, I suggest that these two versions of the principle were directed against two quite different threats to the freedom of the citizens: on the one hand, the possible arbitrary exercise of the judiciary power; on the other, the exorbitant power of the democratic majorities that the American constitutional tradition initially regarded as the

---

[15] This is of course an oversimplification. In America as well as in France there were debates and memorable confrontations between the supporters of the two versions. Nonetheless, it is a fact that the Anti-Federalists were beaten during the ratification of the Constitution of 1787 (see Manin 1994). Likewise it is historical fact that Mounier and the *monarchiens* were defeated in France in the Constituent Assembly (see Pasquino 1990 and 1994). It is worth remembering that Sieyes's proposal in 1795 to establish through the Constitution an organ with powers of judicial review was rejected unanimously by the convention.

210 *Pasquale Pasquino*

most significant threat in a representative government. This latter danger is more important in a majoritarian electoral system such as Italy has recently come to enjoy.

THE JUDICIARY POWER AS "BOUCHE DE LA LOI"

> The dramatic history of Continental Europe in the last two centuries, where the ideal of civil-libertarians was for too long one of strict separation of powers rather than of reciprocal checks, is very instructive. Strict separation brought about a weak judiciary . . . it brought about an unchecked legislator.
>
> Cappelletti 1989, 23

In Europe, one of the central functions of the separation of the judiciary from the legislative and executive powers has always been to limit or prevent the arbitrary exercise of judicial power by the monarch who was already endowed with the two other powers. The Old Regime practice of the *lettres de cachet*, by which the king arbitrarily imprisoned or deprived defenseless citizens of their rights, is well known.[16] The large number of privileges allowed by the monarch, which Sieyes called *privatae leges*, evitiated both the *Rechtssicherheit* as well as the concept of equality before the law. It was during the Enlightenment that the idea of the "rule of law" established itself in the culture of the European continent, prior to its introduction into positive law during the French Revolution. Rule of law means here, in Lockean language, government by public, stable, general, and abstract norms, which apply equally to everyone and thus stand in opposition to the extemporary decrees expressing the mere transient will of the sovereign.[17] However, the rule of law is nothing more than a vague formula unless the judiciary power is rendered distinct from the agencies invested with the other powers, notably the legislative, which otherwise could make and unmake laws with specific regard to the citizens subject to its power.

A judiciary power, separated from the legislative, in an institutional system that distinguishes the organs exercising these two functions as well as the functions themselves, is, in its autonomy, according to Montesquieu's literal phrasing, a *null* power. The judges act as nothing more than the "bouche de la loi." They do not make the law but merely apply it. The judges should also confine themselves to applying a general and abstract norm to concrete cases without any possibility of modifying, in particular instances, the set definition of crimes and punishment. That

---

[16] On that topic, see Farge and Foucault 1982.
[17] See *The Second Treatise of Government*, secs. 136, 142, 144.

definition remains in the hand of the legislator, who must enact laws without considering any influence they might exert when applied to this or that concrete case.

Characterized in this way, the judiciary power also appears as a sort of neutral power that protects citizens from the legislative while depriving both legislators *and* judges of the possibility of modifying the law in response to concrete cases. The judges become accordingly the guarantee of citizens' equality before the law.

Montesquieu was perfectly aware, however, that the person who judges exercises, in a sense, the most worrying power of all. In daily life it is not the legislator who renders judgment or passes sentence, but the judge. Now, the separation of powers guarantees that the judge will pass judgment only on the basis of a norm of which he is not the author but simply the material executor. The judge protects the citizen from the caprices and arbitrary will of the legislator, just as the existence of the law protects the accused from the caprices and arbitrary will of the judge. All that is the substance of the principle of juridical culture called the independence of the judiciary. If this independence is threatened, there is no longer any protection for citizens confronting the possibly arbitrary will of the legislator. The *Rechtssicherheit* would disappear if the judge could pass his judgment without being bound by the existence and the content of a law. Finally, the essential and unavoidable core of this version of the separation of powers lies in the principle of a strict distinction between those who enact the law and those who pass judgments.[18]

Montesquieu's doctrine represents a preconstitutional form of liberalism. That is, his defense of individual liberty and security against despotism – which, again, means the concentration of the three powers – is upheld without invoking the distinction between ordinary and constitutional laws, a distinction that, in fact, Montesquieu never clearly established.[19] From the perspective of modern constitutionalism, which

[18] I do not need to pause here on the well-known circumstance that the belief in a supposedly automatic application of the law revealed itself to be a myth. The inevitably interpretive character of the jurisdiction has been a noncontroversial tenet of the doctrine since the beginning of the century. It is on the other hand quite odd that such an understanding did not put into question the hierarchical conception of the separation of powers specific to French ideology.

[19] From this point of view, his idea is not different from that of Rousseau. Nonetheless in the absence of a doctrine of "popular sovereignty," it does not necessarily lead to the principle of the supremacy of the legislative over the other powers, a principle that indeed characterizes the *Social Contract* model of the separation of powers. In fact Rousseau's model is more utopian than intrinsically despotic. Because, according to him, the laws *are made by all* and *apply to all*, there is a guarantee for the citizens, a guarantee that disappears in representative government where legislation is the monopoly of parliamentary majorities.

212 *Pasquale Pasquino*

imposed itself with the two revolutions of the late eighteenth century and which represented a new guarantee of individual liberties, a simple parliamentary majority can modify only the so-called ordinary laws, but not the constitutional provisions regulating the exercise of the state powers.[20] The ideology of a *null* power of the judges lies at the very formative inception of the version of the separation of powers that imposed itself on the legal and constitutional culture of the European continent through the French Revolution. That version, in its link with a democratic ideology of a Rousseauian type, produced the first model of the relations between the state organs, which is the object of this section. It can be described by the geometrical form of a pyramid. At the top we find the legislative power, as an expression of the popular sovereignty; lower down, the executive; and, at the bottom, the judiciary power, which, like a sort of machine, limits itself to applying the general norms to the concrete cases on which it has to pass a judgment.

The view that the other state powers are strictly subordinate to the *sovereign* legislative is made explicit in Rousseau's *Social Contract*, which justifies this hierarchy by appealing to the popular character of the legislative power. If the laws are enacted by the popular assembly, the other powers cannot challenge the authority of the popular will, and, although they possess specific functions that the first cannot exercise, they occupy a position of subordination and deference like that of a servant before his master. According to that version, the separation of powers takes the form of a division of labor between those who give orders and those who obey them.[21] In representative governments the legislative power is exercised by the parliamentary majority, which often represents, in the limiting cases where a majoritarian electoral system exists, far less than 50 percent of the electoral body.

Rousseau's argument concerning the separation of powers was adapted to the representative form of government thanks to the peculiar doctrine of the "practical syllogism" associated with Condorcet and especially Kant. "A State [*civitas*] is the union of a certain number of people under juridical laws," Kant wrote.

Every state contains three powers, i.e. the universally united will is made up of three separate persons [*trias politica*]. These are the *ruling power* (or sovereignty)

---

[20] This is true at least for the so-called rigid constitutions (like the U.S., French, and Italian) that fix provisions for constitutional amendments beyond the discretionary power of simple majorities and require the agreement of qualified majorities or/and popular ratification.

[21] One should recall that the same conception was explicitly formulated by Engels: "The division of powers is in fact nothing more than a prosaic division of the industrial labor applied to the State mechanism in order to simplify and to control it"; quoted in de Ruggiero 1988, 198.

The Judiciary and the Italian Constitution 213

in the person of the legislator, the *executive power* in the person of the individual who governs in accordance with the law, and the *judicial power* (which allots to everyone what is his by law) in the person of the judge [*potestas legislatoria, rectoria et iudiciaria*]. They can be likened to the three propositions in a practical operation of reason [*Syllogism*]: the major premise, which contains the *law* of the sovereign will, the minor premise, which contains the *command* to act in accordance with the law (i.e. the principle of subsumption under general will), and the conclusion, which contains the *legal decision* (the sentence) as to the rights and wrongs of each particular case. . . . The three State powers are, also, *firstly* co-ordinated . . . but *secondly* they are also *subordinated* one to the other.[22]

In its vulgar form, the Rousseau-Condorcet-Kant interpretation of the separation of powers claims that the judges may not do "politics" – a claim that is at once vague and specious. To be sure, judges and prosecutors do not sit in the parliament and cannot enact laws. On the other hand, it is rash to say that the judiciary, even in countries with a civil law tradition, does not exercise an increasingly important portion of the power vested in the constitutional state.

To end on this point, it shall be enough to say that the model of the "bouche de la loi," which emerged in response to the arbitrariness of a judiciary power directly exercised by the sovereign, runs the risk of giving temporary majorities an overwhelming power, which may turn into a dangerous threat for the *Rechtssicherheit* and the supremacy of the constitution.

AMBITION COUNTERACTING AMBITION

In the United States, Montesquieu's doctrine produced a strikingly different interpretation and application of the constitutional theory of the separation of powers. As an Italian scholar of comparative constitutional law recently observed: "Only a balanced system of reciprocal checks can combine, without dangers to freedom, a strong legislature with a strong executive and a strong judiciary as well. This balance of powers has been the real secret for the undeniable success of the American Constitution" (Cappelletti 1989, 23). The classical statement of this alternative version of the principle of separation can be found in *Federalist* 47–51, written by James Madison. These five essays are actually a short and dense treatise on the rationale and function of the separation of powers, and their analytical power makes it easy to acknowledge the constitutional genius of Madison. For Madison, the problem of the separation of powers is no longer dominated by the challenge of blunting the threat of monarchical

---

[22] Kant [1797] 1977, 138. Condorcet ([1792] 1847) attributed to the executive the simple function "of making a syllogism of which the law is the major premise, a more or less general case the minor premise, and the conclusion the application of the law."

214 *Pasquale Pasquino*

absolutism;[23] rather, the critical issue is to confront the threat of democracy – that is, the political power of the elected majority.

Madison opened his polemic against the Anti-Federalists, who had criticized the American constitution because of its violation of the separation of powers, with an insightful argument about the proper interpretation of Montesquieu's doctrine.[24] His thesis is well known: separation of powers does not mean a strict or rigid division among the three powers; nor does it demand a hierarchy or a lack of reciprocal checks. On the contrary, it is precisely that technology of reciprocal control among the state powers that seems for Madison to be the core of the liberal principle to which his adversaries referred.[25]

Every political-constitutional doctrine (or ideology) has an enemy or, more precisely, a threat that it seeks to avert. For the model of the "bouche de la loi," that enemy is the power of the judges, especially when they are the same person as the legislator. For the second model, the most dangerous threat is represented by democratic majorities, which may act upon their interests and their momentary passions to the detriment of the freedom of citizens and the authority of the constitution.[26] The "super-legality" of the constitution, its possessing a higher normativity than the ordinary laws enacted by the legislator, should protect it from the passions of the latter. Nonetheless, constitutions may amount to mere "parchment barriers" (a favorite phrase of Madison). It becomes necessary to find a mechanism internal to the constitution itself, capable of guaranteeing its protection from democratic majorities that may be tempted to change the rules of the game whenever they find it convenient to do so.

---

[23] The choice of republican government by the American colonies made that problem much less compelling than it was on the European continent.

[24] "The oracle who is always consulted and cited on this subject [the separation of powers], is the celebrated Montesquieu." Madison, *Federalist* 47, 244.

[25] Actually, Madison did not deny in 1787 the de facto supremacy of the legislative power. That is why he was anxious to establish a balance inside the legislative, attributing it to three distinct organs: the House of Representatives, the Senate, and the president ("But experience assures us, that the efficacy of the provision [to mark with precision the boundaries of these departments in the Constitution] has been greatly over-rated; and that some more adequate defence is indispensably necessary for the more feeble, against the more powerful members of the government. The legislative department is every where extending the sphere of its activity, and drawing all power into its impetuous vortex." *Federalist* 48, 250–1).

[26] In 1925, in the very first years of the fascist government in Italy, Guido de Ruggiero wrote in his *Storia del liberalismo europeo*: "l'onnipotenza della maggioranza è il corollario pratico della democrazia [non liberale] . . . il condensamento di un immenso potere a servizio di una maggioranza spesso fittizia è veramente tirannico . . . anzi, è la più grave e pericolosa forma di dispotismo quella che si origina dalla democrazia . . . e non le minoranze soltanto sono tiranneggiate, ma le maggioranze stesse, la cui effettiva consistenza sociale è ben diversa da ciò che figura col loro nome sulla scena politica" (1971, 362).

The Judiciary and the Italian Constitution

From *The Federalist* onward, the central challenge confronting modern constitutionalism was to develop a set of rules for the exercise of state powers that would prove capable of enforcing the superlegality of the constitution to the greatest extent possible.

We know that the solution provided by the U.S. Constitution, which Madison defended during the public debate over its ratification, is what we have ever since called the system of checks and balances. It is pointless to try to sum up Madison's analysis, which is one of the masterpieces of constitutional literature. I will simply quote the salient steps of his argument:

It is agreed in all sides, that the powers properly belonging to one of the departments, ought not to be directly and completely administered by either of the other departments. It is equally evident, that neither of them ought to possess directly or indirectly, an overruling influence over the others in the administration of their respective powers. It will not be denied, that *power is of an encroaching nature*, and that it ought to be effectually restrained from passing the limits assigned to it.

From this formulation, Madison immediately concluded that "the next and most difficult task is to provide some practical security for each against the invasion of the others."[27] To imagine that the legislature would have a natural incentive to maintain the proper separation was a delusion. In support of this proposition, Madison invoked the authority of Thomas Jefferson, who had addressed the problem of legislative overreaching in an important passage of his *Notes on the State of Virginia*. After restating Montesquieu's definition of tyranny as the consolidation of all power "in the same hands," Jefferson had gone on to observe that

173 despots would surely be as oppressive as one. . . . As little will it avail us that they are chosen by ourselves. An *elective despotism*, was not the government we fought for; but one which should not only be founded on free principles, but in which the powers of government should be so divided and balanced among several bodies of magistracy, as that no one could transcend their legal limits, without being effectually checked and restrained by the others.[28]

Because the mere constitutional definition of the role of the three powers will not be enough to guarantee the citizens against the ever possible violation of the limits fixed for each of them, resort must be made to a self-enforcing mechanism capable of maintaining the equilibrium of powers and the basic design of the Constitution.[29]

---

[27] *Federalist* 48, 250 (emphasis added).

[28] Ibid., 252; here Madison is quoting Jefferson.

[29] *Federalist* 49, 258: "We found in the last paper that mere declarations in the written constitution, are not sufficient to restrain the several departments within their legal limits."

216   *Pasquale Pasquino*

The only answer that can be given [Madison concluded], is, that as all these exterior provisions are found to be inadequate, the defect must be supplied, by so contriving the interior structure of the government, as that its several constituent parts may, by their mutual relations, be the means of keeping each other in their proper places. . . . But the great security against a gradual concentration of the several powers in the same department, consists in giving to those who administer each department, the *necessary constitutional means, and personal motives, to resist encroachments of the others.* The provision for defense must in this, as in all other cases, be made commensurate to the danger of attack. *Ambition must be made to counteract ambition. . . .* It may be a reflection on human nature, that such devices should be necessary to controul the abuses of government. But what is government itself but the greatest of all reflections on human nature? If men were angels, no government would be necessary. If angels were to govern men, neither external nor internal controuls on government would be necessary. In framing a government which is to be administered by men over men, the great difficulty lies in this: you must first enable the government to control the governed; and in the next place oblige it to control itself.[30]

The model of separation of powers that Madison suggested in those pages is quite different from the practical syllogism that we considered earlier. "In a society under the forms of which the stronger faction can readily unite and oppress the weaker, anarchy may as truly be said to reign."[31] Anarchy and despotism became the common enemies of freedom. The U.S. Constitution deploys several instruments to prevent democratic majorities from imposing their will against the constitutional provisions. The federal structure,[32] a differentiated bicameral system, the presidential veto on the bills of the Congress, and, finally, the judicial review of legislation all play their parts in maintaining the equilibrium of the constitution.

In *Federalist* 78, another well-known essay, Madison's coauthor Alexander Hamilton observed (after again invoking Montesquieu) that "Liberty can have nothing to fear from the judiciary alone." In fact, Hamilton continued, the contrary is true: "from the natural feebleness of the judiciary, it is in continual jeopardy of being overpowered, awed or influenced by its co-ordinate branches [the legislative and executive]."[33] This remark deserves special stress if we consider that in French (and continental) constitutional culture, the rigid and hierarchical view of the

---

[30] *Federalist* 51, 261–2 (emphasis added).
[31] Ibid., 265.
[32] Ibid., 264: "In the compound republic of America, the power surrendered by the people, is first divided between two distinct governments, and then the portion allotted to each, subdivided among distinct and separate departments."
[33] *Federalist* 78, 394.

separation of powers ended with the attribution of a subordinate role to the judiciary power.[34]

Having reviewed these two basic conceptions of the liberal doctrine of separated powers, I now propose to turn to a third case of pressing contemporary interest, that of modern Italian constitutionalism, which fits neither model.

THE INDEPENDENCE OF MAGISTRATURE IN THE ITALIAN CONSTITUTION

The Constituent Assembly elected in Italy in 1946 following the fall of fascism chose for the republic a peculiar version of the classical doctrine of separation of powers in which the relation between the judiciary power, on one side, and the legislative and executive, on the other, has characteristics significantly different from both of the great constitutional traditions that I have just sketched. This peculiarity has recently become the object of much criticism.[35] Before expressing a judgment, it will be necessary to briefly recount the debates of the Constituent Assembly in order to grasp the meaning and the spirit of this third model.

The discussion concerning the judiciary power took place essentially in the second subcommission of the constitutional committee where the jurist Piero Calamandrei, a member of the small *Partito d'Azione*,[36] played an extremely important role. From his interventions in these debates, it is possible to derive some of the principles that influenced the decisions of the Constituent Assembly. First of all, Calamandrei favored a *nonhierarchical* view of the three powers and notably "the need to put that power

---

[34] See Cappelletti 1989, 194. It is self-evident that this dramatically short presentation of the American constitutional doctrine has no pretension to be a description of the concrete working of the separation of powers and of the judiciary in the American society. My point here is to consider and compare ideologies and models with the hope that it will help us to understand how they redescribe reality. It is worth noticing that in France too, where the judiciary has no strong autonomy and is in part under the control of the executive power, during the last few years the prosecutors have started to lead investigations against politicians despite governmental pressures. See, e.g., "Le réveil des juges," *Le Monde*, October 20, 1994, and Bredin 1994.

[35] The violent polemic against the Italian judiciary was one of the main preoccupations of the defunct, so-called Socialist Party of B. Craxi. The same job has been taken over more recently by Berlusconi and his movement, Forza Italia. In the academic discussion, see notably the conclusion of Guarnieri 1992, 149–62. More recently Guarnieri published with P. Pederzoli a new, less critical book in France (1996).

[36] This party, which did not survive the electoral competitions after the Second World War, gathered together, after the downfall of the fascist regime, the Italian non-Marxist liberal elite (e.g., N. Bobbio, F. Venturi, a.s.o.).

218   *Pasquale Pasquino*

[the judiciary] *on the same level as the other two.*"[37] Second, Calamandrei stressed that the judiciary power should be regarded as "an integral part of sovereignty, which consists of the sum of the three powers."[38] Third, on the crucial question of the recruitment of the members of the judiciary body, Calamandrei supported the "competitive examination" (*concorso*), rather than the elective system for the appointment of the magistrates, because the latter "either did not give good results, or turned (as had been the case in Switzerland) into a constant renewal of the magistrates elected the first time."[39] Under the latter system, one could add, the magistrates appeared to be far more concerned with their reelection than with the administration of justice.

These cursory observations allow us to provide an outline of the Italian constitutional model as it relates to the place of the judiciary in the separation of powers. Its peculiarity consists in establishing a system that eschews the American doctrine of *checks and balances* while simultaneously rejecting the French view of the subordination of judges to the other powers. It is, in fact, a model that implies a strong independence of the magistrature where the judges are subordinated only to the law (a fundamental principle of *Rechtstaat*, and a guarantee of the limitation of the judiciary),[40] but which also establishes the full autonomy of a self-governing power (through the Superior Council of the Magistrature [Consiglio Superiore della Magistratura]) that operates independently of the influence of the executive. Compared with the two models of the "bouche de la loi" and "ambition counteracting ambition," the Italian model appears as a mixed form because it relies neither on the pattern of intervention among the supreme organs of the state, as in *The Federalist*, nor on the ideology of absolute supremacy of the legislative, based on the preeminence of the elected organs. The three state powers are coessential parts of sovereignty,[41] or, to speak the metaphysical language of constitu-

---

[37] *La Costituzione della Repubblica* 1971, 8: 1913: "[Calamandrei] Remarks first of all that in the phrasing proposed by Castiglia the latter spoke of judiciary *functions*. He claims on the contrary that the committee seemed to agree on the expression 'judiciary *power*' ... because of the necessity to put that power *on the same level as the two others*" (translated by the author).

[38] Ibid., 1914: "Remarks that the expression 'emanates' [a previous draft proposed the phrasing "The judiciary power emanates directly from the State sovereignty"] seems to him formally improper, and moreover substantially it could lead to the belief that the sovereignty and the judiciary power are two distinct things. On the contrary, the latter is properly part of sovereignty which consists in the sum of the three powers." (The second reporter, Giovanni Leone (Christian democrat), agreed on that remark; see p. 1914).

[39] Ibid., 1892.

[40] Para. 2 of Art. 101 of the Constitution says "Judges are subject only to the law."

[41] This thesis is not accepted by some authors. In the *Commentario della Costituzione*, concerning the Articles 104–7 (Branca 1986, 6), F. Bonifacio and G. Giacobbe claim that "the

tional doctrine, they stand on their own feet as guarantors of the constitutional order. The independence of the magistrature, which includes judges *and* prosecutors,[42] plays the role of a barrier and of a *negative* check on the two other powers.

The Italian model has another characteristic that, up to a point, makes it resemble the American one. The judges always have the option of referring cases to the Constitutional Court any time they have to apply a law that seems to them to contradict the constitution. On this basis, it is sensible to claim that the judge, subordinated to the law in the first instance, is bound eventually only by his loyalty to the constitution.[43] It is also possible to maintain that the judiciary in Italy participates in the control of the legislative power, control that is the specific function of the Constitutional Court, in a way that is simply not imaginable under the French model of judicial subordination. If we consider that the ordinary judge can set in motion a procedure that ends with a decision of the Constitutional Court, one can hardly claim that the judge is in a position of mere subordination to the will of the parliamentary majority. The wisdom of the Italian Constituent Assembly circumscribed the will of the legislature with several checks,[44] establishing a judiciary power whose strong autonomy now appears quite important during an extremely difficult period of transition in Italian political and constitutional life.

The Italian Constitution was drafted after the Second World War and the Resistance by the Christian Democrats and the Communists,[45] whose

character of sovereignty may and has to be recognized in the acts of legislation; on the other hand the same character cannot be attributed to jurisdictional activity, that, as we already noticed, is only an *indirect* exercise of sovereignty and cannot be defined in itself as sovereign." Now, if it is true that the judge's sentence is subordinate to the law, it is also true that legislation is subordinate to the Constitution and to judicial review by the Constitutional Court.

[42] "The Italian judiciary is organized along lines radically dissimilar to those followed in common law systems. The principle of separation of powers is pushed toward its logical conclusion: the judiciary is not only a separate but also an autonomous branch of government. Judges are appointed, promoted, and supervised by judges. Moreover, the judicial function is deemed to be fundamentally distinct from advocacy; consequently, a judgeship is not the culmination of an advocate's career but a post to be earned by apprenticeship within the judiciary. And in Italy it is the impartial judge, not the fiercy advocate, who is chosen to carry out the prosecutorial function" (Cappelletti, Merryman, and Perillo 1967, 102). Concerning the organization of the judiciary power in Italy, see Pizzorusso 1990.

[43] On that question and from a comparative point of view, see Cappelletti 1979, 97–99; 1971.

[44] According to the Constitution, Art. 87, para. 5, a law cannot be promulgated without the agreement of the president of the Republic.

[45] The text of the Constitution was signed by the Communist Umberto Terracini and the Christian Democrat Alcide De Gasperi.

common will was to avoid a civil war in the aftermath of the destruction of the fascist regime. The two parties agreed on the fundamental choice of a liberal-democratic institutional regime, based on the electoral principle, separation of powers, and the preeminence of the Constitution. The primary political task of the new republic was to guarantee peace and stability in the country (without raising the question of Italian membership in the Western military, political, and economic bloc). The proportional electoral system, without being formally incorporated in the Constitution, was nonetheless also an important element in the postwar political order. After the Christian Democratic victory in the elections of 1948, this electoral system worked reasonably well as an instrument of political integration, allowing citizens of radically different political beliefs to feel themselves members of the same polity. The guarantees provided by proportional representation thus helped to prevent existing political and social conflicts from deteriorating into more ominous forms of conflict.[46]

Over time, however, the initially positive effects of these postwar decisions evolved into a working political system from which Italy is now trying to escape. The inescapable need in the first years of the republic to avoid disruptive conflicts between Communists and moderates gave rise to that form of organizing public life which has recently been called "consociativism" (Pizzorno 1993). By this term I mean a political system where the majority does not impose its will on the minority but tries to secure its agreement, or, in the absence of an agreement, its acceptance of the status quo. In a very divided society this attitude may prove useful to avoiding disruptive conflicts; in a more homogeneous society, such as Italy nowadays, it ends by making it virtually impossible to seek any significant political decision. In fact, one cannot deny that the system of proportional representation also played the role of protecting the constitution from the power of the majority. In my view, "consociativism" has simultaneously operated both as a mechanism for the hidden distribution of political power and as a constitutional check. Contrary to the opinion held by many Italians and even many political scientists, the arrangements of consociativism worked as a defense of the constitution in a country characterized by a weak liberal culture. However, it is no less true that "consociativism" contributed to an increased level of bribery and corruption within the Italian political class.[47]

---

[46] The proportional electoral system, despite various flaws, has under certain circumstances the advantage of defusing social conflicts by moving them into the sphere of political representation where compromises are easier to achieve (either openly or secretly).

[47] Among the numerous analyses on that topic, see Della Porta 1992, including the introduction by A. Pizzorno.

Then, quite suddenly, this apparently overly stable political regime collapsed with the dramatic events of the mid-1990s. The two critical events were the introduction of an electoral system largely structured on a majority basis which was imposed on the Parliament by popular referendum in 1993, followed by the splitting of the Christian Democratic Party, which had represented the moderate-conservative center of the electoral spectrum for the half century since the end of the Second World War. These and other changes that cannot be described here radically modified the Italian political and institutional landscape. Italy is moving slowly toward a bipolar party system which may mark the end of exorbitant power of political parties (*partitocrazia*), manifested in the repeated negotiations required to form new governments, but which urgently raises the question of new checks on the power of majorities.

In a country like Italy, with a very weak liberal tradition, the strong political majorities that the new electoral system may well create represent a potential threat to the constitutional foundations of the *Rechtstaat*. A return to the old system of proportional representation seems out of the question. It is likely that a conservative majority, should it emerge from future elections, will try to discredit the constitutional function of the non-elected organs of the magistrature and the Constitutional Court, insofar as the latter might limit its political will.[48]

In fact, two rival views of a democratic political system are now in conflict in Italy. On one side, we find a sort of populist version of the Westminster model, where the winners of political elections would have something like an unchecked power, concentrating in their hands the legislative and the executive, subordinating the judiciary, and attempting to destroy the legitimacy of the Constitutional Court. On the other side, the few true liberals and some of the social democrats will try to defend a moderate constitutional regime where the nonelected organs will retain the capacity to balance the democratically elected elements of the constitutional system.

REFERENCES

Böckenförde, E.-W. 1991. "Demokratie und Repraesentation. Zur Kritik der heutigen Demokratiediskussion." In *Staat, Verfassung, Demokratie*, 379–405. Frankfurt am Main: Suhrkamp.

Bognetti, G. 1994. *La divisione dei poteri*. Milan: Giuffrè.

Branca, G., ed. 1986. *Commentario della Costituzione*. Bologna: Zanichelli – Roma, Il Foro italiano.

---

[48] The very recent constitutional amendment (passed in November 1999) with the approval of 90 percent of the Parliament represents very likely, notwithstanding the etiquette of "due process" (*giusto processo*), an attempt by the political class to limit the power of the judiciary in the prosecution of (political) crimes.

Bredin, J.-D. 1994. "Un gouvernement des juges?" *Pouvoirs* 68.

Cappelletti, M. 1971. *Judicial Review in Contemporary World*. Indianapolis: Bobbs-Merill.

1979. *Il controllo giudiziario di constituzionalità delle leggi nel diritto comparato*. Milan: Giuffrè.

1989. *The Judicial Process in Comparative Perspective*. Oxford: Clarendon Press.

Cappelletti, M., J. H. Merryman, and J. M. Perillo. 1967. *The Italian System*. Stanford: Stanford University Press.

Chantraine, P. 1968. *Dictionnaire étymologique de la langue greque*. Paris: Keincksieck.

Condorcet, Jean-Antoine-Nicolas de Caritat Marquis de. [1792] 1847. "De la nature des pouvoirs politiques dans une nation libre." In *Ouevres*, 10: 595. Paris: Firmin Didot.

Crouzet, D. 1990. *Les guerriers de Dieu. La violence au temps des troubles de religion (vers 1525–vers 1610)*. Seyssel: Champ Vallon.

de Ruggero, G. [1925] 1971. *Storia del liberalismo europeo*. Milan: Feltrinelli.

de Ruggero, L. 1988. "La legittimazione del portere del giudice oggi in Italia." In Marianna Li Calzi, ed., *Question giustizia oggi*. Caltanissetta-Roma: S. Sciascia.

Della Porta, D. 1992. *Lo scambio occulto*. Bologna: Il Mulino.

Farge, A., and M. Foucault. 1982. *Le désorde des familles. Lettres de cachet des Archives de la Bastille*. Paris: Gallimard.

Guarnieri, C. 1992. *Magistratura e politica in Italia*. Bologna: Il Mulino.

Guarnieri, C., and P. Pederzoli. 1996. *La puissance de juger. Pouvoir judiciaire et démocratie*. Paris: Editions Michalon.

Kant, I. [1797] 1977. *Metaphysics of Morals*. In H. Reiss, ed., *Political Writings*. Cambridge: Cambridge University Press.

La Costituzione della Repubblica nei lavori preparatori della Assemblea Costituente. 1971. Rome: Camera dei desputati.

Locke, J. 1970. *Two Treatises of Government*. Ed. P. Laslett. Cambridge: Cambridge University Press.

Madison. J. 1982. *The Federalist Papers*. New York: Bantam Books.

Manin, B. 1994. "Checks, Balances and Boundaries: The Separation of Powers in the Constitutional Debate of 1787." In B. Fontana, ed. *The Invention of the Modern Republic*, 27–62. Cambridge: Cambridge University Press.

1995. *Les principes du gouvernement représentatif*. Paris: Calmann-Lévy.

Pasquino, P. 1990. "La théorie de la balance du législatif du premier Comité de constitution [1789]." In F. Furet et M. Ozouf, eds., *Terminer la Révolution. Mounier et Barnave dans la Révolution française*, 67–89. Grenoble: PUG.

1994. "The Constitutional Republicanism of Emmanuel Sieyes." In B. Fontana, ed., *The Invention of the Modern Republicanism*, 107–17. Cambridge: Cambridge University Press.

Pizzorusso, A. 1990. *L'organizzazione della guistizia in Italia*. Turin: Einaudi.

Rousseau, J. [1762] 1986. *Du contrat social*. Paris: Maynard.

7

A Political Theory of Federalism

*Jenna Bednar, William N. Eskridge Jr.,
and John Ferejohn*

Multiethnic nations (South Africa, Russia, Nigeria, Rwanda, the former Yugoslavia, to name a few) have sometimes found decentralized political arrangements attractive. Such arrangements – as long as they last – permit peoples who may differ greatly in their conceptions of a good public life to develop and maintain their own separate communities, within the context of a larger and more powerful political economy.[1] Ethnically more homogeneous nations such as the United States, at the time of its founding, or Australia today, often find decentralized modes of policy formation and administration convenient as well. In such nations, geographic distances, diverse economies, regional disparities in preferences, and variations in local historical experience can make decentralized policy-making institutions more efficient and more responsive than national ones.

The advantages of decentralization are realizable, however, only if there are good reasons for the players – ordinary citizens as well as regional and central governments – to believe that others will generally abide by the terms of the federation. That is, all must believe that the regional governments will not try to take advantage of one another and that the center will not try to usurp power from the regions. Without such assurance, frequent disputes and suspicion of foul play would reduce the participants' enthusiasm for the federation, possibly motivating some participating governments to withdraw from the federation altogether. Decentralized

---

The authors gratefully acknowledge support from Stanford's Institute for International Studies and particularly to the George P. Shultz Fund for Canadian Studies. We thank Christopher Eisgruber, Larry Kramer, and Larry Sager for their generous comments without, of course, blaming any of them for any errors we failed to correct.

[1] This view of decentralization parallels the economist's conception in which the value of federal arrangements is that it permits subnational communities to decide autonomously what the mix of public goods and taxes shall be, so that citizens may then sort themselves into jurisdictions whose mixes they find attractive. In both views, it is important that the autonomy of local governments be preserved.

224   *Bednar, Eskridge, and Ferejohn*

political institutions must somehow induce participants to believe that all others will abide by the federation's terms and to act accordingly, by complying as well. That is to say, decentralization, if it is to work, must be credible, an ideal that has proved elusive at times in each of the nations mentioned, each having experienced periods of instability.

Federalism, the division of sovereign authority among levels of government, can be seen as a way of stabilizing, or making credible, decentralized governmental structures. The federal solution, however, is not without its own problems. It is not obvious, for example, that the division of sovereignty is actually possible. Some conceptions of government hold sovereignty to be necessarily unitary; a divided sovereign is, on these accounts, several separate states.[2] Whatever the truth of this theoretical claim, the important question for our chapter is whether practical federal arrangements can sufficiently insulate governmental decisions at all levels to maintain a stable and credible decentralized political structure.

From our viewpoint, then, federalism is at once an attractive and problematic governmental structure.[3] By dividing sovereign authority between a supreme national government and semiautonomous provincial governments,[4] federal arrangements promise to secure the advantages of decentralization. But many federal arrangements (most dramatically, those in Yugoslavia or the antebellum United States) have collapsed in the face of centrifugal forces when provincial entities decided that the benefits of membership in the federation were not worth the cost, in terms of

[2] The idea that federalism is intrinsically unstable can be traced to a Hobbesian conception of the state, according to which sovereignty must ultimately be indivisible. When superficial appearances are stripped away, on this view, federal governments are basically either centralized or are mere alliances of separate states. From this perspective, federal institutions are doomed to succumb either to centrifugal or centripetal forces. However, Hobbes's identification of sovereignty with the "ultimate" location of authority can be misleading, if the conditions under which that location can be reached are sufficiently improbable. Moreover, his focus on the state actors as opposed to the individual officials who act for the state fails to take account of the actual strategic structure of federal systems.

[3] We leave aside, for the present, the ways in which federal arrangements are often normatively problematic, in particular when such arrangements cut against the realization of equality norms.

[4] We use the term "federalism" to denote a state broken up into provinces. Governmental powers are divided between the two levels, with some shared between the two levels, and in at least one domain each level of government is the final authority. With this definition we follow a precedent established by William Riker (1964). Morton Grodzins's (1964) depiction of American federalism as a marbled cake rather than a stratified layer cake is an expression of the fragility of classical federal ideals within American history. Power within the American system is not neatly stratified into federal and state jurisdictions but is shared and overlapping in distinct policy subsystems. Our analysis suggests that, because of the peculiar period in which he wrote, perhaps the high-water mark of centralized federalism in the United States, we think his conclusions were somewhat overstated.

economic health, security, or regional autonomy. Conversely, in some putative federations, decision making has become so concentrated at the center that the provincial governments come to resemble administrative extensions of the central government, rather than autonomous governments.[5] Indeed the apparent success of the American federalism has often been debunked in these terms by those who see national power, at least since the New Deal, as excessively concentrated in Washington (Van Alstyne 1985; Riker 1964).

Elsewhere, two of us have argued that American federalism is not yet dead and that the exercise of state and local power in American federalism has remained robust in the face of profound legal-constitutional transformations (Eskridge and Ferejohn 1994). Indeed, recent developments in the states as well as in the Supreme Court point to continued viability of states as political competitors for authority.[6] While there have been continual adjustments in the legal and constitutional authority of states and of the national government within specific policy areas, the allocation of actual decision-making authority in American federalism seems relatively stable. This feature of U.S. federalism is puzzling in light of the apparently opposite phenomenon in Canada, where for the past two generations aggressive regional interests have attempted to secure more regional autonomy. The failure to win such autonomy has evidently led many Canadians to prefer to divide into separate states rather than to continue their own federal experiment. This difference is particularly notable because in many other respects, American and Canadian societies are similar. Thus, the development of separatist regionalism, which imperils Canadian federalism, and its absence in the United States need some explanation.[7]

The contrast between resilient American federalism and Canada's apparently less stable federal politics inspires the current project, which examines federalist experiments in different Anglo-American countries: Great Britain, the United States, and Canada. Our inquiry is aimed at identifying conditions necessary for federalism to flourish. Our central

---

[5] The connection, if any, between sovereignty and autonomy will not be addressed here. It is not at all clear that the sovereignty of an impoverished Third World nation is any guarantee of its autonomy as a locus of authoritative decisions.

[6] We should also note that the responses of the Senate and president to initiatives enlarging the domain of state authority suggest that the powers of the national government within the federal system remain formidable as well.

[7] This puzzle exists despite the reality of recent efforts to devolve more authority to the American states, especially with respect to welfare policy. These efforts are not, however, based on claims of deep regional difference among states but on a belief that such policies would be better administered at a level nearer the people (taxpayers or beneficiaries). Such efforts are, moreover, statutory and involve no constitutional guarantee of decision-making autonomy. Only a political naif would see in such efforts a realistic prospect of eliminating the congressional role in welfare policy.

thesis is that durable federal arrangements are possible only if two conditions hold. First, national forces must be structurally restrained from infringing on the federal bargain. Second, provincial temptations to renege on federal arrangements must be checked as well, possibly by the application of legal rules enforced by an independent judiciary.[8] This too is only a necessary condition and is no guarantee of the emergence or stability of federal arrangements. We do not offer a prescription of what form these structural restraints actually take and imagine that they may be institutionally embodied in many different ways. What is important, however, is that everyone has good reason to believe that the terms of federal bargain may be reasonably relied upon. In the United States, except for the period prior to the Civil War and for a short period thereafter – roughly, 1840 through 1877 – both conditions have usually been present since the time of founding (although they have exhibited some local variation). Indeed the failure of these conditions to hold during this crucial "middle period" of American political life helps to explain both the shape of the rebellion and reintegration of the southern states during this period. We think that achieving structural guarantees of the kind described here has contributed substantially to the success of the American federal experience and is a key to the development of effective federal arrangements more generally.[9]

CREDIBLE DECENTRALIZATION: THE ADVANTAGES OF FEDERALISM

Decentralized governmental structures offer many advantages over more unified forms. Rational choice theories of politics explain why a decentralized system would best satisfy popular preferences in a polity containing heterogeneous individual preferences.[10] Borrowing from Charles Tiebout and Gordon Tullock, one can suppose that if sixty citizens in a centralized polity prefer policy "A" and forty prefer policy "not-A," the polity will adopt policy A, but with forty dissatisfied citizens (provided

---

[8] The use of judicial checks on the provinces is probably only one method of restraining them. The provinces might themselves develop fragmented systems of power that prevent them from opportunistic behavior. Although such a system might be possible, it seems hard to believe that every province will be sufficiently restrained over the long run, to solve the credibility problem. Structural devices are possible to restrain the provinces, although they are not as likely to be successful, for reasons we discuss in note 15.

[9] We are tempted to argue that the presence of both necessary conditions is sufficient for a stable federalism but cannot do so without a more systematic examination of the full range of empirical cases.

[10] Early works of great consequence include Buchanan and Tullock 1962; Hirschman 1970; Tiebout 1956; and Tullock 1969. Important recent works include Ostrom 1991; Oates 1972; Peterson 1981; 1995; and Trebilcock 1983.

that the practice of A in one region is compatible with not-A nearby). A decentralized polity will usually end up with fewer dissatisfied citizens. For example, where fifty citizens in the first province favor policy A while ten oppose it, and thirty citizens in a second province favor non-A with ten favoring A, each province can adopt different policies, leaving only twenty (rather than forty) dissatisfied citizens. If there is mobility within the polity, citizens can move between the two provinces, and even greater satisfaction is achieved under the decentralized arrangement.

As long as migration is relatively easy, its possibility contributes to greater citizen satisfaction, but also limits the range of tax-service packages that can be offered by provincial rather than national units. Provinces would, for example, be restrained from engaging in extensive wealth redistributions. Programs with such effects would locate at the national level, if indeed they exist at all.[11] The national government would also be better suited to provide services and regulatory regimes where collective action problems (the free-rider problem and the race to the bottom) militate against optimal policies at the state level.

The political economy of decentralization may be understood either normatively or positively. As a normative theory it counsels the adoption of policy formation processes that take advantage of scale economies and permit citizens to sort themselves among jurisdictions according to their tastes for public services. Decentralization permits the allocation of decision-making authority to take account of the economic characteristics of the goods and services being produced. It permits the choice of governmental units capable of internalizing externalities in service provision and recognizes that this usually entails having different units provide each good or service and that taxation be organized at the national level (to ensure that allocational decisions are not tax-induced).

As a positive or predictive theory the political economy of decentralization foresees jurisdictions arising in a manner that responds to technical production and distribution characteristics of the particular public services in question. One would expect the temporary emergence of special districts, each dedicated to producing one kind of public service, and each shifting its size and structure as technical conditions changed. Which jurisdictions actually emerged would depend on contingent technological and population characteristics. One would also expect to see a degree of flux in governmental units as technologies and tastes varied over time. In

---

[11] Attempts to implement programs at the provincial level would trigger "races to the bottom" in which the redistributive elements of the programs effectively disappear. See Peterson 1981. To the extent that the global economy is becoming increasingly interconnected, and movements between countries more like movements between provinces, redistributive programs will be increasingly harmful at the national level as well. See Peterson 1995.

228 *Bednar, Eskridge, and Ferejohn*

establishing jurisdictions, however, the framers of a decentralized arrangement might well reflect linguistic and ethnic differences insofar as these differences affect economic or political transactions costs. It may turn out, therefore, that for some nations, ethnically based jurisdictions will be employed in order to economize on these costs.

These arguments apply directly to multiethnic situations. Decentralized institutional arrangements make it possible for German, French, and Italian citizens of Switzerland to enjoy the benefits of nationally provided services and a common market and, at the same time, to live in relatively homogeneous communities. This kind of self-sorting permits individuals and families to make locational decisions based on considerations of ethnic or linguistic identity as well as economic prospects. Insofar as ethnic identity carries with it preference-related content, such sorting supports the provision of characteristic cultural goods and services associated with various ways of life. Indeed, decentralized institutions might be most valuable in multiethnic states. The reason is not that policy preferences are likely to be more diverse in such states, but that some policy preferences are likely to be bound up with deeply felt identities. If people place a sub-stantial enough weight on ethnic or linguistic identity, it is more likely there will be a relatively stable institutional structure based on these iden-tities. The ethnic communities may not be the optimal scale to provide certain services but they may provide a sufficient improvement over more national arrangements so that they have some sticking power. Multiethnic states may therefore be able to approach the generic incentive problems of decentralization in a distinctively productive way.

Although political-economic theories of decentralization show how improvement over centralized regimes is conceivable as well as beneficial, they ignore a central practical difficulty with constructing and maintain-ing regimes of this sort. That is, the constituted agents of a decentralized regime, the national and subnational governments, will have strong incen-tives and many opportunities to cheat on the arrangement (Bednar and Eskridge 1995; Peterson 1995). The national government is constantly tempted to increase its own power relative to the provinces and to shift to the provinces some of the costs of national programs. The provinces, in turn, have incentives to push costs off onto neighboring states as well as to trespass on national values. Cheating in these ways not only undermines the advantages of the decentralized arrangement but also threatens the viability of the state itself, by inducing the constituent governments to engage in defensive activities aimed at protecting their decisional spheres. These dangers seem especially keen in multiethnic polities.[12] Anticipation

---

[12] The fact that a politics of "identity" is involved in such states makes the stakes of oppor-tunistic behavior higher than they would otherwise be. That it is a province dominated by

A Political Theory of Federalism

of such failure may make the benefits of decentralization politically unavailable at the outset: regions, tribes, or states, acting rationally, will refuse to enter into a federal arrangement if they believe that there is no credible machinery for enforcing it.[13]

Yet rational choice theories of institutions have persuasively maintained that constitutional procedure and structure can limit the collective harms caused by individually rational behavior. The enterprise of this chapter is to consider what constitutional designs might be expected to alleviate the durability problems inherent in decentralized institutional structures. Initially, we suggest theoretical solutions to the problem, then hone as well as illustrate the theory by considering its explanatory value in three different national contexts: Great Britain after 1690; Canada after 1867; and the United States after 1789.

THE FEDERAL SOLUTION

Genuinely federal institutions must be credibly robust against both national and provincial aggrandizements of power. That is to say, federal arrangements must represent a commitment by the parties generally to refrain from trespassing on the rights of their federal partners. How might this commitment problem be solved or managed? The obvious way to manage this problem is to enlist independent courts to force both the states and the national government to respect jurisdictional boundaries. But it has always been difficult to convince skeptics that courts can be made sufficiently independent to provide robust guarantees of such institutional boundaries. Indeed, insofar as courts are institutionally dependent on other national bodies, they tend to be seen as creatures of the national government with little real authority to check its powers on important matters. And, if national courts are not created, state courts would be vulnerable to an analogous suspicion. For this reason we think that judicially enforced federalism, by itself, is probably unworkable.[14]

---

members of a rival ethnic group that is dumping costs onto a neighboring area may add heat to resentment and dispute. Conversely, the fact that identity politics makes the stakes high may permit the establishment of credible restraints on opportunistic behavior that would not generally be available. The fact that otherwise mundane disputes might escalate into deeply felt grievances and be implicated in tragic histories may restrain participants from careless infringements on the claims of their neighbors. The examples that come to mind most easily are, of course, cases in which these restraints failed – in Lebanon, Northern Ireland, Somalia, Yugoslavia, etc. – but successful cases, or, better, successful periods of time, must be much more frequent.

[13] One of us has called the foregoing dilemma the "Federal Problem" – a durability problem that all federal arrangements face. See Bednar 1998a. In another publication, two of us described it as a "commitment problem." Bednar and Eskridge 1995.

[14] The Anti-Federalist Brutus offered another criticism of such a system. In his view national courts were probably completely uncontrollable, and the U.S. Constitution essentially

A better way to address the issue operates at two formally and functionally different levels. Opportunism by the national government is best constrained by fragmenting power at the national level. By making it harder for a national will to form and be sustained over time, these mechanisms will tend to disable national authorities from invading state authority, especially as to controversial political issues (the most tempting target for national cheating on the federal arrangement).[15] The foregoing fragmentation may be accomplished through a formal system of separation of powers and extra requirements (such as bicameral approval and presentment to the chief executive for veto) for legislation; these mechanisms require the cooperation of different institutions, accountable to different constituencies, before significant policy shifts can be made. Fragmentation may also be achieved through an electoral system that limits the capacity of political parties to coalesce. However it occurs, fragmentation of national power inhibits national incursions on state powers, but it also undermines the ability of the national government to regulate state cheating on the federal arrangement. For this reason opportunism by state governments is better constrained by the operation of an independent national judiciary. Federal courts are well situated to monitor local advantage taking, in part because they can act immediately and decisively when outsider interests blow the whistle on state rent seeking and cost shifting, and in part because they are relatively immune from local (as opposed to national) political pressures in the long- as well as short-term. It is in the rational self-interest of federal judges to enforce federalism rules vigorously against state and local cheating, because such enforcement confirms the arbitral, and perhaps policy-making, power of judges without big institutional risks if judges make poor political judgments.

Within a system of separated powers at the national level, decentralization might be implemented by any or a combination of three distinct modalities. The first is *rules*: the actions of national and provincial authorities are formally restricted by judicially enforceable legal rules.

created a system of government by courts. If Brutus is right about this – if neither the national nor state governments can threaten judicial independence – then judicial federalism might be more workable than we argue. In order for judicially maintained federalism to work, the courts must be adequately motivated to draw and enforce federal boundaries, however.

[15] Note that while fragmentation is effective at the national level, it probably cannot be counted on to provide insurance against opportunistic behavior at any subnational level. This is essentially the point that Madison made in *Federalist* 10. Smaller governments are more susceptible to majoritarian capture that can overwhelm internal checks. Furthermore, the national government comprises the provincial interests; each region is represented at the national level. However, no region contains representatives from the other regions or the national level; the success of fragmentation depends on conflicting interests on the federalism question, a condition that fails at the regional level.

A Political Theory of Federalism

Alternatively, decentralized practices may be enforced by a system of informal *norms* where, in place of explicit rules, the various parties understand themselves as obligated to stay within certain zones of activity, whether or not such zones are enforceable by legal institutions.[16] Finally, federal promises might be redeemed by a self-enforcing structure of *incentives* in which the various actors stay within their respective zones of action as a matter of political prudence. Such a structure of incentives could, in turn, support a pattern of practice among the various governments motivated by considerations of power or material interest. For decentralization to be a credible solution to political problems, it must somehow be supported as an equilibrium in one of these three ways. The first two methods involve reliance on a rule of law to enforce decentralized practices, either through explicit rule enforcement or compliance with normative expectations. The last involves the balancing of political opportunities and incentives to stabilize decentralized administration.

Juridical Federalism

The adoption of federalist juridical rules offers one way to enforce the boundaries between national and provincial authority. Juridically, federal governments characteristically distribute decision-making powers among some of its subunits, either through explicit constitutional provision or through the evolution of legal conventions that have the same effect.[17] The possession of some sovereignty powers permits subordinate governments to validate claims against each other as well as against the national government and permits them particularly to mitigate the damage done to their citizens by other provincial governments. Simultaneously, the national government can enforce its legal claims against provincial units.[18]

---

[16] Norms can have a restraining effect on action even when they cannot be judicially enforced, whether the reason for unenforceability is traced to the political incapacity of courts or to problems of identifying judicially administrable rules to implement the norms. That the agents are motivated to interpret and give effect to norms permits decentralization to be sustained as an equilibrium. British constitutionalism is an example of norm-based enforcement. Constitutional norms in that system are not law and are not enforceable by courts, unless they are also statutes, in which case they may be enforced as statutes. For a perspective on American constitutionalism that recognizes the efficacy of nonenforceable norms, see Sager 1978 and Ross 1987.

[17] A good example of the attempt to develop a legal convention is found in Justice O'Connor's efforts to articulate a limit to the congressional authority to regulate local governments; see *Gregory v. Ashcroft*, 501 U.S. 452 (1991); *New York v. United States*, 505 U.S. 144 (1992), and, in more recent federalism decisions by her colleagues on the Court, see *United States v. Lopez*, 514 U.S. 549 (1995); *Printz v. United States*, 521 U.S. 98 (1997); *Seminole Tribe of Fla. v. Florida*, 517 U.S. 44 (1996).

[18] A theory of federalism, as opposed to a theory of decentralization, must explain how subnational institutions can actually be provided with decision-making powers in certain

Its remedial rather than prophylactic nature distinguishes juridical from structural mechanisms for ensuring federalist guarantees. Whereas structural federalism reduces the frequency of opportunism by making it difficult for government to decide to take or implement action that infringes on the federal arrangement, juridical federalism seeks to remedy the consequence of an infringing action. To do so, it relies on legal discourse based on either rules or norms, or both. Insofar as the legal discourse is backed up by an institutional structure that enforces valid claims of this sort, juridical federalism is said to be rule-based: in rule-based federalism, the judiciary can exert power within its domain of authority because legal institutions recognize and enforce such claims. A state has norm-based juridical federalism if its claims are predictably respected by other parts of government whether or not they are enforceable in court.

Although it may seem clear enough that rule-based federalism is properly thought of as juridical, we think norm-based federalism ought to be thought of in this way as well.[19] Judicial institutions can play a critical role in both rule-based and norm-based federalism. In the first case they are charged with identifying violations and enforcing the rules. In the second case, they act to articulate norms and expectations[20] to identify transgressions, relying on less formal methods of enforcement.[21] The most famous example of the latter is the Canadian Supreme Court's chastisement of Prime Minister Pierre Trudeau for attempting to patriate the Canadian Constitution without adequately consulting with the provinces.[22] "Enforcement" of this ruling was left to public opinion or to

domains. Without such an account, federalism is just another word for decentralization. If we are to take seriously the distinction between federalist and decentralized nonfederalist regimes, we need to find a place in the theory for the allocation of powers. Conferring some aspects of sovereignty on subnational units can permit a regime to establish and maintain structures and policies of the sort recommended by the political economy of federalism. The division of decision-making authority can help solve a characteristic "credibility" problem faced by a political regime intent on taking advantage of decentralized policy making and administration.

[19] It is important to see that rule-based federalism cannot be rule based "all the way down." Ultimately, rule-based federalism rests on the acceptance of norms by others in government and by the people requiring that judicial orders are to be respected and enforced.

[20] The distinction between rules and norms that we employ is parallel in some respects to Dworkin's (1985) distinction between rules and principles, which in turn is derivative of Hart and Sacks's distinction between policies and principles. See Hart and Sacks 1994. For all three thinkers, principles, seen as the animating normative ideas "behind" a legal system, have direct force for normatively motivated agents, whether or not they give rise to specific legal rules.

[21] See Milgrom, North, and Weingast 1990.

[22] *Re Resolution to Amend the Constitution* (Patriation Reference) 1 S.C.R. 753 (1981).

Trudeau's own constitutional sensibilities. But even if courts play no role at all, the public discourse of norm-based federalism is juridical in that it is aimed at identifying expectations and principles governing acceptable conduct. Whether federal limits are enforceable in courts, or they evoke compliance for normative reasons, is less important than that they serve as the basis for forming accurate and stable expectations as to how others should and will behave.

A central dilemma for juridical federalism arises from the fact that national courts are asymmetrically situated relative to the national and provincial governments. Their vulnerability to the national legislature may often, or (two of us fear) typically, lead them to develop a deferential jurisprudence toward it that inhibits judicial articulation or enforcement of federal norms aimed at restraining national institutions. Even though no such vulnerability exists toward the provinces, the legitimacy of judicial interventions in the states will be in question if the judiciary is seen as overly deferential to national forces.

Thus, the judiciary can play an effective role in enforcing federal expectations only when it is politically independent of the national legislature.[23] That independence can be facilitated, but not assured, by the fragmentation of powers at the national level. Life tenure and protection against diminution of salary for national judges, difficult procedures for impeachment, and separation of the appointment from the confirmation power may protect federal courts from becoming captives of the national legislative authority. These protections are, however, of diminished consequence in periods when the political branches are ideologically united. They are potentially more important in periods when government is ideologically divided, but their significance depends upon the court's being well motivated to protect the overall federal arrangement rather than to pursue a more shortsighted substantive goal.

Structural Federalism

Federalism recognizes the existence of sovereign authority in any circumstance in which a governmental unit has a reliable prospect of asserting its legally assigned authority and defending it when it is challenged. This definition of sovereign authority is much weaker than the claim that the unit can enforce its will against others in all counterfactual circumstances. The latter idea sees a sovereign as holder of ultimate authority, and this view leads to a conception of sovereignty as necessarily unitary and is

---

[23] Williamson (1996) is skeptical as to how far de facto federalism in the People's Republic of China can go without attaining some juridical status. Our account adds this: such a development requires more than legal rules and norms; it requires political conditions within which judicial independence could be sustained.

famously inconsistent with federalism as we understand it. On our account, a state can have sovereign authority if circumstances are such that it exercises jurisdiction in some domain and is not, for reliable reasons, ever challenged (or is only rarely challenged) by the national government or other states. This circumstance might be based on the existence of a normative structure enforcing compliance with sovereignty claims. Or, in the case of structural federalism, on the balance of resources held by the governmental units, on alliances among political or social forces, or on constitutional arrangements that permit provincial actors or institutions a direct voice in the formation of national majorities, making the formation of such majorities impossible without the concurrence of the provinces or their political agents.

This condition has two parts, one focusing on the government with a sovereignty claim and the other on the governmental units surrounding it. For a government to be sovereign in a domain it must be sufficiently decisive to assert a claim in that domain. Also, it must be the case either that the claim is rarely challenged or, if it is, that the claiming government can usually make its claim stand. In the case of federal arrangements, much of the bite in this definition will arise from the fact that, because of the structural division of powers within the national government, provincial sovereignty claims are rarely challenged. As a consequence, nonjuridically sovereign provinces can usually exercise their powers unchallenged. The danger to provincial sovereignty comes from the assertion of national preemptive power, and the challenge is to regulate the exercise of that power procedurally or structurally.

An apparent mechanism for regulating national preemptive exercises of power is to make it difficult for the national government to act without the acquiescence of the states. One can imagine numerous mechanisms for achieving this goal, though many of the mechanisms, such as a state liberum veto, are too costly to the polity's overall well-being.[24] Less costly mechanisms would include giving the states formal or functional control over membership in at least part of the national legislature, requiring some kinds of national legislation to be ratified by a majority of the states, vesting implementation of national programs in state officers, and so forth. Precisely which mechanisms are best suited for the particular polity may be a relatively ad hoc matter. In some cases, political traditions may evolve in the place of institutional provisions to fragment authority. For example,

---

[24] A liberum veto would allow any state (or a surrogate) to block enactment of a statute or adoption of a new policy. The political weakness of Poland in the eighteenth century, culminating in its being partitioned by Prussia, Austria, and Russia, is widely thought to be a consequence, in part, of a system in which many players could exercise a liberum veto.

A *Political Theory of Federalism* 235

in Canada, voters generally "balance" their national representation by electing candidates from an opposing party to provincial office.[25]

A thesis that emerges from the foregoing theoretical discussion is that horizontal fragmentation of national power is a necessary but not a sufficient condition for robust federalism. Fragmentation directly satisfies the first condition for federal stability: it checks the ability of the federal government to take advantage of the provinces. Fragmentation works indirectly on the second condition; it allows for effective juridical federalism, in which an independent court can combat defections from the provinces. To explore the different ways national power can be fragmented, and some ways in which national power can sometimes be reconsolidated to the detriment of federalism, we turn to our three historical case studies.

THE COLLAPSE OF DE FACTO
FEDERALISM IN GREAT BRITAIN

Perhaps Great Britain is a surprising place to begin a story about federalism.[26] But Douglass North and Barry Weingast (1989) have argued that Britain effectively became a federal state – in which localities were securely in control of their jurisdictions, if only de facto – after the Glorious Revolution.[27] Part of the Settlement of the Glorious Revolution was an agreement by the monarchy to share a substantial part of its authority with Parliament, which consisted of two chambers: the House of Lords, representing the nobility and clergy, and the House of Commons, which was representative of the propertied and commercial interests of the nation at the time. The post-1688 English (after 1707, British) division of national power between the Crown, the Lords, and the Commons – the king-in-parliament model, in which each of the three institutions had veto authority over legislation – successfully fragmented national power. In this new system, obtaining new national legislation was arduous, and parliamentary legislative output was limited compared with that in France in the same period.

Hilton Root has demonstrated some rather remarkable features of this new system. For example, "The King's Council in France was able to produce more legislation in an average four months than Parliament could in the entire reign of George I, more legislation in one year than during

---

[25] We are indebted to Brian Gaines for this suggestion.

[26] That a similar story could be told about decentralized economic development in China can be seen in Montinola, Qian, and Weingast 1995.

[27] Our account of British political development is indebted to that presented in Weingast 1995. Unlike Weingast's account, however, our emphasis on the role of a disorganized party system in providing a foundation for decentralization underlines the fragility of British arrangements in the face of a fundamental partisan realignment.

the reign of George II, and more legislation in any four years than the British Parliament accomplished during the entire sixty-year reign of George III" (Root 1994, 41–2). The difficulty of getting legislation made it imperative that the king and his ministers concentrate their influence, in the famous system of "corruption" by which the monarchy "managed" Parliament, to push bills of major importance to the monarchy, especially those concerning foreign and military policy. "The English Crown's authority fell primarily in the areas of state administration, foreign affairs, and in the management of the army and navy. . . . [R]oyal administrators in England did not have means similar to those of their French counterparts to regulate the economy and divide the nation's commercial and industrial wealth" (1994, 44). Attempts by the crown to enforce monopolies and to introduce excise taxes were repeatedly turned back by the Parliaments of the eighteenth century.[28]

This sclerotic system permitted the local governments a great deal of leeway in setting economic policy. North and Weingast (1989) demonstrate that the fragmentation of power between the king and Parliament effectively prevented the national government from imposing taxes and regulations on commercial enterprises and that such governmental activity occurred instead at local levels. Not only did the localities impose most taxes and regulations, but they were actively engaged in competition with one another for commercial advantage; as a result, taxes and regulation remained relatively light. Lacking a written constitution or a normative articulation of the formal powers of local governments, British federalism remained purely structural rather than juridical. Nonetheless, as our theory suggests, so long as national political power remained fragmented, de facto federal arrangements were stable.

From about 1690 to 1832, British public administration and government were notably local in character.[29] Locally entrenched elites administered their communities largely without interference from Westminster. The preeminence of local government fit well with the characteristics of the public services being produced at the time. Police, sanitation services, and the maintenance of local roads probably did not offer economies of

---

[28] For an example of a failed attempt to impose excise taxes during Walpole's administration, see Price 1983.

[29] Our choice of 1690 as the beginning of a stable era of decentralized administration is somewhat arbitrary; for our purposes, we could just as well have chosen 1700, the year in which the Act of Settlement became law. The 1690s were a period marked by a relatively high level of partisanship and so, one would conjecture, would not be hospitable to sustained localism. Indeed, if one sees the "federal aspects" of British rule as including not only localism but also relations among England, Ireland, and Scotland, it is perhaps not surprising that these "British" relations were under great tension for as long as the partisan organization of British politics sustained itself: roughly until 1715 or so.

scale that would have rewarded more centralized production. Of particular importance, most of the economic regulation that did occur was carried out at the local level. Under this system, competition among localities exerted a steady downward pressure on tax rates and discouraged restrictive regulations.[30] The orientation of the localities to Parliament operated for the most part through private bills for enclosures or other local projects and through patronage seeking by the local member of Parliament, or MP (Cox 1987).

Local governments and parliamentary constituencies remained remarkably constant over this period, and stable electoral practices evolved by which parliamentary seats were claimed and held by the same local elites who administered justice in their communities. As a result, the Parliaments of this period were highly fragmented, their members locally oriented and chronically difficult to organize to achieve any genuinely national project. This period, parts of which historians variously have characterized as the Whig oligarchy, the Namierite system, and the golden age of the MP, was one that saw the emergence of prime ministers capable of organizing, if only for the moment, a fragmented and independent Parliament for purposes of pursuing national policies, principally in foreign affairs.

The Crown's influence in national politics was maintained by bargaining for control of a sufficient fraction of these seats (including the rotten boroughs) in an effort to influence parliamentary proceedings important to its interests. The resulting system was one of publicly recognized "corruption," in which parliamentary seats were bid for by respectable families, ambitious merchants, and crown ministries. Some of the returns from this bidding flowed to the local electorates in the form of improved roads, waterworks, and other local projects. Some of the funds for the bidding came from the ministries, but much of it also came from the private purses of those who aspired to hold parliamentary office (Namier [1928] 1957). Local constituencies often looked forward eagerly to electoral contests, seeing them as an opportunity either to "shake down" some ambitious local elites or to drain some money from the Treasury.

After the period analyzed by North and Weingast, the political conditions for this de facto federalism – the fragmentation of national power – dissipated. The apparent stability of the system of locally oriented government was undermined in the nineteenth century by the growth of

---

[30] North and Weingast (1989) have argued that this situation was behind the vast expansion of British enterprise in the eighteenth century and, subsequently, Britain's becoming a global power. This is, of course, a reversal of the more traditional argument in that it traces the economic transformation to political causes.

238   *Bednar, Eskridge, and Ferejohn*

organized and disciplined parties.[31] Over a period of roughly fifty years, starting in about 1830 and accelerating with the passage of the Second Reform Act in 1867, the largely independent MP, usually elected without serious competition, intent on voting his conscience, and representing the particular claims of his local community, was replaced by the disciplined partisan chosen more often in contested election, focused on enacting his party's program. The system of private member legislation declined rapidly and was replaced by party programs pledging nationally oriented legislation. The norms and practices of cabinet government and party responsibility subsequently began to develop.[32]

As a result, beginning in the mid-nineteenth century, the system of decentralized administration that had characterized British public life became unglued, and Britain entered into a period of unitary governance. The fragility of decentralized political arrangements is well illustrated in modern British history. Increasingly, disciplined parties shifted political action and administration to Westminster on a variety of fronts, under-cutting the system of local patronage-based administration and creating in its place majoritarian parliamentary practices aimed at enacting national legislation and a centralized public administration run by a non-partisan civil service. Not surprisingly, these radical changes in the parti-san organization of the House of Commons reinforced the traditional tension between it and the House of Lords, itself the last line of defense against the emergence of a unitary governmental system, and ultimately undercut the constitutional authority of the upper chamber.[33] Ironically, in view of this chapter's concern with durable decentralization, one of the last occasions on which the Lords was able to block legislation occurred on the Second Irish Home Rule Bill in 1893.[34]

---

[31] Cox (1987) points as well to the attrition of the parliamentary rights of backbenchers and the expansion of cabinet control over the agenda in the Commons, a development that may be partly independent of the development of disciplined parties.

[32] The dating of these phenomena is somewhat imprecise. The important point for us is that the period of the three Reform Acts, 1832 to 1884, was one in which the parties became vastly more coherent and organized and that, as this occurred, the earlier system of par-liamentary rights, privileges, and organization was transformed.

[33] Although we do not pursue the matter here, it is striking how weak the House of Lords and the Crown were in maintaining a semblance of a formal separation of powers. If any-thing, the formal institutional powers of the Crown in the legislative process were supe-rior to those of the American president, and those of the House of Lords were at least comparable with those of the U.S. Senate. Nevertheless, the political legitimacy of both of these bodies declined with the partisan realignment in the House of Commons. The reason for this acquiescence must lie in the absence of any popular base for the authority of these traditional institutions.

[34] The Lords thwarted Liberal-Labour-Irish legislation once again in the 1906–8 period, and followed up by rejecting the budget produced by the Commons in 1909, thereby

A Political Theory of Federalism

With the rise of effective unitary government, what we now call the Westminster model, British courts came to adopt a jurisprudence that fit this new political reality. Only in the mid-sixteenth century did English courts come to treat parliamentary statutes as authoritative "law," and for the next 150 years the courts approached such statutes with great flexibility (Thorne 1942, 67; Cross 1987, 9–11; Corry 1936). Thus judges routinely expanded the reach of some statutes under the "mischief rule,"[35] while constricting other statutes in order to avoid "unreasonable" consequences.[36] This judicial flexibility fit well with the localized nature of British politics during that period. By the mid-eighteenth century, however, courts were discernibly moving toward a more deferential and textual, and less flexible and contextual, attitude toward statutes.[37] As a unitary government developed over the course of the nineteenth century, with the House of Commons at its center, the courts methodically worked toward an astringent textualism, under which parliamentary commands would be taken seriously and applied literally, judges would deny themselves any discretion to alter the terms of the statute's text, and extramural materials (legislative history) were excluded from statutory

challenging one of the most profound constitutional assumptions of the British division of powers. The 1911 Parliament Act, which ended the Lords' veto powers, was the response.

[35] The "office of all the judges is always to make such construction as shall suppress the mischief, and advance the remedy, and to suppress subtle inventions and evasions for continuance of the mischief . . . and to add force and life to the cure and remedy, according to the true intent of the makers of the act." *Heydon's Case*, 3 Co. Rep. 7a, 7b (Ch. Exch. 1584), usefully discussed in Popkin 1999, ch. 1.

[36] In *Stradling v. Morgan*, 1 Plowd. 199, 205, the court reported that "the sages of the law heretofore have construed statutes quite contrary to the letter in some appearance, and those statutes which comprehend all things in the letter they have expounded to extend but to some things, and those which generally prohibit all people from doing such an act they have interpreted to permit some people to do it, and those which include every person in the letter they have adjudged to reach some persons only, which expositions have always been founded on the intent of the legislature which they have collected sometimes by considering the cause and necessity of making the Act, sometimes by comparing one part of the Act with another, and sometimes by foreign circumstances." See also *Dr. Bonham's Case*, quoted and discussed in Thorne 1938.

[37] The development of a more deferential and strictly textual interpretive regime occurred over a long stretch of time. The court in *Colehan v. Cooke*, 125 Eng. Rep. 1231, 1233 (1742), started with a particularly deferential statement of the earlier flexible approach: "When the words of an Act are doubtful and uncertain, it is proper to inquire what was the intent of the Legislature." This was immediately followed with a statement of an even stiffer refusal to countenance judicial flexibility under the new regime of parliamentary sovereignty, "but it is very dangerous for Judges to launch out too far in searching for the intent of the Legislature, when they have expressed themselves in plain and clear words." See also Blackstone 1765–9, 559–62.

240

construction, lest they provide a basis for judicial discretion to rewrite statutes.[38]

Textualism, then as now, was justified on the grounds that statutes provided the best and most accurate expression of the popular will and that any "errors" produced by a literalist approach to statutes could and would be remedied legislatively (see note 38). The features of the Westminster model made this assumption particularly plausible in British circumstances. Parliamentary sovereignty together with unicameralism and majoritarianism permitted Parliament to react quickly to deficiencies the laws revealed in their literal application. In any case, Parliament was not content merely to trust the judiciary to defer to its statutes: in 1850 and 1889 it enacted Interpretation Acts, which attempted to spell out in detail how statutory provisions were to be construed. In addition to its more technical provisions, the 1889 act instantiated part of the transformation that had occurred in British politics. It required courts to construe legislation enacted after 1850 as public rather than private law, and to interpret such statutes broadly and not as private bargains to be narrowly understood.

The textualism of British courts in matters of statutory interpretation stood in contrast to older methods of common-law development and amounted to a public positioning of the judiciary as subservient to the legislature. This renunciation of judicial independence is not best seen as a natural doctrinal development of British law; indeed, it was strikingly inconsistent with the confident and flexible approach judges had taken to statutes in earlier centuries. Instead, judicial self-denial was a recognition of a new political reality in which the House of Commons became the font of institutional legitimacy within British political life and was in fact able to impose its imprint on law with no reliable possibility of institutional resistance.[39]

---

[38] Lord Bramwell's opinion in *Hill v. East and West India Dock Co.*, 9 App. Cas. 448, 464–5 (House of Lords, 1884), is a leading statement of a strictly literalist construction of statutes, even when yielding absurd results. "I think it is infinitely better, although an absurdity or an injustice or other objectionable result may be evolved as a consequence of your construction, to adhere to the words of an Act of Parliament and leave the legislature to set it right than to alter those words according to one's notion of an absurdity." See also Lord Chancellor Loreburn's opinion in *London & India Docks Co. v. Thames Steam Tug & Lighterage Co.* (1909), App. Cas. 15. The exclusionary rule was (apparently) first articulated in *Millar v. Taylor*, 4 Burr. 2303, 2332 (1769), but was not rigidly applied until the late nineteenth century. Even after that point, extrinsic materials could be used to establish a statutory purpose. The House of Lords in *Pepper v. Hart*, 1 All E.R. 42 (1993), abolished the rule and permitted reference to parliamentary materials in many circumstances.

[39] The transition from the purposive regime articulated in *Heydon's Case* (note 35) to the textualist one in the *India Dock* cases (note 38) was somewhat more gradual than might

Historians often explain the transformation of British governmental forms and practices by pointing to evolution in the British economy or to the changing place of Britain in world politics. But these developments had been occurring gradually since early in the eighteenth century, without undermining the localist administrative system. While these developments may well have contributed to a greater "demand" for nationalization, they do not explain the "supply side," namely, the ease and rapidity of the political transformation. This is better explained by the absence of genuine institutional supports for localism. Thus, there was nothing in the British constitutional system to stand in the way of highly organized and disciplined parties once they appeared on the scene. The House of Lords by the middle of the nineteenth century not only lacked institutional legitimacy but had no systematic connection with local administration. The monarchy had its own reasons to support the expansion of national authority in a variety of domains. The judiciary was by then too vulnerable to Parliament, especially to the newly partisan House of Commons, to validate federalist institutions even if they had existed.

The case of Great Britain suggests that the fragmentation of national authority might be a necessary condition for durable federalism. As long as the separation of powers aspects of the British system remained resilient (as they did into the eighteenth century), and as long as the parties were fragmented and disorganized, local authority remained secure. But this security was not based on judicial enforcement of federal constitutional expectations, for such expectations did not exist. Insofar as judges restrained parliamentary intrusions into local and private conflict, they did so in the name of protected common-law rights, not structural constitutional rights. In any case, this line of protection weakened over the course of the eighteenth century. The principal protection of local spheres of action was structural. Parliaments of this period were too fractious and disunified to agree to substantial national regulatory legislation.

The fact that the political basis for British federalism was both fragile and eroding meant that it was not robust to the collapse of the "Namierite" system. The absence of either an explicit federal

---

be inferred from our brief treatment. Moreover, even at the point where literalist deference to Parliament was triumphant, British judges sometimes followed the "golden rule," that the ordinary meaning of statutory words should be followed, "unless when so applied they produce an inconsistency, or an absurdity or inconvenience so great as to convince the Court that the intention could not have been to use them in their ordinary signification, and to justify the Court in putting on them some other signification, which, though less proper, is one which the Court thinks the words will bear." *River Wear Comm'rs v. Adamson*, 2 App. Cas. 743, 764 (House of Lords, 1877) (opinion of Lord Blackburn). See Cross 1987, 15.

bargain or an implicit understanding that laid out separate spheres of decision-making authority, within which different institutions could expect to govern more or less autonomously, meant that there was no juridical impediment to expanding parliamentary claims. Even had such expectations existed, they would not have been judicially enforceable: once Parliament attained a sufficient degree of partisan cohesion, British courts were no longer sufficiently independent to thwart its will. The absence of institutional restraints on the political centralization made possible increasing national demands on localities and removed any real chance of resistance to these demands in court.

Only at the level of the relations among the British states, specifically with respect to Ireland and Scotland, could one discern explicit juridical federal expectations. But the irony of the Irish situation within Britain, a situation in which the Parnellites had become pivotal to the formation of Liberal governments, made home rule an issue that was central to the Liberal agenda. The effect of this was to undermine the independent authority of House of Lords when it tried to block such efforts, thereby increasing the unitary nature of British government. In the absence of legal impediments to concentrated national power, the only recourse was submission to London or political resistance.[40] In our view, this as much as anything else led to the separation of the Republic of Ireland from Great Britain and to the continuing energy of separatism in Northern Ireland.[41]

THE EROSION OF JURIDICAL FEDERALISM IN CANADA

Canadian history underscores the necessity of structural support for federalist arrangements suggested by the British case. Canada has few structural safeguards against national usurpation of provincial domains, but for the first half of its history as a federation, an unusual source of juridical federalism monitored the national government. When an institutional shift eliminated the juridical safeguards protecting the provinces, provincial interests were stimulated to rally against the potential for increased centralization. The Canadian case demonstrates the insufficiency of provincial constraints for assuring a federal arrangement; if stability is to be secured, the national government must also have institutional incentives to respect jurisdictional boundaries.

---

[40] As we write, the Blair government has begun an effort to devolve some authority onto the "nations" and perhaps to recreate British "federalism." Insofar as British national institutions remain effectively unitary – the devolution is merely statutory after all – our analysis suggests skepticism about the prospects for success.

[41] For an illustration of an attempt to overcome the deficiencies of unitary government, see Spiller and Vogelsang 1994.

For the first eighty years after Confederation, an unusual institutional mechanism helped support stability. The legal rules defining the relationship between the national government and the provincial governments were policed in an unlikely juridical forum: the Judicial Committee of the British Privy Council in London, a high court structurally independent from the influence of Canadian politics. As long as the Judicial Committee retained judicial review authority over Canadian statutes, which it held until 1949, the provinces could rely on the courts for protection against federal encroachment, permitting the development of what we call juridical federalism. The Judicial Committee regularly enforced limits on federal power through the application of a set of province-protecting legal rules and doctrines that it developed over the eighty years that it retained appellate authority. Once that appellate authority disappeared, however, the provinces effectively lost the capacity to protect their powers from central incursions through the appeal to legal rules. While the federalist norms that evolved during the Judicial Committee era may have retained some authority, the legal restraints on Ottawa have largely disappeared. As a result, the potential for unchecked action by the federal government has driven the provinces to agitate for change outside the legal system, resulting in chronic and volatile political instability.

Although we emphasize the changing institutional structure to explain the shift in Canadian federalism, another important characteristic of the Canadian polity cannot be ignored. Canada is a state of (at least!) two societies and cultures, and the ethnic tensions between them often seem to be the source of instability of the federalism. Indeed, commentators commonly explain the chronic instability of the Canadian federation in terms of cultural and linguistic conflict. Our account is different. We believe that the intensity and political nature of cultural conflict is best seen as endogenous. The change in institutional rules (the patriation of appellate authority) caused minorities to lose confidence in the protection of their values within the federal system. Faced with this loss of legal protection, the only course left to them was to attempt to erect political barriers.

De Facto Federalism

Both norm-based and rule-based juridical federalism have early roots in Canadian history. The tradition of federalism was established more than twenty-five years prior to the enactment of the British North America (BNA) Act. In law, the Act of 1840 created a union between the two Canadian regions, Upper and Lower Canada, to be governed under one parliament without regard to regions, which it was expected would imply a British domination over the French Canadians. In fact, the British

244 *Bednar, Eskridge, and Ferejohn*

Canadian leadership soon realized that it could not govern without the participation of francophone leaders as well.[42] As early as 1842, Sir Charles Bagot recognized the need to invite a French Canadian leader into his cabinet, and the tradition of dual ministerial appointments continued until confederation in 1867.

The institutions created under the Act of 1840 were ill-suited to manage a de facto federalism, and deadlock and instability were common (Russell 1992, 13–14). Delegates from the provinces of Canada (Upper and Lower) met in Quebec City to propose a structure for the new union. All were in agreement that the new union should be based upon the Westminster system of parliamentary government but modified into a form of federalism to protect the needs of the region's two distinct populations. The anglophones of Upper Canada, led by John Macdonald, were largely in favor of a highly centralized federalism, where primary responsibility for the nation's governance would rest with the general government, while the francophones of Lower Canada argued for a much looser alliance, with much more sovereignty retained at the provincial level. The arguments on either side remain to the present day: anglophones (at least Ontario) believe that only a centralized federalism can promote the stability and coordination necessary to generate growth, whereas French Canadians (occasionally joined by other regionalists) argue that only by retaining most governmental authority at the provincial level can the needs of distinct populations be served.

Juridical Federalism with Bite

The result of several rounds of negotiation, the BNA Act in 1867 created a union between Upper and Lower Canada, together with the maritime provinces. Within the loose structure of the British Empire, the BNA Act became "independent" Canada's de facto constitution. The provisions for juridical federalism were evident in the enumeration of powers, which were a compromise between provincialist and nationalist concerns.[43] Section 91

---

[42] Stanley 1956, 99–102. We maintain that the characteristic gridlock of pre-1867 Canada was probably not corrigible by creating a stronger central government. The recognition that dual ministerial appointments were necessary for governability prior to 1867 was a sign of the wisdom of the governments of that period. Something like the same practice would have to evolve after the adoption of the BNA Act if Canada was to remain viable.

[43] Speaking at the 1865 Confederation Debates, Hector Langevin, solicitor general of Lower Canada, expressed the view of many French leaders: "The Central or Federal Parliament will have the control of all measures of a general character. . . . It will be the duty of the Central Government to see that the country prospers, but it will not be its duty to attack our religion, our institutions, or our nationality, which . . . will be amply protected." Quoted in Cook, Brown, and Berger 1967, 367–8, 105n.

authorized the federal government to regulate trade and to control foreign affairs and taxation, while section 92 granted the provincial governments the last word on matters related to education, hospitals (later interpreted to mean health care), and social services, as well as all matters that did not expand beyond provincial boundaries. Criminal law was to be in the federal domain, although certain administrative duties were to be left with the provinces. Section 91 also left the residual powers to the federal government, contained in the opening clause granting legislative authority for the "peace, order and good government" of all of Canada.[44]

What did not exist, however, were adequate guarantees of structural federalism. The national government was only nominally fragmented. Although it had a bicameral legislature, the upper house was as ineffective in design as the British House of Lords at representing provincial concerns.[45] True to the Westminster model, the legislature and executive were fused. Although the BNA Act formally guaranteed judicial independence, the court was perceived as linked to the national government.[46] We argue that Canada, with little internal structural fragmentation, was dependent

---

[44] The opening text of section 91 reads: "It shall be lawful for the Queen, by and with the advice and consent of the Senate and House of Commons, to make laws, for the peace, order and good government of Canada, in relation to all matters not coming within the classes of subjects assigned exclusively to the Legislatures of the Provinces."

[45] In the text of the London Resolutions (the document that immediately preceded the final BNA Act as passed by the British Parliament), it was written that the Senate appointments would be made from the provincial legislatures, and a strict distribution of the provincial representatives was allotted. But the text of the BNA Act, as adopted by Parliament, granted the governor general the power of senatorial appointments. Although this may be interpreted as a setback for the provincial powers, included in the comments for the change was a note that this was specifically and extensively discussed and agreed to in the London meetings. O'Connor 1939, annex 4.

[46] From the very beginning it appears that the judiciary was intended to be subservient to the national legislature. The text of section 33 of the London Resolutions read: "All courts, judges and officers of the several Provinces shall aid, assist and obey the general Government in the exercise of its rights and power, and for such purposes shall be held to be courts, judges and officers of the general Government." This section was removed before the BNA was written. No minutes were taken of the deliberations of the London Conference to write the BNA, so we do not know with certainty the reasons for the elimination of this section. However, the concordance prepared by the Colonial Office to explain the changes between the (Canadian) London Resolutions and the (British) BNA Act reads: "As to Court and Judges this resolution was dropped. The Judges were bound by their office. As to Officers of the provinces, the Resolution, redrafted, survives as section 130 of the Act." The texts of the Quebec and London Resolutions can be found in Kennedy 1930. A detailed comparison of the transitions from the Quebec Resolutions to the London Resolutions, and from the London Resolutions to the BNA Act itself, can be found in O'Connor 1939, annex 4. Any doubt as to the legal independence of the Supreme Court justices was thereby removed, although some justices may have felt a duty to side with the federal government nonetheless, and we may thereby see some of the rationale for court members' deference to the national legislature.

246   *Bednar, Eskridge, and Ferejohn*

on external juridical mechanisms to support its federation.[47] An oddity of Canada's continuing political link to Great Britain permitted the evolution of a juridical federalism with bite.

Canada's separation from Great Britain was incomplete; it was this lingering connection, we argue, that sustained the Canadian federation. Although the world recognized Canada as a sovereign country, ultimate legal authority still resided in London. The British Parliament alone could approve amendments to the original BNA Act, which was after all a British statute. In matters of interpretation, despite the subsequent creation of a Canadian Supreme Court, the Judicial Committee of the British Privy Council served as the final court of appeals, a forum insulated from Canadian politics, both theoretically and practically, as subsequent events revealed.

For most of the thirty years following the enactment of the BNA Act, nationalistic Conservatives, led by John A. Macdonald, controlled the government. Macdonald's vision of provincial authority was narrow and he worked to establish the political conditions for a genuinely nationalized form of government.[48] Macdonald's government made full use of the powers to disallow provincial legislation. Russell reports that between 1867 and 1896, sixty-five provincial acts were disallowed (Russell 1992, 39), provoking the development of a partisan opposition at the provincial level and of appeals to the judiciary to adjudicate jurisdictional claims. The Canadian Supreme Court, though it was created in 1875 under a short-lived Liberal government, rapidly became the creature of nationalist Conservatives and ruled repeatedly against provincial claims.[49] As a result,

[47] In a succinct analysis of provincialist claims in the Canadian founding period, Vipond argues that all parties understood that a third party would be necessary to resolve jurisdictional disputes, interpreted, most likely, to mean either the courts or an imperial power. See Vipond 1991, esp. 34–5, and the discussion of the political thinking of David Mills, who recognized the importance of the courts to act as umpire over the inevitably blurry jurisdictional boundaries (158–9). Vipond also emphasizes the importance of the Judicial Committee in the early years of federation, which extended beyond its decisions to influencing the actions taken by the governmental agents at both the national and the provincial levels. For a formal analysis of this case, see Bednar 1998b.

[48] Simpson (1988) emphasizes, initially, John Macdonald's extensive use of patronage to build the Conservative Party into a national political party and, subsequently, Wilfred Laurier's development of the Liberal Party using similar tools, first in Quebec and then nationally.

[49] The early decisions of the Supreme Court were nationalist. In *Severn v. The Queen* 2 S. C.R. 70 (1878), the court struck down an Ontario statute licensing brewers as *ultra vires*; two years later, it repeated this interpretation of the trade and commerce clause in *City of Fredericton v. The Queen* 3 S.C.R. 505 (1880). The Supreme Court also seemed hospitable to an expansive reading of the peace, order, and good government clause. In *Severn*, Justice Henry wrote: "*Everything* in the shape of legislation for the peace, order and good government of Canada is embraced" in the clause. "[S]ub-section 29 [of

A Political Theory of Federalism 247

alleged federal usurpation of provincial powers became a partisan issue, embraced by the Liberal Party. Led by Oliver Mowat, the Liberal premier of Ontario, five of seven provinces petitioned the British Parliament to amend the Constitution so as to abolish the federal power to disallow provincial legislation. When this initiative came to nothing, the provinces turned their efforts to judicial appeals to the Privy Council's Judicial Committee. On Ontario matters, Mowat himself sometimes journeyed to London to be present for the appeals.

The Judicial Committee turned out to be remarkably hospitable to provincial claims, and over the next seventy years it evolved a narrow and legalistic reading of the federal residual powers,[50] and construed the national exclusive power over trade and commerce to apply only to international trade and the interprovincial movement of goods.[51] Just as significantly, it construed the provincial authority over property and civil rights as a broad general contracts clause, thereby imposing a limit on national regulatory authority. Of twenty division of powers issues decided by the Judicial Committee between 1880 and 1896, fifteen were resolved in favor of the provinces (Russell 1992, 42).

section 91] goes further and provides for exceptions and reservations in regard to matters otherwise included in the power of legislation given to the Local Legislatures." Finally, "Every constituent, therefore, of trade and commerce, and the subject of indirect taxation, is thus, as I submit, withdrawn from the consideration of the Local Legislatures, even if it should otherwise be *apparently* included" (emphasis in original). 2 S.C.R. at 70.

[50] The Privy Council relied on the peace, order, and good government clause (p.o.g.g.) in *Russell v. The Queen*, 7 App. Cas. 829; I Olmsted 145 (1882), to sustain the Canada Temperance Act. The case offered the Privy Council a chance to review the decision of the Supreme Court in the *Fredericton* case (note 49). Although the Judicial Committee agreed with the Supreme Court that the act was valid, the committee disagreed with the manner by which the Court had reasoned the case. The committee rejected the use of section 91(2), instead using the p.o.g.g. power. In this manner it was able to maintain the narrow construction of the trade and commerce clause established in *Parsons* (note 51). However, the Privy Council became increasingly reluctant to accept arguments based upon such a general grant of power to the federal government and made its narrow conception clear in the Local Prohibition Case of 1896. In upholding a local prohibition statute from Ontario, Lord Watson, writing for the court, gave a narrow construction of the p.o.g.g. clause: "To attach any other construction of the general power which, in supplement of its enumerated powers, is conferred upon the Parliament of Canada by s.91, would . . . not only be contrary to the intendment of the Act, but would practically destroy the autonomy of the provinces." *Attorney General Ontario v. Attorney General Canada* (Local Prohibition Case) A.C. 348; I Olmsted 343 (1896).

[51] In *Citizens Insurance Co. v. Parsons*; *Queen Insurance Co. v. Parsons*, 7 App. Cas. 96; I Olmstead 94 (1881), the Judicial Committee held that insurance contracts fell within the provincial (section 92[13]) authority over "Property and Civil Rights," rather than the national (section 91) powers over trade and commerce, arguing that national powers extended only over international trade and commerce.

248   *Bednar, Eskridge, and Ferejohn*

In so acting, the Privy Council served as the shield for the provincial governments, which lacked any internal structural protection from encroachment of the federal government into their jurisdictions. It is not necessary to argue, as some might, that the Privy Council was biased in favor of the provincial governments over the federal government. The higher number of proprovincial resolutions was partly due to the great number of profederal resolutions at the Supreme Court level. The Privy Council might be better viewed as a balancing element. As modern legal analyst Barry Strayer has written, "our constitution can sustain strong government at either level" (Strayer 1968, 216). It may be true, however, that it was easier for the Privy Council than the Supreme Court to rule against the federal government. Despite its nominal independence as guaranteed by the BNA Act, the Court depended on the rest of the federal government and therefore tended to side with it. Because the Privy Council was removed from Canadian political influence, it was more capable of applying neutral rules of law or of balancing provincial interests with national.

Separation from Canadian politics had its costs as well as its benefits. One might say that the Privy Council was out of synch with Canada in politics and that it doggedly maintained a high level of decentralization even when the dynamics of the federation called for increased centralization. During the Great Depression of the 1930s, the government of Canada proposed legislation that paralleled Roosevelt's New Deal agenda. At this point, the British justices overturned nearly the whole of the Conservative Party's New Deal Program as being *ultra vires* of the Canadian Parliament.[52] In response, the federal government decided to begin action to eliminate appeals to the Privy Council.

There had already been movements throughout the British Empire as well as in Britain itself to limit the right of appeal to London, culminating in the Statute of Westminster of 1931, which established that the power to abolish appeals to the Privy Council now rested with the Dominion parliaments. Court proceedings soon followed. The *British Coal Corp.* case of 1935 abolished Privy Council review of federal laws,[53] but not until 1947, in *Attorney General of Ontario v. Attorney General of Canada*,[54] was appeal to the Privy Council concerning provincial laws abolished. The case

---

[52] Alan Cairns (1971) reports that by 1937, in a series of decisions, the Privy Council invalidated the New Deal legislation of the Bennett government. Cairns notes that most legal observers believed that the legislation struck down was of dubious constitutionality and that, in any case, the Bennett government had been turned out of office in 1935 and his successor evinced little support for the bills.

[53] *British Coal Corp. v. The King* A.C. 500, 520 (1935).

[54] *Attorney General Ontario v. Attorney General Canada* (Privy Council Appeals) A.C. 127 (1947).

A Political Theory of Federalism 249

originally appeared before the Supreme Court in 1940,[55] which decided in the federal government's favor (by 4-2): appeals to the Privy Council regarding provincial law were to be abolished. Four provinces appealed to the Privy Council (British Columbia, New Brunswick, Ontario, Prince Edward Island). In evidence that the federation needed a natural adjustment, two provinces, Manitoba and Saskatchewan, supported the federal government's position. The amendment, which made the Supreme Court of Canada the final court of appeal, was finally enacted in 1949. However, a grandfather clause kept cases in the Privy Council for another decade. The impact of the structural change was quickly felt throughout the country, for in our view it destabilized the federal arrangement in Canada.

Toothless Juridical Federalism

The parliamentary form of Canadian government, together with relatively unified parties, makes it comparatively easy for majorities to form and enact legislation. Moreover, Canadian parties have been highly disciplined and programmatic parties for most of their histories. Our analysis of the British case would suggest, therefore, that Canada was not fertile soil for a durable federalism. But until 1949, when the Canadian Supreme Court became the ultimate appellate authority, the powers of the Canadian Parliament were tightly circumscribed by a politically independent tribunal. The Judicial Committee had systematically acted to provide a secure constitutional basis for broad provincial jurisdiction from 1880 until the end of the Second World War, and as long as its provincialist doctrines remained in force, the federal nature of the Canadian Constitution was preserved.

Since 1949, however, with the patriation of appellate authority, the provinces have steadily lost much of the constitutional ground they had gained under the Judicial Committee. The Canadian Supreme Court, while asserting doctrinal allegiance to earlier decisions, has regularly ruled in favor of expanding national legislative authority. To a great extent, these rulings have come about by means of adopting jurisprudence deferential to Parliament. Unlike the tradition of nineteenth-century British courts, however, Canadian statutory jurisprudence has not taken a textualist form. It did not call for a strengthening of received British judicial traditions but instead proceeded by articulating broader readings of the general peace, order, and good government clause (effectively saying that the national government can deal with any problem having a "national dimension"),[56] and gradually developing a generous construction of national

---

[55] The delay from 1940 to 1947 was due to the war.
[56] See *R. v. Crown Zellerbach Ltd.* (1988) 1 S.C.R. 401: "The national concern doctrine applies to both new matters which did not exist at Confederation and to matters which,

250 Bednar, Eskridge, and Ferejohn

authority over trade and commerce.[57] The court has also found a "dormant" aspect to federal powers over trade and commerce that forbids provincial regulations that discriminate against nonresidents or protect local producers.[58] In these cases, the court not only found an expansive constitutional basis for federal authority, it also stopped showing deference to provincial efforts to regulate in these newly created federal domains. In allowing federal action in antitrust, securities regulation, and environmental protection, for example, the fact that the provinces had been already engaged in regulation in these areas did not stand in the way. That provinces had traditionally acted to regulate in these areas was no impediment to federal intrusion.

The expansive readings of section 91 powers since 1949 echoed the broad readings of the Commerce Clause given by the U.S. Supreme Court after 1937. We can see in retrospect that U.S. Supreme Court deference to Congress in this regard was a temporary phenomenon and can be reversed in the right political climate. In the unitary context of Canadian institutions, however, we doubt that such backsliding is likely. The Canadian

although originally matters of a local or private nature in a province, have since, in the absence of national emergency become matters of national concern." Although some aspects of the national dimensions doctrine had appeared earlier, its development accelerated after 1949. Predictably, some Québécois judges have been apprehensive about these developments. Justice Jean Beetz criticized recharacterizing as national those domains traditionally interpreted as provincial in his dissent in *Reference re Anti-Inflation Act* (1976) 2 S.C.R. 373. Swinton (1992, 126–7) writes, "It is not difficult to speculate as to where this line of reasoning would lead: a fundamental feature of the Constitution, its federal nature, the distribution of powers between Parliament and the provincial legislatures, would disappear not gradually but rapidly."

[57] In *General Motors* (1989) 1 S.C.R. 641, the Court devised a "general regulation of trade" doctrine, "which allows Parliament to create policies aimed at the economy as a unit, rather than at a particular trade or business, despite its impact on intraprovincial business activity" (Swinton 1992, 127). This doctrine permitted the national government to formulate a competition policy based on its authority to regulate trade. Previous competition statutes had rested on the federal power to make criminal laws.

[58] Justice Martland wrote for the Court that "the plan at issue not only affects interprovincial trade in eggs but aims at the regulation of such trade. It is an essential part of this scheme . . . specifically to control and regulate the sale in Manitoba of imported eggs. It is designed to restrict or limit the free flow of trade between provinces as such. Because of that, it constitutes an invasion of the exclusive legislative authority of the Parliament of Canada over the matter of the regulation of trade and commerce." *Attorney General Manitoba v. Manitoba Egg & Poultry Assoc.* S.C.R. 689 (1971). This decision was a clear departure from two Judicial Committee decisions upholding provincial regulatory schemes that had impacts on producers from other provinces, *Home Oil Distributors Ltd. v. Attorney General British Columbia* S.C.R. 444 (1940), and *Shannon v. Lower Mainland Dairy Products Board* A.C. 708 (1938), but reflected the aggressive dormant commerce clause precepts followed in Canada's neighbor to the south, e.g., *Dean Milk Co. v. City of Madison*, 340 U.S. 349 (1951); *Baldwin v. G.A.F. Selig*, 294 U.S. 511 (1935).

A Political Theory of Federalism 251

system lacks the structural bounds that constrain defections in the federal relationship. No formal political institution exists to check the federal government from encroaching on the provinces. Instead, Canada must rely on variations of juridical federalism. In the Privy Council period, legal rules, enforceable through a genuinely independent judicial body, maintained the federal-provincial balance. These rules worked together with federalism norms, especially the convention that the provinces should be consulted on any explicit modifications to the division of powers. Under the Supreme Court but prior to the Charter of Rights and Freedoms, a new document that would guarantee rights for individuals but also extend rights to communities, the nature of the federal relationship was allowed to shift, but was still mildly maintained by the constraint of norms and practice.

One important norm does impose a separation-of-powers-like restriction on federal action. For some major constitutional issues, the prime minister meets with the ten provincial premiers for approval. The importance of this norm was demonstrated in the Patriation Reference, 1981. Objecting primarily to the Charter of Rights and Freedoms, several provinces challenged Prime Minister Trudeau's decision to patriate the constitution, without first gaining the approval of the provinces.[59] The Supreme Court decided that, although Trudeau's plan would alter the nature of the federal relationship, and therefore that a convention of provincial consultation existed,[60] such a norm was not legally enforceable and therefore that the provinces had no recourse to the court for enforcing this convention. The legal effect of the Court's decision was to free up Trudeau to pursue patriation as he had originally intended. However, the Court's declaration that Trudeau would be breaking an established convention placed political pressure on Trudeau, and he no longer felt that it was feasible to ignore the provincial concerns (Russell 1987; Hogg 1992). As a result, the impact of the charter on provincial powers was diminished.[61] Although it worked in

---

[59] The inevitable conflict between guaranteeing rights for individuals and extending rights to communities would without doubt end up on the Supreme Court's docket, and the Court would become very important in deciding what the new constitution meant. Several provinces are leery of any increased role for a court they distrust. For a discussion of the legal complexity of these competing goals, see Swinton 1990, 338–48.

[60] While the Court found that a convention existed in the Patriation Reference, it failed to recognize such a norm in the Senate Reference (1980) 1 S.C.R. 54. In the Senate Reference, the Court did not find a convention that would command the federal government to consult the provincial governments on the proposed amendment to the Senate, even though such an amendment would be "of interest" to the provinces. The Court has thus drawn the line at recognizing the convention of provincial consultation only when the legislative power of the provincial governments is directly at stake. See Monahan 1987.

[61] The most important change was the addition of the notwithstanding clause, which allows Parliament or the provinces to enact legislation notwithstanding the guarantees of rights in the charter. These exemptions expire after five years unless reenacted.

the Patriation Reference, reliance on norm-based federalism to sustain the federal relationship remained an uncertain process, especially in view of the fact that there was little agreement as to what precisely these norms were. For this reason, demands to create structural checks on federal power are increasing.

The Charter of Rights and Freedoms has again upset the balance in the division of powers. The interests of federalism are in tension with individual rights. Indeed, one reason for the establishment of federalism is to protect regional identities, whereas the concept of individual rights implies a more national, or universal, interpretation. With the adoption of the charter, the Canadian Supreme Court has had a grossly expanded docket of complex cases in the demand to define the appropriate interpretation of the charter. At times, this task raises issues that clash with the goals of federalism.

Peter Hogg writes that federalism claims should be superior to charter claims.[62] However, he continues to say that the Court need not decide the federalism issue before the charter issue, when both are raised. In fact, it might choose the charter issue first.[63] In this scenario, federalism questions will be side-stepped as the charter limits are defined, and the federalism question will only be addressed if the Court finds that the case passes the charter test first. Nevertheless, provinces are worried about the potential to sap their power that the charter raises. Despite Hogg's judgment that federalism powers should not be trumped by the charter, the court has been inclined to read the charter broadly.

Of perhaps the greatest concern to the provinces is that the introduction of the charter places the Court in a highly political position, as it works in the next decade to define the limits of the charter, without subjecting it to the same political constraints that provided the only force, however weak, to check the federal government from encroaching upon provincial territory. Still, the charter has not replaced legislators with

---

[62] Hogg's logic is as follows: "It is impossible for a nation to be governed without bodies possessing legislative powers, but it is possible for a nation to be governed without a Charter of Rights. The Charter of Rights assumes the existence of legislative powers, although admittedly it imposes limits on these powers. I conclude that the argument that a law is invalid because it is outside the powers conferred on the enacting body by the federal part of the Constitution is a prior, or more radical, argument than the argument that a law is invalid because it offends a prohibition contained in the Charter of Rights" (Hogg 1992, 373).

[63] Paul Weiler (1973) has argued that prior to the enactment of the charter, the Court often resorted to federalism grounds for overturning legislation that the Court felt violated certain rights, and therefore should not have been invoked.

A Political Theory of Federalism

judges as lawmakers. Although the vast majority of the Court's cases are considerations of the legality, under the charter, of legislation,[64] the Court has been largely unable to come to unanimous decisions (Swinton 1990, 335–7), leaving the Parliament with little guidance and limiting the legitimacy of the Court's rulings. Nevertheless, it is the potential for encroachment that is disturbing to the provinces, and will cause increased demands for institutional reform.

From the rise of regional parties to the perennial demands of Quebec for increased sovereignty, the evidence of instability is pervasive in the Canadian polity. In the summer of 1990, the Senate, traditionally a rubber stamp for House legislation, threatened to veto an important tax bill. Progressive Conservative Prime Minister Brian Mulroney drowned the Senate activism by adding Senators until the Progressive Conservatives had a majority in the upper chamber, in a move that was constitutionally legal but unconventional – a virtual guarantee of damnation in Canada. Because of his support for the unpopular tax, Mulroney's popularity rating had plummeted to a record-setting low of 12 percent; his tampering with the institutional structure so outraged the electorate that it guaranteed that he would not recover.

The prospects for a solution based upon some version of a compact philosophy of the founding have been greatly reduced by the heightened awareness of the multicultural aspects of the Canadian society. Whereas it might have been possible to arrive at a constitutional compromise if Quebec was the only special society demanding recognition (as contemplated at Meech Lake in 1987), the recognition of the indigenous societies as well as the various minority communities, whose claims to privileges have been legitimized by court interpretations of the charter, made such a compromise impossible (as shown at Meech Lake in 1990 and Charlottetown in 1992). Rather than create one society of all Canada, and hence increase the pressure for centralization of power, the newly recognized communities have begun to fight for increased autonomy in ways that defy traditional federal dynamics. Possibly the manner by which the institutions will be redesigned will follow a more consociational, rather than federal, path. But, if that is the case, the sense in which Canada will remain a recognizable state rather than a mere alliance of smaller sovereign entities remains to be determined.

---

[64] See, e.g., Monahan 1987; Russell 1987, 576. Russell estimates that 1,500 cases related to the charter came before the various courts in the first three years of the charter; the diversity of the various provincial courts means that until the Supreme Court can get to them, the charter will mean different things in different parts of the country.

STRUCTURAL AND JURIDICAL FEDERALISM
IN THE UNITED STATES

The U.S. Constitution, as it was formulated in the Philadelphia Convention and ratified by the states, is filled with expressions of federalism norms.[65] What is particularly significant about American federalism, however, is that the framers understood the federal commitment problem and offered both structural and juridical conceptions of federalism as complementary solutions to it.[66] There is no question that Madison and the other framers of the Constitution intended that the Supreme Court would review state legislation. Such legislation represented, for Madison and others at Philadelphia, the most frequent source of unjust laws; perhaps the most important effect of reconstituting American government was to place some restraints on self-dealing by the states. But the founders were certainly less clear about the need or possibilities for judicial restraints on the national government. This is not to take a position on the vexed issue about whether judicial review of federal legislation was "included" in the constitutional scheme, but only to say that the need for such review was seen as less pressing to the framers of the Constitution. Lacking enforcement powers, the judiciary was seen as the weakest of the three branches of the federal government and was unlikely to be willing or able to oppose Congress's will for very long.[67]

Indeed, the opponents of the proposed Constitution were much more worried about the potential powers of the judiciary in the federal scheme. As far as the framers of the Constitution went in providing guarantees for the authority of the states – leaving to the states all unenumerated powers and effectively giving state governments representation in the Senate[68] – it

[65] Starting with enumeration of national powers, U.S. Const., Art. I; continuing through the guarantee clause, Art. IV, sec. 4, and the supremacy clause, Art. VI, sec. 2; and on to the reservation of unexpressed powers to the states, Amend. X, the Constitution remains the classical expression of a normative understanding that the states and the national government would be supreme in their respective spheres.

[66] Alexander Hamilton's *Federalist* 78 articulated a mode of juridical protection for federalism against the states that was implemented by the Supreme Court in *McCulloch v. Maryland*, 17 U.S. 316 (1819). James Madison's *Federalist* 10 and 45–6 articulated structural protection for federalism that was later the basis for *Garcia v. San Antonio Metropolitan Transit Auth.*, 469 U.S. 528 (1985).

[67] Events soon confirmed these suspicions. Witness the Court's meek acceptance, in *Stuart v. Laird*, 5 U.S. (1 Cranch) 299 (1803), of Congress's authority, effectively, to fire sixteen presumptively life-tenured federal judges by repealing the 1801 Judiciary Act.

[68] The fact that senators were to be chosen by state legislatures rather than directly by the electorates and that the Senate shared with the executive the appointment powers for high ministers and the Supreme Court illustrates the formal structural protections provided for states. In *Federalist* 45 and 46, Madison argued that the states had other, extraconstitutional, means to protect themselves from unjust federal legislation. He estimated that the

was not sufficient to convince many of the Anti-Federalists. Brutus presciently offered a powerful critique of rule-based juridical federalism, arguing that it would devolve into an arbitrary government run by judges. Life-tenured judges could not be controlled by the other branches and would soon find ways to escape constitutional fetters. He and the Federal Farmer also criticized the structural protections in the Constitution on the grounds that they would simply be incapable of restraining a Congress determined to make use of what they regarded as the open-ended necessary and proper clause.

These and other concerns led several of the state ratifying conventions to attempt to insist on amending the proposed Constitution to provide explicit protections for state authority. Although those attempts were successfully resisted, Madison and other Federalist leaders agreed ultimately to incorporate some of the proposals as constitutional amendments to be offered by the First Congress. Those first amendments did introduce a number of limits on congressional powers, but the only explicit protection for state jurisdictions was the vague and notoriously truistic Tenth Amendment.

The conventional wisdom among law professors has been that juridical federalism is unworkable – at least the rule-based version of it – and that structural features of the constitutional system must be relied upon to ensure that the federal government and the states keep to their appropriate federal roles (Wechsler 1954; Choper 1981). The conventional wisdom among political historians has been that these constitutional structures have not in fact been able to prevent the creation of a strong national government that has substantially eroded the autonomy of the states (Ostrom 1991; Riker 1955).

Historians are right to argue that there has been an expansion in national authority over the history of the republic and that structural forces have not been sufficient to stop it. Constitutional lawyers are also right to note the Court has been reluctant to attempt to enforce constitutional rules to restrain this evolution. Thus, one might be tempted to conclude that there is nothing in the constitutional system sufficient to maintain federalism. But it seems to us that American federal practices have been enormously robust in the face of massive changes in the nature of the society and the economy. The states and localities are still vibrant sources of policy determination; the federal government, as large as it has become, participates more often as a partner of state and local

---

states could put about a half-million men under arms, compared to thirty thousand or so commanded by Congress. Short of a call to arms, their hold on popular affections would enable the states to provide a reservoir of effective political power as well that would oppose unjust congressional designs.

government than as a central commander. The growth of federal power has in fact been episodic and halting. Congress has only rarely claimed the full extent of authority that seemed theoretically available to it at any particular moment in time. And even when such authority has been claimed, it has usually trickled back to states and localities within the newly created federal programs and sometimes reverted to them outright.

As some of us have argued in detail elsewhere,[69] the nationalization of American government has been neither extreme nor unidirectional and certainly not as rapid as the nationalization of American politics and culture. State authority has remained remarkably resilient in the face of immense reductions in the costs of transportation and communication and resultant increases in cross-border flows of people and things. The major expansions in congressional authority have only come at those rare political moments when the characteristic centrifugal tendencies of American political institutions are defeated by the appearance of cohesive political consensus. Such moments are exceptional in American history[70] and are partially offset by the scaling back that has characteristically followed them.[71] Our theory suggests a robust, albeit evolutive, federalist equilibrium induced by the structures built into the Constitution, as well as by more recent institutional developments, such as the construction of integrated state-federal administrations and political parties.

Our theory also suggests that the Supreme Court can play an effective role in enforcing federalism. The Court has both rule of law and institutional incentives to enforce federalism against both national and state cheating. The rule of law incentives derive from the clear instantiation of federalism in the Constitution and from the fact that the stable exercise of political authority in the far-flung American republic requires a recognition of some degree of local autonomy. The institutional incentives derive from the Court's wish to maintain its role as an arbiter of an evolving federal structure: if the Court could establish and maintain itself as a neutral broker among the states and between the state

---

[69] See Eskridge and Ferejohn 1994 (surveying federalism decisions in U.S. constitutional history).

[70] National consensuses reigned during the Washington administration (1789–97), the Era of Good Feelings (roughly the Monroe administration, 1817–25), possibly the Jacksonian period (1829–37), Reconstruction (1865–77), the McKinley-Roosevelt era (1897–1913), the New Deal and World War II (1933–45), and the Great Society (1964–9). But only during the Washington administration, Reconstruction, the New Deal and World War II, and the Great Society was there a consensus in favor of expanding national power.

[71] The nationalizing agenda of the Washington administration (dominated by Hamilton) was scaled back by the Democrat-Republicans (Jefferson and Madison). The ambitious agenda of Reconstruction was abandoned by the Compromise of 1877. The New Deal and Great Society have been curtailed by deregulationist platforms that have prevailed in all the elections after 1964.

and national governments, it assures its own central importance in our governance.

On our account, the Court has the institutional capacity over time to make and enforce rules restraining the states from interfering unduly with each other or with national values. It is well positioned to articulate and defend constitutional values and rights. It is also sufficiently independent of the state governments to be able to establish and maintain principled rules restricting the states from unfairly discriminating against outsiders. It is far less able, however, to restrain a determined national government from infringing on the federal compact. Such infringements, if they are sustained, are likely to be both deliberate and popular. Judicial attempts at resistance are likely to appear willful and antidemocratic and are therefore dangerous to the maintenance of judicial autonomy. Consider these points in light of American constitutional history (Eskridge and Ferejohn 1994).

The potential for judicial enforcement appeared early in our history. The Supreme Court of Chief Justice John Marshall firmly rebuffed state shirking[72] and attempted incursions on national power.[73] Although the Court gave a broad reading to the enumerated powers of Congress,[74] it was unwilling to restrict state regulation of local matters simply because Congress might regulate those matters.[75] The federal structure was less fortunate under the next chief justice, Roger Taney. Although the Taney Court was more likely to support state authority to regulate even in domains where national authority was claimed,[76] it also invoked national powers to attempt to enforce the Fugitive Slave Act in face of intense local opposition.[77] In its

---

[72] See *Cohens v. Virginia*, 19 U.S. (6 Wheat.) 264 (1821), which established the Court's authority to review state supreme court decisions and reverse them if inconsistent with national rules and norms.

[73] See *McCulloch v. Maryland*, 17 U.S. 316 (1819), which overturned a state attempt to tax the Bank of the United States.

[74] See *McCulloch* (note 73), which found congressional authority to establish the Bank of the United States in the necessary and proper clause, U.S. Const., Art. I, sec. 8, cl. 17, and *Gibbons v. Ogden*, 22 U.S. 1 (1824), which upheld congressional authority to regulate navigation and commerce and to preempt state laws interfering with such regulation.

[75] See *Willton v. Black Bird Creek Marsh*, 27 U.S. 245 (1829), upholding a state authorization for a company to build a dam across a navigable river and rejecting a rigid "dual federalism" in which states were precluded from regulating issues over which Congress might theoretically regulate.

[76] See *Mayor of the City of New York v. Miln*, 36 U.S. 102 (1837), upholding a local law screening immigrants coming into the state from overseas and barring such immigrants likely to become public charges, and *Cooley v. Board of Wardens*, 53 U.S. 299 (1851), upholding a state law requiring vessels entering and leaving the port of Philadelphia to engage local pilots.

[77] Note the attempts of various northern states to nullify that act, attempts firmly rebuffed on supremacy clause grounds in *Ableman v. Booth*, 62 U.S. 506 (1859).

fateful decision in *Dred Scott v. Sandford* (1857)[78] the Court committed a strategic as well as moral blunder that might have ended the American experiment in federalism altogether. By invalidating the Compromise of 1820, which had prohibited slavery in the former Northwest Territories, *Dred Scott* pressed the slavery issue back onto the nation's agenda under circumstances that undermined the credibility of federalism in this context. The decision also called into question the Court's claim to be a neutral arbiter on questions of either federalism or slavery, and undermined Congress's capacity to maintain interregional compromises about the issue (such as the 1820 compromise).[79] In a real sense, the Court's decision in Dred Scott's case helped precipitate a chain of events that culminated in southern secession and civil war.[80]

Federalism might have failed to survive the Civil War period in either of two ways. The southern secession might have succeeded, leaving behind two nations, neither sufficiently diverse to maintain federal institutions. Or the rebellion might have ended with the construction of a national republic institutionally capable of guaranteeing directly constitutional values and liberties. While the war did end with the imposition of national authority on the southern states, this imposition was temporary, and the system soon reverted substantially back to the decentralized ways of the antebellum period. Thus, federalism survived the Civil War and Reconstruction. In quite analogous fashion it also survived the successive nationalizing periods represented by the New Freedom, the New Deal, World War II, and the Great Society. The story in each case is the same.

Each of these events – the Civil War and Reconstruction, Woodrow Wilson's New Freedom, Franklin Roosevelt's New Deal, and Lyndon Johnson's Great Society – was marked by a brief political consensus and domination of Congress and the presidency by a strong majority party which moved rapidly to enact a legislative program without paying much heed to the opposition. But, in each case, both the unity of purpose and the size of the majority contingent were only temporary, and each broke apart in the face of public reactions to these legislative programs. Thus, the unified radical Republicans were unable to keep the northern public with them to transform southern society beyond about 1872.[81] Wilson's

---

[78] *Dred Scott v. Sandford*, 60 U.S. 393 (1857).

[79] Weingast (1994) argues that the pattern of representation in the Senate – particularly what he has called the "balance rule," which kept northern and southern representation in the Senate balanced as new states were admitted – was the key to keeping the Missouri Compromise in place. Other congressional practices such as the "gag rule" in the House turned out to be much more vulnerable to shifting demographics in the antebellum period.

[80] See, generally, Fehrenbacher 1978.

[81] Indeed, as the *Civil Rights Cases*, 109 U.S. 3 (1883) (invalidating those parts of the Civil Rights Act of 1875 that imposed nondiscrimination obligations on private businesses),

A Political Theory of Federalism

New Freedom, produced by much smaller legislative majorities, was much more short-lived, lasting only until the distracting outbreak of European hostilities. The New Deal, of course, lasted longer, perhaps because it was as much a reaction to profound and troubling national crisis as it was a rejection of a divided and exhausted Republican Party. But it too fell apart as southern Democratic representatives increasingly began to make a common cause with Republicans in opposing the extension of national powers into social and some economic issues. Like the support for Wilson's New Freedom, the Democratic unity that lay behind the Great Society collapsed legislatively after only a couple of years as the conservative coalition of southern Democrats and Republicans became able to stop liberal initiatives. This left the legacy of the Great Society to be carried forward administratively or judicially, by friendly executive department officials and judges.

If in retrospect it seems inevitable that the modern revolution in transportation, communication, and warfare would render national regulation increasingly important, it is equally striking how much room was left for the states to pursue their own policies in these areas, partly because of the constitutional hybrid of structural and juridical protections for federalism, but partly too because of the difficulty of maintaining unified national majorities capable of occupying the domain. Reconstruction turned out to be an unprecedented but relatively brief suppression of (southern) state autonomy, and it was followed by a regime of political laissez-faire on race issues and judicial reluctance to interpret the Reconstruction amendments very broadly.[82] After the end of Reconstruction, the Court invoked the due process clause as a basis for reviewing state economic legislation on individual rights grounds, but in cases presenting issues of national-versus-state power, the Supreme Court repeatedly protected state autonomy against infringement by the national government.[83]

A similar scenario can be traced for the New Deal Court constituted by Franklin Roosevelt in 1937–42. On the one hand, the Court retreated

indicated, the Supreme Court began to erode Republican legislative and constitutional gains fairly quickly.

[82] See the *Civil Rights Cases*, 109 U.S. 3 (1883) (described in note 81); *United States v. Harris*, 106 U.S. 629 (1882) (invalidating the antilynching provisions of the Civil Rights Act of 1871, because not aimed at state action). See also *Collector v. Day*, 78 U.S. 113 (1871) (restricting federal taxation of the states).

[83] See *Plessy v. Ferguson*, 163 U.S. 537 (1896) (allowing states to establish "separate but equal" facilities for racial apartheid); *United States v. E. C. Knight Co.*, 156 U.S. 1 (1895) (Sherman Act does not apply to manufacturing, which is "local" and therefore reserved for state regulation); *The Income Tax Case*, 157 U.S. 429 (1895) (striking down federal income tax as a direct tax unequally apportioned among the states); *Hans v. Louisiana*, 134 U.S. 1 (1890) (expansive interpretation of the Eleventh Amendment to prevent lawsuits against states).

260   *Bednar, Eskridge, and Ferejohn*

from the restrictive interpretation of national power in several pre-1937 decisions and upheld every major expansion of national power presented to it. On the other hand, the New Deal was itself highly deferential to state autonomy, and the Supreme Court reaffirmed the authority of the states to engage in economic development and employ traditional police powers without federal interference. Indeed, the New Deal Court insisted on federalism as a sharp limit on the constitutional authority of the national judiciary as well as the legislature.[84] Additionally, the Court developed rules of statutory interpretation to reconcile state allocation and development policies with new federal development and redistribution statutes. Courts must "start with the assumption that the historic police powers of the States were not to be superseded by the Federal Act unless that was the clear and manifest purpose of Congress."[85] Likewise, the Great Society legislation tended to build on and defer to state regulation rather than to displace it completely. When Congress has imposed burdensome obligations directly on the states, the Court has frequently intervened, either directly by constitutional invalidation of the federal statute[86] or by a narrow construction of the federal law.[87]

The Court of Chief Justice William Rehnquist has been more overtly activist in monitoring national infringements on state authority, even as it has vigorously monitored state regulatory policies for infringement of the federal arrangement. On the one hand, the Court has insisted on the integrity of state government and state police powers (i.e., policies protecting public health or safety or promoting economic development) and

---

[84] In *Erie Railroad v. Tompkins*, 304 U.S. 64 (1938), the Court overruled earlier precedent and required federal courts in diversity jurisdiction cases to apply state law rather than federal common law. Justice Louis Brandeis's justification for the overruling rested mainly on constitutional federalism, suggesting that neither Congress nor the Court had the authority to displace state law in such a global manner.

[85] *Rice v. Santa Fe Elevator Corp.*, 331 U.S. 218, 230 (1947). For leading recent statements, see *Ray v. Atlantic Richfield Co.*, 435 U.S. 151 (1978); *Cipollone v. Liggett Group, Inc.*, 505 U.S. 504 (1991); *BFP v. Resolution Trust Corp.*, 511 U.S. 531 (1994).

[86] See *National League of Cities v. Usery*, 426 U.S. 823 (1976), overruled [5-4] by *Garcia v. San Antonio Metropolitan Transit Authority*, 469 U.S. 528 (1985), limiting the federal government's ability to regulate the states qua states; *New York v. United States*, 505 U.S. 144 (1992), forbidding the federal government from "commandeering" the states, applied to state executive officers in *Printz v. United States*, 521 U.S. 98 (1997); *United States v. Lopez*, 514 U.S. 549 (1995), invalidating a federal gun control law as beyond Congress's commerce clause power; *Seminole Tribe of Fla. v. Florida*, 517 U.S. 44 (1996), holding that Congress does not have authority under the commerce clause to abrogate state Eleventh Amendment immunity from lawsuits in federal courts, applied to lawsuits in state courts, *Alden v. Maine*, 119 S.Ct. (June 23, 1999) (no. 98–436).

[87] See Eskridge and Frickey 1992, demonstrating that the Burger and Rehnquist Courts vigorously enforce federalism values through superstrong, clear statement rules presuming against national intrusion into domains of traditional state regulatory competence.

A Political Theory of Federalism · 261

has overridden national efforts to commandeer state officials for national projects.[88] On the other hand, the Court has vigilantly policed state policies that discriminate against interstate commerce; when there is strong evidence that a state is pursuing a policy that pushes costs onto nonresidents, the Court has not been reluctant either to set aside the state laws or authorize congressional action.[89] Juridical federalism has, in this respect, developed in a way that permits the states to be the primary engines of what Paul Peterson (1995) calls "developmental" policies (aimed at improving the state economy) and "allocative" policies (traditional police powers, the day-to-day operation of state services).

The Rehnquist Court has generated publicity and controversy in a series of decisions (collected in notes 85 and 88) that have insisted on limits to the federal Commerce Clause power, denied the national government the ability to commandeer state officials, and even limited citizen access to state as well as federal courts to sue the states. Although these decisions are controversial and closely decided, they do not radically alter the fabric of American federalism and may even be said to reaffirm that arrangement. The Court's new willingness to place limits on national powers amounts, at present, to striking down or limiting authority claimed by Democratic congresses at a time when the Democrats no longer hold majorities. It is not yet clear how robust juridical federalism is in checking national powers when they enjoy the support of contemporary congressional majorities.[90] In any case, it remains clear that the most effective protections for state authority are structural – in the unwillingness or inability of Congress to seek new authority – rather than reliance on the paper-thin majorities by which the current court has been limiting national powers.[91]

---

[88] See *New York v. United States*, 505 U.S. 144 (1992), invalidating congressional efforts to commandeer state legislatures; *Printz v. United States*, 521 U.S. 98 (1997), invalidating congressional efforts to commandeer state and local law enforcement officials; *Alden v. Maine*, 119 S.Ct. (June 23, 1999) (no. 98–436), invalidating congressional efforts to commandeer state courts against the states themselves.

[89] See, e.g., *West Lynn Creamery, Inc. v. Healy*, 512 U.S. 186 (1994), invalidating a nondiscriminatory tax on milk that was used to subsidize the state's dairy farmers and, therefore, indirectly to discriminate against interstate commerce; *C & A Carbone, Inc. v. Town of Clarkstown*, 511 U.S. 383 (1994), invalidating an environmental regulation that discriminated, even if minorly, against interstate commerce.

[90] We may anticipate such circumstances arising in the extension of federal criminal law or perhaps in tort reform. Federal legislation in these areas is likely to conflict with traditional state powers and should help us to understand better the contours of juridical federalism.

[91] It is hardly accidental that the revivification of federalism norms has tracked growing Republican strength in the national government. Presidents Reagan and Bush led the way by appointing federalism-friendly justices, but the Republican strength in Congress has

The contrast with Canada in particular supports the idea that structural restraints are crucially important and that the critical structural variable is the fragmentation of powers at the national level. The formal requirements of bicameral approval and presentment to the president, and the less formal but characteristic incoherence of the national political parties, give the states or their surrogates[92] multiple entries (and vetoes) to the national political process and make it unlikely that Congress will seriously impair the operation of state governments. The system of checks and balances also facilitates the operation of judicial enforcement of federalism rules (through judicial review invalidating congressional enactments) and norms (through statutory interpretations narrowing congressional enactments): Supreme Court justices are protected against extreme national political pressure, because their appointments reflect preferences of both the presidents who appoint them and the Senates that confirm and because their life tenure assures a rolling ideological mixture of justices.

Because the federal courts are substantially independent from state politics and operate through case-by-case adjudication, juridical federalism is most effective in monitoring and preventing states from infringing on other jurisdictions or from unduly favoring their own citizens. Because bicameralism and presentment operate to delay or block federal legislation, structural federalism works best to restrain the national government from overreaching its powers within the federal system.[93] But, it is important to see that the restraints on the federal government work only so long as no cohesive and long-lived majority is formed. If such a majority were to appear and was determined to undermine state authority, the structural protections could probably not resist it for very long. And so, perhaps ironically, American federalism is hostage to the truth of Madison's famous argument in *Federalist* 10: it is particularly difficult to form and maintain cohesive majorities in a large and heterogeneous polity.

CONCLUSION

Stable federal arrangements require that both national and provincial authorities be kept within their proper spheres of activity. Legal rules and norms can, we think, play a part in restraining these governments but cannot be relied upon to do the whole job. Instead, as Madison argued,

---

attenuated nationalist legislative impulses as well. There are exceptions, of course, in the areas of expanding federal criminal law and federal efforts at tort law reform.

[92] Administrators, the president, and national political parties all have incentives to represent the interests of the states on various issues. See Kramer 1994.

[93] This argument is expanded upon in Bednar, "The Federal Problem" (Stanford University, January 1995, unpublished manuscript). See also Bednar and Eskridge 1995.

governmental restraints are more effectively founded on structural configurations of power. In this chapter, we have argued that legal rules and institutions are particularly unlikely to succeed at preventing the national government from predatory jurisdictional expansion. The key to restraining such expansion is in the fragmentation of power within the national government, which can prevent the formation of a legislative will. Fragmentation can be achieved in two ways: formally, by designing institutions that check the exercise of concerted power and, informally, by inhibiting the formation of unified and disciplined political parties.

The cases we have examined have permitted us a limited test – really, more an illustration – of these hypotheses. The Canadian case allowed us to see how a constitutional change reducing the institutional independence of the judiciary led directly to the decline of judicial protection for the provinces. Until 1949 both the United States and Canada enjoyed effective institutional conditions for restraining the national government from intervening extensively in provincial jurisdictions. In both nations a powerful and independent judiciary also acted to restrain the states and provinces from trampling too egregiously on their neighbors. The institutional conditions for judicial independence were greatly weakened in Canada after 1949. This decline was especially significant because there were few effective internal checks on the exercise of national powers, which limited the possibilities for rule-based juridical federalism applied to the national government. It is not surprising, therefore, that since 1949 the Canadian courts have been developing a jurisprudence that is more deferential to the national parliament. The Canadian Supreme Court has evolved constitutional doctrines that permit that government much more latitude to regulate economic and social activity than it previously enjoyed, and there are few fallback protections for provincial autonomy as there are in the United States.

Juridical federalism still regulates what the provinces can do, however, and Canadian courts have been active in enforcing limits to provincial authority when the provinces discriminate against outsiders or infringe on national authority. As this process occurs, the provincial governments and their electorates can be expected to lose confidence in the judiciary as an enforcer of traditional provincial "rights." In turn, we expect to see the development of defensive political and cultural strategies at the provincial level – typically demands for additional special constitutional protections or special status within a looser federation and, occasionally, threats to exit – that promise to inhibit the national government from expanding its authority. Such phenomena have been occurring in recent years, and our theory would predict that Canadian federalism will continue to be troubled and may have to be reconfigured, or may even dissolve, in the future. An implication of our theory is that the obvious reason for Canada's

264   *Bednar, Eskridge, and Ferejohn*

troubled federalism – ethnic and linguistic separatism – is not so much the cause as the consequence of the evanescing political structure. It remains true, however, that norm-based federalism could still play a role in limiting national power, as it did, arguably, in the case of the Patriation Reference. But appeals to norms will work only where there are a robust sense of common purpose and a willingness of all to abide by norms supporting the continued Canadian project.

The British case allowed us to assess the impact of "informal" constitutional change on federal practices. In a series of developments starting at around the enactment of the First Reform Act and continuing for sixty years, the nature of British electoral and legislative practices was profoundly transformed. Although there remains significant disagreement among scholars as to the details, there is little question that the expansion of the electorate led, for whatever reasons, to the formation of disciplined and unified parties that were capable of organizing both electoral and legislative activity. This political transformation undercut whatever constitutional barriers existed (the House of Lords and the monarchy) to the creation of a unified majoritarian government capable of implementing vast and complicated legislative schemes following an election. We have argued that this same transformation significantly undercut the system of localism that had prevailed in Britain for a century and a half.

Finally, the American experience allowed us to examine the relative robustness of federal practices within a system of fragmented powers. In the United States, as in Canada so long as appellate authority remained with the Judicial Committee, the courts have had the opportunity to develop an independent federalism jurisprudence. Although the enforcement of federalist norms and values has been uneven and though courts have sometimes acquiesced to expansionist initiatives from various governments, recent political and legal developments suggest that juridical federalism remains quite resilient. Our emphasis on robustness and resilience and on the importance of a structurally independent judiciary leads us to doubt the pessimistic assessments of federalism's demise that are a staple of both the political science and legal literatures.

We do not doubt that in America as in Britain, if a highly unified and disciplined national political party, bent on undercutting federalist norms, were to gain large and long-lived majorities, our federalist practices could be significantly eroded – at least for a time. But American political history teaches us how rare and difficult this circumstance is compared with its relative ease and frequency in the United Kingdom. The ascendancy of the radical Republicans after the Civil War and the New Deal Democrats offer the only genuine candidates for parties of this kind. It seems safe to say that if the end of Reconstruction did not teach us how fragile and temporary this combination of power and will is in American politics, the collapse of the New Deal coalition should do the job.

REFERENCES

Bednar, Jenna. 1998a. *The Federal Problem*, Ph.D. dissertation, Stanford University.

1998b. "An Institutional Theory of Federal Stability." Paper presented at the annual meeting of the American Political Science Association, Boston, September.

Bednar, Jenna, and William N. Eskridge Jr. 1995. "Steadying the Court's 'Unsteady Path': A Theory of Judicial Enforcement of Federalism." *Southern California Law Review* 68: 1447–92.

Blackstone, William. 1765–9. *Commentaries on the Laws of England.* Oxford: Clarendon Press.

Buchanan, James, and Gordon Tullock. 1962. *The Calculus of Consent: Logical Foundations of Constitutional Democracy.* Ann Arbor: University of Michigan Press.

Cairns, Alan C. 1971. "The Judicial Committee and Its Critics." *Canadian Journal of Political Science* 4 (September): 301–44.

Choper, Jesse. 1981. *Judicial Review and the National Political Process: A Functional Reconsideration of the Role of the Supreme Court.* Chicago: University of Chicago Press.

Cook, Ramsay, Craig Brown, and Carl Berger, eds. 1967. *Confederation.* Toronto: University of Toronto Press.

Corry, J. A. 1936. "Administrative Law and the Interpretation of Statutes." *University of Toronto Law Journal* 1: 286–312.

Cox, Gary. 1987. *The Efficient Secret: The Cabinet and the Development of Political Parties in Victorian England.* Cambridge: Cambridge University Press.

Cross, Rupert. 1987. *Statutory Interpretation.* 2nd ed. Ed. John Bell and Sir George Engle. Reprint, Carlsbad, Calif.: Butterworth Legal Publishers.

Dworkin, Ronald. 1985. *A Matter of Principle.* Cambridge, Mass.: Harvard University Press.

Eskridge, William N., Jr., and John Ferejohn. 1994. "The Elastic Commerce Clause: A Political Theory of American Federalism." *Vanderbilt Law Review* 47: 1355–1400.

Eskridge, William N., Jr., and Philip P. Frickey. 1992. "Quasi-Constitutional Law: Clear Statement Rules as Constitutional Lawmaking." *Vanderbilt Law Review* 45: 593–646.

Fehrenbacher, Don E. 1978. *The Dred Scott Case: Its Significance in American Law and Politics.* New York: Oxford University Press.

Grodzins, Morton. 1964. *American Federalism.* Chicago: University of Chicago Press.

Hart, Henry M., Jr., and Albert M. Sacks. 1994. *The Legal Process: Basic Problems in the Making and Application of Law.* Ed. William N. Eskridge Jr. and Philip P. Frickey. Westbury, N.Y.: Foundation Press.

Hirschman, Albert O. 1970. *Exit, Voice, and Loyalty: Responses to Decline in Firms, Organization, and States*. Cambridge, Mass.: Harvard University Press.

Hogg, Peter W. 1992. *Constitutional Law of Canada*. 3rd ed. Toronto: Carswell.

Kennedy, W. P. M., ed. 1930. *Statutes, Treaties, and Documents of the Canadian Constitution, 1713–1929*. Toronto: Oxford University Press.

Kramer, Larry. 1994. "Understanding Federalism." *Vanderbilt Law Review* 47: 1485–1561.

Milgrom, Paul R., Douglass C. North, and Barry R. Weingast. 1990. "Role of Institutions in the Revival of Trade: The Medieval Law Merchant, Private Judges, and the Champagne Fairs." *Economics and Politics* 2 (March): 1–23.

Monahan, Patrick. 1987. *Politics and the Constitution: The Charter, Federalism and the Supreme Court of Canada*. Toronto: Carswell.

Montinola, Gabriella, Yingyi Qian, and Barry Weingast. 1995. "Federalism, Chinese Style: The Political Basis for Economic Success in China." *World Politics*, 48 (October): 50–81.

Namier, Lewis. [1928] 1957. *The Structure of Politics*. 2nd ed. London: Macmillan.

North, Douglass, and Barry R. Weingast. 1989. "Constitutions and Commitment: The Evolution of Institutions Governing Public Choice in Seventeenth-Century England." *Journal of Economic History* 49: 803–32.

Oates, Wallace. 1972. *Fiscal Federalism*. New York: Harcourt Brace Jovanovich.

O'Connor, W. F. 1939. *Report Pursuant to Resolution of the Senate to the Honourable Speaker by the Parliamentary Counsel* [concerning the BNA Act]. Ottawa: the Queen's Printer.

Ostrom, Vincent. 1991. *The Meaning of American Federalism: Constituting a Self-Governing Society*. San Francisco: ICS Press.

Peterson, Paul E. 1981. *City Limits*. Chicago: University of Chicago Press.

——— 1995. *The Price of Federalism*. Washington, D.C.: Brookings Institution.

Popkin, William D. 1999. *Statutes in Court: The History and Theory of Statutory Interpretation*. Durham, N.C.: Duke University Press.

Price, Jacob M. 1983. "The Excise Affair Re-Visited: The Administrative and Colonial Dimensions of a Parliamentary Crisis." In Stephen B. Baxter, ed., *England's Rise to Greatness, 1600–1763*, 257–322. Berkeley: University of California Press.

Riker, William H. 1955. "The Senate and American Federalism." *American Political Science Review* 49: 452–69.

——— 1964. *Federalism: Origin, Operation, Significance*. Boston: Little, Brown.

Root, Hilton L. 1994. *The Fountain of Privilege: Political Foundations of Markets in Old Regime France and England*. Berkeley: University of California Press.

Ross, Stephen F. 1987. "Legislative Enforcement of Equal Protection." *Minnesota Law Review* 72: 311–65.

Russell, Peter H., ed. 1987. *Leading Constitutional Decisions*. 4th ed. Ottawa: Carleton Library Series.

——— 1992. *Constitutional Odyssey: Can Canadians Become a Sovereign People?* Toronto: University of Toronto Press.

Sager, Lawrence Gene. 1978. "Fair Measure: The Legal Status of Underenforced Constitutional Norms." *Harvard Law Review* 91: 1212–64.

Simpson, Jeffrey. 1988. *Spoils of Power: The Politics of Patronage*. Toronto: Collins.

Spiller, Pablo, and Ingo Vogelsang. 1994. "Regulations, Institutions, and Commitment in the British Telecommunications Sector." Policy Research Working Paper 1241. Washington, D.C.: World Bank.

Stanley, G. F. G. 1956. "Act or Pact? Another Look at Confederation." In Canadian Historical Association, *Report*.

Strayer, Barry. 1968. "The Flexibility of the BNA Act." In Trevor Lloyd and Jack McLeod, eds., *Agenda 1970: Proposals for Creative Politics*. Toronto: University of Toronto Press.

Swinton, Katherine. 1990. *The Supreme Court and Canadian Federalism: The Laskin-Dickson Years*. Toronto: Carswell.

1992. "The Role of The Supreme Court in Canada: Federalism under Fire." *Journal of Law and Contemporary Problems* 55: 121–45.

Thorne, S. E. 1938. "Dr. Bonham's Case." *Law Quarterly Review* 54: 543–52.

1942. Introduction to the critical edition of Sir Thomas Egerton's *A Discourse upon the Exposition & Understandinge of Statutes*. San Marino, Calif.: Huntington Library.

Tiebout, C. M. 1956. "A Pure Theory of Local Expenditures." *Journal of Political Economy* 64 (October): 416–24.

Trebilcock, Michael J., ed. 1983. *Federalism and the Canadian Economic Union*. Toronto: University of Toronto Press.

Tullock, Gordon. 1969. "Federalism: Problems of Scale." *Public Choice* 6: 19–29.

Van Alstyne, William. 1985. "The Second Death of Federalism." *Michigan Law Review* 83: 1709–33.

Vipond, Robert C. 1991. *Liberty and Community: Canadian Federalism and the Failure of the Constitution*. Albany: SUNY Press.

Wechsler, Herbert. 1954. "The Political Safeguards of Federalism: The Role of the States in the Composition and Selection of the National Government." *Columbia Law Review* 54: 543–60.

Weiler, Paul. 1973. "The Supreme Court and the Law of Canadian Federalism." *University of Toronto Law Journal* 23: 307–67.

Weingast, Barry R. 1994. "Institutions and Political Commitment: A New Political Economy of the American Civil War Era." Hoover Institution, unpublished manuscript.

1995. "The Economic Role of Political Institutions: Federalism, Markets, and Economic Development." *Journal of Law, Economics, and Organization* 11 (1): 1–31.

Williamson, Oliver. 1996. "The Institutions and Governance of Economic Development and Reform." In *The Mechanisms of Governance*. New York: Oxford University Press.

PART THREE

CONSTITUTIONAL CHANGE
AND STABILITY

8

Designing an Amendment Process

Sanford Levinson

Imagine two written constitutions.[1] One sets out a standard series of political structures and governmental empowerments and limitations; it concludes with a clause saying: "Anything in this constitution can be changed by the passage of ordinary legislation as spelled out in this constitution." Were this "parliamentary sovereignty" model – found, for example, in the Austrian Constitution[2] – present in the United States Constitution, then constitutional amendments could come about by agreement of majorities in both houses of Congress and assent by the president or by two-thirds vote in each house overriding a presidential veto. Our second constitution comes to a radically different conclusion: "And the Articles of this confederation shall be inviolably observed by every state . . . ; nor shall any alteration at any time hereafter be made in any of them; unless such alteration be agreed to in a congress of the united states, and be afterwards confirmed by the legislatures of every state."[3] Not only does the second constitution require assent by a different institutional layer from that of the national political assembly, in this case, the constituent states of the union; it also requires that this latter act of assent be unanimous. By definition, as with Poland's (in)famous liberum veto, this allows one holdout state to countermand the desire of every other state (and, presumably, the

---

I am grateful to Jim Fleming, Doug Laycock, Hans Linde, Scot Powe, and Eugene Volokh for comments on earlier drafts of this essay. A version of this essay was published as "The Political Implications of Amending Clauses," *Constitutional Commentary* 13 (1996): 107–23.

[1] The adjective is important, for it is obvious that *all* political systems can be said to have "constitutions" in the sense of constitutive conventions of practice and tradition. Yet most – all but seven current states, in fact – have chosen to have *written* constitutions, and this chapter concerns only such systems and some of the problems attached to "putting it in writing."

[2] This appears to be the basic rule adopted in the Austrian Constitution, the easiest of all national constitutions to amend. See Lutz 1995, 260.

[3] Articles of Confederation, Article XIII, in Kurland and Lerner 1987, 26.

272 *Sanford Levinson*

national legislature) for constitutional change. Both of these examples are taken from real political life, even though the latter constitution, the U.S. Articles of Confederation, lasted only six years. Theoretically, though, one can imagine an even stricter constitution, such as John Locke's draft constitution for the Carolinas in which he wrote that "[T]hese fundamental constitutions shall be and remain the sacred and unalterable form and rule of government . . . forever."[4] Such delusions of unamendable grandeur are, however, found in no present constitution. Still, the scheme established by the Articles, or even the substitute structure found in Article V of the Constitution that replaced the Articles, presents a dramatic enough contrast to such relaxed structures as that found in Austria to generate more than enough food for thought.

As to Austria, one might be tempted to say that the polity described really does not have a "constitution" at all, at least if a "constitution" is in some ways supposed to stand "above" and in some sense even "outside" the everyday system of ordinary political decision making. Thus Mark Tushnet has written that "[p]erhaps some degree of institutional stability is required for a system to warrant the name *constitutional*, which suggests that it should not be too easy to amend all of a constitution's provisions, or perhaps any of its basic institutional prescriptions" (Tushnet 1995, 223, 225). Lynn Baker has similarly written that a "constitution is, after all, a fundamental law, which we therefore expect – and want – to be more permanent than the ever-changing, ordinary, statutory law" (Baker 1995, 143, 146). From this perspective, then, Austria may have less of a "constitution," whatever its title, and more of a functional initiating statute that gets the political game underway but is otherwise thoroughly "inside" the ordinary political order that it establishes.

It is "inside" in a double sense: first, its mechanism for change differs not at all from the standard-form politics of legislation; and, second, *only* those already inside the political system – that is, elected officials – participate in the decision-making process. To be sure, even this constitution might in fact be difficult to change insofar as ordinary legislation is itself difficult to pass, as is the case in the notoriously complex system established by the United States Constitution, with its bicameral legislature and independent role for the president (not to mention the political implications of federalism and consequent hindrances to the establishment of a truly united national party system). But one can easily imagine alternatives to our given political structure, which has, indeed, been adopted by no other country in the world. One would, for example, predict both more legislation and more amendment in unicameral than in bicameral systems; similarly, one assumes that passage would be easier if the president (or

---

[4] From *The Fundamental Constitutions of Carolinas*, sec. 120 (drafted by John Locke).

Designing an Amendment Process 273

monarch) played no role, especially if the formal system, as in the United States or France, for example, tolerates the possibility of an executive and legislature controlled by different political parties.

Perhaps even this "minimalist" constitution would have some special prestige because of the identity of its authors that would lead to a certain cultural hesitation to amend it. There is no logical reason why it could not receive the "veneration" thought by James Madison to be so important to the constitutional enterprise (Levinson 1990, 2443), though, as an empirical matter, it may be that such "veneration" is a function of the difficulty of amendment. Cognitive dissonance theory might predict, for example, that one will tend to adjust and even find merit in structures that are in fact difficult to change, and the absence of difficulty might lead to a reduced level of effective commitment.

In any event, this constitution presents no special obstacles to its own change. A bicameral system could, for example, become unicameral if both houses agreed to the change; the presidency could simply be abolished and replaced with a prime minister drawn from the legislature; or life tenure for judges could be eliminated. Should we discover, after a suitable passage of time, that this constitution had remained unchanged we would, I think, be entitled to offer the lack of change as evidence of very high satisfaction, at least on the part of ruling elites, in regard to the original scheme.

The second constitution is, of course, at the opposite extreme. Its unanimity condition makes significant change highly unlikely, at least empirically, outflanked only by the Lockean constitution, which, by making amendment theoretically impossible, means that most modest change – at least where "change" is defined as formal amendment – would presumably require its "overthrow." Evidence of lack of formal change could be plausibly submitted only for the proposition that dissatisfaction had not risen to such a fever pitch that regime overthrow was found to be preferable to continuation of the system established by the constitution. It would, however, be foolhardy to view nonamendment as any more positive an endorsement or reaffirmation than that. (Any such claims, indeed, should be subject to the same discount as given statements by leaders in dictatorial one-party states that the absence of a competing party denotes unproblematic acceptance by the population at large.)

But a system that makes formal change exceedingly difficult (even if not theoretically impossible) forces us to confront a subject of great theoretical importance: how precisely do we identify constitutional amendments? As Stephen Griffin, among others, has well pointed out, an ever present alternative to *formal* amendment is *informal* amendment.[5] Least likely in

---

[5] See Griffin 1995b, 37–62. See also Lutz's (1995) superb essay.

274   *Sanford Levinson*

a dynamic political system is *no* amendment, whether or not these changes take canonical textual form. Noam Zohar, an Israeli philosopher, has analyzed the theoretical problem of amendment within Jewish *halacha*, which is absent any formal process of amendment. After all, *halacha* is based on divine revelation, and it is untenable, both practically and perhaps even theologically, to suppose that God would have committed errors subject to correction by fallible humans. Yet Zohar points out that there is certainly a great deal of significant *change* in Jewish law, though it is almost never described as "amendment" (Zohar 1995).

It is thus problematic to identify "amendment" *only* as formal textual additions (or subtractions). Only the most atheoretical person, I believe, can confidently assert that the U.S. Constitution has exactly twenty-seven amendments.[6] Indeed, one function of such almost literally thoughtless confidence is to blind us to the reality of non–Article V amendments within our own constitutional system.[7] In that sense, emphasis on Article V as the source of *all* amendments is truly *ideological*, reinforcing a certain kind of political understanding and promoting a false consciousness about our political reality.

Bruce Ackerman has been the most notable proponent of the presence of non–Article V (and nontextual) amendments within what any well-trained lawyer would today identify as "the United States Constitution" (see, e.g., Ackerman 1991; 1998). Although he earlier focused on changes in the "domestic" power of the national government surrounding the post–Civil War period and the New Deal, most recently he has turned his attention to foreign affairs. He thus argues that the authorization of the North American Free Trade Agreement and the General Agreement on Trade and Tariffs by majorities of both houses of Congress, rather than by two-thirds of the Senate, where the 1787 Constitution reposed the power to ratify treaties, is evidence of a profound "structural amendment" provoked by World War II and its aftermath.[8]

Still, even if one believes that it is foolish to assert that *only* formal changes count as amendments, it would be perverse to reject the importance of formal amending structures or of the formal additions to, and

---

[6] Professor James Fleming has suggested to me that a theoretical person certainly can suggest this, on the ground that a "bad theory" is, "nonetheless, a theory." There may be something to this. It is the case, though, that most people who offer the "confident" assertion suggested in the text are no theorists at all: they are simply repeating a conventional wisdom that has been insufficiently theorized. At best, they are mindlessly repeating someone else's bad theory.

[7] See Levinson 1995. For our purposes, I put to one side the difficulties in counting the Eighteenth and Twenty-first Amendments and the question of whether the Twenty-seventh Amendment was properly ratified. On this latter issue, see Levinson 1994, 101.

[8] See Ackerman and Golove 1995, 799. Harvard's Laurence Tribe (1995, 1221) scathingly attacks the Ackerman-Golove analysis, and Golove 1998, 1791 replies.

Designing an Amendment Process 275

subtractions from, constitutional text that such structures uniquely allow. At the very least, any legal culture, like that of the United States, that includes *textual argument* among the array of lawyerly rhetorics[9] must appreciate the advantage of being able to refer to specific text rather than have to make what some analysts would dismiss as appeals to unwritten general traditions or conventions. Opponents of President George Bush's policy in the Persian Gulf were certainly helped by the presence of the declaration-of-war clause in Article I of the Constitution, and they would, concomitantly, have been significantly hindered had the "power to declare war" been placed in Article II.

Needless to say, to note the importance of text does not require that one believe either that texts are self-interpreting or that textual argument will necessarily prevail over, say, doctrinal or prudential argument. Still, it is impossible to believe that anyone in our legal culture (or others with written constitutions) believes that text is truly irrelevant. Otherwise why would one *care* whether, for example, a balanced budget amendment or any other proposal was in fact adopted? Similarly, the importance of text in our constitutional tradition presumably explains why supporters of women's rights committed themselves to the equal rights amendment (ERA), even though few were willing to explain precisely what rights it would add beyond those already protected by (their version of) the Fourteenth Amendment. Sophisticated poststructuralist critiques of the sufficiency of text do not in the least serve to negate the practical importance of texts within everyday political life.

Anyone thinking about constitutional design – consider, for example, someone flying to Eastern Europe to offer advice about constitutional design in Eastern Europe and elsewhere – *must* therefore address procedures for amendment every bit as much as the standard topics of institutional design.[10] Indeed, few topics are *more* important, whether as a theoretical or practical matter, than amendment clauses.

I return to our two modal constitutions that establish the two ends of a spectrum. What might lead to adoption of one or the other of these two admitted extremes? To adopt the title of a book that I have edited, *Responding to Imperfection*, let me suggest that the authors of the first constitution would be maximally modest as to their own capabilities and maximally aware of their capacity for imperfect judgments. That is, they would acknowledge the relatively high probability that their notions of proper government, whether one is referring to institutional design or the

---

[9] See Bobbitt 1981; 1991, which develop the notion of American constitutional law being constituted by specific rhetorical *modalities*, one of which is reference to the text of the Constitution.

[10] For an excellent discussion, see Holmes and Sunstein 1995.

276   *Sanford Levinson*

authorization or prohibition of specific powers, are in fact subject to error, given the complexities of political life.

Consider the statement of Virginia's George Mason on June 11, 1787, as he opened the debate in Philadelphia on what amending procedure the delegates should adopt for the Constitution taking form that summer. "[T]he plan now to be formed will *certainly* be defective," he told his fellow delegates. "Amendments therefore will be *necessary*, and it will be better to provide for them, in an easy, regular and Constitutional way than to trust to chance and violence."[11] Indeed, I drew the title *Responding to Imperfection* from a comment by Mason's fellow Virginian George Washington to his nephew, Bushrod Washington: "The warmest friends and the best supporters the Constitution has do not contend that it is free from imperfections, but they found them unavoidable and are sensible if evil is likely to arise there from, the remedy must come hereafter" (Kammen 1986, 83).

Those who accentuate the possibility of imperfection and adopt what might be termed a "statutory" mode of amendment accept the twin likelihoods as well, first, that future generations are likely to recognize the existence of these imperfections *and*, second, that these generations will be sagacious enough to correct them. In turn these successor generations will presumably also be wise enough to realize that they, too, will be imperfect in their political judgments and thus leave it open to *their* successors to engage in the same presumptively progressive response to imperfections, and so on ad infinitum. Thus all successor generations would presumably feel empowered to change the constitutional rules whenever that seemed to be a good idea. Needless to say, such confidence was *not* expressed by Washington or his colleagues in Philadelphia.

The second constitution would presumably be authored by persons who had both an inordinate confidence in their own political wisdom coupled with a perhaps equally inordinate lack of confidence in successor generations. Locke's use of the word "sacred" may be telling, moreover, insofar as it suggests a self-perception by the framers of themselves as (at least) demigods, whose work is entitled to the same awesome respect as that given "real" gods.

Although one might think that the first constitution is *maximally* open to change, that is not the case. One can imagine a third constitution that concludes not only with the postulated sentence but, in addition, states that "this constitution can also be amended by majoritarian popular referendum on initiatives propounded by 5 percent of the population." What political presuppositions might account for this addition?

[11] Farrand 1937, 1:202–3 (emphases added).

One obvious answer is that the framers are familiar with contemporary public choice theory and its concern about agency costs. That is, to limit constitutional amendment only to what gains the assent of those already ensconced within governmental institutions is, almost by definition, to lessen the possibility that the occupants of political office will be amenable to proposals that would significantly affect their interests or, in the language of public choice, diminish the possibility of engaging in successful rent seeking for themselves and their supporters (Boudreaux and Pritchard 1993, 111).

One does not have to be a modern to have this insight. Again one can turn to George Mason, who vigorously opposed initial drafts of Article V that placed exclusive power to initiate amendments in the hands of Congress. "As the proposing of amendments is . . . to depend . . . ultimately, on Congress, no amendments of the proper kind would ever be obtained by the people, if the Government should become oppressive, as he verily believed would be the case" (Kurland and Lerner 1987, 577). It was therefore vital to create alternatives to Congress as the possible progenitors of constitutional amendment. Mason's mirror image was New York's Alexander Hamilton, who trusted the states no more than Mason trusted Congress. After all, said this highest of Federalists, "The State Legislatures will not apply for alterations but with a view to increase their own powers" (ibid.) and, presumably, weaken those of the national government. The solution found in Article V seems to address both of their concerns: Hamilton won the right of Congress to propose amendments, but Mason won the right of states to initiate a new constitutional convention upon petition of two-thirds of the states.

Needless to say, this latter mode of amendment has never in fact been attempted. Most mainstream analysts seem frightened to death by the very possibility, though I confess I do not share this view. In this regard, it would be especially helpful to recognize that the United States in fact includes fifty-one constitutions within its territory and to study the propensity of states to subject their constitutions to the more-or-less frequent scrutiny of constitutional conventions. Some analysts have recently argued that state constitutions are not "real" constitutions precisely because they are so little blessed by the "veneration" visited upon the national constitution, but this obviously begs the question as to how precisely we identify something as a constitution (see, e.g., Gardner 1992, 761; 1993, 927).

It is also worth mentioning in this context the powerful argument of Akhil Reed Amar (1995) that the American idea of popular sovereignty *requires* the possibility that the U.S. Constitution be amendable as well by a majority of voters in a popular referendum, in addition to the supermajoritarian procedures set out in Article V. Even though, as a practical

278 *Sanford Levinson*

matter, Amar's method is not only untried but also, for most Americans, I suspect unthinkable, his argument is noteworthy insofar as it is built on seeing the role of Article V as protecting the people en masse against the corruption of their political agents rather than necessarily endorsing the political status quo itself. Thus for Amar the Article V requirement of extraordinary majorities in both houses of Congress and state legislatures is far less a commitment to the perfection of the existing constitutional scheme than an expression of the deep mistrust of political actors and fear that too-easy methods of change would provide simply a royal road to rent seeking.

Even the Article V possibility of convention-by-call-of-the-states does not entirely overcome the agency problem, for one might imagine circumstances when *all* political officials, regardless of the level of office held, would have interests in common against the civilian populace. Thus perhaps the western states – most (in)famously California – teach an essential lesson by offering the possibility of amendment by direct initiative and referendum of the sovereign people themselves, freed of any requirement to beseech political intermediaries for their substantive approval (though these intermediaries must still presumably agree to place the measures on some official ballot and then to count the votes).[12] For what it is worth, it is not only the fevered states of the American West who have rejected the monopolization of the amendment process by state officials. Switzerland, for many a symbol of boring stability, has been described as "the only nation in the world where political life truly revolves around the referendum. . . . the great political moments of modern Switzerland have occurred not in the following of bold statesmen but in the national debates that have drawn the masses to the polls to decide their country's future" (Kobach 1994, 98).

What must one believe to endorse direct initiative and referendum as a mechanism of constitutional amendment? One possibility is that one possess an unusually high, some might say paranoid, mistrust even of popularly elected agents, who will presumably be corrupted once they take their seats in Washington, Albany, or Budapest, coupled with an equally remarkable, neo-Rousseauian faith in an uncorrupted people. To adopt an initiative-and-referendum system like California's is, in addition, to reject the importance placed by Madison on *representative* government and on multiple filters between the mass of the electorate and ultimate political outcomes. These filters, of course, range from the ostensibly virtuous characters of those likely to be elected to office to the encouragement of certain kinds of deliberation by the rules or practices of our political institutions.

---

[12] See, e.g., California Constitution, Art. II, sec. 8; Arizona Constitution, Art. IV, pt. 1, sec. 1; Montana Constitution, Art. XIV, sec. 9.

Designing an Amendment Process

Indeed, it is just this escape from the filtration of republican deliberation that has led Hans Linde to suggest that the practice of initiative and referendum in the western states at least on occasion violates the "republican form of government" clause in Article IV of the Constitution (Linde 1993, 19).

One response to such arguments is that presented by UCLA professor Eugene Volokh, himself a participant in the political wars over California Proposition 209, by which the electorate prohibited affirmative action in that state. "The legislative process," he argues, will often allow

> minorities who care deeply about a subject to overcome the will of majorities who care less deeply. This might, for instance, be why the anti–affirmative action campaigns are being waged more on the initiative front than the legislative front: If the minority that is pro–affirmative action is very passionate about its support, and the majority that is anti is more lukewarm in its opposition, then a legislator – a repeat player – may prefer to vote for affirmative action and mildly alienate the majority than vote against and strongly alienate the minority. And, of course, the minority will be able to cut legislative deals that it can't with the initiative.
>
> This feature of the legislative process may often be a good thing, but I can see someone arguing that it isn't always – that there ought to be a mechanism for majority sentiments, even those most weakly held, to prevail over strongly held minority sentiments.[13]

There is certainly something to Volokh's argument, which, of course, raises the general issue of the relevance of preference intensity within a democratic theory committed to the formal equality of every voter or, more to the point in this instance, of every representative, even if they owe their actual elections to a particular single-issue constituency that is, in fact, not at all typical of the actual distribution of public opinion. Of course, one criticism of referenda is that they may give great (and presumptively undeserved) advantage to highly intense, well-organized, and well-financed groups as against the ordinary mass of the polity. If one views referenda more as Madisonian nightmares than Jeffersonian dreams, the question is whether the nightmare would be caused by the *theory* of initiative and referendum or, rather, by the empirical circumstances of its *practice* within the United States (as opposed, say, to Switzerland).

My impression – for I confess that I have not sufficiently studied the matter[14] – is that popular referenda have supplanted legislative decision making as the preferred method of constitutional change in California and, perhaps, in others of the western states. Imagine if the U.S. Constitution were like the California Constitution and allowed

---

[13] E-mail from Eugene Volokh to Sanford Levinson, December 6, 1995.

[14] See, though, Cronin 1989.

amendment by popular initiative and referendum in addition to the procedures set out by Article V. What would the likelihood be that proponents of balanced budget or term limits amendments – or, indeed, of any other amendment that profoundly changed the political status quo – would invest in electoral politics of the more-or-less Madisonian variety (i.e., focusing on *representative* government and gaining the required supermajorities at both national and state levels of politics) rather than in what might be called plebiscitarian politics (i.e., focusing on direct, unmediated democracy free of the filters provided by representation or of the particular kinds of deliberation fostered by institutional political processes)? Given the immense difficulty of amendment through Article V procedures – to win the "amendment game," for example, one must win the approval of two national legislative bodies plus no fewer than seventy-five state bodies (assuming that one of them is Nebraska's unicameral legislature) – is it not readily predictable that rational agents would focus their resources on initiatives and referenda? For better or worse, recent displays of congressional consideration of balanced budget amendments might become a thing of the past, as "We the People" instead were summoned to decide about the wisdom of constitutionalizing a particular theory of political economy.

That may as yet be only a dim specter on the horizon, but let me suggest that one highly thinkable outcome of the frustration over failure to gain the final vote needed to propose the balanced budget amendment – or of the earlier failure, in the 1970s, to gain ratification of the ERA in spite of the fact that a majority of the states representing a majority of the population had given it their assent – will be the amendment of Article V itself. The juxtaposition of the ERA with the balanced budget amendment should illustrate, incidentally, that dissatisfaction with the requirements of Article V does not necessarily assume a particular political coloration. What is protected by Article V is the status quo, whether liberal or conservative.

Stephen Griffin has recently suggested that the worst feature of the current U.S. Constitution is indeed Article V, precisely because it makes formal change so inordinately difficult. Amendatory change is often masked as "constitutional interpretation," at immense costs in intellectual cogency or candor. This also gives to judges both responsibility and power that one might well think they are unsuited for, yet another political implication of such a rigorous amending clause. Even worse, perhaps, is that highly desirable change is stifled because one cannot in fact figure out an alternative to use in place of the formal procedures.

Griffin made his comment in a symposium asking only for identification of the worst (or "stupidest") aspect of the Constitution (Griffin 1995a); it did not ask for positive recommendations as to how to cure the suggested defects. But that is clearly the next step for anyone who *does* accept the view that the United States is not well served by its amending procedure. One might even make the radical suggestion that one might find desirable alternatives through study of the constitutions of the American states, not to mention foreign constitutions, none of which have such difficult schemes of amendment. Actually, the preceding sentence is incorrect in one small respect. *One* country did have a more complicated scheme of amendment than that bequeathed us by the Philadelphia Convention of 1787. That country was Yugoslavia.[15]

In any event, I think it is worthwhile to take the next step and to imagine the changes one might advocate for Article V, as well as their political consequences. One set of changes might simply involve greater specification of the answers to a number of important conundrums suggested by our actual political history. The easiest example concerns the right of states to rescind their ratification of a proposed amendment, at least prior to a declaration by the National Archivist that sufficient numbers of ratifications have been received to make the proposed amendment "part of this Constitution."[16] Because the ERA never gained the assent of sufficient numbers of states under *any* theory, we never had to face the question of the constitutionality of Idaho's attempted rescission.

My own view is that a state does indeed have a right to change its mind. Imagine that the balanced budget amendment had been successfully proposed by the 1995 Congress and that several states had rushed to ratify it. (Indeed, New Jersey attempted to ratify such an amendment even *before* proposal, so eager were the legislators to have New Jersey become the first state to endorse it.) Imagine also that, like the ERA, it ran into some trouble, and that the electorate began to realize that a constitutional amendment was unnecessary in order to achieve the goal (and might have significant side costs as well). Does one really want to argue that a state

---

[15] See Lutz 1995, 261. Lutz developed an "Index of Difficulty" based on the complexities of amending procedures. Yugoslavia was highest, at 5.60. The United States follows with 5.10. Next come Switzerland and Venezuela with 4.5. Austria and Sweden have the "easiest" constitutions to amend, with rates, respectively, of 0.80 and 1.00. This does not, obviously, include those few countries that do not have written constitutions, like Great Britain, New Zealand, or Israel.

It would be absurd to argue that the current difficulties in the former Yugoslavia are due to the formal difficulty of constitutional amendment. Can one, however, be entirely confident, in the absence of detailed study, that it played no role in making necessary political changes, following Tito's death, simply too difficult to realize through ordinary political processes? Even if formal constitutional process explains no more than 2 percent of the variance in accounting for contemporary South Balkan politics, is that not still a damning indictment, *unless* the rigidity in fact helped to purchase forty years of relative ethnic peace during the Tito years?

[16] See Article V. On rescission, see Rees 1977, 896.

should not be entitled, as a constitutional matter, to change its collective mind on a matter of such profound import? After all, a vote *not* to ratify does not prevent a future legislature from deciding to endorse a proposed amendment. Why does the option to switch work in only one direction? Whatever one's views on the merits, does one really want to leave this hanging as an open question, to be decided either by Congress or the Supreme Court as one's jurisprudence dictates?[17] The better course, it seems to me, is to come to some decision, while there is no amendment pending, and to codify it in the Constitution itself.

The most spectacular failures of Article V to provide any genuine guidance come in regard to the convention that could be called on petition of thirty-four states. As noted, this is as yet only a theoretical problem, but so long as we wish to leave open this possibility of a convention, it *cannot* be wise to leave open as well such fundamental questions as whether states would vote by unit, as in Philadelphia, or by individual delegates or whether the agenda of the convention could be limited by the states or Congress, on the one (actually two) hand, or only by choice of the "sovereign" convention itself, on the other. As should be obvious, once one gets started, a "corrective" Article V devoted only to filling in some of the blanks – and not even touching, for example, the basic structure of requiring supermajority votes in Congress and ratification by three-quarters of the states – could well turn out to be almost as long as the existing Constitution itself.

But surely the most basic disputes would concern the basic structure of Article V. Griffin's complaint is not merely that Article V has some stunning lacunae in it, but rather that it clearly disserves the polity. So what direction might "reform" of Article V take?

Would anyone, for example, suggest a process by which national-level officials alone could amend the Constitution? Consider, for example, a proposal to allow amendment by vote of two-thirds of each house of Congress *and* presidential approval, *or* by vote of three-quarters of each house (in order to prevent, for example, an absolute presidential veto of modification of presidential power itself). I assume that in fact few of us would be tempted by such a proposal, and I assume that what would animate most of us in our opposition would indeed be the lack of any formal state role and/or the lack of popular participation as through a referendum. But what underlies that mistrust of a national power would, I think, be some version of the agency argument. Otherwise, if one's objection to the present Article V is its role in preventing vitally needed changes,

---

[17] See, e.g., Dellinger 1983, 386, arguing for judicial review of such questions; Tribe 1986, 433, arguing that Congress has "plenary power" to decide on the legitimacy of rescissions.

it is hard to see why one would not endorse simply eliminating the participaton of the states.

If one does endorse continued participation by states, that simply forces one to confront the question of *how many* states should have to endorse an amendment before it is accepted as part of the Constitution? Would anyone seriously defend, as we enter a new millennium, the present system that in essence allows one house of thirteen states to block the desires of the remaining public? That is, the "amendment game" gives victory to those who can win thirteen such houses against the side that prevails in seventy-five houses in thirty-eight states other than Nebraska. Quite frankly, I can think of *no* defense for the present rules of this particular game *unless* one is committed simply to making it as difficult as practically possible to engage in formal amendment.

Does an alternative number suggest itself? One possibility, obviously, is a simple majority of states. The major problem with that is the theoretical possibility that such a majority could be gathered by aggregating states that themselves contain substantially less than a majority of the American public. Is it adequate to overcome this fear to point out that any amendment must first gain the support of two-thirds of the House of Representatives, which is, of course, apportioned on the basis of population? One might respond, of course, that the apportionment is scarcely independent of political factors, ranging from incumbency to race, and one might not really believe that the support of two-thirds of the representatives necessarily translates even into majority support by the public in general.

Unless one is a "high federalist" in a distinctly modern sense – that is, someone who really does accept the metaphysical integrity of Idaho qua Idaho, and so on – it seems hard to argue that actual population ought not play some role in the ratification process. One might well, therefore, adopt a version of the Australian rule, which is to require a majority of the states *and* that this majority include a majority of the national population. Note well, though, that this allows for the possibility that even if a *minority* of states containing a majority of the national population supported an amendment that, by stipulation, has gained the approval of Congress or a national convention, the amendment would nevertheless remain unratified.

At this point, then, we have to ask ourselves why we would care that even a majority of states ratify an amendment. The answer, presumably, would be to return to some of the original debates of 1787–8, where one finds rampant mistrust on the part of small states in regard to the potential conduct of large states. Still, we might ask ourselves why the organization of the Senate, based as it is on formal state equality, does not offer (more than) enough protection to "states qua states." How much protection *are* Wyoming, North Dakota, Alaska, and Rhode Island entitled to against the wishes of, say, California, Texas, Florida, and Michigan? Is it *only* the fact that I am a Texan (of sorts) that makes me unsympathetic to continuing the remarkable power given small states within our political system?

If one remains justifiably suspicious of exclusive national amendment, but is equally suspicious of maintaining the role of states in ratification, is an acceptable alternative the national referendum on amendments first proposed by Congress or by a national convention? Resistance to this notion could be based on fear by, say, people living in Mountain and Upper Midwestern states that they would simply be swamped by their fellow citizens who have chosen life in the mega-city. But, of course, more fundamental objections would be based on some of the earlier-expressed fears either about the corrupting role of money in politics, including national referendum campaigns, or about the inability of ordinary citizens to think reflectively about the kinds of issues appropriate for constitutional placement.

I have, up to now, been assuming the necessity of two-thirds vote in each house of Congress. But why maintain the supermajority requirement at all, especially if one maintains a sufficiently strong role for states in the ratification process to guarantee some kind of barrier against a "rush to judgment"? Or, why not require a congressional supermajority *only* if the president formally opposes the proposed amendment? Otherwise, I'd be inclined to take my chances with congressional majorities *plus* presidential approval *plus* ratification by sufficient states to comprise a majority of the population *or* popular ratification.

I have also been assuming that a constitution establishes a *single* rule for constitutional amendment. There is clearly no necessity that this be the case, as demonstrated by Article V itself, which varies the difficulty of the amendment process with the importance of given issues. Thus the drafters of Article V explicitly exempted two issues from the general rules regarding amendment set out at the beginning of the article. First, *unanimity* is required to change the rule of equal representation of states in the Senate.[18] Second, *any* amendment concerning congressional abolition of the slave trade prior to 1808 appears to be precluded. Whatever one might think of these specific precedents, the latter one of which certainly points to one of the most horrific aspects of the Constitution, they nonetheless point to the possibility of requiring a more difficult process of amendment for things

---

[18] Contrary to what is sometimes asserted, the Senate clause is *not* "unamendable" as a matter of theory, though, as a practical matter, that is almost certainly the case, given the extreme unlikelihood of, say, Wyoming agreeing to give up its excess of power in the Senate. What is less clear is whether Article V could be amended to change the unanimity requirement by less than a unanimous vote. See, e.g., Linder 1981, 717.

Designing an Amendment Process   285

we define as "basic rights of the people" than for all other constitutional provisions.

There may be good reason to require very high supermajorities before limiting rights of freedom of speech and the like. Does any such reason suggest itself in regard to term limits, whether of legislators or the president, or, for that matter, to any other structural feature of the Constitution? For me the question is rhetorical, for I can think of no good reasons to support the formal stasis engendered by Article V. No doubt the adoption of such a two-tier system would lead to significant wrangling about what might count as a "basic right," but such wrangling seems a small price to pay for what would be a distinct improvement in overall constitutional design and the increased possibility of cogently responding to significant structural imperfections.

Ultimately, though, all such discussions take us back to our simplistic, but not, I hope, simpleminded, models outlined at the very beginning of this chapter. That is, to what extent do we first acknowledge the possibility of imperfection and then have faith in our fellow citizens to respond adequately to such imperfections? Our answers to these questions, whether we are conscious of them or not, ultimately dictate where along the spectrum of possibilities we choose to place (and defend) our own procedures for constitutional amendment. I use the words "we" and "ours" on the assumption that most readers are Americans concerned to assess the implications of our own amendment process for the quality of our polity. But it should be obvious that the issues raised go beyond such parochial concerns, whether one is wrestling with the writing of constitutions elsewhere in the world or simply engaging in detached reflection about the consequences for political practice of various institutional designs.

REFERENCES

Ackerman, B. 1991. *We the People: Foundations.* Cambridge, Mass.: Harvard University Press.
    1998. *We the People: Transformations.* Cambridge, Mass.: Harvard University Press.
Ackerman, B., and D. Golove. 1995. "Is NAFTA Constitutional?" *Harvard Law Review* 108: 799–929.
Amar, A. R. 1995. "Popular Sovereignty and Constitutional Amendment." In Sanford Levinson, ed., *Responding to Imperfection: The Theory and Practice of Constitutional Amendment,* 89–115. Princeton: Princeton University Press.
Articles of Confederation. 1987. Reprinted in P. B. Kurland and R. Lerner, eds., *The Founders' Constitution: Major Themes,* 23–26. Chicago: University of Chicago Press.
Baker, L. A. 1995. "Constitutional Change and Direct Democracy." *University of Colorado Law Review* 66: 143–58.

286 *Sanford Levinson*

Bobbitt, P. 1981. *Constitutional Fate.* New York: Oxford University Press.
　1991. *Constitutional Interpretation.* Oxford: B. Blackwell.
Boudreaux, D. J., and A. C. Pritchard. 1993. "Rewriting the Constitution: An Economic Analysis of the Constitutional Amendment Process." *Fordham Law Review* 62: 111–62.
Cronin, T. E. 1989. *Direct Democracy: The Politics of Initiative, Referendum, and Recall.* Cambridge, Mass.: Harvard University Press.
Dellinger, W. 1983. "The Legitimacy of Constitutional Change: Rethinking the Constitutional Amendment Process." *Harvard Law Review* 97: 386–432.
Farrand, M. 1937. *The Record of the Federal Convention of 1787.* 4 vols. New Haven: Yale University Press.
Gardner, J. A. 1992. "The Failed Discourse of State Constitutionalism." *Michigan Law Review* 90: 761–837.
　1993. "Roundtable: Responses to James A. Gardner." *Rutgers Law Journal* 24: 927–56.
Golove, D. 1998. "Against Free-Form Formalism." *New York University Law Review* 73: 1791–942.
Griffin, S. 1995a. "The Nominee Is . . . Article V." *Constitutional Commentary* 12: 171–73.
　1995b. "Constitutionalism in the United States: From Theory to Politics." In S. Levinson, ed., *Responding to Imperfection: The Theory and Practice of Constitutional Amendment,* 37–62. Princeton: Princeton University Press.
Holmes, S., and C. Sunstein. 1995. "The Politics of Constitutional Revision in Eastern Europe." In Sanford Levinson, ed., *Responding to Imperfection: The Theory and Practice of Constitutional Amendment,* 275–306. Princeton: Princeton University Press.
Kammen, M., ed. 1986. *The Origins of the American Constitution: A Documentary History.* New York: Penguin Books.
Kobach, K. W. 1994. "Switzerland." In D. Butler and A. Ranney, eds., *Referendums around the World: The Growing Use of Direct Democracy,* 98–153. Washington, D.C.: AEI Press.
Kurland, P. B., and R. Lerner. 1987. *The Founders' Constitution.* Chicago: University of Chicago Press.
Levinson, S. 1990. "'Veneration' and Constitutional Change: James Madison Confronts the Possibility of Constitutional Amendment." *Texas Tech Law Review* 21: 2443–60.
　1994. "Authorizing Constitutional Text: On the Purported Twenty-seventh Amendment." *Constitutional Commentary* 11: 101.
　1995. "How Many Times Has the United States Constitution Been Amended? (A)<26; (B)26; (C)27; (D)>27." In Sanford Levinson, ed., *Responding to Imperfection: The Theory and Practice of Constitutional Amendment,* 13–36. Princeton: Princeton University Press.
　1996. "The Political Implications of Amending Clauses." *Constitutional Commentary* 13: 107–23.
Linde, H. A. 1993. "When Initiative Lawmaking Is Not 'Republican Government': The Campaign against Homosexuality." *Oregon Law Review* 72: 19–40.

Linder, D. 1981. "What in the Constitution Cannot be Amended." *Arizona Law Review* 23: 717–33.

Locke, J. 1909. *The Fundamental Constitutions of Carolinas*. Reprinted in F. Thorpe, ed., *American Charters, Constitutions, and Organic Laws, 1492–1908*, 5: 2772–86. Washington, D.C.: Government Printing Office.

Lutz, D. S. 1995. "Toward a Theory of Constitutional Amendment." In Sanford Levinson, ed., *Responding to Imperfection: The Theory and Practice of Constitutional Amendment*, 237–74. Princeton: Princeton University Press.

Rees, G. 1977. "Comment, Rescinding Ratification of Proposed Constitutional Amendments – A Question for the Court." *Louisiana Law Review* 37: 896–925.

Tribe, L. 1986. "A Constitution We Are Amending: In Defense of a Restrained Judicial Role." *Harvard Law Review* 97: 433–45.

1995. "Taking Text and Structure Seriously: Reflections on Free-Form Method in Constitutional Interpretation." *Harvard Law Review* 108: 1221–303.

Tushnet, M. 1995. "The Whole Thing." *Constitutional Commentary* 12: 223–5.

Zohar, N. 1995. "Midrash: Amendment through the Moulding of Meaning." In Sanford Levinson, ed., *Responding to Imperfection: The Theory and Practice of Constitutional Amendment*, 307–18. Princeton: Princeton University Press.

9

Constitutional Theory Transformed

Stephen M. Griffin

Theories of constitutional change try to see the U.S. Constitution whole. They attempt to understand how all three branches of government have contributed to the course of constitutional development in the United States. Among recent theorists of constitutional change, Bruce Ackerman deserves great credit for highlighting the importance of this issue and stressing the need to consider the relationships among all the branches of government during three great constitutional moments: Founding, Reconstruction, and the New Deal (1991; 1998).

Whereas Ackerman is primarily interested in exploring the implications of constitutional change for constitutional law, I am interested in what this means for constitutional theory (Griffin 1996). Using the New Deal as my focus, I argue in this chapter that the new concern with constitutional change has the potential to transform American constitutional theory. In particular, I wish to press two related ideas: that because theories of constitutional change are *historicist*, they are not necessarily *interpretive*.[1] Indeed, there is an important sense in which theories of constitutional change are prior to theories of constitutional interpretation.[2]

I am grateful to Barry Friedman, Richard D. Friedman, Michael Klarman, Sandy Levinson, Michael Dorf, and Keith Whittington for commenting on an earlier version. I received helpful research assistance from Richard S. Dukes Jr. This chapter is dedicated to the memory of my father, Clifford S. Griffin, Professor of American History at the University of Kansas from 1959–97.

[1] Here and elsewhere in the chapter, I use "interpretive" and "interpretation" in the specific sense of *legal* interpretation. I do not mean to refer to the much different debate of whether the social sciences should be pursued through an interpretive method.

[2] How is the idea of "change" to be understood? What counts as a change? Some might imagine that I must use an originalist notion of change, according to which whether the Constitution has changed is measured against a baseline composed of evidence of the intent of the framers. In this and in my earlier work (Griffin 1996), however, I am not using an originalist baseline but a historicist one. The baseline for determining whether a constitutional change has occurred is not a relatively discrete set of statements by important

288

This perspective on constitutional change is inspired in part by the methodology of "historical institutionalism" in political science. Historical institutionalism is often called a "state-centered" approach because it takes the concept of the state seriously and focuses on its halting evolution through American history. Perhaps the most important contribution of historical institutionalism has been its emphasis on the autonomy of the state. As historian Alan Brinkley describes, the main thesis of this state-centered approach is that "[t]he state and the institutions surrounding it . . . are themselves crucial factors in determining the outcome of political struggles, indeed often more influential than social forces or the efforts of popular interest groups" (Brinkley 1995, 11). The point is that the state does not simply provide the arena in which various interests struggle for dominance. The state also writes the rule book, polices the field, decides the winners, or even changes the game in the middle of play. The structure of the state and, especially, the decisions made before the players take the field, has a real and continuing influence on policy outcomes.

My point of departure is how constitutional law accounts for the New Deal, surely one of the most crucial periods of constitutional change in American history. I initially confront the best-known, most widely accepted, and most implausible account – that the New Deal involved no real change as such, but was simply a restoration of the wisdom of the Marshall Court. Ackerman notes that lawyers tell themselves a story about the New Deal "which denies that anything deeply creative was going on. This view of the 1930's is obtained by imagining a Golden Age in which Chief Justice Marshall got things right for all time by propounding a broad construction of the national government's lawmaking authority" (1991, 42). What I call the restoration thesis or restorationism is still very much alive.

Ackerman is correct that the restoration thesis still serves as the primary way for lawyers and scholars to integrate the New Deal into the larger story of American constitutionalism. But the importance of the restoration thesis goes far beyond this. It is a key prop in maintaining traditional, ahistorical approaches to constitutional law and theory. In effect, the thesis asserts that our constitutional world is meaningfully related to the world of the early republic, the world of James Madison, Alexander Hamilton, and John Marshall. The thesis maintains continuity with the past,

members of the founding generation issued during the period surrounding the adoption of the Constitution as well as statements by framers of its subsequent amendments. It is rather the historical context in which those statements were made. More specifically, the baseline for assessing change is composed of the institutional structures and state capacities created by the Constitution. We can study constitutional change by observing the continuities and discontinuities as these structures develop through time.

290   *Stephen M. Griffin*

reassuring lawyers that there is an unbroken American constitutional tradition. It thus prevents scholars from gaining a more perspicuous view of the process of constitutional change by denying that overwhelmingly significant changes have occurred since 1787 in the structure of American government.

Before we can gain a better understanding of the New Deal and the process of constitutional change, then, the restoration thesis must be debunked. In the first section I set out the restoration thesis as it has been advocated by scholars and the Supreme Court and critique it for being implausible as a matter of history. I do not criticize restorationism for being an incorrect interpretation of the Constitution or for misunderstanding original intent. My critique is offered from a historicist perspective, using the methodology of historical institutionalism. Its focus on the development of state institutions provides the context that is missing every time lawyers invoke *McCulloch v. Maryland*, 17 U.S. 316 (1819), *Gibbons v. Ogden*, 22 U.S. 1 (1824), or some other Marshall Court case to justify the kind of government we have today.

The problems with restorationism are not confined to its understanding of the Marshall Court. Precisely because it is an interpretive rather than a historicist response to the New Deal, restorationism fails to understand the new constitutional order that emerged out of the crisis of the Great Depression. I describe the constitutional changes of the New Deal along four dimensions: with respect to the alterations it made to American democracy, to constitutional doctrine, to constitutional institutions such as the presidency and federalism, and as a challenge to American constitutional ideology.

My own theory of constitutional change is intended to avoid not only the mistakes of restorationism, but of all similar interpretive or legalistic theories. It therefore does not offer an alternative interpretation of the Constitution but a historicist, state-centered perspective on the development of constitutional institutions. I argue that the attempt of the founding generation to create a permanent constitutional order based on enduring principles produced an impasse once the national state became truly activist in response to the Great Depression. The difficulty of formal amendment under Article V forced most constitutional change "off-text." Further, most of this change was not expressed in a legalistic manner through the development of Supreme Court precedent, but rather occurred in the course of ordinary political change. To track the changes brought on by the activist state, both during the New Deal and after, we must have a way of specifying the rules, practices, and institutions that operate as the functional equivalent of the rules contained in the text of the Constitution. Again, historical institutionalism is helpful. By directing our attention to the development of state institutions, it frees us from having to rely solely on constitutional amendments and Court precedents as markers of change. We can then view our constitutional order as a whole and ask new questions about the changing relationships among legal and political institutions in the post–New Deal period.

The critique of restorationism thus cuts very deep into traditional approaches prevailing in constitutional theory. It implies that no conventional theory of interpretation can justify the constitutional changes that occurred during the New Deal. Because these changes are usually thought to constitute the very foundation of the contemporary regulatory-welfare state, the stakes here are quite high. At issue is our understanding of the origins of the current arrangement of state institutions and of their legitimacy in a constitutional sense. The critique of restorationism is thus intended to suggest that in order to understand our constitutional world we must transform constitutional theory by turning our attention from interpreting the Constitution to understanding the relationship between the Constitution and the historical development of state institutions.

I explore the idea of a transformed constitutional theory in the second section, beginning with Ackerman's theory of transformative amendment. Ackerman's theory of constitutional change is similar to my own in that he recognizes the need to adopt an explicitly historicist approach (Ackerman 1991, 16–33; Griffin 1996, 164–9), although this has not been recognized by many of Ackerman's critics. But Ackerman attempts to account for constitutional change within a framework that remains ultimately legalistic. Ackerman argues that Reconstruction and the New Deal gave birth to unconventional amendments that have the same legal status as amendments made through Article V. His theory has trouble coming to grips with the more political aspects of constitutional change, especially how that change is produced frequently by ordinary political struggles. For all its historical sophistication, Ackerman's theory is advanced in a legalistic mode that is not helpful in understanding twentieth-century constitutional change.

I then argue that the main theories of constitutional interpretation are not historicist theories, no matter what claims they make to historical backing. I begin by describing some specific criticisms historians make of the use of history in constitutional interpretation. These criticisms may be familiar because they have been employed in the debate over originalism. But my purpose in emphasizing a few particular criticisms is to make the largely overlooked point that they apply across the board to all theories of constitutional interpretation, originalist or not. This is because theories of constitutional interpretation accept an essentially ahistorical view about the role the constitutional principles of the early republic can and should play in the complex democracy of the present. The emphasis in these theories, characteristic of American constitutionalism from

292   *Stephen M. Griffin*

the beginning, on the fundamental principles adopted by the founding generation and how contemporary constitutional problems can be solved through a theory that will specify how those principles can be applied in the present, is completely implausible from a historicist perspective.[3]

Suppose constitutional theory did take historicism seriously. What result? I provide an account of what a historicist constitutional theory would look like. A "contextualized" constitutional theory would involve pairing normative constitutional theory with the study of the development of the fundamental institutions, practices, and rules that structure American politics. Normative constitutional theory would thus be informed by a historicist perspective, not a purely legalist one. The ahistorical, anachronistic questions that are often the focus of interpretive theory would be avoided. We would then have the ability to pose and answer new questions about the structure of American government that have never received a proper hearing in mainstream constitutional theory.

THE NEW DEAL "RESTORATION" AND THE THEORY OF CONSTITUTIONAL CHANGE

Restorationism Reconsidered

The restoration thesis holds that decisions of the Marshall Court, particularly *Gibbons v. Ogden*, 22 U.S. 1 (1824) and *McCulloch v. Maryland*, 17 U.S. 316 (1819), provided a complete constitutional justification for the legislation enacted during the New Deal. Constitutional controversy over legislation enacted by Congress centered on the Commerce Clause, providing that Congress has the power "[t]o regulate Commerce with foreign Nations, and among the several States, and with the Indian Tribes" (U.S. Const., Art. I, sec. 8, cl. 3). One particular paragraph in *Gibbons* interpreting this clause proved irresistible for partisans of the New Deal. Here Marshall defined the commerce power as "the power to regulate; that is, to prescribe the rule by which commerce is to be governed" (*Gibbons*, 196). Marshall continued, "[t]his power, like all others vested in Congress, is complete in itself, may be exercised to its utmost extent, and acknowledges

---

[3] In a widely noted article, Robert Gordon argued that historicism, which he defined as "the recognition of the historical and cultural contingency of law," still had not been absorbed by legal scholars because it was a threat to the standard ways of doing legal scholarship (1981, 1017). Gordon contended that the evasion of this threat had limited the "intellectual options and imaginative range" of legal scholarship (1981, 1017). Although Gordon used some examples drawn from constitutional law, he did not explore the consequences of his thesis for constitutional theory in any detail. As the argument in this chapter shows, I believe that Gordon was largely correct.

no limitations, other than are prescribed in the constitution" (ibid.). Then, in his most suggestive remark, Marshall stated:

If, as has always been understood, the sovereignty of Congress, though limited to specified objects, is plenary as to those objects, the power over commerce with foreign nations, and among the several States, is vested in Congress as absolutely as it would be in a single government, having in its constitution the same restrictions on the exercise of the power as are found in the constitution of the United States. (*Gibbons*, 197)

The word "plenary" was especially comforting to those searching for constitutional bases for New Deal legislation. To New Dealers, the word implied that Congress had a broad power to regulate the national economy as it saw fit. This argument was made, not simply after hours or in political speeches, but in the legal briefs submitted to the Supreme Court to justify New Deal legislation (Irons 1982, 137–8). In a famous article, Robert Stern (who worked in the solicitor general's office throughout the Roosevelt administration) argued that New Deal legislation regulating national economic activity was justified under "the fundamental concepts which guided those men who prepared the Constitution and to the principles which the Supreme Court has professed since the days of John Marshall" (1934, 1337). As Peter Irons (1982, 92–3, 137–8, 295) has shown, government lawyers cited *Gibbons* repeatedly in litigation as a precedent that justified New Deal legislation. In the wake of the Court's 1937 shift, Attorney General (soon to be Justice) Robert Jackson summarized the constitutional meaning of what had occurred: "[t]he unifying principle running through all of our constitutional litigations has been the recognition that the Constitution contemplated a really effective government. It has been in the nature of a Constitutional Renaissance – a rediscovery of the Constitution itself" (1941, xiv–xv).

Although government lawyers and constitutional scholars have advanced the restoration thesis, its most influential proponent has been the Supreme Court itself. When the Court began consistently upholding the validity of New Deal legislation after 1937, *Gibbons* provided the foundation for the Court's approach to the commerce clause. In *United States v. Darby*, 312 U.S. 100 (1941), Justice Stone cited *Gibbons* prominently in upholding the Fair Labor Standards Act and overruling *Hammer v. Dagenhart*, 247 U.S. 251 (1918). In relying on the paragraph from *Gibbons* quoted earlier, Stone referred to "the plenary power conferred on Congress by the Commerce Clause" (*Darby*, 115) and contended, *Hammer* excepted, that this had been the consistent policy of the Court since Marshall's time. In *Wickard v. Filburn*, 317 U.S. 111 (1942), the case that completed the Court's shift away from its pre-1937 jurisprudence, Justice Jackson echoed the arguments made in his book and again invoked *Gibbons*, claiming that "[a]t the beginning Chief Justice Marshall described the federal commerce power with a breadth never yet exceeded" (120). Jackson characterized Court opinions upholding broad interpretations of the commerce power as "bring[ing] about a return to the principles first enunciated by Chief Justice Marshall in *Gibbons v. Ogden*" (122).

Commerce Clause decisions that came after the close of the New Deal era echoed the theme of restoration set out in *Darby* and *Wickard*. In *Heart of Atlanta Motel v. United States*, 379 U.S. 241 (1964), the case that upheld Title II of the Civil Rights Act of 1964, the Court quoted several long passages from *Gibbons* and stated that although "conditions of transportation and commerce have changed dramatically," nonetheless "the principles which we apply today are those first formulated by Chief Justice Marshall in *Gibbons v. Ogden*" (251). Finally, in *Perez v. United States*, 402 U.S. 146 (1971), the Court quoted *Gibbons* as encapsulating a broad view of the commerce power. The Court continued, "[d]ecisions which followed departed from that view; but by the time of *United States v. Darby* . . . and *Wickard v. Filburn* . . . the broader view of the Commerce Clause announced by Chief Justice Marshall had been restored" (*Perez*, 151).

Restorationism is not simply an enthusiasm confined to the Court or to the New Deal era. As Ackerman argues, it remains the leading organizing idea that contemporary lawyers and judges employ in understanding how the New Deal fits into the larger narrative of the American constitutional tradition. This is nowhere better illustrated than by the reaction of some leading Harvard doctrinalists to Ackerman's criticism of restorationism. The responses of Charles Fried and Laurence Tribe contain more than a whiff of the idea that the post-1937 Court was simply returning to the path laid down by Marshall (Fried 1995; Tribe 1995). With respect to the Marshall Court, Fried states that its decisions "gave significant support to a broad reading of the extent of the national power over the economy" (1995, 33) and thus, of course, to the New Deal itself. Tribe writes that "the Supreme Court's New Deal shifts were matters of legitimate if controversial constitutional interpretation. They simply did not entail any sort of architectural alteration that would require a textual change in the Constitution" (1995, 1295).

The restoration thesis allows constitutional lawyers to maintain a narrative of continuity when telling the tale of the American constitutional tradition. The constitutional structures and precedents of today are thus represented as having more than just a family resemblance to the institutions and understandings of the founding generation. The possibility that this makes little sense from a historical point of view is not raised because the restoration thesis is more of an "as if" belief than an argument based on a serious examination of the world of the early republic. Once a concern for historical context enters the picture, the restoration thesis collapses.

Recent historical scholarship on the Marshall Court has cast serious doubt on the restoration thesis simply by placing the Court in the context of its own time. In his comprehensive history of the later Marshall Court, G. Edward White opens the discussion of such cases as *Martin v. Hunter's Lessee*, 14 U.S. 304 (1816), *Cohens v. Virginia*, 19 U.S. 264 (1821), *McCulloch v. Maryland*, 17 U.S. 316 (1819), and *Gibbons v. Ogden*, 22 U.S. 1 (1824), by saying that these rulings have "often been loosely characterized and sometimes patently misunderstood" (1988, 486). He continues, "[t]he cases have often been identified as decisions promoting 'nationalism,' but ... [t]he 'nationalism' inherent in those decisions was not a nationalism in the modern sense of support for affirmative plenary federal regulatory power; the Court's posture can more accurately be described as a critique of reserved state sovereignty" (1988, 486).

White does note that twentieth-century scholars have been more than willing to describe the Court in nationalistic terms, but "to the extent that the cases took on additional implications, such as the implication that the economic and political growth of the nation would be accompanied by a growth in the regulatory powers of the federal government, the Marshall Court cannot fairly be identified with those implications" (1988, 487). The Marshall Court was simultaneously trying to carve out a place for itself and for the federal government as a whole while at the same time attempting to defend itself from political attack (Ackerman 1991, 62). Under these conditions, Marshall's theory of broad federal power articulated in *McCulloch* and *Gibbons* was "more of a preservationist theory in its emphasis than a theory designed to foster an affirmative federal regulatory presence" (White 1988, 519).

Herbert Johnson concurs in his own recent study of the Marshall Court. It is true that "[t]he Court's emphatic rejection of the compact theory of Union ... marked it as a force for national unity.... On the other hand, the Marshall Court justices never conceived that plenary federal power would be as pervasive as it has become in twentieth-century America" (1997, 73). Charles Hobson, the editor of Marshall's papers, argues with respect to *McCulloch* that it should "not be understood as a prescient anticipation of the modern liberal state, in which a federal government of vastly augmented powers has assumed primary responsibility for regulating the economy and promoting social welfare." The "nationalism" of *McCulloch* "is more accurately defined in negative or defensive terms ... [t]he opinion purported not to enhance the powers of the federal government but to enable that government to exercise its powers effectively and to prevent state encroachments upon its legitimate operations." Marshall certainly "did not intend to suggest that Congress, in addition

296 *Stephen M. Griffin*

to its delegated powers, could tap a vast reservoir of other powers that were not expressly granted but could be implied because Congress was the legislative branch of the national government" (Hobson 1996, 123).

With respect to *Gibbons*, Howard Gillman (1994) has recently pointed out that the opinion itself contains clear indications that Marshall could never accept the kind of broad reading of federal power advanced by the restorationists. Marshall showed that he believed in a bright line between interstate and intrastate commerce by saying that the power of Congress to regulate does not extend to "commerce, which is completely internal, which is carried on between man and man in a State, or between different parts of the same State, and which does not extend to or affect other States" (*Gibbons*, 194). Further, in discussing state inspection and health laws, Marshall remarked that while they "may have a remote and considerable influence on commerce" (*Gibbons*, 203), they cannot be based on any power to regulate commerce. Why? Because "[t]hey act upon the subject before it becomes an article of foreign commerce, or of commerce among the States. . . . No direct general power over these objects is granted to Congress; and, consequently, they remain subject to State legislation" (*Gibbons*, 203). Marshall thus implies that any product goes through a series of stages (such as production or manufacturing) before it can become an article of interstate commerce subject to congressional regulation. This further implies, of course, that Congress may not regulate products in these precommerce stages. This is fatal to the kind of regulatory power the New Dealers claimed for the federal government on the basis of *Gibbons*.

Although these conclusions may seem surprising, these historians are not interested in undermining the legitimacy of the New Deal. Instead, they want to understand the Marshall Court in the context of the circumstances that existed in early nineteenth-century America. In those circumstances, the fight over the nature and limits of federal regulatory power was not about whether to establish a powerful welfare state (Rakove 1996, 177–202). On Marshall's side at least, it was an effort simply to establish the legitimacy of the federal courts and the federal government as a whole; an effort to win respect for the national government from the states.

Restorationism asserts a certain relationship between decisions of the Marshall Court and the governmental structure of the early republic. Marshall was a "nationalist" and decisions of his Court confirmed that the federal government had broad powers to develop and regulate the American economy in order to achieve ends legitimate under the Constitution. The historical works just reviewed make it clear that none of the justices of the Marshall Court shared this vision. More important, examining the structure of the early national state makes it clear that no one could have conceived of a New Deal–style role for the national government in regulating the economy. A historical and institutionalist approach makes apparent the limits of relying on extremely general terms such as "nationalist," "activist," and "regulation" to describe in common the kind of state that existed during Marshall's era, the New Deal, or our own (Ackerman 1991, 62).

McCulloch and *Gibbons* were decided against the background of what is usually termed the Jacksonian era in American politics. This era was not characterized by a steady accretion of power by the federal government, as is often implied by restorationist accounts that focus on the Supreme Court. In fact, one of the chief characteristics of the Jacksonian era was a sharp movement away from dreams of national development guided by a beneficent state. Moreover, throughout the entire antebellum period, the national state was extremely weak and simply unable to shoulder any of the tasks putatively assigned to it by the Marshall Court.

The weakness, indeed incompetence, of the national state during this period is a theme common to both political scientists and historians. Whether we consult the older studies of Leonard White on American public administration (1948; 1951; 1954), the insightful work of James Sterling Young on how the government operated (or failed to operate) in Washington (1966), or the more recent work of Stephen Skowronek (1982), scholars in different academic fields and using different methodological approaches all agree that the national state in the early republic often barely had a pulse.

In Skowronek's influential formulation, the nineteenth-century American state was one of "courts and parties" (1982, 24). The federal-state court system and political parties were the only institutions capable of coordinating government action. In the absence of a federal bureaucracy that had the infrastructural capacity to penetrate to local levels of government, the federal courts and the network of state parties had the ability to address issues of importance, distribute government benefits, and organize citizens for politics. As Charles Bright notes, "[t]he federal state was institutionally weak throughout the [nineteenth century], and it was getting relatively weaker after 1830. . . . Under the Jacksonian presidencies, powers accumulated at the national level by federalist statemakers were given up again" (1984, 121).

One of the great political dramas of the Jacksonian era was the rejection of the "American System" of federal government support for roads, canals, and internal improvement put forward by Henry Clay, John Quincy Adams, John C. Calhoun, and many others (Feller 1995, 53–60, 66–75, 162–8). When put into practice, however, the desire for improvements that could bind the nation together turned out to pit section against section and state against state. President Jackson killed the American System,

298 *Stephen M. Griffin*

thinking that it was better to "abjure developmental powers altogether than to see them subserve, as they always did, the interests of the privileged against the unprivileged, the few against the many. . . . Government's 'true strength,' said Jackson in 1832, 'consists in leaving individuals and States as much as possible to themselves'" (Feller 1995, 168).

In light of these developments, it cannot be credibly maintained that Supreme Court decisions of this period established the legitimacy of widespread national government intervention in the economic order. American politics was running in the opposite direction. The Jacksonian state was not being built up but torn down in favor of the maximum possible release of energy by the enterprising American people. As we have seen, the language of *Gibbons* and other Marshall Court decisions was not really to the contrary. From the Court's perspective, its task was not to suggest a policy agenda for a rising national state. It was rather to preserve a limited sphere of federal power against insistent attempts by the states to dismantle it altogether (Goldstein 1997; Graber 1995). This task was entirely consistent with the tentative quality of the nascent American state.

At this point I must take notice of a conceptual complication in this apparently straightforward argument. Does a historicist account of the Marshall Court really refute restorationism or simply change the subject? Restorationism, after all, is a serious interpretation of the Constitution and Court precedents, put forward by knowledgeable lawyers and justices and supported by perfectly conventional arguments. One might think it misguided, but showing where it goes wrong would surely involve advancing yet another interpretation. It is therefore important to appreciate that the historicist argument I have just made is not an interpretation of the Constitution as that is ordinarily understood.

All interpretations of the Constitution tend to abstract from historical context. They do so partly to avoid being bogged down in unnecessary detail, but also to retain the capability to resolve the contemporary issues to which they are addressed. But a given interpretation cannot abstract entirely from historical context without losing its status as an interpretation of the Constitution rather than of some other historical document. Constitutional interpretation is always backward-looking in this sense. It draws on the past in order to provide legal authority to the present. Even as it abstracts from historical context, then, constitutional interpretation is dependent on it for its status as law. If the authority sought in the past is not there to be found, the interpretation is debunked.

That is what the foregoing argument accomplished with respect to restorationism. Its status as law has been debunked because the context it presumes did not exist in the early republic. I debunked it, moreover, by employing a historicist argument rather than a competing interpretation. This raises the possibility that the same argument could be made of any interpretive attempt to justify the New Deal. This raises the stakes a bit higher. The issue is not the abandonment of some outmoded theory pursued by a few naive New Deal lawyers. It is rather whether *any* interpretive argument can suffice to justify the constitutional changes that occurred during the New Deal and after. Pursuing this line of inquiry involves coming to a better understanding of just what constitutional changes occurred after Franklin Roosevelt took office in 1933.

The New Deal as a Constitutional Revolution

The New Deal was indeed a constitutional revolution, one that can be traced in three dimensions of constitutional change: in the doctrines of constitutional law, the institutions of American government, and the ideology of American constitutionalism. A fourth distinct dimension to the New Deal is that it represented a change in American democracy. This last dimension is the key to understanding all the others and also makes clear why the New Deal was not simply a significant but incremental development. After all, didn't independent regulatory agencies exist before the New Deal? Wasn't national regulatory power clearly recognized in certain areas, such as over the railroads and monopolies? Hadn't Theodore Roosevelt and Woodrow Wilson articulated new conceptions of the presidency?

All this is true, and beside the point. To see why, we need to remind ourselves of one obvious feature of the New Deal – it was a response to a *crisis*. The Great Depression was one of the most serious political and economic crises in American history (Garraty 1987; Leuchtenburg 1963). Such crises create unique opportunities for state building and FDR and the Democratic Congress exploited the opportunity as far as they were able. But the president and Congress were able to go as far as they did because they had the backing of the democratic authority provided by some of the greatest electoral victories in American politics. The American people confirmed over and over again, particularly in the presidential elections of 1936 and 1940, that they wanted the government to have the constitutional power necessary to alleviate the Depression and to prevent future economic disasters (Ackerman 1998, 279–382).

As Louis Seidman and Mark Tushnet have suggested, at the base of these New Deal electoral mandates lay a public belief that the national government should be held accountable not only when it acts, but when it fails to act – as when it fails to respond to a national economic emergency (1996, 26–71). Once the federal government was held responsible by the American people for its failures to act, however, the entire idea of limited constitutional government was thrown into question. A government comprised of officials who know that they will be held accountable for failing to prevent significant harms to the American public is a government that is necessarily affirmative rather than limited, a government that constantly seeks out problems with which citizens are concerned in order to "solve" them and address their needs generally. It is a welfare state in a literal sense.

These democratic electoral mandates thus created an entirely different dynamic for the national state – one that had no precedent in American history. Never before had there been a consistent electoral mandate for the assumption of permanent national power over the entire economy. Certainly before the New Deal the federal government was involved in the regulation of economic activity. But it was a question of the regulation of this or that industry, such as the railroads, or this or that specific harm, such as impure food or monopolies. The Great Depression was a crisis in which it became necessary to contemplate regulation of the *entire* economy, *all* economic activity, no matter what its form. It is not surprising that the only precedent New Dealers could find to justify such a course of action was the kind of command and control regulation exerted by the government during World War I (Leuchtenburg 1995, 35–75).

The new dynamic created by the provision of democratic authority for economic intervention provided the impetus and justification behind the New Deal revolution in the constitutional order. Besides the often discussed changes in constitutional doctrine overseen by the Supreme Court, there were two additional dimensions to the revolution that were just as important: changes in the structure of state institutions, and the death of a constitutional ideology that had important ties to the republican ideology of the early republic. In each dimension, the changes were fundamental rather than incremental because, although each change had its progenitors, the democratic backing for state intervention created a new, permanently different context for the exercise of state authority. I discuss each of these three dimensions in turn.

The New Dealers were going beyond piecemeal regulatory efforts to formulate a plan for reviving the entire economy. Any measures necessary in this revival would surely be constitutionally justifiable, at least as far as they were concerned. But this kind of comprehensive planning ran afoul of several specific lines of Supreme Court precedent. Not everything done in the name of the New Deal was found unconstitutional by the Court. Nevertheless, what was unconstitutional devastated the general purpose of the New Deal – to assume responsibility for addressing what was wrong with the American economy as a whole. The New Dealers won several different electoral mandates to do just that. The course set by the Court in cases such as *Railroad Retirement Board v. Alton Railroad*, 295 U.S. 330 (1935), *Schechter Poultry v. United States*, 295 U.S. 495 (1935), *United*

States v. Butler, 297 U.S. 1 (1936), and *Carter v. Carter Coal*, 298 U.S. 238 (1936) guaranteed a political conflict with the New Deal.

The fundamental departure made by New Deal legislation in terms of doctrine had to do with the sheer scale of the control FDR and Congress wished to exercise over the economy. The National Industrial Recovery Act (NIRA) alone contemplated state control of *all* prices, wages, and conditions of labor in the United States (Ackerman 1998, 286–9). Although there were pre–New Deal precedents giving the federal government the power to influence certain prices, particular wages, and some working conditions, the very idea of total control had never entered the Court's (or anyone else's) mind and had no basis in the constitutional thought of the founding generation.

According to Kenneth Finegold and Theda Skocpol, if the NIRA and the Agricultural Adjustment Act had succeeded, "the United States might have emerged from the Great Depression as a centralized system of politically managed corporatist capitalism. The state would have been directly involved in planning price and production levels and in allocating income shares to capitalists, farmers, and workers" (1995, 20). This was not exactly the kind of limited republican order envisaged in the 1787 Constitution. In reaction to this radical policy shift, a majority of the Court committed itself to a point of view that divided legislation affecting the economy into distinct categories. If the main purpose and effect of the legislation was to regulate production or conditions of labor, then the legislation did not regulate commerce and, in addition, violated the powers reserved to the states under the Tenth Amendment (*Railroad Retirement Board*, 367–8; *Butler*, 63–4, 68–78; *Carter Coal*, 297–310). The role of the Court in making such distinctions was to preserve the constitutional order so as to avoid a centralized government.

The Court thus made impossible the kind of close regulation of production and government involvement in labor relations that was one of the hallmarks of the New Deal. From *National Labor Relations Board v. Jones & Laughlin Steel Corp.*, 301 U.S. 1 (1937), to *Darby*, 312 U.S. 100 (1941) and *Wickard*, 317 U.S. 111 (1942), the Court did not merely reverse course and abandon the categories it had tried to maintain. It also articulated a new standard of deference to Congress that ensured it would be very difficult to challenge any legislation enacted to regulate some aspect (no matter how local it first appeared) of the national economy. Whether the Court was following the 1936 election returns, reacting to FDR's Court-packing plan, simply changing as its membership changed after 1937, or some combination of all three, political forces outside the walls of the Marble Temple drove the transformation of constitutional doctrine that resulted. The Court's opposition to important forms of regulatory legislation engendered political opposition and split the legal elite. The political and legal circumstances produced by the Court's long opposition to various forms of regulatory legislation made it easy for FDR to recruit new justices who could be counted on to support the New Deal.

The two most obvious changes in state institutions accomplished by the New Deal were made with respect to the presidency and the structure of American federalism. The power of the presidency was enhanced dramatically by Roosevelt's leadership during the Great Depression. The presidency became a new kind of constitutional office, offering the potential for a president to surmount the separation of powers and become the de facto head of the federal government, if not the nation as a whole (Leuchtenburg 1995, 1–34). Historian Michael Parrish's summary echoes the conclusions of many scholars: "[FDR's] mastery of the radio, his superb political skills, and the Executive Reorganization Act of 1939 enormously enhanced the prestige of the presidency. With Roosevelt's tenure the White House became the focus of popular dissatisfaction with the nation's economy, foreign policy, and moral tone" (1984, 727).

The Great Depression also forced a significant alteration in American federalism. To an extent that is difficult to appreciate today, state governments were largely ineffectual in responding to the armies of poor and unemployed that required assistance (Patterson 1969). This inability to respond had a constitutional dimension in that many state constitutions made it very difficult for state governments to do anything (Griffin 1996, 41–2). This left a vacuum of power that was filled at the national level. The national state of the New Deal was built on assuming tasks that local and state governments had previously shouldered alone. What resulted was a complex system in which there were a few programs for which the national government was solely responsible; many more programs for which the national and state governments shared responsibility, typically with the federal government providing funding and the states providing administration; and some policies that the federal government encouraged the states to adopt on their own through use of grants-in-aid and other carrots and sticks. The federal government led the way but the states were an indispensable partner.

Finally, the constitutional revolution of the New Deal had an important ideological dimension. The central assumptions of American legal and constitutional thought were antithetical to the principles the New Dealers had to develop to justify their proposals. These assumptions included the following:

1. Some economic regulatory measures were beyond the power of legislatures to enact. An important example was legislation passed to benefit a particular class of citizens (Gillman 1993).

Constitutional Theory Transformed 303

2. Individuals and corporations had vested property rights that originated in the Constitution and could not be violated absent compelling reasons (Wiecek 1998).
3. Government measures could not have the redistribution of property as their primary object – there could be no "taking the property of A and giving it to B" (Wiecek 1998).
4. The separate state governments retained sovereignty in the federal system as equals of the national government, as guaranteed by the Tenth Amendment (Benedict 1979, 41–2).
5. The role of the federal government should be strictly limited and any additional duties taken on should be of a temporary nature (as during a war) or should be understood as clear exceptions to the normal rule of nonintervention.

Of course, these assumptions overlapped and there were many interconnections among them. The important point is that they were understood to be interwoven with the Constitution itself. The New Deal ran counter to all of them. Given the emergency conditions created by the Depression and the secure backing of the democratic public authority provided by their electoral victories, New Dealers simply did not pay much attention to any of these assumptions. The necessity of the emergency justified ignoring these no doubt outmoded ideas, based as they were on notions of a static, unchanging Constitution. New Deal legal thinkers publicized the arrival of the dynamic, living Constitution, which changed as social and economic needs demanded (Gillman 1997; White 1997). It was absurd to think that constitutional ideals formed in an age without modern transportation, communications, and monopolistic corporations should rule in the more complex environment of the 1930s. It is difficult to overstate how completely the New Dealers were alienated from these assumptions, once an unquestioned part of the American constitutional tradition.

The conclusive proof that the New Deal embodied a constitutional revolution relates to the belief of the New Dealers that the Depression constituted a serious national emergency. The idea that the emergency justified New Deal legislation competed with restorationism as a legal argument offered in the courts (Irons 1982, 52–4, 93). But the rationale of emergency also served as a much broader political and constitutional justification for the New Deal. Arguably, it was FDR's justification of choice. Even before he gained the Democratic nomination in 1932, he was invoking the idea of emergency and the analogy to war to prepare his audience for the kind of activist government that would be necessary (Roosevelt 1938, 1:631). In his inaugural address, FDR made the wartime analogy explicit. FDR claimed that the American people understood "that if we are to go forward, we must move as a trained and loyal army"; he offered a pledge to "bind upon us all as a sacred obligation with a unity of duty hitherto evoked only in time of armed strife" (Roosevelt 1938, 2:14). If Congress failed this challenge, however, and was unable to pass needed legislation, "I shall ask the Congress for the one remaining instrument to meet the crisis – broad Executive power to wage a war against the emergency, as great as the power that would be given to me if we were in fact invaded by a foreign foe" (Roosevelt 1938, 2:15).

Historians have noted the importance of the wartime analogy to the justification of the New Deal (Karl 1983, 119–21; Leuchtenburg 1995, 33–75). FDR and his supporters called on the experience with command-and-control government during World War I with several purposes in mind: to prepare the American people for what might be necessary, to for-mulate a plan of action, and to justify the far-reaching government intrusions into the economy necessary to address the Depression. Yet the rationale of emergency and the use of the wartime analogy point toward a troubling feature of the New Deal revolution. Much like the Civil War, the New Deal discredited a specific legal ideology without replacing it with a broader political justification for consistent government activism. The wartime analogy purchased justification at a price. FDR and his successors could obtain decisive action from Congress only by invoking the kind of authority that was appropriate in an emergency where the sur-vival of the country was at stake. But this kind of authority could not be sustained. The wartime analogy implied that presidential authority and the measures taken under it would always be temporary (Griffin 1996, 81–5; Karl 1983).

From a constitutional perspective the question that must be asked is why the rationale of emergency was necessary. After all, from a restora-tionist point of view, FDR should have simply declared his allegiance to the principles of *McCulloch* and *Gibbons*. But FDR never embraced restorationism or any other approach that resembled what we now call originalism. Old constitutional rationales were unavailable and new ones were slow to form. The invocation of the rationale of emergency thus dis-credits not only restorationism but any theory of constitutional change that represents American constitutionalism as a narrative of continuity. Like the Civil War, the New Deal marked a sharp break, a discontinuity in American constitutionalism. The New Deal created a hole in the con-stitutional world (Gillman 1993, 201–2).

In addition, the rationale of emergency and the appeal to the kind of government power exercised during World War I show clearly why the New Deal was not an incremental development in the history of American state building. If it were really the case that a competent national state had been established in the Progressive Era, no such argument would have been necessary. The national state would have already had the institutions and justifications required to deal with the Great Depression. Of course this was not the case (Karl 1983, 119). The crucial element of state capacity was missing. It had to be supplied not simply through developing new agencies and infusing Washington with a new cadre of administrative experts, but through fundamentally new constitutional and political justifications.

The different dimensions of change arising from the New Deal pose a crucial challenge for any theory of constitutional change. Of course, none of these changes occurred through the amendment process specified in Article V of the Constitution. Further, it should be clear by now that the Supreme Court did not have the primary role in initiating or carrying through all of the dimensions of change. Even with respect to changes in constitutional doctrine, the Court was more at the mercy of events than it was their master. It therefore does not make much sense to understand the dimensions of change as occurring through the legalistic process of constitutional interpretation. This opens the door to an approach that is historicist, political, and state-centered.

A Political Theory of Constitutional Change

The shock of the New Deal revolution created two distinct spheres in the complex political practice we call American constitutionalism (Griffin 1996, 26–58). The first and smaller sphere was that of the legalized Constitution, which was under the nominal control of the Supreme Court. In this sphere, constitutional change did proceed more or less as traditionally understood; that is, it occurred not only through formal amendments but also through the Court's development of precedent. So in stressing a more general perspective on constitutional change, I certainly do not mean to deny that the Court enforces the Constitution and adapts it to changing conditions. Ultimately, however, it does so only with the permission or acceptance of the political branches. The sphere of the legalized Constitution is necessarily much smaller than the sphere of American constitutionalism as a whole.

In the larger sphere of what might be called the political Constitution, constitutional change did not occur through formal amendment, Supreme Court decisions, or legalistic interpretations of the constitutional text. Instead, it occurred through ordinary political change. Here the president and Congress directed constitutional development. This development, of course, did not end with the New Deal. It continued through World War II, the Cold War, and the extraordinary period of government activism and regulation that began with President Johnson's Great Society (Griffin 1996, 81–7, 194–201).

306 *Stephen M. Griffin*

There is a sense in which the limits on the legally enforceable Constitution were programmed into the constitutional system from the beginning. This did not become obvious, however, until the federal government became a truly activist state in the New Deal. In the era in which the activity of the national state was extremely limited (which existed for most of American history), one could imagine that the entire constitutional structure was being guided by decisions of the Supreme Court. Consider, however, the nature of the agency required to keep up with constitutional change once the state becomes activist. Because any state action has the potential to change or violate the Constitution, the state's entire sphere of action must be available to scrutiny. The agency in charge of maintaining the Constitution must constantly monitor and scrutinize the flow of policy change. It must stand ready to intervene at any moment to prevent unconstitutional action.

The Supreme Court has never possessed this kind of power. Early on, the Court decided that it must indeed act *as a court* if it was to have any legitimacy at all. This move was successful – the Court established a base of power around the idea that in reviewing state and national legislation, it was performing a function well suited to courts. So, for example, the Court had to wait for litigation to develop before it could decide any constitutional question. It drew a line between law and politics and placed itself on the law side of the boundary. "Political questions" could not be entertained (*Marbury v. Madison*, 5 U.S. 137, 166–7 [1803]). The Court thus could not control the total flow of constitutional change.

In the context of the activist state, the Supreme Court would have to be the most powerful branch of government in order to monitor successfully the flow of constitutional change. All actions of the national state would have to pass the tests set by the Court. There would be no evasion of review, no unlitigated issues, and no political questions. Because it is inefficient to inform the other branches of the unconstitutionality of actions after they have already been taken, the Court would have to issue advisory opinions routinely. These are the sort of actions that would be necessary to make the sphere of the legalized Constitution coextensive with the sphere of the political Constitution.

Nothing like this occurred during the New Deal or after. The Supreme Court responded to the advent of the activist national state and the new power of the presidency not by increasing its own power, but by getting out of the way.[4] How could it have been different? As long as the changes

---

[4] The exception, of course, is in the area of civil liberties and civil rights. Even here, however, most of the Court's jurisprudence concerned actions of the state governments, not the national government. Furthermore, in the new democratic context produced by the New Deal, it is a mistake to say simply that the Court responded by increasing its power to

Constitutional Theory Transformed   307

in view were approved by a large majority of the public, presidents could always find justices who agreed with the implicit limits on the legalized Constitution. In any case, in order to keep up with the activist state, the Court would have had to abandon the idea that it was solely a legal body and create a new institutional order. Not only was there never any political support for doing this, but the option of becoming something other than a court and thus having to abandon the law-politics distinction never even occurred to the justices or the legal elite on whose support they depended.

To illustrate this point further, what would have been required for the sphere of the legalized Constitution to keep up with the pace of constitutional change? How could the changes of the New Deal and after been deliberated about and legalized in a way that would preserve a meaningful link with the 1787 Constitution? There is only one answer within the structure of the Constitution – a constitutional convention. The only way to "adapt" the Constitution in a way that ensures the entire document is legally enforceable is by involving elites and the public in a common process that creates a new constitutional order adequate to the demands of the twentieth century. It is ironic that this option is just the one most likely to be rejected by those who revere the Constitution and seek to maintain its legalized form.

The aspiration of the founding generation to create a permanent constitutional order based on enduring principles thus produces an impasse when it is set in the context of the activist national state. Such a state produces a flow of continuous constitutional change that cannot be controlled by any court. The activist state creates a set of new, fundamental structuring rules, practices, and institutions that have the same function as those contained in the text of the Constitution, but without any pedigree in either Article V or judicial precedent. The parts of the Constitution not overseen by the Supreme Court on a regular basis begin to dissolve into the structure of the state. The text of the Constitution tells us less and less about the way the government actually operates and what rules, practices, and institutions are key elements of the constitutional order.

In a polity with an old Constitution that has not been updated through amendments that respond to the activist state and cannot be updated through judicial precedents, seeing the Constitution whole necessarily involves taking proper account of constitutional change that has occurred outside conventionally accepted ways of making such changes. As I have been suggesting, the best way to do this is by employing a historical

---

oversee the branches in the area of rights. The question should rather be posed as follows: why was it in the interest of the political branches for the Court to handle these kinds of issues?

approach that focuses on the rules, practices, and institutions that are the functional equivalent of those in the Constitution. These rules may be informal (in the sense of not being enacted) or formal (expressed in statutes, regulations, and so on). Because we cannot work from an authoritative text in the case of these functionally equivalent rules, we must use an interdisciplinary perspective to sift through history, politics, and key events to find those rules that have appeared most crucial to structuring policy processes and outcomes. The study of these rules can guide us in building a model of our present constitutional order that should enable us to better understand that order, anticipate future developments, and formulate proposals for improvement.

The hole the New Deal created in the constitutional world is the gap between the historical world of the founding generation and the very different world created by the need to respond to the crisis of the Depression. Whereas the founding generation had a number of years to consider the problems of the 1780s, FDR did not have this luxury. During the New Deal the constitutional system had to be edited on the fly. The scale and ad hoc character of this constitutional change means that it is extremely unlikely that any theory of constitutional interpretation can account for it. Restorationism clearly cannot. But the problems of restorationism extend to all interpretive theories. All plausible theories of constitutional interpretation maintain a link with the past through the text. None of them can account plausibly for the constitutional changes set in motion by the New Deal.

If interpretive theories cannot be our guide to this new constitutional universe, how are we to proceed? In the next section, I explore how to transform constitutional theory in order to better understand the Constitution we have.

HISTORY, INTERPRETATION, AND CONSTITUTIONAL THEORY

Ackerman's Theory

In different ways, both Ackerman and I are attempting to develop historicist theories of constitutional change. It is telling that this is one of the points on which Ackerman has been most misunderstood. Legal scholars have difficulty even recognizing historicist theories for what they are. To these scholars, historicist theories look "originalist" at best and nonsensical at worst (Sherry 1992, 923–8). Before I launch into my critique of Ackerman, I should therefore say that he deserves great credit in three areas: (1) highlighting the importance of the general issue of constitutional change; (2) emphasizing the study of American constitutionalism as a series of regimes (1991, 58–130), which means concentrating on changes in all three branches of government over time (and thus providing an opening for historical institutionalism); and (3) adopting an explicitly historicist approach to the different moments in constitutional history (1991, 16–33).

In his latest volume, Ackerman improves the general argument for his theory in several respects. He usefully contrasts his theory with that of "hypertextualist" readings of Article V that cannot account for the questions surrounding Article V, the legitimacy of the Reconstruction Amendments, or the New Deal (1998, 71–95). This is intended to put his critics on the defensive and may well succeed (if they pay attention to his specific historical evidence). Ackerman also makes it much clearer that he is not offering a kind of originalist argument to justify his theory. In *Foundations* this was left uncertain, despite Ackerman's appeal to historicism, because he employed a detailed argument from *The Federalist* to justify his theory (Ackerman 1991, 165–99). In *Transformations*, Ackerman makes it apparent that he is offering a historical and structural argument that attempts to show American citizens facing the same challenges every time they try to amend the Constitution in a fundamental (transformative) way (1998, 12, 66–8).

Ackerman situates his theory of constitutional change between two misguided alternatives. One is hypertextualism, the literalists who believe the only way the Constitution can change is through Article V (and perhaps Supreme Court precedent). The other is the view that constitutional change outside of these normal legal means must be understood as a form of revolutionary politics, which can only succeed or fail (1998, 11–12). In describing this latter alternative, Ackerman loads the dice somewhat by thinking only of what happens during truly significant episodes of constitutional change such as the Founding, Reconstruction, and the New Deal. The reasoning here is that because these moments are so epochal, the alternative to justifying them legally must be some sort of theory of revolutionary change that sees everything as "just politics." Ackerman does not consider the idea that the flow of constitutional change may be continuous, yet occurring through ordinary political struggles.

Ackerman understandably spends most of his time refuting the view that Article V settles how valid constitutional amendments can occur. As Ackerman (1998, 70, 115) notes, this theory has the greatest acceptance among lawyers. And in both *Foundations* and *Transformations*, Ackerman takes pains to appeal to lawyers and judges, not just legal scholars. He remarks that "America is a legalistic country" (1998, 12) and clearly wants to produce a legal theory that can be *used* by lawyers and citizens, not just studied.

310 *Stephen M. Griffin*

The problem here is that trying to turn unconventional constitutional change into "the functional equivalent of formal constitutional amendments" (1998, 26) threatens the entire enterprise of the legalized Constitution. It opens the Constitution to political considerations and fluid arguments that appear arbitrary to doctrinalists and lack the security provided by Article V. In *Transformations*, Ackerman tries harder to convince mainstream scholars that his theory poses no real threat to their legalistic enterprise (1998, 91–5). He stresses again and again that he is making careful, lawyerly arguments to justify his position (1998, 17, 66, 70, 93–5). Unfortunately, unconventional but legal amendment of the Constitution through Ackerman's five stages cannot be admitted to the canon of constitutional law without threatening the legalistic quality of the canon as a whole. Ackerman's theory blurs the law-politics distinction in a way that mainstream lawyers and scholars cannot tolerate.

We are still left with Ackerman's instances of unconventional change: Founding, Reconstruction, and the New Deal. How are we to understand the constitutional situation that prevailed during such periods? Ackerman's account of these three crises ignores the role of constitutional politics conceived as a *structural politics of fundamental values*, not as an alternative means of amendment or legal change (Griffin 1996; Whittington 1999). Each crisis produced a dynamic political situation in which departures from normal legal practice became not only thinkable but also absolutely necessary. This dynamic sort of politics, present in some degree in every American constitutional crisis, rapidly left behind any legalistic efforts to capture and tame it.

In the case of the Founding, Ackerman's own evidence demonstrates this quite clearly. Ackerman's account does not show legalistic Anti-Federalists clashing over the legality of the proposed Constitution with equally legalistic Federalists. To be sure, some opponents of the Constitution cared about legalistic arguments and some Federalists did as well. But arguments about legality did not dominate the debate – if they had, it is likely that the Constitution would not have made it past the Confederation Congress. Ackerman's evidence shows that most Federalists turned aside legalistic arguments with an appeal to the practical realities that faced the struggling republic. He remarks that in the Philadelphia Convention, "[w]ith the exception of Madison, the nationalists were strikingly unconcerned with legal technicalities" (1998, 50). Edmund Randolph's statement was characteristic: "he 'was not scrupulous on the point of power. When the salvation of the Republic was at stake, it would be treason to our trust, not to propose what we found necessary'" (in Ackerman 1998, 50). In other words, the political crisis made questions of legality beside the point. Americans were at least willing to entertain the idea of abandoning the Articles of Confederation for an entirely new scheme of government with new rules of adoption and amendment.

In the case of the Civil War and Reconstruction, Ackerman rules out looking for similar evidence of the role of practical considerations by defining the alternatives to his theory in terms of a choice between Article V literalism and the "grasp of war" theory, saying "the entire point of this book is to reject this dichotomy between legalistic perfection and lawless force" (1998, 116). But these are not the only options presented by the historical record. A more generous reading of the events surrounding the Civil War and Reconstruction supports the idea that these crises created a dynamic political-constitutional situation in which measures like the forced acceptance of amendments became thinkable, necessary, and legitimate (Benedict 1999, 2028–9).

To support his legalistic reading of the war, Ackerman endorses Lincoln's theory of the indissoluble Union, which held that because secession was unconstitutional, the southern states were still in the Union (1998, 113–14). This creates the dilemma Ackerman uses to undermine the Article V literalists (1998, 99–113). Because the southern states never left the Union, their free assent was required to ratify the Thirteenth and Fourteenth Amendments. When this assent was not forthcoming, congressional Republicans departed from Article V and forced their ratification through a nationalistic process that was a legally valid instance of higher law making (1998, 120–252).

This account ignores certain political realities and, more important, misses entirely the profound moral and political significance of the Civil War. With regard to Lincoln's theory, for example, historian James McPherson notes that "[i]n a practical sense, however, the Confederate states were unquestionably *out* of the Union" (1992, 404). The southern states had seceded using all the legal formalities at their command (McPherson 1992, 131–6). Lincoln may have hoped that they were still in the Union in spirit, but in the meantime he was fighting the bloodiest war in American history to force them to return. Further, Lincoln's understanding of the constitutional and political aspects of the war changed over time. He expressed his sense of the realities of the situation by telling an Interior Department official that when the Emancipation Proclamation took effect on January 1, 1863, "'the character of the war will be changed. It will be one of subjugation. . . . The [old] South is to be destroyed and replaced by new propositions and ideas'" (McPherson 1988, 558).

To Ackerman, the kind of view I am advocating implies that "the Civil War amendments emerge from the guns of the Union Army" (1998, 115), instead of a legal and constitutionally legitimate process. Here Ackerman overreaches and misses the point. From a northern perspective, the Civil War was just, moral, legal, and democratic – in short, the War was

312 *Stephen M. Griffin*

politically legitimate. Despite troubling violations of civil liberties, it was not conducted by a military overlord but by a democratically and constitutionally elected government. Indeed, a free and fair presidential election was held in 1864 while the war was going on. This means that the war had the potential to settle far more than the illegality of secession. The grim progress of the War created a political situation in which it was legitimate to force the ratification of constitutional amendments in order to secure the revolution it brought to the South and the nation as a whole. The war had this power not because of the guns of the Union army but because of the sacrifices the army had made and who the army was – the legitimate instrument of a democratic government.

Like Ackerman and unlike most constitutional scholars, I do not want to blink away the unique circumstances surrounding the ratification of the Thirteenth and Fourteenth Amendments. On the other hand, I see no reason to adopt Ackerman's five-stage theory of functional amendment to explain the legitimacy of the amendments unless there is clear historical evidence in its favor. Here is where Ackerman's theory encounters insuperable problems. Did participants in the debates over the Founding, Reconstruction, and the New Deal self-consciously agree that they were creating a several-stage sequence of higher law making that supplemented the procedure provided by Article V? This is what is required for Ackerman to meet conventional understandings of what is necessary to create law. Without self-conscious understanding, Ackerman still has a historical narrative that greatly deepens our understanding of how constitutional change has occurred through essentially political means. But he does not have evidence of a *legal* process. If Ackerman had such evidence, he would be able to show New Dealers, for example, saying something like the following: "Thank heavens for the precedent of Reconstruction. We don't have to go to the states to get amendments approved! We can do it through the nationalistic means created by the 1866 Republican Congress."

Of course, nothing like this was ever said. If it had, we would have heard about it before Ackerman began his research. The legitimacy of the Thirteenth and Fourteenth Amendments can be explained as the outcome of a complex process that is best understood as an instance of structural politics – a sort of politics that is uniquely focused on fundamental constitutional values and how best to realize them. The circumstances surrounding their ratification were an excellent example of this kind of politics in action.

Once shorn of the five-stage sequence and the notion of functionally equivalent amendments, much remains in Ackerman's invaluable account. In discussing the unique constitutional-political circumstances in which Americans found themselves at the end of the Civil War, Ackerman shows

Constitutional Theory Transformed 313

how Congress struggled to formulate new constitutional ideas to deal with a highly unusual political situation. But he does not show that they self-consciously adopted a new method of amendment that supplemented the procedure found in Article V. In trying to make this case, Ackerman is reaching for something that the legalism he admires will not let him have. Giving a proper constitutional account of the Founding, Reconstruction, and the New Deal means accepting the necessity of moving back and forth across the shifting border between law and politics without embracing either.

Historicism and Constitutional Interpretation

We are in the midst of a recognition by constitutional theorists that "we are all originalists, we are all non-originalists" (Kramer 1999, 677). This observation is accurate to the extent that scholars of many different persuasions have been driven to acknowledge that legal and constitutional interpretations inevitably draw on the past to give light to the present (Dorf 1997). Unfortunately, this has also led legal scholars to suppose that in using the past to interpret the Constitution, they have the same perspective as historians (Prakash 1998), which is clearly not the case.

Constitutional interpretation involves creating narratives of continuity. Restorationism is a good example, one that relies on language carefully selected from foundational precedents while ignoring their political and institutional context. It thus creates a false continuity between the Jacksonian era and the New Deal. What is important to see, however, is that any effort to validate the New Deal by conventional means of legalistic constitutional interpretation will have to do the same thing. Whether such interpretations are based on more robust evidence of original intent or on an approach that emphasizes the abstract character of the constitutional text, the result will be a narrative of continuity that disables us from a more realistic appreciation of the discontinuities of American constitutional history. In many ways, a historicist understanding of constitutional development is at odds with the interpretive perspective.

While historicism means different things to different historians, what is important in and common to the historicist perspective emerges sharply when they comment on the use of history in constitutional law. As Robert Gordon (1996, 340) has observed, for lawyers the past is a source of authority, identity, and inspiration. But when constitutional lawyers engage in determined attempts to reconstruct the past, they run into a paradox. The lawyer "is likely to find herself in an alien and unrecapturable social and conceptual world" (Gordon 1996, 341). The more the past is revealed, the more its usefulness in addressing the problems of the present recedes.

The paradox is intensified by the fact that constitutional lawyers, judges, and scholars are interested usually in just two periods of American history: Founding and Reconstruction. The great concentration on these two periods means that the dynamic qualities of history are lost as these periods are studied as if they were isolated islands in the American experience. After performing what are frequently immense labors studying the late eighteenth century and the middle nineteenth century, scholars time-jump to the contemporary world to announce their findings. They do not bother to check whether their findings would be altered by studying what has happened *since* the Founding and Reconstruction. They have no model, similar to that offered by historical institutionalism, to understand American political development or changes in the national state over time.

In trying to avoid the paradox and ensure that their labors yield results, constitutional scholars run into a number of difficulties. The most significant are well summarized by William E. Nelson in his important work on the Fourteenth Amendment. First, scholars tend to ask "questions of twentieth-century significance that cannot be answered by historical inquiry" (Nelson 1988, 6). Questions presented by contemporary Supreme Court cases may never have even occurred to the founding generation or the framers of the Reconstruction amendments. Such questions are nonetheless asked and records ransacked, although there is no conceivable historical evidence that could answer them. Second, "scholars have inquired about how the framers would have resolved issues they did consider but in fact never resolved" (Nelson 1988, 6). The need for answers forces scholars to contort the available evidence until it yields a particular result.

I call this second difficulty "the missing third alternative." Legal scholars are driven by the need to solve issues raised by a case, and each case has only two sides. Scholars thus frame the historical issue around two polar alternatives: either the plaintiff or defendant is right. The idea that the evidence may show that *neither* is right is typically not considered. It is the serious consideration of this third alternative that most clearly distinguishes a historicist perspective such as Nelson's from the interpretive perspective prevalent in constitutional law. As Nelson says, the proper task of historical scholarship is to identify "the meaning which the amendment had for its proponents, even if that meaning is not dispositive of the issues pending in the courts today" (1988, 6). For him, "[t]he essence of history is the identification of continuities and discontinuities between past and present" (1988, 10). If historical evidence shows a discontinuity, this must not be blinked away.

Michael Les Benedict usefully expands on Nelson's points. Benedict criticizes legal scholars for simply focusing on a particular event rather

Constitutional Theory Transformed 315

than the continuous process of historical change. Benedict comments that "[h]istorians are particularly concerned with how institutions and ideas have changed over time: A key purpose of history is to describe how past ideas and institutions differed from those of the present. Change is to be described and explained, not judged" (1992, 379). Benedict recognizes that lawyers and judges may have other purposes in view. The need to decide a given case does not go away simply because the evidence is ambiguous. Courts thus employ special rules, often drawn from statutory construction, to sort out and filter the evidence so that meaning can be ascertained and the case decided (Benedict 1992, 380).

Unfortunately, when courts engage in this kind of filtered history the results are unconvincing from a historicist point of view (Kelly 1966; Wiecek 1988; Richards 1997). The meanings and ambiguities uncovered by historians compete with and undermine the conclusions trumpeted with such certainty by judges and scholars. As Eric Foner comments with respect to discussions of the history of the Fourteenth Amendment: "[t]oo often they [legal scholars] restricted themselves simply to an exegesis of selected quotations from the Congressional debates rather than examining the full historical context, without which these quotations lack real meaning" (1992, 243–4). This may seem an abstract point, but that is why I began by debunking restorationism. Restorationism is an example of an acontextual legal history that indeed has *some* basis in the historical evidence – Justice Marshall did write those broadly worded opinions, didn't he? Any use of Marshall's opinions to validate the New Deal, however, involves the claim that Marshall meant to endorse the general sort of governmental power necessary to enact New Deal legislation. As the historical evidence shows, this was not the case. To invoke Marshall's authority in the context of the New Deal is completely anachronistic. There is no relevant similarity between the two periods that would allow us to even begin exploring what Marshall would have thought about the New Deal.

The example of restorationism shows that while legal rules can be used to generate historical certainties, the evidence produced by historicist inquiry cannot be willed away. The Supreme Court's consideration of the questions raised by constitutional change in *Planned Parenthood of Southeastern Pennsylvania v. Casey*, 505 U.S. 833 (1992) is illustrative. In *Casey*, Justices O'Connor, Kennedy, and Souter argued that the Court's most famous changes in view were the result of changes in the facts. With respect to the demise of *Lochner*, the key factor was that "the interpretation of contractual freedom . . . rested on fundamentally false factual assumptions about the capacity of a relatively unregulated market to satisfy minimal levels of human welfare" (*Casey*, 861–2). The other shift was the transition from *Plessy v. Ferguson*, 163 U.S. 537 (1896) to *Brown*

316   *Stephen M. Griffin*

v. Board of Education, 347 U.S. 483 (1954). Here the decisive factor was that "[s]ociety's understanding of the facts upon which a constitutional ruling was sought in 1954 was thus fundamentally different from the basis claimed for the decision in 1896"; both changes were justified because "each rested on facts, or an understanding of facts, changed from those which furnished the claimed justifications for the earlier constitutional resolutions" (*Casey*, 863).

The motto of the Ursuline Academy, a venerable Catholic school for young women in New Orleans, is: "Times change, values do not." Apparently, this could serve as well for the Court. What I call the "Casey fallacy" is thus assuming that significant constitutional changes are solely a matter of changes in facts, rather than changes in values. Any reputable history of these doctrinal shifts makes it very plain why the *Casey* Court was mistaken. With respect to *Lochner*, the Court gives the game away by using value-laden terms such as "contractual freedom" and "human welfare." The *Lochner* majority was surely aware that many Americans at the turn of the century were not well off. This did not bother the justices in the majority because they presumably believed that the operation of constitutional doctrines such as substantive due process were part of a total system that ultimately worked to the benefit of all Americans. This was, of course, a value judgment that the justices appointed by FDR did not share. They believed that state legislatures had a role in acting directly to increase human welfare through detailed laws regulating conditions of labor.

The change in values is, if anything, even more apparent in the case of *Plessy*. As Michael Klarman has recently reminded us, the turn of the nineteenth century was a time in which the supremacy of the white race was taken for granted (1998, 886–95). To the Court, state-imposed segregation was a reasonable means of ensuring that members of two different races would not be forced into a situation of social equality before they were ready (*Plessy*, 551–2). That these laws were part of a system designed to keep blacks in their place was simply ignored. The decision the Court made in *Brown* not to ignore this reality reflected a change in values. In the restrained phrasing of Morton Horwitz, the *Casey* Court "did not explore the dynamic nature of social or legal consciousness" (1993, 92). Times change, and facts and values change with them.

In recent years, some legal scholars have begun defending the idea of a "usable past" and suggesting that this justifies a lawyerly approach to history. Cass Sunstein argues that although history does impose constraints on constitutional lawyers, the lawyers' role differs from that of the historian: the lawyers' project is "*to make the best constructive sense out of historical events associated with the Constitution*" (1995, 602). Whereas the historian tries to "reimagine the past . . . the constitutional lawyer is trying to contribute to the legal culture's repertoire of arguments and political/legal narratives that place a (stylized) past and present into a trajectory leading to a desired future" (1995, 605).

I do not object to this view to the extent that it is a program for constitutional lawyers. It is evident from Sunstein's remarks, however, that he thinks this approach to history is also suitable for scholars. He distinguishes the advocate who "begins with a preestablished conclusion" (1995, 603) from the constitutional lawyer who seeks the truth. But the real-world experience with "law office" history has shown that Supreme Court justices and constitutional lawyers inevitably tend to act as advocates rather than lawyers, to use Sunstein's terms. I would distinguish justices and lawyers as advocates interested in persuasion, on the one hand, and scholars, on the other.

From a scholarly point of view, Sunstein makes no allowance for anachronism, the asking of questions of history that history cannot answer. With respect to the "missing third alternative," presumably he would say that we should not contort the evidence when it is too ambiguous. Unfortunately, this would eliminate a wide swath of the appeals to history that are standard in constitutional lawyering. The most important difficulty is that Sunstein does not come to grips with the reality that *all* of American history is potentially relevant to his project. The events "associated with the Constitution" almost always turn out to be the Founding and Reconstruction, not the rest of American history. It is what has happened *since* the Founding and Reconstruction that will largely determine whether any contested constitutional practice makes sense today. Recall that the point of this procedure is to cast light on the present and point the way to the future. Given my analysis of constitutional change, there is no way to do this without taking account of all events in American history that bear to a significant degree on the development of the state.

In addition, Sunstein does not appreciate the extent to which the historicist perspective competes with the goal-directed approach he prefers. He defends the practice of giving "special weight to the convictions of those who ratified constitutional provisions" (1995, 604) but does not take account of Foner's argument that understanding what the framers and ratifiers meant depends on a larger historical inquiry that can easily undermine the certain conclusions judges and lawyers wish to reach. Finally, Sunstein underestimates the role history can play in criticizing and destabilizing the restricted sets of options that constitutional law often presents. He notes that constructing a usable past necessarily means bypassing aspects of constitutional history that are not useful for present purposes; slavery and the narrow conception of free speech prevalent in the founding era are his two examples (1995, 605).

318 *Stephen M. Griffin*

This serious error illustrates very well the difference I wish to draw between the Sunstein-inspired lawyer, on the one hand, and the historicist scholar, on the other. This also demonstrates how a preference for narratives of continuity can lead scholars to ignore the discontinuities in American constitutional history. Without a historicist perspective, we cannot meaningfully confront the view of Justice Thurgood Marshall that the Constitution devised by the founding generation "was defective from the start, requiring several amendments, a civil war, and momentous social transformation to attain the [present] system of constitutional government" (1987, 2). The project of looking to the best constructive use of the past encourages the bad habit that lawyers and judges already have of ignoring the dark side of American constitutionalism. Tragedies and discontinuities such as slavery, the Civil War, Reconstruction, and the New Deal are part of the American constitutional story and must be confronted honestly if we are to understand the contemporary constitutional world.

As I indicated earlier, I accept the idea that lawyers and historians have different tasks.[5] As Laura Kalman reminds us, "historians still favor context, change, and explanation . . . [whereas lawyers] value text, continuity, and prescription" (1996, 180). Although the Court clearly recognizes the validity of what Philip Bobbitt calls "historical argument" (1982, 9–24) as a method of constitutional interpretation, it is history done the Court's way. In order to win cases, lawyers must conform to the standards of this mode of argument. The Court's influence, however, extends far beyond the lawyers who appear before it. Indeed, its antihistorical orientation pervades American constitutionalism.

Studying the Court's pronouncements on history and building narratives of continuity in order to resolve current and future constitutional controversies is clearly an appropriate and valuable task for academic lawyers. What is problematic is the idea that, in so doing, they are conforming with the requirements of sound scholarship. If the Court believes in narratives of continuity such as restorationism, lawyers will tend to go along, if only to ensure that their arguments have some influence with the justices. By contrast, scholarship involves a commitment to seeking the truth, wherever it may lead. A corollary scholarly virtue is critical distance,

---

[5] In drawing the distinctions in this section, I do not wish to be misunderstood. I am not arguing that historians pursue a purely descriptive project without the need to assume a normative point of view. The difference between historians and lawyers is not that the former are interested solely in description or explanation, whereas the latter are interested solely in prescription. Although historians do focus on description and explanation, the crucial difference is that they bring a much broader normative perspective to bear on historical evidence. To oversimplify, lawyers are interested in resolving cases by building narratives of continuity. Historians are not so limited and specifically tend to focus on the discontinuities between the present and the past.

which means being willing to question your own assumptions as well as commonly held beliefs (Kahn 1999). This implies an attitude of skepticism and a willingness to search for contrary evidence. One might say that scholars seek an ideal of discussion and debate in which the only standard is the force of the better argument (Habermas 1975, 107–8).

So while I agree that the paths of the lawyer and historian are different and in some sense equally valid, I do not accept the idea that the paths of the lawyer and the constitutional scholar are the same. Scholarship involves a commitment to questioning, if warranted, the necessary fictions of constitutional law. If arguments are available that undermine a strictly legalist perspective and its narratives of continuity, then those arguments cannot be avoided without compromising intellectual honesty. The reality that the Court adheres to mistaken historical views such as restorationism or the idea that only facts change, not principles and values, provides no reason why scholars must accept them.

In specifying a path for a transformed constitutional theory then, I hope I have made it clear that this is constitutional theory understood as scholarship, not as an aid to constitutional lawyering. Constitutional theory should assume a historicist perspective and take seriously the problems posed by constitutional change. As I hope to show, these commitments would have a dramatic impact on both the scope and content of American constitutional theory.

Constitutional Theory Transformed

A historicist perspective allows us to develop what I call a contextualized constitutional theory. When a clause of the Constitution, Supreme Court precedent, or constitutional practice or institution is at issue, it must first be set in historical context before a theoretically sound constitutional argument can be made. As I have argued, the most appropriate general context for understanding the Constitution is that suggested by historical institutionalism. We begin with the concept of the state and the problem of the relation of the Constitution to American political development. We then work out a theory of constitutional change to explain this relation and provide the context for more specific inquiries.

This means that the theory of constitutional change is prior to the task of constitutional interpretation. All theories of constitutional interpretation, not just originalism, depend on a historical baseline to get their arguments off the ground. The only way to justify what baseline to start from is through a historicist theory of constitutional change. I have sought to illustrate this point by critiquing restorationism. The justices who employed restorationism, such as Jackson and Douglas, were not originalists as that term is usually defined. Their justification for the New Deal, however, necessarily turned on an appeal to history because that was the only way to preserve the continuity of American constitutionalism.

The general form of the argument against restorationism allows us to do something that is fairly rare and very underrated in contemporary constitutional theory – debunking a normative argument by critiquing the descriptive-explanatory grounds of that argument. Here, restorationism is the normative argument. It asserts the legitimacy of something that happened in the 1930s and is, in some sense, still with us by referring us to authoritative pronouncements made in the distant past. When we examine the historical context, we discover that it is not plausible to maintain that those who made such statements were endorsing practices that resemble those of our own time. Further, when we take care to specify the institutional context in which those statements were made, we find that practices resembling those of our own time simply did not exist. It becomes apparent that asking the past to validate episodes such as the New Deal is to ask questions of history that history cannot answer. This debunks the normative claim at the heart of restorationism by taking away its basis in history. Without historical plausibility, restorationism becomes a purely doctrinal argument that statements in the past resemble statements we would like to use in the present to endorse certain contested practices.

Debunking restorationism raises the question of how many other normative arguments commonly made in constitutional law could stand up to a similar historicist test. Originalist arguments may appear to be obvious candidates for debunking, but I am interested primarily in the far more widespread and casual use of appeals to various kinds of precedents in the early republic. For example, it is common in both administrative law and federal courts jurisprudence to take some founding era pronouncement as given without asking whether current practices are so different as to make the statement irrelevant (Amar 1985, 210–16; Sunstein 1987, 467). To ask this question in a meaningful way, of course, we must have a baseline from which to judge founding era institutions against our own. This is where historical institutionalism makes a useful contribution. Instead of relying on uselessly general terms to describe the early American state, we focus with more precision on the structure of government institutions and whether they were able to wield authority effectively.

I stress that the point of doing this is not primarily to assist the Supreme Court or constitutional lawyers in their important tasks. I do not assume or expect that either lawyers or the Court will adopt a historicist perspective. That is why I emphasized the differences between lawyering and constitutional scholarship. This point extends to the development of contextual theories of judicial review and constitutional interpretation, which should be developed in accordance with scholarly values, not the values of lawyering or judging.

The difference a historicist approach can make to the traditional questions of constitutional theory can be dramatic. With respect to theories of judicial review, Judge Posner provides a recent example by referring to the contention that judicial review is undemocratic; he argues that this "begs the question" because "[t]he Court is part of the Constitution, which in its inception was rich in undemocratic features" (1998, 6). To assess this common argument and rejoinder in an appropriate scholarly way, however, we would have to explore what has happened *since* the adoption of the Constitution. We would have to do this not simply with reference to changes in the text but to the development of democracy in the United States as a historical phenomenon and its relation to the evolution of state institutions. For example, Morton Horwitz (1993, 57–65) has argued that the growing prestige of democracy in the twentieth century had a substantial impact on the Supreme Court even as the text of the Constitution stood still. This means that it is Posner who is begging the question. The political or nonlegalized aspects of the Constitution developed in a more democratic direction in the twentieth century and thus influenced the Court. It is anachronistic to refer to the 1787 Constitution as settling the question of the relation between judicial review and democracy because that governing order is no longer with us (Griffin 1996, 88–124).

Similarly, the most obvious difference a historicist perspective makes to the development of theories of constitutional interpretation is the avoidance of debates that are anachronistic. Ackerman makes this apparent when he argues that *Lochner* should be viewed in the context of its own time (1991, 63–6). The context that Ackerman provides is his own, and certainly not all historians would agree with it. But the general point is clear enough. It is pointless to ask, for example, whether there is a difference between *Lochner* and *Roe* (Griffin 1996, 168). This does not mean we should bring back the *Lochner* era, only that we should recognize that contemporary constitutional law and *Lochner*-era jurisprudence are both products of the unresolved political and legal conflicts of their time.

A historicist perspective does not favor any of the contending theories of interpretation, whether originalist or nonoriginalist. Whether these theories are best understood as modes of constitutional argument grounded in different sources of law or as interpretive proposals backed by more general theories of law and moral-political philosophy, they are all equally ahistorical. This is not a criticism but simply a fact of life. To be credible to an audience that is assumed to consist of academic lawyers and federal judges, these theories have to work within the Court's parameters. As I have argued, those parameters do not include a historicist perspective on the past. This means that when it comes to theories of interpretation, contextual constitutional theory and conventional theories do not share the same goals. The goal of contextual constitutional theory is to understand

322   *Stephen M. Griffin*

where American constitutionalism has been, where it is now, and where it is going. The resolution of specific cases is a task for lawyers, not theorists engaged in a scholarly inquiry.

The issues that should concern constitutional theorists have to do with the relation of the Constitution, understood as the fundamental institutions, rules, and practices that structure politics, to the contemporary challenges facing the United States. In other words, constitutional theory should be placed in contact with American politics. This certainly does not exclude discussion of the Supreme Court and fundamental rights. In a contextualized constitutional theory, however, these discussions would take place against the backdrop of the efforts of all branches and levels of government to deal with the politics of rights. Any issue of rights or interpretation of the Constitution would have to be set in a broad historical and institutional context before progress could be made in understanding or debating it. Any normative proposal regarding a constitutional right would have to take account of this broad backdrop before it could be regarded as plausible.

Besides Ackerman, Seidman and Tushnet (1996), Klarman (1996), Levinson (1995), Flaherty (1995), and Friedman and Smith (1998) have all adopted a historicist perspective in their recent work. In discussing the debate over the Court's ability to protect minority rights, for example, Klarman calls for constitutional historians (by my way of thinking, constitutional scholars in general) to "situat[e] constitutional disputes within their complex historical contexts . . . [and] identify the sorts of background forces – political, social, economic, cultural, ideological – that render possible dramatic shifts in constitutional doctrine" (1996, 31–2). The goal here is to understand "the parameters within which judicial review actually operates" (1996, 32). Here, Klarman provides an excellent example of precisely the sort of inquiry constitutional scholars should undertake and a model for how they should proceed.

In political science, the scholars whose views come closest to my own (besides historical institutionalists interested in constitutional law) are those associated with the Committee on the Political Economy of the Good Society (Elkin and Soltan 1993). They refer to their work as the new constitutionalism because it focuses attention on "the perspective of an institutional designer" (Soltan 1993, 3). The point is to study the design of the political order as a whole with a view toward diagnosing problems of that order and considering whether reforms can be made.

This viewpoint is useful also because it serves to answer a question some scholars may have about the historicist project. That is, if the purpose of contextualized constitutional theory is not to help the Court, then what is its purpose? The example of restorationism and my remarks on judicial review and constitutional interpretation may answer these concerns to some extent. There are normative claims worth debunking, and once they are debunked, we may see a way clear to a better theory. But theory for what?

My interest in constitutional change and a historicist perspective on American constitutionalism is motivated by the sense that the United States is in a period of unusual challenges to its governing institutions (Griffin 1996, 194–201). At the same time, the concepts and vocabulary bequeathed to us by our constitutional tradition seem singularly inappropriate to address those challenges. This state of affairs calls for a constitutional theory that gives us the ability to understand how we arrived at this situation and a sure grasp of the problems and capabilities of American government. And understanding is the best way to characterize the goal of constitutional theory. The purpose of constitutional theory is not merely to describe, explain, evaluate, or justify; it is to reach the best possible understanding of the distinctive political practice we call American constitutionalism.

CONCLUSION

It is both interesting and ironic that 1998–9 saw a classic demonstration of constitutional change occurring outside the Supreme Court. I refer, of course, to the impeachment and trial of President Clinton. Constitutional scholars witnessed the only grand jury investigation in American history aimed directly and exclusively against a sitting president and the only impeachment of a president initiated by a detailed report from an independent counsel.

There were numerous differences between the Clinton impeachment and that of President Nixon, its closest analog in the post–New Deal period. The Nixon impeachment investigation established a number of constitutional practices that were not followed in Clinton's case. The House Judiciary Committee did not conduct a thorough investigation of the charges contained in the independent counsel's report and did not call material witnesses. Most important, Henry Hyde, chairman of the Committee, deliberately decided to proceed in the absence of bipartisan agreement on the importance of the charges and the appropriate remedy for the president's misdeeds. As a final touch, the Senate decided to hold one of the few impeachment trials in American history without witnesses.

All of these events amounted to constitutional change from my point of view. It is perfectly possible that they will not outlast the turn of the century, given the public opprobrium heaped on the heads of the House impeachment managers. But they did happen and they could make a difference. In any case, they are now part of the constitutional landscape and deserve appropriate attention from scholars.

324 *Stephen M. Griffin*

Whether they will receive it is an open question. To many legal scholars, I imagine the Clinton impeachment looked as the stuff of pure politics. The events were related to constitutional provisions to be sure, but they did not exactly constitute the stuff of normal constitutional science. From my point of view, that is all the more reason we should be interested in understanding the practices and fundamental political structures that made Clinton's impeachment possible. How has the constitutional system been affected by the politics of scandal? Why did so many firebreaks in the system seemingly fail so consistently? Answering these questions requires not only an analysis of constitutional doctrine but the kind of historicist and institutionalist approach I have advocated here. It requires seeing the Constitution whole.

REFERENCES

Ackerman, Bruce. 1991. *We The People: Foundations*. Cambridge, Mass.: Harvard University Press.

1998. *We The People: Transformations*. Cambridge, Mass.: Harvard University Press.

Amar, Akhil Reed. 1985. "A Neo-Federalist View of Article III: Separating the Two Tiers of Federal Jurisdiction." *Boston University Law Review* 65: 205–72.

Benedict, Michael Les. 1979. "Preserving Federalism: Reconstruction and the Waite Court." *Supreme Court Review* 1978: 39–79.

1992. Book review. *Law and History Review* 10: 377–83.

1999. "Constitutional History and Constitutional Theory: Bruce Ackerman on Reconstruction and the Transformation of the American Constitution." *Yale Law Journal* 108: 2011–38.

Bobbitt, Philip. 1982. *Constitutional Fate*. Oxford: Oxford University Press.

Bright, Charles C. 1984. "The State in the United States in the Nineteenth Century." In Charles Bright and Susan Harding, eds., *Statemaking and Social Movements*, 121–58. Ann Arbor: University of Michigan Press.

Brinkley, Alan. 1995. *The End of Reform: New Deal Liberalism in Recession and War*. New York: Knopf.

Dorf, Michael C. 1997. "Integrating Normative and Descriptive Constitutional Theory: The Case of Original Meaning." *Georgetown Law Journal* 85: 1765–1822.

Elkin, Stephen L., and Karol Edward Soltan, eds. 1993. *A New Constitutionalism: Designing Political Institutions for a Good Society*. Chicago: University of Chicago Press.

Feller, Daniel. 1995. *The Jacksonian Promise: America, 1815–1840*. Baltimore: Johns Hopkins University Press.

Finegold, Kenneth, and Theda Skocpol. 1995. *State and Party in America's New Deal*. Madison: University of Wisconsin Press.

Flaherty, Martin S. 1995. "History 'Lite' in Modern American Constitutionalism." *Columbia Law Review* 95: 523–90.

Constitutional Theory Transformed

Foner, Eric. 1992. "The Supreme Court's Legal History." *Rutgers Law Journal* 23: 243–7.

Fried, Charles. 1995. "Foreword: Revolutions?" *Harvard Law Review* 109: 13–77.

Friedman, Barry, and Scott B. Smith. 1998. "The Sedimentary Constitution." *University of Pennsylvania Law Review* 147: 1–90.

Garraty, John A. 1987. *The Great Depression*. Garden City, N.Y.: Anchor Books.

Gillman, Howard. 1993. *The Constitution Besieged: The Rise and Demise of Lochner Era Police Powers Jurisprudence*. Durham, N.C.: Duke University Press.

    1994. "The Struggle over Marshall and the Politics of Constitutional History." *Political Research Quarterly* 47: 877–86.

    1997. "The Collapse of Constitutional Originalism and the Rise of the Notion of the 'Living Constitution' in the Course of American State-Building." *Studies in American Political Development* 11: 191–247.

Goldstein, Leslie Friedman. 1997. "State Resistance to Authority in Federal Unions: The Early United States (1790–1860) and the European Community (1958–94)." *Studies in American Political Development* 11: 149–89.

Gordon, Robert W. 1981. "Historicism in Legal Scholarship." *Yale Law Journal* 90: 1017–56.

    1996. "The Past as Authority and as Social Critic: Stabilizing and Destabilizing Functions of History in Legal Argument." In Terrence J. McDonald, ed., *The Historic Turn in the Human Sciences*. Ann Arbor: University of Michigan Press.

Graber, Mark A. 1995. "The Passive-Aggressive Virtues: *Cohens v. Virginia* and the Problematic Establishment of Judicial Review." *Constitutional Commentary* 12: 67–92.

Griffin, Stephen M. 1996. *American Constitutionalism: From Theory to Politics*. Princeton: Princeton University Press.

Habermas, Jürgen. 1975. *Legitimation Crisis*. Boston: Beacon Press.

Hobson, Charles F. 1996. *The Great Chief Justice: John Marshall and the Rule of Law*. Lawrence: University Press of Kansas.

Horwitz, Morton J. 1993. "Foreword: The Constitution of Change: Legal Fundamentality without Fundamentalism." *Harvard Law Review* 107: 30–117.

Irons, Peter H. 1982. *The New Deal Lawyers*. Princeton: Princeton University Press.

Jackson, Robert H. 1941. *The Struggle for Judicial Supremacy*. New York: Knopf.

Johnson, Herbert A. 1997. *The Chief Justiceship of John Marshall, 1801–1835*. Columbia: University of South Carolina Press.

Kahn, Paul W. 1999. *The Cultural Study of Law: Reconstructing Legal Scholarship*. Chicago: University of Chicago Press.

Kalman, Laura. 1996. *The Strange Career of Legal Liberalism*. New Haven: Yale University Press.

Karl, Barry D. 1983. *The Uneasy State: The United States from 1915 to 1945*. Chicago: University of Chicago Press.

Kelly, Alfred H. 1966. "Clio and the Court: An Illicit Love Affair." *Supreme Court Review* 1966: 119–58.

326 *Stephen M. Griffin*

Klarman, Michael J. 1996. "Rethinking the Civil Rights and Civil Liberties Revolutions." *Virginia Law Review* 82: 1–67.

   1998. "Race and the Court in the Progressive Era." *Vanderbilt Law Review* 51: 881–952.

Kramer, Larry D. 1999. "Madison's Audience." *Harvard Law Review* 112: 611–79.

Leuchtenburg, William E. 1963. *Franklin D. Roosevelt and the New Deal, 1932–1940*. New York: Harper and Row.

   1995. *The FDR Years: On Roosevelt and His Legacy*. New York: Columbia University Press.

Levinson, Sanford, ed. 1995. *Responding to Imperfection: The Theory and Practice of Constitutional Amendment*. Princeton: Princeton University Press.

Marshall, Thurgood. 1987. "Reflections on the Bicentennial of the United States Constitution." *Harvard Law Review* 101: 1–5.

McPherson, James M. 1988. *Battle Cry of Freedom: The Civil War Era*. Oxford: Oxford University Press.

   1992. *Ordeal by Fire: The Civil War and Reconstruction*. New York: McGraw-Hill.

Nelson, William E. 1988. *The Fourteenth Amendment: From Political Principle to Judicial Doctrine*. Cambridge, Mass.: Harvard University Press.

Parrish, Michael E. 1984. "The Great Depression, the New Deal, and the American Legal Order." *Washington Law Review* 59: 723–50.

Patterson, James T. 1969. *The New Deal and the States: Federalism in Transition*. Princeton: Princeton University Press.

Posner, Richard A. 1998. "Against Constitutional Theory." *New York University Law Review* 73: 1–22.

Prakash, Saikrishna B. 1998. "Unoriginalism's Law without Meaning." *Constitutional Commentary* 15: 529–46.

Rakove, Jack N. 1996. *Original Meanings: Politics and Ideas in the Making of the Constitution*. New York: Knopf.

Richards, Neil M. 1997. "Clio and the Court: A Reassessment of the Supreme Court's Uses of History." *Journal of Law and Politics* 13: 809–91.

Roosevelt, Franklin D. 1938. *The Public Papers and Addresses of Franklin D. Roosevelt*. Vols. 1 and 2. New York: Random House.

Seidman, Louis Michael, and Mark Tushnet. 1996. *Remnants of Belief: Contemporary Constitutional Issues*. Oxford: Oxford University Press.

Sherry, Suzanna. 1992. "The Ghost of Liberalism Past." *Harvard Law Review* 105: 918–34.

Skowronek, Stephen. 1982. *Building a New American State: The Expansion of National Administrative Capacities, 1877–1920*. Cambridge: Cambridge University Press.

Soltan, Karol Edward. 1993. "What Is the New Constitutionalism?" In Stephen L. Elkin and Karol Edward Soltan, eds., *A New Constitutionalism: Designing Political Institutions for a Good Society*, Chicago: University of Chicago Press.

Stern, Robert L. 1934. "That Commerce Which Concerns More States Than One." *Harvard Law Review* 47: 1335–66.

Sunstein, Cass R. 1987. "Constitutionalism after the New Deal." *Harvard Law Review* 101: 421–510.

1995. "The Idea of a Useable Past." *Columbia Law Review* 95: 601–8.

Tribe, Laurence H. 1995. "Taking Text and Structure Seriously: Reflections on Free-Form Method in Constitutional Interpretation." *Harvard Law Review* 108: 1221–1303.

White, G. Edward. 1988. *The Marshall Court and Cultural Change, 1815–1835*. New York: Macmillan.

1997. "The 'Constitutional Revolution' as a Crisis in Adaptivity." *Hastings Law Journal* 48: 867–912.

White, Leonard D. 1948. *The Federalists: A Study in Administrative History*. New York: Macmillan.

1951. *The Jeffersonians: A Study in Administrative History, 1801–1829*. New York: Macmillan.

1954. *The Jacksonians: A Study in Administrative History, 1829–1861*. New York: Free Press.

Whittington, Keith E. 1999. *Constitutional Construction: Divided Powers and Constitutional Meaning*. Cambridge, Mass.: Harvard University Press.

Wiecek, William M. 1988. "Clio as Hostage: The United States Supreme Court and the Uses of History." *California Western Law Review* 24: 227–68.

1998. *The Lost World of Classical Legal Thought*. Oxford: Oxford University Press.

Young, James Sterling. 1966. *The Washington Community, 1800–1828*. New York: Harcourt, Brace.

10

Constitutional Economic Transition

Russell Hardin

> A constitution is not intended to embody a particular economic theory, whether of paternalism and the organic relation of the citizen to the State or of laissez faire
>
> Justice Holmes, dissent in *Lochner v. New York*

A NEUTRAL CONSTITUTION

In his short but sharp dissent in *Lochner v. New York*, 198 U.S. 45 (1904), Justice Oliver Wendell Holmes declared that a constitution is neutral on economic policy. He was wrong in general because some constitutions have gone very far toward embodying particular economic theories. Even the U.S. Constitution embodies a limited degree of laissez-faire, enough to give capitalism at least an advantage over any other economic organization of the society, if Adam Smith's theory is roughly right. What capitalism mainly needed was free markets, and the U.S. Constitution went very far toward providing that markets would not be trammeled by the states acting for narrow interests against farmers and producers in other states.

Holmes was right, however, in the sense that the Constitution of 1787 would allow various economic theories to prevail. One of three systems of economic organization favored by different groups was plantation agrarianism. Although not constitutionally bound to fail, plantation agrarianism failed economically on its own in the face of overpowering capitalism. But the framers of the Constitution did not intentionally put capitalism

---

Prepared for discussion at the conferences on Constitutions and Constitutionalism, at the Murphy Institute, Tulane University, New Orleans, February 18–20, 1994, and March 11–12, 1995. This chapter has benefited from discussions with Elaine Swift and the participants at the Murphy Institute conferences. Its writing has been supported by New York University and by the center for Institutional Reform and the Informal Sector (IRIS), University of Maryland.

into the Constitution. They merely designed an economically almost neutral – at least neutral between plantation agrarianism and capitalism – national government, which was virtually all that capitalism needed. And they arguably did even that without much understanding. In the cockiness of their belief in their different views, the two economic groups that colluded in designing the constitution – plantation agrarians and the party of commerce, industry, and finance – thought merely ending state-level interference in their markets was enough for their views to prevail.

Was that an unintentionally wise choice? In a fundamentally important sense, it was wise for the longer-run workability of the Constitution, as the government faced massive economic transitions over the subsequent centuries. A government too narrowly defined to handle one set of economic conditions can be a disaster when it must handle dramatically different conditions. The problem of the eastern socialist nations in the 1980s is that they had been designed essentially to handle the mobilization of backward economies to make them more productive quickly. Indeed, they had been designed to manage the Russian transition after World War I. When the economies of these nations ceased to benefit from centrally controlled mobilization to do what was already well done elsewhere, their Communist governments were an obstacle to developing in other ways. The mercantilism of the eighteenth century in France, England, and other European nations had similarly been an obstacle to economic development in the early decades of the new industrial age, as the quasi mercantilism of the U.S. states was an obstacle to general development in the United States under the Articles of Confederation after the War of Independence.

The fundamentally important element in the design of constitutions that will enable rather than hinder economic transitions that are not well understood in advance is the lack of an embodied economic theory that might fit ill with dynamic transitions. In the American constitutional experience, the necessary move was to break the hold of a mix of crude mercantilism and beggar-thy-neighbor competition at the level of the individual states and, thereby, to create a large, diverse, and relatively free market. In the current constitutional redesign of the formerly socialist nations of the East, the necessary move is likely also to be to create relatively free markets. But, in these nations, this will have to be accomplished by demolishing a vast array of institutions for controlling production, distribution, and even consumption. Relatively simple coordination on a national regime sufficed for the American states. A far more dramatic transformation is required for the eastern nations.

Holmes supposed that a constitution could be economically neutral so that government might choose economic policy without severe constraint.

He was wrong in fact: Anti-Federalist communitarianism is partially an economic system that was definitively ruled out by the U.S. Constitution. And he was arguably wrong in the abstract for two broad classes of economic systems. It is hard to conceive a meaningful constitution that would be completely neutral as between state-controlled and non-state-controlled economic systems. While, as Holmes remarked, nothing so specific as Herbert Spencer's social statics was built into the U.S. Constitution, something vaguely approaching the free market was. At the very least, the constitution enabled capitalism, a system not well understood by the framers of the constitution, and stood in the way of a centralized command economy. It also enabled plantation agrarianism by protecting slavery, although plantation agrarianism could not finally survive the coming economic changes that would make agriculture a minor part of the economy, and it was destroyed before that by the Civil War.

In standard capitalist economics, a central concern is stability of expectations that will give incentive to investment. Any constitution that can create stable expectations in a context of entrepreneurial freedom especially enables capitalism. There might be an economic system in which stability of expectations would not play a strong constructive role in motivating people to improve their lives, but it is hard to imagine that economies geared to production can function well without relatively stable expectations. Part of the ideology of communism was the possibility of creating a new socialist human being, who would be motivated by social or moral commitment rather than by incentives of personal gain. Part of the method of slavery in many contexts has been the use of force and terror to motivate. Neither moral commitment nor terror seems likely to induce widespread creativity and innovation, but if either of them or if some other system not dependent on stable expectations and incentives could be made to work, then much of what I say might be irrelevant.

In what follows, I discuss the role of expectations and constitutional stability in economic relations. Next I consider the conflicting economic and political visions in the United States in the constitutional era, the Commerce Clause, and its object – freeing trade from petty interferences by the states and foreign powers – and the working of the constitutional regime with subsequent general problems of growth and economic transition. Then, turning to Eastern Europe, I discuss the contradictory symbolic vision of economic relations in the era of the hammer and sickle, the peculiarly complex problem the eastern regimes face in combining democratic and economic transitions, and the role that demographic changes have had and could have in economic change. I conclude with some general comparisons of the American and eastern experiences and prospects, including elements of luck in the apparent success of their constitutional regimes. In both the American and the eastern cases, the focus will be on

Constitutional Economic Transition 331

the workings of the constitutional order rather than on the politics of bringing it about.[1]

EXPECTATIONS AND CONSTITUTIONAL STABILITY

Nations commonly go through substantial economic transitions. Many nations today are facing merely a grander than usual transition as they attempt to move from central planning to relatively free-market organization. Large economic transitions, perhaps the most important challenges for constitutions, might be managed without grievous difficulty by a political regime that is stable. But many of the transitions today are coupled with at least temporarily destabilizing constitutional transitions from autocratic to relatively democratic forms of government. The problems of some of these are complicated further by ethnic conflict.[2]

Stable expectations are conspicuously important in economic contexts, because investment (in capital, skills, reputation) will commonly be higher if, for a given level of average expected benefit from the investment, variance in results is less. If you can double your current wealth or lose it all on the toss of a fair coin, you are likely to prefer not to make the gamble. In social contexts, the gamble is often even worse than this, because the potential losses stagger the potential gains. For example, suppose the peasants of Vietnam can switch from one strain of rice to another to increase their average annual yields of rice – but only at the risk of a greater likelihood of complete failure and starvation in any given year. They might then reasonably opt for the less productive strain (Scott 1976; Popkin 1979). Similarly, a firm that might have its access to a market in a neighboring state barred from one year to the next may invest less in increasing production for that market. With such truncated expectations, one has far less reason to bank on the future.[3]

Reputedly, unstable expectations about the general future in Central Europe and the former Soviet Union have led people to have far fewer children than before – indeed, fewer than enough to reproduce the population in Russia (*New York Times*, March 6, 1994, I.1, 18). Unstable expectations can themselves be disruptive enough to bring about the lower range of possibilities. Introducing stability of expectations can therefore

---

[1] For a discussion of the politics of bringing about the U.S. Constitution, see Hardin 1999, ch. 2.

[2] This may commonly be, in large part, a matter of failed economics. See Hardin 1995, 56–9, 142–7.

[3] Such problems might be overcome. For example, if the government could convincingly guarantee to provide minimal levels of rice even in the worst years, it could, at very low average annual cost, stimulate a substantial increase in rice production. That increase could be taxed enough to pay for the occasional rice distributions, thereby making everyone better off.

332 *Russell Hardin*

substantially stimulate future-oriented actions. A working constitutional order that stabilizes expectations is therefore enormously important to economic productivity and welfare. To stabilize expectations over the longer run, such an order must enable economic developments – or at least not block them.

The long-run success of the U.S. Constitution arguably came from its fit with the developing economy. The object of the Commerce Clause, while important to the original thirteen states and the reason for the constitutional convention of 1787, is central to the possibility of large-scale economic organization without government control.[4] It is almost the doctrine of laissez-faire defanged and made operational rather than ideological, at least for the domestic economy. The proponents of the Constitution and its Commerce Clause wanted uniform national tariffs to make their then current relations work better, especially in the context of Great Britain's divide-and-conquer trade policies with the states. Perhaps there were thinkers who had the foresight to imagine what prodigious economic changes were in store during the century after adoption of the constitution, but it seems likely that no one argued for the Commerce Clause and national government on the claim that these would enable revolutionary changes in the world the constitutional generation knew. That what they designed worked through this eventual revolution of the economy was largely a matter of chance.

ECONOMIC AND POLITICAL VISIONS
IN THE EARLY UNITED STATES

In contest for the future of the United States during the constitutional era, there were three defining visions about the nature of the society that would follow creation of a national government: the plantation agrarian vision of Thomas Jefferson, the commercial vision of Alexander Hamilton, and the communitarian vision of the rural Anti-Federalists. The last of the three played the central role in the ratification debates in many states, especially in New York, but was effectively crushed by the creation of a relatively strong national government. Because it was of little political significance once the Constitution of 1787 was ratified, I do not discuss it here (but see further Hardin 1999, ch. 2). Although Jefferson and Hamilton each wanted many things, it makes sense to restrict the labels that their names provide to central parts of their views. Each had implicit theories of how society might work once it was properly governed, but

---

[4] See various documents in Kurland and Lerner 1987, 477–528. In 1785 Madison argued especially strenuously that the national government must be made able to accomplish the ends of the eventual Commerce Clause, if necessary by replacing it with a different government (Kurland and Lerner 1987, 481).

these theories need not be included in their visions. For example, Jefferson seemed to think it possible that the world could continue to be organized by agrarian concerns, and Hamilton generally believed that commercial progress depended on massive state action on behalf of business. The central, defining parts of their visions were their different views about the nature of the economy that would prosper.

Another vision, more nearly structural and not substantive, was that of James Madison. This impressionist's vision of a unified nation that could respond to the world it faced in essence carried the Philadelphia convention that designed the constitution. It then became Holmes's neutral arbiter between the economic visions of Jefferson and Hamilton, while it wrecked the hopes of the Anti-Federalist vision of small communities and independent farmers.

Conceptually, the striking thing about the constitution that Jefferson, Hamilton, and Madison all supported in the end is that it could have accommodated either Hamilton's or Jefferson's vision – and in this it clearly fulfilled Madison's vision. Factually, the most striking thing about the constitution is that in some compelling sense it worked, especially in getting the new nation started. Explaining a successful constitutional regime raises two quite separate issues: successful establishment of the constitution over roughly its first generation, and its success in guiding and constraining government in the longer run of many generations. In this era of numerous constitutional transitions, the more urgent of these two issues is the first. Many constitutional transitions have largely or utterly failed over the few decades immediately after the constitution's adoption. Adoption of a successful constitution is typically a matter of coordination (Hardin 1989; 1999, ch. 2), but longer-run success also depends on the subsequent coordination of a polity on stable expectations, perhaps especially economic expectations.

How can a constitution have accommodated two such opposing economic visions as those of Hamilton and Jefferson? Largely, it did so because the Jeffersonian plantation agrarian society and the Hamiltonian urban commercial society both required national organization of their markets and because the constitution did not attempt to control general economic developments beyond establishing national markets. Because theories of economic developments have generally been poor and even perverse, the saving grace of the Constitution is not to have enshrined any such theory. Jefferson's vision eventually *failed* because his theory was wrong. Hamilton's eventually *succeeded* because his theory was wrong. Madison's vision was a more or less neutral referee in the economic transitions that followed the Constitution. Because of the general lack of understanding of economic futures, of what the future alignment of interests and their weights would be, the neutral Constitution was relatively easily agreed to. Moreover, it was likely to be more stable than a more definite one would have been. Adam Przeworski has observed that "Institutions adopted when the relation of forces is unknown or unclear are most likely to last across a variety of conditions" (1991, 88). But this observation should be qualified. A constitution is more likely to last if it does not embody a misfit economic theory. It may be less likely to embody any theory if the relation of forces is not well understood. Hence, the direct correlation between unclarity and longevity of institutions may be spurious.

After twelve years of tentative government, Jefferson and the Jeffersonians came to power in the United States under the still new Constitution. At the time, this must have seemed to be the success of a Cincinnatus who could guarantee the stability of the agrarian party. From our retrospective vision, this would have been – at least economically – a disaster. In the long run of a century or so, business was sure to become the dominant force, and Jefferson's farmers were bound almost to disappear, although no one need have understood this trend during Jefferson's lifetime. The remarkable fact is that Jeffersonism controlled the early government, perhaps down through the presidency of Martin Van Buren (1837–41), while business interests have seemingly controlled much of the policy of American government in this century. C. E. Lindblom (1977) argues that the interests of business are now so much in tune with what government must want that business need not even overtly exert itself. The transformation of the economy from an agrarian society to an industrial society was wrenching, although the twists in people's lives were spread out over generations and often appeared to be individual rather than group or national and, therefore, personal rather than political.

With slight differences in the political makeup of the new nation, Hamilton and the Hamiltonians might have gained the dominant position in the government, a position they very briefly held under President John Adams and that they perhaps shared with agrarian interests under the less clearly defined presidency of George Washington. Would Hamiltonian hegemony have meant a less stable constitutional regime? Perhaps. But it seems plausible that stability of either party in office would have produced a stable constitutional regime in the longer run. The U.S. constitutional order came to work in part because one party gained hegemony for several decades. It might not have mattered very much whether the Hamiltonians or the Jeffersonians gained such hegemony. But it might have mattered whether *neither* had gained it, whether there had been consequential fighting and better definition of the partly latent conflicts. Then each party in office might have put great energy into preempting the other party to secure its own vision through any interregnum.

In particular, the two opposing groups might have tried to impose their wrong economic theories on the government, making it less able to handle the economic transitions that violated both theories. John Adams's midnight appointments to federal offices as he and the Federalists left office in 1801 are merely a hint of what might have happened with real competition thereafter. The instability of expectations in the United Kingdom wrought by several postwar flip-flops between socialization and privatization of various industries is more indicative of the harms that an early ideological fight between Jeffersonians and Hamiltonians might have caused. In the United Kingdom, each side thought its vision was correct and the other's wrong. But both should retrospectively have agreed that frequent reconsideration was worse than stability under either regime. Early American Democracy may oddly have benefited from the relative lack of competition. Stability per se and not particular Jeffersonian policies may have been the supreme value of Jeffersonian hegemony. And that value could as well have been supplied by Hamiltonian hegemony. Because they were continuously in power, except for the ambiguous interregnum of John Quincy Adams (1825–9), the Jeffersonians could be confident of their own leadership and could forgo trying to put institutional obstacles in the way of any nonagrarian vision.

Why can stability lead to stability? Other things equal, stability over a long period reduces *expected* variance, which leads to greater investment in future returns, which leads to enhanced future production, which confirms and reinforces positive expectations. Stability of a constitutional order becomes self-confirming as the order endures. Of course, other things need not always be equal, and there might be external or internal shocks that upset the trend of expectations. For example, by about 1850 the U.S. constitutional order began to be undermined by the prevalence of the Hamiltonian vision over the Jeffersonian. Industrial production in the growing cities of the northeast and farm production without slavery in the new western states tipped the political balance away from what was previously the relatively even balance of slave and nonslave states.

The success of the Hamiltonian vision might have undermined the order even more than it did, but that vision needed no party to lead it to triumph. Under relatively weak government, it would succeed on its own. Business as such has got little advantage from any party, although individuals and individual firms have often gotten enormous advantages, sometimes through graft and special favor, sometimes through more general policies. At the extremes in the late nineteenth century, the 1920s, and the 1980s, these advantages have been sweeping, especially in making large numbers of people rich and inadvertently strengthening a bit of the Hamiltonian vision by severely undercutting subsequent government capacity.

THE COMMERCE CLAUSE

The Commerce Clause – assigning the federal government power to regulate interstate and foreign commerce – has been seen through many lenses to do many different, sometimes contrary things. It reputedly empowered the federal government, disempowered it, and did little or nothing. Perhaps, with the proper nuances, all these claims are true. This is the clause in its simplicity: "The Congress shall have Power . . . To regulate Commerce with foreign Nations, and among the several States, and with the Indian Tribes" (U.S. Constitution, Art. III, sec. 8). It sounds like an empowerment. But it is instructive to recall that, in its time, the Commerce Clause bothered many people primarily because it took power from the states and gave it to the national government, not because it created government power at all. As exercised by the states, that power had been destructive. States attempted to generate their public revenues from taxation on trade from other states and from tariffs.

The Commerce Clause implies that the federal government has the power of taxation on commerce. But it also implies the end of selective taxation on domestic commerce that happens to cross state boundaries, leaving only general excise taxes and taxation on foreign trade. Even for the latter, the government can only tax particular categories of imports uniformly, so that it cannot differentially affect competing business incentives in two or more states. For commercial interests, the constitution turned the United States into a single market.

There had been extensive prior agitation for measures to improve economic prospects by equalizing tariffs, harmonizing currencies, and developing joint waterways. Many documents leading up to the Philadelphia convention articulate concern with the disruptive trade practices of the states under the Articles of Confederation.[5] A relatively typical delegate to the Philadelphia convention, Roger Sherman of Connecticut, asserted that regulating trade was one of the few principal objects of the convention – along with defense against foreign attack, prevention of the use of force among the states, and making international treaties (Farrand 1937, 3:133). Even more singular than the claims for the need for national regulation of the market, however, is the strongest objection to the convention's purpose. Rhode Island refused to send delegates and two of New York's three delegates withdrew from the convention early in the proceedings in July 1787 (the convention continued until September 17). Madison attributed the obstinance of New York and Rhode Island to their opposition to the object of the Commerce Clause. Under the Articles of Confederation, these two states benefited from the beggar-thy-neighbor

---

[5] See several documents in Kurland and Lerner 1987, 3:477–83.

uses of their ports to extract wealth from neighboring states, especially Massachusetts and New Jersey (Farrand 1937, 3:474 [Rhode Island], 547 [New York]). Supporters and opponents alike knew the object of the convention: to end such disruptive practices.

In many respects, the Commerce Clause can be seen as reducing overall government power over the economy. Instead, at the time, it was criticized as an overreaching of federal power. But this response was an artifact of the nature of the debate, which was whether powers of the states should be transferred to the federal government. The clause was an imposition, after all, *on the states, not on economic enterprises.* Indeed, it may have reduced overall government power in principle and it did reduce overall impositions on business and trade in actual practice. It made the states considerably weaker without making the federal government very strong.[6] Because state power was economically disruptive in its exercise in the years before the constitution, eliminating it with the Commerce Clause would serve business more than it would serve the federal government. When he wanted to vest such power in the Congress under the Articles of Confederation, even the ultimate Hamiltonian described it as public power to do good things. Against those who argued that trade would take care of itself, he should have argued that it would – but only if the states were stopped from interfering with it. Instead, he argued that, to prosper, trade needs the regulating hand of government (Kurland and Lerner 1987, 2:477–9). He was wrong. It was only the states that needed the uniformly regulating hand of national government if trade was to prosper.

The misguided nature of some of the U.S. constitutional debate is being relived today as many nations of Europe object to giving up power to the European Community. In its chief respect, this is not what those nations are doing. Rather, they are reducing overall government power over their economies. The European Community has weaker economic powers than the member nations have given up. *The chief transfer of power is from politicians at any level to business and its customers.* As the Community develops and as its court interprets its powers, it may take on far greater powers, as the U.S. government and many others have done over time. But initially, its role is to reduce government power over commerce.

The Commerce Clause sounds nearly vacuous today. It does not say that states do not have power to regulate commerce, merely that the federal government does. One might suppose it virtually a logical inference to conclude that the states have no such power, because the federal government can clearly override their actions. But they do seem to have that power until the

---

[6] It did, however, set up the possibility of later accretions of power, such as those of the Civil War, the two world wars, the Cold War, and the welfare state.

338   *Russell Hardin*

federal government does override. The federal government has trumping power but it does not have the only power. Part of the reason the clause sounds so vacuous today is that its point was so well understood that no one needed to state it more fully. The reason for calling the Constitutional Convention in Philadelphia was to establish national power over commerce, especially foreign commerce, but also commerce between the states. This seemed to be an urgent issue because most of the states favored a uniform tariff policy but, under the single-state veto of the Articles of Confederation, they could not adopt such a policy. Hence, states that were hard on imports from Great Britain simply lost British commerce to some other state, which might then transship British goods to the first state.[7]

There could not have been significant misunderstanding of the import of the Commerce Clause among those who knew the Continental Congress, the Philadelphia Convention, or the later state ratifying conventions. *This is not a normative argument from original intent to rightness*; it is merely an explanatory argument about how the clause came to be and how it was actually understood at the time. What mattered for the initial success of the Constitution was whether it coordinated positive expectations. In the matter of the Commerce Clause, expectations were already coordinated, and the Constitution principally played the role of setting up institutions that could live up to those expectations. Hence, it was not the actual operation of the Commerce Clause, as in later court decisions, that mattered but merely the institutional fact of putting the power over tariffs in national as opposed to state hands.

The central point of the Commerce Clause, the Constitutional Convention, and the larger Constitution itself was to stop the states from exercising the commerce powers that were assigned to the federal government by the Constitution. This was so thoroughly taken for granted that it was not even explicitly written. In part, this seeming oversight follows from the haughty view the Constitution has toward the prior government under the Articles of Confederation; it largely ignores that government as though the nation were being created de novo by its future citizens. There is a thesis in constitutional history that national arrogation of commerce powers was accomplished by the Court in a series of cases that gave increasing power to the federal government. In this view, the Commerce Clause is held originally to have been a barrier to federal power. It is reputedly the "dormant powers" of the Commerce Clause that were slowly awakened by Court action.[8] But the doctrine of these "dormant

---

[7] Madison attributed Rhode Island's obstinate refusal to take part in the Philadelphia Convention to its wish to continue this practice (Farrand 1937, 3:546–7).

[8] See Eskridge and Ferejohn 1994 for a brief discussion. They cite case book treatments of Gunther 1991, chs. 2–5; Farber, Eskridge, and Frickey 1993, ch. 7; and Stone 1991, chs. 3–4.

powers" is a later embellishment that was used as justification of the Court's rulings, not explanation of them.

An alternative reading of these cases is that they made more clearly explicit what was the broad understanding of what the government could do. Part of that understanding probably was that the federal government was not to have as capricious power over commerce as the individual states had had. Essentially, the federal government was to be relatively laissez-faire. Specific empowerment of that government to be proactive in the economy, as the mercantilist Hamilton wanted it to be, was deliberately denied at the Constitutional Convention. Hence, the view that the Commerce Clause limited the national government is not ungrounded. But its limits on that government are clearly not stated in the clause itself. As is true of much of the U.S. (and presumably any other) Constitution, much of it is unwritten. The ostensibly written U.S. Constitution is only different in degree from the unwritten British Constitution. What later came to be called the dormant powers of the Commerce Clause and the general doctrine of laissez-faire were both well understood and plausibly both taken for granted by the constitutional generation. It is in this sense that, as Samuel Beer says, capitalism was there in the Constitution.[9]

If a constitution is essentially a start-up measure rather than a compelling guide forevermore, it follows that well-understood interpretations of its meaning need not be written into it in order for it to work to establish an initial order. If initial understandings change, a partially unwritten constitution may lose its clarity over time. But, in any case, it may also cease to be an important guide to expectations, which may be increasingly grounded in extant institutions and arrangements. Many of the latter may have been given their initial form by the Constitution, but they may evolve very far from their initial form (Griffin, Chapter 9, this volume; Hardin 1999, ch. 4).

In guiding our own decisions, it is likely to be more important to most of us to look to the extant institutions than to their presumed genesis. It would then be true to say that the original constitutional arrangements affect us forever after, but this is a trivial point. For example, the resolution of the small-versus-large-states conflict was, in part, to give states equal representation in the Senate. That this was not an important part of the resolution is suggested by the fact that the Senate was relatively unimportant during the first generation of its life. If the small-versus-large-states conflict had been urgent, the Senate would surely have assumed an important role at once. Instead, it was not even an attractive venue for a political career, and major contenders for national leadership mainly came

---

[9] Oral comments at the second Murphy Institute conference on Constitutions and Constitutionalism, Tulane University, New Orleans, March 11–12, 1995.

340 *Russell Hardin*

from the House of Representatives instead of the Senate. The Senate rose to importance as the result of dramatic leadership efforts toward the end of the Virginia hegemony over the presidency (Swift 1993). For example, Henry Clay rose to prominence in the House of Representatives. But when, after holding national office, he later returned to Congress, he chose the newly important Senate as his home.

That the Senate exists is now an important fact of American political life. Indeed, if it had not been included in the constitutional arrangements, no one now living in the United States might have been born and the American citizenry would be completely different people. Both these facts are of little interest for constitutionalism, but what is important for constitutionalism would be the success of the later Senate in managing the conflicts that lay behind the constitutional debates if these conflicts continued or, alternatively, the success of the Constitution in getting the nation out of the small-versus-large-states conflict altogether. On the latter score, the creation of the Senate under the Constitution was important in making the document work as a start-up device, although it was not otherwise important in resolving the large-versus-small-states conflict, which simply vanished once there was national government to block military conflict between large and small states. The important fact for the resolution of the once potential conflict is not how the Senate has worked to defuse the conflict (it has not done so), but in the way the existence of a genuinely national government has made it no longer an issue at all. Just as with the interest in making trade policy uniform, the issue of peaceful cooperation between the states was a matter of consensual coordination by almost all.

The original consensus on laissez-faire was not as broad as that on stopping states from intruding into commerce. As implied earlier, Hamilton wanted not laissez-faire but an economically activist national government that would invest in harbors and waterways and that would help in financing and managing business expansion. In *Federalist* 85 he claimed that the antimercantilist views of "a very ingenious and sensible writer" – presumably Adam Smith – had been exaggerated. Part of the great appeal of laissez-faire to many people, including the plantation agrarians, was that it would force business to make it on its own without subsidy from agrarian interests. They did not want government to favor business. The Madisonian constitution was a compromise seemingly more to the favor of the agrarians than of commercial interests. It gave the plantation agrarians almost all they could expect from national government but not the protection against their eventual economic decline that they might have wanted if they had foreseen the decline. And it gave commercial interests a national market through limits on capricious state governments and not the activist government that at least Hamilton wanted.

Oddly, both groups seem to have misread the future in which commercial interests needed little more than laissez-faire to enable them to dominate the nation. What the unwritten rule of laissez-faire did for commerce was enable it to lead the grand economic transition from a rural agrarian to an urban industrial economy and polity. That transition might have been harder during the decades in which declining but still dominant agricultural interests might have used greater constitutional powers over the economy to block or slow the transition. Farmers were disempowered in large part because the elitist Jeffersonian agrarians had preemptively and perhaps unwittingly disempowered every group in favor of relatively unconstrained individual initiative.

ECONOMIC GROWTH, ECONOMIC TRANSITION

The Commerce Clause was of immediate value to both the plantation agrarians and the commercial interests, and therefore they could coordinate in creating the Constitution. While they were united in creating a national government that benefited both southern plantations and northern traders and financiers, they had dramatically different philosophical visions of the ideal future of the new nation. Hamilton foresaw cities and banks, although his vision was still tainted with the mercantilism that Smith had only recently reviled. Jefferson foresaw farms, although his vision from the crest of his little mountain of Monticello distorted these into plantations. Each group must fully enough have understood the vision of the other. Their difference was one of values and tastes, openly acknowledged.

Of course, both groups thought their own visions superior in complex causal ways as well. For example, the agrarians believed that government should be republican and that only farmers could be civic republicans, and the Hamiltonians believed government should make things work well for business. However, their debate never ascended to the heights of the debate over the communitarianism of the Anti-Federalists, perhaps because no immediate choices of significance turned on the difference of views. As time passed, the agrarian vision was sorely tarnished by its seeming association with plantations, which were grounded on slavery.[10] The difference between slave and nonslave states, which was causally correlated with the difference between plantation agrarianism and urban commercialism, was itself a recognized potential conflict, as noted by Madison during the convention (Farrand 1937, 1:486). But, although it inspired some debate at the convention and may have lain behind some southern doubts about the new Constitution, the slavery difference remained a minor issue to be

---

[10] Some of the debate is represented in Norton 1986.

managed by temporizing compromise. After all, the slave states needed open domestic and international commerce – they could not consume their own produce and prosper. The Jeffersonian agrarian vision was shattered by the Civil War and was then remade in the image of western subsistence farmers. Its career fell rapidly thereafter and it has finally been reduced to the trivializing dogma of the benefits of the family-owned farm in our time, Cincinnatus having long since died.

Oddly, neither the Hamiltonians nor the Jeffersonians may have understood the causal nature of their eventual conflict, which would turn mortal. Both seemingly thought – incorrectly – that it was a matter of choice which way the nation went. Commerce was sure to crush the agrarians economically if the agrarians did not first defeat commercial interests politically. In the constitutional period there may have been no one who grasped the accelerating trend out of agriculture and into the larger economy. In the constitutional period, commerce and agriculture had potential conflicts, but these were not significantly different in kind from the conflicts between certain industries or between certain agricultural interests. For example, they had the usual conflict over who should bear the brunt of the tariffs that funded the government.

The fundamental change that the United States faced was astonishing growth in wealth and consumption. There was, of course, no need for radically greater consumption of foodstuffs after 1788. Hence, the growth came from greater productivity of labor, which meant that labor could be moved off the land and into other forms of production. This trend would be the ruin of agrarian visions. Yet the larger agrarians, especially the plantation owners, needed what the urban commercial interests needed – the Commerce Clause with its easy, stable access to domestic and foreign markets.

Because the agrarian vision, for all its appeal, had any chance only in plantation society, Jefferson's generation of agrarians held views that could not remain tenable together in the longer run. Jeffersonian views were simultaneously conservative, in supposing that the agrarian life could be maintained, and romantic, in supposing that such life would be good and beautiful. Jefferson's inherently elitist agrarian views conflicted oddly with his egalitarianism. The grand estates of Jefferson and his plantation colleagues did not represent the conditions of the agrarian life for most farmers and farm workers in Jefferson's time. Most farmers struggled to achieve subsistence; they did not enjoy the cultured leisure of Jefferson and his library at Monticello. Most of these subsistence farmers had nothing to gain from the Commerce Clause in their daily lives; if they benefited from the clause, it was through the longer-run reformation of the economy and its opportunities. But this was a benefit that many of them – perhaps almost all of them – would have opposed, because it was a benefit that came via the destruction of their way of life. Most farmers in Jefferson's America were like many workers in the failing industries and farms of the Eastern European and former Soviet nations. Given a chance to veto the changes brought on by the industrial revolution and the Commerce Clause, they might have done so. Their veto would have had huge intergenerational effects because it could have worked only by trapping the next generations in subsistence farming.

The Philadelphia Convention focused on the conflict between large and small states. The nation and its press during the ratification debate and many constitutional scholars since then focused on the conflict between Federalists and Anti-Federalists. But the inescapable and overriding conflict was that represented by Hamilton and Jefferson, two eminences who were largely missing from the constitutional convention. In this conflict, Jefferson seemingly triumphed. Hamilton went to an ignominious early death in his duel with Aaron Burr, while Jefferson created the party that held hegemony over U.S. politics until it was broken by the slavery issue in the 1850s. But, by the time he died on July 4, 1826, the fiftieth anniversary of the Declaration of Independence, Jefferson might have been able to read from the changing facts of the nation and its demography that his agrarians were doomed. They were doomed by the eventually crossing trend lines of relatively decreasing employment in agriculture and increasing employment in all else.

Jefferson was an agrarian living off the surplus production of his plantation. Such agrarians can be mistaken for communitarians. Some of the prosperous farmers of upstate New York, New England, and Pennsylvania genuinely were communitarians. But Jefferson the plantation agrarian was not communitarian. With many communitarians the Jeffersonian agrarians shared a belief in the political goodness of a society organized at the level of the local community. Such a society could support the open debate and extensive participation of civic republicanism. But, in their desire for a national economy that would let them prosper despite specializing in agricultural production, they differed from the communitarian Anti-Federalists. Many of the southern plantation owners may have preferred small-society government all else being equal, but they could not have lived well with it unless they secured open trade with other societies. Nothing short of a national constitution with a commerce clause could fit their interests, which were for open economic arrangements and security from military attack. Between their interests and their vague ideals of civic republicanism, they went with their interests.[11]

---

[11] North Carolina balked until its choice was complete independence or full submission to the Constitution. With the romanticism of myriad possibilities from which to choose finally closed off when all but Rhode Island had voted for the Constitution, North Carolina submitted.

Suppose government had been more important in people's lives than it was two centuries ago in the United States. Perhaps we could imagine what participation and life might have been like for large numbers of people, who would have become active as Jefferson, Hamilton, James Madison, and many others did. But in reality, it seems utterly implausible that there could have been many more of these people. Someone had to produce things, food especially, but also the wigs these men wore and the paper on which they wrote. These active participants in governing were a leisure class – Hamilton perhaps much less than the others, which may be why they soon finessed him out of power.

Then what would civic republicanism have meant to that society? It cannot have meant Philadelphia writ large across the life of the nation. National government did not have much to do until the Civil War and then not again until the First World War and the Depression. Outside of wartime and before the past sixty years, citizens regularly encountered national government only in the person of the local postmaster. Indeed, A. J. P. Taylor noted that, before World War I, "a sensible, law-abiding Englishman could pass through life and hardly notice the existence of the state, beyond the post office and the policeman" (Taylor 1965, 1). Since World War II national government has invaded our lives. In the age of Jefferson, most men could have participated heavily in politics only at the local level, which is to say, only in a relatively small-scale communitarian organization of the society. What a dismal thought – squandering the talents of Jefferson and even lesser politicos on very small local politics.

It would be false to claim that whether agrarian or business interests prevailed initially was a matter of chance. The coordination on agrarian control was not a matter of random tipping. There were many features of the situation of the late eighteenth and early nineteenth centuries that gave the agrarians great advantages. Foremost was the sheer number of independent landowners among the initial electorate. Commercial society was still nascent and business owners were few. The spectacular rise of cities was still in the future, although New York, Philadelphia, and Boston gave hints of what might come. Moreover, once Jefferson came to power, he and the Jeffersonians could extend the vote to incorporate many new voters into their party and thereby increase the chance that they could win future elections. And the opening of new lands to the west generally meant the expansion of farming.

Similarly, the later change to the predominance of business interests followed demographic changes. The rise of business in the economy meant that workers' interests partly coincided with those of business against those of farmers. And the demographic decline of farmers has almost removed them from the electorate altogether. (Less than 3 percent of American employed persons now gain their living from farming.) The Jeffersonian move to extend the suffrage to all white males was complete by about 1820. That increased the proportion of farmers in the electorate and seemingly, therefore, secured the agrarian hold. That this was not the result in the longer run may be suggested by the very undemocratic form government took in the southern plantation states, where the oligarchy of plantation barons held control enough to take the region into the Civil War. They constituted no more than 10 percent of the vote but virtually all of the government of the region. Small, especially subsistence, farmers were of little political consequence in the South.

From our retrospective it appears that in the early days of the U.S. Constitution, business needed little more than domestic laissez-faire from government, protection of the large domestic market from regional or state barriers, and uniform foreign trade prospects. The Commerce Clause largely gave it all of these. Additionally, business could have benefited from stable monetary policy (again, decreasing variance in expectations increases investment) and favorable tariffs for international trade and protection. Here, of course, agrarian and business interests generally conflicted. Farmers wanted freer money with its inflationary tendencies and they wanted high tariffs on agricultural imports and no tariff on industrial goods. But the constitution gave business so much of what it wanted that it could prosper under Jeffersonian government. Indeed, it could virtually explode into wealth and innovation in an industrial revolution that outpaced those of Europe.

In essence, the Hamiltonians won the constitutional convention. But because the trend from agriculture to business was driven by forces that went well beyond deliberate political and governmental plans, they were likely to win the economic contest eventually in any case. The stability of the U.S. constitutional order may therefore have depended on the constitutional protections that eased the way for business. Those protections were far short of interventions on behalf of business per se. They were just as much protections of farmers who could produce for markets outside their states and abroad. But they were more important for business than for farming just because business had the greater prospect of expansion.

HAMMER AND SICKLE

The crossed hammer and sickle of the Soviet Union and its followers was the symbol of the union of workers' and farmers' interests in the Communist Party. It was an illogical symbol because it represented an essentially impossible union. Urban industrialization would bring about

346   *Russell Hardin*

the ruin of agricultural life for most farmers and their progeny. By the time the symbol flew on a flag over Moscow, this fate must have been recognized as economically determined. When Jefferson believed in his elitist variant of the agrarian vision, the signs of its impossibility were not yet clear. By 1917, when the leading industrial nations had begun to leave agriculture behind and farmers had left the land in large numbers, the impossibility of the nonelite agrarian vision was transparent. The symbol lay in tatters at the Russian parliamentary elections of December 1993, when the residual Communist Party had split into the main Communist Party and the rump Agrarian Party.[12]

The contradictory symbolism in the Soviet Union did not matter because agricultural interests were not constitutionally empowered. Similarly, Jefferson's agrarian vision did not matter very much because it was also not constitutionalized beyond protection of the right to own slaves, perhaps because he and other agrarians took the vision for granted as merely a description of the natural state of affairs. In the U.S. case, *the best constitution was one that left the Jeffersonian and Hamiltonian visions to be fought out in the economy rather than in the polity.* Politics could hardly affect the outcome but politics could be wrecked by the effort to affect it.

The biggest economic transition that nations typically make is that from agricultural life to greater general prosperity. It is the move that makes for modern nationhood, the move that any ardent Marxist or capitalist must want. Yet Marxism in our time perversely became the ideology of peasant rebellions. In the United States, the agricultural work force has fallen from over 80 percent of the total work force to less than 3 percent. This change occurred over about two centuries, but its modal period was the era of populism, when farmers fell from majority status and took Jefferson's party down with them. Populism was a variant of Poujadist movements that rise when a group's fate is clearly determined and its aspiring leaders make a last ditch effort to interrupt the downward trend. The greenback or easy-money fight in the populist era was essentially a hopeless fight against the implications of the falling relative value of agricultural production.

In retrospect, one might readily conclude that the dramatic change in the relative values of agricultural production and all other forms of production was one of the greatest benefits in human history. But at the time, it was a source of great pain for those whose opportunities in agriculture fell. Because they could not recapture the government, they could not force their momentary interests into law.

---

[12] Together the two parties took about 20 percent of the vote (*New York Times*, December 26, 1993, sec. I, p. 18).

Agrarian visions and interests were central to political debate and conflict in virtually all nations until very recently. They were at the heart of the French revolutionary constitutional debates and perhaps all the great nineteenth-century constitutional efforts. For example, Argentine constitutional efforts repeatedly faltered over conflicts between agrarian interests and financial and shipping interests until the efforts finally succeeded in the 1850s. Then the Argentine Constitution was broken during the period of agrarian malaise around 1930 that may have been stimulated by protectionist tariffs in the United States that led to European tariffs. Revolutions from Mexico to China to Vietnam have been based on agrarian interests and peasant fighters. The astonishing thing about all these revolutions is that they were openly contradictory. Their agrarian focus was opportunistic and, if the revolutions were to succeed in the long run, that focus had to be betrayed. Still, peasants today back movements that, once in power, could do little for peasants other than slow down their painful transition, primarily by detaining their children in rural poverty.

It seems unlikely that constitutional debates in advanced industrial states today would spend much time on agrarian issues, although agrarian concerns are often the sore point of European Community debates. As Jefferson may have thought these issues were settled in his time, most people in advanced economies today plausibly think they are settled in our time – merely that now they are settled against Jeffersonian agrarianism. Contemporary defenses of the agrarian ideal and the so-called land ethic sound more nearly quaint and irrelevantly romantic than politically of interest (e.g., Berry 1993). That ideal could become real today only after the radical reduction of the per capita national product to less than a tenth its present level and the elimination of vast urban populations. That sounds like a prescription for a heavy dose of Pol Pot.

DEMOCRACY AND TRANSITION

The striking difference between the current Russian constitutional challenge and the earlier American challenge is that the changes to be wrought in the Russian economy may be guided by deliberate government intervention, whereas the American economic developments followed very nearly from government laissez-faire. In Russia today, a regime of economic liberalism must be brought into existence by illiberal, central determination. In the U.S. case, the economic changes were not extensively foreseen and could more or less overtake the populace. In the Russian case, the economic changes that would be the result of successful introduction of the market can be extensively foreseen and they can overtake the populace only against substantial opposition.

In the transformation of the Russian and other eastern economies there is heated debate over so-called shock therapy. In shock therapy, the transformation is done instantly with one big change rather than being spread out over many years with small, piecemeal changes. There is immediate privatization of most public firms through sale or free distribution of stock in them, immediate distribution to individual farmer-owners of publicly held collective farms, immediate currency reform, and immediate closure of many government agencies whose functions had been to direct the economy. The initial effect is unemployment and declining production in many areas. Expectations are initially shattered, but this result is supposed to be partially beneficial because the prior expectations were often of the wrong things. Thereafter, expectations are left to stabilize over the next several years as no further shocks are necessary.

The initial losses of welfare from shock therapy might be substantial, but supposedly the aggregate losses of welfare from piecemeal therapy would be even greater. Relatively depressed expectations would last for many years under piecemeal therapy. Hence, investment would tend to lag below the optimal level for many years, and the effects of low investment in early years would be multiplied through subsequent years. On the other hand, positive expectations would begin to develop soon after shock therapy; hence, investment would soon begin to reach a level that would reinforce positive expectations. Among those whose expectations matter are, of course, foreign investors, who will more readily invest if they expect high rates of return – which are more likely after shock therapy than during the long period of piecemeal therapy. But even more important are the investments in personal training and careers by Russians, on whose efforts the economy must mostly build. Hence, shock therapy and economic growth do not require bootstrapping efforts to invest resources that do not yet exist; they require primarily the investment of time to create the resources of skill and reputation, and such investment will happen if expectations for return on it are good.

Shock therapy has in common with the Commerce Clause that it sounds like economics when it is actually politics. Shock therapy is not a device for politically organizing the economy; it is a device for *ending* the political organization of the economy. Any alternative to shock therapy is necessarily a program that uses government to run the economy to some extent – perhaps to a very large extent.

Unfortunately, the debate over the merits of shock therapy and of piecemeal reform in parts of the former Soviet Union is complicated by a logically unrelated but empirically associated problem: the destabilization of the political regime. The destabilization is not merely the initial destabilization of creating a new order but is, further and more profoundly for the economy, the ongoing destabilization of democratic vacillation over how to go. It is possible that most of the Eastern European nations currently attempting economic conversion will face constant turnover of regimes and policies. Hence, one inclined to invest time and resources in developing skills, facilities, or reputation may think it optimal to do as well as possible in the short run and to leave the longer run for later worry – because the longer run is too unpredictable to risk the present for it.

Oddly, the focus on the short run invites a variant of the position of the English Luddites, the American populists, and the French Poujadists. These groups wanted to stop economic change in order to maintain their positions as they were. They all lost the day because the changes were too massively beneficial to others to be stopped and, in any case, while groups wanted to stop the changes, their individual members and their children often chose to join in the changes. What the reorganization of the formerly Soviet-type economies involves in many cases is a combination of Luddite, Poujadist, and populist groups in agreement on one thing: stopping the transition for the time being, roughly for the life of the current generation. The chief argument for shock therapy is that only such a dramatic move can take the focus off politics and put it on economic opportunity for roughly the life of the current generation. Active politics is useful in stimulating political change, as in ending autocracy in much of Eastern Europe and the former Soviet Union. But it can also be a drain on economic activity. It is a drain that is exacerbated in many of these nations by the current lack of demographic growth to allow quicker expansion of new enterprises through intergenerational shifts into them.

There are serious objections to shock therapy. The most widely discussed is its harm to many in the present generation, which seems unjust. But economic transitions generally entail harm for some. The transition to cheap personal computers hurt IBM stockholders and workers. Should it therefore have been blocked or slowed down? Piecemeal therapy merely spreads this effect out over a much longer period, plausibly exacerbating it in the aggregate. A second problem is that shock therapy may have a perverse political effect. When an industry slowly declines, workers lose their jobs a few at a time and they may tend to hold themselves personally responsible. When a firm closes outright, workers are less likely to hold themselves responsible and to hold the firm and the government responsible. Shock therapy in Russia has arguably created a large block of politicized people ready to vote for a Vladimir Zhirinovsky to undo the transitional order.

The problem for government in the West has not been how to manage or control or cause various major transitions but how not to interfere destructively in them. In part just because the full scope of the transition from agrarian to urban life was not understood, at least not at the level of active politics, governments in England and the United States stumbled through the transition without wrecking themselves on it. The problem of the formerly Communist states is that they attempted to control various transitions, especially that from agrarian to urban life. It seemingly requires government action to undo government action. We may have some evidence that strong, autocratic government can stimulate industrialization, as in the Asian Tigers and perhaps in the Soviet Union during its early decades. But we have no evidence that democratic government can deliberately manage such a transition. And, because democratic government is unlikely to be consistent in its policies, we have reason to doubt that it can micromanage a long-term transition without destabilizing expectations. That is the chief argument for shock therapy in the newly liberalizing nations that are simultaneously democratizing.

Solid expectations are not mandatory for economic growth, which can happen even in the face of short-term or shaky expectations. For example, there is a McDonald's in Moscow, put there at some risk while things were very much in flux. But the McDonald's can do very well in the short run. And, in truth, its expectations may be genuinely better than those of a Russian entrepreneur without relevant foreign backing. The McDonald's enjoys the privileged position Lindblom attributes to American business in the United States. Its interests coincide with the interests of the Russian government in maintaining good relations with the United States and foreign investors more generally. Oddly, an unstable domestic regime may therefore give foreign investors large advantages over domestic entrepreneurs because it gives them relatively better, more stable expectations. Of course, all investors and entrepreneurs would be better served by better, more stable expectations, without which the economic transition is apt to be slower, perhaps much slower, enough so to reduce political expectations in the new regime.

ECONOMIC TRANSITION AND DEMOGRAPHIC GROWTH

Consider a simplistic model of economic transition with and without demographic growth. Suppose careers are fifty years. Without demographic growth there are, say, a million people in each decade: those who are in their twenties, thirties, forties, fifties, and sixties. With 10 percent demographic growth per decade, there are, say, 1,100,000 in their twenties, 1,000,000 in their thirties, 910,000 in their forties, 830,000 in their fifties, and 760,000 in their sixties. (Ten percent population growth per decade implies a doubling of population in a little over seventy years.) Suppose every new worker moves into new enterprises, which enjoy productivity gains of 10, 20, or 30 percent per decade while old enterprises have stagnant productivity.

Constitutional Economic Transition

Table 10.1. Increase in Production after Two Decades (%)

% Productivity Growth per Decade	0% Work Force Growth per Decade	10% Work Force Growth per Decade	
	Absolute and per Capita	Absolute	Per Capita
0	0	20	20
10	8	32	26
20	18	44	37
30	28	58	48

From this simple model it follows that economic productivity during a transition into new directions (either of organizational form or of sectors of production) enjoys a tremendous multiplier effect from growth in the work force, as shown in Table 10.1. Productivity growth in new enterprises of 20 percent per decade produces *44 percent growth in total production* in two decades with 10 percent growth in the work force. Against this, there would be only *18 percent production growth* with no growth in the work force. The Soviet regime took most of the benefits from economic transition from agriculture to industry and from demographic growth, and now the new Russian regime must survive popular scrutiny while gaining little benefit from the general sectoral transition or from demographic growth, which has nearly stopped.

When there is no growth of the work force, absolute growth of production is identical to per capita growth. When the work force is expanding, absolute growth exceeds per capita growth, which, however, still *exceeds* production growth without work force growth. Hence, demographic growth contributes to economic transition and transformation in several ways. First, it produces a per capita surplus that can be taxed to provide greater public benefits. Second, it helps the new forms come to quicker dominance over old forms and raises the optimism of expectations, hence stimulating further contributions to the transformation. It should therefore come as no surprise that rapid economic growth often fades with declining demographic growth. Declining birthrates may be caused, as is often argued, by the economic prosperity, but they also contribute to slowed economic growth. These reciprocal motors make growth rates partially self-limiting.

In the model, the effects of production growth follow from two kinds of source. First, productivity growth in new enterprises and, second, the multiplier on this effect from work force growth. The first of these kinds of source takes at least two distinctively different forms. First, there are the standard transitions from old to new sectors of economic activity, among which the largest historical example is the transition from agriculture to manufacturing and other productive activities. Second, there is the apparent gain in productivity that could come from transformation of a centrally controlled economy to a market economy. Here, there need be no transition from one sector to another, but there may be many transitions from old and inefficient enterprises to new entrepreneurial enterprises.

Consider the high rate of productivity growth of the South Korean economic expansion from about 1960 to the present day. Much of the productivity increase in South Korea came from the transition of its economy from agricultural and rural to industrial and urban production. China is now enjoying the overall production growth that follows from such a transition. Most of that transition has already happened in Russia, although part of the possible gains were forgone in stifling control of the economy.[13] That previously forgone part of the gains is now much of what is available to the Russian people for growth over the next couple of decades of predictable work force stability. The rest of what is available is transition out of heavy industry and inefficient farming into more productive sectors, which is merely the ongoing transition of the developed economies. Hence, even with successful policies, Russia is unlikely to achieve South Korean or Chinese rates of growth. And, if it proceeds year by year through low rates of growth, it will depress expectations, thereby depressing investment in growth.

Finally, captured in the model are implications for the welfare of those who are not part of the intergenerational shift. Their per capita gains from their production alone are 0 percent in all decades in all conditions. They are relative losers in the changes if their productivity does not rise to match the gains of the new enterprises. If they are relative losers, they are likely also to be absolute losers insofar as many of the things they currently consume and want may become, relative to their wages, more expensive as patterns of demand change. But they could also benefit from the changes through rising government investment in public works, welfare programs, and education and retraining for displaced workers. If the transition is not merely intergenerational but is pushed via closing or reduction of older firms, many people may be absolutely worse off as a direct result even while the economy in the aggregate booms. These people are potential Luddites

---

[13] It is commonly asserted that the Soviet regime coerced peasants off the land and into factories. In actual fact, the rates of movement from the land to cities in the Soviet Union were comparable with those during periods of comparable development in the United States and many other Western nations. Apart from its murderous treatment of kulaks, the Stalin regime was plausibly not so much brutal as inefficient in its rate of encouraging movement off the land. Because it had the economy under central control, perhaps it should have encouraged faster movement off the land.

in further political moves. Taken together across many kinds of industry and enterprise, from agriculture to manufacturing to bureaucratic organizations, they may constitute a blocking group for economic reform. If the next and future generations had votes, reform would win hands down. But it is the present generation that votes, and the interests of many in the present generation, especially those who are older, are not well served by reform.[14]

In some of the former republics of the Soviet Union, economic transition through restructuring by hiring new workers into new firms rather than by closing old firms would be facilitated by demographic growth. But some of these areas are now sidetracked into destructive ethnic groupism, into fighting over shares of the current resources and over control of political office. They may therefore pass the opportune moment for restructuring their economies, the moment when restructuring could come more quickly through intergenerational shifts. If they do pass that moment, and demographic growth continues to slow its rate, they may later face a harsher, more conflictual prospect of transition without the benefits of the multiplier of demographic growth. And they may face it from a condition of greater relative poverty than they suffer today.

One reason for the slow success of the industrial revolution in France is that France had a virtually stable population with little or no demographic growth during the nineteenth and early twentieth centuries. The German population grew relatively rapidly during the same period. Hence, that long period, which started with France as the dominant power of Europe, ended with Germany the dominant power. Germany's dominance came not only from its greater numbers available for military service but also from its quicker move during the latter half of the period into modern industries that generated national wealth and contributed to national power. The United States and Australia both benefited from rapid demographic growth that enabled relatively free development of varied economic enterprises. The American reputation for innovativeness may owe much to the demographics of immigration, which allow for relatively easy shifting of workers into new areas. People do not have to leave old jobs to work on building the railways or programming computers; they can leave old countries.

Demographic change might work as well in centrally planned as in market economies. But the way it generally works its largest effects is through the growth of new industries and firms that gradually replace

---

[14] Demographic growth may be more important for a democratic regime undergoing economic transition than for a nondemocratic regime. With demographic growth, the number of those who benefit from the transition rises faster to become a majority of the working population.

or substitute for old, established industries and firms. Aluminum and plastics displace steel. The microchip displaces wires, tubes, and other electronic components, and electronic equipment replaces mechanical equipment. The steel industry does not have to reorganize itself to help us through a beneficial transition. If it fails to change, it need merely fail to mobilize government to protect it against the future. In moments of such transitions, a government that cannot easily be mobilized is a great benefit.

Rapid demographic growth can create problems for constitutional order, as it perhaps does in Kenya and Bangladesh today. But it can dramatically ease the way for economic transitions that involve shifting the proportions of the work force in various occupations and industries. In general such transitions happen intergenerationally. The young move into new enterprises, leaving declining and outmoded enterprises to the older generations, who may suffer economic decline. The computer world offers a conspicuous if rarefied example of dominance by the next generation. That world is peopled by perhaps the largest number of wealthy young entrepreneurs the world has ever seen. That world is also more open than perhaps any other in the United States to people from new immigrant groups and their children. It is sometimes supposed that Asian Americans have greater natural abilities in that world, and they may have. But it may be more important for them that opportunities are inherently best in an expanding world and the expanding world of the moment is electronics.

AMERICAN AND RUSSIAN COMPARISONS

The broad U.S. constitutional experience generalizes only to nations with diverse economies, or potentially diverse economies. A nation whose best returns in the international market are from a single or few specialties would get little advantage from a commerce clause or near equivalent. But there is a more general lesson to draw. The actual import of the Commerce Clause was to reduce the power of the states over economic development and not to empower the national government. To put it perversely, perhaps the greatest strength of the U.S. Constitution in managing economic relations is its weakness. It does not empower government to do very much in economic life. In particular, it does not empower government to do much more than plead with business.[15] Much of the seemingly strong power it

---

[15] Many economists hold that the federal corporate tax is a major distorter of economic activity in the United States. Ironically, that tax initially assumed its importance because of the supposed interest states had in controlling taxes levied on individuals. Yet again, it was politics and not economics that failed. And yet again, the problem that needed to be resolved was ending state-level control of part of the economy.

has in facing business is the kind of power business would want it to use, just as citizens must almost all welcome the imposition of power to make traffic flow well. The extraordinary strength of the constitution or the government or the society is in government's *inability* to override the weaknesses of its empowerment from the flimsy constitution.

In the face of uncontrollable and poorly understood economic transitions, among the most important provisions of a constitution, especially as it affects business and the economy, must be those that eventually restrain government, not those that enable it. This is not an a priori claim but merely a generalization from the experience of many societies, a generalization sitting uncomfortably on too few cases. The original Commerce Clause and the larger Constitution that was opportunistically wrapped around it was written not to weaken the authority of national government in the United States but to weaken the authority of the individual states, an authority that had enabled them collectively to bring themselves to the edge of economic ruin. If its purpose was to be achieved, the Commerce Clause had to be vested in a moderately capable central government, and therefore an adequate government was designed for it. The Commerce Clause virtually secured the national government for commercial interests. Lindblom's thesis, cited earlier – that business is substantially in control of government without having to exert control because government needs its cooperation in governing the society – is already faintly written into the Constitution.

Although government in the United States has grown enormously more powerful over its two centuries, central politics in the United States has continued to be too weak to strike very hard at business even when adversary interests have controlled the government. Central politics in Russia is dramatically different; it still has much of the character of earlier Soviet politics. Russian leaders can ignore constitutional constraints with relative impunity, as Boris Yeltsin did in disbanding the national parliament. Moreover, the contemporary threat to commerce in Russia is not the threat of localities to impose tariffs; therefore, a mere commerce clause would be inadequate to protect entrepreneurial efforts. The central threat is the possibility of national, not local, intervention. Hence, constitutional constraint to protect economic institutions in their investment in their futures cannot readily look effective enough to stimulate long-term positive expectations unless that threat is blocked.

The United States in the 1780s needed a constitution that would break the power of the states over commercial relations. The Commerce Clause made federalism safe for business. Russia needs a constitution that will break the power of the national state over production and distribution. The Soviet past requires strong Russian action to establish new expectations. The Russians have a much harder task than the Americans had. As

Madison observed already of the easier problem, "From the trials of which I have been a witness I augur that great difficulties will be encountered in every attempt to prevail on the Legislature to part with power" (Kurland and Lerner 1987, 2:482). Tell it to Yeltsin.

A final benefit of shock therapy is the possibility that quick building down of the state apparatus of commercial control would make intervention thereafter much harder by weakening the government. Lacking a government that can willy-nilly intervene in business dealings helps to stabilize expectations. This tendency is not enough to justify weakened government. One might still suppose there are moments when it would be better if the state could intervene. Hence, one must balance the potential costs and benefits of greater and lesser state power. It seems overwhelmingly likely that the former Soviet Union would benefit from substantially weaker central government. Strong central government failed to make its economy prosper not merely because it was socialist in particular but because it was controlling in general.

Perhaps, as Madison feared, it is implausible that politicians will write a constitution that weakens the possibilities of political control. But, with its embedded culture of willful intervention, Russia has special need of a government that cannot intervene easily. A simple constitution investing government with very limited powers is, for the short run of a generation and plausibly for the longer run of many generations, the only sensible response to the current style of strong control, a style that Yeltsin follows even in the name of stopping government. But a weak constitution per se is inadequate to demobilize authoritarian government. Such a constitution could be given force by dismantling most of the remaining system of directing the economy. Giving it such force would dramatically enhance expectations for economic rebuilding, not least because it would mean that changing from, say, Putin to Zhirinovsky would not easily wreck the economic trends.

There may be one other general lesson to draw from comparative constitutional experiences. Guaranteeing the market in the early United States may well have helped secure democracy, and perhaps this lesson can be followed up in newly democratizing nations. But guaranteeing the market in general may undermine the prospects for greater domestic equality. Equality evidently requires government power in industrial societies. Indeed, equality is almost by definition a centralized concept. If economic productivity requires government weakness, productivity and equality are in conflict. This conclusion is at a more general level than that commonly discussed in economics under the rubric of the conflict between equality and efficiency (Okun 1975; Hardin 1992 and 1999, ch. 4). It is not merely a conflict between a particular policy to achieve greater productivity or equality. *It is a conflict between the kind of government that lacks the power*

*to block great productivity in general and the kind that has the power delib-
erately to manage equality.* Even if we could overcome the incentive effects
that put efficiency into conflict with equality, we might reasonably still
forgo having the kind of government that could secure equality.

The growth of the modern U.S. government has been driven by military and welfare concerns, and eventually it may acquire the power to trade
productivity for equality on a grand scale. Soviet governments failed to
achieve either efficiency or equality, although they may sometimes have
done better than the United States and many other nations at the latter.
Perhaps the only systematically successful societies at achieving equality
have been primitive, extremely unproductive societies. In the face of this
vast and distressing failure, however, many Russians might still seek to
create an order that promises greater equality rather than one that
promises greater productivity. If they ally with the variant Poujadists cling-
ing to past economic structures, they can probably be led to support strong
government, which might be democratically unstoppable. As supporters
of the quasi-fascist Zhirinovksy and those of Yeltsin agreed in voting for
a constitution with strong presidential powers in the constitutional referendum in Russia in late 1993, so these disparate groups may produce
a government none of them would want if it were controlled by any
group other than itself. Because a generation of hegemony such as the
Jeffersonians enjoyed may be out of the question in a democratic Russia,
the adopted constitution may be a disaster if it lasts.

During the constitutional debates, Washington fretted that, while
arguing over what was the ideally best way to put out the fire, his fellow
citizens were at risk of letting the whole building burn down. What
was needed, Washington thought, was any solid national government.
Madison, who entered the Philadelphia Convention in 1787 with clear
ideas on what would be best, soon enough focused on what would be workable. The Russians may finally suffer from not having a Madison focused
only on achieving a workable national government.

The debate over shock versus incremental therapy recalls the earlier
quarrels in the United States. The incrementalists (not the theorists but
the practitioners) may constantly reconsider what is the best rule. But "the
best" may be an empty category. As Washington urged, it is more important to settle on a rule and let the economy get on with it than to try to
design a perfect government or, we may add, in the absence of perfect
theory, to design one that could manage the economy perfectly from day
to day. Dozens of rules might be good if they were applied consistently.
The most successful rule might therefore be the one that cuts government
control. Then the government could focus on welfare policies that would
directly ease the lives of individuals who lose in the transition rather than
on policies that *indirectly* ease their lives by interfering with the transition.

358 *Russell Hardin*

The transition might be stopped but likely only by stopping the Russian people.

If the model of Table 10.1 is roughly correct, then demographic growth at the right time can contribute to the growth of positive expectations under the new order. More generally, economic boom time is especially propitious for establishing a new constitution. To create a new order to face immediate economic failure invites negative expectations and enhances the prospects for the failure of the order, as in the United States under the Articles of Confederation before the 1787 Constitution, in Weimar Germany, and possibly today in Russia, Romania, Serbia, and several other nations. The accidental association of negative economic expectations with a new regime may affect expectations for the regime itself. Many revolutionary regimes and juntas were able to come to power because the old regimes faced devastating crises. The new regimes have often then understandably failed to manage the crises and have been tarred with low expectations of their capacities.

The reverse may also be true: propitious conditions can help a regime become established. The creation of the U.S. version of the modern welfare state with large, permanent government, which came into being in the 1930s under Franklin Roosevelt, is often called a second American revolution. That government may have gained its acceptance in part merely from the fact that it was there at the time of completion of a successful, popular war and at the time of resurgent economic prosperity. The lore of that government is that it became legitimate in the eyes of the people because it worked to rescue the economy. It may, rather, have become legitimate because of its accidental association with positive trends. The new regimes in Russia and other democratizing nations would benefit from similar associations.

CONCLUDING REMARKS

In the face of our generally poor economic understanding of the future, we should read Holmes's comment that a constitution "is not intended to embody a particular economic theory" as rather a prescription than a theoretical, descriptive claim. There may be contexts in which the short-term requirements for a constitution to be adopted successfully run against the long-term requirement that it be economically enabling rather than commanding. In those contexts, we can plausibly expect eventual failure of the constitutional order. For example, there have been many revolutionary contexts in which a constitution that did not require relatively egalitarian results, a specific theocratic social and economic order, or other particular social dispensation, such as an antidemocratic or ethnic hierarchy, might not have been acceptable. Such a constitution could not long be the

Constitutional Economic Transition

effective guide of a successful polity in a hard-driving, competitive economic world. If, however, it did successfully regulate government structure and policy through dramatic economic transitions, it could do so only at substantial social and economic cost, such as the Communist political orders suffered.

REFERENCES

Berry, Wendell. 1993. *Sex, Economy, Freedom, and Community: Eight Essays.* New York: Pantheon.

Eskridge, William, and John Ferejohn. 1994. "The Elastic Commerce Clause: A Political Theory of American Federalism." *Vanderbilt Law Review* 47 (October): 1355–1400.

Farber, Daniel A., William N. Eskridge, and Philip P. Frickey. 1993. *Cases and Materials on Constitutional Law: Themes for the Constitution's Third Century.* St. Paul, Minn.: West.

Farrand, Max. 1937. *The Records of the Federal Convention of 1787.* 3 vols. Rev. ed. New Haven: Yale University Press.

Griffin, Stephen M. 1995. "The Problem of Constitutional Change in the United States." Paper presented at the conference on Constitutions and Constitutionalism, Murphy Institute, Tulane University, New Orleans, March 11–12.

Gunther, Gerald. 1991. *Constitutional Law.* 12th ed. Westbury, N.Y.: Foundation Press.

Hardin, Russell. 1989. "Why a Constitution?" In Bernard Grofman and Donald Wittman, eds., *The Federalist Papers and the New Institutionalism*, 100–20. New York: Agathon Press.

1992. "Efficiency vs. Equality and the Demise of Socialism." *Canadian Journal of Philosophy* 22: 149–61.

1993. "Altruism and Mutual Advantage." *Social Service Review* 67: 358–73.

1995. *One for All: The Logic of Group Conflict.* Princeton: Princeton University Press.

1999. *Liberalism, Constitutionalism, and Democracy.* Oxford: Oxford University Press.

Kurland, Philip, and Ralph Lerner, eds. 1987. *The Founders' Constitution.* 5 vols. Chicago: University of Chicago Press.

Lindblom, C. E. 1977. *Politics and Markets.* New York: Basic Books.

Norton, Anne. 1986. *Alternative Americas: A Reading of Antebellum Political Culture.* Chicago: University of Chicago Press.

Okun, Arthur M. 1975. *Equality and Efficiency: The Big Tradeoff.* Washington, D.C.: Brookings.

Popkin, Samuel L. 1977. *The Rational Peasant: The Political Economy of Rural Society in Vietnam.* Berkeley: University of California Press.

Przeworski, Adam. 1991. *Democracy and the Market: Political and Economic Reforms in Eastern Europe and Latin America.* Cambridge: Cambridge University Press.

Schneewind, J. B. 1990. "The Misfortunes of Virtue." *Ethics* 101: 42–63.
Scott, James C. 1976. *The Moral Economy of the Peasant: Rebellion and Subsistence in Southeast Asia.* New Haven: Yale University Press.
Stone, Geoffrey. 1991. *Constitutional Law.* 2nd ed. Boston: Little, Brown.
Swift, Elaine. 1993. "The Making of an American House of Lords: The U. S. Senate in the Constitutional Convention of 1787." *Studies in American Political Development* 7: 177–224.
Taylor, A. J. P. 1965. *English History, 1914–1945.* Oxford: Oxford University Press.

11

Institutionalizing Constitutional Interpretation

Jack Knight

When a constituent assembly or other constitution-making body convenes in order to draft a constitution, the members of that assembly face a complex task. Their main goal is to agree on a constitution that will serve as the basis for a government for the present and, presumably, future generations. The constitution must establish a framework for the administration of government as well as enumerate the principles that will govern the relationship between the government and the citizenry. This is essentially a process of creating political institutions that will structure the behavior of the members of that society, a set of rules that will guide them toward a particular set of substantive political and economic goals.

In order to accomplish this task the members of such a body must come to the negotiations with some sense of which rules will best achieve their substantive goals. Because the rules will affect future outcomes, constitution makers want to create constitutional provisions that will produce the future outcomes they prefer given their expectations about the future conditions relevant to those outcomes. Thus, their preferences over constitutional provisions will be a function of their substantive preferences over future outcomes. But constitution making is a political process and these initial preferences must be modified by two primary concerns. First, they want to propose provisions that will achieve the assent of a sufficient number of additional constituent members to enact their proposals. In this *politics of constitution making*, they must take account of the compromises that must be made in order to garner the support of those who do not share their basic interests. Second, they want to create provisions that will be respected and complied with by future generations. In this *politics of constitutional enforcement* special attention must be given to the ways in which the interests of future generations may differ from those of the drafters of the constitution.

Most analyses of constitution making focus either on the politics of the initial agreement embodied in the constitution or on the effects of

361

362 *Jack Knight*

questions of future compliance on the initial decision-making process. In this chapter I focus on a related, but distinct, question that has received little explicit attention. The question arises from a fact about any attempt to establish rules to govern future behavior: rules are inherently ambiguous and inevitably subject to future interpretation. Thus the question: what is the effect of this fact on the process of constitution making?

From the perspective of the individual drafter, the process of constitution making is analogous to the problem of contracting for future circumstances (Macneil 1980).[1] She desires to create a contract, a set of rules, that will structure her future interaction with others with whom she is involved in a collective endeavor. She prefers a contract that will protect her present and future interests. But determining the future effects of these rules is a complex task: these effects depend in large part on future actions and circumstances that are beyond her present control. And she will often be uncertain about these future events. Thus, the best that a contractor can do is to select those rules that she thinks will protect her interests in the future, given her present expectations about what will happen in the future.

Because rules are always subject to interpretation, however, the future effects of the provisions of the contract are in part a function of the ways in which the provisions will be subsequently interpreted. Eskridge and Ferejohn (1994) note the importance of this issue in their analysis of the effects of Supreme Court decision making on congressional law making. They argue that legislators need a theory of judicial statutory interpretation in order to enact legislation that will further their long-term goals. Without such a theory legislators may enact legislation that will produce unintended consequences because the expectations upon which they base their actions might be flawed. On the Eskridge-Ferejohn account, the more legislators are able to predict accurately the ways laws will be interpreted, the better they will be able to fashion legislation that will achieve their future goals.

Here I want to apply a similar logic to the constitution-making process. If constitution makers want to affect the future, they will need to establish expectations about how the rules might be interpreted in the future. Incorporating this idea into the contracting-for-future-circumstances framework, we can identify the primary factors that should affect the decisions of constitution makers: (1) their preferences over present and future substantive outcomes and (2) their expectations about how the rules

---

[1] I do not mean to say here that constitutions are contracts. In fact, I disagree with many of the implications of conceiving of constitutions as contracts. See Knight 1992. But the process by which actors initially establish their preferences over constitutional provisions is analogous to what one would do if he were anticipating entering into a contract.

Constitutional Interpretation

instantiated in the constitution will affect those outcomes. These factors together determine the constitution makers' preferences over constitutional provisions. What is most important for my analysis are the ways in which expectations about future circumstances (such as constitutional interpretation) affect expectations about how the rules will influence the future.

In the remainder of this chapter I analyze how the fact of constitutional interpretation might affect both the preferences and expectations of drafters of a constitution. I have rather limited goals here. I do not pretend to offer a comprehensive account of constitution making grounded merely in the potential effects of constitutional interpretation. What I want to focus on is a stage prior to the actual constitution-making process. It is the stage of preference and expectation formation prior to the actual process of negotiation and bargaining. This is, of course, a necessary but often neglected aspect of any explanation of constitutions as a product of contracting, bargaining, and negotiation.

In this analysis I attempt in the chapter's third section to assess how my conclusions about preferences and expectations relate to several examples, both historical and contemporary, of constitution making. But my goal there is merely to see if the analysis lends support to certain empirical claims about the types of constitutions that we would expect to be preferred in different social contexts. Clearly much more detailed analysis of the actual processes of constitutional negotiations will be necessary to provide an adequate explanation of the empirical cases.[2]

PREFERENCES AND EXPECTATIONS

Given the logic of contracting for future circumstances, a constitution maker needs to assess the relationship between her present preferences and the future preferences of those who will interpret the constitution. Here there are two sets of preferences to be considered. The first, and primary, set of preferences are those of the judiciary (or the constitutional council, if a separate body is to be established to focus explicitly on questions of constitutional interpretation.) When I speak of the preferences of the judiciary, I use the concept of preferences broadly. There is considerable debate in both the legal and social-scientific literature over the actual motivations of judges, and I have no desire or need to take a narrow stance on this question.[3] Rather, I intend preferences of future interpreters here to encompass the underlying principles or criteria that judges use in interpreting a constitution. Each interpreter has a set of principles,

---

[2] I am presently engaged in such a project with my colleagues, Lee Epstein and Olga Shvetsova.

[3] See Epstein and Knight 1998 for a general discussion of judicial motivations.

364   *Jack Knight*

which Eskridge and Ferejohn (1994) call "interpretive regimes," that provide a reason for offering an interpretation of a particular constitutional question.

The task for the members of a constitution-making body is to assess the relationship between their own substantive preferences over future outcomes and the effects of a judiciary that employs some set of reasons for interpreting the constitution. For simplicity of discussion here I treat these reasons as the future preferences of the judiciary. If the effect of the judiciary's reasons is to affectuate the goals of the original designers, then we can say that the preferences of the designers will be the same as the preferences of the judiciary. To the extent that the effect of the judiciary's reasons is to produce consequences that deviate from the outcomes preferred by the designers, we should say that the preferences of the designers differ from the future preferences of the judiciary. If expectations of the effects of future constitutional interpretation affect the process of constitution making, then the constitution maker's assessment of this preference relationship should have an important influence on how they attempt to institutionalize constitutional interpretation and change.

The second set of preferences are those of the legislature.[4] These preferences are relevant to expectations about interpretation in the following indirect way. The task is to consider the effects of future preferences of legislators on the future effects of constitutional provisions. The preferences of legislators are relevant to the substantive effects of the provisions. If the constitution maker believes that these future preferences will correlate positively with his own present preferences, he will seek to establish a particular relationship between legislation and constitutional review, presumably granting the legislature broad autonomy. If, rather, the designer anticipates divergence with the preferences of future legislatures, then that is one factor that might influence the establishment of broad constitutional review. In the end the effects of future expectations about interpretation on constitutional preferences should be a product of beliefs about both future legislators and future judges.

I focus in this analysis on three main features of a constitution that may be affected by concern over interpretation: (1) in the drafting of the substantive provisions themselves, (2) in the drafting of the procedures for constitutional amendment, and (3) in the crafting of institutional constraints on the interpretive process itself. It is helpful to conceptualize the problem facing constitution makers vis-à-vis each of these features in terms of the effects of an expected divergence between the present preferences of constitution makers and the future preferences of those who

---

[4] I thank John Ferejohn for insisting that the preferences of legislators were a necessary part of this analysis.

affect interpretation. The relevant issue in regard to substantive detail is: to what extent will the divergence of present and future preferences affect the extent to which constitution makers create open-ended versus closed and detailed provisions? Here we might focus on both provisions structuring the form and nature of government activity and provisions enumerating individual and collective rights. The relevant issue in regard to ease of amendment is: to what extent will the divergence of present and future preferences affect the complexity of the mechanism created for constitutional amendment? The relevant issue in regard to the institutionalization of the interpretation process is: to what extent will the divergence of present and future preferences affect efforts to institutionalize both the scope and the process of constitutional interpretation? This last question is the most important for my purposes because it represents an explicit effort to affect the influence of future preferences on the future effects of constitutions. It involves the consideration of questions of both the scope of review (what issues are to be considered) and the process of review (both who participates in the process and who ultimately decides the interpretive question.)

My analysis proceeds in stages. First, I analyze the effects of expectations about future interpretation on the present constitutional preferences of an individual constitution maker. I distinguish three categories of expectations for analysis: (1) one's present preferences will be the majority (or dominant) preference in the future, (2) one's present preferences will be the minority (or dominated) preference in the future, and (3) uncertainty about future preferences. Because there are two sets of future preferences to consider, the analysis of possible effects is a complex one. To simplify the exposition I consider the effects of expectations about the future preferences of the judiciary and the legislature separately and then consider the possible interactive effects to produce a weighted conception of the overall effect of future expectations on present constitutional preferences. Then, I turn to an analysis of how different distributions of substantive preferences and expectations within a constitutional assembly might affect a drafter's expectations about the future.

Preferences

The following propositions about the rationality of constitutional design follow from the basic logic of contracting for future circumstances (Macneil 1980). For the present I want to focus on the effects of future expectations on the present constitutional choices of a drafter who believes that his preferences will dominate in the politics of constitution making – that is, that his preferred constitutional provisions will be those chosen by the constituent assembly. I later consider what effects, if any, there are if

366   *Jack Knight*

it turns out that he is in the minority in the constituent assembly. First, if you expect that the dominant future preferences will be the same as yours are now, then you will choose principles and procedures that will best further the goals of those in the future majority. The exact form that these principles should take depends on the particular issue at stake. Second, if you expect that the dominant future preferences will be different from what yours are now, you will seek to minimize the adverse effects of future actions on your interests. There are two ways of doing this. You can attempt to constrain institutionally the effects of future actors by leaving as few issues open to future consideration as possible. But, given the fact that there are limits to how much constraint one can place on the future, you can also seek to maximize the likelihood that the future minority who shares your preferences will have some influence over whatever future decisions are made. The reasoning here is simple: whenever you think that those who share your preferences are in the minority, you will value decision-making procedures that allow for the greatest input from the greatest range of interests.

Third, if you are uncertain about the future, so that you do not know the relationship between your present preferences and the dominant preferences in the future, the effect of this uncertainty on your constitutional choices depends on how risk accepting you are. The more risk accepting you are, the more you will prefer a constitution that favors majority interests in the future. Given the fundamental importance of the constitution, I think that it is more reasonable to assume, following the logic of Rawls (1971), that uncertainty would cause you to be more risk adverse and choose provisions and principles that reflect a concern for the less fortunate, thus similar to the choices of someone whose expectations are that his present preferences will be in the future minority.

Judiciary

With this general logic in mind, let us turn now to the specific analysis of the effects of future expectations about the judiciary. If a drafter expects that his present preferences will be the majority preferences of the judiciary in the future, he will seek to establish rules and procedures that enhance the likelihood that these preferences will determine future outcomes. This has the following implications for the three features of the constitution. On the dimension of substantive detail, expectations of future dominance create a preference for *general* and *open-ended* provisions. When one is contracting for the future, one cannot always anticipate future circumstances that might affect the achievement of one's goals. Contractual provisions that would achieve goals in one context might thwart these goals in another. Thus, achievement of future goals requires flexibility to adapt to future unforeseen circumstances. As long as one reasonably believes that he will have the power to exercise the authority that flexibility provides, the best means of achieving these goals through a contract is to create an open-ended framework that sets broad constraints but that can be fleshed out in the future. Control of the judiciary and thus the interpretation process is one important source of authority over the future.

On the dimension of amendment procedures, expectations of future dominance create a preference for *difficult* amendment procedures. Here the argument is slightly more indirect. There are basically two ways of changing a constitution, short of abandoning it and implementing a new one. One way is through the amendment process. The other is through the process of constitutional interpretation.[5] Control of the judiciary guarantees control of one of the mechanisms of constitutional change. Absent expectations that one has control over the other mechanism, it reasonably follows that the best way of controlling future constitutional change is to establish procedures that make change through amendment difficult.

On the dimension of interpretation, expectation of future dominance creates clear preferences over the institutionalization of constitutional review. The best means of effecting future outcomes, given control of the judiciary, is to establish *broad* scope of review, but *narrow* participation. The reason for broad scope is obvious. The reason for narrow participation follows from the desire to maximize the influence of those who share one's own preferences. On this reasoning, the narrower the range of participation, the more likely the preferences of the dominant interests will be instantiated in judicial decisions. Thus, influence is enhanced by broadening the range of issues under consideration by the judiciary, while narrowing the range of interests that participate in the process.

If a constitution maker expects that his present preferences will be the minority preferences of the judiciary in the future, he will seek to establish quite different rules and procedures. We can readily see this by considering the implications of the previous arguments for the interests of future minority groups. On the dimension of the substance of provisions, flexibility for future interests to determine the effects of constitutional provisions is unlikely to be in the interests of those who are presently in the majority but destined to be in the minority in the future. Drafters with such expectations will prefer, rather, to constrain the effects of future actions. Thus, they will prefer *specific* and *detailed* constitutional provisions. On the amendment dimension, lack of control over the judiciary diminishes the effectiveness of interpretation as a means of constitutional

---

[5] See Levinson 1995 for a persuasive argument in support of the idea that constitutional interpretation is often a form of constitutional change.

change. Absent specific expectations about the status of one's preferences in the legislature, constitution makers who anticipate minority status in the judiciary might reasonably prefer to create other mechanisms for change. This entails a preference for *easy* amendment procedures that would increase the availability of alternative ways of changing the constitution.

On the interpretation dimension, the lack of dominance on the judiciary alters the preferences for institutional procedures governing constitutional review. Lack of judicial control creates an incentive to *narrow* scope and *broaden* participation. If one believes that constitutional provisions will be interpreted in ways that deviate from the original interests, then the task is to constrain the effects of such interpretations – thus the efforts to narrow the scope of such interpretations. At the same time, given the fact that the effectiveness of constraints on scope is at best incomplete, minority interests will seek to exert whatever influence they can on the decision-making process. From this it reasonably follows that expectations of minority status in the judiciary will lead to a preference for review procedures that expand the range of interests that participate in that review process.

For the reasons stated earlier, the constitutional preferences of a constitution maker who is uncertain about the relationship between his present preferences and the future preferences of the judiciary will depend on his attitude toward risk. The more risk averse he is, the more his preferences will mirror the preferences of someone who expects to be in the minority in the future.

Legislature

The previous arguments about the importance of flexibility and access to mechanisms of change and participation apply as well to the effects of expectations about the future preferences of the legislature, but the implications are somewhat different. Expectations about the legislature relate to expectations about the effect of future interpretation in an indirect way: the focus here is on the effects of future actors on the enactment of substantive policy, on the laws and policies that will be subject to constitutional scrutiny. Whether one controls the enactment of substantive policy is an important factor in assessing whether one wants that policy to be subject to minimal or extensive review.

Consider first the expectations that one's present preferences will be the majority preferences in the future. In this case the goal of a constitutional drafter is to enhance the capacity of future actors in the legislature to foster the basic goals that they share. Here flexibility is desired and thus dictates *general* and *open-ended* provisions. Similarly, absent evidence of control of the judiciary, these expectations foster a preference for minimal constitutional review, thus *narrow* scope and participation. The implications of these expectations for the dimension of amendment procedures are the most difficult for me to determine. Here there is a close correlation between preference for change and the certainty of expectations. Flexibility is enhanced by amendment procedures that make change *easy*, but it seems that such a preference would require expectations near certainty that one's preferences will clearly dominate in the future. This is a remarkably stringent threshold. If a drafter has any reasonable doubt about these expectations, then a preference for more *difficult* amendment procedures may be implied.

Assessing the implications of expectations of future minority status is more straightforward. The task in such a case, as I have previously argued, is to constrain the effects of future actions by the legislature and to maximize whatever influence minority interests can have on those effects. This entails a preference for the following constitutional features: *specific* and *detailed* provisions, *difficult* amendment procedures, and *broad* scope and participation in the constitutional review process. Note that the specific and detailed nature of the constitutional provisions should be most evident in the enumeration of individual and collective rights. Members of the constituent assembly who expect that they might be in the legislative minority in the future will prefer a more substantively detailed statement of the constitutionally protected rights of the minority. Also, the preference for broad constitutional review rests on a couple of important premises. In terms of scope, minority interests will seek an expansive protection of their constitutionally protected rights. Historically, this has been one of the most important justifications of constitutional constraints on democratic decision making (Ely 1980). In terms of participation, such interests will seek to maximize their chance to influence the future. If they lack control of the legislature, they will look to other sources of influence over constitutional matters. Absent evidence of whose interests control the judiciary, lack of control of the legislature should push interest in the direction of broader influence of the judiciary.

As in the case of the judiciary, attitudes toward risk should affect the constitutional preferences of a constitution maker who is uncertain about the future preferences of the legislature. For the reasons offered previously, I think that there is good reason to expect an uncertain drafter to favor the preferences of a constitution maker who expects to be in the future minority.

Overall Effect of Expectations

To assess the overall effect of these expectations on the constitutional preferences of an individual member of a constitution-making body, I

Jack Knight

Table 11.1. Preferences

| | | Constitutional Feature | | |
Expectations	Provisions	Amendment	Interpretation Scope	Interpretation Participation
I. Judiciary/ legislature	Open-ended	*Difficult*/easy	Broad/*narrow*	Narrow
II. No judiciary/ legislature	Detailed/ *open-ended*	Easy	Narrow	*Broad*/narrow
III. Judiciary/no legislature	Open-ended/ *detailed*	Difficult	Broad	*Narrow*/broad
IV. No judiciary/ no legislature	Detailed	*Easy*/difficult	Narrow/*broad*	Broad
V. Uncertain	Detailed	*Easy*/difficult	Narrow/*broad*	Broad

Note: For significance of italics, see text.

have collected the implications of the arguments of the last two sections in Table 11.1, which presents five cases of future expectations. The cases range from expectations that one's future interests will dominate in both branches of government (case I) through expectations of being in the minority in either one (cases II and III) or both (case IV) to uncertainty about the future (case V). In half of the preference categories the preferences dictated by the two sets of expectations are the same, making the determination of overall effect easy. For example, belief that your future interests will dominate in both the legislature and the judiciary (case I) implies a preference for narrow participation in the interpretation process. In the other half of the preference categories the expectations have conflicting implications for constitutional preferences. For example, the same belief (case I) implies conflicting preferences for the scope of interpretation: control of the judiciary implies a broad scope, whereas control of the legislature implies a narrow one.

How these conflicting preferences get resolved in the various categories depends on how the constitution maker weighs the two sets of preferences in a particular case. Different drafters may apply different weighting schemes to resolve these conflicts. There are, however, weighting schemes that follow, I think, from the arguments about flexibility and access to influence. The issue of the substantive nature of constitutional provisions is really a question of how much flexibility one wants to give to future interests in the development of laws and policies. This is primarily the responsibility of the legislative branch of government. This suggests that legislative expectations might deserve greater weight in regards to the question of open-ended versus detailed provisions.

Similarly, the issue of the scope of constitutional interpretation rests on the question of how much influence one gives to the judiciary in determining the substantive nature of future laws and policies. Here I think that the arguments for flexibility and access cut in different directions. Judicial review can be conceptualized as a constraint on the flexibility of the legislature. Thus, one might argue that legislative expectations should govern on the grounds that the determinate factor should be the extent to which one wants to constrain the control of the legislature over future decisions. On the other hand, judicial review can be seen as a question of the access of the judiciary to influence over substantive laws and policies. On this conceptualization one might argue that judicial expectations should govern on the grounds that the determinate factor should be the nature of the influence that might be exercised by the courts. In the end, I think that, on the issue of scope, the argument that judicial review is primarily a question of constraint on the flexibility of the legislature is the more persuasive, rendering the legislative expectations determinate on this issue. This is consistent with the standard view of the courts as a protector of constitutional rights. But I admit to some uncertainty on this question.

The other two dimensions, amendment process and the nature of participation in the interpretation process, are clearly issues of access to influence over both substantive policy and constitutional change. Preferences over access hinge primarily on one's expectations about the likelihood that there are other sources of control over the future. That is, if you think that you will control the judiciary, you will prefer to restrict other mechanisms of constitutional change. Similarly, if you expect to be in the minority in the judiciary, but think that you cannot constrain the influence of the judiciary over future events, you will prefer to institutionalize extensive participation in the interpretation process in order to enhance the likelihood that your interests might affect the process. Given that questions of access beyond the legislative process (which presumably is open to everyone in a democratic society) rest mainly on the availability of influence in the judiciary, I think that the more reasonable weighting of expectations on these dimensions is to give predominance to judicial expectations.

These proposed weightings (the implications of which are designated by italics in Table 11.1) produce the following general preference patterns. Expectations of future majority status (case I) imply a preference for a constitution of general and open-ended provisions (including general statements of individual rights), which institutionalizes restrictive mechanisms of interpretation and change (minimal judicial review and difficult amendment procedures). As expectations of future control over the branches of government diminish, preferences will shift toward constitutions with more specific and detailed provisions that institutionalize broader access to effective mechanisms of interpretation and change for minority interests. In the extreme, expectations of lack of control (case IV) imply a constitution with a detailed provision of procedures and individual rights as well as amendment procedures with low thresholds for change and institutional procedures allowing for broad and extensive constitutional review.

Although it is easy to identify how the preferences about provisions and amendments are instantiated in constitutions, identifying the implications of the institutions of judicial review is a more difficult task. A few questions about different review procedures must be addressed. How do we interpret the establishment of specific constitutional tribunals distinct from the regular judicial system? Separating the authority over constitutional review from the functions of the regular judiciary is a common feature of European constitutional systems (Jackson and Tate 1990; Shapiro and Stone 1994). If constitutional review is limited to this special court as opposed to all courts, it has potential effects on both the scope and the nature of participation in the interpretation process. Special constitutional tribunals are often restricted in terms of both the types of issues that they can consider and the types of people who have standing to bring questions of interpretation to the court. Specifications of scope are generally rules establishing whether the tribunal can engage in either abstract or concrete review. Given the fact that this is an issue that can affect courts other than special tribunals, I briefly postpone discussing how we should interpret such scope rules. It is sufficient to say that the creation of a special tribunal has no per se implication for the breadth of constitutional review.

Special constitutional tribunals are often restricted in terms of who can place a question on the tribunal's docket. This raises an interesting question about participation: does the fact that standing to raise constitutional questions is limited to politicians and government officials constitute a restriction on the participation of interests as I have defined it? I think that the answer depends on whether the restrictions on standing truly diminish the prospects for certain interests to influence the interpretation process. A number of mechanisms can serve to broaden the range of interests subject to consideration – for example, standing rights for any member of the legislature so that he can file a constitutional challenge to a bill before the legislature, or the right of a judge in the regular court system to raise constitutional questions on behalf of the parties to regular judicial proceedings. The existence of these liberal standing rules that allow a government official to initiate a case on behalf on any possible interest would seem to offset the apparent restriction on participation by individual private citizens found in various systems.

Constitutional Interpretation 373

How do we interpret institutional constraints on either abstract or concrete review? Abstract review provides for an analysis of the constitutionality of bills as they are enacted by the legislature. Such review may occur as the bill is being considered (a priori review) or after the bill is enacted (a posteriori review). Concrete review provides for an analysis of the constitutionality of a law as it applies to particular cases. Clearly a system that institutionalized both abstract and concrete review would constitute the broadest scope of review. The German Constitutional Court is representative of such a system (Currie 1994). It is more difficult to discern whether abstract or concrete review alone constitutes the broader form. Limitations of judicial systems to abstract review diminish scope in the sense of not allowing for the consideration of interests affected by a fact situation that cannot be anticipated in advance of actual applications of laws and policies.[6] But abstract review also has an expansive effect relative to judicial systems restricted to concrete review in that it expands the role of constitutional interpretation in the initial decision-making process. Given the significance placed on issues of separation of powers and questions of the legitimacy of judges (especially nonelected judges) intervening in the democratic process, there is reason to believe that most constitution-making bodies conceive of abstract review within the legislative process as the more expansive and invasive form of constitutional interpretation.

In terms of overall effect, there is evidence that abstract review significantly influences the politics of law making. Shapiro and Stone (1994) argue that abstract review not only expands the role of constitutional review in the initial decision-making process, but also affects the nature of decision making in the legislature. The existence of a mechanism of abstract review can affect the strategic politics of the legislature in that it opens up a mechanism that, through the process of anticipated reaction, might prevent legislatures from passing legislation that is questionable on constitutional grounds. They also argue that abstract review can diminish the likelihood that legislators pass laws merely for political purposes.

But there are conflicting arguments as to what are the net substantive effects of these changes in the politics of law making. Stone (1992) argues that this judicialization of politics has made law making in Western Europe (though his analysis is primarily on France) more principled, on the one hand, but more resistant to reform and change, on the other. Landfried (1985) argues that the effect in Germany has been more negative. She suggests that the existence of the German Constitutional

---

[6] See Gunther 1993 for an instructive discussion of the impossibility of anticipating in advance all of the possible applications for an individual law.

374 *Jack Knight*

Court has served to exacerbate ideological conflict. Thus, although the substantive effects are debatable, the evidence of significant effect seems substantiated.

How should we interpret institutional procedures that allow for the easy overrule of tribunals conducting constitutional review? Some countries, such as the United States, provide for only one mechanism for overruling the Supreme Court's interpretation of the constitution: the process of constitutional amendment. In other countries, such as in Eastern Europe, some of the new constitutions provide mechanisms by which the legislative branch can overrule the decisions of their Constitutional Courts.[7] For example, Poland established a provision that through a two-thirds vote of the primary legislative chamber, constitutional decisions can be overturned. Similarly, Romania established a two-thirds threshold in either chamber of its parliament. Schwartz (1992, 760) argues that such mechanisms serve as constraints on judicial review. He points out that in the Romanian case the threshold for overturning decisions of the Constitutional Court is lower than the threshold for constitutional amendment.[8] In such cases he describes the overrule mechanism as a "true intrusion of the finality of constitutional decisions."

An alternative interpretation of these thresholds is suggested by the efforts of the Reagan administration (and especially Attorney General Edwin Meese) in the 1980s in the United States to assert a right of constitutional review for the nonjudicial branches of government. Given the lack of explicit treatment of the interpretation question in the U.S. Constitution, Meese and others argued that the historical assertion of the primacy of judicial review as the arbiter of constitutional questions did not preclude independent authority over such questions for the other branches. On the Meese logic, these thresholds for constitutional overrule might be interpreted, not as constraints, but rather as an expansion of the role of constitutional interpretation in the decision-making process. Although I tend to agree with the Schwartz interpretation of such mechanisms, I would admit that the effect of the mechanism in the Eastern European countries is to expand the number of actors who potentially participate in the interpretation process. The problem with this, from the perspective of a concern for separation-of-powers issues, is that, to the extent that these additional interpreters are the actors whose earlier decisions are

---

[7] Such a mechanism was proposed by Madison in the U.S. Constitutional Convention during the debate over a proposal to establish a Council of Review with powers of abstract review (Butzner 1941, 56). The proposal for the mechanism was dropped when the effort to establish the council failed.

[8] The threshold is the same for both in the Polish case.

the object of analysis, the net effect will quite possibly be to minimize the influence of the judiciary on the overall process.[9]

Expectations

Expectation formation is obviously a complex process, affected by a variety of factors. Here I want merely to consider two potential effects on the expectations of constitution makers that are directly related to their ability to achieve both their short-term constitutional and long-term substantive preferences. One set of expectations concerns an individual drafter's beliefs about the likelihood that she will achieve her constitutional preferences: how confident is she that the enacted constitutional provisions will reflect her own institutional preferences? The second set of expectations concerns an individual drafter's beliefs that future judges and legislators will share her substantive policy preferences and provides the central question of my analysis of constitutional preferences: will future actors enact and interpret laws in such a way as to achieve my own preferred political and economic outcomes? Although a number of factors might affect these expectations, one factor that should be prominent is the present distribution of substantive interests in the constituent assembly. If we distinguish constituent assemblies in terms of the degree of heterogeneity in the substantive interests that are represented at the assemblies, we can offer some tentative claims about the effects of different distributions on the relevant expectations of constitution makers. This should, according to the logic of contracting for the future, affect their preferences over constitutional provisions.

Heterogeneity might affect the expectations of the individual constituent members in a number of distinct, but related, ways. Consider first the effect on their expectations about short-term success in the constitution-making process. The politics of constitution making involves bargaining and compromise, and the constitution that is produced by this process will be some mix of the various preferences represented in the assembly. The exact nature of that mix will be a function of a number of factors, the most important of which will be the distribution of bargaining power among the constituent members (Knight 1992). But I think that it is easy to identify a relationship among the heterogeneity of preferences, the strength of these various effects, and present and future expectations. If a constituent assembly consists of members with homogeneous preferences, then the effects of bargaining power and the pressure for

---

[9] This last issue may be relevant to an analysis of the implications of the French constitutional provision (Article V of the 1958 Constitution) that authorizes both the president and the National Assembly to assess the constitutionality of laws (Stone 1992).

376 *Jack Knight*

compromise will be minimal and the resulting constitution will closely mirror the substantive preferences of the individual members. In such circumstances an individual drafter will place a high probability on ultimately achieving her own constitutional preferences.

If, rather, a constituent assembly is characterized by a wide range of disparate preferences, the effects of bargaining power and the pressure for compromise will be great and the resulting constitution will reflect this compromise, producing a document whose substantive provisions will deviate from the substantive preferences of any particular member. To the extent to which heterogeneity increases the influence of bargaining power and the pressure for compromise, it should affect a drafter's expectations of short-term success as well as her basic commitment to the particular substantive goals instantiated in the constitution. And this might have an affect on her constitutional preferences: to the extent that the constitution instantiates substantive goals that vary from her own ideal preferences, she will be less willing to constrain the future to the perpetuation of those goals. In such a case, the constitution makers should be more willing to allow the interests of the future to influence the direction of constitutional effects.

Now consider two effects of heterogeneity on expectations about the preferences of future actors. Although the strength of these effects may vary in terms of the exact number of members who hold the different substantive interests, they should tend to push expectations and, thus, the nature of constitutional preferences in a similar direction. First, the existence of a wide range of preferences might affect the individual member's perception of the likelihood that he will be in the minority in the future. On this account, the greater the diversity of preferences represented in the constituent assembly, the more likely the existence of expectations that one could be in the minority in the future. Second, the existence of a wide range of preferences might affect the confidence with which a drafter holds his expectations about the future. That is, the greater the diversity of preferences in the assembly, the more uncertain one could be about the exact status of one's preferences in the future. To the extent to which heterogeneity increases both expectations of minority status and uncertainty about those expectations, it would affect both a drafter's basic conception of which rules he must establish to produce his preferred outcomes and which rules will most likely compel compliance in the future, thus producing a preference for a constitution that will protect the interests and the potential influence of the minority in the future.

If this argument about the tendency for heterogeneity to affect expectations and preferences is correct, it suggests the following predictions about the types of constitutions that will be most preferred by various constitution-making bodies. Members of homogeneous constituent

Constitutional Interpretation

assemblies will prefer constitutions that are characterized by the features of case I expectations: *general* and *open-ended* provisions, *difficult* amendment procedures, and *narrow* constitutional review. As the heterogeneity of the substantive preferences in the constituent assemblies increases, the tendency will be to prefer constitutions that are characterized by the features of cases IV and V: *specific* and *detailed* provisions, *easy* amendment procedures, and *broad* constitutional review.

HISTORICAL CASES

An analysis of several cases of constitution making lends support to these arguments. The first task of such an analysis is to determine the nature of the distribution of substantive interests among the participants in the constitutional process. Ascertaining the degree of diversity in a particular distribution of interests is a complex empirical problem about which there may be considerable debate. I believe that there are ways of systematically addressing this question. But I also think that it is sufficient for my purposes here merely to assess the relative degree of heterogeneity of the historical cases that I consider. Given that the argument is cast in terms of tendencies toward particular sets of constitutional preferences, an analysis in terms of the relative degree of heterogeneity should allow us to assess the level of empirical support for the argument.

Let me begin by proposing a relative ranking of the historical and contemporary cases that I want to consider, ranking them from least to most heterogeneous: the United States (federal constitution), United States (state constitutions), France, Germany, Italy, and countries in Eastern Europe. While acknowledging that others might assess the degree of heterogeneity somewhat differently in some of these cases, I think that they offer a reasonable measure of the relative levels of diversity in the various cases. A number of factors should be considered in assessing the degree of heterogeneity of substantive interests. In proposing this relative ranking, I rely on three relevant indicators, none of which are sufficient alone but each of which provides some evidence of the degree of heterogeneity.

First, we should consider the existence of actual conflicts of interests within the constitution-making process. Evidence of conflict is one primary source of evidence of diversity. The historical evidence of the process of constitution making in the countries under consideration shows that there were important issues over which serious conflict arose in every case. But evidence of conflict should be considered relative to the extent of agreement within the body. Conflict can often arise even among homogenous groups because of disagreement over the best means of achieving shared goals. So the evidence of conflict should be assessed in the context of the range of issues addressed in the constitution as a whole. The relevant measure here should be the range of issues in the constitution over which there was substantive conflict relative to the total range of issues addressed in the document. Here I think that the historical evidence supports the relative ranking that I propose. Although there were some major sources of conflict among the delegates to the U.S. Constitutional Convention (an obvious example being the issue of slavery), the range of issues on which the delegates agreed was far greater than that which can be found in the negotiations over constitutions in Western and Eastern Europe (Wood 1972; 1993). Similarly, when we look at the history of constitution making at the state level in the United States, we find greater conflict over the substantive provisions of these constitutions than is found in the federal negotiations (Friedman 1988; Griffin 1995).

But evidence of actual conflict in the constitution-making process alone is insufficient evidence of the relevant level of heterogeneity of interests. Participants in the constitution-making process may take account of interest conflicts that extend outside the process itself. For this reason we should consider as a second indicator the existence of political conflict in the society at large. This level of conflict provides evidence of the diversity of interests within the society: the greater the political conflict, the greater the heterogeneity of interests in the society. In the post-Communist transition period in Eastern Europe the degree of political and economic uncertainty is quite high. This uncertainty has produced a wide range of ideas and interests about how the post-Communist societies should and would develop. This has been reflected in a high level of political conflict in the constitution-making process in these countries (Lijphart 1992; Klingsberg 1992; Schwartz 1992; Elster 1993).

In the post–World War II development of constitutions in Western Europe, a wide range of social and economic problems in most of these societies, combined with memories of experiences of political instability in the prewar period, produced a high level of political conflict as well as considerable uncertainty in terms of what the dominant political preferences would be in the future (Stone 1992; Currie 1994; Volcansek 1994). Contrast the European experience with that of the United States. The conditions under which the founders met to draft the U.S. Constitution were quite different from either of the European periods, as the founders, despite their internal differences, were much more certain that their basic political preferences would persist in the foreseeable future. They represented a considerable range of interests, but they were unrepresentative of many segments of American society in the postrevolutionary period (Wood 1972).

In fact, the U.S. case suggests a third measure of the level of diversity in the constitution-making process. The existence of general political conflict provides a referent by which to analyze the degree of diversity within the constitutional process itself. If the level of general political conflict is high, but the level of conflict within the constitution-making process is low, this is potential evidence of the unrepresentative nature of the constitutional body and thus evidence of a lower degree of heterogeneity than might be possible. Thus, we should also consider the relationship between the range of interests represented in the constitution-making process itself and the range of interests that actually exist in the society at large. The greater the discontinuity between represented and actual interests, the greater the limitation on diversity in the constitution-making process.

In the United States of the late eighteenth century, political representation was restricted by various social and economic factors so that a significant number of political interests was excluded from the negotiations over the constitution (Wood 1972). In Western Europe, after World War II, formal restrictions were established in some countries to restrict explicitly the access of various politically extreme interests from participating in the drafting of the constitutions (Currie 1994). In Eastern Europe, the post-Communist emphasis on new political representation created considerable pressure against constraints on participation and in favor of an inclusive representation of interests (Schwartz 1992). Restrictions on representation are reflective of the power differentials that characterize many societies. As such they are evidence of the present dominant status of particular substantive interests and might be evidence of expectations of continued dominance by these groups.

An analysis of the relevant features of the different constitutions and of some of the political conflict surrounding the enactment of those provisions can offer additional support for this ranking and for its relevance for explanations of constitutional preferences. Because my primary concern is with the ways in which the various constitutions address the question of constitutional interpretation, I focus primarily on the dimension of the institutionalization of constitutional review. Fortunately, the ways in which the different constitutions treat the issues of the nature of the substantive provisions and the criteria of amendment are clear and easy to assess in terms of the arguments about the relevance of heterogeneity and future expectations.

In these conditions of heterogeneity European constitution-making bodies produced a set of rather detailed constitutions with extensive bills of rights and complex governmental structures. The constitution makers in Germany developed a lengthy and detailed bill of rights (the first eighteen articles in the Basic Law) and a complex distribution of power scheme (Currie 1994). Extensive charters of rights were enacted in Italy and Austria (Shapiro and Stone 1994, 410). The 1946 constitutional negotiations in France produced an extensive debate over the inclusion of detailed

380   *Jack Knight*

statements of rights in the constitution. The debate culminated in a decision to incorporate several sets of principles in the preamble to the constitution (Stone 1994). Contrast these with the U.S. Constitution, with its more general and open-ended provisions. In the U.S. context, the use of constitutions to establish substantive policy provisions is much more prevalent in state constitutions. Consistent with this analysis, these provisions, which Friedman calls "superlegislation" (1988, 35–7), are more prevalent in those states in which the political alignments were less stable. In fact, state political actors have been much more willing to rewrite their constitutions as political alignments have changed (Griffin 1995).

Similar historical evidence supports the claims about the effect of uncertainty on the drafting of amendment criteria. The most difficult amendment procedures are found in the U.S. Constitution (two-thirds of the members of both houses of Congress and a majority of the members of three-fourths of the state legislatures.) The amendment procedures instantiated in state constitutions in the United States vary, but they are clearly less stringent than the federal standards (Ordeshook and Shvetsova 1995). Griffin (1995) argues that the more lenient criteria are related to the fact that state constitutions are more often the source of conflictual policy debates than is the federal document. The criteria for amendments are least stringent in those European societies where the level of uncertainty was greater for the authors of constitutions – for example, Germany, Article 79 (2): two-thirds vote of the Bundestag and of states represented in the Bundesrat (Currie, 1994, 171); France: a majority of both chambers of the National Assembly (Stone, 1992, 58); Poland: two-thirds vote of the Sejm, the primary legislative chamber (Schwartz 1992, 760).

As we turn to a more extensive analysis of the historical evidence on the ways in which constitution makers have treated the institutionalization of judicial review, the expected relationship between heterogeneity, future expectations, and the breadth of judicial review is supported. The treatment of judicial review ranges from narrow review in the United States to increasingly broader procedures in the European countries. This variation is consistent with an explanation in terms of the differences in expectations about the effects of constitutional interpretation on the interests, present and future, of the participants in the constitution-making process. An analysis of the politics that underlies the establishment of procedures governing judicial review reveals the importance of both the range of interests participating in the process and the effects of changes in expectations on efforts to alter existing procedures.

Judicial review in the U.S. federal system has been the product not of explicit institutionalization in the Constitution but rather of an evolutionary process (Knight and Epstein 1996). The evolved system is more restrictive than those found in European systems. It is limited to concrete

Constitutional Interpretation 381

review, an assessment of the constitutionality of laws as they apply to particular cases. But it is a feature of all courts and not just special tribunals, and standing to challenge the constitutionality of statutes and government decision making generally rests with any private citizen who is involved in an active legal dispute.

That the founders would not explicitly develop a mechanism for judicial review in the U.S. Constitution is consistent with my arguments about the effect of future expectations on the institutionalization of constitutional interpretation. At the time of the drafting of the Constitution, judges in the United States were very political actors, often serving in other more explicitly political offices while sitting on the bench (Wood 1993, 323–4). Although early state constitutions provided for separation of powers with a distinct judicial branch, their independence was constrained by the fact that the legislature controlled the length of their terms in office, set their salaries and fees, and established the procedures for removal from office (Wood 1972, 161). But during the same period there was a rise in concern about the unconstrained power of the legislatures. State judiciaries in New Jersey, Virginia, New York, Rhode Island, and North Carolina entertained arguments in support of judicial review in cases in which they sought to constrain the enactment of laws by their state legislatures (Wood 1972, 454–5).

There was significant debate in the Constitutional Convention over the appropriateness of judicial review. There were precursors of abstract review in the United States prior to the drafting of the constitution. The Pennsylvania Constitution of 1776 had a Council of Censors to review constitutional behavior. The first New York State Constitution established a Council of Revision, consisting of the governor, the chancellor, and the supreme court judges, that reviewed the constitutionality of legislative bills (Friedman 1988, 39). In the Constitutional Convention, Madison, among others, endorsed the establishment of a Council of Revision, to consist of the president and the justices of the Supreme Court. The council, based on the New York procedures, would be empowered to review congressional enactments to assess whether they were either unconstitutional or "unwise and unjust" (Farrand 1966, 2:73–8, 109–10). If the Council ruled against an enactment, Congress would have the right to overturn the decision by a two-thirds vote of both houses. In the end the proposal was rejected on the grounds that it was a violation of separation of powers and an excessive grant of power of the courts over the legislature (Butzner 1941, 54–7, 147–52).

As to the intentions of the framers on the appropriateness of concrete review, there is some historical question on this point. Wood (1972, 549–52) argues that the framers were split on the wisdom of institutionalizing judicial review. He suggests that while Madison offered arguments against judicial review on the grounds that it would undermine the fundamental principle of legislative supremacy, others argued that judicial review was necessary to control the powers of the legislature. Rakove (1996, 175, 186–7) argues that the delegates intended their enumeration of the powers of the judiciary to entail that judicial review would apply to the actions of both the national and, more controversially, the state legislatures. For my purposes here, either historical account supports the basic proposition that, to the extent that the framers of the U.S. Constitution sought to institutionalize constitutional review, it was of the more narrow, concrete review, variety.

If we contrast the U.S. case with those of Western and Eastern Europe, we see how an increase in the heterogeneity of interests in the constitution-making process may affect the treatment of judicial review. Historically, judicial review lacked support in Europe because of the ideological commitment to the primacy of the legislature (Shapiro and Stone 1994, 400). For example, there was no explicit provision concerning judicial review in either the French Constitution of 1791 or the 1871 Bismarck Constitution in Germany (Stone 1992; Currie 1994). One might speculate as to whether the opposition to judicial review grounded in ideology was reinforced by the substantive preferences of the dominant groups in these countries, given the fact that there were clear restrictions on the political participation of many social groups into the twentieth century. As long as control of the legislature remained within the hands of a few dominant groups, there was no need for the alternative sources of influence offered by judicial review. On the one hand, such speculation ignores that fact that there was significant political conflict even among those groups that did have access to the legislative process. On the other hand, however, support for this view can be found in the response among European legal scholars and some judges to the increased influence of previously disenfranchised groups in the late nineteenth and early twentieth centuries.

Stone (1992, 227) argues that judicial review began to gain support among legal scholars in the early twentieth century, especially as the elites began to criticize legislative action produced by the growing influence of unions and working-class political parties. In addition to this support among scholars, there is evidence of early efforts to implement such constitutional review. Hans Kelsen drafted a constitution that was enacted in the Austrian Republic in 1920 that provided for a special constitutional tribunal to resolve conflicts over constitutional matters. But this tribunal came under constant and increasingly severe attack by factions of the right throughout the 1920s and was dissolved by government edict in 1933 (Stone 1992, 230). Similarly, the Supreme Court of Weimar Germany, which had been granted authority to resolve constitutional conflicts among Reich officials and between the Reich and the individual states

Constitutional Interpretation

(Hucko 1989, 152), exercised the authority to annul various statutes as unconstitutional that were contrary to the interests of dominant business interests (Stone 1992, 228). The level of support for judicial review continued to grow so that by the time that new constitutions were drafted in the post–World War II period constitutional drafters throughout Europe included explicit provisions establishing special constitutional tribunals that have exclusive jurisdiction over constitutional questions.

Today the European model of judicial reform takes many forms, providing various combinations of abstract and concrete review. Consider these variations. From the perspective of standard mechanisms of judicial review, France has enacted the strictest institutional constraints on its Constitutional Council to be found in Europe (Stone 1992; 1994). The council, on which career politicians serve as justices for nine-year terms, only conducts abstract review of bills passed by the National Assembly during the period of time between passage and promulgation. The 1958 Constitution limited standing to refer bills to the council to members of the government in power, but an amendment in 1974 extended the right of referral to any coalition of at least sixty opposition deputies. But, an interesting feature of the 1958 Constitution, Article V, extends the authority to assess the constitutionality of laws to both the executive and the legislative branches. Thus, while France has the most restrictive constraints on abstract review in Europe, it has expanded the range of actors who have the authority to interpret laws for their constitutional validity. In the aftermath of the 1974 amendment, the Constitutional Court has been quite an activist one. Stone (1994, 449) reports that, since the late 1970s, almost every major bill has been referred to the court and, since 1981, more than half of those bills have been rejected as unconstitutional.

Germany and Italy, on the other hand, have limited review authority to constitutional courts, but have provided those courts with much broader powers of review. The German Basic Law of 1949 established a special court with two separate Senates, one for questions of constitutionality arising from ordinary litigation and another for questions arising from interbranch conflict (Currie 1994). This court has the power of both abstract and concrete review, accepting referrals from government officials, the regular judiciary, and individual private litigants. The judges, originally career politicians and now increasingly legal professionals who serve twelve-year terms, have the power not only to declare laws unconstitutional but to declare them incompatible with the Basic Law, leaving them in effect for a period of time during which the legislature can attempt to amend them in terms of the court's decision (Kommers 1989, 60–1). The court has also garnered extensive authority to review the constitutionality of both bureaucratic and executive action (Currie 1994, 162–3). This system is similar to the one established by the Italian Constitution of 1948

(Volcansek 1994). This constitution created the Constitutional Court, which has exclusive power to determine the constitutionality of legislation. The court, consisting of fifteen members, most of whom are explicit representatives of the major political parties, has the authority not only to find laws unconstitutional but also to render decisions that, in fact, rewrite the laws in terms that they find constitutionally acceptable.

Finally, the institutions of judicial review established by the new Eastern European constitutions are generally modeled after the German system. Schwartz (1992) offers a comprehensive analysis of the various approaches to judicial review institutionalized in the constitutions of Bulgaria, Hungary, Poland, Romania, and Russia. Each constitution establishes a Constitutional Court with authority of abstract review of legislation upon referral by a government official and concrete review of laws upon referral by judges in the regular court system. Appointments to these courts are by political authorities for fixed, nonrenewable terms, except in Hungary where the terms are renewable. In addition to this basic scheme, the authority of these courts is expanded to various degrees in Hungary, Russia, and Romania. In each of these countries the Constitutional Court can initiate abstract review on its own initiative. Also, individual citizens have broad powers to initiate concrete review in Hungary and more limited authority in Russia.

This institutionalization of extensive judicial review in countries long opposed to it can be explained by the uncertainty engendered by significant political conflict in the post–World War II period. Consider three examples. In France political conflict over judicial review has been intimately related to conflict over the substantive content of the provisions. In the 1946 Constitutional Assembly there was significant debate over the nature of the preamble to the Constitution (Stone 1992, chs. 1 and 2). The representatives of the left advocated that the preamble consist of a set of principles that enumerated an extensive list of social, economic, and political policies. The right proposed as an alternative the 1789 Declaration of the Rights of Man and a set of rules called the Fundamental Principles Recognized by the Laws of the Republic. Both the left and the center parties accepted the rights of due process and legal equality in the 1789 text, but they opposed the provisions governing rights to private property. In the end the parties compromised and established a preamble that incorporated each of the three texts. What the parties to the 1946 compromise did not anticipate was the 1971 decision by the Constitutional Council to incorporate this preamble (as reenacted in the 1958 Constitution) into the substantive provisions of the Constitution.

This decision started a concerted effort on the part of the various political interests to convince the Constitutional Council to give priority to one of the three preamble texts. Throughout the 1970s the parties of the left attempted unsuccessfully to establish the priority of the 1946 principles. After 1981 the Socialists changed their strategy and began to instantiate these principles in legislation, only to find that the parties of the right, using their referral power for abstract review, persuaded the council to overturn much of this legislation (especially the socialist economic policies). In overturning this legislation the council effectively granted priority to the 1789 Declaration, arguing that the 1946 principles merely supplemented the 1789 text. In partial response to these decisions by the council, President Mitterand introduced a constitutional amendment in 1990 that would establish concrete review by referral from individual citizens. The Senate, controlled by the parties of the center and the right, rejected the proposal and argued that a new bill of rights would have to be established before they would consider concrete review. Stone (1992, 58–9) argues that the center-right parties strongly opposed the Mitterand amendment because the Socialists controlled the future appointments to the council.

In Germany the Basic Law of 1949 established the Federal Constitutional Court with broad powers of judicial review. There were three main factions in the constitutional debates: the Christian Democrats, the Social Democrats, and the delegates from the German states represented in the Bundesrat. They negotiated the Basic Law in the shadows of the Weimar period and World War II, so there was substantial support across the political spectrum for constitutional limitations on the power of democratic majorities. Each group had interests that they thought could best be protected in the long run by judicial review: the basic right of private property for the Christian Democrats, the rights of minority political groups in parliament for the Social Democrats, and guarantees of German federalism for the member states. Although there were significant conflicts among these groups over the substance of the basic constitutional provisions, they readily agreed over the broad authority of the Federal Constitutional Court to protect constitutional rights and guarantee the autonomous authority of the various German states (Kommers 1994, 471–2).

In Italy there were similar divisions: the Christian Democrats (seeking protection for personal liberties and the rights of the Catholic Church), the left parties (Socialist and Communists, seeking protection for mass parties), and the minority parties (neofascist, liberal, and republican, seeking protection for minority rights). The debates at the Constitutional Assembly on the establishment of the Constitutional Court "were essentially about how to divide power among the parties" (Volcansek 1994, 493–4). That the various political parties saw judicial review as a protection against the political actions of the majority party is clear from an analysis of these debates. When the Christian Democrats feared that they

386 *Jack Knight*

would be in the minority, they advocated judicial review in the face of opposition from the left parties who thought that they were in position to take over the government. Eventually provisions for the Constitutional Court were included in the Constitution. After the first parliamentary elections produced a surprising victory for the Christian Democrats, the parties switched their positions of judicial review and the Christian Democrats were able to postpone implementation of the court for eight years. In the end of this conflict, the establishment of an informal formula to divide court seats in a manner proportional to the distribution of political affiliations in the legislature was the key to the ultimate implementation of the Constitutional Court in Italy (Volcansek 1994).

I can summarize the argument in regard to the effects of heterogeneity and political uncertainty on the institutionalization of judicial review by emphasizing the effects of the broad review of the European variety. The overall effect has been to increase the political efficacy of those actors who have been less successful in the legislative arena (Stone 1992; Landfried 1985, 1994; Kommers 1994; Volcansek 1994). This expansion of the range of political preferences that influence democratic outcomes is exactly what a constitutional drafter who believes that the future political fortunes of those who share her political preferences will be in the minority would seek to implement. Judicial review has done this not only through the most often cited way, protecting the political rights of minorities (a main effect of the more restrictive American system), but also through its effects on the substance of political decision making.

Two main points should be reiterated. First, it has resulted in the judicialization of politics to use Stone's phrase (1994, 446). By this he means to describe "the general process in which legal discourse – norms of behavior and language – penetrate and are absorbed by political discourse." Part of this effect has been to push political discourse in the legislature in the direction of justificatory arguments based on constitutional norms. Second, broad judicial review has had the effect of blocking and/or modifying many legislative initiatives. For example, Stone (1992; 1994) shows how the court through abstract review has been used in France and Germany as a resource for opposition parties to block nonincremental reform. He shows that we find a high level of judicial activism in abstract review in cases in which the legislative majority seeks to enact nonincremental reform and in cases in which the political distribution of power in the legislature does not match the political distribution of authority in the court.

This effect highlights the importance of the distribution of political preferences on the constitutional courts when abstract review is a part of the constitutional system. The historical evidence offered here demonstrates that advocacy of broad judicial review by constitution makers was

Constitutional Interpretation

contingent on their belief that their substantive political interests would be adequately represented on the constitutional councils. Similar stories can be told about the development of constitutional courts in the emerging Eastern European democracies (Schwartz 1992).

IMPLICATIONS

My analysis suggests that expectations about future constitutional interpretation can significantly affect the preferences of constitution makers for both the substantive and procedural aspects of their constitutions. The relationship between expectations and constitutional preferences is summarized in Table 11.1. Although some of the expectations imply conflicting preferences, the general thrust of the relationship can be stated as follows: the more that members of a constitution-making body either believe that their preferences deviate from the preferences of future interpreters of the constitution or are uncertain about the future, the more likely they are to prefer a constitution that is characterized by detailed substantive provisions, easy amendment procedures, and broad scope and participation for judicial review.

Given this relationship between expectations and preferences, I argued that there is a relationship between the distribution of substantive interests in a society and the types of constitutions that a member of a constitutional assembly will prefer. This relationship is based on two implications of heterogeneity in interests on the process of constitution making. First, there is a tendency for diverse interests to produce greater compromise in terms of the substantive interests instantiated in the constitution and thus to diminish the commitment of any individual member to the particular interests embodied in the constitution. Second, there is a tendency for heterogeneity to increase an individual member's uncertainty that his substantive preferences will be the dominant preferences governing future interpretation and thus to modify his constitutional preferences in the direction of case V in Table 11.1. Together these two implications of heterogeneity produce a tendency in the process of constitution making toward constitutions that are characterized by cases IV and V.

Heterogeneity of interests is a fundamental characteristic of modern culturally diverse societies. My analysis suggests that the members of such societies, when motivated primarily by a concern for their own substantive preferences, will prefer constitutions that institutionalize ease of amendment and extensive judicial intervention in the democratic process. This raises important questions about efforts to establish constitutions that will foster economic growth and political stability. Much of our conventional wisdom about the efficacy of constitutional democracy rests on the idea that the system works best when amendment is difficult and a

388   *Jack Knight*

precise separation of powers is maintained. But what are the implications for the long-term success of the constitution-making process when the interests of the individual constitution makers work against the creation of a constitution with these features? Let me close by highlighting two issues that reflect the tension between the politics of constitution making and the potential efficacy of constitutional democracies.

First, on the issue of ease of amendment, there is a possible conflict between the implications of easy amendment procedures and the efficacy of many governmental policies, both in terms of political and economic activity. The problem for the government as a collective actor is the following. The success of many governmental policies rests on the ability of state actors to commit themselves credibly to promises that they make to their own citizens and to other states (Holmes 1988; North and Weingast 1989). The state as a collective actor persists, but individual political actors change. To the extent that the actions of the state are a product of the preferences and actions of a changing group of politicians, a promise made by the state at one point in time may not be honored by a state controlled by a different set of politicians at a later moment. Constitutions serve to constrain these changes in behavior by prohibiting certain actions and guaranteeing the protection of others. Through these contraints they enhance the credibility of the promises made by state actors at any single point in time. Thus, a constitution that cannot be easily changed can increase the efficacy of state action in this credibility-enhancing way.

However, the process of constitution making in a heterogeneous society can lead to a potentially perverse outcome. Societies characterized by a wide range of substantive interests are likely to be the ones in which the credibility of a particular government's promises is open to most serious doubt. But, if it is the case that heterogeneous societies will be less likely to enact constitutions with difficult amendment procedures, then those culturally diverse societies that most need strong government support for economic growth and prosperity and for the guarantees of broad political rights and representation will be least likely to produce it.

Second, the feature of broad and extensive judicial review may challenge the underlying legitimacy, and thus possibly the stability, of democratic institutions. The classic formulation of the relationship between judicial review and democracy has been the countermajoritarian objection: action by nonelected judges who alter the will of the legislature is contrary to fundamental democratic principles and thus normatively illegitimate (Hamilton, Madison, and Jay 1961). On this account the legitimacy of the democratic process rests on the close relationship between the interests of society and the collective outcomes of the democratic decision-making process (Knight and Johnson 1994). To the extent that the interpreters of the constitution fail to represent the relevant interests of society and thus break this connection between interests and democratic outcomes, the effects of constitutional interpretation on the democratic process undermine the legitimacy of those outcomes.

The most widely accepted response to the countermajoritarian objection is that offered by Dahl (1989) and Ely (1980) among others: judicial review that protects fundamental political rights is not undemocratic and is in fact democracy-enhancing and thus essential to a functioning democracy. There is considerable empirical evidence that this has actually been the main effect of judicial review in some European societies. Shapiro and Stone (1994, 410) argue that "the constitutional review activity of virtually all national European constitutional courts is dominated by rights issues." Ninety percent of the case loads of the constitutional courts in Germany and Spain involve individual claims of rights violations (Stone 1992, 86–7), while in France "nearly every important legislative invalidation by the council has been enabled by its reading of rights provisions" (Shapiro and Stone 1994, 410).

But this democracy-enhancing response to the countermajoritarian objection will not satisfy the challenge when applied to judicial intervention over nonpolitical controversies. When constitutional interpreters intervene in the democratic process on other social and economic issues, an alternative argument in support of the legitimacy of that intervention must be found. Whatever form such an argument might take, it seems that it must, at a minimum, address the question of the relationship between the interests of the intervening interpreters and the interests of the members of society (Knight and Johnson 1996). One possible solution to this problem might be the election of judges. Another possibility might rest on the types of informal mechanisms established in several European systems that guarantee a proportional representation of the interests of the major political parties on the Constitutional Courts. Without such mechanisms the underlying legitimacy of constitutional review may be in question. But, given the necessity of interpretation in any constitutional system, a resolution of this question is at the forefront of the issues facing any constitution-making body.

REFERENCES

Butzner, Jane. 1941. *Constitutional Chaff*. New York: Columbia University Press.
Currie, David P. 1994. *The Constitution of the Federal Republic of Germany*. Chicago: University of Chicago Press.
Dahl, Robert. 1989. *Democracy and Its Critics*. New Haven: Yale University Press.
Elster, Jon. 1993. "Constitution-Making in Eastern Europe: Rebuilding the Boat in the Open Sea." *Public Administration* 71: 169–217.
Ely, John H. 1980. *Democracy and Distrust*. Cambridge, Mass.: Harvard University Press.

390 *Jack Knight*

Epstein, Lee, and Jack Knight. 1998. *The Choices Justices Make*. Washington, D.C.: CQ Press.

Eskridge, William, and John Ferejohn. 1994. "Theories of Statutory Interpretation and Theories of Legislatures." In Ian Shapiro, ed., *Nomos: The Rule of Law*. New York: New York University Press.

Farrand, Max. 1966. *Records of the Federal Convention of 1787*, 265–94. 3 vols. Rev. ed. New Haven: Yale University Press.

Friedman, Lawrence M. 1988. "State Constitutions in Historical Perspective." *Annals* 496: 33–42.

Griffin, Stephen M. 1995. "Understanding American Constitutionalism." Paper presented at the conference on Constitutions and Constitutionalism, Tulane University, New Orleans, March 11–12.

Gunther, Klaus. 1993. *The Sense of Appropriateness*. Albany: SUNY Press.

Hamilton, Alexander, James Madison, and John Jay. 1961. *The Federalist Papers*. Ed. Clinton Rossiter. New York: New American Library.

Holmes, Stephen. 1988. "Precommitment and the Paradox of Democracy." In Jon Elster and R. Slagstad, eds., *Constitutionalism and Democracy*, 195–240. Cambridge: Cambridge University Press.

Hucko, Elmar M. 1989. *The Democratic Tradition: Four German Constitutions*. Oxford: Berg Publishers.

Jackson, Donald, and C. Neal Tate, eds. 1990. "Symposium: Judicial Review and Public Policy in Comparative Perspective." *Policy Studies Journal* 19 (1).

Klingsberg, E. 1992. "Judicial Review and Hungary's Transition from Communism to Democracy." *Brigham Young University Law Review* 41: 41–144.

Knight, Jack. 1992. *Institutions and Social Conflict*. Cambridge: Cambridge University Press.

Knight, Jack, and Lee Epstein. 1996. "On the Struggle for Judicial Supremacy." *Law and Society Review* 30(1): 87–120.

Knight, Jack, and James Johnson. 1994. "Aggregation and Deliberation: On the Possibility of Democratic Legitimacy." *Political Theory* 22: 277–96.

1996. "Political Consequences of Pragmatism." *Political Theory* 24: 68–96.

Kommers, Donald P. 1989. *The Constitutional Jurisprudence of the Federal Republic of Germany*. Durham, N.C.: Duke University Press.

1994. "The Federal Constitutional Court in the German Political System." *Comparative Political Studies* 26: 470–91.

Landfried, Christine. 1985. "The Impact of the German Constitutional Court on Politics and Policy-Outputs." *Government and Opposition* 20: 522–41.

1994. "The Judicialization of Politics in Germany." *International Political Science Review* 15: 113–24.

Levinson, Sanford. 1995. "How Many Times Has the United States Constitution Been Amended? (A) <26; (B) 26; (C) 27; (D) >27: Accounting for Constitutional Change." In Sanford Levinson, ed., *Responding to Imperfection: The Theory and Practice of Constitutional Amendment*, 13–36. Princeton: Princeton University Press.

Lijphart, Arend. 1992. "Democratization and Constitutional Choices in Czechoslovakia, Hungary and Poland, 1989–91." *Journal of Theoretical Politics* 4: 207–24.

Macneil, Ian. 1980. *The New Social Contract: An Inquiry into Modern Contractual Relations*. New Haven: Yale University Press.

North, Douglass, and Barry Weingast. 1989. "Constitutions and Commitments: The Evolution of Institutions Governing Public Choice in Seventeenth-Century England." *Journal of Economic History* 49: 803–32.

Ordeshook, Peter, and Olga Shvetsova. 1995. "Russia, Federalism and Political Stability." Social Science Working Paper No. 882. California Institute of Technology, Pasadena, Calif.

Rawls, John. 1971. *A Theory of Justice*. Cambridge, Mass.: Harvard University Press.

Rakove, Jack. 1996. *Original Meaning: Politics and Ideas in the Making of the Constitution*. New York: Knopf.

Schwartz, Herman. 1992. "The New East European Constitutional Courts." *Michigan Journal of International Law* 13: 741–85.

Shapiro, Martin, and Alec Stone. 1994. "The New Constitutional Politics of Europe." *Comparative Political Studies* 26: 397–420.

Stone, Alec. 1992. *The Birth of Judicial Politics in France*. Oxford: Oxford University Press.

1994. "Judging Socialist Reform: The Politics of Coordinate Construction in France and Germany." *Comparative Political Studies* 26: 443–69.

Volcansek, Mary L. 1994. "Political Power and Judicial Review in Italy." *Comparative Political Studies* 26: 492–509.

Wood, Gordon S. 1972. *The Creation of the American Republic*. New York: W. W. Norton.

1993. *The Radicalism of the American Revolution*. New York: Vantage Books.

Name Index

Ackerman, Bruce, 8, 33, 34, 65, 66, 104–5, 111nn2,3, 112, 115n4, 138, 149n2, 274, 288, 289, 291, 294, 295, 297, 299, 301, 308–13, 321, 322
Adair, Douglass, 43–4, 45, 56
Adams, John, 64n34, 334, 335
Adams, John Quincy, 297, 335
Amar, Akhil Reed, 29n21, 60n29, 65, 111nn2,3, 115n4, 149n2, 277–8, 320
Arato, Andrew, 71n4, 74, 76n13
Arrow, Kenneth, 163n12
Ash, Timothy Garton, 71n3

Bagehot, Walter, 71, 79–80, 97, 103
Bagot, Sir Charles, 244
Bailyn, Bernard, 47
Baker, Keith Michael, 6n7
Baker, Lynn, 272
Banning, Lance, 58n28, 181n25
Barber, Sotirios A., 170n2, 176
Beard, Charles A., 43, 61
Bednar, Jenna, 31–2, 223–67, 228, 229n13, 246n47, 262n93
Beer, Samuel H., 56, 181n25, 339
Beetz, Justice Jean, 250n56
Benedict, Michael Les, 303, 311, 314–15
Bennett, W., 248n52
Bentham, Jeremy, 148
Berger, Carl, 244n43
Berluoconi, S., 217n35
Berry, Wendell, 347
Blackburn, Lord, 241n39
Blackstone, William, 46, 53, 239n37
Blair, Tony, 242n40
Block, Robert, 84n26
Bobbio, N., 217n36
Bobbitt, Philip, 275n9, 318
Böckenförde, E.-W., 206n5
Bognetti, G., 208n13

Bonifacio, F., 218–19n41
Bork, R. H., 45n10
Botev, Nikolai, 82n23
Boudreaux, D. J., 277
Bourke, Paul F., 43
Bowen, John, 77n15, 78n18, 85n27, 89n35
Bramwell, Lord, 240n38
Branca, G., 218n41
Bredin, J.-D., 217n34
Brandeis, Louis, 260n84
Brennan, Geoffrey, 99
Bright, Charles, 297
Brinkley, Alan, 289
Brown, Craig, 244n43
Brown, J. F., 71n2, 73, 74n10, 75, 76, 88, 89n35, 96n49
Brown, John, 170, 178
Brutus (Anti-Federalist), 229–30n14, 255
Brzezinski, Mark, 94
Buchanan, James M., 17n12, 99, 149, 162, 226n10
Bulow, Jeremy, 25n19
Bunce, Valerie, 73
Burke, Edmund, 53
Burr, Aaron, 343
Burt, Robert A., 177n15
Bush, George, 192n36, 261n91, 275
Butzner, Jane, 374n7, 381

Cairns, Alan, 248n52
Cairns, Huntington, 153n4
Calamandrei, Piero, 217–18
Calhoun, John C., 5, 20, 29n20, 297
Calvert, Randall, 92, 93, 100n56, 101
Cannadine, David, 80
Cappelletti, M., 213, 217n34, 219nn42,43
Carey, John M., 165n14
Carter, Jimmy, 195n39
Casper, Gerhard, 99

393

394   *Name Index*

Chantraine, P., 206n3
Choper, Jesse, 255
Clay, Henry, 24, 297, 340
Clinton, William, 44n3, 323, 324
Cohen, Anthony, 76
Coke, Edward, 24
Condorcet, Marquis de, 212, 213
Cook, Ramsay, 244n43
Cooke, Jacob E., 156, 170n1
Corry, J. A., 239
Cox, Gary, 237, 238n31
Craxi, B., 217n35
Cronin, T. E., 279n14
Cross, Rupert, 239, 241n39
Crouzet, D., 207n11
Csanadi, Maria, 73
Currie, David P., 373, 378, 379, 380, 382, 383

Dahl, Robert A., 43, 44, 45, 56, 190n33, 192n35, 389
De Gasperi, Alcide, 219n45
de Ruggiero, Guido, 214n26
de Ruggiero, L., 212n21
Della Porta, D., 220n47
Dellinger, W., 282n17
Diamond, Martin, 1, 2, 26, 27, 43, 44, 45, 56
Dicey, A. V., 17, 18
Donia, Robert, 77n15, 81n22, 82n23, 83n25, 94n45, 96n48
Dorf, Michael C., 313
Douglas, S., 319
Drankulic, Slavenka, 84, 85
Drewry, Gavin, 173
Dworkin, Ronald, 18, 19, 97–8, 192n35, 232n20

Eisgruber, Christopher, 136n6
Elkin, Stephen L., 322
Elkins, Stanley, 3n2
Elster, Jon, 26, 71n4, 72n5, 94, 98n54, 102n63, 103n65, 378
Ely, John Hart, 19, 369, 389
Engels, Friedrich, 212n21
Engeman, T. S., 44
Epstein, D., 45n9
Epstein, Lee, 363nn2,3, 380
Erler, E. J., 44
Eskridge, William N., Jr., 31–2, 182, 183n27, 186, 233–67, 225, 228, 229n13, 256n69, 257, 260n87, 262n93, 338n8, 362, 364
Everett, Edward, 171n4, 181

Farber, Daniel A., 338n8
Farge, A., 210n16

Farrand, Max, 49n15, 50, 55n24, 60n30, 62n32, 64n33, 178n16, 179nn18,19, 194, 195n40, 198n43, 276n11, 336, 337, 338n7, 341, 381
Fehrenbacher, Don E., 258n79
Feller, Daniel, 297, 298
Fendall, Philip R., 171n4, 181n23
Ferejohn, John, 31–2, 97n52, 182, 183n27, 186, 223–67, 225, 256n69, 257, 338n8, 362, 364
Fine, John, 77n15, 81nn22,23, 83n25, 94n45, 96n48
Finegold, Kenneth, 301
Flaherty, Martin S., 322
Fleming, James E., 170n2, 176, 274n6
Foner, Eric, 3, 15, 317
Foucault, M., 210n16
Frickey, Philip P., 260n87, 338n8
Fried, Charles, 294
Friedman, Barry, 322
Friedman, Lawrence M., 378, 380, 381
Friedrich, Carl, 99

Gaines, Brian, 235n25
Gardner, J. A., 277
Garraty, John A., 299
Geertz, Clifford, 77–8, 85n28, 93n42
George I, 235
George II, 236
George III, 236
Gerry, Elbridge, 44n6
Giacobbe, G., 218–19n41
Gillman, Howard, 296, 302, 303, 304
Glenny, Misha, 71n2, 76, 82, 83n24, 85, 88n34, 89n35
Goldstein, Leslie Friedman, 298
Golove, D., 274n8
Gordon, Robert, 292n3, 313
Gordon, Scott, 165n14
Graber, Mark A., 298
Graham, H. D., 54n20
Griffin, Stephen M., 33–4, 35, 273, 280, 282, 288–327, 288, 291, 302, 304, 305, 310, 321, 323, 339, 378, 380
Grodzins, Morton, 224n4
Guarnieri, C., 217n35
Gunther, Gerald, 338n8
Gunther, Klaus, 373n6
Gyani, Gabor, 91

Habermas, Jürgen, 319
Hamilton, Alexander, 3, 42–3, 44, 45, 56, 63–4, 66, 171–2, 216, 254n66, 256n71, 277, 289, 332, 333, 334, 339, 340, 341, 343, 344, 388
Hamilton, Edith, 153n4
Hardin, Russell, 34–5, 88n33, 93n42, 100,

101, 102n62, 103, 328–60, 331nnl,2, 332, 333, 339, 356
Hare, Thomas, 167
Harsanyi, John C., 149–50, 152, 154, 156, 157n5, 158, 159, 160, 161–2, 166
Hart, H. L. A., 11, 121
Hart, Henry M., Jr., 232n20
Hayden, Robert, 86, 96, 97
Hedges, Chris, 85
Hellman, Joel, 88n31
Henkin, Louis, 194n38
Henry, Justice, 246n49
Henry, Patrick, 61
Hirsch, Alan, 29n21, 149n2
Hirschman, Albert O., 226n10
Hobbes, Thomas, 224n2
Hobsbawm, Eric, 78, 79, 91n37, 97
Hobson, Charles F., 180, 295–6
Hodson, Randy, 82–3n23
Hofeller, T. B., 44
Hogg, Peter W., 251, 252
Holmes, Oliver Wendell, 328, 329–30, 333, 358
Holmes, Stephen, 25n19, 99, 275n10, 388
Horwitz, Morton, 316, 321
Howard, A. E. Dick, 72n5, 75n12, 102n63
Hucko, Elmar M., 383
Hume, David, 43, 46
Hunt, Gaillard, 181n24
Hyde, Henry, 323

Ickes, Harold, 190n34
Ilonszki, Gabriella, 94
Irons, Peter H., 293, 303

Jackson, Andrew, 177n12
Jackson, Donald, 372
Jackson, Justice Robert, 293–4, 297–8, 319
James I, 24
Jaworski, Rudolf, 91n37
Jay, John, 61, 388
Jefferson, Thomas, 3, 4n3, 5, 17, 51, 53, 57, 59, 60, 65, 66, 67, 177nn12,15, 180n21, 181, 215, 256n71, 332, 333, 334, 341, 342–3, 344, 346, 347
Jensen, M., 64n33
Johnson, Herbert, 295
Johnson, James, 28, 71–109, 71n1, 81, 92n39, 100n56, 101, 388, 389
Johnson, Lyndon, 258, 305

Kahn, Paul W., 319
Kalman, Laura, 318
Kames, Lord, 53
Kaminski, J., 64n33
Kammen, Michael, 276
Kant, Immanuel, 212–13

Kaplan, Robert, 77
Karl, Barry D., 304, 305
Katyal, Neal, 65n36, 111nn2,3
Kelly, Alfred H., 315
Kelsen, Hans, 121, 382
Kennedy, Justice Anthony, 315
Kennedy, W. P. M., 245n46
Kesler, C., 44n4
Kiss, Elizabeth, 73n9, 78, 82n23
Klarman, Michael J., 316, 322
Klingsberg, E., 378
Knight, Jack, 35, 100n58, 101, 361–91, 362n1, 363n3, 375, 380, 388, 389
Kobach, K. W., 278
Kommers, Donald P., 383, 385, 386
Kornhauser, L. A., 138n8
Kramer, Larry D., 42n1, 206n7, 262n92, 313
Kubik, Jan, 99
Kurland, Philip B., 53n19, 271n3, 277, 332n4, 336n5, 337, 356
Kydland, Finn, 25n19

Laba, Roman, 99
Laitin, David, 89n35, 95n47
Landfried, Christine, 373, 386
Langevin, Hector, 244n43
Laski, Harold, 43
Laurier, Wilfred, 246n48
Lazare, D., 68n39
Leone, Giovanni, 218n38
Lerner, Ralph, 53n19, 271n3, 277, 332n4, 336n5, 337, 356
Leuchtenburg, William E., 190, 299, 300, 302, 304
Levinson, Sanford, 33, 35, 271–87, 322, 367n5
Lieberman, D. M., 53
Lijphart, Arend, 165n14, 172n9, 185n29, 378
Lincoln, Abraham, 177n12, 311
Lindblom, C. E., 334, 350, 355
Linde, Hans, 279
Linder, D., 284n18
Linz, Juan, 83n23, 87n30
Locke, John, 46, 272, 276
Loreburn, Lord Chancellor, 240n38
Lukes, Steven, 79
Lutz, Donald S., 181, 271n2, 273n5, 281n15

Mach, Zdzislaw, 76
McCormick, R. P., 55n23
McCoy, Drew R., 53n17, 61, 181nn23,25
McDonald, Forrest, 3n2
Macdonald, Sir John A., 244, 246
McKay, Richard, 65

Name Index

McKinley, William, 256n70
McKitrick, Eric, 3n2
Macneil, Ian, 362, 365
McPherson, James, 311
Madison, James, 2, 3–6, 7, 17, 20n16, 27–8,
30–1, 31n23, 41, 42–3, 44, 45, 47–50,
51–6, 57–63, 64–7, 156, 170–1, 172,
173–4, 176–8, 179, 180, 181, 188, 189,
190, 191, 192, 193–4, 195n40, 197, 198,
201, 209, 213–14, 215, 216, 230n15, 254,
255, 256n71, 262–3, 273, 278, 289, 310,
332n4, 333, 336, 338n7, 341, 344, 356,
357, 374n7, 381–2, 388
Manin, B., 205n1, 209n15
Mansfield, H., 53
Marshall, Chief Justice John, 1, 171n3,
257, 289, 292–3, 294, 295, 296, 297
Marshall, Thomas, 190n33
Marshall, Justice Thurgood, 315, 318
Martin, Luther, 44n6
Martland, Justice, 250n58
Mason, George, 44n6, 55, 178n16, 276, 277
Massey, Rath, 82n23
Meese, Edwin, 374
Merryman, J. H., 219n42
Meyers, Marvin, 170, 171n4, 178, 179,
181n23, 189n31
Michelman, F. I., 138n8
Milgrom, Paul R., 232n21
Mill, John Stuart, 171n5, 173, 189n31
Miller, Gary, 103n65
Mills, David, 246n47
Mishler, William, 190n33, 192n36
Mitterand, F., 385
Monahan, Patrick, 251n60, 253n64
Monroe, James, 179, 256n70
Montesquieu, Baron, 43, 45, 46, 208–9,
210, 211, 214, 215, 216
Montinola, Gabriella, 235n26
Morris, Gouverneur, 178n16, 195n40
Mostov, Julie, 78, 91n37
Mowat, Oliver, 247
Mueller, Dennis C., 99, 162, 163–5
Mulroney, Brian, 253
Murphy, Walter F., 170n2, 176,
177nn12,15, 180n22, 194n38
Myerson, Roger, 162n10

Namier, Lewis, 237
Nedelsky, Jennifer, 45n9, 53n17, 178
Nelson, William E., 46, 314
Niederhauser, Emil, 78n19
Nixon, Richard, 323
North, Douglass C., 99n55, 232n21, 235,
236, 237, 388
Norton, Anne, 341n10
Norton, Philip, 185n28

Oates, Wallace, 226n10
O'Connor, Justice Sandra, 231n17, 315
O'Connor, Mike, 95n47
O'Connor, W. F., 245nn45,46
O'Donnell, Guillermo, 73
Offe, Claus, 72, 86, 87–90, 92, 93, 102n64
Okun, Arthur M., 356
Ordeshook, Peter C., 96, 100, 102n64,
162n10
Ost, David, 74n10, 88
Ostrom, Vincent, 226n10, 255

Parrish, Michael, 302
Pasquino, Pasquale, 28, 31, 205–22,
209n15
Patterson, James T., 302
Peden, W., 65n37
Pederzoli, P., 217n35
Perez-Diaz, Victor, 91–2
Perillo, J. M., 219n42
Peterson, Paul E., 226n10, 227n11, 228,
261
Pizzorno, A., 220
Pizzorusso, A., 219n42, 220
Plato, 153
Pognay, Istvan, 74, 75n11, 100n57
Pope, Alexander, 64
Popkin, Samuel L., 331
Popkin, William D., 239n35
Posner, Judge Richard, 321
Prakash, Saikrishna B., 313
Prescott, Edward, 25n19
Price, Jacob M., 236n28
Pritchard, A. C., 277
Przeworski, Adam, 75n12, 85n28, 88, 104,
334
Putin, Vladimir, 356
Putnam, Robert, 79n20

Qian, Yingyi, 235n26

Rae, Douglas W., 162
Rakove, Jack N., 2n1, 5nn4,5, 22n18, 27,
41–70, 42n1, 43n2, 44n6, 48n12, 51n16,
54n21, 55, 61, 62, 64n33, 65n36, 171n3,
178, 181n25, 189, 296, 382
Randolph, Edmund, 57, 65, 310
Ranger, Terence, 79
Rasmussen, Eric, 201n44
Rawls, John, 149, 366
Reagan, Ronald, 192n36, 261n91, 374
Rees, G., 281n16
Rehnquist, William, 260, 261
Reid, J. P., 53n19
Richards, Neil M., 315
Riker, William H., 162n10, 189n32, 224n4,
225, 255

Name Index

397

Riley, Jonathan, 28, 30–1, 43n3, 147–69, 161n9, 166, 167, 170–204
Rives, William C., 171n4, 181n24
Roane, Spencer, 171n4
Rogoff, Kenneth, 25n19
Rohr, John A., 31n22, 172n9, 202n45
Roosevelt, Franklin D., 177n12, 190n34, 195n39, 248, 258, 259, 299, 301, 302, 303–4, 308, 316, 358
Roosevelt, Theodore, 256n70, 299
Root, Hilton, 235–6
Rosenberg, Gerald N., 192n35
Ross, Stephen F., 231n16
Rousseau, Jean-Jacques, 205–6, 211n19, 212, 213
Rudolph, Lloyd, 77n15, 78n18, 82n22
Rudolph, Susanne Hoeber, 77n15, 78n18, 82n22
Russell, Peter H., 244, 246, 247, 251, 253n64
Rutland, Robert A., 49n14, 51n16, 53nn17,18, 54n21, 57n26, 58n27, 60n29, 61n31, 65n37, 180

Sacks, Albert M., 232n20
Sager, Lawrence G., 13, 28–9, 33, 35, 110–44, 113, 138n8, 139, 231n16
Saladino, G., 64n33
Sartori, Giovanni, 162n10, 165, 172n9
Scharf, Fritz, W., 194n38
Schechter, Stephen L., 178n17, 179n20, 197n41
Schelling, Thomas, 80, 92, 93, 101n59
Schlesinger, Arthur, Jr., 185n29
Schmitter, Phillip, 73
Schopflin, George, 74
Schwartz, Herman, 374, 378, 379, 380, 384, 387
Scott, Dred, 258
Scott, James C., 331
Seidman, Louis Michael, 299, 322
Sekulic, Dusko, 82n23
Selten, Reinhard, 159n8
Sen, Amartya K., 150n3, 163n12, 167n15
Shapiro, Ian, 104n66
Shapiro, Martin, 372, 373, 379, 382, 389
Sheehan, Reginald S., 190n33, 192n36
Sherman, Roger, 336
Sherry, Suzanna, 308
Shils, Edward, 79
Shugart, Matthew S., 165n14
Shvetsova, Olga, 363n2
Sieyes, A., 206n8, 209n15, 210
Simpson, Jeffrey, 246n48
Skocpol, Theda, 301
Skowronek, Stephen, 297
Slonim, S., 55n22

Smith, Adam, 328, 340, 341
Smith, Scott B., 322
Soltan, Karol Edward, 322
Sorenson, Leonard R., 181n25
Souter, Justice David, 315
Spencer, Herbert, 330
Spiller, Pablo T., 186n30, 194n38, 242n41
Spitzer, Matthew L., 186n30
Stanley, G. F. G., 244n42
Starr, S. Fredrick, 95n46
Stein, Eric, 94
Stepan, Alfred, 83n23, 87n30
Stern, Robert, 293
Stone, Alec, 372, 373, 375n9, 378, 379, 380, 382, 383, 384, 385, 386, 389
Stone, Geoffrey, 338n8
Stone, Justice Harlan, 19n15, 293
Storey, Joseph, 43n2
Stourzh, G., 64n34
Strayer, Barry, 248
Street, Alfred B., 178, 197n41
Strotz, Robert, 25n19
Sunstein, Cass R., 275n10, 316–17, 318, 320
Swift, Elaine, 340
Swinton, Katherine, 250nn56,57, 251n59, 253

Taney, Roger, 257
Tate, C. Neal, 372
Taylor, A. J. P., 344
Taylor, Michael, 93n43
Ten, C. L., 99
Terracini, Umberto, 219n45
Thorne, S. E., 239
Tideman, Nicolaus, 167n16
Tiebout, Charles, 226
Tiller, Emerson H., 186n30, 194n38
Tismaneanu, Vladimir, 74, 77n16
Tito, M., 88n34, 281n15
Tocqueville, Alexis de, 148
Trebilcock, Michael J., 226n10
Tribe, Laurence, 274n8, 282n17, 294
Trudeau, Pierre, 232, 233, 251
Tudjman, Franjo, 88n34
Tullock, Gordon, 149, 162, 226
Tushnet, Mark, 272, 299, 322

Van Alstyne, William, 225
Van Buren, Martin, 334
Venturi, F., 217n36
Verdery, Katherine, 73n8, 83n25, 85, 88, 92n40
Vipond, Robert C., 246n47
Vogelsang, Ingo, 242n41
Volcansek, Mary L., 378, 384, 385, 386
Volokh, Eugene, 279

Name Index

Wallace, Caleb, 189n31
Walpole, R., 236n28
Walzer, Michael, 72, 73, 75, 76, 88, 91n37, 105
Washington, Bushrod, 276
Washington, George, 3, 57, 63, 256n70, 276, 334, 357
Watson, Lord, 247n50
Watson, Richard A., 195n39, 197n41
Webster, N., 72
Wechsler, Herbert, 255
Weiler, Paul, 252n63
Weingast, Barry R., 99n55, 232n21, 235, 236, 237, 258n79, 388
White, G. Edward, 295, 303
White, Leonard, 297
Whittington, Keith E., 310
Wiecek, William M., 303, 315

Williamson, Oliver, 233n23
Wills, Garry, 48n13, 170n2, 176, 177n14, 178, 198n42
Wilson, James, 44n6, 49, 54, 178n16, 180n21, 195n40, 198n43
Wilson, Woodrow, 189n31, 258–9, 299
Wood, Gordon S., 46, 48n13, 54, 378, 379, 381
Woodward, Susan, 71n2, 76, 77n15, 82, 83, 85, 86, 88n33, 89n36, 101n61

Yeltsin, Boris, 355, 356, 357
Young, Crawford, 77nn15,17
Young, James Sterling, 297

Zagarri, Rosemarie, 50
Zhirinovsky, Vladimir, 349, 356, 357
Zohar, Noam, 274

Subject Index

absolute power, 12, 151, 153–4, 156, 160
absolutism, 207, 214
Act of Settlement, 236n29
act utilitarianism, 152, 153, 157, 160
activist state, 290, 303–4, 306–7
adventurer, 23
agency, 150–1; distribution of, 131, 132
agency costs, 277
agency problem, 278, 282–3
agrarian interests, 344–5
Agrarian Party (Russia), 346
agrarian-to-urban transition, 349–50
agrarian vision, 341, 342, 343, 346, 347
Agricultural Adjustment Act, 301
agriculture, 346
agriculture to industry transition, 351, 352
Alien and Sedition Acts, 2, 4, 5
ambition counteracting ambition, 209,
  213–17, 218
amending structures, 274–5
amendment(s), 10, 21–2, 34–5, 66, 135,
  143, 148–9, 159, 172, 180–1, 190, 255,
  291, 313, 374; of amendment provisions,
  139–42; in Articles of Confederation,
  29; circumventing requirements for,
  139–40; Civil War, 311–12; clauses, 275;
  and constitutional change, 25–6, 33,
  116–18; designing process for, 271–87;
  difficulty of, 112–13, 131–2, 133, 137,
  290; by direct initiative, 278–80; drafting
  of procedures for, 364–5, 367–8, 369,
  371, 372, 377, 380, 387–8; extra-Article
  V, 115, 117, 126–9, 274; identifying,
  273–5; limiting, 277; machinery for,
  114–16; provisions for, 125–6; by
  referendum, 277, 278–80, 282, 284;
  requirements for, 29–30, 116;
  supermajoritarian procedures, 164, 167;
  terms of, 121, 123–4; transformative,

291; unanimity vote for, 164;
  unconventional, 310; voting protocols,
  125
America, 208; *see also* United States
American constitutionalism, 7–8, 14, 21–2,
  35, 68, 291–2, 322, 323; and Madison,
  2–8, 27–8, 41–68, 170–202, 213–16; *see
  also* American democracy;
  constitutionalism
American democracy, 172, 174–6, 178,
  180, 182, 183–4, 186, 190–3, 194, 195,
  197, 198–201, 321, 335; and New Deal,
  290, 299, 305–8; series of regimes in,
  308–9; *see also* democracy,
  constitutional
"American System" (Henry Clay), 24,
  297–8
amoral agents, 148, 150, 181
Annals of Congress, 176
Anti-Federalism, 3, 23–4
Anti-Federalists, 21–2, 46–7, 64n33, 214,
  255, 310, 343; and communitarianism,
  330, 332, 333, 341; and popular
  sovereignty, 65, 66
appellate authority, 249, 264
Argentine Constitution, 347
Article I (U.S. Constitution), 275
Article II, 275
Article IV, 279
Article V, 29, 30, 32–3, 34, 41, 111, 114–16,
  117, 123, 125, 126, 143, 181, 272, 274,
  277, 280, 284, 285, 291, 305, 307, 312;
  changes for, 281; circumventing, 125–9;
  democratic objections to, 130–5;
  difficulty of amendment under, 290;
  extraordinary majorities requirement,
  277–8; hypertextualist readings of, 309;
  literalism, 311; requirements of, 112–13;
  structure of, 282–3

399

400 *Subject Index*

Article V revisionists, 114–15, 116–17, 126
Article VII, 110, 123, 125
Articles of Confederation, 41, 61, 64, 65, 66, 143, 329, 358; abandoning, 310–11; amendment, 29, 110, 111, 271, 272; single-state veto, 338; as status quo, 102; trade practices under, 336–7
Asian Tigers, 350
assurance effects, 156, 161
Attorney General of Ontario v. Attorney General of Canada, 248–9
Australia, 223, 353
Australian rule, 283
Austria, 234n24, 379
Austrian Constitution, 271, 272
Austrian Republic, 382
authority: of constitutions, 2, 6; decentralization of, 15; devolution of, 225n7; of government, 11–12, 15, 16, 21

balanced budget amendment, 280, 281
Balkans, 74, 76, 77
Bangladesh, 354
bargain(s), 194; constitution as, 20–2, 24, 26, 103; federal, 226, 241–2
bargaining (game), 183, 184
bargaining power, 150, 151
beginnings, constitutional, 27–30
bicameralism, 49, 193n37, 195, 216, 262, 272, 273
Bill of Rights, 5, 22
bills of rights, 4
Bismarck Constitution, 382
birth logic of democratic constitution, 29, 110–44
Bosnia-Herzegovina, 81–7, 92, 93, 94–5
Boston, 344
"bouche de la loi," 209, 214, 218; judiciary power as, 210–13
boundaries, enforcing, 229, 231, 242
branches of government, 34, 309; in constitutional development, 288; division of power, 176–7; expectation of future control over, 371–2; right of constitutional review, 374
breakdown, constitutional, 115, 139–42, 143
Britain, *see* Great Britain
British Coal Corp. case, 248
British Columbia, 249
British Constitution, 16, 18n13, 339; dignified and efficient parts of, 79–80, 97; *see also* English Constitution
British constitutionalism, 13, 235–42
British Empire, 244, 248–9
British North America (BNA) Act, 243–4, 245, 246, 248

British Privy Council: Judicial Committee, 32, 243, 246, 247–9, 251, 264
Brown v. Board of Education, 315–16
Bulgaria, 384
Burkean ideal, 48–9
business, 340; and government, 354–5
business interests, 334, 335, 337, 344–5

California, 278, 284; Proposition 209, 279
California Constitution, 279–80
Canada, 32, 235; Charter of Rights and Freedoms in, 251–3; decentralization, 229; erosion of juridical federalism in, 242–53; as exemplary constitutional government, 15; federalism, 225, 262, 263–4; Parliament, 248, 249, 253
Canada Temperance Act, 247n50
Canadian Constitution, 232, 249
Canadian Supreme Court, 232–3, 246, 248, 249, 251, 252, 253, 263
capitalism, 328–9, 330, 339
cardinal utility, comparisons of, 165–6
Carter v. Carter Coal, 301
"Casey fallacy," 316
Central Europe, unstable expectations in, 331
charisma (concept), 93n42
Charlottetown, 253
Charter of Rights and Freedoms (Canada), 251–3
cheating, 256; in decentralization, 228, 230
checks: in council arrangement, 196; on legislature, 193–8; in parliamentary democracy, 195
checks and balances, 23, 24, 31, 41, 147, 148, 150, 155, 156–7, 161, 165, 167, 209, 215, 218, 262; in American democracy, 174–6; in Madisonian democracy, 176–81; in parliamentary democracy, 173–4, 195; systems, comparisons of, 182–202
China, 235n26, 352
choice, constitutional, 111, 133, 142, 143
Christian Democrats (Italy), 219–20, 221
cities, rise of, 344
citizenry, participation of, 15, 369, 372
civic republicanism, 343, 344
civil liberties/rights, 306n4
Civil Rights Act of 1875, 258n81
Civil Rights Act of 1964, 54n20; Title II, 294
Civil War, 8, 14, 258, 304, 330, 337n6, 342, 344, 345; and constitutional change, 311–13, 318
code, constitutional, 30, 147, 148, 149, 150, 151, 152, 154–5, 156, 162, 181; design of,

166; in two-stage model, 158, 159, 160, 161
cognitive dissonance theory, 273
Cohens v. Virginia, 295
Cold War, 305, 337n6
Commerce Clause, 116, 117, 250, 261, 293–4, 296, 330, 332, 336–43, 345, 348; controversy over, 292–6; import of, 354, 355
commercial interests, 336, 340–1, 342, 355
commercial vision, 332, 333
commitment capacity, 25, 26
committee of postponed parts, 55
Committee on the Political Economy of the Good Society, 322
communism, 87, 330
Communist Party (Moscow), 345, 346
Communist regimes, 74
Communists (Italy), 219–20
communitarian vision/communitarianism, 330, 332, 333, 341, 343, 344
compliance, 101–2, 103
Compromise of 1820, 258
Compromise of 1877, 256n71
compromises, 361, 376, 387
Confederation (Canada), 243, 244
Confederation Congress, 310
conflicts of interest: in constitution making, 377–9
Congress, 31, 50, 64, 66, 255, 258, 262, 274, 301; and amendment, 277, 282, 284; in American form of constitutional democracy, 174–6; authority of, 256; checks on, 171–2, 195, 197; commerce power, 292–3, 296; and constitutional change, 305, 313; constitutional interpretation, 198; decision making under uncertainty, 198–201; and election, 54, 55; executive and, 3; law-making authority of, 187–8; in Madisonian democracy, 177, 179–80, 181; New Deal agenda, 116, 117, 299; power of, 2, 257; small states in, 62; Supreme Court and, 260; and veto, 191, 192, 193; veto on state laws (proposed), 59
conscience, rights of, 60
consensus option, 164
consent, 122, 123
conservatism: in Madison, 66
Conservatives (Canada), 246, 248
consociational path (Canada), 253
consociativism (Italy), 220
constituent assemblies, 375–7
constitution(s): amendment of, 271–4, 275–7, 284–5 (*see also* amendment); as bargains, 20–2, 24, 26; defined in

abstract, 17; democratically deficient, 139–42; and economic theory, 358–9; identifying, 15–18; optimal, 161–8, 182; in political economy, 34–5; resistant to change, 123–4, 136, 138–9; restraints on government in, 208, 355, 356; revoked/changed, 113–14; and separation of powers, 208–10; sovereignty of, 209; Soviet-style, 102, 103; as start-up measure, 339; status of, 65; superlegality of, 214, 215; supremacy of, 206–7, 213, 220; written, 206; *see also* United States Constitution
constitution making, 1, 2, 104, 124–5, 361–3; goals in, 366–7, 368, 376; heterogeneity of interests in, 382, 387–8; historical cases, 377–87; politics of, 71–2, 92n41, 95, 103; in post-Communist states, 98n54, 99; preferences and expectations in, 363–77, 388; strategic structure of, 99–103
constitutional breakdown, 139–43
constitutional change, 25–6, 32–5, 67–8, 110–14, 115, 125–6, 140, 141, 323; access to influence over, 371; amendment and, 116–18; and constitutional theory, 288, 319–21; democracy and, 129–36; and federalism, 263, 264; majority rule for, 116; mechanisms of, 367, 368; New Deal and, 289, 290, 291, 292–308, 309, 310, 312, 313, 318, 319–20; non-Article V, 117–18; political theory of, 305–8; theories of, 288–92
Constitutional Convention, *see* Philadelphia Convention
constitutional court(s), 31n23, 374, 383, 384, 385–7; Italy, 31, 219, 221, 384, 385–6; *see also* council(s) of revision
constitutional democracy, *see* democracy, constitutional
constitutional government, *see* constitutional political system(s)
constitutional interpretation, *see* interpretation of constitution(s)
constitutional law, 310, 319; distinction between ordinary law and, 206, 211–12; and New Deal, 289; use of history in, 313
constitutional order, 308, 331, 334; demographic growth and, 354; permanent, 307; and stable expectations, 332; stability of, 139–43, 335, 345
constitutional phase (higher track), in two-track model, 147–8, 158, 166, 181
constitutional political system(s), 10, 12, 45, 46; comparing, 147–68, 182, 225–6,

402 *Subject Index*

constitutional political system(s) (*cont.*)
271–5, 363; dividing constitutional from
ordinary law, 9–10; and politics of
scandal, 324
constitutional problematics (c. 1787), 41–70
constitutional regime(s), 1, 2, 3–4, 35, 96,
105, 333; democratic provenance of, 126;
establishment of, 28; problems of growth
and economic transition, 330, 341–5;
revocation of, 29, 139–43; *see also*
constitutional political system(s)
constitutional review, *see* review,
constitutional
constitutional rules, 11–12, 13, 16, 17, 29,
30, 31, 123–4, 147–8, 149, 150, 151, 153,
154, 181, 182, 308, 361, 376; for
amendments, 284–5; choosing a code of,
147–61, 188–9; deviation from, 161; in
federalism, 31–2, 230, 232–3, 257, 262–3;
as higher-order rules, 9–10, 15, 16–17;
see also constitutional political system(s)
constitutional theory, 10, 11, 16, 18–20, 42;
of Ackerman, 308–13; of Buchanan,
17n12; *Federalist* and, 42–6; history,
interpretation, and, 308–23; of Madison,
2–8, 27–8, 41–68, 170–202, 213–16;
originalist, 20–2; transformed, 288–327
constitutionalism, 9, 10, 11, 14–15, 16–17,
20, 22, 134, 139, 340; American, 7–8, 14,
21–2, 35, 68, 291–2, 322, 323; British, 13,
231n16; and cultural context, 75n12; and
democracy, 22–7; essence of, 99; ethnic
nationalism and, 102; French, 31n23;
Italian, 217–21; legal/normative, 12–13,
14; modern liberal, 206, 207, 209,
211–12, 215; New Deal revolution and,
305–8; originalist account of, 112;
political theory of, 1–2; politicized, 6; in
politics of possibility, 72; as social
process of interpretation, 8–10; *see also*
constitutional political system(s); and
democracy, constitutional
contextualized constitutional theory, 292,
319, 321–2
continence/self-control problem, 26
Continental Congress, 57, 61, 110, 338
continuity: of American constitutionalism,
289–90, 294–5, 320; narratives of, 313,
318, 319
contract(s), constitutions as, 20–1, 23,
99–100, 101; *see also* bargain(s)
contracting for future circumstances, 362,
363, 365
coordination, 333
coordination problem, 100–1, 102, 103, 104
corruption, system of (Great Britain), 236,
237

council(s) of revision, 31, 178, 188–9,
193–5, 197–8, 201, 374n7; executive and
judiciary united in, 194, 195; and judicial
supremacy, 191; vetoes of, 188, 194, 195,
198, 201
countermajoritarian objection, 388–9
court "packing" schemes, 190
courts, 13–14, 139, 297; Canadian, 263;
in constitutional theories, 19; English,
239, 240, 242; federal, 233, 262; and
federalism, 229, 233, 264; independent,
229, 235; and interpretation, 8, 174–5,
191–2; and judicial supremacy, 194;
national, 233; power of obstruction, 190;
as protector of rights, 371; *see also*
constitutional court(s)
critical distance, 318–19
Croatia/Croats, 82n23, 83, 84, 87, 97
cultural confict, 243
cultural context of constitutionalism,
75n12
cultural pluralism, 77n15
cultural traditions, 28, 155
culture, constitutional, 2, 6–7, 10–15, 16,
18, 26, 27; and constitutional theory, 18,
19
Czech republic, 74
Czechoslovakia, 74, 94, 102

decentralization, 223–4; in Canada, 248;
credible, 224, 226–9; in Great Britain,
238; modalities of, 230–1
decision making, 147–8, 366, 374; abstract
review and, 373; ongoing, 135; popular
constitutional, 112–13, 123
decision-making authority: allocation of,
227; in Britain, 242; distribution of, 231;
in U.S. federalism, 225
decision-making costs, 162, 163, 164
decision making under uncertainty,
198–201
Declaration of Independence, 56
Declaration of the Rights of Man, 384,
385
democracy(ies), 35, 43, 96, 113–14, 121,
122, 127, 128, 137–8, 205–6; defined,
205n3; and economic transition, 347–50;
Rousseau's theory of, 205–6; threat of,
214; *see also* American democracy;
democracy, constitutional
democracy, American, *see* American
democracy
democracy, constitutional, 8, 22–7, 29,
30–1, 387–8; birth logic of, 110–43; and
constitutional amendments, 271–85; and
constitutional change, 129–39, 288–324;
and constitutional interpretation,

361–89; in Eastern Europe, 71, 72, 73, 74, 75, 76, 81, 94; and economic development, 328–59; efficacy of, 388–9; forms of, 172, 177–8, 179, 181, 182, 201–2; judicial review in, 186–9, 372–89; Madison and, 2–8, 41–68, 170–202; as two-stage game, 147–68, 181–2; *see also* American democracy; United States Constitution

Democrat-Republicans, 6, 7, 256n71; *see also* Jeffersonians

democratic community, 133; features of, 129–30, 131

democratic constitution, birth logic of, 110–44

democratic threshold, 136–7, 139

Democrats/Democratic Party, 259, 261, 264

demographic changes: and economy, 330, 344–5

demographic growth: economic transition and, 350–4; and expectations, 358

departmentalism, 177nn12,15, 180n22

derived coordination problem, 93

design, constitutional, 30–2, 163n12, 164–5, 177–8, 229, 275, 285, 329; optimal constitution, 161–8; rationality of, 365–6; sources of uncertainty and contingency in, 42, 47–8

despotism, 208–9, 211, 216

direct democracy, 206

direct initiative, amendment by, 278–80

"dormant powers" doctrine, 338–9

Dred Scott v. Sandford, 190, 258

due process, 116, 259

dynamic planning, 25n19

Eastern Europe, 28, 71–3, 81, 101, 102, 103, 104, 343, 374; constitution making in, 377, 378, 379; constitutional courts in, 387; economics in, 88, 329, 330, 345–7; ethnic attachments in, 76–8; judicial review in, 382, 384; traditions in, 78–81; tribalism in, 73–8

economic growth, 96, 330, 341–5

Economic Interpretation of the Constitution (Beard), 43

economic policy: Constitution neutral on, 328–31; in Great Britain's federalism, 236–7

economic systems, 328–9, 330

economic theory, 329, 333, 334, 335, 358–9

economic transition, constitutional, 328–60; democracy and, 347–50; and demographic growth, 350–4; harm from, 349–50

economic visions, early U.S., 330, 332–5

economy: government in/and, 34, 35, 52, 293, 297, 298, 300–2, 304, 337, 339, 347, 354–5, 356, 357–8

Eighteenth Amendment, 17, 274n7

election(s), 7, 49–50, 54–5, 189, 205, 280

electoral college, 55

electoral mandates: New Deal, 299–300, 303

election systems, 161, 162, 164; proportional (Italy), 220, 221

Eleventh Amendment, 259n83

encroachments, 4, 5; by federal government (Canada), 251, 252, 253; legislative, 28, 48, 51, 52, 54, 67; by state governments, 180

enforcement, constitutional, 361

English Constitution, 22, 24, 209; *see also* British Constitution

Enlightenment, 210

epistemic claim for majority vote, 130, 131

Equal Employment Opportunity Commission, 54n20

equal-intensity assumption, 162–3n12, 165, 166–7

equal membership requirement, 129, 131–2, 134, 137, 138

equal rights amendment (ERA), 275, 280, 281

equality, productivity and, 356–7

equality before the law, 210, 211

equilibrium(a), 100–1, 102, 103, 216; decentralization as, 231; ethnic violence as, 95n47; federalist, 256; Nash, 159, 181, 182, 183n27; in postconstitutional games, 182–3, 184, 185, 187, 188, 191, 192, 197; in two-stage model, 159

Era of Good Feelings, 256n70

Esprit des lois (Montesquieu), 208, 209

establishment clause, 99

ethnic attachments: as primordial, 76–8, 81, 82, 85

ethnic conflict, 331

ethnic groups: in former Soviet Union, 353

ethnic identity, 228

ethnic nationalism: alternatives to invented traditions of, 90, 91–2; in Bosnia-Herzegovina, 82–7; and constitutionalism, 102; Eastern Europe, 72, 74, 75, 81, 88–9, 90, 95–6, 97; manipulated by political leaders, 87

ethnic tribalism, 28

ethnicity, 102, 103; in Canada, 243, 264; political salience of, 96, 97

Europe: constitution making in, 379–80; judicial review in, 382–6, 389; mercantilism in, 329; political power in, 207–8; separation of powers in, 210; *see also* Eastern Europe

404 *Subject Index*

European Community, 20n16, 337, 347
European Convention on Human Rights, 136n7
executive department, 3, 4, 7, 28, 47, 48, 209, 212–13, 273; in Italian constitution, 217; legislative encroachment on, 51, 52, 54; relative to legislature, 53–4, 55; veto power of, 194–5, 196–7; *see also* presidency/president; prime minister
Executive Reorganization Act of 1939, 302
expectation effects, 160, 161
expectations, 41, 233, 361; constitution as guide to, 339; in constitution making, 101; and constitutional stability, 330, 331–2, 358; coordinated, 338; demographic growth and, 351, 358; and economic growth, 350; about future interpretation, 365, 387; about interpretation, 380; and preferences, 369–77; and preferences, in constitution making, 362–77, 387–9; role of, in economic relations, 330; in Russia, 355; security of, 198; in shock therapy, 348; stability of, 330, 331, 333, 335, 345; value of secure, 156–7, 161; weighting of, 371–2
expectations regimes, 201n44
external costs, 162, 164

faction(s), 4, 41, 216; Madison's theory of, 52; problem of, 45, 56–63
Fair Labor Standards Act, 293
fatalism, 28; in Eastern Europe, 72, 74–5, 76, 78–9, 81, 85–6, 87, 89, 90, 94, 95, 103, 104; rationalist grounding for, 87–90
Federal Act, 260
Federal Convention, *see* Philadelphia Convention
federal government: accountability for failure to act, 299–300; activist state, 306–7; in Canada, 243, 248, 249, 251–2; expansion of, 255–6; legitimacy of, 296; in New Deal, 302; power of, 295–6, 297; power over economy, 300–2; power to regulate commerce, 336–41; president de facto head of, 302; role of, 303; *see also* national government
"Federal Problem," 229n13
federal republic, theory of, 41–2, 223–65
federalism, 23–4, 31–2, 41, 47, 57, 60, 216, 229–35; advantages of, 226–9; American, 224n4, 225–6, 264–5, 272, 290, 302; in Canada, 243–4, 245, 262, 263–4; conditions necessary for, 225–6; in Great Britain, 235–42, 264; intrinsically unstable, 224n2; juridical, 231–3;

Madisonian, 3; political theory of, 223–65
Federalist, The, 1, 170, 215, 218, 309; Madison's contributions to, 2, 27, 42; and pure theory of Constitution, 42–6
Federalist 10, 42–4, 45, 52, 56–7, 59, 62, 63, 230n15, 262
Federalist 37, 47, 52
Federalist 46, 5
Federalist 47–51, 57, 213–14
Federalist 48, 51, 174
Federalist 49, 51, 66, 67
Federalist 50, 66
Federalist 51, 4, 45, 66, 174, 189, 193, 209
Federalist 62, 50
Federalist 68, 64
Federalist 78, 44, 56, 216–17
Federalist 81, 175
Federalist 85, 340
Federalist Party/Federalists, 3, 4, 5, 6, 7, 21–2, 46–7, 56, 61, 63, 255, 310, 335, 343; and popular sovereignty, 65–6
First Amendment, 9, 180; establishment clause, 99
First Reform Act of 1832 (Great Britain), 264
flexibility, 35, 368, 369, 370, 371
followers, distinction between founders and, 1, 2
Foundations (Ackerman), 309
founders, distinction between followers and, 1, 2; *see also* framers
founding generation, 29, 124, 142–3, 292, 308, 314, 318; continuity with understandings of, 294; permanent constitutional order, 290, 307; political heterogeneity of, 35
founding period, 22, 28, 44, 115, 314, 317; constitutional change in, 309, 310–11, 312, 313; normative argument from, 116; relationship among branches of government in, 288
Fourteenth Amendment, 13, 21n17, 60, 275, 311, 312, 314, 315
fragmentation of powers, 233, 234–5, 262, 263; in Britain, 235, 236, 237–8, 241; in Canada, 245–6; in federalism, 230, 264
framers, 21–2, 28–9, 43, 44, 46, 138–9, 153; and amendment process, 114, 115; confidence of, 276; and economic neutrality, 328–9; and federalism, 254; and institutionalizing judicial review, 381–2; intentions of, 41–2, 182–3; and judicial versus legislative supremacy, 171, 176–7; and presidency, 54, 55–6
France, 208, 273, 277, 373; Constituent Assembly, 205n2; constitution making,

377, 379–80; Constitution of 1791, 206, 209, 382; Constitution of 1958, 383; Constitutional Assembly 384; Constitutional Council, 31nn22, 23, 383, 384–5; Fifth Republic, 31nn22, 23, 165, 172, 201–2; industrial revolution in, 353; judicial review, 383, 384–5, 386, 389; King's Council, 235–6; National Assembly, 6, 375n9; preamble to Constitution, 384–5; revolutionary constitutional debates, 347; separation of powers, 31n22

free markets, 328, 329, 330, 331

freedom of speech, 285, 317

freedom(s): in liberal democratic constitution, 164, 166; value of, 152–5, 156, 161

French Canadians, 243–4

French Declaration of Rights, 208

French Revolution, 3, 6, 206, 209, 212

Fugitive Slave Act, 257–8

functional theory, 17, 18

Fundamental Principles Recognized by the Laws of the Republic (France), 384

future generations, 26, 113, 361; and amendment, 114, 276

future preferences, 362, 363–5; of judiciary, 364, 365, 366–8; of legislature, 364, 365, 368–9

game(s): constitutional democracy as two-stage, 147–69; cooperative, 147–9, 158–9; noncooperative, 147–9, 159; postconstitutional, 181–9

game theory, 24, 25n19, 30, 161, 167–8, 188, 201, 202

General Agreement on Trade and Tariffs, 274

"general regulation of trade" doctrine, 250n57

German Constitutional Court, 373–4

Germany: Basic Law of 1949, 383, 385; constitution making in, 377, 379, 380; demographic growth of, 353; judicial review in, 383, 385, 386, 389

Gibbons v. Ogden, 290, 292–4, 295, 296, 297, 298, 304

global constitution, 155

Glorious Revolution, 235

governance: democratic, 137–8; machinery of, 122, 123

government, 11–12, 15–16, 64; check against arbitrary, 190–1; in Constitution, 134–5; constitutional, 10–15, 16, 18; in constitutionalism, 22–3, 24–5; forms of, 208; levels of, 47, 155; participation in, 344; power of people to remake, 126–7,

128, 133; restraints on, 99–100; role in economy, 34, 35, 52, 293, 297, 298, 300–2, 337, 339, 347, 354–5, 356, 357–8; role of, 341; in Russia, 356; see also federal government; national government; representative government; state governments

government activism, 305–6

government officials: checks and balances, 148, 155; incentives and assurances, 156, 157; power sharing, 165

government regulation: New Deal, 300–2

Great Britain, 32; Canada's link to, 246; collapse of de facto federalism in, 235–42; decentralization, 229; federalism, in, 225, 264; governance structure, 136–7; imports from, 338; parliamentary system, 173 (see also Parliament [Great Britain]); trade policies, 332

Great Depression, 34, 117, 248, 305, 344; and constitutional change, 302, 303–5; as national emergency, 299, 300, 301, 303–5, 308; new constitutional order emerging from, 290; New Deal response to, 299

Great Society, 24, 256nn70, 71, 258, 259, 260, 305

Greek federations, 20n16

"Grundnorm," 121

Gulf of Mexico, 61

halacha, 274

Hamiltonians, 334, 335, 337, 341, 342, 345, 346

hammer and sickle, 345–7

Hammer v. Dagenhart, 293

Heart of Atlanta Motel v. United States, 294

heterogeneity: of founders, 35; of preferences/expectations, 375–7

heterogeneity of interests, 378, 379–80, 382, 386–8

historical context, 319, 320, 321, 322

historical institutionalism, 289, 290–1, 314, 319, 320

historicism/historicist theory, 26, 290, 291–2, 298–9, 308–13, 320, 321–3, 324; and constitutional interpretation, 313–19

history: and constitutional theory, 41–68, 71, 308–23

House Judiciary Committee, 323

House of Commons, 53, 173, 235, 238, 239, 240, 241

House of Lords, 235, 238, 241, 242, 245, 264

Subject Index

House of Representatives, 3, 4, 50, 55, 135, 283, 340
Huguenots, massacre of, 207
Human Rights Act of 1998 (Great Britain), 136n7
Hungary, 94, 96n49, 102, 384
hydraulic thesis, 72, 75, 76, 81–7, 90
hypertextualism, 309

Idaho, 281
idealist position, 103, 104
identity, politics of, 228–9n12
ideology, constitutional: New Deal changes in, 290, 299, 300, 302–3, 304
impeachment, 190, 323–4
imperative mandates, 205, 206
implementation effects, 159, 161
impossibility theorem, 163n12
impoverishment thesis, 72, 73, 75, 76, 81, 89, 90, 91, 94, 100
incentive effects, 156, 161
incentives, 231
incorporation doctrine, 60
indeterminacy, 73, 83
indeterminate circumstances, 89, 92–3
industrial revolution, 345, 353
industrialization, 350
institutional constraints on interpretation, 364–5, 366, 367, 369, 373, 374
institutions, constitutional, 112, 113; New Deal changes in, 290, 299, 300, 302, 305
intergenerational effects, 343; of economic transition, 352–3, 354
Interpretation Acts (Great Britain), 240
interpretation of constitution(s), 6, 8, 10, 23, 27; abstraction from historical context, 298; amendatory change masked as, 280; in Canada, 246; by Congress, 31, 198; and constitutional change, 25–6, 33, 305; and constitutional theory, 308–23; constitutionalism as social process of, 8–10; contextual theories of, 320; control over, 170–2, 191–2, 195, 198; control over, in American democracy, 174–6, 177–8; control over, in Madisonian democracy, 178–81; control over, in parliamentary democracy, 173–4; and democratic process, 389; historicism and, 313–19; institutionalizing, 361–91; judicial, 34, 135; and judicial supremacy, 186; legal, 97–8; and legislative supremacy, 201; necessity of, 389; originalism in, 21–2; public opinion and, 189; Supreme Court, 14, 186, 187; themes of constitutional change prior to theories of, 288, 319–21; theories of, 290,

291–2, 308, 321; will of past constitutional majorities in, 112
interpretive argument, 114, 115, 299, 314
interpretive canons, 7, 14
interpretive regimes, 364
investment(s), 198, 331, 335, 345, 348; government, 352
Ireland, 236n29, 242
Italian Constitution of 1948, 31, 208, 383–4; independence of judiciary in, 205–22
Italy: constitution making in, 377, 379; Constituent Assembly in, 217–18, 219; Constitutional Assembly in, 385; Constitutional Court in, 31, 291, 221, 384, 385–6; judicial review in, 383–4, 385–6; Parliament in, 221

Jacksonian era, 256n70, 297–8, 313
Jeffersonians, 6, 7, 256n71, 334, 335, 341, 342, 343, 344, 346; see also Democrat-Republicans
Jeffersonism, 334, 335
judges, 56, 210–11, 233, 375; British, 239–40, 241; election of, 389; federal, 230; in Italy, 219; legitimacy of, 373; life tenure for, 255, 273; null power of, 212; and politics, 231, 381; power of, 211, 214, 280
judicial activism, 188–9, 192, 386
judicial decision making, 112
judicial enforcement, 226, 257–8, 262
judicial obstructionism, 188–9, 190
judicial reform, European model of, 383–4
judicial review, 13–14, 24, 56, 133–4, 136, 182, 183, 191, 193, 207, 216, 371; in Canada, 243; in constitutional democracy, 186–9; constraints on, 374–5; contextual theories of, 320, 321, 322; and council(s) of revision, 176–81; in Federalist, 44, 174–6; institutionalization of, 372–89; lacking in parliamentary democracy, 174, 201; and legitimacy of democracy, 388–9; and separation of powers, 59–60, 186–202; see also judicial supremacy
judicial supremacy, 188, 191, 194, 201; doctrine of, 170–2; legislative supremacy versus, 173–81; Madisonian critique of, 192–3; rule of law and, 198; of Supreme Court, 186
judicial understandings of Constitution, change in, 116–18
judiciary department, 28, 34, 35, 47, 48, 56, 60, 209, 212, 213, 216–17, 254–5; and authority over constitutional choices,

133, 134; as "bouche de la loi," 210–13; Canada, 263; constitutional, 139; federal, 7, 31, 113, 131, 135; future preferences of, 365, 366–8, 370, 371; in Great Britain, 240, 241; independence of, 32, 56, 208–9, 226, 230, 263, 264; independence of, in Italian Constitution, 205–22; legislative encroachments on, 51, 52, 54; and popular sovereignty, 130; preferences of, 363–4; state, 381; veto power of, 194–5, 196–7, 198; *see also* interpretation of constitution(s); judicial review

juridical federalism, 231–3, 235, 242, 254–62, 264; in Canada, 242–53, 263

jurisdictions, 227–8; ethnically based, 228

jurisprudence: in Canada, 249–50, 263; in federalism, 264; in Great Britain, 239–40

justice, 19–20, 25, 35, 112, 113, 115, 130, 134, 182; and enduring constitution, 124, 125, 127, 136–7; and liberal democratic constitution, 147–57; normative claim for, 114–15; values of, 135–6

justiciability, doctrines of, 13–14

Kentucky, 178

Kentucky Resolutions, 2–3, 5

Kenya, 354

king-in-parliament model, 235

Kosovo, 76

laissez-faire, 328, 332, 339, 340–1, 345, 347

large states, 55, 62, 64, 283

law: forms of, 48; and restorationism, 298–9; *see also* constitutional law; ordinary law

lawmakers, superior class of, 48–9

law making, 53; American, 188–9, 195, 196, 198–201; American/Madisonian/parliamentary, 190–3; Madisonian, 192, 195; politics of, 373–4

law-making game, 182–6

law-politics distinction: Supreme Court, 306, 307, 310

legalistic perspective, 34, 319

legalistic theories: of constitutional change, 290, 291

legislation, 64; New Deal, 292, 293, 301–2, 315; politics of, 272

legislative department, *see* legislature

legislative despotism, 197

legislative initiatives: blocked by judicial review, 386

legislative supremacy, 170, 191, 197, 201,

382; versus judicial supremacy, 173–81; supermajoritarian, 182, 189–93

legislative voting rules, 161, 162

legislators, 48–9, 50–1; future, 375

legislature, 4, 47, 51–6, 209–13, 215, 273; decision making in, 373; effective checks on, 193–8; encroachment by, 28, 48, 51, 52, 54, 67; in federalism, 233; future preferences of, 365, 368–9, 370, 371; in Italian Constitution, 217, 219; preferences of, 364; simple majority decision making in, 167; *see also* state legislatures

legitimation: and ratification, 63–8

lettres de cachet, 210

liberal democratic constitution, 151–7, 161, 164

liberal democratic politics: Eastern Europe, 75, 78–9, 89–90

Liberal Party (Canada), 246–7

liberal rationalists, 104–5

liberalism, 207, 211–12

liberties, 23, 25; collective, 155; individual, 211–12

liberum veto, 64, 234, 271

linguistic identity, 228, 264

local governments, 255–6; in Great Britain, 236–8, 241

local power: in American federalism, 225

localism: in Great Britain, 241, 264

Lochner v. New York, 116, 315, 316, 321

logic of rational political nihilism, 72, 87, 90

London Resolution, 245nn45,46

Lower Canada, 243, 244

Luddites, 349, 352

McCulloch v. Maryland, 290, 292, 295, 297, 304

Macedonia, 97

Madisonian forms of constitutional democracy, 27–8, 172, 176–81, 182, 186, 189–201

magistrature: independence of, in Italian Constitution, 217–21

Magna Carta, 20

majoritarian view, 29–30, 149, 164

majorities, 112, 113, 148, 216, 220, 262; in amendment, 127–8, 277–8, 280, 284, 285; in Canada, 249; checks and balances and, 156; checks on powers of, in Italy, 221; factious, 3, 4; legislative, 162–3, 164, 173, 178, 179, 181, 195, 198; limitations on power of, in Germany, 385; popular, 193, 194; power of, 209–10, 213, 214; of states, in amendment, 283

408 *Subject Index*

majority rule, 122, 163n12, 166–7; for constitutional change, 116; in ratification, 111; *see also* simple majority rule; supermajority

Manitoba, 249

Marbury v. Madison, 306

Marshall Court, 34, 289, 290, 292–4, 295–7, 298

Martin v. Hunter's Lessee, 295

Marxism, 346

Massachusetts, 66, 337

Massachusetts Constitution of 1780, 65

Massachusetts Declaration of Rights, 208

Meech Lake (Canada), 253

member of Parliament (MP), 237, 238

mercantilism, 329, 341

minorities, 24, 25, 86, 138, 148, 164, 192, 195; and amendment, 279; in Canada, 243, 253; future, 367, 368, 369, 372, 376; protection of, 96, 156–7, 322, 386

minority rule, 4, 162n11, 163

"mischief rule," 239

misrule, check on, 51, 161, 193–4

"missing third alternative," 314, 317

Mississippi controversy of 1786, 61

Missouri Compromise, 258n79

mixed constitution, 20

mixed government, 45

mixed regimes, 205n1

moderate regime(s), 208–9

monarchy, 79, 80, 208, 241, 264; sharing authority with Parliament, 235, 236; privileges allowed by, 210

monetary policy, 345

moral agent, 147–8, 149, 150, 151, 152, 154–5, 156, 157, 158, 161–2, 166–7, 181

moral choice, 161

moral exhortation, 92, 93–4

moral reading, 18

moral saints, 151, 152–3, 154, 155, 157, 160

moral theory, 19

Mostar, 87, 93, 95

multiculturalism (Canada), 253

multiethnic states, decentralization in, 223, 228–9

Muslims, 82n23, 83, 84–5, 87

Namierite system, 237, 241

Nash bargaining, 150, 152

Nash equilibrium, 159, 181, 182, 183n27

national dimensions doctrine, 250n56

national government: in Canada, 245–6, 247, 249–50, 263; and capitalism, 329; changes in power of, 274; and commercial interests, 355; and economy, 332; and factions, 58, 59; in federalism, 224–5, 227, 228–9, 230, 231, 233, 234,

262–3; growth of, 259, 260, 356, 357; intervention in states, 60; judicial restraints on, 254, 255, 257, 260–1, 262; large states and, 64; in Madisonian form of constitutional democracy, 180–1; role of, 344; states' advantages over, 64; *see also* federal government

National Industrial Recovery Act (NIRA), 301

National Labor Relations Board v. Jones & Laughlin Steel Corp., 301

national security powers, constitutional allocation of, 7

national supremacy (principle), 65

nationalism: constitutional, 96–7; Eastern Europe, 72, 75

nationalization, 256, 258

Nebraska, 280, 283

New Brunswick, 249

New Deal, 4, 24, 34, 116, 117, 190, 248, 256nn70,71, 258, 259, 260, 264, 265, 274, 309, 315; activist government in, 306; and constitutional change, 289, 290, 291, 292–308, 309, 310, 312, 313, 318, 319–20; as constitutional revolution, 299–305; conversion of Supreme Court, 115n4; relationship among branches of government in, 288

New Deal Court, 259–60

New Freedom (Woodrow Wilson), 258, 259

New Hampshire Constitution of 1784, 65

New Jersey, 281, 337, 381

New York (city), 344

New York (state), 336–7, 381

New York Constitution of 1777: council of revision, 178, 179n20, 197n41, 381

nihilism, 89, 92

Ninth Amendment, 13

normative argument, 114–16, 126, 292, 320

norm-based (juridical) federalism: in Canada, 243–4, 251, 252, 264

norms: cultural, 12, 30; in federalism, 231, 232–3, 254; higher-order, 15; substantive/procedural, 18, 19; two-level structure of, 10, 11

norms, constitutional, 1, 2, 9–10, 11, 15, 16, 17, 22–3, 41; enforcement of, 13–14

North (the), 61

North American Free Trade Agreement, 274

North Carolina, 343n11, 381

Northern Ireland, 242

Northwest Territories, 258

Notes on the State of Virginia (Jefferson), 66, 215

null power, 210, 212

Subject Index

nullification, 5, 179, 191, 192, 194, 198, 201; *see also* "South Carolina heresy"

Old Regime, 210
Ontario, 249
optimal constitution, 182; designing, 161–8
ordinary law, 10, 11, 12, 14; distinction between constitutional law and, 206, 211–12
originalism/originalists, 20–2, 46, 112, 291, 304, 309, 313, 319, 320, 321

parchment barriers, 4, 5, 23, 214
Pareto-efficient, 183
Pareto-optimality, 150, 166
Parliament (Canada), 248, 249, 253
Parliament (Great Britain), 12, 32, 136, 235, 236, 237, 240, 241, 242, 246, 247; power of, 207n10
Parliament Act of 1911 (Great Britain), 239n34
parliamentary democracy, 173–4, 182, 183–6, 191–2, 193, 195, 197, 201
parliamentary sovereignty model, *see* Westminster model
parliamentary statutes, 239–40
parliamentary system, 139, 165, 192–3; in Canada, 249
Parnellites, 242
participation of citizens, 15, 344, 369, 372
Partito d'Azione, 217
party systems, 63, 164, 221, 272
past (the), 46; continuity with, 289–90; in interpretation, 313; usable, 316–18
Patriation Reference (Canada), 251, 252, 264
peace, order, and good government, 247n50, 249
Pennsylvania Constitution of 1776, council of censors, 381
people (the), 26, 28, 137, 175, 179; Article V and, 126–9; constituting, 121–5; constitutional appeals to, 65, 67; in constitutional change, 140, 141–2; in constitutional theory, 20, 21; and judicial obstructionism, 190, 192
Perez v. United States, 294
Persian Gulf, 275
pessimists, 90–1, 92, 94, 95, 103, 104, 105
Philadelphia, 344
Philadelphia Convention, 2, 30–1, 47, 58, 171, 177, 254, 281, 282, 310, 333, 336, 338, 339, 343, 357, 374n7; conflict in, 178n16, 378; debate about judicial review in, 179n19, 381–2
Planned Parenthood of Southeastern Pennsylvania v. Casey, 174, 315, 316

plantation agrarianism, 328, 329, 330, 332–4, 340–1, 343
plebiscitarian politics, 280
Plessy v. Ferguson, 315, 316
pluralist theory of democracy, 43
Poland, 94, 96n49, 97, 98–9, 102, 234n24, 374, 380, 384; and liberum veto, 234, 271
policy: distinct from constitutional interpretation, 179; influence of judiciary on, 186–7; in law-making games, 182–3
political community, 133–4, 137–8, 139; and amendment, 125–6, 128; and constitutional change, 140, 142; expression of popular will, 135; formation of, 122–5; voting protocols, 124–5, 128–9
political conflict, 378–9; and judicial review, 382, 384
political economy of decentralization, 227–8, 328–59
political justice, *see* justice
political order, 198, 272–3
political parties, 256, 262, 273, 297; in Canada, 249; and constitutional courts, 389; and federalism, 263, 264; in Great Britain, 238, 241, 264; in Italy, 221; *see also* party systems
political question doctrine, 14, 194n38
political regime, destabilization of, 348–9
political system(s), 159, 160; constitutional, 10, 11–12, 15
political traditions, 334–5; Eastern Europe, 95; inherited, 75, 76, 78–81, 104; invented, 73, 91, 104
political visions: early U.S., 330, 332–5
politics, 1, 6, 284, 309, 346, 349; and Constitution, 3, 6, 7, 24, 27, 28, 67; of constitution making, 71–2, 92n41, 95, 103, 361, 365–6, 375, 388–9; constitutional, 16–17, 66, 88, 99, 149, 291, 310; of constitutional enforcement, 361; constitutional theory and, 322–3; of constitutionalism, 73, 81; in Eastern Europe, 73; electoral, 280; and federalism, 32; interest-group, 34; judicalization of, 386; of lawmaking, 373–4; machinery of, 121; participation in, 344; popular, 138, 139; revolutionary, 309; in Russia, 355; structural, 312
politics of possibility, 71–3, 86–7, 92, 93, 95, 103; in Bosnia-Herzegovina, 83
popular sovereignty, 65–6, 112, 126–7, 130, 172n7, 211n19, 212; and amendment, 277–8
populism/populists, 49, 52, 346, 349
positive law, 206, 210
positivist account, 112, 117–18

Name Index

postconstitutional games, 181–9
postconstitutional phase (lower track), of two-track model, 147–8, 150, 152, 155, 158, 161, 162, 165–6, 167, 181–2
Poujadists, 346, 349, 357
power: abuse of, 5; allocation of, 10, 16; in constitution making, 100–1; distribution of, 134–5; hierarchical ordering of, 209, 212–13; shared, 165; of the state, 207–8
practical syllogism doctrine, 212–13
precedent, 7, 305, 309, 319, 320
Preface to Democratic Theory, A (Dahl), 43
preferences, 279, 386; distinct from judgments, 138; distribution of, 386–7; and expectations, in constitution making, 363–77, 387–9; and interpretation, 387; in postconstitutional games, 182–3, 184–5, 186–7, 188, 197; present and future, 362, 363–5, 368; weighing, 370
presidency/president, 7, 34, 135, 272–3; and constitutional change, 305; constitutional form, 54–6; New Deal changes in, 290, 299, 302, 304; Virginia hegemony over, 340; veto power of, 182, 183, 187, 192, 193, 194–5, 196–7, 198, 216; *see also* executive department
prime minister (PM), 173, 184–6, 237, 273; in Canada, 251; *see also* executive department
primordial attachments, 77–8
Prince Edward, 249
proceduralist theory, 18–19, 26–7
production, change in relative values of, 346
productivity, 342, 350–2; and equality, 356–7
Progressive Conservatives (Canada), 253
property rights, 58, 60, 61, 198, 303
proportional representation (PR), 164, 165, 167
Progressive Era, 303
protective nationalism, 96n49
Protestants, 60, 62
provinces, 32, 228; restraint on, 226n8, 227
provincial governments, 245, 246–50, 251, 252–3, 263; in federalism, 224–5, 231, 233, 235, 236, 262–3
provincial interests (Canada), 242, 243, 244
provincial sovereignty, 234
public choice, popular control over, 135–6, 137
public choice theory, 277
public good, 151, 154–5, 157, 161

Publian theory, 45
pure theory of constitution, 41–2, 59–60, 67

Quebec, 253

Railroad Retirement Board v. Alton Railroad, 300, 301
ratification, 10, 28–30, 44, 59, 110, 111, 112, 114, 118, 125, 177n14; Article V requirement, 131; Article VII requirement, 116; legitimation from, 63–8; of proposed amendments, 281–2, 283–4; terms of, 121–3
ratification debates, 56, 332, 343
ratifying conventions, 29
rational agent/actor(s), 150, 162, 167, 181, 183, 186–7
rational choice theories, 226, 229
rational devils, 151, 152, 153, 154, 160
rational nihilism, 72–3, 90
rationalist fatalism, 72–3, 89–90
Rawlsian criteria, 167–8
Rechtssicherheit, 210, 211, 213
Rechstaat, 206, 218, 221
Reconstruction, 8, 256nn70,71, 258, 259, 264–5, 288, 314, 317; and constitutional change, 291, 309, 310, 311, 312, 313, 318
Reconstruction Amendments, 115n4, 309
referendum, amendment by, 277, 278–80, 282, 284
Reform Acts (Great Britain), 238n32
Reformation, 207
regional identities, 252
regional interests, 20, 62; in Canada, 225
regions, 61, 223
regulatory power, 296–7, 299
Rehnquist Court, 261
religious liberty, 59
religious wars, 207, 208
rent seeking, 277, 278
Report of 1800 (Virginia), 5
representation, 50, 51; based on size, 62; equal, in Senate, 339–40; proportional, 220, 221; restrictions on, 379
representative government, 205–6, 211n19, 278, 280; elections check against misrule in, 189; legislative power in, 212–13; threat in, 210
representatives, 49, 51–2, 62; power of, 205
republic, 4, 42, 43, 44, 45, 47, 172; division of power in, 172, 177; factions in, 57, 59; legislative power in, 51, 172; Madisonian, 53, 171n6, 181, 198; within the states, 58–9
Republic of Ireland, 242

Republic of Serbia, 76
"republican form of government" clause, 279
republican ideal, 48–9
republicanism, 60, 61
Republicans/Republican Party, 258, 259, 261n91, 264; *see also* Democrat-Republicans; Jeffersonians
Responding to Imperfection (Levinson), 275, 276
restoration thesis/restorationism, 289–90, 291, 303, 304, 308, 313, 315, 318, 319–20, 322; reconsidered, 292–9
review, constitutional, 372–3; abstract/concrete, 373, 381–2, 383, 386–7; institutionalization of, 372–89; legitimacy of, 389; preferences regarding, 377; scope and process of, 365, 367, 368, 369, 372; *see also* constitutional courts; council(s) of revision; judicial review
revolution, constitutional: New Deal as, 299–305
Revolutionary War, 53, 206
revolutions: agrarian interests in, 347
Rhode Island, 64–5, 284, 336–7, 338n7, 381
rights, 23, 96, 158–9; in Canadian federalism, 251, 252; constitutional, 17, 163–4, 165, 167, 195, 365, 369, 379–80; constitutional, in Germany, 385; in French Constitution, 384; judicial protection of, 59; judicial review and, 60, 389; of minorities, 386; politics of, 322; protecting, 24, 25, 207, 241
rights, basic, 33, 147, 148, 152, 155, 156, 157, 164, 165; violations of, 194, 197
Robinson Crusoe economy, 25n19
Romania, 358, 374, 384
rule of law, 189, 210; stable, 198–201
rule of law incentives, 256
rule of recognition, 11, 12, 121
rule utilitarians, 157n5, 161, 162
rule-based juridical federalism, 255; in Canada, 243–4, 251, 263
rules: first-order (or lower level), 9–10, 16, 17; higher-order, 9–10, 15, 16–17; preconstitutional, 118; regime of, 121; two-level structure of, in a constitutional political system, 10, 11; *see also* constitutional political system; constitutional rules
Russia, 223, 234n24, 347–8, 350; constitutional experience of, compared with the United States, 354–8; economic transition, 351, 352; judicial review in, 384; shock therapy in, 349

Sarajevo, 87, 93, 97
Sarajevo massacre, 96n48
Saskatchewan, 249
Schechter Poultry v. United States, 300
Scotland, 236n29, 242
secession, 258, 311, 312
Second Irish Home Rule Bill, 238
Second Reform Act, 238
sectional balance/sectionalism, 57, 61–2, 63
selective incentives, 92n42
self-determination, collective, 155
self-interest, 148, 149–50, 154
semipresidential system, 165, 172
Senate, 55, 60, 62, 135, 180, 174, 283; discussed by Madison, 49–50, 51; equal representation in, 284, 339–40; impeachment of Clinton, 323; and presidency, 55, 56; representation in, 254, 258n79
senators: electing, 49–50
separation of powers, 4, 23, 24, 32, 41, 156, 181, 201, 206, 207, 302, 373, 374, 381, 388; discussed by Madison, 44, 51–2, 54, 170–202, 213–17; in Canada, 251–2; constitution and, 208–10; in Europe, 212–13; in France, 31nn22,23; in Great Britain, 238n33, 241; and independence of judiciary in Italian Constitution, 31, 205–22; judicial review in, 59–60; and judiciary, 211; in parliamentary democracy, 173–4; in representative government, 212–13; Rousseau's model of, 211n19; in states, 45n8, 381
separatist regionalism: in Canada, 225
Serbia/Serbs, 82n23, 83, 84, 87, 96n48, 97, 358
service provision, 227, 228, 236–7
shock therapy, 348, 349, 356, 357
simple majority rule, 119–21, 122, 131, 133, 162–3, 165, 166; amendment by, 126, 128–9; for constitutional change, 116; in ratification, 123; and requirements of democratic community, 130
slave codes, 59
slave states, 62, 335, 341, 342
slave trade, 284
slavery, 61, 62–3, 258, 317, 318, 341–2, 343, 346, 378; protected in Constitution, 330
Slovak republic, 74
Slovenia, 97
small states, 61–2, 283–4
small-versus-large states conflict, 339–40, 343
social choice theoretic problems, 189n32

412 *Subject Index*

Social Contract (Rousseau), 212
Social Contract model of separation of
powers, 211n19
social justice, *see* justice
social value: maximizing, 152–3
Solidarity, 98
South (the), 61
"South Carolina heresy," 5n6, 180
South Korea, 352
southern states, 226, 258, 311
sovereign authority: in federalism, 233–4
sovereign debt problem, 25n19
sovereignty: division of, 224; of the
people, 172n7; state, 218–19; in
Yugoslavia, 86
Soviet Union, 331, 345–6, 348–9, 350,
351, 353; *see also* Russia
Spain, 61, 91–2, 389
stability, constitutional, 32–5, 41;
expectations and, 330, 331–2, 358
stalemate, 119, 120
standing, 13, 372, 381
state, 317; activist, 290, 303–4, 306–7;
autonomy of, 289; constitutional, 208;
credibility of promises of, 388;
Hobbesian conception of, 224n2; in
Kant, 212–13; in New Deal, 302; new
dynamic for, 300; origin and necessity of,
207–8; threatened by cheating, 228;
weak, 297
state authority/power: in American
federalism, 225; judicial enforcement of,
257–8; limitation of, 207
state-centered approach, 288, 290
state constitutions, 54, 65, 277, 281, 380;
amendment of, 110, 111; reform of, 57,
58; separation of powers in, 381
state governments (U.S.), 32, 362;
advantages over national, 64; and federal
government, 47, 255–6; and Great
Depression, 302; national infringement
on, 260–1; power of, 180; sovereignty of,
303
state institutions: democracy and, 321;
development of, 290, 291; New Deal
changes in, 302, 305
state laws: Congress power over, 2–3,
59, 180; Supreme Court reviewing,
254
state legislatures, 4, 5, 7, 29, 58, 65, 381,
382; and amendment of Articles of
Confederation, 110; discussed by
Madison, 49, 50
state powers, 254, 255, 256, 259, 260; in
Italian constitution, 217–21; relations
among, 212, 215–16, 217–19, 242
states: commerce powers of, transferred to

federal government, 336, 337–8, 339–40,
354, 355; and constitutional amendment,
277; and electoral law, 50; factional
misrule within, 57–9; in federalism, 230;
legitimacy of judicial interventions in,
233; and ratification, 110, 123, 284; and
republican form of government, 45; right
to rescind ratification of proposed
amendments, 281–2, 283, 284; sovereign
authority, 234
states rights theories, 3, 5, 180
status quo, 102, 199–200; in
postconstitutional games, 182, 183, 184,
185, 186, 187, 188, 191, 192; protected in
Article V, 280
Statute of Westminster, 248
structural federalism, 232, 233–5, 236, 263;
in Canada, 245–6; in the United States,
254–62
structural politics, 312
structural restraints, 226, 262
structure, constitutional, 30–2, 124; *see also*
constitutional political system(s);
constitutional rules
subgame perfect equilibrium, 182–3, 187
substantive interests, 387, 388
substantive provisions, 121; drafting of,
364–7, 368–9, 370, 371, 372, 377, 380,
387
substantive theory, 18–19, 26–7
suffrage, 60, 345
supermajoritarian formula, 138, 149, 167
supermajoritarian legislative supremacy,
178, 179, 181, 182, 189–93
supermajority rule, 119, 122, 123, 132–3,
163, 164, 190, 195
Supreme Court, 117, 133, 178, 182, 225,
250, 255, 307, 314, 317, 320, 321, 322;
and amendment, 282; appointment of
justices to, 135; authority to interpret
Constitution, 174, 176; and
constitutional change, 290, 291–7, 298,
300, 301–2, 305, 306, 309, 315–16, 318,
319; decision making on constitutional
law making, 362; decision making under
uncertainty, 198–201; and federalism,
256–8, 259–61; judicial supremacy,
186–7, 191, 192; jurisdiction, 13, 14; in
Madisonian democracy, 179; New Deal
conversion of, 115n4; overruling
interpretation by, 374; protection from
political pressure, 262; reluctance to
invalidate acts of Congress, 194–5n38;
repudiated substantive due process
tradition, 116; and restoration thesis,
290; Roosevelt's Court-packing plan,
190; and state legislation, 254

Subject Index

Switzerland, 218, 228, 278, 279
symbol: and strategy, 71, 80, 83, 86, 87, 90, 91–2, 93, 95, 103, 105

talent, filtration of, 46–51
Taney Court, 257–8
tariffs, 332, 336, 338, 342, 345, 347
taxation on commerce: power of, 336
Tenth Amendment, 13, 255, 303
text, 8, 10, 15, 16, 23, 42, 307, 313, 321; amendment/interpretation, 9, 25; of Article V, 114–15; and contents, 18–19, 139; difficult to change, 32–3; founding, 66; importance of, 275; link to past through, 308; meaning of, 31, 48; ratification of, 112
textual construction, 8–9
textualism: in British courts, 239–40
Thirteenth Amendment, 311, 312
three-fifths clause, 62, 63
trade regulation, 336–7
traditions, constitutional, 79, 99; inventing, 71–109; see also political traditions
transactions cost approach, 30, 162–5; variation on, 165–8
Transformations (Ackerman), 309, 310
transitions, constitutional, 27–30, 333
tribalism, 72, 73–7, 78; assumptions regarding, 76–81; confounding, 81–7
tribunal(s), constitutional, 372–3, 374, 381, 382, 383; see also constitutional court(s); council(s) of revision
Twelfth Amendment, 174n10
Twenty-first Amendment, 274n7
Twenty-seventh Amendment, 274n7
two-stage game: constitutional democracy as, 147–68, 181–2, 202
tyranny of the majority, 137

unanimity rule, 119–20, 148–9, 163, 164, 284
uncertainty, 366; decision making under, 198–201; in Eastern Europe, 73, 87; effects of, on judicial review, 378, 380, 384, 386–7
unicameral system, 272, 273
union (the), 47, 61, 62, 63, 311
unitary government (Great Britain), 238, 239, 242
United Kingdom, 12, 15, 136n7, 264; instability of expectations in, 335; see also Great Britain
United States: antebellum, 224; constitution making, 377, 378–9, 380–2; constitutional experience of, compared with Russia, 354–8; constitutional

problematics of, circa 1787, 41–68; decentralization, 229; demographic growth, 353; economic and political visions in early, 330, 332–5; economic relations in, 354; as exemplary constitutional government, 15; federalism, 32, 225, 226, 264–5; homogeneity in, 223; structural and juridical federalism in, 254–62; three great constitutional moments in, 288
United States Constitution, 18, 31, 101, 102, 103, 206, 272; assumptions about origins of, 41–2; authority of, 3, 6; birth lessons of, 113–16; birth of, 110–13, 142–3; and contemporary challenges, 322–3; control over interpretation of, 170–2; federalism in, 254–5, 256; Federalist and pure theory of, 42–6; fit with developing economy, 332; flaw in, 170, 177; guarantee clause, 12–13; illegality in inception, 111n2; influence of Madison's writings on commentaries on, 27–8; legality of, 310–11; legalized, 305–8, 310; legitimacy of, 42, 112; neutral on economic policy, 328–31, 333–4; obdurate to change, 130, 138–9; partially unwritten, 339; political, 305, 306; ratification, 28–30; ratification to legitimation, 63; replacement/ amendment, 111 (see also amendment); separation of powers in, 209, 213–17; slavery provisions of, 17; supremacy clause, 59; theories of, 19; theories of change, 288–92
United States v. Butler, 300–1
United States v. Darby, 293, 294, 301
Upper Canada, 243, 244
usable past, 316–18
utilitarian constitution, 165
utilitarianism, 166–7
utility information, 165–6
utility-maximizers, 150, 162

values: in constitutional change, 41, 316
veil of ignorance, 1, 147, 149–50, 151, 152, 154, 155, 158, 181
veto, 179, 182, 183, 189, 192, 193; congressional, 180; council of revision, 188, 194, 195, 198, 201; executive and judicial, 194–5, 196–7, 198, 201; Supreme Court, 187; see also liberum veto
"Vices of the Political System of the United States" (Madison), 57
Virginia, 381
Virginia assembly, 57
Virginia Plan, 178n16, 180n21

Virginia Report of 1800, 5
Virginia Resolutions of 1799, 2–3, 5, 180
virtuous motives, 149–50
voice requirement, 129, 131, 133, 134, 137, 139
votes: differential weighing of, 131, 132
voting rules/protocols, 122, 124–5, 131, 164–5; choosing, 118–21, 128–9; disfavoring persons/positions, 132–3; legislative, 161, 162; optimal, 162; in ratification, 123

Weimar Germany, 358; Supreme Court of, 382–3
welfare state, 135, 296, 300, 337n6, 358
Western Europe, 373; constitutions in, 378, 379; judicial review in, 382

western states, 63, 278, 279
Westminster model, 221, 239, 240, 244, 245, 271; *see also* Parliament (Great Britain); parliamentary democracy
Whig ideology, 47
Whig oligarchy, 237
Wickard v. Filburn, 293–4, 301
World War I, 300, 337n6, 344; command-and-control government during, 304
World War II, 256n70, 258, 274, 305, 337n6

Yugoslav Communist Party, 89–90
Yugoslavia, 77n15, 83n24, 84, 90, 92, 95, 96, 97, 103, 207, 224; constitution, 281; ethnicity in, 85–6, 87, 89–90; intermarriage in, 82n23

For EU product safety concerns, contact us at Calle de José Abascal, 56–1°, 28003 Madrid, Spain or eugpsr@cambridge.org.

www.ingramcontent.com/pod-product-compliance
Ingram Content Group UK Ltd.
Pitfield, Milton Keynes, MK11 3LW, UK
UKHW011329060825
461487UK00005B/430